Warriner's
English Grammar
and Composition

LIBERTY EDITION

Complete Course

Warriner's English Grammar and Composition

LIBERTY EDITION

John E. Warriner

Complete Course

 Harcourt Brace Jovanovich, Publishers

Orlando   San Diego   Chicago   Dallas

THE SERIES:

English Grammar and Composition: First Course
English Grammar and Composition: Second Course
English Grammar and Composition: Third Course
English Grammar and Composition: Fourth Course
English Grammar and Composition: Fifth Course
English Grammar and Composition: Complete Course

Annotated Teacher's Edition, Part I; Teacher's Edition, Part II, for each above title.

CORRELATED SERIES:

English Workshop: First Course
English Workshop: Second Course
English Workshop: Third Course
English Workshop: Fourth Course
English Workshop: Fifth Course
English Workshop: Review Course

Composition: Models and Exercises, First Course
Composition: Models and Exercises, Second Course
Composition: Models and Exercises, Third Course
Composition: Models and Exercises, Fourth Course
Composition: Models and Exercises, Fifth Course
Advanced Composition: A Book of Models for Writing, Complete Course

Vocabulary Workshop: First Course
Vocabulary Workshop: Second Course
Vocabulary Workshop: Third Course
Vocabulary Workshop: Fourth Course
Vocabulary Workshop: Fifth Course
Vocabulary Workshop: Complete Course

John E. Warriner taught English for thirty-two years in junior and senior high schools and in college. He is chief author of the *English Grammar and Composition* series, coauthor of the *English Workshop* series, general editor of the *Composition: Models and Exercises* series, and editor of *Short Stories: Characters in Conflict.* His coauthors have all been active in English education.

Printed in the United States of America
ISBN 0–15–311805–9

To the Student

Now you are probably thinking, "Here we go again—another English class, another textbook." You are, of course, quite right. Since almost everything you do involves the use of language, schools make the study of English a required subject in every year, and in any English class, a textbook is an essential tool.

This textbook is designed to help you master the skills required for the effective use of standard English. Although the book will help you to *speak* better, its primary purpose is to help you to *write* better.

You have been learning to write almost as long as you have been going to school, which, at this point, may seem to you to be a very long time. To be sure, you have already studied many composition skills. This book reviews those skills while it carries you further into the study of more advanced skills which lead to better writing.

As your experience increases, your ideas become more sophisticated and consequently more difficult to express. Additional skills are needed. This textbook provides instruction in these skills and the opportunity to practice their use. Practice is important because you learn to write by writing. No one ever learned to write in any other way.

Your textbook is also designed as a useful reference book: it offers the solution to almost any writing problem you are likely to encounter. By familiarizing yourself with the contents and organization of the book, and by using the index freely, you can easily find out what you need to know, whether it is a question about punctuation or usage or sentence structure, or a suggestion about the form of an outline, of a bibliography, or of a business letter. Keep this book nearby whenever you write. Develop the habit of looking up the answers to questions that arise concerning the use of standard English.

J.W.

CONTENTS

4. The Clause   67

THE FUNCTION OF CLAUSES

Part Two: USAGE

8. Correct Use of Pronouns   156

NOMINATIVE AND OBJECTIVE CASE; SPECIAL
PROBLEMS

Part Three: COMPOSITION: Writing and Revising Sentences

18. Sentence Conciseness 322
AVOIDING WORDINESS AND OVERWRITING

19. Sentence Combining and Revising 333
VARIETY, INTEREST, EMPHASIS

20. Sentence Revision 355
PRACTICE EXERCISES

Part Four: COMPOSITION: The Writing Process

22. Writing Paragraphs   407

STRUCTURE AND DEVELOPMENT OF
PARAGRAPHS

23. Writing Expository Compositions 463

INFORMATIVE AND EXPLANATORY
COMPOSITIONS

25. Writing Persuasive Compositions 574

LANGUAGE AND LOGIC

26. Expressive and Imaginative Writing 626

PERSONAL NARRATIVES, STORIES,
DRAMA, POETRY

28. Writing Business Letters 709

STANDARD PRACTICE IN BUSINESS
CORRESPONDENCE

29. Effective Diction 729
APPROPRIATE CHOICE OF WORDS

Part Five: MECHANICS

33. Punctuation   815

OTHER MARKS OF PUNCTUATION

Part Six: AIDS TO GOOD ENGLISH

35. Reference Books 863
SPECIAL SOURCES OF INFORMATION

36. The Dictionary 878
CONTENTS AND USES OF DICTIONARIES

37. Vocabulary   892
MEANING THROUGH CONTEXT AND
WORD ANALYSIS

38. Spelling 922

IMPROVING YOUR SPELLING

39. Test-Taking Skills 943

COLLEGE ENTRANCE AND OTHER
EXAMINATIONS

Warriner's
English Grammar
and Composition
LIBERTY EDITION

Complete Course

PART ONE

GRAMMAR

CHAPTER 1

The Parts of Speech

THEIR IDENTIFICATION AND FUNCTION

By this time in your education, you understand the importance of being able to speak and write effectively. A principal goal of instruction in English is to increase your competence in speaking and writing. Every year your English courses take you further toward achieving that goal.

Since English is a cumulative subject, some things that you encounter each year are bound to be familiar. Among these is grammar, which you have probably been studying since elementary school. There is a good chance that by now you already know enough English grammar to meet your needs. You may, however, find your knowledge of grammar somewhat tarnished and in need of polishing.

Grammar is important. By giving names to the kinds of words and the parts of a sentence, it provides the terminology you need in your study of language. By making you aware of the basic patterns of English sentences, it helps you to develop a varied and interesting style. You should, therefore, find out early in the school year whether your knowledge of grammar is adequate. The way to do this is to test yourself and then review what you still need to learn.

Chapter 1 deals with the fundamentals of grammatical knowledge —the parts of speech, or the classification of words according to their function in the sentence.

DIAGNOSTIC TEST

Identifying the Parts of Speech of Words. Number your paper 1–20. Write the numbered words in the following passage and write what part of speech each of the words is, using these abbreviations: *n.* (noun), *pron.* (pronoun), *adj.* (adjective), *v.* (verb), *adv.* (adverb), *conj.* (conjunction), *prep.* (preposition), *interj.* (interjection). Base your answers on the way each word is used in the sentence.

EXAMPLE   Writing can be (1) *inventive* and original.
    1. *inventive, adj.*

For less than five dollars (1) *you* can get to know yourself better! How can such a wonder be accomplished? Purchase a (2) *blank* notebook (3) *and* begin to keep a personal journal. Within a short time you will be amazed to see what you (4) *learn* (5) *about* yourself.

Keeping a journal is (6) *simple.* There is only one rule: Date all entries. Entries may be as short as a sentence or as long as many paragraphs. (7) *Usually* your mood will determine length. Use a variety of entries. One type is the (8) *daily* log, in which you record (9) *what* you did and how you felt on a particular day. Another is a (10) *record* of favorite songs and poetry. (11) *Most* important are those entries that have nothing to do with your (12) *"outer* life," but which (13) *record* your "inner life": your dreams, your thoughts, your questions, your goals, and especially, your feelings. (14) *Because* the journal is a personal book, which no one else reads, it becomes a "free place" where you can say (15) *anything* you want. Most people find that writing at least four or five entries a week is a realistic goal. Rereading your entries weeks and months (16) *later* will give you a portrait of the way you were at a particular time in your life.

Does the journal really work? (17) *Wow!* You bet it does! One girl in (18) *Connecticut* wrote to her teacher that keeping a journal was "the closest I've come to knowing myself." The journal is an adventure (19) *in* self-awareness. (20) *Try* keeping one yourself.

THE NOUN

1a. A *noun* is a word used to name a person, place, thing, or idea.

Nouns may be classified in three ways: *proper* or *common; abstract* or *concrete;* and *collective.*

A *proper noun* names a particular person, place, or thing and is capitalized: *Ann, New Mexico, Sears Tower.*

A *common noun* does not name a particular person, place, or thing. Common nouns are not capitalized: *woman, district, chair.*

An *abstract noun* names a quality, a characteristic, an idea: *peace, civilization, honor, justice.*

A *concrete noun* names an object that can be perceived by the senses: *star, whisper, flame, cinnamon.*

A *collective noun* names a group: *jury, band, family.*

☞ **NOTE**   A *compound noun* is a noun of more than one word: *County Savings and Loan Association, roller coaster.*

August 27, 1993

EXERCISE 1. Identifying and Classifying Nouns. On your paper, write in order the nouns in the following sentences, placing before each the number of the sentence in which it appears. After each noun, indicate its classification: proper or common.

1. Last summer our family drove to Chicago in our new van.
2. Because of their intelligence and athletic ability, Karen Cornell and Leonard Johnson were named "Scholar Athletes."
3. In one afternoon the crew carefully checked and repaired eleven helicopters.
4. We purchased delicious tomatoes, lettuce, and corn grown by local farmers.
5. The Congress debated the merits of a new tax bill late into the night.
6. My goal is to visit every state in the United States within the next ten years.
7. When they saw the beauty of the snow-capped Rockies, the hikers paused and silently enjoyed the scene.
8. Her fresh ideas and her valuable experience as last year's class treasurer convinced a majority of the students to vote for her for class president.
9. Blunt honesty, quick wit, and fierce loyalty are the qualities I most admired in Huck Finn.
10. The crowd roared enthusiastically as Chip sank the winning basket just one second before time ran out.

WRITING APPLICATION A:
Defining Abstract Nouns

An important dimension of being human is the ability to think in abstract terms about abstract ideas. An abstract noun usually does not refer to something that can be pictured or heard or felt.

EXAMPLES   hope, freedom, awe, regret, success

Writing Assignment

Great writers usually focus on abstract ideas. For example, William Shakespeare explores the quality of *mercy* in *The Merchant of Venice*, *ambition* in *Macbeth*, and *indecision* in *Hamlet*. Select an abstract noun that particularly interests you. Define it in a clear, specific way and think of an anecdote or illustration that helps to make it meaningful for your readers.

THE PRONOUN

1b. A *pronoun* **is a word used in place of a noun or of more than one noun.**

EXAMPLES   The commuters complained to the mayor about the fare increase. **They** said that **he** had not warned **them** about **it.** [The pronouns *they* and *them* take the place of the noun *commuters.* The pronoun *he* takes the place of the noun *mayor.* The pronoun *it* takes the place of the noun *increase.*]
An umbrella and a book were left in the cafeteria. **They** have not been claimed. [The pronoun *they* takes the place of the nouns *umbrella* and *book.*]

Sometimes a pronoun takes the place of another pronoun.

EXAMPLE   **One** of the film projectors is broken. **It** has been sent out for repair. [The pronoun *it* takes the place of the pronoun *one.*]

The word to which a pronoun refers (whose place it takes) is the *antecedent* of the pronoun. In the preceding example *one* is the antecedent of *it.*

Pronouns are classified as: *personal, reflexive, intensive, relative, interrogative, demonstrative,* and *indefinite.*

Personal Pronouns

I, me	he, him	it	they, them
you	she, her	we, us	

Possessive Forms of Personal Pronouns

my, mine	his	its	their, theirs
your, yours	her, hers	our, ours	

Some of the possessive forms—*my, your, his, her, its, our, their*—are used before a noun in the same way that adjectives are used to limit the meaning of a noun: *my* parents, *your* home, *her* coat, etc. They are possessive pronouns functioning as adjectives. In this book these words are called pronouns. Your teacher may, however, prefer to have you call them possessive adjectives. Follow your teacher's instructions in labeling these words.

Reflexive and Intensive Pronouns

myself	ourselves
yourself	yourselves
himself, herself, itself	themselves

Personal pronouns combined with *–self, –selves* may be used in two ways:

1. They may be used *reflexively.*

   Miranda explained **herself.**

2. They may be used *intensively* for emphasis.

   Miranda **herself** made the explanation.

Relative Pronouns

who	which	whose
whom	that	

Relative pronouns are used to introduce subordinate clauses (see Chapter 4, page 71).

EXAMPLES   The student *who* won the scholarship is in my class.
The college *that* I chose is in Texas.
Do you know the woman *whose* writing was mentioned?

Interrogative Pronouns

who	which	what
whom	whose	

Interrogative pronouns are used in questions.

EXAMPLES   **Who** borrowed my pen?
            Which do you prefer?

Demonstrative Pronouns

this   these   that   those

Demonstrative pronouns are used to point out persons or things.

EXAMPLES   **That** is an excellent question.
            This is the correct answer.

Most Commonly Used Indefinite Pronouns

all	everybody	no one
another	everyone	one
any	few	other
anybody	many	several
anyone	most	some
both	neither	somebody
each	nobody	someone
either	none	such

Pronouns that do not usually refer to a specific antecedent are called *indefinite pronouns.* Most indefinite pronouns express the idea of quantity: *all, few, none.*

EXAMPLES   **Most** of the members have voted.
            Everyone favors a weekly meeting.

EXERCISE 2. Identifying Pronouns.   Number your paper 1–10. After the number of each sentence, write in order the pronouns in the sentence.

1. Last year our school gave two photography courses, neither of which had been offered before.
2. The course that I took dealt with the ways in which people perceive their environment.
3. Most of us block out our everyday surroundings, ignoring details that we have learned to take for granted.
4. You can prove to yourselves how blind all of us become to our surroundings.
5. Which of you, upon returning home from a trip, suddenly notices how different all of the rooms look to you?

6. Some of your possessions may look unfamiliar to you, and a few of them may seem totally alien.

7. Eventually, the impression of newness wears off, and your house takes on its familiar appearance.

8. Each of us can regain the ability to see freshly if we make full use of our sense of sight.

9. We must see the objects themselves as shapes instead of thinking about their function.

10. According to Claude Monet, a French impressionist painter whose works are world-famous, in order to see as an artist, we must forget the names of the things that we are looking at.

THE ADJECTIVE

1c. An _adjective_ is a word used to modify a noun or a pronoun.

To modify means "to limit," or to make more definite the meaning of a word. Adjectives may modify in any one of three different ways:

1. By telling _what kind:_

    green apples, **small** car, **capable** student

2. By pointing out _which one:_

    this woman, **that** play

3. By telling _how many:_

    some birds, **two** squirrels

As the preceding examples show, the normal position of an adjective is directly before the word it modifies. Occasionally, for stylistic reasons, a writer may use adjectives after the word they modify.

EXAMPLE The hikers, **tired** and **hungry,** straggled into camp.

A _predicate adjective_ (see Chapter 2, pages 37–38) is separated from the word it modifies by a verb.

EXAMPLES Deborah is **practical.**
He looks **thoughtful.**
His stew tasted **delicious.**
She appeared **confident.**

Articles

The most frequently used adjectives are *a, an,* and *the.* These little words are usually called *articles.*

A and *an* are indefinite articles; they refer to one of a general group.

EXAMPLES   **A** book fell down.
Margaret ate **an** orange.
We worked **an** hour.

A is used before words beginning with a consonant sound; *an* is used before words beginning with a vowel sound. Notice in the third example above that *an* is used before a noun beginning with the consonant *h,* because the *h* in *hour* is not pronounced. *Hour* is pronounced as if it began with a vowel (like *our*). Remember that the *sound* of the noun, not the spelling, determines which indefinite article should be used.

The is the definite article. It indicates that a noun refers to someone or something in particular.

EXAMPLES   **The** book fell down.
Margaret ate **the** orange.
The hour passed quickly.

The Same Word as Adjective and Pronoun

A word may be used as more than one part of speech. This rule is especially true of the words in the list below, which may be used both as pronouns and as adjectives.

all	either	one	these
another	few	other	this
any	many	several	those
both	more	some	what
each	neither	that	which

ADJECTIVE   **These** books are overdue. [*These* modifies the noun *books.*]
PRONOUN   **These** are overdue. [*These* takes the place of a noun previously mentioned.]

ADJECTIVE   We chose **neither** candidate. [*Neither* modifies the noun *candidate.*]
PRONOUN   We chose **neither.** [*Neither* takes the place of a noun previously mentioned.]

Nouns Used as Adjectives

Nouns are sometimes used as adjectives.

sofa cushion	**hotel** lobby
bread pudding	**glass** beads

When you are identifying parts of speech and you encounter a noun used as an adjective, label it an adjective.

EXERCISE 3. Identifying Adjectives and the Words They Modify. On your paper, write in order the adjectives in the following sentences, placing before each the number of the sentence in which it appears. After each adjective, write the word(s) modified. Do not list articles (*a, an,* and *the*).

1. The first person to walk on the moon was Neil Armstrong, the American astronaut.
2. Young people admire the sleek look of a new car.
3. Nine players are needed to form a baseball team.
4. "That engine will work perfectly for many years," said Mr. Sanchez.
5. On a sultry July afternoon we enjoyed sitting under the branches of a beautiful willow tree.
6. The rich soil of Kansas accounts for the high agricultural yield of that state.
7. A thousand fans waited in line for several hours to purchase tickets for the rock concert.
8. In 1936 Jesse Owens made Olympic history by winning four gold medals.
9. On an ordinary day the major television networks offer serious and comic programs.
10. Sharon made a narrow vase, a deep bowl, and a coffee mug in her pottery class; she was proud of these accomplishments.

EXERCISE 4. Identifying Nouns, Pronouns, and Adjectives. Some of the nouns, pronouns, and adjectives in the following sentences are italicized. For each sentence, write the italicized words in order in a column, numbering them as in the example. After each word, tell what part of speech it is. If a word is an adjective, write in parentheses the word that the adjective modifies. Do not list articles (*a, an,* and *the*).

EXAMPLE 1. *Everyone* in English class is writing a poem about a *famous*
American.
1. *Everyone pron.*
famous adj. (*American*)
American n.

1. *Some* students are writing *theirs* about well-known Presidents;
others have chosen *military* heroes as *their* subjects.
2. *Most* of *us* are writing about *someone whom* we admire.
3. *Those* who do otherwise may find *themselves* writing a poem *that* is
uninspired.
4. The *aviator* Amelia Earhart is a *popular* subject; *another* choice is
Harriet Tubman, the *courageous* woman who led *many* people to
freedom on the Underground Railroad.
5. *Both* of *these* women have made lasting impressions in their time.
6. On Earhart's attempted around-the-world *flight, radio* contact
aboard her plane was broken and never resumed.
7. Despite the unlikelihood of her survival, *speculation* about the
nature of Earhart's flight continues; *many* are convinced that she
was on an *intelligence* mission for the *Navy.*
8. Tubman was *one* of *many* former slaves *who* devoted their lives to
the *cause* of freedom and to the *advancement* of their people; the
abolitionist John Brown referred to her as *"General Tubman."*
9. Although *she* eventually became *free,* she could not be happy while
even *one* member of her family remained a *slave;* once she brought
as many as *twenty-five* slaves to freedom in a *single* band.
10. *Nobody* in our class seems *unhappy* with his or her choice of a
subject; all will be relieved, however, when their *poems* have been
successfully completed.

WRITING APPLICATION B:
Replacing Drab Adjectives with Fresh, Lively Ones

You use adjectives constantly in your speech and writing to make nouns
and pronouns more definite. Adjectives tell what kind, which one, and
how many. Your responsibility to your reader is to replace the old worn-
out adjectives with fresh, sometimes startling ones. For example,

Gerard Manley Hopkins uses fresh, vivid adjectives to describe a falcon in his poem "The Windhover": ". . . *dapple-dawn-drawn* Falcon . . . how he rung upon the rein of the *wimpling* wing . . ."

Writing Assignment

Many writers write about meaningful experiences from their childhood. Select a childhood experience that had particular meaning for you. As you describe this experience, try to use fresh, lively adjectives.

THE VERB

1d. A *verb* is a word that expresses action or otherwise helps to make a statement.

All verbs help to make a statement. Some help to make a statement by expressing action. The action expressed may be physical, as in such verbs as *hit, play, move,* and *run,* or it may be mental, as in *think, know, imagine,* and *believe.*

Transitive and Intransitive Verbs

Action verbs may or may not take an *object*—a noun or pronoun that completes the action by showing *who* or *what* is affected by the action. Verbs that have an object are called *transitive.* The verbs in the following examples are transitive:

EXAMPLES   Winslow Homer **painted** seascapes. [*Seascapes* is the object of *painted.*]
The rain **lashed** the windows. [*Windows* is the object of *lashed.*]
My cousin **bought** a new car. [*Car* is the object of *bought.*]

Verbs that express action without objects are called *intransitive.*

EXAMPLES   Winslow Homer **excelled.**
The rain **fell.**
My cousin **drove.**

Although some action verbs are transitive only (*ignore, complete*) and some intransitive only (*arrive, exist*), most verbs in English can be either.

EXAMPLES　The chorus **sang** patriotic songs. [transitive]
　　　　　The chorus **sang**. [intransitive]
　　　　　The delegates **applauded** them. [transitive]
　　　　　The delegates **applauded**. [intransitive]

☞ NOTE　Most dictionaries group the meanings of verbs according to whether they are transitive (*v.t.* in most dictionaries) or intransitive (*v.i.*). Remembering the difference will help you to find readily the meaning you want.

Linking Verbs

Some verbs help to make a statement not by expressing action but by expressing a state or condition. These verbs link to the subject a noun, a pronoun, or an adjective that describes or identifies the subject. They are called *linking verbs*. The word that is linked to the subject is called a *subject complement*.

EXAMPLES　The author **is** our guest. [The subject complement *guest* refers to the subject *author*.]
　　　　　This **is** she. [*She* refers to the subject *this*.]
　　　　　She **looks** serious. [*Serious* refers to the subject *she*.]

The subject complement always refers to the subject of the linking verb. It may identify the subject, as in the first two examples, or describe the subject, as in the third one.

The most common linking verb is the verb *be*[1], which has the following forms: *am, is, are, was, were, be, being, been* (and all verb phrases ending in *be, being,* or *been,* such as *can be, is being,* and *could have been*). Other common linking verbs are listed below.

Common Linking Verbs

appear	grow	seem	stay
become	look	smell	taste
feel	remain	sound	

Many of the verbs in the preceding list can also be used as action verbs—that is, without a subject complement.

[1] The verb *be* can also be followed by certain adverbs and adverb phrases: We were *there;* the men were *at work.* In this situation, *be* is not considered a linking verb.

LINKING   The singer **appeared** nervous.
ACTION   The singer **appeared** on television.

In general, a verb is a linking verb if you can substitute for it some form of the verb *seem*.

EXAMPLES   The singer **appeared** [seemed] nervous.
The audience **looked** [seemed] sympathetic.
The singer gradually **grew** [seemed] more relaxed.

The Helping Verb and the Verb Phrase

A *verb phrase* is made up of a main verb and one or more *helping verbs* (sometimes called *auxiliary verbs*). Helping verbs are so called because they *help* the main verb to express action or make a statement. The helping verbs in the following phrases are printed in boldfaced type:

> **has** played   **will be** coming
> **should have** paid   **must have been** injured

In other words, a verb phrase is a verb of more than one word.

Common Helping Verbs

am	has	can (may) have
are	had	could (would, should) be
is	can	could (would, should) have
was	may	will (shall) have been
were	will (shall) be	might have
do	will (shall) have	might have been
did	has (had) been	must
have	can (may) be	must have
		must have been

The parts of a verb phrase may be separated from one another by words; i.e., the helping verb may be separated from the main verb.

EXAMPLES   **Did** you **see** Lorraine Hansberry's play?
We **have** not **seen** it yet.
I **will** eventually **write** for tickets.

EXERCISE 5. Identifying and Classifying Verbs and Verb Phrases.

Write in order the verbs and verb phrases in the following sentences, placing before each the number of the sentence in which it appears. After each verb, tell whether it is transitive, intransitive, or linking. You may use abbreviations: *v.t., v.i.,* or *l.v.* (linking verb). Be sure to list all words in a verb phrase.

1. The Statue of Liberty, which has become a major American landmark, may well be the best-known structure in the world.
2. It possesses a twofold magic: It symbolizes human liberty, and it unfailingly moves the imaginative visitor.
3. Moreover, it has never fallen down and has survived everything that wind and weather can throw at it.
4. Although Frederic-Auguste Bartholdi designed the statue, the supporting framework came from the drawing board of Alexandre-Gustave Eiffel, an engineering genius whose most famous work is the Eiffel Tower in Paris.
5. The statue is made of copper, with an intricate inner network that supports Liberty's somewhat awkward pose.
6. The statue itself was a gift from the people of France, but Americans were asked for contributions toward the construction of its pedestal.
7. In newspaper editorials, Joseph Pulitzer persuaded the American people that they needed this statue.
8. Seemingly they agreed, and in 1886 the Statue of Liberty was dedicated on what was then Bedloe's Island in New York Bay.
9. Bartholdi had used his mother's features for Liberty's face.
10. Those features have remained symbols of perseverance and quiet determination.

WRITING APPLICATION C:
Selecting Precise Verbs

Both grammatically and semantically, the verb is a vital part of the sentence. The particular verb you choose can transform a vague, imprecise meaning to a highly specific, keen idea. Notice the shades of meaning suggested by the following verb changes: He *talked—negotiated—chattered* for an hour.

Writing Assignment

A small incident that on the surface seems unimportant may eventually be quite significant. Write a journal entry describing such a recent event. Make a distinct effort to use fresh, specific verbs.

THE ADVERB

1e. An *adverb* **is a word used to modify a verb, an adjective, or another adverb.**

The adverb is used most commonly as the modifier of a verb. It may tell *how, when, where,* or *to what extent* (how often or how much) the action of the verb is done.

EXAMPLES   She reads **quickly.** [*Quickly* tells *how* she reads.]
She reads **early** and **late.** [*Early* and *late* tell *when* she reads.]
She reads **everywhere.** [*Everywhere* tells *where* she reads.]
She reads **continually.** [*Continually* tells *to what extent* she reads.]
She reads **frequently.** [*Frequently* tells *how often* she reads.]

Some adverbs, such as *really, actually, truly, indeed,* are used mostly for emphasis. Classify these adverbs as adverbs of extent.

EXAMPLES   Rosa can **really** skate. [*Really* emphasizes the fine quality of Rosa's skating.]
She can **actually** fly over the ice. [*Actually* emphasizes the fact that she can fly over the ice, which is apparently a surprise to the speaker.]
She is **truly** a fine skater. [*Truly* emphasizes the fact that she is a fine skater.]

An adverb may modify an adjective.

EXAMPLE   She is a **really** intense competitor. [*Really* modifies the adjective *intense,* telling to what extent she is competitive.]

An adverb may modify another adverb.

EXAMPLE   She skated **very** well. [The adverb *very* modifies the adverb *well,* telling how well she skated.]

☞ **NOTE**   The word *not* is classified as an adverb. Because it occurs so frequently, especially in contractions, you may ignore it in doing the exercises on parts of speech.

Nouns Used as Adverbs

Some nouns may be used adverbially.

My parents left **yesterday.**
I am joining them **tomorrow.**
We will return **Saturday.**

In identifying parts of speech, label nouns used in this way as adverbs.

EXERCISE 6. Identifying Adverbs and the Words They Modify.
On your paper, write in order the adverbs in the following sentences, placing before each the number of the sentence in which it appears. After each adverb, write the word or words it modifies, and state whether the adverb tells how, when, where, or to what extent.

1. Dr. Rosalyn Yalow is an American physicist who helped develop an extremely sensitive biological technique.
2. Radioimmunoassay is now used in laboratories here and abroad and can readily detect infinitesimal biological substances that had previously defied measurement.
3. In an essay, Dr. Yalow writes: "If you ever have a new idea, and it's really new, you have to expect that it will not be widely accepted immediately."
4. In other words, unlike Archimedes, scientists do not leap excitedly from the bath crying, "Eureka!"
5. Dr. Yalow and her colleague accidentally discovered radioimmunoassay while observing two patients.
6. They then carefully interpreted their observations and correctly arrived at their exciting discovery.
7. Although her collaborator was deceased, the Nobel Prize Committee promptly excepted its rule and awarded Dr. Yalow the undeniably prestigious Nobel Prize for Medicine.
8. Radioimmunoassay was an unquestionably important discovery; it soon became a scientifically sound tool for investigation in widely different areas of medicine.
9. According to Dr. Yalow, the technique was not quickly accepted because people ordinarily resist change.
10. She is convinced that progress cannot be obstructed forever and that eventually a highly original idea is accepted.

EXERCISE 7. Identifying the Parts of Speech of Words. Write the numbered, italicized words. After each word, tell what part of speech it is; then after each adjective or adverb, tell what word or words it modifies.

Lizards may be sleek, slender, and (1) *graceful;* or they may be (2) *fantastically* ugly, with grotesque (3) *horns,* spines, and frilly collars. (4) *They* have startling habits. They may snap off (5) *their* tails when they are seized. (6) *Some* may rear up and run (7) *away* on their hind legs. (8) *Certainly,* there is nothing (9) *commonplace* about lizards.

(10) *Warmer* portions of the earth (11) *have* the (12) *greatest* number and variety of lizards, but (13) *they* are (14) *also* found in temperate latitudes. There are about 125 (15) *different* kinds in the United States. (16) *One* of the most familiar is the little chameleon, also called the anolis. (17) *It* (18) *belongs* to the iguana family and is (19) *quite* different from the (20) *true* chameleon family of Africa. (21) *Both* families are interesting for their (22) *ability* to change color. The chameleons' (23) *large,* powerful relatives, the iguanas, (24) *dwell* in the jungles of Mexico, Central and South America, the (25) *West Indies,* and the Galápagos Islands.

THE PREPOSITION

1f. A *preposition* is a word used to show the relation of a noun or pronoun to some word in the sentence.

In the following sentences the prepositions are shown in boldfaced type. The words between which the prepositions show relationships are underscored.

> The first speaker **on** the program is my mother.
> Her cousin will teach **in** San Diego next year.
> The two **of** us edited the article **for** the magazine.

Object of a Preposition

A preposition always appears in a phrase, usually at the beginning (see Chapter 3, page 47). The noun or pronoun that comes at the end of a prepositional phrase is the *object* of the preposition that begins the phrase.

EXAMPLES   before **lunch**   at the **game**

Commonly Used Prepositions

about	between	over
above	beyond	past
across	but (meaning "except")	since
after	by	through
against	concerning	throughout
along	down	to
amid	during	toward
among	except	under
around	for	underneath
at	from	until
before	in	unto
behind	into	up
below	like	upon
beneath	of	with
beside	off	within
besides	on	without

A group of words may act as a preposition: *on account of, in spite of.*

EXERCISE 8. Writing Sentences with Prepositions. Write ten sentences, each containing a different one of the following prepositions. Draw a line under the phrase that each preposition introduces, and draw a circle around the object of each preposition.

1. above	3. below	5. during	7. into	9. until
2. against	4. by	6. for	8. of	10. up

THE CONJUNCTION

1g. A *conjunction* is a word that joins words or groups of words.

In the following sentences, the conjunctions are printed in boldfaced type; the words or groups of words that the conjunctions join are underscored.

Jim **and** his brother are backpacking in the Rockies.
The bear turned **and** lumbered off into the woods.
We can use a pickup truck **or** a jeep.
We called your office, **but** nobody answered.
She helped **both** Carrie **and** me with our applications.
They will **either** drive **or** go by bus.
The doctor will call back **after** he has studied the X-rays.
We left early **because** the roads were slippery.

There are three kinds of conjunctions: *coordinating* conjunctions, *correlative* conjunctions, and *subordinating* conjunctions.

Coordinating Conjunctions

and　　　but　　　or　　　nor　　　for　　　so　　　yet

as sometimes

Correlative conjunctions are always used in pairs.

EXAMPLES　These shirts are available **not only** in small sizes **but also** in outsizes.
The speech was **neither** eloquent **nor** convincing.

Correlative Conjunctions

either . . . or	not only . . . , but (also)
neither . . . nor	whether . . . or
both . . . and	

*$5.00
72.
×25
360
1440
18.00*

Subordinating conjunctions are used to begin subordinate clauses (see Chapter 4, pages 78–79), usually adverb clauses.

In the following sentences the subordinate clauses are printed in boldfaced type, and the subordinating conjunctions that introduce them are underscored.

This computer is even better **than we had anticipated.**
The sun had already set **when we reached Grand Canyon National Park.**
Let's go to a museum **unless you have other plans.**

A subordinating conjunction does not always come between the sentence parts that it joins. It may come at the beginning of the sentence.

If the price is right, I will buy your bicycle.
Since you can't help me, I will do it myself.

Commonly Used Subordinating Conjunctions[1]

after	before	provided	unless
although	how	since	until
as	if	than	when
as much as	in order that	that	where
because	inasmuch as	though	while

---

[1] Some of these words may be used as prepositions: *after, before, since, until;* others may be used as adverbs: *how, when, where. That* is often used as a relative pronoun.

EXERCISE 9. Identifying and Classifying Conjunctions.
Number your paper 1–10. After each number, write the conjunction(s) in the sentence. Then classify the conjunction(s) as coordinating, correlative, or subordinating.

1. The auto mechanic said the car might need either a valve job or a new engine.
2. "Before you submit your research paper, you will be required to submit an outline," stated Mr. Jackson.
3. I don't know whether I'll take physics or economics next year.
4. Taritha excels not only as a swimmer but also as a musician.
5. After I had read the novel *The Return of the Native,* I became a Thomas Hardy fan.
6. Workers in New York City pay city, state, and federal income taxes.
7. Because the Tsang family had installed a smoke detector in their home, their lives were saved.
8. Both Mike and Sue work at the same supermarket.
9. Are you going to the movies or not?
10. When I looked in my wallet, I was amazed to find five dollars I hadn't noticed.

THE INTERJECTION

1h. An *interjection* is a word that expresses emotion and has no grammatical relation to other words in the sentence.

EXAMPLES   Oh!   ·   My goodness!   Hurry!   Ah!   Ouch!

THE SAME WORD AS DIFFERENT PARTS OF SPEECH

You have already learned that there are many words in English which may be used as more than one part of speech. For example, *these* may be an adjective (these books) or a pronoun (I want these); *blue* may be an adjective (the blue car) or a noun (Blue is my favorite color); *Tuesday* may be a noun (Tuesday is my birthday) or an adverb (Come Tuesday). There are thousands of words like these that can be classified by part of speech only when you see them in sentences.

EXAMPLES   The **plant** was growing in a terrarium. [*Plant* names a living thing; it
is a noun.]
We usually **plant** tomatoes in the spring. [*Plant* expresses action; it
is a verb.]
Bacteria cause many **plant** diseases. [*Plant* modifies *diseases;* it is an
adjective.]

EXERCISE 10. Identifying the Parts of Speech of Words.   This
is an exercise in identifying the same word used as different parts of
speech. Write on your paper the italicized words in the following
sentences. After each word, write what part of speech it is. Be prepared
to explain your answers.

1. We found an unusual *bargain* on the *bargain* table.
2. We *left* the hotel, turned *left* onto Main Street, and found the
   theater, the second building on the *left*.
3. I must return my *library* books to the school *library* this afternoon.
4. Every holiday we *set* the table with our best *set* of china.
5. Everyone leaned *forward* as the *forward* made one dazzling play
   after the other.

REVIEW EXERCISE. Identifying the Parts of Speech of Words.
In a column on your paper, write in order the italicized words in the
following paragraphs. Carefully consider the use of each word, and
write after it what part of speech it is.

One summer (1) *night* (2) *several* years ago I was (3) *suddenly*
awakened (4) *by* the noisy clatter of garbage cans. I quickly ran (5)
outside (6) *where* I heard scratching noises from inside the large can (7)
that held (8) *most* of our garbage. I cautiously removed the lid and (9)
out popped a (10) *family* of raccoons.

Every night (11) *that* month those visitors of (12) *ours* (13) *returned*.
I piled (14) *heavy* bricks on top of the can (15) *and* attached all sorts of
clamps to the lid. (16) *No one* could open the can except the mother
raccoon.

Since then I have learned that (17) *one* raccoon myth is (18) *untrue:*
raccoons (19) *are* not (20) *fastidious*. True, they (21) *wash* their food
before they eat (22) *it*. The purpose, however, is not improved hygiene
(23) *but* improved taste. Moreover, raccoons will greedily eat (24)
everything in sight. (25) *Among* their favorite dishes are berries, small
birds, and, of course, garbage.

CHAPTER 1 REVIEW: POSTTEST 1

Identifying the Parts of Speech of Words. In a column on your paper, write the numbered words in the paragraphs below. Next to each word, write what part of speech it is.

(1) *"Wow!* Wait until you see your picture! It's great!" Every (2) *year* at high schools throughout America, excitement (3) *is* the overwhelming response of students as they get their (4) *first* glimpse of the yearbook. Also known as the annual (5) *or* classbook, the yearbook is published in May or June and is regarded (6) *by* seniors as a sure sign that graduation is no longer a dream but a reality. (7) *Although* the yearbook may seem to appear almost (8) *magically,* (9) *it* is the (10) *product* of a year's labor for a dedicated group of students.

Planning for the yearbook (11) *begins* in the spring: Editors are chosen, themes are decided, and budgets are set. When school opens for the fall semester, the staff moves at (12) *top* speed. A (13) *flurry* of activity marks September and October: Organize the senior section, cover sports and clubs, shoot candids (14) *of* students and faculty, run the advertising campaign. Frazzled (15) *but* wiser, the staff members meet their first deadline and move into the (16) *winter* months, during (17) *which* they must accomplish the bulk of their work. Deadlines come faster, meetings get longer, friendships (18) *grow* deeper. Then, (19) *usually* (20) *by* mid-March, work is finished. The waiting begins.

Finally, weeks and weeks later, (21) *someone* says, "The books are here!" (22) *As* the staff members (23) *turn* the pages of the new (24) *yearbooks,* (25) *they* take pride in a job well done.

CHAPTER 1 REVIEW: POSTTEST 2

Identifying the Parts of Speech of Words. Number your paper 1–25. Each of the following sentences contains at least one word of the kind specified before the sentence. Find these words and write them next to the appropriate number. Base your answers on the way each word is used in the sentence.

EXAMPLES 1. *Nouns* I have an interesting job.
      1. *job*
      2. *Verbs* Did they hunt and fish yesterday?
      2. *hunt, fish*

1. *Adjectives*   Dr. Samuel Johnson compiled the first dictionary in the English language.
2. *Pronouns*   Did Elizabeth's parents want her to try out for the squad?
3. *Prepositions*   My keys were sitting on the table, but I was convinced that I had lost them in the yard.
4. *Nouns*   Although she was blind and deaf, Helen Keller learned to communicate effectively with other people.
5. *Conjunctions*   At the end of the game, neither the coach nor the team members could account for the lopsided score.
6. *Verbs*   Because we thought we knew our way, we blithely ignored street signs and went miles out of our way.
7. *Adverbs*   Drivers in the Indianapolis 500 must stay continuously alert and be extremely skillful.
8. *Nouns*   How can you prepare yourself best for an effective interview?
9. *Adverbs*   The ads for the movie *Summer Mystery* ironically promised that the film would be "a chilling thriller."
10. *Conjunctions*   We wanted to take the trip, but we couldn't afford the plane fare.
11. *Prepositions*   John Updike's novels have met with success from critics and public alike.
12. *Pronouns*   Sharon said, "I'd like to arrive a day later, if you don't mind."
13. *Adjectives*   Mr. and Mrs. Lopez enjoyed the three years they spent in Vermont.
14. *Verbs*   After her successful concert, Heidi said that the praise of her teacher, Ms. Hawkins, was her greatest reward.
15. *Adverbs*   The evening air felt rather cool as we opened the door of the densely packed gymnasium and stepped outside.
16. *Prepositions*   A man with a full beard slipped a note to a sinister looking character during the first intermission of the show.
17. *Pronouns*   Anyone who knows anything about music would enjoy these songs.
18. *Nouns*   The ad for the movie promised "the intense emotional experience of both sorrow and joy."
19. *Verbs*   The detectives thought that there might have been a burglary when they noticed that the lock had scratch marks around it.

20. *Conjunctions* If either Ann or Maria calls, please say that I still have their notes and will return them tomorrow.
21. *Adjectives* This antique clock chimes a soulful note every hour.
22. *Adverbs* The chorus usually meets on Tuesday evenings, but sometimes very short rehearsals are held on Fridays.
23. *Pronouns* "This is one short story that you will really enjoy," Mr. Evers told us.
24. *Verbs* When I had finished the test, I handed Ms. Martello my paper, returned to my seat, and became calmer.
25. *Prepositions* At the start of the movie I wondered about the sound effects that came toward me from all sides.

CHAPTER 1 REVIEW: POSTTEST 3

Writing Sentences with Words Used as Specific Parts of Speech. Write twenty sentences according to the following guidelines. Use the dictionary for help.

1. Use *yesterday* as an adverb.
2. Use *today* as a noun.
3. Use *when* as a subordinating conjunction.
4. Use *though* as a subordinating conjunction.
5. Use *am* as a helping verb.
6. Use *sound* as a noun.
7. Use *work* as a noun.
8. Use *all* as a pronoun.
9. Use *fire* as a verb.
10. Use *leather* as an adjective.
11. Use *or* as a conjunction.
12. Use *terrific* as an interjection.
13. Use *with* as a preposition.
14. Use *either* as an adjective.
15. Use *hard* as an adverb.
16. Use *which* as a pronoun.
17. Use *both* as an adjective.
18. Use *seem* as a verb.
19. Use *fare* as a noun.
20. Use *remains* as a verb.

SUMMARY OF PARTS OF SPEECH

Rule	Part of Speech	Use	Examples
1a	noun	names	man, Iowa, corn, wealth, team
1b	pronoun	takes the place of a noun	you, we, herself, them, this, who
1c	adjective	modifies a noun or pronoun	red, large, two
1d	verb	shows action or helps to make a statement	is, does, have, wanted, seems
1e	adverb	modifies a verb, an adjective, or another adverb	rapidly, well, somewhat, too
1f	preposition	relates a noun or a pronoun to another word	into, below, from, of
1g	conjunction	joins words or groups of words	and, but, or, for, after, as, until
1h	interjection	shows strong feeling	Ow!

CHAPTER 2

The Parts of a Sentence

SUBJECTS, PREDICATES, COMPLEMENTS

In order to achieve an understanding of English sentences, you should be familiar with certain terms used in referring to the basic parts of the sentence. With only two terms—*subject* and *predicate*—you could begin to describe most sentences. After you had started, however, you would find out that you also need to know the name and function of some other important sentence elements: *object, predicate nominative,* and *predicate adjective,* to name only the most important. You have met all of these terms in previous English classes. To find out how well you remember them, take the following diagnostic test to see which terms, if any, you need to review.

DIAGNOSTIC TEST

Identifying Subjects, Predicates, and Complements. Number your paper 1–20. For each sentence, identify the italicized word using these abbreviations: *s.* (subject), *v.* (verb), *d.o.* (direct object), *i.o.* (indirect object), *p.n.* (predicate nominative), *p.a.* (predicate adjective).

EXAMPLE 1. Jim's *sarcasm* made him unpopular with the other members of the class.
1. *s.*

1. *Some* of your classmates will attend.
2. This experience taught me a valuable *lesson.*
3. Out of the darkness came a huge, lumbering *creature.*
4. To everyone's surprise, Jane and I *were* not late.
5. The water in the bay seemed very *cold.*
6. The only people in the water were the *children.*
7. This morning the mail carrier *left* this letter for you.
8. He gave *me* this one, too.
9. Lee Trevino is an excellent *golfer.*
10. Mechanics had just assembled and checked all *parts* of the motor.
11. Cheryll gave *me* her paper to proofread.
12. Yolanda is the *valedictorian* of her class.
13. Please put the *dishes* away.
14. Yesterday seemed rather *dreary.*
15. I *wrote* that essay in less than an hour.
16. Examples of religious music are *Gregorian chants, church hymns,* and *gospel singing.*
17. "There are only fifteen *problems* for tonight's assignment," said our math teacher with a wry smile.
18. Please do not omit any necessary *punctuation.*
19. Brian told *Arnie* some very funny stories.
20. In the middle of the road was a large *patch* of ice.

2a. A *sentence* **is a group of words expressing a complete thought.**

SENTENCE   The significance of the computer as a message carrier is often ignored.

NOT A SENTENCE   The significance of the computer as a message carrier

SENTENCE   A computer can instantly scan its entire library for documents of interest to the user.

NOT A SENTENCE   A computer instantly scanning its entire library for documents of interest to the user

SUBJECT AND PREDICATE

2b. **A sentence consists of two parts: the** *subject* **and** ~~the~~ *predicate.* **The** *subject* **of the sentence is the part about which something is being said. The** *predicate* **is the part that says something about the subject.**

SUBJECT	PREDICATE
Computers and electronic calculators	can solve problems quickly.
PREDICATE	SUBJECT
Ahead of us may lie	a universal computer language.

A subject and a predicate may consist of a single word or of many words. The whole subject is called the *complete subject;* the whole predicate, the *complete predicate.* However long a subject or predicate may be, it always has a core, or an essential part.

The Simple Subject

2c. The *simple subject* is the principal word or group of words in the subject.

EXAMPLES   The most distinguished participant at the ceremonies was the President. [subject: *The most distinguished participant at the ceremonies;* simple subject: *participant*]
The Memorial Coliseum in Los Angeles was filled to capacity. [subject: *The Memorial Coliseum in Los Angeles;* simple subject: *Memorial Coliseum*]

☞ NOTE   Throughout this book the term *subject,* when used in connection with the sentence, refers to the simple subject; the term *verb* refers to the simple predicate.

The Simple Predicate, or Verb

2d. The principal word or group of words in the predicate is called the *simple predicate,* or the *verb.*

EXAMPLE   The athletes were greeted with cheers. [predicate: *were greeted with cheers;* simple predicate: *were greeted*]

Compound Subjects and Verbs

2e. A *compound subject* consists of two or more subjects that are joined by a conjunction and have the same verb. The usual connecting words are *and* and *or.*

EXAMPLE   Jomo and Ahmed wore long, flowing robes. [compound subject:
           Jomo . . . Ahmed]

2f. A *compound verb* **consists of two or more verbs that are joined by a
conjunction and have the same subject.**

EXAMPLE   Mary McLeod Bethune founded Bethune-Cookman College and
           served twice as its president. [compound verb: *founded . . .
           served*]

How to Find the Subject of a Sentence

To find the subject of a sentence, first find the verb (the simple
predicate); then ask yourself the question "Who or what . . .?" For
instance, in the sentence "Outside the wall walked an armed guard,"
the verb is *walked.* Ask the question, "Who or what walked?" The
answer is *guard walked. Guard* is the subject of the sentence.

   In addition to this simple formula for locating the subject, here are
some other facts you should keep in mind:

   1. In sentences expressing a command or a request, the subject is
always *you,* even though the word *you* may not appear in the sentence.

(You) Proofread your report after typing it.
(You) Please submit a cover sheet with your report.

   2. The subject of a sentence is never in a prepositional phrase.

Neither of these books has an index. [verb: *has.* What has? *Neither. Neither*
is the subject. *Books* is not the subject. It is in the prepositional phrase *of
these books.*]
The rules of punctuation are sometimes frustrating. [verb: *are.* What are?
Rules. Rules is the subject. *Punctuation* is not the subject. It is in the
prepositional phrase *of punctuation.*]

   3. To find the subject in a question, turn the question into statement
form.

QUESTION   What subject did you choose for your speech?
STATEMENT   You did choose what subject for your speech? [subject: *you;* verb:
            did choose]

   4. *There* and *here* are not usually the subjects of a verb. Except in a
statement like the previous sentence, *there* and *here* are either adverbs
or expletives.

Here is your pencil. [verb: *is;* subject: *pencil.* In this sentence the word *here* is an adverb telling where.]
There are several good points in your argument. [verb: *are;* subject: *points.* In this use *there* is called an *expletive,* a word used to get the sentence started. The word *it* may also be used as an expletive: *It is senseless to leave.*]

EXERCISE 1. Identifying Subjects and Verbs. Number your paper 1–20. Write after the proper number the subject and the verb in each sentence. Underline subjects once and verbs twice. Be careful to include all parts of compound subjects and verbs, as well as all words in a verb phrase.

1. Researchers at Harvard and Stanford universities studied the exercise patterns of 17,000 subjects and reported the results.
2. Participants climbed stairs, walked, and engaged in sports.
3. Careful records of these activities were coupled with other information about height, weight, history of heart disease, etc.
4. Even mild exercise, according to this study, can be beneficial.
5. High blood pressure and cardiovascular disease have been blamed on the lack of physical fitness.
6. Now scientists from Harvard and Stanford urge regular exercise.
7. Even brisk walks four times a week may prevent serious diseases.
8. Until now no scientific proof had been offered of the link between exercise and fitness.
9. A research report from doctors in Dallas confirms the study.
10. Both the Harvard-Stanford report and the Dallas study were published in the *Journal of the American Medical Association.*
11. The Department of Medicine at the University of Oregon has found a link between weight lifting and cholesterol reduction.
12. The editor of the *Journal of the American Medical Association* considers these studies extremely important.
13. They may well connect physical fitness with prolonged life.
14. The real discovery of this research is the presence of cardiovascular disease in sedentary people.
15. For years physicians have been aware of this connection but have not always convinced their patients of it.

16. Uncertainty and even skepticism have existed as to the benefits of physical activity.
17. Will a direct relationship between fitness and life span become clearer in the minds of the sedentary?
18. Doctors can now point to these studies as proof of the beneficial effects of physical activity.
19. Carefully consider your own physical activities.
20. There will likely be some changes in your approach to physical fitness.

COMPLEMENTS

Some sentences express a complete thought by means of a subject and verb only.

S V   S V
She won.   The spectators cheered.

Most sentences, however, have in the predicate one word or more that completes the meaning of the subject and verb. These completing words are called *complements*.

She won	the **race.**
Someone sent	**me** a **plant.**
She is	the **mayor** of our town.
The ripest ones are	**those.**
They seem	**industrious.**
He called	**me overconfident.**
Who made	**you boss?**

☞ **NOTE** An adverb modifying the verb is not a complement. Only nouns, pronouns, and adjectives function as complements.

Dr. Ames is **here.** [The adverb *here* modifies the verb *is*. It is not a complement.]

Dr. Ames is an **internist**. [The noun *internist* is a complement.]
Dr. Ames is **brilliant**. [The adjective *brilliant* is a complement.]

Direct and Indirect Objects

Complements that receive or are affected by the action of the verb are called *objects*. They are of two kinds: the *direct object* and the *indirect object*.

2g. The *direct object* of the verb receives the action of the verb or shows the result of the action. It answers the question *What?* or *Whom?* after an action verb.

We drove **Jim** to the train station. [We drove *whom?*]
He was carrying a large **suitcase**. [He was carrying *what?*]

Except when it ends in *–self (myself, himself),* the object of a verb never refers to the same person or thing as the subject.

☞ **NOTE** The diagrams are included as an aid to those students who have already studied diagraming. No attempt is made in this book to teach diagraming or to give practice in diagraming. However, a review explanation may be appropriate. Sentence diagrams are "pictures" of the structure of a sentence—that is, they illustrate ways of placing the words of a sentence into a pattern, so that their functions can be more easily seen. On the main horizontal line the subject comes first, then a vertical line crossing the main line, then the verb. Between the verb and the direct object is a vertical line that does not cross the main line. Between the verb and a predicate adjective or a predicate nominative (see pages 37–38) is a similar line slanted to the left. The indirect object occupies a lower horizontal line joined to the verb by a slanted line. Single-word modifiers slant downward from the words they modify.

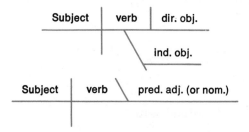

2h. The *indirect object* of the verb precedes the direct object and usually tells to whom or for whom the action of the verb is done.

If the word *to* or *for* is used, the noun or pronoun following it is part of a prepositional phrase; it is not an indirect object. Like subjects, objects of verbs are never part of a prepositional phrase.

> Mr. Bates promised me a job. [*Me* is an indirect object.]
> Mr. Bates promised a job to me. [*Me* is part of the phrase *to me*.]

EXAMPLES   He gave **us** his permission. [gave *to* us]

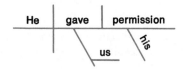

Bob made his **mother** a writing desk. [made *for* his mother]

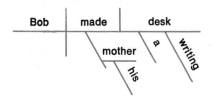

Objects of the verb may be compound.

> Mrs. Spiers praised the stage **crew** and the **cast**.

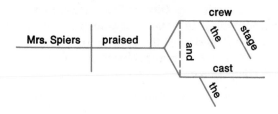

She gave **George** and **me** several suggestions.

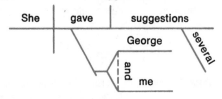

The Objective Complement

To complete their meaning, some action verbs require an additional complement following their objects. This additional complement is called an *objective complement* because it refers to the object; it may be a noun or an adjective.

> They elected Mary **chairwoman.** [The noun *chairwoman* refers to the direct object *Mary* and helps to complete the meaning of the verb *elected.* It is an objective complement.]

They	elected	Mary \ chairwoman

> You made her **angry.** [The adjective *angry* modifies the direct object *her* and helps to complete the meaning of the verb *made.* It is an objective complement.]

You	made	her \ angry

Only a few verbs meaning "make" or "consider" take an objective complement: *elect, appoint, name, choose, render, make, consider,* etc.

> The cat licked its paws **clean.** [*made* its paws clean]
> We painted my room **green.** [*made* my room green]
> I thought the joke **tasteless.** [*considered* the joke tasteless]

EXERCISE 2. Identifying Direct Objects, Indirect Objects, and Objective Complements.

Number your paper 1–10. Write after the proper number the objects of the verb or verbs in the sentence. After each object, write *i.o.* for indirect object, *d.o.* for direct object, or *o.c.* for objective complement.

1. Computers may have created the automobile revolution of the 1980's.

2. A spokesperson for the industry showed reporters several examples of computerized cars.
3. One car has a computer display for its speedometer and its turn signals.
4. Another makes trips a pleasure with computerized travel information.
5. Some cars have seven computers on board.
6. A voice synthesizer in one car warns the driver of drowsiness.
7. According to engineers, computers can give us an amazing amount of detailed and accurate information about a car.
8. Car computers are already making predictions about engine failure.
9. One computer even makes a car burglarproof.
10. On the negative side, some safety experts consider colorful computer panels a driving hazard.

Subject Complements

Complements that refer to (describe, explain, or identify) the subject are *subject complements*. There are two kinds: the *predicate nominative* and the *predicate adjective*.

Subject complements follow linking verbs only. The common linking verbs are the forms of the verb *be* (see page 14) and the following verbs: *become, seem, grow, appear, look, feel, smell, taste, remain, sound, stay*.

2i. A *predicate nominative* **is a noun or pronoun complement that refers to the same person or thing as the subject of the verb. It follows a linking verb.**

New York is our largest **city**. [*City* refers to the subject *New York*.]

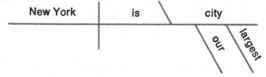

My favorite authors are **Austen** and **she**. [Compound predicate nominative: *Austen* and *she* refer to the same people as the subject *authors*.]

2j. A *predicate adjective* **is an adjective complement that modifies the subject of the verb. It follows a linking verb.**

This book is **dull**. [The predicate adjective *dull* modifies the subject *book*.]

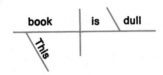

His speech seemed **repetitious** and **tiresome**. [Compound predicate adjective modifying the subject *speech*.]

In the normal order of an English sentence, complements follow the verb. However, a complement may precede the verb.

This **song** he wrote in 1980. [*Song* is the direct object of the verb *wrote*.]
Fortunate are those who can learn from their mistakes. [*Fortunate* is a predicate adjective modifying the subject *those*.]

EXERCISE 3. Identifying Predicate Nominatives and Predicate Adjectives. Number your paper 1–20. After the proper number, write any predicate nominatives or predicate adjectives in the sentence; identify each complement with the abbreviation *p.n.* or *p.a.* Some sentences contain more than one complement.

1. Her nominating speech was both effective and convincing.
2. In 1817, Monroe became the fourth U.S. President from the state of Virginia.
3. That story sounds suspicious to me.
4. Iago grew increasingly more ruthless and cunning.
5. The police officer's account of the accidents seems plausible.
6. The cats appeared nervous during the storm.
7. Pablo Casals was not only a famous cellist but also a conductor.
8. The spray tasted salty, and the wind felt cold.
9. In my opinion Pip's anonymous benefactor is either Miss Havisham or he.
10. The bite of a tarantula is not usually fatal, but it can be painful.
11. I sometimes feel jumpy before a game.
12. A college degree can become a lifelong asset.
13. The practice session will be long and strenuous.

14. Thiamin is an essential vitamin.
15. This week has been unusually chilly and rainy.
16. The rooms in the restored guardhouse smelled musty.
17. This is my new address.
18. Thomas Edison was a brilliant inventor.
19. Those strawberries look ripe and delicious.
20. That reflector was once the most powerful telescope in the world.

REVIEW EXERCISE. Identifying Subjects, Verbs, and Complements. Number your paper 1–20. Write after the proper number the subject, the verb, and any complements in the sentence. After each complement, tell what kind it is, using abbreviations as follows: direct object, *d.o.;* indirect object, *i.o.;* predicate nominative, *p.n.;* predicate adjective, *p.a.;* objective complement, *o.c.*

1. Mark Twain is the pseudonym of the American writer Samuel Langhorne Clemens.
2. He became famous for his stories about the Mississippi.
3. As the result of his own days as a riverboat pilot, Twain wrote about the river with authority.
4. His adventurous life was almost unbelievably dramatic.
5. For him both success and failure were equally spectacular.
6. Through his writings he has given us homespun pictures of America and some exaggerated tales of life in the mining camps of the West.
7. At his death in 1910, many critics considered him the most prominent American writer of his generation.
8. Everyone eagerly awaited the eventual publication of his autobiography.
9. Twain, however, had some curious notions about his life story.
10. Over the years those ideas became even more curious.
11. He once told William Dean Howells the scheme of his autobiography.
12. That scheme was apparently a haphazard one.
13. At first Twain composed sections by hand and ended with cryptic notations.
14. In 1885 he dictated a series of recollections and of entertaining impressions of his meetings with General Grant.

15. Five years later he wrote some memories of his mother.
16. Not until 1898 did he write the memorable chapter about the early days on his uncle's farm.
17. As a result, the first published autobiographies were fragmentary and imperfect.
18. In 1959 Charles Neider added 40,000 words of text to the earlier versions.
19. He painstakingly arranged events in their proper sequence.
20. The result is a magnificent document of value as both literature and entertainment.

WRITING APPLICATION:
Using Complete Sentences in Your Writing

If you are always predictable in your writing, you might also be uninteresting. One way to add variety is to experiment with the placement of subjects and verbs.

EXAMPLE   Deep within the misty darkness, swaying and undulating around a steaming pot, were three filthy witches. (The verb *were* and the subject *witches* are at the end of the sentence.)

Writing Assignment

In literature, an *epiphany* is a sudden realization. Experiencing an epiphany is like turning a light on in a darkened room. Suddenly, you see what you didn't see before, perhaps about your own strengths and weaknesses. Write about an epiphany—either yours, a friend's, or a fictional character's. At some point, vary subject and verb placement.

CHAPTER 2 REVIEW: POSTTEST 1

Identifying Subjects, Verbs, and Complements.   Number your paper 1–25. For each sentence, identify the italicized word using one of the following abbreviations: *s.* (subject), *v.* (verb), *d.o.* (direct object), *i.o.* (indirect object), *p.n.* (predicate nominative), or *p.a.* (predicate adjective).

EXAMPLE   1. Studying the map carefully, we *decided* on the shortest route.
            1. *v.*

1. Terry is *captain* of the gymnastics team.
2. *Robert Frost* became famous as a poet.
3. The desk *was moved* to a corner of the room.
4. My little sister has an interesting coin *collection*.
5. Was much *damage* done by the tornado?
6. The directions on the package were *clear*.
7. Rob gave *her* a smile.
8. The home economics class hosted a *luncheon* for their parents.
9. I *read* the newspaper for news of sales and bargains.
10. Margaret received a ten-speed *bicycle* for her birthday.
11. My sister had successful eye *surgery* last year.
12. The factory owner gave his *employees* a raise in pay.
13. Each spring, millions of people *watch* the Academy Awards on television.
14. The parents of the award winner felt *proud*.
15. One of the most valuable experiences of my life was *scouting*.
16. Did you give *Ming Chin* directions to the beach?
17. Abraham Lincoln is *one* of the most beloved American Presidents.
18. My grandfather got a *part* in an amateur play.
19. After work, will *you* call me so that we can make plans?
20. I felt *energetic* after my exercise workout.
21. Eventually Margo became a well-known *musician*.
22. *Place* the disk in the disk drive first.
23. Leroy started his *business* in Kansas.
24. My mother is *taller* than any of her four sisters.
25. Without warning, out jumped a *mouse*!

CHAPTER 2 REVIEW: POSTTEST 2

Identifying Subjects, Verbs, and Complements.   Number your paper 1–25. Next to the appropriate number, identify the part of the sentence indicated in italics.

EXAMPLES   1. *Subject*   After school, I am going to work.
            1. *I*

            2. *Verb*   Who succeeded Harry Truman as President?
            2. *succeeded*

1. *Predicate nominative*   The Koran is the sacred scripture of the Muslim faith.
2. *Subject*   Dawn is planning a career in diplomacy.
3. *Direct object*   The college offered special courses for high-school seniors.
4. *Verb*   A new area of research involves study of the right and left halves of the human brain.
5. *Indirect object*   The mayor awarded firefighter Ed Jenkins a medal of honor for bravery.
6. *Predicate adjective*   Abbott and Costello, famous movie comedians of the forties and fifties, were very popular.
7. *Subject*   In her spare time, Janell loves to read.
8. *Direct object*   Our softball team played an exciting game.
9. *Predicate nominative*   Vast areas of wilderness are part of Alaska's scenic beauty.
10. *Subject*   Most major cities in the United States have at least one symphony orchestra.
11. *Verb*   President Franklin D. Roosevelt introduced many reforms during the 1930's.
12. *Direct object*   Attorney Rosemary Jackson explained the process of jury selection to our social studies class.
13. *Subject*   An electrical power failure disrupted everyone's day.
14. *Predicate adjective*   Tina looked rather calm during the debate.
15. *Indirect object*   In auto class, Ms. Dodd gave us directions for inspecting brake linings.
16. *Verb*   A revolution is occurring in communications technology.
17. *Predicate nominative*   Managing money is a challenging task.
18. *Indirect object*   Our local newspaper gave Senator Cramer praise for her work on behalf of education.
19. *Direct object*   Several students from our school will visit England next summer.
20. *Verb*   The campers discovered fresh deer tracks near their campsite.
21. *Predicate adjective*   Courage under stress is essential for a competitive athlete.

22. *Subject* John Irving and Alice Walker are popular American novelists.
23. *Predicate adjective* The Indiana dunes on the southern shore of Lake Michigan are surprisingly similar to the Cape Cod dunes in Massachusetts.
24. *Direct object* Flaming reds and oranges marked the sunset.
25. *Verb* The audience cheered and applauded the cast during three curtain calls.

CHAPTER 2 REVIEW: POSTTEST 3

Writing Sentences. Write your own sentences, one of each of the following kinds, and underline the subjects and verbs.

1. A sentence with a compound subject and a compound verb
2. A sentence with a direct object and an indirect object
3. A sentence with a direct object and an objective complement
4. A sentence with a predicate nominative
5. A sentence with a predicate adjective

SUMMARY OF SENTENCE PATTERNS

You have learned that every sentence has two basic parts—subject and predicate. Within the subject there is a simple subject, commonly called the subject; within the predicate there is a simple predicate, commonly called the verb. The pattern of some sentences consists of subject and verb only.

$$\overset{\text{S}}{\text{Artists}} \quad \overset{\text{V}}{\text{paint.}}$$

Modifiers may be added to the subject and verb without changing the basic pattern of such a sentence.

$$\overset{\text{S}}{\text{Several artists}} \text{ from the neighborhood Senior Citizen Center } \overset{\text{V}}{\text{paint}} \text{ in the nearby mountains.}$$

You have learned also that certain additions to the predicate create other sentence patterns. These additions are complements, which complete the meaning begun by the subject and verb. The different kinds of complements produce the different sentence patterns. The seven common sentence patterns are as follows:

```
   S        V
Artists    paint.
```

```
   S        V          D.O.
Artists    paint    landscapes.
```

```
   S        V      I.O.       D.O.
  She      gave    them     supplies.
```

```
   S        V          D.O.     OBJ.COMP.(ADJ.)
 These     made     the artists     happy.
```

```
   S        V         D.O.    OBJ.COMP.(NOUN)
 They      named      her     resident artist.
```

```
   S       V                    P.N.
  She      is     their resident artist.
```

```
   S        V         P.A.
  She      seems    talented.
```

CHAPTER 3

The Phrase

KINDS OF PHRASES AND THEIR FUNCTIONS

Words in a sentence act not only individually but also in groups. The grouped words act together as a unit that may function as a modifier, a subject, a verb, an object, or a predicate nominative. The most common group of related words is the phrase. In Chapter 1 you learned about the verb phrase, which is a verb of more than one word (*is coming, might have been*). This chapter provides a review of the makeup and function in the sentence of other kinds of phrases.

DIAGNOSTIC TEST

Identifying Phrases.   Number your paper 1–20. Next to each number, identify the kind of phrase italicized in each of the following sentences. Write *adj.* for a prepositional phrase used as an adjective, *adv.* for a prepositional phrase used as an adverb, *part.* for a participial phrase, *ger.* for a gerund phrase, *inf.* for an infinitive phrase, or *appos.* for an appositive phrase. Do not identify separately any phrases within a larger italicized phrase.

EXAMPLE   1. We had a tossed salad *with fresh tomatoes* at lunch.
　　　　　　1. *adj.*

　1. Marnie made an appointment *to audition for a part in the play.*

2. For a split second, the football sat balanced *on the goal post bar.*
3. Dr. Martin, *the pediatrician,* has advertised for a receptionist.
4. *Sitting in the sun for three hours* gave Rebecca a headache.
5. *Smiling broadly,* the television commentator praised the work of the 4–H Club.
6. I saw the beautiful bouquet *of roses* on the table.
7. William Golding, *the British novelist* who wrote Lord of the Flies, was awarded the Nobel Prize for literature in 1983.
8. The members of the biology class had mixed emotions about *dissecting the frog.*
9. Kai's ambition is *to drive a tractor-trailer truck.*
10. Shakespeare's plays are performed *in numerous languages* throughout the world.
11. *Moving their cars to the right,* the drivers allowed the ambulance to pass quickly.
12. Marianne and Fred intend *to run for class offices.*
13. *Filled with joy and happiness,* the bride and groom greeted their family and friends after the wedding ceremony.
14. Two clowns *from the circus* gave a benefit performance at the Municipal Theater.
15. My friends *Alecca and Leon* sent me a postcard from Rome, the capital of Italy.
16. You can get help in an emergency by *dialing the operator.*
17. Donya wants to ride her bicycle from Washington, D.C., *to Seattle, Washington.*
18. The public library is a valuable resource for anyone who wants *to do research.*
19. My social studies teacher recommended a book *about the Industrial Revolution.*
20. We watched three experts *discussing the economy on television.*

3a. A *phrase* is a group of words not containing a verb and its subject. A phrase is used as a single part of speech.

Five kinds of phrases are explained on the following pages: *prepositional phrases, participial phrases, gerund phrases, infinitive phrases,* and *appositive phrases.*

THE PREPOSITIONAL PHRASE

3b. A *prepositional phrase* is a group of words beginning with a preposition and usually ending with a noun or pronoun.

for Lisa and you	**in** the park
after the game	**to** the store

The noun or pronoun that concludes the prepositional phrase is the object of the preposition that begins the phrase.

on the **way**	from **Angela** and **me**
with a **shout**	for **Grandmother** or **Grandfather**

Prepositional phrases are usually used as modifiers—as adjectives or adverbs. Occasionally, a prepositional phrase is used as a noun:

Before lunch will be convenient. [The prepositional phrase is the subject of the sentence; it is used as a noun.]

The Adjective Phrase

3c. An *adjective phrase* is a prepositional phrase that modifies a noun or a pronoun.

Tucson has been the locale **of many Westerns.**

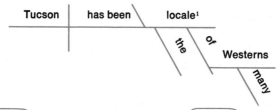

Tourists **from the East** visit the old frontier towns **in the West.**

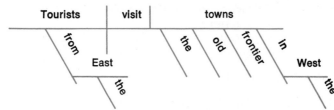

[1] In a diagram the preposition that begins the phrase is placed on a line slanting downward from the word modified. The object of the preposition is placed on a horizontal line extending to the right from the line with the preposition. Single-word modifiers are diagramed in the usual way.

Many **of the tourists** like historical places.

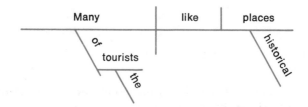

EXERCISE 1. Identifying Adjective Phrases and the Words They Modify. After each sentence number, list the adjective phrases in the sentence. Next to each phrase, write the noun modified.

1. The rivers of New Guinea are now popular areas for rafting enthusiasts.
2. A series of nearly continuous rapids crosses jungles of primeval beauty.
3. Twenty-eight major rapids on the Tua River make it a course for rafters with experience and courage.
4. There are butterflies with brilliant colors, and the metallic whine of cicadas almost drowns out the roar of the river.
5. The banks are a chaos of tumbled boulders and uprooted trees.

The Adverb Phrase

3d. An *adverb phrase* **is a prepositional phrase that modifies a verb, an adjective, or another adverb.**

The following sentences show the ways in which an adverb phrase can modify a verb.

Tina exercises **with care.** [*how* Tina exercises]
She exercises **before a meet.** [*when* she exercises]
She exercises **in the gym.** [*where* she exercises]
She exercises **for months.** [*to what extent* she exercises]
She exercises **for her health.** [*why* she exercises]

Note the following diagram.

In the following sentence, the adverb phrase modifies a predicate adjective.

He was true to his word.

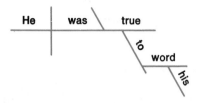

The following sentence illustrates the placement of an adverb phrase that modifies an adverb.

He threw the ball far to the left.

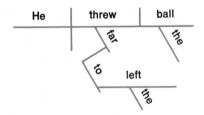

EXERCISE 2. Identifying Adverb Phrases and the Words They Modify.   Number your paper 1–10. After the appropriate number, list the adverb phrases in the sentence. After each phrase, write the word(s) the phrase modifies.

1. Nothing in Dutch memory compares with the flood of February 1953.
2. Some 50,000 houses were swept out to sea; 70,000 people were evacuated from their homes.
3. As a result of that deluge, engineers are erecting a massive coastal barrier.
4. Work on the barrier was not begun until 1978 but should be completed by 1990.
5. By that time this masterpiece of engineering will have cost Dutch taxpayers nearly three billion dollars.
6. From a distance the odd-looking structures resemble skyscrapers.
7. They are located near the Dutch town of Zierikzee and symbolize Holland's centuries-old struggle against the sea.

8. The barriers will be positioned between two islands and will reach from shore to shore.
9. These massive pillars were constructed in dry dock and will be moved into place by a special ship.
10. With the pillars firmly in place, Holland may remain safe from the sea forever.

EXERCISE 3. Writing Sentences with Adjective and Adverb Phrases. Demonstrate your understanding of the way a prepositional phrase functions as an adjective or adverb by writing complete sentences as indicated.

EXAMPLE 1. with great fluency [Use as an adverb phrase.]
1. *Hilda speaks English with great fluency.*

1. with unexpected emotion [Use as an adverb phrase.]
2. on the speaker's platform [Use as an adjective phrase.]
3. for her contribution [Use as an adverb phrase.]
4. without preparation [Use as an adverb phrase.]
5. with extraordinary talent [Use as an adjective phrase.]
6. of unusual bravery [Use as an adjective phrase.]
7. about art [Use as an adjective phrase.]
8. by hard work [Use as an adverb phrase.]
9. of the story [Use as an adjective phrase.]
10. after the election [Use as an adverb phrase.]

PHRASES CONTAINING VERBALS

Less common than the prepositional phrase but still very useful to a writer are verbal phrases: the *participial phrase,* the *gerund phrase,* and the *infinitive phrase.* These phrases are called verbal phrases because the most important word in them is a verbal. Verbals are so called because they are formed from verbs and, in some respects, act like verbs. Verbals may express action; they may have modifiers; and they may be followed by complements. In one important respect, however, verbals are not like verbs; verbals do not function as verbs in a sentence. They function as nouns, as adjectives, or as adverbs.

Before you can understand verbal phrases, you must understand the verbals on which the phrases are based. On the following pages you will find an explanation of each kind of verbal, followed by a discussion of the verbal as it is most commonly used—in a phrase.

The Participle and the Participial Phrase

3e. A *participle* is a verb form that can be used as an adjective.

The rapidly **developing** storm kept small boats in port.
Developing rapidly, the storm kept small boats in port.
The storm, **developing** rapidly, kept small boats in port.

In these sentences, *developing,* which is formed from the verb *develop,* is used as an adjective, modifying the noun *storm.*

In the following sentence the participle *crying,* formed from the verb *cry,* is used as an adjective, modifying the pronoun *him.*

I found him **crying.**

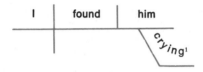

There are two kinds of participles: *present participles* and *past participles.* A present participle, like those in the preceding examples, ends in *–ing.* A past participle may end in *–ed, –d, –t, –en,* or *–n:* ask*ed,* sav*ed,* deal*t,* eat*en,* see*n.*

PRESENT PARTICIPLE   We watched the puppies **playing.**
PAST PARTICIPLE   The puppies, **exhausted,** collapsed in the grass.

Although participles are formed from verbs, they are not used alone as verbs. A participle may, however, be used with a helping verb to form a verb phrase.

PARTICIPLE   The **barking** dogs followed the colts into the barn. [**Barking** modifies **dogs.**]
VERB PHRASE   The dogs **were barking** excitedly. [The verb phrase *were barking* consists of the helping verb *were* plus the present participle *barking.*]

When participles are used in verb phrases, they are considered part of the verb and are not considered adjectives.

---

[1] In a diagram the participle is written on a bent line drawn downward from the word the participle modifies.

3f. A *participial phrase* is a phrase containing a participle and any complements or modifiers it may have.[1]

Removing his coat, Jack rushed to the river bank. [The participial phrase is made up of the participle *removing* and the complement *coat,* which is the direct object of *removing.* Like verbs, participles may take an object.]

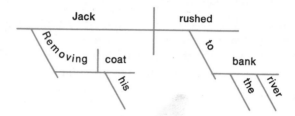

Hesitating there for a moment, he quickly grasped the situation. [The participial phrase is made up of the participle *hesitating* plus its modifiers—the adverb *there* and the adverb phrase *for a moment.*]

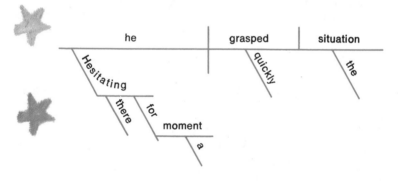

The participle usually introduces the phrase, and the entire phrase acts as an adjective to modify a noun or pronoun.

We saw Carl Lewis **receiving his first gold medal** in the 1984 Olympics.

Swaying hypnotically, the snake raised its head.

Spread with white linen, the table glowed in the candlelight.

[1] For work on the participial phrase as a sentence fragment, see pages 272–73. For exercises on the dangling participle, see pages 305–307.

EXERCISE 4. Identifying Participial Phrases and the Words They Modify. Write on your paper the participial phrases in the following sentences. Be sure to include all complements and modifiers. Before each phrase, write the number of the sentence in which it appears. After each phrase, write the word the phrase modifies.

1. High-school graduates <u>replying to a questionnaire about their college courses</u> often mention freshman English as the course giving them the most trouble.
2. Facing college standards, the graduates realize that they did not work hard enough on the themes assigned in high school.
3. Statistics reported by the National Education Association revealed that the vast majority of American colleges offer remedial English classes emphasizing composition.
4. Handicapped by their writing deficiencies, graduates seeking employment or advancement in their occupations are often denied desirable opportunities.
5. Recognizing the importance of practice, teachers of composition, imitating the athletic coach, conduct regular practice sessions.

WRITING APPLICATION A:
Recognizing the Value of Participial Phrases

Participial phrases contribute to sentence variety while supplying pertinent information for the reader.

EXAMPLE   *Reflecting a deep love of Ireland,* the poems of William Butler Yeats were awarded the Nobel Prize.

Writing Assignment

What does the word *heroic* mean to you? Are there any modern American heroes? Does a hero have to be someone famous, rich, or prominent, or can it be an ordinary person? Define what you think a hero is, and then illustrate this definition with an example. Use at least three participial phrases. Underline these phrases.

REVIEW EXERCISE A. Identifying Participial Phrases, Adjective Phrases, and Adverb Phrases. For each of the following sentences, write the numbered and italicized phrases in order on your paper. Place each phrase and its number on a separate line. After each phrase, write the word it modifies, and tell whether it is a *participial* phrase, an *adjective* prepositional phrase, or an *adverb* prepositional phrase. Do not list separately the prepositional phrase within a larger italicized phrase.

EXAMPLE   (1) *Living far from the city,* I developed an interest (2) *in nature* (3) *at an early age.*
   1. *Living far from the city, I, participial*
   2. *in nature, interest, adjective*
   3. *at an early age, developed, adverb*

a. (1) *Having studied hard,* Karen walked rapidly (2) *to school,* confident that she would do well on her test (3) *in chemistry.*

b. (4) *By next week* all of the students (5) *trying out for the soccer team* will have heard (6) *from the coach or his assistant.*

c. Those (7) *going on the field trip in the morning* will meet (8) *either at Debbie's house at eight-thirty or at the school at nine o'clock.*

d. Today's newspaper, (9) *printed last night,* made no mention (10) *of this morning's traffic tie-up.*

e. Many (11) *of the articles* (12) *written for a newspaper* are based (13) *on news-wire reports.*

f. (14) *Annoyed by the mosquitoes,* Mr. Sims, (15) *slapping at his neck and face,* went (16) *into his house* (17) *for a while.*

g. (18) *Rinsed with hot water,* the dishes were stacked in the sink, (19) *waiting to be washed.*

h. The gift (20) *given to our principal, Mrs. Scott,* was a necklace (21) *made of silver and turquoise.*

i. (22) *Addressing her audience,* the principal spoke words (23) *of encouragement.*

j. At the end of the speech we heard some people (24) *clapping politely in the front rows* and others (25) *cheering hoarsely from the balcony.*

The Gerund and Gerund Phrase

3g. A *gerund* is a verb form ending in *–ing* that is used as a noun.

Walking is healthful exercise. [**Walking** is formed from the verb *walk* and, as the subject of the sentence, is used as a noun.]

A gerund is a verbal noun. It may be used in any way that a noun may be used.

Good **writing** comes from much practice. [gerund used as subject]

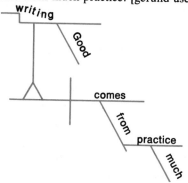

They do not appreciate my **singing.** [gerund used as object of verb]

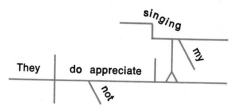

By **studying** you can pass the course. [gerund used as object of a preposition]

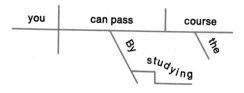

3h. A *gerund phrase* is a phrase consisting of a gerund and any complements or modifiers it may have.

Carrying coals to Newcastle is a traditional example of the unnecessary. [The gerund *Carrying* has *coals* as its direct object and is modified by the adverb phrase *to Newcastle.*]

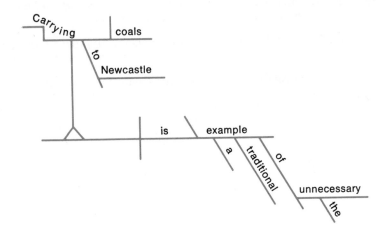

Like the gerund alone, the gerund phrase may be used in any way that a noun may be used.

> **Writing that letter** was a good idea. [gerund phrase as subject]
> My cousin enjoys **working as a lifeguard.** [gerund phrase as direct object]
> We were fined for **parking there.** [gerund phrase as object of preposition]
> Her most publicized achievement was **winning three gold medals.** [gerund phrase as predicate nominative]

EXERCISE 5. Identifying Gerund Phrases and Their Functions.

Number your paper 1–10. For each sentence, identify the gerund phrase and write it next to the appropriate number. Then identify its function as subject, predicate nominative, direct object, indirect object, or object of a preposition.

EXAMPLE   1. Learning how to type is one of the most practical things I have
   ever done.
   1. Learning how to type—subject

1. Solving crossword puzzles is one of Geraldo's favorite pastimes.
2. Sylvia's method of making decisions reveals a great deal about her personality.
3. My grandparents enjoy walking briskly.
4. "In making any changes, please notify our secretary, Ms. Erikson," said Ms. Hanley.

5. Producing a movie for Mr. Hisoka's cinematography course requires the ability to organize and communicate.
6. Ms. Sanapaw finished writing her paper.
7. Gaining the vote for women was the goal of Susan B. Anthony's lifework.
8. One of the most interesting characteristics of bees is their dancing to communicate the location of distant food sources.
9. Hector earns money on the weekends by giving guitar lessons.
10. My brother's singing in the shower adds mirth and music to our morning routine.

WRITING APPLICATION B:
Using Gerund Phrases in Describing a Process

A gerund phrase is a phrase consisting of a gerund and any complements or modifiers it may have. Gerund phrases are particularly useful in describing a process because a process involves action.

EXAMPLE You can improve your vocabulary by *keeping a notebook, writing down new words, and making an effort to use these words.* (The gerunds *keeping, writing,* and *making* introduce three gerund phrases.)

Writing Assignment

Jot down the steps a person should follow to complete a process you are familiar with. Plan to use gerund phrases in the topic sentence. Write the process. Underline your gerund phrases.

The Infinitive and the Infinitive Phrase

3i. An *infinitive* is a verb form, usually preceded by *to,* that can be used as a noun or a modifier.

to study   to write   to hope   to be

An infinitive is generally used as a noun, but it may also be used as an adjective or an adverb.

The infinitive used as a noun:

> **To leave** would be rude. [infinitive as subject]
> No one wants **to stay.** [infinitive as direct object]
> Her goal is **to win.** [infinitive as predicate nominative]

The infinitive used as an adjective:

> She is the candidate **to watch.** [The infinitive modifies *candidate.*]

The infinitive used as an adverb:

> We came **to cheer.** [The infinitive modifies the verb *came.*]

☞ **NOTE** Do not confuse the infinitive, a verbal of which *to* is a part, with a prepositional phrase beginning with *to,* which consists of *to* plus a noun or pronoun.

INFINITIVES	PREPOSITIONAL PHRASES
to go	to them
to sleep	to bed

The word *to,* called the sign of the infinitive, is sometimes omitted.

The clowns made her [to] **laugh.**
Help me [to] **clean** the car.

3j. An *infinitive phrase* **consists of an infinitive and any complements or modifiers it may have.**[1]

> They promised **to return soon.** [*Soon* is an adverb modifying the infinitive *to return.*]
> We have time **to walk to the concert.** [The prepositional phrase *to the concert* modifies the infinitive *to walk.*]
> I saved enough money **to buy a car.** [*Car* is the object of *to buy.*]

Like infinitives alone, infinitive phrases can be used as nouns or as modifiers.

> We tried **to reason with her.** [The infinitive phrase *to reason with her* is the object of the verb *tried.*]

[1] For exercises on the use of the infinitive phrase to reduce wordiness, see pages 323–29.

To save money became her obsession. [*To save money* is the subject of the sentence.]

There must be a way **to solve this problem.** [The infinitive phrase modifies the noun *way.*]

I am too busy **to go to the movies tonight.** [The infinitive phrase modifies the adjective *busy.*]

His plan is **to go to college for two years.** [The infinitive phrase is a predicate nominative, referring back to *plan.*]

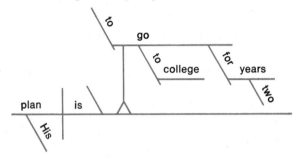

The Infinitive Clause

Unlike other verbals, an infinitive may have a subject as well as complements and modifiers.

Everyone expected **Gina to win the nomination.** [*Gina* is the subject of the infinitive *to win.*]

We asked **her to lead the discussion.** [*Her* is the subject of the infinitive *to lead.*]

We believe **the winner to be Andrew.** [*Winner* is the subject of the infinitive *to be; Andrew* is a predicate nominative referring back to *winner.*]

I found **it to be difficult.** [*It* is the subject of the infinitive *to be; difficult* is a predicate adjective referring back to *it.*]

When an infinitive has a subject, as in the preceding examples, the construction is called an *infinitive clause.* Notice that the subject of an infinitive is in the objective case.[1]

EXERCISE 6. Identifying Infinitive Phrases and Their Functions. Number your paper 1–10. Identify the infinitive phrases in the following sentences and indicate whether the phrase is used as a noun, an adjective, or an adverb. If the phrase is used as a noun, identify its function as the subject, direct object, predicate nominative, or object of a preposition.

[1] For rules concerning the use of the objective case, see pages 161–63.

EXAMPLE   1. I like to compose music for the guitar.
          1. to compose music for the guitar, noun, direct object

1. To win an Olympic gold medal is the dream of every member of the women's ski team.
2. The candidate had the courage to speak honestly on a controversial issue.
3. We went to Florence, Italy, to see Michelangelo's statue, 'the *David*.
4. The Key and Keyette Clubs try to work together on school service projects.
5. Martin Luther King's dream was that all people should be free to exercise their human rights.
6. Louis Pasteur experimented for years to discover a method for preventing rabies.
7. The ability to speak distinctly is an advantage in job interviews.
8. To open the box required a hammer and a crowbar.
9. Alana's hobby is to spend hours each day developing original computer programs.
10. Marvella has always wanted to learn about horseback riding.

REVIEW EXERCISE B. Identifying Prepositional, Participial, Gerund, and Infinitive Phrases.   Number your paper 1–20. In the following sentences most prepositional, participial, gerund, and infinitive phrases are numbered and italicized. Study the entire phrase, and after the corresponding number on your paper, write what kind of phrase it is. If it is a prepositional phrase, tell whether it is an adjective phrase or an adverb phrase. Do not identify separately the prepositional phrase within a larger italicized phrase.

a. (1) *Having read several poems by Robert Frost,* I suddenly saw the difference between (2) *enjoying prose and enjoying poetry.*
b. (3) *Reading poetry* does not require the same kind (4) *of skill* as reading prose.
c. Inexperienced readers (5) *of poetry* try (6) *to find* "messages."
d. Many readers race (7) *through a poem* (8) *to seek* that elusive nugget (9) *of wisdom.*
e. It is misleading (10) *to equate the enjoyment of a poem* with (11) *finding its central thought.*

f. (12) *Enjoying a poem to its fullest* is somewhat like (13) *watching a baseball game.*

g. (14) *During a game,* most fans are eager (15) *to participate vicariously in the pleasure* of (16) *hitting a home run* or of (17) *making a double play.*

h. (18) *Awaiting the outcome of a game,* the average fan also responds to the total experience of the game itself.

i. (19) *To read a poem for meaning alone* can be compared to (20) *attending a baseball game and watching the scoreboard.*

THE APPOSITIVE[1]

3k. An *appositive* is a noun or pronoun—often with modifiers—set beside another noun or pronoun to explain or identify it.

> My cousin **Maria** is an accomplished violinist.
> Riboflavin, a **vitamin,** is found in leafy vegetables.

An *appositive phrase* is a phrase consisting of an appositive and its modifiers.

> My brother's car, **a sporty red hatchback with bucket seats,** is the envy of my friends.

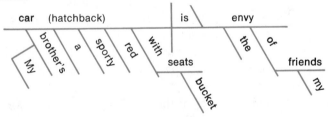

An appositive phrase usually follows the word it explains or identifies, but may precede it.

> Once a pagan **feast,** Valentine's Day is now celebrated as a day of love.

REVIEW EXERCISE C. Identifying Phrases. Number your paper 1–25. In the following sentences most of the phrases have been numbered and italicized. Write after its number on your paper the name of the phrase: prepositional, participial, gerund, infinitive, or apposi-

---

[1] For rules on the punctuation of appositives, see page 803. For the use of the appositive in subordination of ideas, see page 290.

tive. In the case of a prepositional phrase, write whether it is an adjective phrase or an adverb phrase. Do not identify separately the prepositional phrase within a larger italicized phrase.

a. Altamont Pass, (1) *an area of grassy hills* (2) *surrounding San Francisco Bay,* is producing a new cash crop.
b. (3) *Called the epitome of marginal land,* the Altamont is valued (4) *at ten dollars an acre* for grazing.
c. Now, however, energy entrepreneurs are hurrying (5) *to lease wind rights on acreage* (6) *throughout the Altamont.*
d. One rancher owns several hundred acres (7) *of range land* (8) *dotted with tall white wind machines.*
e. (9) *Standing in rows on the windswept hills,* this crop is expected (10) *to produce electricity.*
f. Such wind farms are part of an experiment (11) *marked by financial and technical difficulties.*
g. (12) *With any luck,* however, the wind-power industry may soon spread (13) *to other parts* of the country.
h. The temperature differences (14) *between the cool coast and the hot valley* can create air surges (15) *funneling inland through natural gaps* (16) *like the Altamont.*
i. According to some energy experts, there will be several hundred wind machines (17) *producing thirty million kilowatts per year,* the power (18) *used by 4,800 homes.*
j. (19) *An economist and a trained engineer,* John Eckland has advocated (20) *generating electricity* by (21) *using these updated windmills.*
k. Not until the oil shortages of the 1970's did a serious effort begin (22) *in the United States* (23) *to develop a wind industry.*
l. Today there are several companies (24) *offering small wind machines.*
m. Modern wind turbines may someday become as numerous (25) *in the United States* as windmills are in Holland.

WRITING APPLICATION C:
Using Appositives and Appositive Phrases in Your Writing

Appositives and appositive phrases are useful in your writing because they identify or explain the noun or pronoun they follow. As you read the following sentences, notice that the appositive and appositive phrases add important information.

EXAMPLES   My mother, **Lillian,** is a very warm person.
Joe, **the treasurer of our class,** collected the money for the yearbook.
The press spoke to Dr. William C. Devries, **the famous heart surgeon.**

Writing Assignment

Write five sentences using appositive phrases. Vary the positions of the phrases in the sentences.

CHAPTER 3 REVIEW: POSTTEST 1

Identifying Phrases.   Number your paper 1–25. For each sentence, write the italicized phrase. Then identify it as a prepositional, participial, gerund, infinitive, or appositive phrase. If it is a prepositional phrase, indicate whether it is used as an adjective or an adverb. Do not identify separately any phrases within a longer italicized phrase.

EXAMPLE   1. The sunlight shimmering *on the lake* was beautiful.
1. *on the lake, prepositional, adverb*

1. Juanita likes *to take candid pictures of her friends.*
2. *Arriving late at school,* Bill stopped in the office to get a pass.
3. The sound *of the band* made everyone want to dance.
4. *Speaking before a large audience,* the President delivered an important foreign policy speech.
5. Made *in Ireland,* Waterford crystal is admired throughout the world.
6. By *inventing the telephone,* Alexander Graham Bell assured himself a place in history.
7. Try *to finish your work before dinner.*
8. Luciano Pavarotti, *the great Italian tenor,* received a standing ovation at the end of his concert.
9. Ruth's secret ambition is *to do research in space.*

10. My grandmother enjoys *knitting sweaters for her friends and her family.*

11. We stood on the deserted street *looking in vain for a taxi.*

12. Raul has the talent *to sculpt and design beautiful objects.*

13. Francine's hobby is *collecting earrings;* she has more than twenty pairs!

14. As Captain Williams stood *on the deck of the boat,* he scanned the horizon.

15. For great performers, *interpreting music* is an art as well as a skill.

16. *Having suffered through three days of a heat wave,* we decided to purchase an air conditioner.

17. In Cleveland, we visited our friend Barbara, *a prosecuting attorney.*

18. While the witness gave her testimony, the members *of the jury* listened carefully.

19. At the rodeo, I always enjoy *watching the courageous riders.*

20. Karen went to the Upper Peninsula in Michigan *to swim in Lake Superior.*

21. "It is a pleasure to be with you today," remarked the mayor *at the beginning of her talk.*

22. Swaggering cowboys and daring sheriffs are stereotypes that appear *in many old western movies.*

23. Dr. Acevedo, *a noted cardiologist,* assured the patient's family that the operation had been successful.

24. Many pioneer women kept diaries and journals *of their experiences* settling the American wilderness.

25. *To speak freely on any issue* is guaranteed to all Americans by the Bill of Rights.

CHAPTER 3 REVIEW: POSTTEST 2

Identifying Phrases. Number your paper 1–25. Each of the following sentences contains one or two phrases of the kind specified before the sentence. Find these phrases and write them next to the appropriate number. Include any phrase within a larger phrase.

EXAMPLES 1. *Infinitive* When we went to the store, we were surprised to see so many items on sale.
1. to see so many items on sale

2. *Prepositional*   We were annoyed by the noise of the television set.
2. by the noise, of the television set

1. *Infinitive*   The young actress, a graduate of Northwestern University, was delighted to have a role in the new play.
2. *Participial*   Working in the garden, the gardener seemed happy.
3. *Infinitive*   I intend to repair this flat tire.
4. *Prepositional*   During the cold weather some people use their fireplaces.
5. *Gerund*   Taking inventory is a tedious but important task for owners of stores and factories.
6. *Participial*   Needing money for the weekend, we went to the bank and cashed our paychecks.
7. *Gerund*   When I was in the hospital recently, the doctors made me feel comfortable by keeping me informed.
8. *Appositive*   The Concorde, a jet plane, arrived on time.
9. *Infinitive*   The purpose of the NATO alliance is to safeguard the freedom of its members.
10. *Gerund*   Because she is outgoing, Ms. Turner enjoys selling insurance.
11. *Participial*   Perched on the outdoor telephone wires, the birds resembled notes on a musical scale.
12. *Infinitive*   To complete the new room before October was the contractor's goal.
13. *Infinitive*   Never one for small projects, my sister Kyle wants to climb Mount Everest.
14. *Prepositional*   Doug always writes with care.
15. *Gerund*   Believing you is difficult.
16. *Infinitive*   To keep a friend's secret is not difficult for me.
17. *Prepositional*   Snow is expected to fall across Montana today.
18. *Gerund*   Shaping flowers from molten glass demands precision and skill.
19. *Prepositional*   Our local radio station is noted for its excellent coverage of the news.
20. *Prepositional*   Each of the workers tried to repair the clock.
21. *Infinitive*   "Have you always had such a strong desire to teach?" my interviewer asked me.

22. *Gerund*   By budgeting carefully we were able to double our savings in a year.
23. *Participial*   Located in Cambridge, Massachusetts, Harvard is one of the most prestigious universities in the United States.
24. *Appositive*   Marcia, an excellent chess player, was determined to win the game.
25. *Prepositional*   If the laundry is dry, please take it off the line and put it into the basket.

CHAPTER 3 REVIEW: POSTTEST 3

Writing Sentences with Phrases.   Write your own sentences according to the following guidelines:

1. Use *with patience* as an adverb phrase in a sentence.
2. Use *for my friend Margaret* as an adverb phrase in a sentence.
3. Use *from Chicago* as an adjective phrase in a sentence.
4. Use *with vegetables* as an adjective phrase in a sentence.
5. Use *looking from a distance* as a participial phrase in a sentence.
6. Use *studying hard* as a gerund phrase that is the object of a preposition in a sentence.
7. Use *writing letters* as a gerund phrase that is the subject in a sentence.
8. Use *to dream* as an infinitive phrase that is the object of a verb in a sentence.
9. Use *to study the piano* as an infinitive phrase that is the subject in a sentence.
10. Use *our local newspaper* as an appositive phrase in a sentence.

CHAPTER 4

The Clause

THE FUNCTION OF CLAUSES

As you have been reminded in Chapter 3, most sentences are made up not only of single words functioning as parts of speech but also of word groups functioning as single parts of speech. The phrase is one such word group; the clause is another. Knowledge of the subordinate clause, which you will review in this chapter, is essential for all those wishing to improve their writing.

DIAGNOSTIC TEST

Identifying Clauses; Classifying Sentences. Identify each italicized group of words as an independent or a subordinate clause. If it is a subordinate clause, identify it as an adjective clause, an adverb clause, or a noun clause. Classify each sentence as simple, compound, complex, or compound-complex and then as declarative, interrogative, imperative, or exclamatory.

EXAMPLES   1. *As he cruised along the tranquil beach on his bicycle,* Warren could hear the waves beating on the rocky shore.
　　　　1. *subordinate clause—adverb clause*
　　　　　complex—declarative
　　　　2. Is the tumor malignant or *is it benign?*
　　　　2. *independent*
　　　　　compound—interrogative

67

1. American Indian culture, *which is rich and interesting,* is not sufficiently familiar to most Americans.
2. Why is it that I can never find a pencil *when I need one?*
3. On your way here, *did you meet a group of strange people wearing space-age outfits?*
4. As we walked along the road, *we saw the wheat waving in the wind.*
5. I don't care *what you think!*
6. Do you know *that Dr. Robert Goddard was the pioneer of the liquid-fuel rocket?*
7. Set in the rural South, *Flannery O'Connor's short stories present an assortment of odd characters.*
8. Given to the United States by France in 1886, *the Statue of Liberty stands in New York Harbor and is regarded as a symbol of American freedom.*
9. I'm so happy *that I could dance and sing!*
10. *Because his art work received wide recognition,* Pablo Picasso became famous and wealthy.
11. I have concluded *that personal freedom involves both self-realization and service to others.*
12. *The pitcher read the catcher's signals* and then struck out the hitter with a fastball.
13. Please do not talk *while the test is in progress.*
14. Did the coach realize *that she was looking at her strongest softball team in years?*
15. As the lights dimmed in the theater, *a hush fell over the audience,* and the overture began.
16. *"Mitosis" and "meiosis" are technical terms for most people,* but they are merely everyday words for cellular biologists.
17. Having had a job as a chef for six months, *Jerome hopes to own his own restaurant in the future.*
18. The Realtor said *the price of the house has been lowered by $100,000.*
19. Is it true that Jack, *who lives in Sacramento, California,* works in San Francisco?
20. *After the hurricane had destroyed many homes,* the townspeople bravely began a difficult clean-up operation.

4a. A *clause* is a group of words containing a subject and a predicate and is used as part of a sentence.

Clauses are classified according to grammatical completeness. Those that can stand alone if removed from their sentences are called *independent clauses.* Those that do not express a complete thought and cannot stand alone are called *subordinate clauses.*

INDEPENDENT CLAUSES

When removed from its sentence, an independent clause[1] makes complete sense. Written with a capital at the beginning and a period at the end, it becomes a simple sentence. It is an independent *clause* only when combined in a larger sentence with one or more additional clauses, independent or subordinate.

When two or more independent clauses are joined together into a single sentence, the usual connecting words are *and, but, or, nor,* and *for.*

EXAMPLES   It was a hot, sunny weekend, **and** all the beaches were packed. [The conjunction *and* joins two independent clauses.]
The soup was delicious, **but** the main course tasted bland. [The independent clauses are joined by *but.*]

SUBORDINATE CLAUSES

Subordinate clauses,[2] which cannot stand alone as sentences, are used as nouns or modifiers in the same way as single words and phrases. A subordinate clause is always combined in some way with an independent clause. The following examples are subordinate clauses.

whoever knows the song
which is my favorite song of the West
as she has always insisted

Combined with an independent clause, each of these subordinate clauses plays its part in a sentence:

Whoever knows the song may join in.
We sang "Green Grow the Lilacs," **which is my favorite song of the West.**
As she has always insisted, Mother will not sing at parties.

---

[1] Independent clauses are sometimes called *main* clauses.
[2] Subordinate clauses are sometimes called *dependent* clauses.

EXERCISE 1. Identifying Independent and Subordinate Clauses. In each of the following sentences, a clause is printed in italics. If the italicized clause is an independent clause, place *I* after the proper number. If it is a subordinate clause, place *S* after the proper number.

1. Egyptology is the branch of learning *that is concerned with the language and culture of ancient Egypt.*
2. *Until the Rosetta Stone was discovered in 1799,* the ancient Egyptian language was an enigma to scholars.
3. Boussard, *who was a captain in the engineers under Napoleon,* found the stone in the trenches near Rosetta, a city near the mouth of the Nile.
4. Before the French had a chance to analyze its inscriptions, *the stone was captured by the British.*
5. Because the stone contained the same message in two kinds of Egyptian writing and in Greek script, *it provided the needed key for deciphering the Egyptian language.*
6. *When the Rosetta Stone was found,* part of the hieroglyphic portion was missing.
7. Scholars could easily read the Greek inscription, *which was nearly complete.*
8. *In 1818 Thomas Young succeeded in isolating a number of hiero- glyphics* that he took to represent names.
9. *The message* that was written on the stone *was not very exciting in itself.*
10. Since the priests of Egypt were grateful for benefits from the king, *they were formally thanking the king for his generosity.*

The Adjective Clause

Like a phrase, a subordinate clause acts as a single part of speech—as an adjective, an adverb, or a noun.

4b. An *adjective clause* **is a subordinate clause that, like an adjective, modifies a noun or a pronoun.**

EXAMPLES He visited his home, **where he was warmly welcomed by the mayor.**

She is someone **who has shown remarkable courage.**

This book, **which I read for my history report,** is about Africa.

Since a subordinate clause, like a sentence, has a verb and a subject and may contain complements and modifiers, it is diagramed very much like a sentence. Adjective and adverb clauses are placed on a horizontal line below the main line. An adjective clause is joined to the word it modifies by a slanting broken line drawn from the modified word to the relative pronoun at the beginning of the clause.

EXAMPLES   Students **whose work represents their second-best** are not real students. [The subordinate clause *whose work represents their second-best* modifies the noun *students.*]

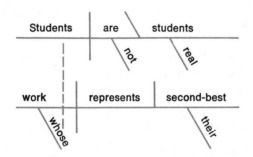

Bob spent on an old car all the money **that he had earned during the summer.** [The subordinate clause *that he had earned during the summer* modifies the noun *money.*]

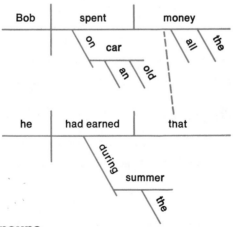

Relative Pronouns

Adjective clauses often begin with the pronouns *who, whom, whose, which,* or *that.* These pronouns refer to, or are *related* to, a noun or pronoun that has come before.

4c. A *relative pronoun* is a pronoun that begins a subordinate adjective clause and is related to a noun or a pronoun already mentioned or understood. The word to which the relative pronoun is related is its *antecedent*.

A relative pronoun does three things:

1. It refers to a preceding noun or pronoun:

   Let's listen to a weather forecaster **whom we can trust.**

   The amplifier was one **that we had seen before.**

2. It connects its clause with the rest of the sentence:

   Ms. Lopez is a counselor **who never betrays a confidence.** [The relative pronoun *who* joins the subordinate clause to the independent clause.]
   You should find a source **that is more up-to-date.** [The subordinate clause is joined to the independent clause by the relative pronoun *that.*]

3. It performs a function within its own clause by serving as the subject, object, etc., of the subordinate clause:

   The principal appointed George, **who is a reliable student.** [*Who* is the subject of the verb *is* in the adjective clause *who is a reliable student.*]

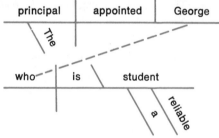

Show me the book **that you read.** [*That* is the object of the verb *read* (read *what?*).]

These are the assignments **for which you are responsible.** [*Which* is the object of the preposition *for.*][1]

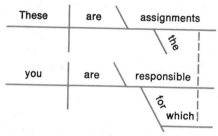

An adjective clause may also begin with the relative adjective *whose* or with the relative adverb *where* or *when.*

He is a coach **whose record has been amazing.** [*Whose,* the possessive form of the relative pronoun *who,* functions as an adjective modifying *record.*]

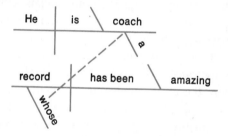

Do you remember the restaurant **where we ate lunch**? [*Where* acts as an adverb modifying *ate,* the verb in the clause. The antecedent is *restaurant.*]

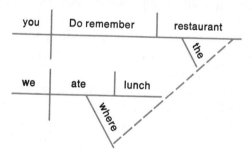

[1] In this sentence two words—*for* and *which*—begin the clause. Other two-word combinations of a preposition and a relative pronoun to begin a clause are *in which, by whom, for whom, from whom,* etc.

EXERCISE 2. Identifying Adjective Clauses and the Words They Modify. On your paper, write in order the adjective clauses in the following sentences. Before each clause, write the number of the sentence in which it appears. After each clause, write the noun or pronoun that the clause modifies. Your teacher may ask you to indicate whether the word that begins the clause is used as a subject, an object of a verb, an object of a preposition, or a modifier.

1. The Mars of the nonscientist is a planet of the imagination, where an ancient civilization has left its mark and where maps blossom with romantic place names like Utopia and Elysium.
2. Earthlings, who were awed by the planet's red glow in the evening sky, looked on Mars as a home for aliens who might someday cross cosmic barriers and visit planet Earth.
3. Such thinking was encouraged by an Italian astronomer who observed the planet through a telescope and saw a series of fine lines that crisscrossed its surface.
4. He called the lines *canali,* which is Italian for *channels;* the word was erroneously translated into English as *canals.*
5. A planet where there are canals must, of course, be inhabited by people who are capable of building not only canals but also the cities that presumably sprang up at their intersections.
6. Later Percival Lowell, the astronomer who founded the reputable Lowell Observatory in Flagstaff, breathed life into the Martian myths with several nonscientific observations that most astronomers disputed.
7. According to the eminent astronomer, the canals on Mars were built by inhabitants who belonged to an advanced civilization whose origins remain a mystery.
8. Lowell reported a total of 437 canals, of which a large number were discovered by his own team of astronomers.
9. A writer whose interest was drawn to Mars was Edgar Rice Burroughs, whom we remember as the creator of Tarzan; in his Martian books, Burroughs recounts the adventures of John Carter, who could transport himself to Mars by standing in an open field and wishing.
10. Burroughs' best-known literary successor is· Ray Bradbury, who wrote *The Martian Chronicles,* published in 1950.

The Noun Clause

4d. A *noun clause* is a subordinate clause used as a noun.

In diagraming, a noun clause is pictured as a unit by placement at the top of a vertical line rising from the part of the diagram (subject, object, predicate nominative) to which the clause belongs.

EXAMPLE   **Whoever wins the election** will have many problems.

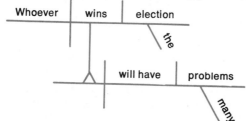

The entire noun clause *whoever wins the election* is the subject of the verb *will have*. Study the following pairs of sentences to see how a noun clause functioning in the same way that a noun functions may be a predicate nominative, an object of a verb, or an object of a preposition.

This is the **solution**. [*Solution* is a noun used as a predicate nominative after the linking verb *is*.]
This is **what we have been looking for**. [*What we have been looking for* is a noun clause used as a predicate nominative.]

We learned an interesting **fact**. [*Fact* is a noun used as the object of the verb *learned*.]
We learned **that she is a physicist**. [*That she is a physicist* is a noun clause used as the object of a verb.]

Here is a draft of my **proposal**. [*Proposal* is a noun used as the object of the preposition *of*.]
Here is a draft of **what I am proposing**. [*What I am proposing* is a noun clause used as the object of a preposition.]

A noun clause may begin with an indefinite relative pronoun—*that, what, whatever, who, which, whoever, whichever*. Unlike a (definite) relative pronoun, an indefinite relative pronoun does not have an antecedent in its sentence.

EXAMPLE   He gave me **whatever I wanted**.

A noun clause may also begin with an indefinite relative adjective —*whose, which, whatever*—or an indefinite relative adverb—*where, when, how*, etc.

I know **whose car this is.**

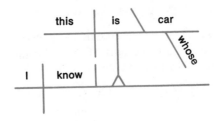

I know **where she went.**

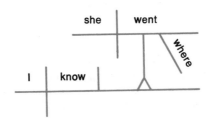

> ☞ **NOTE** Adjective and noun clauses are sometimes used without an introductory word. Note that the introductory word is omitted in the second sentence in each of the following pairs:

I.M. Pei is an architect **whom most critics praise.**
I.M. Pei is an architect **most critics praise.**
She says **that James Earl Jones was once a pre-med student.**
She says **James Earl Jones was once a pre-med student.**

EXERCISE 3. Identifying Noun Clauses and Their Functions.

On your paper, write the noun clauses in the following sentences. Before each clause, write the number of the sentence in which it appears. After each clause, write its function in the sentence: *subject, direct object, predicate nominative, object of a preposition.*

EXAMPLE 1. I don't know what to think.
   1. *what to think—direct object*

1. The problem is that my finances don't quite allow me to live in style; in fact, I'm broke!

2. Do you know what the referee says to the opponents at the start of a boxing match?
3. What I like most about Harriet is that she never complains.
4. Scientists disagree about why dinosaurs died out.
5. Sometimes I am amused and sometimes I am amazed by what I read in the newspaper's advice column.
6. Through scientific research, psychologists have learned that everyone dreams during sleep.
7. What the dancers Agnes de Mille and Martha Graham did was to create a new form of American dance.
8. Can you tell me where the Museum of African Art is located?
9. Do you know whether Sakima has tried out for the track team?
10. I know how you are feeling, and I am happy for you.

EXERCISE 4. Identifying Adjective and Noun Clauses. Each of the following sentences contains at least one subordinate clause. Write the clauses in order on your paper. Before each clause, place the number of the sentence in which it appears. After each clause, tell what kind it is—adjective or noun. Be prepared to tell what word each adjective clause modifies and how each noun clause is used in the sentence.

1. A person has found that toys are not meant only for children.
2. Athelstan Spilhaus, an oceanographer, admits he has sometimes been unable to distinguish between his work and his play.
3. Some of the toys he collects are simply to be admired; his favorites are those that can be put into action.
4. Some of his collectibles are put into intensive care, where he skillfully replaces parts that have been damaged or lost.
5. Dr. Spilhaus says that a toy is anything that enables us to tarry during the fast whip of ordinary life.
6. What is appealing about some toys is that they can make us laugh.
7. Someone once suggested that many physical principles began as playthings.
8. For example, the toy monkey that is activated by squeezing a rubber bulb uses the same principle as the jackhammer that digs up our streets.
9. Only those who have lost touch with childhood question what a toy is worth in dollars and cents.
10. Ask someone who knows toys what their enchantment is worth.

The Adverb Clause

4e. An *adverb clause* is a subordinate clause that, like an adverb, modifies a verb, an adjective, or an adverb.

In the following examples each adverb clause illustrates one of the typical adverbial functions of telling *how, when, where, why, to what extent,* or *under what conditions.*

She practices **as though her life depended on it.** [*how* she practices]
She practices **whenever she has time.** [*when* she practices]
She practices **wherever the team travels.** [*where* she practices]
She practices **because she wants to win.** [*why* she practices]
She practices more **than anyone else does.** [*how* much more]
She practices on weekends **if her schedule permits.** [*under what conditions* she practices]

In diagraming, an adverb clause is written on a horizontal line below the main line of the diagram. The subordinating conjunction beginning the clause is written on a slanting broken line which links the verb of the clause to the word the clause modifies.

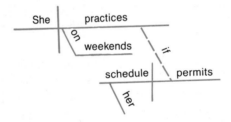

Adverb clauses may also modify adjectives and other adverbs.

She is certain **that she will make the team.** [The adverb clause *that she will make the team* modifies the adjective *certain.*]
He runs faster **than I do.** [The adverb clause *than I do* modifies the adverb *faster.*]

The Subordinating Conjunction

Adverb clauses often begin with a word like *after, because,* or *when* that expresses the relation between the clause and the rest of the sentence.

4f. A conjunction that begins an adverb clause is called a *subordinating conjunction.* It joins the clause to the rest of the sentence.

The following words are subordinating conjunctions. (Many may also be used as other parts of speech.)

Common Subordinating Conjunctions

after	because	so that	whenever
although	before	than	where
as	if	though	wherever
as if	in order that	unless	whether
as long as	provided that	until	while
as though	since	when	

The Elliptical (Incomplete) Clause

Sometimes in our writing and speaking, we do not complete an adverb clause.

EXAMPLES   I am much taller **than you [are].**
            While [I was] running for the bus, I dropped my books.

In these adverb clauses the part of the clause given in brackets has been omitted. The missing part, however, could be readily provided by a reader or listener. Such incomplete clauses are said to be "elliptical."[1]

EXERCISE 5. Identifying Adverb Clauses.   Write on your paper the adverb clauses in the following sentences. Before each clause, write the number of the sentence in which it appears. Draw a line under the subordinating conjunction that introduces the clause. After each clause, write what the clause tells: *how, when, where, why, to what extent, under what conditions.*

1. Because company was coming for dinner, Lola Gomez and her father prepared a special treat of Cuban black beans.
2. After Lola had soaked a pound of black beans overnight, she drained them and covered them with fresh water.
3. Before she lit the stove, she added chopped onion and green pepper, a bay leaf, coriander leaves, oregano, and salt pork to the beans.
4. While the mixture was simmering, Mr. Gomez prepared the sofrito.

---

[1] The definition of *ellipsis,* as applied to grammar, is an omission of one or more words obviously understood but necessary to make the expression grammatically complete. For the correct usage of pronouns in elliptical clauses, see page 170.

5. Whenever a recipe calls for sofrito, you finely chop some onion, green pepper, and garlic.
6. Then you fry these vegetables in a little oil until they are tender.
7. As soon as the sofrito was ready, Mr. Gomez added it to the bean mixture.
8. He then crushed some of the beans against the side of the pot so that the bean mixture would become thicker.
9. When the mixture was thick, Lola put in some vinegar and sugar.
10. Although this dish is usually served with rice, Lola and her father prepared a green salad instead.

WRITING APPLICATION A:
Using the Adverb Clause to Express Cause-and-Effect Relationships

One of the most important skills of reasoning is the ability to determine *why* something happens or *why* people act the way they do. Once the question has been answered, the answer usually includes an adverb clause. In addition to telling *why*, adverb clauses also tell *how, when, where, how much,* and *under what conditions.*

EXAMPLE   Frank Lloyd Wright's building was the only large building standing in Tokyo after the earthquake of 1923 *because he used steel and concrete and floated it on a sea of mud.* (In this cause-and-effect sentence, the cause is placed in a subordinate adverb clause.)

Writing Assignment

It is usually a sign of intelligence to ask questions. One type of question that is often asked begins with *why*. Think of a *why* question that you would like to answer. Either do the research or conduct interviews to find the answer. In your topic sentence use an adverb clause to express this cause-and-effect relationship. Some ideas are the following:
1. Why are some scientists concerned about a "greenhouse effect"?
2. Why are high levels of cholesterol dangerous?
3. Why do students take Latin, which is called a "dead" language?
4. Why are some people able to face adversity with a positive attitude?
5. Why can't anything travel faster than the speed of light?

REVIEW EXERCISE A. Identifying Adjective, Noun, and Adverb Clauses.   Each of the following sentences contains at least one subordinate clause. Write the clauses in order on your paper. Before each, write the number of the sentence in which it appears. After each, write what kind it is—adjective, noun, adverb.

1. When a group of scholars first applied computer science to the study of literature, their colleagues expressed what can only be described as polite skepticism.
2. What, they asked, would the computer do?
3. Enraged scholars argued that measuring the length of Hemingway's sentences was dreary enough when it was done without computers.
4. Would precise mathematical profiles of style determine if Thomas More wrote one of Shakespeare's plays?
5. Because initial studies were indeed made along these lines, they provided controversy when published.
6. Although such controversy raged for years, computers have gradually won increasing support that has become more and more impressive.
7. Researchers use the computer whenever a project involves such mechanical tasks as compiling an index or a bibliography.
8. Since all of ancient Greek is now available on computer tape, scholars can make analyses that shed light on etymology.
9. There are certain elements in literary research that computers can pick up faster than readers.
10. Many eminent scholars believe that the use of the computer as a literary tool has already produced results that are both significant and intelligible.

SENTENCES CLASSIFIED BY STRUCTURE

4g. Classified according to their structure, there are four kinds of sentences: *simple, compound, complex,* and *compound-complex.*

(1) A *simple sentence* is a sentence with one independent clause and no subordinate clauses.

Great literature stirs the imagination.

literature | stirs | imagination

Great *the*

(2) A *compound sentence* is a sentence composed of two or more independent clauses but no subordinate clauses.[1]

Great literature stirs the imagination, and it challenges the intellect.
Great literature stirs the imagination; moreover, it challenges the intellect.

☞ **NOTE** Do not confuse the compound predicate of simple sentences with the two subjects and verbs of compound sentences.

Study the following diagrams.

Great literature **stirs** the imagination and **challenges** the intellect. [simple sentence with compound predicate]

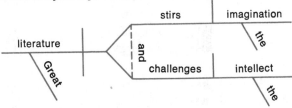

Great **literature stirs** the imagination, and **it challenges** the intellect. [compound sentence with two subjects and two verbs]

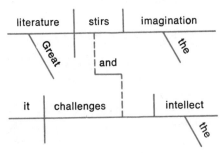

[1] For rules concerning the punctuation of compound sentences, see pages 795 and 817–18.

Independent clauses are joined by coordinating conjunctions:

and	but	nor	or	for	yet	so

or by conjunctive adverbs:

also	furthermore	nevertheless	therefore
besides	however	otherwise	thus
consequently	moreover	then	still

(3) A _complex sentence_ is a sentence that contains one independent clause and at least one subordinate clause.

Great literature, which stirs the imagination, also challenges the intellect.

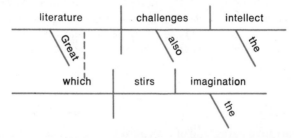

(4) A _compound-complex sentence_ is a sentence that contains two or more independent clauses and at least one subordinate clause.

Great literature, which challenges the intellect, is sometimes difficult, but it is also rewarding. [The independent clauses are _Great literature is sometimes difficult_ and _it is also rewarding_. The subordinate clause is _which challenges the intellect_.]

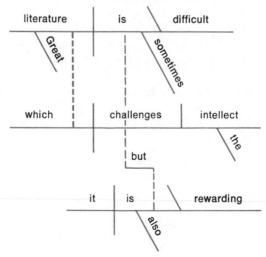

WRITING APPLICATION B:
Using a Variety of Sentence Structures to Enliven Your Writing

When you use a variety of sentence structures, you enliven your writing. Notice in the following paragraph that the writer has used a variety of sentence structures to add vitality to his writing.

> When he was far up toward the top, he lay down and slept for a little while. (CX) The withered moon, shining on his face, awakened him. (S) He stood up and moved up the hill. (S) Fifty yards away he stopped and turned back, for he had forgotten his rifle. (CD) He walked heavily down and poked about in the brush, but he could not find his gun. (CD) At last he lay down to rest. (S) The pocket of pain in his armpit had grown more sharp. (S) His arm seemed to swell out and fall with every heartbeat. (S) There was no position lying down where the heavy arm did not press against his armpit. (CX)
>
> JOHN STEINBECK

Writing Assignment

Write a narrative paragraph of a memorable experience in your life. Use a variety of sentence structures to enliven your writing. When you revise your narration, check to see that you have used a variety of sentences.

SENTENCES CLASSIFIED BY PURPOSE

4h. Classified according to their purpose, there are four kinds of sentences: *declarative, imperative, interrogative,* and *exclamatory.*

(1) A *declarative sentence* is a sentence that makes a statement.

Homes should be made safer for the elderly.

(2) An *imperative sentence* is a sentence that gives a command or makes a request.

Close that book and pay attention.
Please lower the volume.

(3) An *interrogative sentence* is a sentence that asks a question.

What was the name of that song?

(4) An *exclamatory sentence* **is a sentence that expresses strong feeling.**

How happy I am!

EXERCISE 6. Classifying Sentences According to Structure and Purpose. Number your paper 1–10. After the proper number, classify the sentence in two ways: (1) according to its structure and (2) according to its purpose.

EXAMPLE   1. Look at this article I'm reading.
          1. *complex   imperative*

1. Are you aware that there is a worldwide demand for butterflies?
2. Millions are caught and sold each year to museums, entomologists, private collectors, and factories.
3. The plastic-encased butterflies that are used to decorate ornamental objects such as trays, tabletops, and screens are usually common varieties, most of which come from Taiwan, Korea, and Malaysia.
4. There is a difference, however, between what goes on there and what goes on in Papua.
5. Papua, which was administered by Australia until it gained its independence in 1975, is taking advantage of a growing interest in tropical butterflies.
6. Here butterfly ranchers gather, raise, and sell high-quality specimens that are accompanied by scientific data.
7. Because biologists have not yet detailed the life cycles of the Papuan butterflies, the villagers have become the experts; and as a result butterfly ranching has improved the economy in many otherwise impoverished villages.
8. Some Papuan butterflies are quite small, but others are larger than an adult human hand.
9. As you examine these photographs, observe that a carefully stocked pasture of butterflies looks like a flower garden.
10. What rich, vibrant colors Papuan butterflies have!

REVIEW EXERCISE B. Identifying Clauses; Classifying Sentences. Identify each italicized group of words as an independent or a subordinate clause. If it is a subordinate clause, identify it as an adjective clause, an adverb clause, or a noun clause. Classify each sentence as simple, compound, complex, or compound-complex and then as declarative, interrogative, imperative, or exclamatory.

EXAMPLE   1. *Whenever I need a piece of golfing equipment,* I know that the To a Tee Shop is certain to have it in stock.
           1. *subordinate   adverb   complex   declarative*

1. Do you know that imaginative teachers *who are enthusiastic about their work* can make school pleasurable for their students?
2. Last year, *when I took a social studies elective,* Law and Order, I found myself looking forward to fourth period each day.
3. *What our teacher, Ms. Schiavone, did to enrich our course* was to bring the outside world into the classroom.
4. In addition to assigning reading, homework, and tests, *she invited guest speakers to share their experiences with us.*
5. By the end of three months, the class had met with a defense attorney, a prosecutor, and several local police officers; and *we had interviewed the first FBI agent* we had ever met.
6. In addition, Ms. Schiavone arranged to have four prisoners, accompanied by police, speak to us about *how they were coping with life in prison.*
7. *After we had listened to these men and women telling of their experiences,* everyone in the class agreed that a career in crime is definitely not attractive!
8. In addition to bringing these people and experiences into the classroom, Ms. Schiavone set up a schedule of field trips, and *she then took the classroom "into the world."*
9. For example, on one day we visited the local jail; and on another, *when we attended a session of a jury trial,* we spoke personally with the judge.
10. I am grateful that I was a member of Ms. Schiavone's class, and I was not surprised *when she was voted "Outstanding Educator of the Year" by the senior class.*

CHAPTER 4 REVIEW: POSTTEST 1

Identifying Clauses; Classifying Sentences.   Identify each italicized group of words as an independent or a subordinate clause. If it is a subordinate clause, identify it as an adjective clause, an adverb clause, or a noun clause. Classify each sentence as simple, compound, complex, or compound-complex and then as declarative, interrogative, imperative, or exclamatory.

EXAMPLE 1. *While we were talking on the telephone,* our conversation was drowned out by noise on the line.
  1. *subordinate   adverb   complex   declarative*

1. *Tamara applied for the job last Monday,* and each day since then she has been waiting for a call from the company.
2. Do you think *that your parents will approve of your spending so much money for a stereo?*
3. *Please give me a break.*
4. Amelia Earhart, *who was the first woman to fly solo over the Atlantic and Pacific Oceans,* had great courage.
5. *Though he was a paraplegic because of injuries sustained in an auto accident,* Mr. Benoit was the best coach at Central High School.
6. As you wait for the signal, concentrate only on *what you have to do to win.*
7. Since last year Maureen and Jim have been rotating household tasks, and as a result, *each has become more understanding and more helpful.*
8. *If you study patterns of stock market transactions,* you will notice that prices often fall as interest rates rise.
9. How was I ever going to get the parts of the engine reassembled *before my father got home?*
10. *I won a soccer ball* when I was ten because I had raked more leaves than my brother or sister did in a "contest" devised by our clever parents.
11. Tired from a long day in the hot sun, the lifeguard reported *that there had been no accidents.*
12. In high school, Consuela Garcia set an all-city scoring record in basketball, and *she later went to college on a scholarship.*
13. Can you tell me *why there is still famine in parts of the world?*
14. After World War II, *President Harry Truman authorized the Marshall Plan,* a massive program designed to speed economic recovery in Europe.
15. The night *when I was home alone for the first time* I read Poe's "The Tell-Tale Heart," and I could feel my heart beating faster as the story progressed.

16. *Even though it has been years since his death,* Elvis Presley's records still show good sales.
17. *Where are you going in such a hurry* that you have forgotten to put on your shoes?
18. Please proceed to the auditorium with your homeroom class, and *take the seats assigned to you.*
19. President Lyndon B. Johnson, a Texan, is credited with the passage of the Civil Rights Act of 1964, *which is a landmark piece of legislation.*
20. *This morning the bank approved our loan,* and this afternoon we began work on the new solar addition to our house.
21. As the molten lava moved down the sides of the mountain, residents *who lived within a ten-mile radius* were asked to evacuate their homes.
22. I am so relieved *because the ordeal is over at last!*
23. My friend Kaya likes to solve puzzles that are challenging; cryptograms are *what he enjoys most.*
24. When Bart says *he will arrive at noon,* I know I can expect him at any time between one o'clock and four.
25. Sometimes, on rainy Sunday afternoons, *Carmen enjoys watching an old movie on television.*

CHAPTER 4 REVIEW: POSTTEST 2

Identifying Subordinate Clauses; Classifying Sentences.
Most of the following sentences have one subordinate clause or more.
First, write the subordinate clause(s). Then, identify the clause(s) as an adjective clause, an adverb clause, or a noun clause. Classify each sentence as simple, compound, complex, or compound-complex and then as declarative, interrogative, imperative, or exclamatory.

EXAMPLE 1. When I was a sophomore, I read only the sports pages, but now I read front page news and some movie reviews as well.
   1. *When I was a sophomore*
      adverb   compound-complex   declarative

1. I love to hear my grandparents tell stories about how they fell in love and got married.

2. Kevin was never very interested in science until he took a chemistry course with Mr. Gutierrez.
3. Most large American cities do not have subway systems but rely instead on buses for public transportation.
4. The project, which had started out so easily, became more complicated with each passing day.
5. What will you do with the television antenna on your roof when your cable wires are installed?
6. Although Wyatt said very little during class, he leaned forward and listened intently to each speaker.
7. You won't believe what I'm about to tell you!
8. William Miller, Edmund Muskie, Sargent Shriver, and Robert Dole may not be familiar household names, but each of these men ran unsuccessfully for the vice-presidency between 1964 and 1976.
9. Though she has only lived in the United States since she was nine years old, Pilar speaks and writes English well.
10. Let's go on the picnic, despite the forecast of rain!
11. That it would cost him enormous effort to conquer weeds was the last thing on Tomas' mind when he planted a "small" half-acre garden last spring.
12. The British novelist Margaret Drabble has a special talent for creating characters who, though they live ordinary lives, are absorbing for the reader.
13. Alcoholism, which is widely misunderstood, is a disease.
14. Did you know that El Paso, Texas, is on the Mexican-American border?
15. To appreciate the exhibits at the Museum of Science and Industry in Chicago requires more than one visit.
16. The Grand Canyon, one of the most spectacular sights on the North American continent, has been carved out of rock by the forces of nature.
17. At the assembly, the concert and jazz bands gave performances that had the student body clapping, cheering, and calling for encores.
18. Because the hospital emergency team worked so brilliantly helping the accident victims, Governor Ortega sent them a special letter of commendation.

19. Maura has always taken delight in words such as *bark, sighed, rib, eye,* and *ewe,* which have double meanings.
20. As the first raindrops fell, Eric and Pablo continued their match; but when the thunder roared, they left the court in a hurry!
21. During the monsoon season in India, heavy rain falls every afternoon, flooding fields and towns.
22. Last year, many farmers in the Southwest suffered crop failures due to drought.
23. The Vietnam Memorial, a black granite wall engraved with the names of those who died in the Vietnam War, was designed by Maya Lin when she was a student at Yale University.
24. Has Earline decided whether she is going to ask for a raise?
25. The highways of America, built under mountains, over rivers, and through deserts, are engineering wonders.

CHAPTER 4 REVIEW: POSTTEST 3

Writing Sentences.   Write your own sentences, one of each of the following kinds:

1. A complex sentence with an adjective clause beginning with the relative pronoun *where*
2. A complex sentence with a noun clause used as the subject of the sentence
3. A complex sentence with a noun clause used as the object of the verb of the sentence
4. A complex sentence with an adjective clause beginning with the relative pronoun *who*
5. A complex sentence with an adverb clause beginning with the subordinating conjunction *because*
6. A complex sentence with an adverb clause beginning with the subordinating conjunction *while*
7. A compound-complex sentence
8. A complex sentence with an elliptical clause
9. An interrogative compound sentence
10. An imperative sentence

GRAMMAR
MASTERY REVIEW: Cumulative Test

A. THE PARTS OF SPEECH. The following paragraph contains fifteen numbered, italicized words. Number your paper 1–15; next to each number, identify the part of speech of the corresponding italicized word or words. Use the following abbreviations: *n.* (noun), *pron.* (pronoun), *adj.* (adjective), *v.* (verb), *adv.* (adverb), *conj.* (conjunction), *prep.* (preposition), *interj.* (interjection).

EXAMPLE   1. The newspaper ran the election results in a (1) *banner* headline.
1. *adj.*

(1) *One* of the best-kept secrets (2) *in* America is that the economy depends to a (3) *great* extent on the work of (4) *teen-agers*. For instance, if every teen-ager in America were to strike for a day, what (5) *would happen*? Without doubt, fast-food restaurants would (6) *immediately* have to close for the day. Supermarkets, grocery stores, (7) *and* department stores would have to close many of their checkout counters. Lines would form (8) *at* gas stations as mechanics would be pressed into service at the pumps. Restaurant tables would remain uncleared because of absent waiters and waitresses. Messenger (9) *delivery* services would be in (10) *turmoil*. And, (11) *alas,* a multitude of parents would have to cancel social commitments (12) *because* there would be almost no available baby sitters. The majority of working teen-agers (13) *perform* their work productively and (14) *maturely;* (15) *they* deserve recognition for their economic contribution to our society.

B. SUBJECTS AND VERBS. Number your paper 16–20. For each sentence, identify the simple subject and the verb. Be sure to include all parts of a verb phrase and all parts of a compound subject or a compound verb.

EXAMPLE   1. On page one, a picture and a lengthy article featured the happy winner of the election.
1. *picture, article*
featured

16. In hot weather, people invent a variety of ways to keep cool.
17. Powered by hand and wrist, newspapers and magazines are sometimes employed as modern versions of the age-old handheld fan.

18. Electric fans of all sizes provide welcome, if artificial, breezes in many homes.
19. Another, more costly electrical device, the air conditioner, continues to grow in popularity.
20. During a heat wave, Americans have been known to resort to the oldest coolant of all: a plunge into cool water.

C. COMPLEMENTS. Number your paper 21–25. Next to each number, write the complement (or complements) contained in the corresponding sentence and identify the kind of complement each is. Use the following abbreviations: *d.o.* (direct object), *i.o.* (indirect object), *p.n.* (predicate nominative), *p.a.* (predicate adjective).

EXAMPLE   1. Will you give me a minute of your time, please?
　　　　　　 1. *me, i.o.*
　　　　　　　 minute, d.o.

21. Margaret Mead, the great American anthropologist, pioneered new methods of studying human culture.
22. Mead's writing about the people of the South Pacific gave the public a clearer understanding of the origins of human behavior.
23. For one of these groups, a demonstration of love and kindness is the most important responsibility of parents.
24. In sharp contrast, another group with a different attitude toward life were not affectionate toward their children.
25. According to Mead's conclusion, people learn kindness and cruelty through their culture.

D. THE PHRASE. Each of the following sentences contains an italicized phrase. Number your paper 26–35. Next to each number, identify the kind of phrase in the corresponding sentence. Use these abbreviations: *appos.* (appositive), *ger.* (gerund), *inf.* (infinitive), *part.* (participial), *prep.* (prepositional).

EXAMPLE   1. I will buy Duran Duran's new album *for you* for your birthday.
　　　　　　 1. *prep.*

26. Two years ago, Anthony, *a friend of mine since the first grade,* spent hours teaching me how to make a delicious tomato sauce.
27. It is a versatile sauce, which can be used in *making spaghetti, chicken cacciatore, and many other dishes.*

28. *Specially created many years ago,* this Italian recipe came from Anthony's grandmother, Mrs. Rossi.

29. Anthony was firm in *warning me* that I must use all the ingredients and spices: tomatoes, tomato paste, basil, garlic, pure olive oil, spicy Italian sausage, salt, and pepper.

30. And, he insisted, *under no circumstances* was I to simmer the sauce for less than four hours.

31. *Having followed the recipe exactly,* I was delighted with the results.

32. My first taste of my own Italian sauce almost made me forget how hard I had worked *to produce it.*

33. Thanks *to Anthony and Mrs. Rossi,* I have received many compliments from family and friends and have earned quite a reputation as a cook.

34. Last summer, when I first had the pleasure of meeting Mrs. Rossi, *a woman now in her sixties,* I told her enthusiastically how grateful I was to have her recipe.

35. Imagine my surprise when she responded, "Oh, I'm too busy *to make sauce the old-fashioned way these days.* I always buy mine in the supermarket."

E. THE CLAUSE. In the following passage, there are ten italicized clauses. Number your paper 36–45. For each item, identify the clause as adjective (*adj.*), adverb (*adv.*), noun (*n.*), or independent (*ind.*). If the clause is an adjective clause or an adverb clause, write after it the word(s) the clause modifies. If the clause is a noun clause, indicate whether it is used as a subject (*subj.*), direct object (*d.o.*), indirect object (*i.o.*), predicate nominative (*p.n.*), or object of a preposition (*o.p.*).

EXAMPLES 1. *If a class is boring,* students do not learn efficiently.
1. *adv., do learn*
2. This is *what the critic had to say about the project.*
2. *noun, p.n.*

At the beginning of the third marking period, our English teacher, Mr. Jefferson, told us (36) *that we would be responsible for doing an original project.* (37) *After our moans and groans had subsided,* Mr. Jefferson went on to say that we could work alone or in groups of two or three students. Since we had a three-week deadline, (38) *most of us spent only a few days procrastinating and then got down to work.*

We were amazed at the results. Floyd Brown and Marshall Davis made a hilarious sound film, (39) *which satirized the student body.* Ming Chin Kwan and Chee Draper invented a game, "Mystery Guests," in which class members had to ask questions of another student who played the part of a person, place, or thing from literary works (40) *we had studied.* Another successful project was one (41) *that involved the class in one of our most heated debates.* In this project, Roberto Seda and Gabriel Aguilar directed discussion of issues that must be considered (42) *before people marry.* Among class members, the "realists" and the "romantics" quickly took opposing positions, and (43) *everyone became involved in sharing facts, opinions, and ideas.*

This experience taught me much about how I can research and organize material and about (44) *how I can present my ideas to my classmates.* I gained self-confidence, I learned a lot, and (45) *I grew to respect the imaginative strengths of my classmates and my teacher.*

F. THE CLASSIFICATION OF SENTENCES. Number your paper 46–50. Next to each number, indicate the structure of the sentence, using these abbreviations: *s.* (simple), *cd.* (compound), *cx.* (complex), *cd-cx.,* (compound-complex). Then indicate the purpose of the sentence, using these abbreviations: *decl.* (declarative), *int.* (interrogative), *imp.* (imperative), *excl.* (exclamatory).

EXAMPLE   1. Within minutes after the accident, the Red Cross workers were giving assistance to the injured.
     1. *s., decl.*

46. Is there anyone who has never heard of the Red Cross?
47. An international organization headquartered in Geneva, Switzerland, the Red Cross was established in 1864.
48. The original purpose of the organization was to assist the wounded in wartime, but the purpose has been expanded to the assistance of people during any kind of natural disaster.
49. Red Cross workers are courageous, and they often work in situations where bullets are flying and volcanoes are erupting nearby!
50. American Red Cross volunteers have saved countless lives and offered comfort to countless numbers of people in times of need.

PART TWO

USAGE

CHAPTER 5

Levels of Usage

STANDARD AND NONSTANDARD ENGLISH

Because we are all part of one society, there are a number of matters we do not have to decide independently for ourselves. Instead, we more or less unconsciously comply with social conventions—the customary ways in which groups of people behave together. The styles of clothing we wear derive from such conventions; so do our styles of etiquette. This chapter is about the conventions that govern our uses of language. But before considering conventional language, consider the more obvious and familiar conventions that affect the way we dress.

Although everyone knows the expression "clothes make the man," few really believe it. We like to think that we can recognize the admirable qualities in people whether they are wearing bathing suits or business suits. Yet we cannot truthfully say that people's clothes make no impression on us at all. We pay no particular attention to what people wear so long as their clothes are more or less what we would expect under the circumstances. We expect to see bathing suits at the beach and business suits at the office. We would notice a business suit at the beach or a bathing suit at the office. In other words, it is only when clothing is obviously singular or inappropriate that we are drawn to notice it emphatically and forced to consider the motives of its wearer.

Appropriate Language

It is much the same with the language a person uses. As long as it is appropriate—"fits in" with what others use—we do not pay special attention to the way in which people form their sentences or to the vocabulary they use. However, when a person's use of language strikes us as clearly unsuitable to the situation, we become distracted from *what* is being said and begin to think mainly about *how* it is being said. Language that deliberately calls attention to itself gets in the way of communication instead of making communication easier. However, there is a great variety within appropriate language; no single form of English usage can be the only correct one for every situation.

Language conveys more than mere ideas. It also conveys the speaker's own personality. If you speak stiffly, you may give the impression of being standoffish, whether you mean to be or not. If you speak as casually with a prospective employer as you do in conversation with close friends, the impression you create of yourself may lose you the job. In conversational use of the language you would probably say, "No one knew who the President had chosen." In a formal written report, however, you would write, "No one knew *whom* the President had chosen."

THE VARIETIES OF ENGLISH

We can distinguish several different kinds of English, all by the differing situations in which each is used. In general, we can distinguish two broad areas of English usage: *standard* and *nonstandard.*

Standard English

Standard English is the kind of English usage developed over the centuries and is most widely used. It is the language of most educational, legal, governmental, and professional documents. Although standard English differs, as we shall see, in different situations, it has certain conventions regularly observed by all who use it. And because well-educated people are taught to use standard English, their language conventions are respected. That is why this variety of English is called *standard*—a term that denotes an example or model which others may follow.

One of the reasons that standard English is taught in schools and in textbooks such as this one is that many occasions, such as a job interview or the writing of a business letter, require standard English. Learning the conventions of standard English, therefore, is an important task for every student.

Nonstandard English

Standard and nonstandard English are not, of course, different languages. While there are some words that appear only in one or the other, most English words can appear in either. The main differences appear in the use of pronouns and certain verb forms. A user of standard English would use *brought* where a user of nonstandard English might use *brung*. Similarly:

STANDARD	NONSTANDARD
He did it **himself**.	He did it **hisself**.
You and **she** fight all the time.	You and **her** fight all the time.
He **doesn't** trust me.	He **don't** trust me.
She **ran** right into me.	She **run** right into me.

Sentences like those in the right-hand column above are spoken by thousands of native speakers of English. It has always been a major technique of literature to create characterization through the device of having characters use recognizably nonstandard speech. Eudora Welty and William Faulkner are among the great artists admired for their ability to capture the special lilt of certain dialects of nonstandard English. Occasionally it happens that a speaker of nonstandard English makes a style of usage a popular trademark. Dizzy Dean, a famous pitcher for the St. Louis Cardinals and later a radio and television announcer, made his own nonstandard speech a great asset, as did Casey Stengel, when he was manager of the New York Yankees and, later, the New York Mets. The following excerpt from an interview in the *New York Times* gives an idea of what nonstandard English in the Dizzy Dean style is like (as well as offering Mr. Dean's personal opinions about usage):

> And I reckon that's why that now I come up with *ain't* once in a while, and have the Missouri teachers all stirred up. They don't like it because I say that Marty Marion or Vern Stephens *slud* into second base. What do they want me to say—*slidded*?
> Me and Paul [Dizzy's brother, also a pitcher for the Cards] didn't have to worry about that sort of stuff when we were winning games for the old Gas House Gang. And I don't know why I should get a sweat up now.

Paul, he'd win one game and I'd win the next.

Didn't nobody come around after the game and ask whether we'd throwed or threw the ball in there to make a play.

We won 'em, no questions asked.

There are so many varieties of nonstandard English—as there are standard and nonstandard varieties of all living languages—that it seems best to describe it simply as the observance of conventions that are recognizably different from those of the standard language.

Language may vary according to audience and occasion. Standard English is the medium of communication certain to reach the broadest audience of speakers of English and find a hearing. Nonstandard English is by definition, as its name suggests, a form of usage proper to a smaller group than the whole of the English-speaking world. The more general the audience one is trying to reach, the more one tends to use the standard language. The more personal and informal the occasion, the less one needs to be conscious of the conventions and rules applying to standard usage.

TWO KINDS OF STANDARD ENGLISH

Standard English is used in so many different situations—ranging from casual telephone conversations to formal speeches—that it would be impossible to name a particular kind appropriate for each situation. But we can distinguish two domains of standard English: *formal* and *informal*. However, most standard usage tends to fall somewhere between these two varieties.

Formal English

Formal English, like formal dress and formal manners, is language for special occasions. Sometimes referred to as "literary" English, it is the language of all serious writing. It should be used in formal essays, essay answers to examination questions, formal reports, research papers, literary criticism, scholarly writings, and addresses on serious or solemn occasions.

As you might expect, formal English is likely to include words that rarely come up in ordinary conversation. The sentences are likely to be more elaborately constructed and longer than those of ordinary writing. Contractions are rarely used. Formal English pays close attention to refinements in usage and seldom admits any slang. It is language in formal dress.

In the following example of formal English, note the long and carefully constructed sentences. Notice also the extremely formal vocabulary: *colossus, infidel, grandeur, promontory.*

Formidable and grand on a hilltop in Picardy, the five-towered castle of Coucy dominated the approach to Paris from the north, but whether as guardian or as challenger of the monarchy in the capital was an open question. Thrusting up from the castle's center, a gigantic cylinder rose to twice the height of the four corner towers. This was the *donjon* or central citadel, the largest in Europe, the mightiest of its kind ever built in the Middle Ages or thereafter. Ninety feet in diameter, 180 feet high, capable of housing a thousand men in a siege, it dwarfed and protected the castle at its base, the clustered roofs of the town, the bell tower of the church, and the thirty turrets of the massive wall enclosing the whole complex on the hill. Travelers coming from any direction could see this colossus of baronial power from miles away and, on approaching it, feel the awe of the traveler in infidel lands at first sight of the pyramids.

Seized by grandeur, the builders had carried out the scale of the *donjon* in interior features of more than mortal size: risers of steps were fifteen to sixteen inches, window seats three and a half feet from the ground, as if for use by a race of titans. Stone lintels measuring two cubic yards were no less heroic. For more than four hundred years the dynasty reflected by these arrangements had exhibited the same quality of excess. Ambitious, dangerous, not infrequently ferocious, the Coucys had planted themselves on a promontory of land which was formed by nature for command.

BARBARA TUCHMAN

Informal English

Informal English is the language most English-speaking people use most of the time. It is the language of magazines, newspapers, books, and talks intended for general audiences.

The conventions of informal English are less rigid than those of formal English. Sentences may be long or short, and they are likely to sound more like conversation than the stately rhythms of formal English. Contractions often appear in informal English and sometimes a slang expression is admitted. Here is an example of written informal English:

One day General Littlefield picked our company out of the whole regiment and tried to get it mixed up by putting it through one movement after another as fast as we could execute them: squads right, squads left, squads on right into line, squads right about, squads left front into line, etc. In about three minutes one hundred and nine men were marching in one direction and I was marching away from them at an angle of forty-five degrees, all alone. "Company; halt!" shouted General Littlefield. "That man is the only man who has it right!" I was made a corporal for my achievement.

The next day General Littlefield summoned me to his office. He was swatting flies when I went in. I was silent and he was silent too, for a long time. I don't think he remembered me or why he had sent for me, but he didn't want to admit it. He swatted some more flies, keeping his eyes on them narrowly before he let go with the swatter. "Button up your coat" he snapped. Looking back on it now I can see that he meant me, although he was looking at a fly, but I just stood there. Another fly came to rest on a paper in front of the general and began rubbing its hind legs together. The general lifted the swatter cautiously. I moved restlessly and the fly flew away. "You startled him!" barked General Littlefield, looking at me severely. I said I was sorry. "That won't help the situation!" snapped the general, with cold military logic. I didn't see what I could do except offer to chase some more flies toward his desk, but I didn't say anything. He stared out the window at the faraway figures of co-eds crossing the campus toward the library. Finally, he told me I could go. So I went. He either didn't know which cadet I was or else he forgot what he wanted to see me about. It may have been that he wished to apologize for having called me the main trouble with the university; or maybe he had decided to compliment me on my brilliant drilling of the day before and then at the last minute decided not to. I don't know. I don't think about it much any more.

JAMES THURBER

EXERCISE 1. Distinguishing Different Kinds of English.
Read each of the following passages carefully and identify the type of English to which it belongs—formal, informal, or nonstandard. Note the particular words and constructions that cause you to label the passage as you do.

1

In a few weeks, you will each receive a copy of the treasurer's report. Anyone who wants to gripe about the way we're spending the club's money will get a chance at next Saturday's business meeting.

2

If I'd of known they was goin' to let you feed the elephants I'd of went with you.

3

Those actions of his former subordinates that the General was now powerless to oppose, he elected to support. In his eagerness to anticipate any new mischief that might occur to the junta, he promulgated a series of new laws, each more harshly repressive than the last, which even the most rabid of the young officers would not have dared to propose.

4

One thing is, she don't take long walks like she used to. Every morning we used to see her out there, takin' those brisk steps. Just as fast! You'd of thought there was something after her. And if you was to meet her, she'd never stop to say nothing to you. Just bob her head at you and go right on. Now that she ain't comin' by anymore, we sort of miss it. When you get used to something, you kind of want it to keep on.

5

I passed all the other courses that I took at my university, but I could never pass botany. This was because all botany students had to spend several hours a week in a laboratory looking through a microscope at plant cells, and I could never see through a microscope. I never once saw a cell through a microscope. This used to enrage my instructor. He would wander around the laboratory pleased with the progress all the students were making in drawing the involved and, so I am told, interesting structure of flower cells, until he came to me. I would just be standing there. "I can't see anything," I would say. He would begin patiently enough, explaining how anybody can see through a microscope, but he would always end up in a fury, claiming that I could *too* see through a microscope but just pretended that I couldn't . . . .[1]

---

[1] From "University Days" from *My Life and Hard Times*, copyright 1933, © 1961 by James Thurber. Published by Harper & Row. Originally printed in *The New Yorker.* (Published in Great Britain as *Vintage Thurber*, copyright © 1963 by Hamish Hamilton, London.) Reprinted by permission of Hamish Hamilton Ltd. and Helen Thurber.

EXERCISE 2. Revising Passages for Specific Circumstances.
Each of the following brief passages is written, as indicated, in a kind of
English typical of certain circumstances. Revise each of the passages by
using English suited to the circumstances specified.

1. Nonstandard English used in an oral summary of an article. Revise
   by using standard informal English.

   The President finally got his dander up and told them Russians to get
   their stuff out of Cuba fast or else! He said the Navy would search ships
   headed for Cuba and if they didn't stop they'd be sorry.

2. A student reports to her friends in the lunchroom a conversation
   she has had with the school principal. Revise by using language she
   would use if reporting the same conversation to her class.

   Yeah, old Sherlock Holmes told me that any kids caught sneaking out of
   assembly would get kicked out of school.

3. Nonstandard English used in relating an incident. Revise by using
   standard informal English.

   When Mom and me come home, we seen right away they'd been
   somebody messing around with the car.

4. The mayor talking informally to the City Commission. Revise by
   using the kind of English the mayor would use in making the same
   explanation to an audience of citizens.

   In a couple of weeks you'll all receive the report recommending a new
   high school. You can bet that there'll be plenty of moaning from those
   people up on the Hill.

WRITING APPLICATION:
Acquiring Flexibility in Levels of Usage

Some people have more than one set of dishes in their households. One
set is used for everyday eating, while the other set is reserved for special
occasions or company. You also have at your command two kinds of
standard English. Like the everyday dishes, informal English is what
you use most of the time. It is more conversational. Formal English, like
special china, is reserved for particular occasions. It is the language of
formal essays, reports, and so on. Notice the formal English in the first
example below, followed by a more conversational, informal version of
the same material.

EXAMPLES
1. In cinema, an extraordinary new genre called scientific fantasy has been developed. Using formality of language and vividness of imagery, this genre portrays the universal theme of benevolence pitted against malevolence. Through the heroic and often macabre intergalactic confrontations, the struggle is waged for the ultimate purpose of establishing moral equilibrium.
2. There's a new kind of movie called science fantasy. The characters use big, scientific words. Some of the scenes are awesome. It's usually good versus evil. There are a lot of bloody battles out in space. In the end, good wins out.

Writing Assignment

You should be able to switch naturally from informal to formal English. Keep in mind that formal English is the level used in serious writing unless the assignment directs otherwise. Write two paragraphs illustrating your ability to use both informal and formal English. Either give an explanation or describe something. Like the example above, use formal English in the first paragraph and informal English in the second paragraph.

IMPROVING YOUR USAGE

While we can speak generally about three kinds of English—formal standard, informal standard, and nonstandard—the lines between them are not always easy to draw. One kind of usage shades into another; an expression we think of as being informal may turn up in a formal address; a slang word that originates in nonstandard English may become an acceptable part of the informal vocabulary; many words and constructions that we think of as belonging to standard speech may come into use among speakers of nonstandard English. The great majority of our words and our ways of putting them together are common to all three.

Sources of Usage Information

If your usage habits conform to the conventions of standard English, your main concern will be in suiting your language to the occasion in which you speak or write. If you are in a conversation, the usage of those you are talking with will give you valuable clues. If you are writing, keeping your audience in mind should help.

There will be times, however, when you cannot be sure whether a particular word or expression is suitable for a particular situation. Or there may be a few nonstandard forms that you habitually use in your writing and speaking. You can deal with these questions by studying a textbook like this one, by referring to a dictionary, or by consulting a special book on usage like those listed on page 107. And most important of all, you can develop habits of noticing the usage preferences of careful users of English.

You will find the rules of grammar a useful but not invariably reliable guide to usage. Grammar describes the system of a language; usage is concerned with appropriate forms of expression. The two are not always the same, for language is a living and growing thing, and life and growth are not always logical. Changes are brought about by the people who use a language, and grammar rules, which can only be stated when the changes have occurred, necessarily come afterward. The rules of grammar describe the way the language works. When the system changes, the rules change.

The Importance of Good English

Using English according to the conventions established by educated users of the language and adapting it to the circumstances in which we use it will not, of course, make us effective speakers and writers. Conventional usage is only one of the qualities of good speech and good writing. Perhaps it is not even the most important. It is not so important, for example, as clarity or forcefulness of expression. It is not so important as honesty or originality or freshness. Yet good usage is important, nevertheless. We like to be noticed for things that are worthwhile and admirable, not just for things that are different. The person who is out of step in a parade attracts more attention than all the rest of those marching, but we do not usually seek that kind of notice.

People will judge you by your usage. If you deviate from the conventions of standard English, they will think more about how you are expressing yourself than they will about what you are saying.

EXERCISE 3. Solving Usage Problems. The words and expressions listed below present usage problems that trouble some people. Look them up in this and whatever other textbooks are available to you—most of these problems will be listed in the index. Consult also the usage books listed below.

1. *It's me*. [pronoun usage]   5. *between* or *among*
2. *shall* or *will*   6. *(the) reason* is *because*
3. *imply* or *infer*   7. split infinitive
4. double negatives   8. *due to*

Guides to Usage

The following books contain accurate information about usage problems. You will find additional information on usage in your dictionary (see page 886). Neither the books in the following list nor your dictionary can tell you exactly what to say or write in a particular situation. What they can do is help you to make up your own mind.

American Heritage Dictionary of the English Language: New College Edition, Boston, Houghton Mifflin Company, 1978.

Bernstein, Theodore M., *The Careful Writer: A Modern Guide to English Usage*, New York, Atheneum, 1979.

Bryant, Margaret M., *Current American Usage*, New York, Funk & Wagnalls, 1962.

Copperud, *The Consensus*, New York, Van Nostrand Reinhold, 1979.

Evans, Bergen and Cornelia, *A Dictionary of Contemporary American Usage*, New York, Random House, 1957.

SUMMARY: STANDARD AND NONSTANDARD ENGLISH

Standard English	Typical Uses	Typical Features
Formal	research papers, serious speeches, books and articles for special occasions	words little used in ordinary speech; longer sentences; complex constructions; few contractions; no slang
Informal	conversations of educated people; most writing in books, newspapers, and popular magazines; lectures to general audiences; political speeches; most textbooks	wide variety of sentence length; less difficult vocabulary than formal; sentences that sound like good conversation, even when written; contractions; some slang

Nonstandard English	*Typical Uses*	*Typical Features*
	conversations which include dialect, phrasing, words, or expressions that are not included in standard English; dialogue intended to represent local dialects in movies, books, comic strips, radio, and television	verb and pronoun forms not appearing in standard English (*you was, he don't, hisself,* etc.); adverbs without the *-ly* ending (She sings *bad*); frequent use of slang words and localisms

CHAPTER 6

The History of English

ORIGINS AND DEVELOPMENT OF THE LANGUAGE

English is a member of one of the largest and most widespread language families in the world. It is related to nearly all of the languages of Europe and to a number of those of South Asia, including Persian, Afghan, and several of the chief languages of India. This circumstance is the result of a long sequence of historical events. In examining this history, we become conscious of the fact that language is a part of the culture of those who speak it and that, just as all societies are in a constant state of change, so the languages that they use are also constantly changing. We do not speak exactly like our parents, and we speak even less like our grandparents. With the passage of long periods of historical time, small differences become greater. One group of speakers influences another or even displaces it; groups break up and separate, until changes have become so great that speakers of what was originally one language can no longer understand one another. In this way, then, does it come about that from one language, spoken thousands of years ago, a far-spreading family of related languages has developed. The history of English properly begins with the story of this great family of which it is a member.

INDO-EUROPEAN

About six thousand years ago a seminomadic people wandered in tribes which even then were fairly widely spread over eastern Europe or western Asia. We surmise from the vocabulary of their descendants that they herded flocks of sheep, kept horses and dogs, knew cold and snow; and from their subsequent history we guess that they were good fighters and good travelers. Probably at least as early as 4000 B.C., groups or tribes of this people began a series of migrations that were ultimately to spread the later forms of their language over half the globe. This language, as we reconstruct it from the records of its descendant languages, we call Proto- (first or earliest) Indo-European. The large family of languages that descends from it we call the Indo-European family.

Early Branchings

One of these tribes that split away from the parent group moved, doubtless in successive waves, over western Asia and Asia Minor eastward, ultimately to northern India by way of the Iranian plateau. Today, in some of the modern languages and in surviving examples of the ancient literatures of India and Persia, we may see the distinct yet closely related languages which developed from the dialects spoken by this people. Another early migration moved southward or westward into Greece, the adjacent islands, and the coastal area of Asia Minor. Successive waves of invasion resulted in several varieties, or dialects, of the language, though modern Greek descends from only one of these, the dialect of Athens. The following table gives the words for *ten* and *three* in some important Indo-European languages. Notice the similarities. Where differences exist, notice that the variations tend to be consistent within a single branch. Thus, all Germanic languages have initial *t* where the others have *d* in the word for *ten*. This kind of resemblance is a mark of close relationship within a branch of the language family.

	English	*ten*	*three*
	Saxon	*tehan*	*thrie*
	Old Norse	*tiu*	*thrir*
Germanic	Swedish	*tio*	*tre*
	Danish	*ti*	*tre*
	Norwegian	*tie*	*tre*
	Gothic	*taihun*	*thrija*

Italic	Spanish	diez	tres
	Italian	dieci	tre
	French	dix	trois
Slavic	Old Slavonic	desja	triye
	Russian	desyat	tri
	Welsh	deg	tri
	Greek	deka	treis
	Sanskrit	dasa	trayas

Another migration westward carried into Italy a group of dialects, one of which was the ancestor of Latin. Centuries after this, as a result of the conquests of the Roman Empire, dialects of Latin were spread over much of Europe, and it is from these that the modern Romance languages, including French, Spanish, Italian, Portuguese, and Romanian, descend. Two other important language groups which migrated away from the Indo-European homeland are Celtic and Balto-Slavic. After a very great expansion over much of Europe and even into Asia Minor, the Celts were gradually conquered and their language largely displaced by dialects of Latin and Germanic. The most important surviving Celtic languages are Welsh, Breton, and Irish, with its Scottish dialect, Scots Gaelic. Balto-Slavic comprises two closely related groups including Lithuanian and Latvian and the Slavic languages of the Balkans from Bulgaria to Poland as well as the various dialects of Russian.

Germanic

In addition to several less well-known languages, one more group of major importance descends from Proto-Indo-European. This group is Germanic, one of whose most important members is English. In the first centuries of our era, the great expansion of Germanic peoples began, northward to the Scandinavian countries and on to Iceland, eastward into the Baltic territory, westward into what is now France, Spain, and England, and even southward to North Africa. The modern Germanic languages include many, though of course not all, of the languages of these areas. Best known are German in its various forms, Dutch, Norwegian, Danish, and Swedish, as well as English.

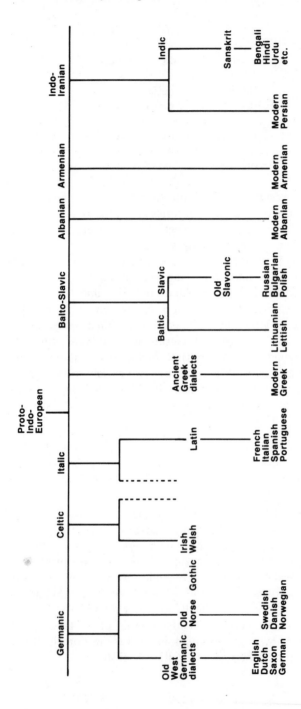

This chart shows the branches of the Indo-European family that have living modern descendant languages. In some instances, important ancient languages also appear. The two empty sub-branches under Celtic and Italic indicate ancient languages that have no important descendants.

The migration of Germanic tribes into the British Isles was the event that marked the beginning of English as a separate language. In the fifth century the Roman colony of Britain was a relatively peaceful and civilized community, the principal languages of which were one or more varieties of Celtic, though many important persons also spoke Latin. Beginning in the fifth century, there descended upon this island waves of Germanic invaders, coming by sea from the lands along the North Sea coast of modern Germany, Denmark, and the Low Countries. During more than a century of fighting, these relatively primitive and warlike tribes drove the Britons back until only a comparatively small part of their country was left to them, chiefly the western and northern mountainous areas of the island. With the displacement of the Celtic-speaking Britons, the language of the new country was henceforth the Germanic speech of the conquerors. This language and the new country which they had founded came relatively soon to be called *Englisc* and *Engla land*, or "land of the Angles," after the largest of the invading tribes.

EXERCISE 1. Plotting the Migration of Indo-European Languages. Find in a dictionary or encyclopedia a detailed chart of the Indo-European family of languages (there is a good one in *Webster's Third New International Dictionary* at the entry "Indo-European languages"). With the help of the chart and the material of this chapter, plot the migration of the various IE languages on an outline map of Europe and Asia. Begin at a point somewhere east of the Black Sea and north of the Caspian Sea and draw in the movements, east and south to Iran and India, west and south to Greece, etc. Be sure to include the Romance languages and, above all, the movement of peoples that resulted in the establishment of a Germanic language in England.

THE DEVELOPMENT OF ENGLISH

English was the first of all modern European languages to reach the status of a literary language. There are in existence documents containing written English from as early as the seventh century, and from the eighth century we have a considerable body of surviving literature. But, as may be imagined, very great changes have taken place in English in the 1,300 years of its recorded existence, as they certainly also did during the prehistoric period. For the purpose of studying the history of these changes, we divide the language into three periods: Old English (or Anglo-Saxon), from the arrival of the Jutes, Angles, and Saxons in Britain to about A.D. 1100; Middle English from 1100 to about 1450; and Modern English from 1450 to the present. The languages of each of these periods differ considerably in sounds of speech, in grammar, and in vocabulary, these being the three features by which languages are usually described.

Old English

During the very long Old English period, considerable change naturally took place in the language, clearly distinguishing it from the western Germanic dialects from which it originated. To the end of the period, however, it retained most of the features characteristic of an early Germanic language. From the point of view of language history, the most significant of these features were grammatical. Old English, like the other members of the Indo-European family, was an inflected language. This means that the relationship between the words of a sentence was usually shown by endings added to the roots of words. Thus each noun in Old English had a set of endings the presence of which might signal that it was subject, direct object, indirect object, a possessive, a singular, or a plural. Also adjectives and articles or demonstratives like *the* or *this* had complete sets of endings to assist in the process of showing relationship. This is to be contrasted with Modern English, in which these relationships are shown almost entirely by word order and by otherwise almost meaningless signaling words like articles and prepositions. The contrast may be seen in the following sentence from the Old English poem *Beowulf*:

> *Thone sithfaet him snotere ceorlas lythwon logon.*

Literally and word for word, this translates, "That journey him wise men not at all criticized." This translation, without the word order and other signaling devices of Modern English, is badly confused. However, the inflectional devices of Old English make it perfectly clear. Among other indications, the ending *–ne* on *thone* marks the following noun as a direct object; the third word is marked by the ending *–m* as a dative, usually to be translated as "to him"; the ending *–as* on the fifth word marks a plural subject; and the last word is marked as a past tense plural verb by the form of the stem and the ending *–on*. Thus the meaning signaled by these devices is seen to be "the wise men criticized that journey to him not at all." Modern English makes these signals almost entirely without the aid of inflectional endings. The subject is signaled by position before the verb and by the presence of *the*. The verb, identified by its ending, is placed after the subject. The position of the noun *journey* (identified as a noun by the presence of *that*) immediately after the verb signals that it is a direct object. The sense of the old dative is signaled by the preposition *to* before *him*. The difference between the older inflectional system and the new way of showing grammatical relationships is very great.

A second grammatical feature in which Old English resembles the other members of the Indo-European family is its possession of gender. In accordance with this system, the nouns of Old English are divided into three groups, or genders: masculine, feminine, and neuter. The adjectives and other modifying words each have three sets of endings, one for each gender. Each noun must be accompanied by a form of the adjective, demonstrative, article, or pronoun having an ending suited to the gender of the noun to which it refers. This feature adds greatly to the grammatical complexity of any language, for it means that each noun, wherever it occurs, must be properly classified and matched with the appropriate form of the adjective, article, or pronoun. We may see this system in modern European languages such as German, where *die Hand, der Fuss*, and *das Auge* are respectively marked as feminine, masculine, and neuter by the varying forms of the definite article, *die, der, das*. In Old English, too, these words appear as *seo hand, se fot*, and *thaet eage*—masculine, feminine, and neuter; but in Modern English, where this feature is almost entirely lost, all are what we may call common gender, and the article is invariable: *the hand, the foot*, and *the eye*.

EXERCISE 2. Identifying Grammatical Features of Latin and English.   Latin is one of the best-known languages with a fairly full set of inflections. In this respect it resembles Old English, as well as other early forms of Indo-European languages. In the following sentences *agricola* means "farmer" and *puella* means "girl." Identify the grammatical features which distinguish subject from direct object in the Latin. Do the same for the English translations.

> Agricola puellam vocat. [The farmer calls the girl.]
> Agricolam puella vocat. [The girl calls the farmer.]

EXERCISE 3. Understanding Grammatical Gender Features of Latin. You now know something about the subject and object forms of this class of nouns. In addition to this, the grammatical gender system of Latin classifies *agricola* as masculine and *puella* as feminine. The adjective *bon–* meaning "good" has in this system a set of forms for use with masculine nouns and another for use with feminine: thus, for subject case *agricola bonus* but *puella bona*, and for object case *agricolam bonum* but *puellam bonam*. Notice that Latin adjectives usually come after the nouns they modify.

Try writing the following sentences in Latin. Since Latin does not use articles in the way that English does, simply ignore the word *the* whenever it occurs.

> The good boy [*puer*, masc.] calls.
> The good queen [*regina*, fem.] calls.
> The good boy calls the good queen.

EXERCISE 4. Explaining Inflectional Features of Old English. In the following Old English sentence *hund* "dog" is masculine and *wylf* "wolf" is feminine; *sliehth* means "kills." The remaining four words are forms of the demonstrative "the": *se* and *thone* are subject and object forms of the masculine, *seo* and *tha* are subject and object forms of the feminine. Explain how the inflectional system signals the meaning in the two sentences.

> Se hund tha wylfe sliehth.
> Thone hund seo wylf sliehth.

Like the grammar, the Old English vocabulary was almost entirely Germanic, except for a relatively small number of words borrowed from Latin. Modern English is quite different; more than three quarters of our present-day vocabulary consists of words borrowed from French, Latin, and other languages. Modern English is, in fact, remarkable for the ease with which it adopts words from other languages. Old English, in its resistance to this kind of borrowing, resembles more the other members of the modern Germanic family. Generally, the Germanic system of filling new needs in vocabulary is to form new words out of native materials, usually by compounding. Modern German, for example, has formed from common German elements the compound *Fernsehen*, literally "far-seeing," in order to name the invention that English calls *television*. Modern English, however, instead of using the native English word stock, has freely and quite typically borrowed the word from French, in which it was formed from the Greek element *tele* "far" and the Latin element *vision*; thus three foreign languages are combined in one English word. Similarly, to give a name to a person who can speak in such a way as to disguise the nature and source of his voice or, as we say, "throw his voice," English borrows the very hard word *ventriloquist* from Latin, which forms it from the Latin words for "belly" and "speak." Norwegian, however, instead of borrowing the Latin word, translates it into native Norwegian elements, producing *buktaler* from Norwegian *buk* "belly" and *taler* "speaker." This, too, is characteristic of Germanic methods of word formation.

This, then, is the way of Old English. Sample Old English compounds are *laececraeft* "the science of medicine," from *laece* "physician" plus *craeft* "art, skill, or craft"; *tungolcraeftiga* "astrologer, magician," from *tongol* "star" plus *craeftiga* "one skilled in a craft." Typical of the Germanic method of translating Latin words into native elements is the Old English word for the Trinity. Modern English, characteristically, borrows its word from the Latin *trinitas*, related to Latin *tres, tria* "three." Old English, however, like Norwegian in the example above, translated the Latin into English elements, producing *thrines,* from Old English *thri* "three" plus *nes*, which is equal to Modern English *-ness*, meaning "state of being."

EXERCISE 5. Finding the Etymologies of Words. In the course of its history, English has acquired new words through two important processes: borrowing from other languages and formation from native elements. Look up the etymology of the following words in a dictionary that traces each element to its ultimate origin. Which words are formed of native elements and which are borrowed? Some of these words are similar in meaning to one or more of the others, though having different origins. Which are these?

advocate	eyeglass	lunatic	retain
canine	firebug	nostril	spokesman
dogtooth	foresee	pyromaniac	withhold
doomsday	loony	resist	word-hoard

Toward the end of the Old English period, there began to appear grammatical developments of the type that in later centuries greatly altered the nature of the language. These developments were reinforced by the historical events of the late Old English and early Middle English periods.

These events began with the Norman Conquest. In the year 1066, the last king of the royal English line of Alfred the Great died. At his death there arose three powerful claimants to the English throne. By law, however, the English council of state was empowered to choose a successor, and they chose, naturally enough, the one of the three who already had the power of England pretty much in his grasp. This was Harold Godwinson, who had been the most powerful of the late king's officers. In the succeeding months Harold prepared for battle against his rivals, and in October he met and defeated the second claimant, Harald, King of Norway. Almost immediately after this battle, however, and before Harold could gather sufficient new troops, the third claimant, William, Duke of Normandy, landed in England with a great army. Near the town of Hastings on October 14, 1066, Harold met William and was defeated and killed. The throne of England thus passed to a line of foreign kings, a significant event in the development of the English language.

In the eleventh century The Duchy of Normandy was a large and powerful state occupying most of the lands along the French coast of the English Channel. Although the Normans were originally pirates from Scandinavia, the language of the Duchy was a variety of French. When William took the English throne, he also took into his hands the high offices of the land and gave them, together with many of the great estates of England, to his French-speaking followers. This process of replacing the native English governing classes with men whose native language was French continued until, in a relatively short time, an entirely new French-speaking ruling class was created.

For most of the first 150 years after the Conquest, we may safely say that French was the native, and often the only, language of most of the upper classes and that it was very probably spoken by many of the merchant classes as well. By 1200, however, the situation was changing, and during the succeeding century, while French continued to be spoken by great numbers of Englishmen, especially of the upper and educated classes, English was increasingly the common language of all. By the fourteenth century, almost everywhere French was in England a language to be learned only from schoolbooks, while English was again becoming the language of literature, of the law courts, of the schools, and of business.

Middle English

Despite this long interruption in the use of English by the governing classes, we must remember, however, that it always remained the language of the great majority of Englishmen. And during all this time the familiar processes of change continued to be at work upon the language: changes of pronunciation, of grammar, and above all, of vocabulary. The dialects of the various parts of England, already different in Old English, continued to develop differently, each in its relative isolation. This, as we have seen already, is the natural way of languages, one which has always gone on and which always will go on so long as they are used by living and changing societies. Yet there has probably been no other equivalent period of time in the history of English when change has been so great and so rapid.

Probably the most important factor contributing to this extraordinary change was the contact—we might almost say conflict—of the two languages, English and French. We have seen that for a long time French was the language of the upper classes, of government and law, and of education. We have seen too that there was a long period in which the usage of these classes and these activities was in transition between French and English. When we see, therefore, that the Middle English vocabulary of these areas of discourse was almost entirely borrowed from French, it is not hard to guess what had happened. During the period of French dominance, English was not used at all in these areas, and, accordingly, the English vocabulary necessary to them was forgotten. Then, as English gradually began to reestablish itself, it became necessary, in the absence of English terms, either to invent new terms or to borrow from French. Since the classes occupied with these activities were obviously intimately familiar with the traditional French vocabulary of the areas, nothing could be more natural than for them to adapt the French terms to English.

French borrowings were, however, by no means concentrated in the political or educational area. Many, in fact, are among the most common words in the language: *city, close, chair, catch, chase, sure*, and many others. In addition, most of our terms of rank or social place are French. The vocabularies of religion and the church, of the arts and sciences, of military affairs, and especially of social life, clothes, manners, and food—all are heavily French. It is interesting to observe that in the latter category the division of the social classes of medieval England is reflected in the distribution of French and English vocabulary.

Words for the animals of the field, for example, are commonly of English origin, for English was of course the language of the country-man: the peasant, the herdsman, and the small farmer. Thus *cow, calf, sheep*, and *swine* are English. But when the meat of these animals is brought to the table as food, it becomes of interest to the upper classes as well, and hence it appears in both Middle and Modern English as French derivatives: *beef, veal, mutton,* and *pork*.

EXERCISE 6. Finding the Etymologies of Words. Look up the etymologies of the following words in a good dictionary. What do they tell you about the history of the English language and the roles of English and French?

authority	herb	paper	sermon
bacon	herdsman	peasant	servant
baron	holy	pen	sir
beauty	hound	pity	song
boil	house	plow	speak
castle	jail	poet	stomach
constable	judge	porch	story
court	manor	prayer	study
dinner	meal	private	tale
earl	medicine	public	taste
feast	music	roast	tower
grammar	noun	saint	write
gruel	pain	sausage	wound

We have noted above that at the end of the Old English period there were already appearing certain grammatical developments that in the Middle English and Modern periods were to change completely the nature of English. One important cause of these developments was a feature that had appeared at a very early time in Germanic, before it had begun to separate into different languages. This was the fixing of a strong stress accent on the first syllable of each word, with the exception of certain prefixes. The result of first syllable stress was, inevitably, the weakening of stress on the remaining syllables and after many centuries their eventual loss. Thus the prehistoric Germanic word that might be written *findanan* turned up in Old English as *findan*, in late Middle English as *finde*, and appears today as *find*, having been reduced from three syllables to one.

The grammatical endings of Old English were not stressed (since they were endings, they could not at the same time be first syllables). Most often, they were distinguished one from the other by differences of vowel. In late Old English, they were more weakly stressed and thus less clearly pronounced; the vowel differences which distinguished them gradually disappeared. For example, in Old English the nominative plural case of many nouns ended in *–as*, and the genitive (or possessive) singular ended in *–es*. In the line from *Beowulf* on page 114, we see an example of the plural subject in *ceorlas* or "men"; the genitive singular of this noun would be *ceorles* or "man's." By Middle English times the distinction between these endings had disappeared and both had become *–es*. This is, of course, still true in Modern English, where there is no distinction in sound between these forms of most nouns (e.g., *boys/boy's; churches/church's*).

This disappearance of the distinctions between the various grammatical forms of words was speeded by another force which very commonly operates in languages. This force is called analogy, and we may perhaps describe it as our desire to make new or irregular words behave according to whatever pattern is already most familiar to us. Thus a child, knowing that for more than one cat we say *cats*, and knowing also *roots, cans, pans, coats*, etc., reasons—quite unconsciously, of course —that when we mean "more than one" we add *–s* to a word. Accordingly, when he uses the word *foot* or *man* he forms, by analogy, the plurals *foots* and *mans*. Though in these particular instances the child may be incorrect, this kind of logic is very important in languages generally. We may see it operating in English today as we fit new words, easily and without any conscious application of "rules," into our grammatical system. Thus when we create such new terms as *slimnastics* or *scuzzy* or when we borrow *sputnik* from Russian, there is never any problem about selecting a special plural form for the creations or any question of adopting the Russian plural *sputniki*. Instead, everyone quite naturally fits them all into the normal English pattern and simply adds *–s*. This is analogy at work in language.

In the rather complex grammar of Old English, there were several different classes of nouns, adjectives, and verbs. Some nouns formed the nominative plural by adding *–a* or *–e* to the stem, like *aex* "ax" and *wylf* "wolf," the plurals of which were *aexa* and *wylfa*. Some changed *–e* to *–u*, like *spere/speru* "spear"; some added *–n*, like *oxa/oxan* "ox," *blostma/blostman* "blossom"; some added *–ru*, like *cild/cildru* "child"; some changed the vowel of the stem, like *boc/bec* "book," *fot/fet* "foot," *toth/teth* "tooth," *cu/cy* "cow"; and some added nothing, like *sceap/sceap* "sheep," *hors/hors* "horse," *word/word* "word," etc. But the largest class of all was that which added *–as*, like *stan/stanas* "stone," *giest/giestas* "guest." We may see among these classes some words which in Modern English have kept their old nominative plural forms: *ox* still adds *–n* in the plural *oxen, foot* still becomes *feet, sheep* still adds nothing, and we may see the added *–r* in *children*. But most nouns have changed classes to become like *stone* and *guest*. This is the result of analogy. The most common way to form plurals was by the addition of *–as*, which by Middle English times had become *–es*. Hence, more and more, people began forming the plurals of nouns by this most familiar means, whether or not the particular word had formed its plural in this way in the older language. The result is that by the end of Middle English times, a very small proportion of English nouns remained in the old special classes.

A similar development took place in the adjectives and verbs of Old English. Partly as a result of the reduction of unstressed syllables and partly as a result of analogy, the only surviving adjective ending in the Middle English period was a final *–e*, and even this completely disappeared by the end of the period. The verbs in Old English, as in Modern English, were divided into two large classes, strong verbs such as *singan* "sing" and weak verbs such as *fyllan* "fill." These were distinguished then, as now, principally by the method of forming the past tense and past participle. The strong verbs formed these by means of a vowel change (*sing, sang, sung*) and the weak by the addition of *–d* or *–t* (*fill, filled, filled*). In Old English the weak verbs were very much the more numerous, and the principal development in Middle English was the change of considerable numbers of strong verbs into weak. This again was the process of analogy, the more common pattern attracting to itself numbers of words originally belonging to the less common one. This development continues to the present time, with a number of verbs still in the process of moving from one class to the other. The past and past participle forms of *crow*, for example, may be the strong forms *crew, crown* or the weak form *crowed*. The past participle of *swell* may be either *swelled* or *swollen*, that of *shave* either *shaved* or *shaven*. These and many more verbs were strong in Old English but have become, or are in the process of becoming, members of the larger and "regular" class.

EXERCISE 7. Tracing the Development of Verb Forms. The following verbs are, and in many cases have long been, in the process of shifting from one class to the other. In some, both the past tense and the past participle are shifting—or at least have developed double forms. In others, only the past participle has changed, and in some cases the double forms of the participle have developed different meanings, one for the verbal use and one for the adjective.

Look up these words in a good dictionary (i.e., one with full treatment of the principal parts). Determine exactly what development the past tense and past participle forms have undergone.

abide	hang	hide
forget	heave	sew
chide	mow	work
knit	speed	
shear	bite	
awake	shine	
get	hew	
dive	plead	
light	thrive	
show	dig	
bid	strike	

Modern English

As has already been suggested, the almost complete loss of grammatical endings in Middle and early Modern English had a very important effect on English grammar as a whole. We have seen earlier that Old English, like the other languages of the Indo-European family, showed the relationship between words of a sentence primarily by means of an elaborate set of inflectional endings. As these endings were lost, it was necessary for the language to rely more upon other means of showing relationship between sentence parts such as adjective and noun, subject and verb, verb and object, etc. The means which developed was, of course, that of Modern English. The subject came to be indicated primarily by the verb; nouns began to be identified less by their endings and more often by the noun-marking or signaling words that preceded them, such as *the, a, some, his*, etc.; prepositions increased in importance and took over more of the task of signaling relationships that formerly had been shown also by the cases of nouns.

An additional result was the complete loss of grammatical gender. Gender had always depended on the endings of nouns and the masculine, feminine, and neuter forms of the accompanying adjectives and demonstratives. With the loss of these endings and the reduction of the demonstratives to a few forms (*the, that, those*), there were no longer any distinctions to mark genders. Except for the relation between the form of the personal pronoun and the sex of its antecedent, gender in English simply disappeared. (In connection with the last two paragraphs, you should refer to the discussion of inflection and gender on pages 114–15.)

By the end of the Middle English period, then, the grammar of English was essentially that of Modern English. In the modern period there were some additional developments in the grammar of the verb, particularly in verbs with auxiliaries such as the progressive tenses. Other minor changes took place also, such as the loss of the second person singular personal pronouns *thou, thee, thy, thine*, but the main grammatical developments were complete in Middle English.

A short quotation from a work from the last quarter of the fourteenth century will illustrate how far the changes from Old English had gone. Except for the spelling and a few words that have changed somewhat in meaning, the passage might almost be Modern English. No really significant difference of grammar or word order is to be found.

> Myda hadde, under his longe heres,
> (Midas had, under his long hair,)
>
> Growynge upon his heed two asses eres,
> (Growing upon his head two ass's ears,)
>
> The whiche vice he hydde, as he best myghte,
> (Which deformity he hid, as best he might,)
>
> Full subtilly from every mannes sighte.
> (Most artfully from every man's sight.)

After the Middle English period the most important changes were in pronunciation. These were very sweeping in their effect on the language but were much too complex to explain here in any detail. The changes in pronunciation were so extensive that an oral reading of the foregoing passage in the pronunciation of Chaucer would be very difficult for us to understand, even though the vocabulary and grammar are relatively familiar. Some idea of the changes that took place in Modern English can perhaps be briefly suggested. In Middle English the *i* of *nice* or *vice* was an "ee" sound, like the modern vowel of *teeth*. The *e* of *meet* or *see* was in Middle English an "ay" sound, like the modern vowel of *late*. The *a* of *name* or *late* was in Middle English an "ah" sound, like the modern vowel of *father*. The *oo* of *tooth* or *moon* was an "oh" sound, like the modern vowel of *coat*. Early in the Modern English period, extensive changes brought all of these and most of the other vowels of Middle English fairly close to the quality that they have at present.

As we might expect, however, vowel changes differed considerably in the various dialects of English. In some dialects, for example, *er* remained more or less as it had been in Middle English, eventually becoming the "urr" sound heard in the usual American English pronunciation of *servant*. In others, however, it changed to *ar*, as in Modern English *parsley*. In the course of time, as more or less standard pronunciation developed, a mixture of dialects resulted in some of these words having –*ar* and some –*er*. Even in present times we still find words of this group that are pronounced differently in various parts of the English-speaking world. Most, like *far, carve, harbor, farm*, are consistently pronounced as *ar*. Many others have remained *er*, like *perfect, perch, sermon, verse, verdict*. At least one, *sergeant*, is spelled with *er* but always pronounced *ar*. But a considerable number are, or have until recently been, pronounced differently in different dialect areas: *learn, servant, serpent, virtue*, for example, were in the last century very commonly pronounced in many areas "larn," "sarvent," "sarpent," "vartue." The Modern English *varsity* survives as a shortened form of a similar pronunciation, "univarsity." In England the word *clerk* and the place names *Derby* and *Hertford* are always pronounced in the standard dialect as if they were "clark," "Darby," and "Hartford." The spellings of the names *Clark* and *Hartford* are representations of this pronunciation, just as the names *Carr* and *Kerr* are spelling representations of two dialect variants of the same personal name.

A great many other English words that differ in pronunciation from one dialect or region to another are traceable to the sound changes that took place in various dialects in the earlier centuries of the Modern English period. Some examples, with the variant pronunciation respelled in quotation marks, are *deaf*/"deef"; *head*/"haid"; *either*/ "eyether"; *home*/"hum"; *roof*/"ruf" (i.e., with a vowel like that of *foot*). Many of the strange-looking rhymes in older poetry also represent dialect variants of earlier stages through which the pronunciation of English has gone. Samuel Pepys (1633–1703) rhymed *root*/*foot*/*dispute*; Alexander Pope (1688–1744) rhymed *head*/*paid*/*shade*; Philip Freneau (1752–1832) rhymed *deaf*/*relief*. Pope, John Milton (1608–1674), and Robert Herrick (1591–1674) regularly rhymed *home*/*come*; and rhymes of *home* with *from, some*, etc., were very common in the seventeenth and eighteenth centuries.

These variations in the pronunciation of both early and recent Modern English are, of course, part of the explanation for the inconsistency of English spelling. The very period during which these various changes were taking place in the dialects of English was also the time when English spelling was beginning to be fixed in something like its present form. Thus, in many instances, the modern spelling reflects a pronunciation that is no longer in ordinary use. A simple example is the curious fact that the vowels of *meat, great*, and *dead* are all spelled with *ea*, yet all are differently pronounced. In Middle English these belonged to a large class of words pronounced with an "eh" sound like the lengthened vowel of Modern English *there*. In the late Middle English this vowel developed differently in various dialects that contributed to the standard language, so that the original turned up in early Modern English usually as a sound like the vowel of Modern English *meat*, but in a few words like that of *great*, and in a good number of words it was modified very slightly to the sound heard in Modern English *dead*. Thus these three words survive as representatives of each of these three developments.

The spelling and pronunciation of English may be seen, then, as a record of particular events in the history of our language. The other characteristic features of Modern English are, of course, also the product of the historical process. The virtual absence of grammatical inflections is the result of a gradual loss that has been going on for thousands of years. In their place has grown up a system of identifying noun, verb, adjective, and adverb, and of relating one word or word group to another, by means of more or less fixed word-order and by a set of function words like *the, of, may, if*, etc. The change that has taken place has often been referred to as *grammatical simplification*. It is very doubtful, however, if this term is entirely accurate.

It is obviously true that the Modern English inflectional system is simpler than that of Old English. This is not the same thing as saying, however, that the total system of Modern English is simpler than one based on full grammatical inflection. We have only to consider a few of the many complexities of our system. The order of the various types of adverbs and adjectives in English, for example, is flexible, but only within very definite limitations. The order of the adjectives in "the little new red ranch-type house" and the adverbs in "slowly walks upstairs now" may be rearranged within limits, but we are not likely ever to see or hear such an order as "the ranch-type little red new house" or "upstairs walks slowly now." We may note the difficulties involved in the idiomatic use of verb-adverb combinations like *bring to* and *look up*. We may see, for example, that these two behave similarly in the sentences "the unconscious girl was hard to *bring to*" and "the information was hard to *look up*." And the elements of both can similarly be separated in "*bring* her *to*" and "*look* it *up*." But while we may say "*Look up* the information," we do not say "*Bring to* the girl." Again, we may note the complication of the differing orders of subject and verb in independent and subordinate clauses after words like *where, why, what*, etc. Unlike many languages, English reverses the order of subject and verb in an independent interrogative structure like "where *are you* going." Can we truly say that these patterns are simpler—easier to learn—than a system of grammatical endings would be? Probably not, and it may well be that they are actually harder. Whatever their relative difficulty, however, these and the other syntactical patterns of English are the system which the events of our language history have produced for us.

So far we have already considered *spelling, pronunciation*, and *grammar*. Another major feature of English that we have examined is its vocabulary. Here, too, special characteristics provide a record of the history of the language. One of the most prominent characteristics of our vocabulary is the great number of words borrowed from other languages. As we have seen, many French words entered our language as a result of the Norman Conquest. Latin, too, because of its great importance as the international language of learning, has been the source of much word-borrowing from the earliest times to the present. Contacts with other European languages have resulted in borrowings which very often show in themselves something of the nature of the contact between the nations. For example, some Spanish words have been borrowed as a result of commercial contacts between Spain and England (*vanilla, brocade, embargo*), and others have come into American English through contacts in the Southwest of the United States (*corral, rodeo, alfalfa*). Italian words appear in English especially in the field of the arts (*stanza, violin, studio*) and, in the United States, in the names of a few foods (*pizza, ravioli*). German has contributed words in some of the sciences, the names of some foods, and a small miscellaneous group (*quartz, sauerkraut, delicatessen, hamburger, kindergarten, loafer*).

Contacts between the English-speaking peoples and nations beyond the borders of Europe have resulted in many other borrowings, especially in more recent times. As early as the Middle Ages, however, contacts with the great Arabic civilizations resulted in the importation into many of the languages of Europe of words for new things and new concepts in the field of knowledge (*cipher, algebra, sugar*). Later expansion in both the East and the West brought new words to English from, among others, various African languages (*gumbo, voodoo, banjo, juke*), American Indian languages (*squash, hominy, moccasin, raccoon*), Australian languages (*kangaroo, boomerang*), and Indic languages (*punch, afghan, jungle, calico*).

We have now summarized very briefly something of the history of the pronunciation, spelling, vocabulary, and grammar of English. This summary should at the very least suggest one general observation. The English language, like all languages, is the product of an almost infinitely complex series of events, of the interaction of innumerable forces and influences. Modern English is likely to seem to a native speaker of another language enormously complex and exceedingly inconsistent. True enough, it is; so, indeed, are all languages. We may see, however, that much of the interest of language study comes from our recognition that within this apparent complexity there is much that can be ordered, rationalized, and explained. If we can know enough, each inconsistency and all the complexities become examples to us of the processes of language and the events of language change and language history.

EXERCISE 8. Finding the Etymologies of Words. Look up the etymologies of the following words in a good dictionary. You may cooperate with several friends, each looking up one column, and pool your results. Arrange them in groups according to the language of origin. What do they tell you of the history of English?

agenda	comedy	orange	skirt
alarm	cyclotron	ouch	snoop
alcohol	devil	piano	spaghetti
alibi	dock	poodle	stampede
animal	dumb	pope	syrup
atomic	extra	posse	take
balcony	frankfurter	potato	tattoo
barbecue	freight	priest	tea
black hand	gingham	propaganda	they
boss	giraffe	pump	umbrella
bungalow	gorilla	sandal	veto
cafeteria	knife	Santa Claus	wiener
camel	macaroni	scream	yam
church	manual	semester	zero
clan	opera	shanty	zinc

EXERCISE 9. Writing About the English Language. Write a composition of about 500 words on the effect of historical forces on the English language. As this is a very large subject, it will be best to limit your discussion to some particular feature of language, such as vocabulary, or to some particular period of time. Illustrate your more important points by using well-chosen examples drawn from this chapter, from the list of words in the foregoing exercise, or from your own reading or investigation.

CHAPTER 7

Agreement

SUBJECT AND VERB, PRONOUN AND ANTECEDENT

Some words in English have matching forms to show grammatical relationships. Forms that match in this way are said to *agree*. For example, a subject and a verb agree if both are singular or both are plural. Pronouns also agree with their antecedents, which are the words the pronouns stand for.

DIAGNOSTIC TEST

Selecting Verbs That Agree with Their Subjects and Pronouns That Agree with Their Antecedents. Number your paper 1–20. After the proper number, write the word in parentheses that correctly completes the sentence. Follow the practices of formal usage.

EXAMPLE   1. Neither of the pitchers (was, were) able to stop the Seagulls from winning the baseball game.
    1. *was*

1. Each of the air traffic controllers (was, were) communicating with departing and arriving pilots.
2. Both of your answers (is, are) correct.

3. A team with too many superstars (has, have) trouble working as a unit.

4. "(Is, Are) mumps contagious?" I asked when my twin sister contracted the disease two days before I was to star in our school play.

5. Laura is one of those students who always (takes, take) good notes in class.

6. Luis' greatest problem before a race (is, are) nerves.

7. Ms. Caplice, in addition to Mr. Ruiz and Ms. Rogers, (was, were) asked to attend the conference.

8. Many a financial investor (has, have) a headache on a day when the stock market drops.

9. An adventure novel, *The Three Musketeers* (has, have) been made into a movie many times.

10. Kathy (doesn't, don't) look like her sister Missy at all.

11. Each of the students had brought (his, their) notes to the meeting.

12. When we got to the picnic grounds, we discovered that neither Fred nor Bill had brought (his, their) radio.

13. The number of people seeking jobs in the computer industry (is, are) rising rapidly.

14. Jane or the twins (is, are) sure to be home when you call.

15. At the dance, some of the food served during the breaks (was, were) home cooked.

16. Our city is proud of (its, their) cultural activities.

17. My mother thought that twenty-five dollars (was, were) too much to pay for the designer T-shirt.

18. As I shaded my eyes from the bright orange, yellow, and green plaid material, Doug said, "(Here's, Here are) my new trousers. What do you think?"

19. One of the women hurt (her, their) foot in the race.

20. The twin towers of the World Trade Center in New York City (is, are) an awesome sight.

AGREEMENT OF SUBJECT AND VERB

7a. A word that refers to one person or thing is *singular* in number. A word that refers to more than one is *plural* in number.

SINGULAR	PLURAL
car	cars
ox	oxen
this	these
either	both
he, she, it	they

7b. A verb agrees with its subject in number.

(1) Singular subjects take singular verbs.

A young **woman lives** next door.
This bake **sale was sponsored** by the Pep Club.

(2) Plural subjects take plural verbs.

Young **women live** next door.
These bake **sales were sponsored** by the Pep Club.

You will find it helpful to remember that *is, was, has,* and most verbs ending in a single *s* are singular: he *thinks,* she *works,* it *counts,* etc. *Are, were, have,* and most verbs not ending in a single *s* are plural: they *think,* they *work,* they *count.* The exceptions, which should cause you little difficulty, are verbs used with *I* and singular *you*: I *think,* you *work,* etc.

Notice that all the verbs given as examples in the preceding paragraph are in the present tense. All past tense verbs have the same form in the singular and plural except for the verb *be,* which has a special form *was* that is used with *I, he, she,* and *it,* and all singular nouns.

SINGULAR	PLURAL
I threw	they threw
he applied	we applied
I was	we were
it was	they were

If English is your native language, you probably have little trouble in making verbs agree with their subjects when they directly follow the subjects as in the examples above. You will encounter sentences, however, in which it is not so easy to identify the subject correctly or determine whether it is singular or plural. These constructions, which create most agreement problems, are taken up separately on the following pages.

Intervening Phrase

7c. The number of the subject is not changed by a phrase following the subject.

A phrase that comes between a singular subject and its verb can easily mislead you if it contains a plural word. Remember that the verb agrees with its subject, not with any modifiers the subject may have.

EXAMPLES   The **counselor was** very helpful.
The **counselor** for the senior students **was** very helpful.
[*Counselor*, not *students*, is the subject of the sentence.]

A **solution has been found**.
A **solution** to these problems **has been found**. [*solution has*, not *problems have*]

In formal writing, singular subjects followed by phrases beginning with *together with, as well as, in addition to*, and *accompanied by* take singular verbs.

EXAMPLE   The **singer**, as well as the musicians, **was** pleased with the recording session.

EXERCISE 1. Selecting Verbs That Agree with Their Subjects.

Number your paper 1–10. Write after the proper number the subject of the sentence. After the subject, write the one of the two verbs in parentheses that agrees in number with the subject. Check your answers.

1. The theory of plate tectonics (has, have) explained causes of earthquake activity throughout the world.
2. Enormous plates of rock (is, are) moving constantly beneath the earth's surface.
3. The movements, in addition to the pressure of molten rock, (causes, cause) the plates to collide.
4. The pressure of colliding plates (forces, force) the rock to bend until it breaks.
5. A ridge of these breaks (is, are) called a fault.
6. The cause of most earthquakes (is, are) the release of stress along a fault.
7. The Richter scale, as well as other measurements, (has, have) been used to record the magnitude of earthquakes.

8. The tremors of the great San Francisco earthquake (was, were) estimated to have measured 8.3 on the Richter scale.
9. California, with the San Andreas and Garlock faults, (has, have) about ten times the world average of earthquake activities.
10. The scientific community, especially seismologists and geologists, (is, are) studying the effects of earthquakes.

Indefinite Pronouns as Subjects

Pronouns like *everybody, someone, everything, all,* and *none,* all of which are more or less indefinite in meaning, present some special usage problems. Some of them are always singular, some are always plural, and some others may be singular or plural, depending on the meaning of the sentence. In addition, such pronouns are often followed by a phrase. Therefore, you must first determine the number of the pronoun and then remember the rule about phrases that come between subjects and verbs.

7d. The following common words are singular: *each, either, neither, one, no one, every one, anyone, someone, everyone, anybody, somebody, everybody.*

EXAMPLES   **Each does** his own cooking.
          Each of the boys **does** [not *do*] his own cooking.
          Everyone enjoys the summertime.
          Every one of the campers **enjoys** [not *enjoy*] the summertime.

7e. The following common words are plural: *several, few, both, many.*

EXAMPLES   **Several** of the students **were** transferred.
          Few on the committee **attend** meetings.
          Both of the teams **play** very well.
          Many were impressed by the guest speaker.

7f. The words *some, any, none, all,* and *most* may be singular or plural, depending on the meaning of the sentence.

Usually, when the words *some, any, none, all,* and *most* refer to a singular word, they are singular; when they refer to a plural word, they are plural.[1] Compare the examples on the following page.

---

[1] Since the word referred to appears in a phrase following the subject, this rule is an exception to rule 7c.

Some of the show **was** hilarious. [*Some* is singular because it refers to *show*, which is singular.]

Some of the actors **were** hilarious. [*Some* is plural because it refers to *actors*, which is plural.]

All of the workout **seems** simple.
All of the exercises **seem** simple.

Most of the program **was** new to me. [an indefinite part of the program]
Most of the programs **were** new to me. [a number of separate programs]

Is any of the salad left?
Are any of the shirts clean?

None of the story **makes** sense.
None of the movies **were** exciting.

☞ **USAGE NOTE**   *Was* could have been used in the last example, but modern English usage prefers a plural verb in this situation. If you want the subject to be singular in such a sentence, use *no one* or *not one* instead of *none*.

WRITING APPLICATION A:
Observing Agreement Rules in Recording Observations

Indefinite pronouns can be tricky. They can be singular, plural, or either, depending upon the meaning of the sentence. Words like *each* are singular; words like *several* are plural; and words like *some* may be singular or plural, depending on the sentence.

EXAMPLES   *Each* of the companies *has* tried to build factories away from population centers.

Several of the industrial-safety problems *involve* the transportation of chemicals.

Some of the regulations *have come* about as a result of disasters.

Some of the missing material *is* here.

(*Some* is considered singular because it refers to *material*, which is singular.)

Writing Assignment

Pretend you are an eyewitness to an important event. It could be a disaster, an impressive ceremony, or any other striking situation.

Record your observations, observing agreement rules carefully. In your written account, include at least four indefinite pronouns (such as *each, all, several, both, many,* etc.) used as subjects.

EXERCISE 2. Selecting Verbs That Agree with Their Subjects.
Number your paper 1–10. Write after the proper number on your paper the subject in each sentence. After it, write the one of the two verbs in parentheses which agrees in number with the subject.

1. Each of the pictures (was, were) in a silver frame.
2. One of my friends (play, plays) the tuba.
3. All of our belongings (is, are) still unpacked.
4. Some of these rare books (has, have) leather covers.
5. None of the people in the theater audience (was, were) pleased with the film.
6. Every one of these jeans (is, are) too small.
7. A few in my class (was, were) asked to help out.
8. The lack of funds (present, presents) a problem.
9. Everybody living in Lewis Heights (go, goes) to George Washington Carver High School.
10. A band with two trumpet players and thirty-five clarinetists (sound, sounds) terrible.

EXERCISE 3. Writing Verbs That Agree with Their Subjects.
Revise these ten sentences, following the instructions that appear in brackets after each of them. Sometimes the addition will affect agreement. Be sure to make the subject and verb of the new sentence agree. Underline each subject once and each verb twice.

EXAMPLE 1. Each of the contestants was confused by the question. [Change *Each* to *Several.*]
1. Several of the contestants were confused by the question.

1. All of the fruit has spoiled. [Change *fruit* to *oranges.*]
2. Each of my friends was angry about the election. [Change *Each* to *Many.*]
3. Has anybody joined the choir? [Change *anybody* to *any of the new students.*]
4. The class leaves tomorrow on the field trip. [Add *accompanied by two chaperones* after *class.* Put a comma before and after the added phrase.]

5. Our team is going to Austin for the debate tournament. [Add *Three members of* before *Our team.*]

6. Most of the classrooms were equipped with new microcomputers. [Change *Most* to *None*.]

7. The pitcher was disappointed in the coach's decision. [Add *as well as the other players* after *pitcher.* Set off the addition with commas.]

8. Every one of the smoke detectors was broken. [Change *Every one* to *All but two.*]

9. Both of them usually expect the worst to happen. [Change *Both of them* to *Everyone.*]

10. Some of her plan has been approved. [Change *plan* to *suggestions.*]

EXERCISE 4. Determining Subject-Verb Agreement. Number your paper 1–20. Read each of the following sentences. If the verb in a sentence agrees with its subject, write a + after the proper number on your paper; if the verb does not agree, write the correct form of the verb on your paper.

1. The mayor, as well as her aides, were in the parade.
2. Neither of the groups follow parliamentary procedure.
3. Some of the essay wasn't coherent.
4. The cause of the recent fires are being investigated.
5. Each of the computers run a different program.
6. None of the students has disagreed with my suggestion.
7. Only a few on any committee do all the work.
8. Luckily every one of the students have passed the test.
9. Most of his lectures holds my interest.
10. Everybody, especially on Mondays, seem to be tired in the morning.
11. Both of the parties sound like fun.
12. Either of your ideas seems reasonable.
13. The captain, together with volunteer teammates, are repairing the damaged windows.
14. Not one of the stores is open on Tuesday night.
15. Anyone in the cooking classes is eligible to win.
16. Most of our project has already been finished.

17. The bus driver, as well as the passengers, was not hurt in the accident.
18. All of the books on history in the library has been checked out.
19. Several of Terry's stamps are valuable.
20. One of the tickets for the concert series are available.

COMPOUND SUBJECTS

As you will recall from Chapter 2, two words or groups of words may be connected to form the subject of a verb. These words, usually joined by *and* or *or*, are called a *compound subject*. Compound subjects may take singular or plural verbs, depending on whether the words joined are singular or plural and what the connecting word is.

7g. Subjects joined by *and* take a plural verb.

EXAMPLES   A **horse and** an **elephant are** mammals.
The **records and** the **tapes were** stacked on the shelf.
Hannah and Dot have been friends for years.

EXCEPTION When the parts of a compound subject are considered as a unit or when they refer to the same thing, a singular verb is used.

EXAMPLES   **Bread and butter comes** with every meal.
Fruit and cheese is my favorite dessert.
Joe's **brother and** best **friend is going** to college in New Mexico.

7h. Singular subjects joined by *or* or *nor* take a singular verb.

EXAMPLES   A **jacket or** a **sweater is** warm enough at night.
Either **Becky or Diane is planning** the meeting.
Neither the **coach nor** the **trainer was** sure of the starting time.

7i. When a singular and a plural subject are joined by *or* or *nor*, the verb agrees with the nearer subject.

ACCEPTABLE   Either the singer or the musicians are off-key.

It is usually possible to avoid this awkward construction altogether:

BETTER   Either the singer is off-key, or the musicians are.

Another reason for avoiding this construction is that the subjects may be different in person. If this is so, the verb must agree with the nearer subject in person as well as number. In the following example, the verb must not only be singular to agree with *I*, but it must also have the form (am) that matches *I* as a subject.

ACCEPTABLE   Neither my girl friends nor I am working part-time at the store.
BETTER   My girl friends are not working part-time at the store, and neither am I.

☞ USAGE NOTE   The rules in this chapter are consistently followed in standard formal English but are often departed from in informal speaking and writing. Formal usage is likely to call for a singular verb after a singular subject in a strictly logical way. Informal usage, on the other hand, often permits the use of a plural verb, whatever the logical number of the subject, if the meaning is clearly plural.

FORMAL   Neither Ellen nor Lola has a video camera.
INFORMAL   Neither Ellen nor Lola have a video camera. [Although joined by *nor*, which strictly calls for a singular verb, the meaning of the sentence is essentially plural: both Ellen and Lola are without video cameras.]

FORMAL   Every one of the winners is celebrating.
INFORMAL   Every one of the winners are celebrating. [Strictly speaking, the subject *one* is singular and takes a singular verb. However, the meaning is essentially the same as that expressed by "All the winners are celebrating." Informal usage permits a plural verb in such circumstances.]

FORMAL   The conductor, as well as a soprano and many stagehands, was trapped in the theater fire.
INFORMAL   The conductor, as well as a soprano and many stagehands, were trapped in the theater fire. [Although the construction logically calls for a singular verb, the meaning is clearly plural—all of them were trapped, not just the conductor. It is usually wise to avoid constructions that set up a conflict between logic and meaning. The example would be better if it were written as "The conductor, a soprano, and many stagehands were . . ."]

   In some of the exercise sentences in this chapter, you will encounter such differences between formal and informal usage. For the purposes of these exercises, follow the rules of formal usage.

EXERCISE 5. Determining Subject-Verb Agreement. Number your paper 1–25. Read each of the following sentences. If the verb in a sentence agrees with its subject, write a + after the proper number. If the verb does not agree, write the correct form of the verb on your paper. Follow the practices of formal usage.

1. One of the most precious resources in the nation is water.
2. The abundance and use of water vary greatly among the regions of the United States.
3. The water supply for all the states come from either surface water or underground water.
4. Unfortunately, neither overuse nor contamination of water supplies has stopped completely.
5. Not one of the water sources are free from pollution.
6. After years of study, pollution of lakes, rivers, and streams continue to be a serious problem.
7. Some of the efforts to clean up surface water has been successful.
8. Lake Erie, as well as the Potomac and Cuyahoga Rivers, have been saved by these efforts.
9. Pollution of ground water, especially in dry regions, is another serious problem.
10. The government, in addition to environmentalists, are worried about the quality and abundance of ground water.
11. Many scientists throughout the country are currently studying aquifers.
12. Aquifers, a source of ground water, is layers of rock, sand, and soil that hold water.
13. About 88 billion gallons of water is pumped out of the ground each day.
14. In some regions, the drinking water for hundreds of people come from aquifers.
15. Every one of the recent studies of aquifers has revealed contamination to some degree.
16. The causes of contamination are varied.
17. Salt for melting ice on city streets cause pollution.
18. The chemicals that sometimes leak out of a sewer system or waste dump contaminates aquifers.
19. Fertilizers used on a farm also add pollutants to the water.
20. All of these pollutants seep through the rock and soil until they reach the water.

21. The extent of the damages from contamination are not known.
22. Another problem, according to scientists, is uncontrolled use of water sources.
23. Ground water in some areas are being used faster than the supply can be renewed.
24. A few states in the nation controls the use of water.
25. Each one of the fifty states have a stake in preserving sources of water.

Other Problems in Subject-Verb Agreement

7j. **When the subject follows the verb, as in questions and in sentences beginning with** *here* **and** *there,* **be careful to determine the subject and make sure that the verb agrees with it.**

NONSTANDARD How's Al and Roberta feeling?
 STANDARD How **are Al and Roberta** feeling?

NONSTANDARD There's seven vegetables in the salad.
 STANDARD There **are** seven **vegetables** in the salad.

7k. **Collective nouns may be either singular or plural.**

A collective noun names a group: *crowd, committee, jury, class.* A collective noun takes a plural verb when the speaker is thinking of the individual members of the group; it takes a singular verb when the speaker is thinking of the group as a unit.

The **audience were entering** the theater. [The speaker is thinking of the individuals in the audience.]
The **audience was** one of the best. [The speaker is thinking of the audience as a whole, a single unit.]
The **committee were writing** five reports for the president.
The **committee was scheduled** to meet in the library.
The **team have voted** eighteen to three to buy new uniforms.
The **team has won** the semifinals.

SOME COMMON COLLECTIVE WORDS

army	crowd	orchestra
audience	flock	public
class	group	swarm
club	herd	team
committee	jury	troop

7l. Expressions stating amount (time, money, measurement, weight, volume, fractions) are usually singular when the amount is considered as a unit.

EXAMPLES   **Five years has been** a long time to wait.
Twenty pounds seems a lot to gain in a month.
Two thirds of the day is spent in school.

However, when the amount is considered as a number of separate units, a plural verb is used.

EXAMPLES   **The last six miles were** the most scenic.
There are thirteen days left in the month.
Two thirds of the holidays fall on a Friday or a Monday.

7m. The title of a book or the name of an organization or country, even when plural in form, usually takes a singular verb.

EXAMPLES   *Lilies of the Field* **is** on the late show tonight.
Friends of the Earth has held a membership drive.
The United States was represented at the summit conference.

EXCEPTION   Some names of organizations (Veterans of Foreign Wars, New York Yankees, Chicago Bears, etc.) customarily take a plural verb when you are thinking of the members and a singular verb when you mean the organization.

The **Veterans of Foreign Wars attend** this meeting.
The **Veterans of Foreign Wars is** a large organization.

7n. A few nouns, such as *mumps, measles, civics, economics, mathematics, physics,* although plural in form, take a singular verb.

EXAMPLES   The **mumps** usually **lasts** three days.
Nuclear **physics is** a controversial branch of science.

The following similar words are more often plural than singular: *athletics, acoustics, gymnastics, tactics.* The word *politics* may be either singular or plural, and *scissors* and *trousers* are always plural.

For more information on the use of words ending in –*ics,* look up –*ics* in your dictionary.

7o. When the subject and the predicate nominative are different in number, the verb agrees with the subject, not with the predicate nominative.

ACCEPTABLE   The last **act** featured **was** the singers and dancers.
ACCEPTABLE   The **singers and dancers were** the last act featured.
BETTER   The **singers and dancers were** featured last.

Although the first two examples are acceptable, the third is clearly better. Avoid writing sentences in which the subject and predicate nominative are different in number.

7p. *Every* or *many a* **before a word or series of words is followed by a singular verb.**

EXAMPLES   **Every waitress, busboy,** and **cashier was** pleased with the new schedule.
Many a young **runner finishes** the grueling race in less than five hours.
Many a candidate running for office **has** spent a sleepless night before the election.

7q. *Don't* and *doesn't* **must agree with their subjects.**

With the subjects *I* and *you,* use *don't* (*do not*). With other subjects, use *doesn't* (*does not*) when the subject is singular and *don't* (*do not*) when the subject is plural.

EXAMPLES   **I don't** like her painting.
You don't talk too much.
It [He, She, This] doesn't work anymore.
They don't agree.

By using *doesn't* after *it, he,* and *she,* you can eliminate most of the common errors in the use of *don't.*

7r. In formal English, verbs in clauses that follow *one of those* **are almost always plural.**

Even though informal usage often permits a singular verb in the clause following *one of those,* the plural verb is almost always correct. The only time that a singular verb is called for is when *one of those* is preceded by *the only.*

EXAMPLES   This is **one of those** assignments that **require** research in the library.
Naomi is **one of those** players who **are** good losers as well as good winners.
Ron is the **only one of those students** who **has** permission to leave early.

WRITING APPLICATION B:
Observing Agreement Rules for Clauses Using *One of Those*

In writing about literature, you may find similarities in characters, plots, settings, and themes, especially when you study several works by the same author. When this happens, you might need to use a construction involving *one of those*. This construction is often used in a topic sentence. When you use such a construction, remember that verbs in clauses that follow *one of those* are almost always plural.

EXAMPLE   Hamlet, Prince of Denmark, is *one of those* Shakespearean characters who *suffer* from a particular tragic flaw. (Notice that the verb
suffer is plural; it follows the *one of those* construction.)

Writing Assignment

Select a poem, play, short story, or novel that appeals to you. Write a paragraph focusing on the major characteristic(s) of this work. In your topic sentence, use the *one of those* construction, as illustrated in the example above. Observe the agreement rule.

7s. The word *number* when followed by the word *of,* is singular when preceded by *the;* it is plural when preceded by *a*.

EXAMPLES   **The number** of volunteers **is** surprising.
A number of volunteers **are** signing up right now.

EXERCISE 6. Selecting Verbs That Agree with Their Subjects.

Number your paper 1–25. After the proper number, write the correct one of the two verbs in parentheses in the sentence.

1. The audience of businesswomen (was, were) enthusiastic.
2. Neither the knife nor the scissors (was, were) sharp enough to cut the rope.
3. Forty dollars (is, are) too much to pay for jeans.
4. (Where's, Where are) her coat and boots?
5. Many a gymnast (dreams, dream) of participating in the Olympic Games.
6. The problems of raising a family (was, were) discussed.
7. There (seems, seem) to be something for everyone.
8. Every one of her quilts (has, have) been sold.

9. The captain of the football team and the president of the senior class (represents, represent) the students.
10. Macaroni and cheese (is, are) on the menu again.
11. *A Tale of Two Cities* (was, were) made into a movie for television.
12. The Chicago Cubs is one of those teams that (rallies, rally) in the late innings.
13. Neither civics nor mathematics (is, are) his best subject.
14. Each of the packages (contains, contain) a surprise gift.
15. The mumps (becomes, become) more dangerous as you grow older.
16. Every volunteer in the city's hospitals (is, are) being honored at the banquet.
17. Only a few of the countries in the world (is, are) sending their best athletes.
18. One half of the receipts (was, were) found in a shoe box.
19. The Society of Procrastinators (has, have) postponed the annual meeting.
20. That was one of those jokes that (offends, offend) everyone.
21. None of the peaches (was, were) bruised in shipping.
22. The acoustics in the auditorium (has, have) been improved.
23. Not one of the accusations (was, were) ever proved in court.
24. *Alternate* and *alternative* (has, have) different meanings.
25. She is one of those people who (has, have) energy to spare.

REVIEW EXERCISE A. Determining Subject-Verb Agreement. Number your paper 1–10. If the verb in a sentence agrees with its subject, write + after the proper number. If the verb does not agree, write the correct form of the verb on your paper.

EXAMPLES 1. Here's two letters for you.
     1. *Here are*
    2. The display in the auto dealer's showrooms represents more than $150,000 worth of cars.
    2. +

1. Each year, a faculty member and a student talks to the student body during an assembly on the opening day of school.
2. In the United States of America, there are a wide variety of ethnic groups in the population.

3. Can you believe that Leo don't go anywhere without his pocket calculator?
4. My sister Latrice is one of those people who make guests feel at ease.
5. As employers demand more skills from employees, the importance of studies after high school are evident to most seniors.
6. Some of the criticism aimed at children's cartoons are perceptive and accurate.
7. From my experience with team sports, I know that when neither the coach nor the team members has the will to win, there is little chance of victory.
8. The number of accidents that happen at home is surprisingly large.
9. The musical *Cats* was based on a group of poems by T. S. Eliot.
10. Every morning during swim season, each of the girls on the team were at the pool by 6 A.M.

WRITING APPLICATION C:
Writing Sentences with Subject-Verb Agreement

Writers make "agreement errors" when they do not see the *true* subjects of their sentences. You should always analyze your sentences for the *true* subjects so that you can make the verbs agree with their subjects.

INCORRECT   The players, as well as the coach, was disappointed.
CORRECT   The players, as well as the coach, **were** disappointed.
[*Players,* not *coach,* is the subject of the sentence.]

Writing Assignment

Write ten sentences, each beginning with one of the following expressions. When you proofread your sentences, make sure that the verbs agree with the subjects of the sentences.

1. *Great Expectations*
2. Five dollars
3. Neither of the sofas
4. The critics' reviews

5. The man who is speaking with the salespeople
6. Many a doctor
7. My grandmother and grandfather
8. Some of the salespeople
9. Peanut butter and jelly
10. Everyone in the contests

AGREEMENT OF PRONOUN AND ANTECEDENT

7t. A pronoun agrees with its antecedent in number and gender.[1]

All that you have learned about agreement of subject and verb will be useful to you in making pronouns agree with their antecedents. The antecedent of a pronoun is the word to which the pronoun refers. Study the following examples, in which the antecedents and the pronouns referring to them are printed in boldfaced type. Notice that as a rule the pronoun is singular when the antecedent is singular, and plural when the antecedent is plural. Notice, too, that the pronoun is masculine (*he, him, his*) when the antecedent is masculine; feminine (*she, her, hers*) when the antecedent is feminine; neuter (*it, its*) when the antecedent is neither masculine nor feminine. This kind of agreement is agreement in *gender.*

> **She** should have done it **herself.**
> **You** missed **your** chance to see the show.
> **Keith** hit **his** first home run today.
> **Mrs. Davis** played **her** guitar.
> **Tom** finished writing **his** report.
> The **Fishers** returned from **their** fishing trip.
> The **company** advertises **its** products on television.

(1) The words *each, either, neither, one, everyone, everybody, no one, nobody, anyone, anybody, someone, somebody* **are referred to by a singular pronoun—***he, him, his, she, her, hers, it, its.*

The use of a phrase after the antecedent does not change the number of the antecedent.

---

[1] Pronouns also agree with their antecedents in *person* (see page 158). Agreement in person rarely presents usage problems.

EXAMPLES **Each** of the women designed **her** own pattern.
Neither of the men left **his** coat on the seat.
One of the girls took **her** umbrella with **her.**

☞ USAGE NOTE Sometimes the antecedent may be either masculine or feminine; sometimes it may be both. Some writers use the masculine form of the personal pronoun to refer to such antecedents. Other writers prefer to use both the masculine and feminine forms in such cases.

EXAMPLES Everyone has handed in **his** paper.
Everyone has handed in **his or her** paper.

You can often avoid the awkward *his or her* construction by rephrasing the sentence in the plural.

The **students** have handed in **their** papers.

In conversation, you may find it more convenient to use a plural personal pronoun when referring to singular antecedents that can be either masculine or feminine. This form is becoming increasingly popular in writing as well and may someday become acceptable as standard written English.

EXAMPLES If **anyone** calls, tell **them** I'll call back.
Someone left **their** umbrella.

Strict adherence to the general rule of agreement between pronoun and antecedent may lead to a construction so absurd that no one would use it:

ABSURD Did *everybody* leave the dance early because *he* wasn't enjoying *himself*?

In instances of this kind, use the plural pronoun or recast the sentence to avoid the problem:

BETTER Did **everybody** leave the dance early because **they** weren't enjoying **themselves**?

or

Did the **guests** leave the dance early because **they** weren't enjoying **themselves**?

(2) Two or more singular antecedents joined by *or* or *nor* should be referred to by a singular pronoun.

Neither **Sue** nor **Maria** left **her** books on **her** desk.

(3) Two or more antecedents joined by *and* should be referred to by a plural pronoun.

Sue **and** Maria presented **their** reports.

☞ NOTE   Like some of the rules for agreement of subject and verb, the rules for agreement of pronoun and antecedent show variations between formal and informal usage. Standard informal usage follows meaning rather than strict grammatical agreement. The sentences below marked "informal" are acceptable in informal writing and speaking. In exercises, however, follow the practices of formal English.

FORMAL   **Neither** of the women carried **her** purse with **her.**
INFORMAL   Neither of the women carried their purses with them.
FORMAL   **Every one** of the contestants was instructed to place **his** scorecard on the table in front of **him.**
INFORMAL   Every one of the contestants was instructed to place their scorecards on the table in front of them.

WRITING APPLICATION D:
Making Pronouns Agree with Their Antecedents

When you write, you often use pronouns to avoid repeating nouns. When you proofread your writing, you should check to make sure that the pronouns agree with their antecedents. Use the rules on pages 147–49 to help you.

Writing Assignment

Write a narration about a humorous or light-hearted incident in which you and a friend or you and a relative were involved. Wherever appropriate, use pronouns to avoid repeating nouns. When you proofread your narration, check to see that the pronouns agree with their antecedents.

EXERCISE 7. Determining Pronoun-Antecedent Agreement.
This exercise covers errors in agreement of pronoun and antecedent.
Number your paper 1–10. If a pronoun in a sentence does not agree with
its antecedent, write the pronoun on your paper and next to it write the
correct form. If a sentence is correct as it is written, write a + after the
proper number. Follow the practices of formal usage.

EXAMPLES   1. Neither Elena nor Barbara made any errors on their chemistry
test.
1. their—*her*
2. Neither Stan nor Len wanted to endanger themselves.
2. themselves—*himself*

1. Each of the skiers waxed their skis before leaving the lodge.
2. All of the senior citizens enjoyed their trip to Boston, where they
walked the Freedom Trail.
3. Every one of the reporters at the press conference asked their
questions too quickly.
4. I believe that anybody should be free to express their opinion.
5. No one brought their camera to the party.
6. Neither of the male soloists pronounced their words very clearly.
7. Neither of the newborn kittens seemed very steady on its feet.
8. If anyone loses their way while exploring Salt Lake City, they
should use the special street maps available from the tour guide.
9. As far as I could see, neither of the women made a mistake while
presenting their argument during the debate.
10. One of the interesting quirks of American history is that neither
President Gerald Ford nor Vice-President Nelson Rockefeller was
elected to his high office.

**REVIEW EXERCISE B. Determining Subject-Verb Agreement
and Pronoun-Antecedent Agreement.** This exercise covers errors in
agreement of verb and subject and of pronoun and antecedent. Number
your paper 1–25. If a sentence is correct, write a + after the proper
number; if it is incorrect, write the correct form of the verb or pronoun.
One error makes a sentence incorrect.

1. The number of accidents have been startling.
2. Most of the short stories were humorous.

3. Each one of the terrorists were captured in a daring rescue attempt.
4. How's the heat and the humidity in Florida?
5. Has either of the brothers traveled before?
6. This is one of those cars that has a fuel injection system.
7. Anyone who speaks a foreign language increases their chance for a high-paying job.
8. Neither of the restaurants serves customers who aren't wearing shoes.
9. The experience of sailing the Great Lakes builds character in the young women.
10. Every part-time employee at the store was thanked for their help in taking the inventory.
11. ~~She is one of the engineers who is working on the space shuttle.~~
12. When the bank's computer breaks down, every one of the tellers holds their breath.
13. The increase in taxes have met resistance.
14. A person who admits his mistakes is respected by all.
15. Three fourths of the audience always stay until the last note is played.
16. Your offer to baby-sit for the five children seem courageous.
17. Each student needs a chance to think for himself.
18. Is there film and batteries in the camera?
19. All but three games in the final round was held at the community center.
20. A large number of scientists is studying the 843 pounds of rock and soil from the moon.
21. When one of the teachers retire, the students give him an engraved plaque.
22. The factory of the future will have robots working on its assembly line.
23. The questions asked by the president of the student council has been answered by the school board.
24. Anyone in the audience who talked during the performance should be ashamed of themselves.
25. Anybody who comes from a large family appreciates the need for privacy.

REVIEW EXERCISE C. Writing Verbs That Agree with Their Subjects. Revise the following sentences according to the directions given for each. Be sure to make changes or additions in verb forms, pronouns, etc., if necessary.

1. Some famous sports stars have made television commercials. [Change *Some famous sports stars* to *Many a famous sports star.*]
2. Where's my book? [Add *and my pen* after *book.*]
3. Both of the candidates have promised to reduce taxes. [Change *Both* to *Neither.*]
4. She writes neatly. [Add *is one of those students who* after *She.*]
5. Our basketball team has won the championship. [Add *Neither our football team nor* at the beginning of the sentence.]
6. People need friends to confide in. [Change *People* to *A person.*]
7. An application blank is required by the state university. [After *blank* add *together with a recent photograph and an autobiographical essay.* Put a comma before *together* and after *essay.*]
8. The tigers are growling ferociously. [At the beginning of the sentence, add *Either the lion or.*]
9. The movie screen is hard to see. [At the beginning of the sentence, add *The captions on.*]
10. A day in the library is all the time I need to finish my research. [Change *A day* to *Two days.*]

CHAPTER 7 REVIEW: POSTTEST 1

Selecting Verbs That Agree with Their Subjects and Pronouns That Agree with Their Antecedents. Number your paper 1–25. After the proper number, write the word in parentheses that correctly completes the sentence. Follow the practices of formal usage.

EXAMPLE 1. Ham and eggs (doesn't, don't) need ketchup on it.
          1. *doesn't*

1. The student council (is, are) to take a vote in fifteen minutes.
2. Some of the tour group (was, were) planning to visit the Bureau of Indian Affairs.
3. (Here's, Here are) five dollars for a new reflector.

4. On the first day of school, every one of the freshmen found it difficult to find (his, their) way to so many new classrooms.
5. Neither Mark nor Lou has finished (his, their) assignment yet.
6. It is one of those diseases that (is, are) considered incurable.
7. Economics (provides, provide) many insights into how the money supply affects all of us.
8. When someone asks you a question, always try to answer (him, them) clearly.
9. Poe's "The Bells" (uses, use) many poetic devices.
10. Neither the members of the Board of Finance nor Mayor Martinez (is, are) opposed to the new zoning law.
11. Here (is, are) the scissors you said you needed.
12. The number of women attending both meetings (was, were) more than two thousand.
13. Many a wanderer lost in the desert found (himself, themselves) walking in circles.
14. If it (doesn't, don't) rain today, I am going out to the park.
15. I wear this shirt quite often, but neither the collar nor the cuffs (is, are) frayed.
16. The Alps (appeals, appeal) to mountain climbers, skiers, and sightseers.
17. Because few if any of the buyers (understand, understands) his jargon, that salesperson will find it difficult to win contracts from them.
18. (Has, Have) any of the livestock been fed today?
19. An ingredient used in a number of Chinese dishes (is, are) tree ears.
20. George Washington Carver showed that one of the most versatile foods, with many uses, (is, are) peanuts.
21. None of the batters in today's game (has, have) hit a home run.
22. Our class trip to northern California, where we saw the giant redwood trees, (was, were) among the best experiences of my life.
23. The Lexington Avenue Five, our neighborhood basketball team, just won (its, their) first all-city championship.
24. The model XEF II is one of those cameras that (does, do) almost everything for you automatically.
25. Mary Ann thought some of the prices at what had been advertised as "The Sale of the Year" (was, were) no bargain at all.

CHAPTER 7 REVIEW: POSTTEST 2

Determining Subject-Verb Agreement and Pronoun-Antecedent Agreement. This posttest covers errors in agreement of verb and subject and of pronoun and antecedent. Number your paper 1–25. If a sentence is correct, write a + after the proper number; if it is incorrect, write the correct form of the verb or pronoun. One error makes a sentence incorrect.

EXAMPLE 1. In September, the new teacher was delighted because the class were enthusiastic and cooperative.
1. *was*

1. One of the South's great ecological treasures are the estuary and flatlands of Galveston Bay.
2. Twenty miles are too far for someone to walk unless he can stop and rest frequently.
3. Neither Melinda nor Greta answered their phone when I called yesterday.
4. During the five hours of deliberation, the jury was often in disagreement.
5. Public relations and advertising is exciting but often stressful work.
6. Anyone earning such a low salary will have trouble paying their bills.
7. Everyone who was at the tennis championship saw Chris Evert Lloyd and Martina Navratilova play their best match ever.
8. Is there any milk and apple pie in the refrigerator?
9. A completed application, in addition to a full financial statement, are required of students seeking college scholarships.
10. Every file cabinet, bookcase, and desk drawer were crammed with books and papers.
11. Where there's people and excitement, you're sure to find the twins Kazuo and Yori.
12. Not one of those nature programs that were shown on television this year have dealt with walruses.
13. Some of the information found in reference books need to be updated every year.
14. You might be surprised to know that many a city dweller grows vegetables in their own small yard.

15. Is Dolores one of the cheerleaders who are receiving a school letter at the sports banquet?

16. Each of the boys called home for a ride after their work was completed.

17. The Murphy family has made plans to visit relatives in West Virginia.

18. Did you know that the city of Savannah, Georgia, has their own spectacular parade on St. Patrick's Day?

19. "Neither of the movies seem to have much hope of making the millions the producers want," commented the film critic.

20. All of the battalion was transferred to Fort Bliss in Texas.

21. Are the Lesser Antilles near Puerto Rico?

22. None of the competitors knew what his own chances of winning were.

23. A gentle snowfall is one of those winter events that is guaranteed to put me into a peaceful mood.

24. The number of people investing in companies that manufacture robots is increasing.

25. One junior, as well as four seniors, have been invited to attend the Milford Youth Council each month.

Correct Use of Pronouns

NOMINATIVE AND OBJECTIVE CASE; SPECIAL PROBLEMS

DIAGNOSTIC TEST

Selecting Pronouns to Complete Sentences. Number your paper 1–20. From the parentheses, select the pronoun that correctly completes the sentence and write it after the proper number on your paper. Base your answers on formal standard usage.

EXAMPLE 1. Jose and (her, she) completed the math test first.
     1. *she*

1. Greg and (I, myself) got our driver's licenses on the same day.
2. My Uncle Bill, (who, whom) I greatly admire, worked in the Peace Corps for two years after he had finished college.
3. As we waited at the starting line, I knew in my heart that the race was really going to be between Ted and (I, me).
4. At the town meeting, Ellen McCarthy asked, "If (we, us) voters don't vote, how can we expect the situation to change?"
5. I thought Manuel was in Kansas City; so when he walked into the restaurant, I could hardly believe it was (he, him).
6. Even though we are twins, Julie has always been taller than (I, me).
7. Does anyone in this group know (who, whom) was using the computer after school yesterday?

8. Sometimes my parents have a low tolerance for (me, my) playing rock music, even though my stereo is in my bedroom.
9. "May I help you?" asked the receptionist. "(Who, Whom) do you wish to see?"
10. The school bus driver greeted (us, we) students with a smile each morning.
11. Owen said that for the first time the soccer team had elected co-captains, Mario and (he, him).
12. When you get to the airport, give your ticket to the person (who, whom) is at the check-in counter.
13. I remember (us, our) exploring the rocky coast of Maine when I was fifteen, and I have wanted to return there ever since.
14. Many people, adults as well as teen-agers, waste time worrying about (who, whom) is more popular in their social group.
15. "Does anyone dance better than (she, her)?" I wondered, as I watched Twyla Tharpe on the stage.
16. "When you and Regina were young children," said my grandfather, "I used to enjoy watching you and (she, her) playing Monopoly."
17. Knowing Noel and Bruce, I knew it had to be (they, them) who had played the practical joke on me.
18. Do you know that Stacy and (me, I) applied for the same job?
19. The President-elect knew exactly (who, whom) he wanted to appoint as Secretary of State.
20. I was so happy to see the new car that I could only gasp to my friend Danielle, "These wheels were made for you and (I, me)!"

The function of a pronoun in a sentence is shown by the case form of the pronoun. Different functions demand different forms. For instance, a pronoun that acts as a subject is in the *nominative case*; a pronoun that acts as an object is in the *objective case*; and a pronoun that shows possession is in the *possessive case*. The following examples illustrate these three functions of pronouns.

PRONOUN AS SUBJECT   **We** called the doctor.
PRONOUN AS OBJECT   The doctor called **us.**
POSSESSIVE PRONOUN   **Our** call was an emergency.

Observe that the pronoun has a different form (*we, us, our*) in each case.

☞ **NOTE**   Since they are used in the same ways that pronouns are used, nouns may also be said to have case. The following sentence illustrates the three cases of nouns.

The *sculptor's statue* won an *award*.
sculptor's   noun in the possessive case
statue   noun in the nominative case—subject
award   noun in the objective case—direct object

However, since nouns have identical forms for the nominative and objective cases and form the possessive in a regular way, case presents no problems as far as nouns are concerned.

8a. Learn the case forms of pronouns and the uses of each form.

Personal pronouns are those pronouns that change form in the different persons. There are three persons—first, second, and third—which are distinguished as follows:

First person is the person speaking: *I* (*We*) work.
Second person is the person spoken to: *You* are working.
Third person is a person or thing other than the speaker or the one spoken to: *He* (*She, It, They*) will work.

Personal Pronouns

Singular	NOMINATIVE CASE	OBJECTIVE CASE	POSSESSIVE CASE
FIRST PERSON	I	me	my, mine
SECOND PERSON	you	you	your, yours
THIRD PERSON	he, she, it	him, her, it	his, her, hers, its

Plural	NOMINATIVE CASE	OBJECTIVE CASE	POSSESSIVE CASE
FIRST PERSON	we	us	our, ours
SECOND PERSON	you	you	your, yours
THIRD PERSON	they	them	their, theirs

Since *you* and *it* do not change their forms, ignore them. Memorize the following lists of nominative and objective forms.

NOMINATIVE CASE	OBJECTIVE CASE
I	me
he	him
she	her
we	us
they	them

USES OF NOMINATIVE FORMS

8b. The subject of a verb is in the nominative case.

This rule means that whenever you use a pronoun as a subject, you should use one of the pronouns from the left-hand column on page 158. Ordinarily, you do this without thinking about it. When the subject is compound, however, many persons do make mistakes in their selection of pronouns. Whereas they would never say "Me am seventeen years old," they will say "Myra and me are seventeen years old." Since the pronoun is used as a subject in both sentences, it should be in the nominative case in both: *"Myra and I* are seventeen years old."

(1) To determine the correct pronoun in a compound subject, try each subject separately with the verb, adapting the form as necessary. Your ear will tell you which form is correct.

NONSTANDARD   Her and me are teammates. [*Her* is a teammate? *Me* am a teammate?]

STANDARD   **She** and **I** are teammates. [*She* is a teammate. *I* am a teammate.]

NONSTANDARD   Either Joe or him was in the gym. [*Him* was in the gym?]

STANDARD   Either **Joe** or **he** was in the gym. [*He* was in the gym.]

(2) When the pronoun is used with a noun (*we girls, we seniors,* etc.), determine the correct form by reading the sentence without the noun.

EXAMPLE   **We girls** painted the house. [*We* (not *Us*) painted the house.]

8c. A predicate nominative is in the nominative case.

A predicate nominative is a noun or pronoun in the predicate that refers to the same thing as the subject of the sentence. For the present purpose, think of a predicate nominative as any pronoun that follows a form of the verb *be*.

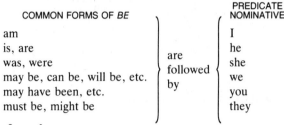

EXAMPLES   I am **she.**
Can it be **he**?
It might have been **they** in the store.

☞ USAGE NOTE   It is now perfectly acceptable to use *me* as a predicate nominative in informal usage: *It's me.* (The construction rarely comes up in formal situations.) The plural form (*It's us*) is also generally accepted. However, using the objective case for the third person form of the pronoun (*It's him, It's them*) is still often frowned on in standard English. When you encounter any of these expressions in the exercises in this book or in the various tests you take, you will be wise to take a conservative attitude and use the nominative forms in all instances.

EXERCISE 1. Using Pronouns in the Nominative Case.
Number your paper 1–20. After the proper number, write the personal pronoun that can be substituted for each italicized expression. In those sentences calling for [1st person pron.], use the appropriate one of the following pronouns: *I, we.*

EXAMPLES   1. Carl and *Sue Ann* are always happy.
            1. *she*
            2. Terri and [1st person pron.] were at the picnic.
            2. *I*

1. Jorge and *Mike* are tied for third place.
2. *Donna* and her parents have moved to San Antoni
3. [1st person pron.] seniors will take the exam.
4. Can it be *some choir members* in that picture?

5. Either Ellen or *Sally* will be in charge.
6. The team and *Mr. Knight* have chartered a bus.
7. [1st person pron.] varsity men earned our trophies.
8. Both *Ms. Ayala* and I wear bifocals.
9. Neither *Carolyn* nor Michele has change for the bus.
10. Did you know that Greg and [1st person pron.] are leaving?
11. I am sure it was *Ed* and you on the dance floor.
12. Will you or *your cousin* be here when I return?
13. It was dark when she saw the burglars, so she isn't sure it is *the burglars* in the lineup.
14. Helen and *Sharlene* have learned from their mistakes.
15. He thought that *Ron's brothers* owned the motorcycle.
16. The managers and [1st person pron.] mechanics repaired thirty cars today.
17. Only *the Washingtons* and the Millers left early.
18. Is it true that *Lillian* will compete in the rodeo?
19. It was *Frank* on the phone when you tried to call.
20. Did you ever expect that [1st person pron.] could type this fast?

USES OF OBJECTIVE FORMS

8d. The object of a verb is in the objective case.

The object of a verb answers the question "What?" or "Whom?" after an action verb.

EXAMPLE   We thanked **her.** [Thanked whom? Answer: *her*, which is the object.]

As their name suggests, the objective forms (*me, him, her, us, them*) are used as objects.

EXAMPLES   I helped **him** with the report.
She surprised **us** last night.
Him I have always admired.

Since both direct and indirect objects are in the objective case, there is no point in distinguishing between them in applying this rule.

EXAMPLES   They hired **her.** [direct object]
They gave **her** a present. [indirect object]

Like the nominative forms of pronouns, the objective forms are troublesome principally when they are used in compounds. Although you would hardly make the mistake of saying, "I helped *he* with the report," you might say, "I helped *Rod and he* with the report." Trying each object separately with the verb will help you to choose the correct pronoun for compound objects: "I helped *him* with the report."

Remember that when a pronoun is used with a noun (*we girls, us girls*), we determine the correct form by omitting the noun.

It annoys **us** runners. [It annoys *us*, not *we*.]

EXERCISE 2. Using Pronouns in the Objective Case. Referring to the list of objective forms, supply the correct pronouns for the italicized words in the following sentences. In sentences calling for [1st person pron.], use the appropriate one of the following: *me, us.*

1. Did you tell the superintendent or *Ms. Marshal*?
2. Carla and *Dave* I would never doubt.
3. Leave [1st person pron.] girls alone for a while.
4. Michelle will be inviting both you and [1st person pron.].
5. Did you see Lois or *Andy* today?
6. I sent the admissions director and *her assistant* a letter.
7. The coach chose Joan and *Carmen and me.*
8. The principal should have notified *Sven* and Gail.
9. Ron just passed Tina and [1st person pron.] in the hall.
10. Please don't ask [1st person pron.] athletes about last Saturday's game.

EXERCISE 3. Selecting Pronouns in the Nominative or Objective Case to Complete Sentences. This exercise covers the use of personal pronouns as subjects of verbs, predicate nominatives, and objects of verbs. Number your paper 1–20. After the proper number write the correct one of the two forms in parentheses in each sentence.

1. The guests thanked Rita and (she, her).
2. Gloria and (I, me) have matching outfits.
3. That's (he, him) standing on the corner.
4. (We, Us) girls are studying self-defense.
5. What were you telling Chuck and (we, us) earlier?
6. Of course, I remember Monica and (she, her).

7. We knew it was (he, him).
8. Did Jean and (he, him) sing in the musical?
9. Give (we, us) girls the message as soon as possible. _____ I O
10. My grandparents took Donna and (I, me) to the symphony.
11. Who will tell Georgia and (I, me) the truth?
12. I didn't hear the teacher and (they, them) arrive.
13. Jana and (she, her) are active members.
14. It's either you or (he, him).
15. I will call Jody and (they, them) tomorrow.
16. The teacher gave her friend and (she, her) more homework.
17. We are glad it wasn't Edna and (she, her) in the accident.
18. The volunteers and (I, me) distributed the posters.
19. You and (he, him) have been practicing every day.
20. I thought it was (she, her) on the stage.

8e. **The object of a preposition is in the objective case.**

Prepositions, as well as verbs, take objects. The noun or pronoun at the end of a prepositional phrase is the object of the preposition that begins the phrase. In the following prepositional phrases the objects are printed in boldfaced type:

| from **Los Angeles** | at the **bottom** | to **them** |
| outside the **house** | toward the **center** | for **us** |

Errors in the use of the pronoun as the object of a preposition, like those made when it is the object of a verb, usually occur when the object is compound. Since you would not say "I gave the ticket to *she*," you should not say "I gave the tickets to *Jenny* and *she*." By omitting the first of the two objects in a compound object, you can usually tell what the correct pronoun should be.

NONSTANDARD   I will speak after Laura or she.
STANDARD   I will speak **after** Laura or **her.** [after *her*]
NONSTANDARD   We got the keys from Len and he.
STANDARD   We got the keys **from** Len and **him.** [from *him*]
NONSTANDARD   Dwayne sat behind Norman and I.
STANDARD   Dwayne sat **behind** Norman and **me.** [behind *me*]

EXERCISE 4. Selecting Pronouns in the Objective Case to Complete Sentences.   Number your paper 1–10. Select the preposition from each sentence, and write it after the proper number on your paper. After the preposition, write the correct one of the two pronouns in parentheses. Remember to choose the objective form.

1. The chess team sent a challenge to Don and (he, him).
2. The slide show was presented by my sister and (I, me).
3. We are planning to leave with (they, them) and Alice.
4. I dedicated my poem to both Marcia and (she, her).
5. Frank arrived right after Juanita and (I, me).
6. The responsibility has fallen upon (we, us) students.
7. Were you sitting near Tony and (she, her)?
8. The matter is strictly between Ms. James and (they, them).
9. Consuelo has been asking about you and (she, her).
10. Would you draw a cartoon for the girls and (we, us)?

REVIEW EXERCISE A. **Selecting Pronouns in the Nominative or Objective Case to Complete Sentences.** Number your paper 1–25. Select the correct one of the pronouns in parentheses in each sentence and write it after the proper number on your paper. After each pronoun, write its use in the sentence, using these abbreviations: s. (subject of a verb), p.n. (predicate nominative), d.o. (direct object), i.o. (indirect object), and o.p. (object of a preposition).

EXAMPLE   1. Leave the pamphlets with Kim and (he, him).
      1. *him, o.p.*

1. The coach chose Darrell and (he, him).
2. Luckily, the Smiths and (we, us) missed the heavy traffic.
3. I haven't heard from Mark and (she, her) in ages.
4. Is it really (she, her) walking down the road?
5. Mr. Weaver chaperoned the boys and (we, us).
6. It could be (they, them) across the street.
7. My brother gave (I, me) his old skis.
8. Ms. Grant, the Dodges, and (she, her) went to the reunion.
9. During the busy season, the boss relies on (we, us) workers.
10. The mayor granted (she, her) an interview.
11. If we wait for (he, him), we'll miss the show.
12. (We, Us) science students did our experiment at the fair.
13. (She, Her) and Heather always sit in the last row.
14. Keiko had a dream about (they, them).
15. Mrs. Lemon said that (we, us) girls inspired her.
16. Would you please stop bothering Marla and (I, me)?

17. Adele painted a picture for (they, them) and (we, us).
18. Who is running toward (he, him)?
19. Neither the Spartans nor (we, us) Cougars play today.
20. Flora visited (she, her) and (I, me) in the hospital.
21. They didn't listen to (I, me).
22. I thought it was Rob and (they, them) in the center aisle.
23. The team and (they, them) work well together.
24. I have read everything written by (she, her).
25. The referee gave Manny and (he, him) a warning.

USES OF *WHO* AND *WHOM*

Like the personal pronouns, the pronouns *who* and *whoever* have three different case forms:

NOMINATIVE	OBJECTIVE	POSSESSIVE
who	whom	whose
whoever	whomever	whosever

Who and Whom as Interrogative Pronouns

Who and *whom* are interrogative pronouns when they are used to ask a question. The four rules on pages 159–163 governing the case forms of the personal pronouns apply also to *who* and *whom*.

EXAMPLES **Who** broke his leg? [The nominative form is required because *who* is the subject of *broke.*]
Whom did Nora choose? [The objective form is required because *whom* is the object of *did choose.*]

You may find it helpful, at first, to substitute *he, she—him, her* for *who—whom,* respectively. If *he* or *she,* nominative, fits the sentence, then *who,* also nominative, will be correct. If *him* or *her* fits, then *whom* will be correct.

EXAMPLES (*Who, Whom*) broke his leg? [**He** broke his leg. Hence, **Who** broke his leg?]
(*Who, Whom*) did Nora choose? [Nora did choose **him.** Hence, Nora did choose *whom.* **Whom** did Nora choose?]

Interrogative pronouns appear in both direct and indirect questions. A direct question uses the exact words of the speaker and is followed by a question mark. An indirect question does not use the exact words of the speaker and is not followed by a question mark.

DIRECT QUESTION **Who** washed the dishes?
INDIRECT QUESTION Joni asked **who** washed the dishes.
DIRECT QUESTION **Whom** did she see?
INDIRECT QUESTION I asked **whom** she had seen.

When the interrogative pronoun is used immediately after a preposition, *whom* is always the correct form.

EXAMPLES **On whom** does it depend?
          For whom did you bake the bread?

☞ USAGE NOTE In informal usage, *whom* is not usually used as an interrogative pronoun. *Who* is used regardless of the case.

INFORMAL **Who** were you calling?
          Who did the club elect?

In formal usage, the distinction between *who* and *whom* is still recognized:

FORMAL **Whom** were you calling? [*Whom* is the object of the verb *were calling.*]
       Whom did the club elect? [*Whom* is the object of *did elect.*]

Who and *Whom* as Relative Pronouns

When *who* and *whom* (*whoever* and *whomever*) are used to begin a subordinate clause, they are relative pronouns. Their case is governed by the same rules that govern the case of a personal pronoun. Although *whom* is becoming increasingly uncommon in spoken English, the distinction between *who* and *whom* in subordinate clauses is usually observed in writing. Study the following explanations and refer to them whenever you need help with relative pronouns in your own writing.

8f. The case of the pronoun beginning a subordinate clause is determined by its use in the clause that it begins. The case is not affected by any word outside the clause.

In order to analyze a *who—whom* problem, follow these steps:

    1. Pick out the subordinate clause.

2. Determine how the pronoun is used in the clause—subject, predicate nominative, object of verb, object of preposition—and decide its case according to the rules.

3. Select the correct form of the pronoun.

PROBLEM   Harry Houdini, (who, whom) was born in Hungary, performed daring escape tricks.

Step 1   The subordinate clause is (*who, whom*) *was born in Hungary.*

Step 2   In this clause the pronoun is used as the subject of the verb *was born;* as a subject, it should be, according to the rule, in the nominative case.

Step 3   The nominative form is *who.*

SOLUTION   Harry Houdini, **who** was born in Hungary, performed daring escape tricks.

PROBLEM   Harry Houdini, (who, whom) audiences adored, performed daring escape tricks.

Step 1   The subordinate clause is (*who, whom*) *audiences adored.*

Step 2   In the clause the subject is *audiences;* the verb is *adored;* and the pronoun is the object of the verb *adored.* As an object it is in the objective case, according to the rule.

Step 3   The objective form is *whom.*

SOLUTION   Harry Houdini, **whom** audiences adored, performed daring escape tricks.

PROBLEM   Do you remember (who, whom) the escape artist was?

Step 1   The subordinate clause is (*who, whom*) *the escape artist was.*

Step 2   In the clause, *artist* is the subject and *was* is the verb; the pronoun is a predicate nominative. As a predicate nominative it is in the nominative case, according to the rule.

Step 3   The nominative form is *who.*

SOLUTION   Do you remember **who** the escape artist was?

In writing the sentence above, one might tend to use *whom,* thinking it the object of the verb *remember,* but *remember* is outside the clause and cannot affect the case of a word in the clause. The object of the verb *remember* is the entire clause *who the escape artist was.*

PROBLEM   I do not remember (who, whom) I lent the book to. [Following the three steps, you will find that the pronoun here is used as the object of the preposition *to*; it should be in the objective case, hence *whom.*]

SOLUTION   I do not remember **whom** I lent the book to.

SOLUTION   I do not remember **to whom** I lent the book.

☞ USAGE NOTE   In determining whether to use *who* or *whom*, do not be misled by a parenthetical expression like *I think, he said*, etc.

EXAMPLES   We are the only ones **who**, I think, are taking jazz dance. [*who* are taking jazz dance]
She is the student **who** Mr. Hines thinks should be a chemist. [*who* should be a chemist]

EXERCISE 5. Selecting the Correct Case Form of *Who* and *Whoever* to Complete Sentences. Number your paper 1—20.

Using the three steps described on pages 166–67 for determining the case of a relative pronoun, determine the pronoun's correct form for each of the following sentences and write it on your paper after the proper number. Take plenty of time. Do not guess.

1. At the party the two people (who, whom) I enjoyed most were Willy and Angela.
2. Someone called you last night, but I did not know (who, whom) she was.
3. The announcer said that (whoever, whomever) finishes in the top ten can compete in the final round.
4. Since we did not hear (who, whom) the principal had named, we asked her to tell us again.
5. Anybody (who, whom) orders now will receive a free gift.
6. Neither of the two pianists was the musician (who, whom) the audience cheered.
7. She is the teacher (who, whom) the secretary thinks will be our substitute.
8. The science club wants to find an astronomer (who, whom) will be an exciting guest speaker.
9. They are curious about (who, whom) you were talking to so angrily.
10. Harriet Tubman was a woman (who, whom) we should remember.
11. The pedestrian (who, whom) the car hit suffered only minor cuts and bruises.

12. The police still have not caught the person (who, whom) stole my bicycle.
13. Several of the women (who, whom) had served on committees were considered for the position.
14. Anyone (who, whom) she can corner will be treated to a lecture on buying a home computer.
15. Allen is the only person in school (who, whom), I believe, has lived in a foreign country.
16. She gave us permission to use her car after she had found out (who, whom) the driver would be.
17. It does not matter (who, whom) wins, as long as you know you have done your best.
18. I have been looking for the person to (who, whom) I can deliver this package.
19. The player's reaction was to shout at the referee (who, whom) charged him with the penalty.
20. Ralph Bunche was a man (who, whom) many people respected.

WRITING APPLICATION A:
Using *Who* and *Whom* Correctly in Subordinate Clauses

When you are writing about characters in imaginative literature, you are usually using formal English. In formal English, the distinction is still made between *who* and *whom*. These pronouns often introduce subordinate clauses in complex sentences that discuss literary characters. Whether you select *who* or *whom* depends upon the pronoun's use in the clause.

EXAMPLES The character **whom** the people hate in *An Enemy of the People* is Dr. Thomas Stockmann. (The pronoun *whom* is used because it is the object of the verb *hate* in the subordinate clause.)
The son **who** closely resembles Willy Loman in *Death of a Salesman* is Happy. (The pronoun *who* is used because it is the subject of the verb *resembles* in the subordinate clause.)

Writing Assignment

Imaginative literature refers to short stories, poetry, plays, and novels. Select a work you have read and discuss one or more of its important characters. At some point, use *who* and *whom* correctly in subordinate clauses. Underline these pronouns.

PRONOUNS IN INCOMPLETE CONSTRUCTIONS

An "incomplete construction" occurs most commonly after the words *than* and *as*. To avoid repetition, we say "The tenor sang louder than he." (*Sang* is omitted.) "Are they as prepared as she?" (as she *is*). The interpretation of the sentence may depend upon the form of the pronoun used.

EXAMPLES   We trust Jane more than **she.** [than she trusts Jane]
We trust Jane more than **her.** [than we trust her]

8g. After *than* and *as* introducing an incomplete construction, use the form of the pronoun you would use if the construction were completed.

EXERCISE 6. Selecting Pronouns in Incomplete Constructions.   Number your paper 1–10. Write after the proper number the part of each sentence beginning with *than* or *as*, using the correct pronoun and completing the sentence to show that the pronoun is correct. In several sentences either pronoun may be correct, depending on how the sentence is completed.

EXAMPLE   1. Nolan has worked longer than (he, him).
          1. *than he has worked*

1. Have you lived in this city as long as (they, them)?
2. I don't know Brenda as well as (she, her).
3. Eva is shorter than (I, me).
4. The senior class scored higher than (they, them).
5. Mr. Cranley was more generous than (he, him).
6. Is she six months older than (I, me)?
7. The results show that I do better on multiple-choice tests than (he, him).
8. Can they hit safely as often as (we, us)?
9. I understand him better than (she, her).
10. Can Ms. Edwards tutor Paula as well as (I, me)?

REVIEW EXERCISE B. Identifying and Correcting Errors in Pronoun Usage.   Number your paper 1–10. Each sentence contains

an error in pronoun usage. After the proper number, identify the incorrectly used pronoun and write it on your paper; next to it, write the correct form of the pronoun.

EXAMPLE 1. Do you know who they gave the money to?
1. *who—whom*

1. The two students whom the committee nominated were Genevieve and me.
2. Geraldine announced to Joe and me that Cleon and her would do the inventory.
3. If you can't trust Ed and her, who can you trust?
4. "We kids are better than the kids on Central's team," Phil said. "So why aren't we doing better than them?"
5. Brenda sat between Sheryl and I.
6. The two people whom you can always rely on are Dave and her.
7. Oscar, whom I believe is the smartest member of our family, shares the evening newspaper with Tammy and me.
8. When Ann and I were young, us kids used to love to ride the tractor with my father.
9. When Laura told Greg and I that Ms. Cohen was going to retire, all three of us seniors felt sad.
10. When Andy and I study together, nobody in our class does better than us.

MINOR PROBLEMS IN THE USE OF PRONOUNS

8h. In standard formal English the pronouns ending in *–self, –selves* are usually used only to refer to another word in the sentence or to emphasize another word.

EXAMPLES I hurt **myself.** [*Myself* refers to *I.*]
She planned the party **herself.** [*Herself* emphasizes *she.*]
The **boys themselves** invented the game. [*Themselves* emphasizes *boys.*]

Avoid the use of pronouns ending in *–self, –selves* in place of other personal pronouns if the pronouns do not refer to or emphasize another word in the sentence.

EXAMPLES Joanne and **I** [not *myself*] are club members.
Ms. Markham gave skating lessons to Al and **me** [not *myself*].

8i. An appositive is in the same case as the word with which it is in apposition.

NONSTANDARD   Two seniors, Abe and her, made the best speeches.
   STANDARD   Two seniors, **Abe and she,** made the best speeches.

Abe and *she* are in apposition with *seniors,* the subject of the sentence. Since the subject of a verb is nominative, the appositive is also nominative; hence, *she* is correct.

STANDARD   For the leads in the play, the director chose two people, **Abe and her.**

In apposition with *people,* which is the object of *chose, Abe* and *her* are also in the objective case; hence, *her* is correct.

8j. Use the possessive case of a noun or a pronoun before a gerund.

This use of the possessive case will appear reasonable if you understand that a gerund is a noun form.

EXAMPLES   We were flattered by the **critic's praise.**
   We were flattered by the **critic's giving** such praise.

   Did you object to **my comments**?
   Did you object to **my making** the comments?

Sometimes a participle ending in *–ing* may be confused with a gerund. Use the objective case before a participle.

EXAMPLE   I followed **him hiking** through the woods.

The use of the possessive *his* in this sentence would change the meaning to a far less likely idea: *I followed his hiking through the woods.*

Whether or not you should use the possessive form of a word preceding a word ending in *–ing* often depends on which word you wish to emphasize. If you wish to emphasize the action in the *–ing* word, you use the possessive. If you wish to emphasize the preceding word, you do not use the possessive.

What did they say about Mary's jogging? [In this sentence the emphasis is on the kind of jogging Mary does.]
Can they imagine Mary jogging? [In this sentence the emphasis is on Mary, who apparently is not a jogger.]

WRITING APPLICATION B:
Using the Possessive Form Before a Gerund

In both your speech and your writing, you often use gerunds, even though you may not be aware of it. Gerunds are simply verb forms used as nouns. Gerunds end in –*ing*. Participles ending in –*ing* can therefore be confused with gerunds. You must decide whether the –*ing* word is a participle or a gerund in determining whether to use the possessive form in front of it. Look at your sentence, and judge whether you wish to emphasize the *action* in the –*ing* word. If you do, use the possessive form of the noun or pronoun that precedes it.

EXAMPLES I saw *him* taking the ACT this morning. (The word emphasized is *him*, not *taking;* therefore, the possessive form is not used before the –*ing* word.)

There is some question about *his* taking the ACT again to improve his score. (The word emphasized is *taking;* therefore, the possessive form is used before the –*ing* word.)

Writing Assignment

An important characteristic of mature people is the ability to listen carefully to advice, to weigh its merits, and then to decide whether or not they should follow it. Think of some advice that you have been given. How did you feel about it? Did you follow it or not? What has been the result? Write a summary of this important incident in your life. Illustrate the use of the possessive form before a gerund. Underline the possessive.

EXAMPLE I resented their urging me to watch the football game every Sunday.

EXERCISE 7. Identifying and Correcting Errors in Pronoun Usage. Some of the following sentences contain errors in pronoun usage. Number your paper 1–10. Write + after the proper number for each correct sentence; write 0 for each incorrect sentence. After each 0, write the correct form of the pronoun.

1. The store's being closed annoyed the shoppers.
2. Both Ruth and myself take piano lessons.
3. We all looked forward to her singing.
4. The coach tried to understand Dave striking out.

5. My close friends, Alicia and her, joined the choir.
6. After him promising to drive us, his car broke down a mile from our house.
7. Someone, either Irene or he, talked to the doctor.
8. They had not been told about us staying overnight.
9. The reporters interviewed his uncle and himself.
10. Their dancing thrilled the audience.

CHAPTER 8 REVIEW: POSTTEST 1

Selecting Pronouns to Complete Sentences Correctly.
Number your paper 1–25. Select the correct one of the pronouns in parentheses in each sentence and write it after the proper number on your paper. Be prepared to explain your answers.

1. Mr. McKay and (he, him) gave a demonstration.
2. The lightning almost struck Julie and (I, me).
3. I should have known it was (they, them).
4. The new student is taller than (she, her).
5. (Who, Whom) do you think Ms. Foster will choose?
6. (She, Her) and (I, me) studied all night for the test.
7. The woman, (who, whom) advertised in the paper, finally sold her house.
8. The bout between Max the Crusher and (he, him) is tonight.
9. I wish I were as lucky as (he, him).
10. Can the police be sure (who, whom) the right one is?
11. His parents were proud of (him, his) entering the Special Olympics.
12. Two debaters, Geri Ann and (she, her), researched the topic thoroughly.
13. If you have any problems, tell them to the sales manager or (I, me).
14. Neither Ms. Vasquez nor (I, me, myself) graded the tests.
15. I wonder (who, whom) the people will elect.
16. Rudy and (he, him) went fishing for trout.
17. We were the riders (who, whom) Mr. Van Hosen trained in show jumping.

18. What bothers all of us most is (they, them, their) always being late.
19. I met Harriet and (she, her) in the parking lot.
20. We introduced (we, us, ourselves) to their parents.
21. In an emergency (we, us) volunteers must work fast.
22. I am one of those people (who, whom) are allergic to pollen.
23. Irv doesn't recall (who, whom) he saw that movie with.
24. The farmers were happier about the rain than (we, us).
25. He said that Rhonda and (I, me) showed the most improvement.

CHAPTER 8 REVIEW: POSTTEST 2

Selecting Pronouns to Complete Sentences Correctly.
Number your paper 1–25. From the words in parentheses, select the pronoun that correctly completes the sentence and write it after the proper number on your paper. Base your answer on formal standard usage.

EXAMPLE   1. After a pause, I heard Tara say into the phone, "Yes, this is (she, me)."
   1. *she*

1. Last summer, my friend Megan and (I, me) worked in a factory that produces microchips for computers.
2. Before we began, we made a pact that (we, us) teen-agers would show the adults that we were responsible workers.
3. For the first two weeks, everything ran smoothly because our supervisor, Mr. Karas, was a person (who, whom) we thought was firm and just.
4. In fact, we were surprised by (him, his) showing interest in our progress and going out of his way to train us.
5. When Mr. Karas went on vacation, we doubted that his assistant, Ms. Sullivan, would be as firm as (he, him).
6. Our first mistake was in thinking that Mr. Karas and (she, her) would have different sets of standards.
7. Also, we thought wrongly that (she, her) sitting in for him would decrease our work load.
8. Well, I'm sure you can guess (who, whom) the situation taught a lesson to.

9. We started giving (us, ourselves) ten extra minutes during our morning break just a week after Ms. Sullivan took over.

10. One morning Ms. Sullivan walked up to us at our job stations and said, "Megan and Rick, until now I had thought you were workers (who, whom) took pride in your work."

11. "In fact, I received a post card from Mr. Karas this morning, and he asked if (his, him) being away has affected your work in any way."

12. "Between you and (I, me)," she said, "he'll never know you failed a test this morning by taking extra time during your morning break."

13. "If you're late again," Ms. Sullivan said calmly, "we, Mr. Karas and (I, me), will be looking for two other trainees for this station after he gets back."

14. It's funny how even an assistant supervisor can make her meaning clear to people like (us, ourselves) in just a few sentences.

15. For the rest of that morning, you couldn't find two other workers concentrating as well as Megan and (I, me).

16. (Who, Whom) do you think we talked about during our lunch break? Right!

17. We, Megan and (I, me), agreed that we had made not just one but several mistakes.

18. First, (us, our) deliberately taking extra time was wrong.

19. Second, we had let Mr. Karas down because it was (he, him) who had hired us, trained us, and trusted us.

20. Third, we had stereotyped Ms. Sullivan, thinking that because she was a woman she wouldn't do her job as well as (he, him).

21. Fourth, we had let (us, ourselves) down by failing to do our best.

22. (Who, Whom) had we been kidding when we had said that we wanted to prove to the adults that teen-agers were mature and responsible?

23. In the two weeks that followed, Megan and (I, me) did our work conscientiously and punctually, keeping our goal in mind.

24. We also watched how Ms. Sullivan did her job, and we soon saw that Mr. Karas and (she, her) shared many of the same strengths we had admired in Mr. Karas.

25. Shaking hands with Mr. Karas and Ms. Sullivan at the end of the summer, (we, us) two agreed that we had earned good money, and that we had also learned important lessons for life.

Correct Form and Use of Verbs

PRINCIPAL PARTS; TENSE, VOICE, MOOD

DIAGNOSTIC TEST

Using Verbs Correctly. The sentences in this exercise contain problems with verbs that will be discussed in this chapter. Number your paper 1–20. After the proper number, write the correct form of the verb in parentheses.

EXAMPLE 1. In a hurry to go to work, I couldn't remember where I had (laid, lain) my keys.
1. *laid*

1. During the political rally, several balloons filled with helium (burst, bursted) as they rose from the ground.
2. Whenever Joan sits down to watch television, her Samoyed puppy (lies, lays) down at her feet.
3. If I (was, were) President, I would make world peace my first priority.
4. When I (finished, had finished) reading my first novel by F. Scott Fitzgerald, I was eager to read another.
5. Mary Ann (swam, swum) the hundred-meter race in record time.
6. If I (had, would have) told the truth in the first place, the situation would have been much easier to handle.
7. (Cooking, Having cooked) a delicious Thanksgiving meal together, the newlyweds received many compliments from their guests.

8. When the math team came in second in the competition, the team members were upset because they (hoped, had hoped) to take first place.

9. On hot, humid summer nights we (sit, set) outside until the mosquitoes drive us indoors.

10. It is better to have loved and lost than never (to love, to have loved) at all.

11. Because we failed to add the proper amount of yeast, the loaves of bread failed to (raise, rise).

12. The tree died because it (was hit, had been hit) by a bolt of lightning.

13. The five riders are pleased (to qualify, to have qualified) for the equestrian team.

14. After I had (wrote, written) my autobiographical essay for my college application, I heaved a sigh of relief.

15. I wished that there (was, were) a good movie playing in town.

16. Because he had starred in four high-school productions, David hoped (to pursue, to have pursued) an acting career.

17. After running six miles, Nick said he could have (drank, drunk) a gallon of water.

18. (Lie, Lay) your work aside and relax for a few minutes.

19. In 1984, Joaquim Cruz, whose right leg is slightly shorter than his left leg, was happy when he (won, had won) Brazil's first gold medal in the 800-meter run.

20. They (began, begun) the trip at 5 A.M., just as dawn was breaking.

A verb is a word that expresses action or otherwise helps to make a statement.

KINDS OF VERBS

All verbs help to make statements about their subjects. Those that do so by expressing action, either physical or mental, are called *action verbs*.

ACTION VERBS Arthur **dashed** across the busy street.
Marla **drove** the car slowly over the bumpy gravel road.
She **wondered** about their strange behavior.

Some verbs help to make statements by linking the subject with a word in the predicate that explains, describes, or in some other way makes the subject more definite. Such verbs are called *linking verbs.*

LINKING VERBS   Their future **looked** bright. [*Bright*, an adjective, modifies the subject *future.*]
Elsa **is** my friend. [*Friend*, a noun, identifies Elsa.]
Vernon **became** an accountant. [*Accountant* identifies Vernon.]

Some verbs can be either action verbs or linking verbs:

ACTION VERB   They **felt** the snake's smooth, dry skin. [*Felt* expresses action.]
LINKING VERB   I **felt** tired today. [This time, *felt* links the subject, *I*, with a word that describes it, *tired.*]

There are many fewer linking verbs than action verbs. (You will find a list of the most common linking verbs on page 14.) The verb used most often as a linking verb is *be*, whose forms are *am, is, are, was, were*, and all verb phrases ending in *be, being*, or *been: may be, was being, has been*, etc.

In addition to functioning as a linking verb, *be* can also be followed by an adverb or adverb phrase:

Rachel was **here**.
The cottage is **in the north woods**.

Although it resembles an action verb in this use, *be* is not generally classified as one. Just remember that *be* is always a linking verb except when followed by an adverb.

THE PRINCIPAL PARTS OF A VERB

Every verb has four basic forms called principal parts: the *infinitive, present participle, past*, and *past participle*. All other forms are derived from these principal parts.

INFINITIVE	PRESENT PARTICIPLE	PAST	PAST PARTICIPLE
talk	(is) talking	talked	(have) talked

The words *is* and *have* are given with the present participle and past participle forms to remind you that these forms are used with a helping verb: *am, is, are, was, were, has been, will be, have, has, had*, etc.

Regular Verbs

A regular verb is one that forms its past and past participle by adding –*d* or –*ed* to the infinitive form.

INFINITIVE	PAST	PAST PARTICIPLE
care	care**d**	(have) care**d**
jump	jump**ed**	(have) jump**ed**

Irregular Verbs

An irregular verb is one that forms its past and past participle in some other way than the way a regular verb does.

This "other way" may involve changing the spelling of the verb or making no change at all.

INFINITIVE	PAST	PAST PARTICIPLE
drive	drove	(have) dri**ven**
ring	rang	(have) r**ung**
set	set	(have) set

The major problem in the correct use of verbs is the choice of the correct past and past participle forms of irregular verbs. Since irregular past tenses and past participles are formed in a variety of ways, you must know the principal parts of each irregular verb.

Three principal parts of common irregular verbs are given in the following alphabetical list. Use this list for reference. For the principal parts of other irregular verbs, consult a dictionary. Drill exercises on irregular verbs frequently misused are given following the list.

Principal Parts of Irregular Verbs

INFINITIVE	PAST	PAST PARTICIPLE
bear	bore	(have) borne
beat	beat	(have) beaten *or* beat
begin	began	(have) begun
bite	bit	(have) bitten
blow	blew	(have) blown
break	broke	(have) broken
bring	brought	(have) brought
burst	burst	(have) burst
catch	caught	(have) caught
choose	chose	(have) chosen
come	came	(have) come

INFINITIVE	PAST	PAST PARTICIPLE
creep	crept	(have) crept
dive	dived[1]	(have) dived
do	did	(have) done
draw	drew	(have) drawn
drink	drank	(have) drunk
drive	drove	(have) driven
eat	ate	(have) eaten
fall	fell	(have) fallen
fling	flung	(have) flung
fly	flew	(have) flown
freeze	froze	(have) frozen
get	got	(have) got *or* gotten
give	gave	(have) given
go	went	(have) gone
grow	grew	(have) grown
know	knew	(have) known
lay	laid	(have) laid
lead	led	(have) led
lend	lent	(have) lent
lie	lay	(have) lain
lose	lost	(have) lost
ride	rode	(have) ridden
ring	rang	(have) rung
rise	rose	(have) risen
run	ran	(have) run
say	said	(have) said
see	saw	(have) seen
set	set	(have) set
shake	shook	(have) shaken
shine	shone *or* shined	(have) shone *or* shined
sing	sang *or* sung	(have) sung
sink	sank *or* sunk	(have) sunk
sit	sat	(have) sat
speak	spoke	(have) spoken
steal	stole	(have) stolen
sting	stung	(have) stung
swear	swore	(have) sworn
swim	swam	(have) swum
swing	swung	(have) swung

[1] Informal, *dove.*

INFINITIVE	PAST	PAST PARTICIPLE
take	took	(have) taken
tear	tore	(have) torn
throw	threw	(have) thrown
wear	wore	(have) worn
write	wrote	(have) written

9a. Learn the principal parts of common irregular verbs.

To help you learn the correct use of irregular verbs, those which are commonly misused are presented on the following pages in four groups. Memorize the principal parts of the verbs in each group and do the exercises. In doing the exercises, remember that the past participle is used with helping, or auxiliary, verbs: *is, are, was, were, have, has, had, have been,* etc. As you say the principal parts, place *have* before the past participle: *begin, began, have begun.*

Group I

INFINITIVE	PAST	PAST PARTICIPLE
beat	beat	(have) beaten *or* beat
begin	began	(have) begun
blow	blew	(have) blown
break	broke	(have) broken
burst	burst	(have) burst
choose	chose	(have) chosen
come	came	(have) come
do	did	(have) done

EXERCISE 1. Using the Past and the Past Participle Forms Correctly. Number your paper 1–20. After the proper number, write either the past or the past participle of the verb given at the beginning of each sentence, whichever will fill correctly the blank in the sentence.

EXAMPLE   1. *do* I——nothing yesterday.
       1. *did*

1. *begin* They had——to argue.
2. *blow* Has anyone——out the candles?
3. *come* Richie——to our party yesterday.
4. *choose* Have they——a captain yet?
5. *beat* You——me at tennis last Friday.
6. *do* Has Erica——her chores yet?

7. *break* Milt has ——— the school track record.
8. *burst* Last March, the water pipes ——— .
9. *do* They ——— cartwheels on the lawn.
10. *begin* We have ——— our exercise program.
11. *blow* John's shed had been ——— over in the storm.
12. *choose* I ——— the album I wanted to hear.
13. *burst* The balloon had ——— in the air.
14. *come* We ——— early to help you fix dinner.
15. *choose* They have ——— a new class president.
16. *break* She ——— our date for tonight.
17. *come* They ——— as soon as they heard the news.
18. *do* The dancers ——— their warm-up exercises.
19. *begin* I was so scared that I ——— to tremble.
20. *come* Jennifer has ——— to spend the weekend.

Group II

INFINITIVE	PAST	PAST PARTICIPLE
draw	drew	(have) drawn
drink	drank	(have) drunk
drive	drove	(have) driven
fall	fell	(have) fallen
fly	flew	(have) flown
freeze	froze	(have) frozen
give	gave	(have) given
go	went	(have) gone

EXERCISE 2. Using the Past and Past Participle Forms Correctly. Number your paper 1–20. Complete each sentence by writing either the past or the past participle of the given verb.

EXAMPLE 1. *go* I hadn't——far when the car stalled.
          1. *gone*

1. *drink* We have——spring water for years.
2. *fall* My ring has——into the dishwater.
3. *freeze* They have——a peck of beans for next winter.
4. *go* Michael has——to the library twice today.

5. *give* She——me sound advice yesterday.
6. *fly* Have you——in a helicopter?
7. *drive* Ellie has never——a jeep.
8. *draw* Toni——pictures on the wall when she was two.
9. *go* Becky has——to the rodeo with friends.
10. *give* They——me the keys last night.
11. *freeze* The ice cubes are not——yet.
12. *fly* They——to Japan in a jumbo jet.
13. *draw* I have never——a portrait.
14. *drink* I worked hard, but he——more water than I did.
15. *drive* We have——more than 500 kilometers today.
16. *fall* Margie——down, but she finished the race.
17. *give* Frank——me one of the puppies.
18. *drive* Whenever I have——the truck, something has always happened.
19. *go* He——out the door before I could stop him.
20. *give* We should have——Donna a surprise party.

EXERCISE 3. Using the Past and Past Participle Forms Correctly. *This exercise covers the verbs in Groups I and II.* Write a + for each sentence in which the italicized verb is correct; if the verb is incorrect, write the correct form of the verb.

EXAMPLE 1. They *have* often *drove* to the mountains.
   1. *have driven*

1. I *gave* her my last dime.
2. They *should have went* to Hawaii for vacation.
3. The guests *have drank* all the punch.
4. It was so cold in the basement, the water *had froze.*
5. Kathy *came* to the conclusion that friends are important.
6. Henry *done* his best yesterday.
7. The teacher *has give* us permission to use his computer.
8. Some of the sketches *were drew* with pen and ink.
9. She wondered if she *had chose* the right one.
10. Why *have* you *came* home so early?
11. We *drove* carefully through the thick fog.
12. During the cold weather the water pipe *had bursted.*
13. Mr. Donahue *flew* to Africa last summer.
14. One of the children *could have fell* down the rickety stairs.
15. The thunder crashed and the lights *begun* to flicker.

16. Our team *has* not *beat* them in three years.
17. *Has* Ms. Gibbs really *give* us another chance?
18. I'll never know why he *done* it.
19. The crystal vase *has broke* in a million pieces.
20. They never *would have begun* if you hadn't helped them.
21. The wind *blowed* gently through the pines.
22. At last we *have chosen* a mascot for our club.
23. They *come* a long way just to see you.
24. We *gone* beyond the exit ramp on the highway.
25. The farmer *has drived* that old tractor for twenty years.

Group III

INFINITIVE	PAST	PAST PARTICIPLE
grow	grew	(have) grown
know	knew	(have) known
ride	rode	(have) ridden
ring	rang	(have) rung
run	ran	(have) run
see	saw	(have) seen
sing	sang *or* sung	(have) sung
speak	spoke	(have) spoken

EXERCISE 4. Using the Past and Past Participle Forms Correctly. Number your paper 1–20. Complete each sentence by writing either the past or the past participle of the verb at the beginning of each sentence.

EXAMPLE *sing* 1. The soprano has——the aria.
    1. *sung*

1. *ring* The fire alarm has——.
2. *run* The shortstop——toward third base.
3. *sing* Have you ever——a round before?
4. *speak* We had——to the plumber about the leak.
5. *see* The science club——a filmstrip yesterday.
6. *ride* Have you ever——on a burro?
7. *know* No one could have——the outcome.
8. *grow* Our baby hamster has——rapidly.
9. *see* We——the parade on television.
10. *know* No one——the formula for baking soda.
11. *ride* A few of us had——on the roller coaster.
12. *grow* My dog Finn has——old.
13. *speak* Have you——to them about it?
14. *sing* We had never——this song before.

15. *run*   When I washed my new shirt, the dye——.
16. *ring*   Has the bell——yet?
17. *speak* She hasn't——to anyone about the party.
18. *see*   I——a flash of lightning just now.
19. *ring*   If my clock hadn't——, I would still be sleeping.
20. *run*   She——all the way to the bus stop.

Group IV

INFINITIVE	PAST	PAST PARTICIPLE
spring	sprang *or* sprung	(have) sprung
steal	stole	(have) stolen
swim	swam	(have) swum
swing	swung	(have) swung
take	took	(have) taken
tear	tore	(have) torn
throw	threw	(have) thrown
write	wrote	(have) written

EXERCISE 5. Using the Past and Past Participle Forms Correctly. Number your paper 1–20. Complete each sentence by writing either the past or the past participle of the verb at the beginning of the sentence.

EXAMPLE 1. *tear* I'm sorry I——your jacket.
          1. *tore*

1. *spring* The rabbit had——out of the bushes.
2. *swim*   We have——in the ocean many times.
3. *tear*   Why have they——up the newspapers?
4. *write*   Has Penny——the editorial for the next issue?
5. *throw* Dee——him out at first base.
6. *take*   She——it to the shop for repairs.
7. *swing* While the photographer loaded the camera, the monkeys——from tree to tree.
8. *steal*   Someone has——our sack lunches!
9. *throw* Connie finally——away her old tennis shoes.
10. *write* Jesse——a story about the early pioneers.
11. *tear*   Someone has——a page from the photograph album.
12. *swim* She should not have——so soon after lunch.

13. *spring* Mr. Dodge——out of his seat and cheered loudly for his favorite player.
14. *take* I wish I had——your advice.
15. *swing* The trapeze artists——high above the crowd and performed daring acrobatic feats.
16. *steal* Why would anyone have——your notebook?
17. *write* We have——to five companies for information.
18. *swim* The children were like fish; they——for hours.
19. *throw* Make a wish after you have——a coin into the well.
20. *write* The poems you——will be published soon.

EXERCISE 6. Using the Past and Past Participle Forms Correctly. *This exercise covers the verbs in Groups III and IV.* Write a + for each sentence in which the italicized verb is correct; if the verb is incorrect, write the correct form of the verb.

EXAMPLE 1. The bells *rung* loudly two hours ago.
  1. *rang*

1. I *have ran* too far to turn back now.
2. *Had* the children *rang* the bell as a prank?
3. Little Tommy *has growed* two inches taller than I.
4. Ms. Owens *seen* the hit-and-run accident.
5. The choir *has sung* the national anthem at every game.
6. He *has tore* his shirt on that rusty nail.
7. *Had* she *knew* they were here, she would have stayed home.
8. You *should* not *have took* the biggest slice for yourself.
9. Jory Ann *swung* the lariat and roped the calf.
10. Are you sure he *swum* fifty lengths of the pool?
11. They're sorry they *had* not *spoke* up sooner.
12. He *has* always *rode* the bus to school.
13. I'm afraid the pool *has sprang* a leak.
14. How many times *has* Bobby *stole* second base?
15. Sheila *wrote* that letter to the editor.
16. Mrs. Kowalski *throwed* the javelin in the 1964 Olympics.
17. The startled burglar *sprang* out of the window.
18. *Has* Gladys ever *sang* a cappella?
19. I *seen* that movie twelve times.

20. Sam *would have wrote*, but he misplaced his address book.
21. The children's choir *sung* as well as could be expected.
22. Who *throwed* out my old comic books?
23. We *were torn* between the two candidates.
24. Keith *swinged* his partner so hard that she fell.
25. I think I *have sprang* the lock on my diary.

EXERCISE 7. Using the Past and Past Participle Forms Correctly. *This exercise covers the verbs in Groups I–IV.* Number your paper 1–50. Complete each sentence by writing either the past or the past participle of the verb at the beginning of the sentence.

EXAMPLE   1. *run*   I have——out of ideas.
                  1. *run*

1. *burst*   The firefighters——open the door.
2. *freeze*   Waiting for the bus, we almost——.
3. *break*   Have the movers——anything?
4. *fly*   They could have——to Dallas in two hours.
5. *blow*   A sudden gust of wind——out all the candles.
6. *fall*   She could not have——more than two meters.
7. *begin*   The networks——the new season last Monday.
8. *know*   We have——them since grade school.
9. *beat*   They——us fair and square.
10. *ring*   I opened the door, but no one had——the bell.
11. *drive*   We were——by our sense of justice.
12. *ride*   Carlton has finally——in a trolley car.
13. *drink*   During the recent flood, we——bottled water.
14. *run*   They——five miles yesterday evening.
15. *do*   Edith and I——much better than we had hoped.
16. *swim*   Holly has——the 100-meter butterfly race.
17. *come*   Shortly after you called, Rudy——home.
18. *steal*   She discovered that the microfilm had been——.
19. *choose* We should have——seats closer to the stage.
20. *sing*   I have——professionally since I was ten.
21. *grow*   The number of entrants has——tremendously.
22. *speak*   We have——to the judges on your behalf.
23. *go*   I arrived early, but Gloria had already——.
24. *see*   Do you think he——us buying his gift?

25. *give* What in the world——them such a crazy idea?
26. *take* Brenda could have——a longer vacation.
27. *tear* I have——the coupons out of the magazine.
28. *throw* Greg was furious when Billy——the golf clubs into the swimming pool.
29. *tear* The photograph had been——in half.
30. *write* Thomas Hardy——many novels and poems.
31. *throw* The pitcher has——six curve balls to me.
32. *go* I——to my friend's recital last Sunday.
33. *see* Haven't you——the abstract art exhibit?
34. *freeze* Frost had——on the inside of the window.
35. *run* Time has——out on the deadline.
36. *come* When I was sick, Maria——to the hospital.
37. *write* How many postcards have you——?
38. *drink* Someone——the last glass of orange juice.
39. *know* Iris was never——for her singing.
40. *break* The children——their promise to behave.
41. *begin* As soon as the play started, Lynne——to cough.
42. *swim* It was so hot, the adults——in the "kiddy" pool.
43. *fall* We were told that Don had——off the ladder.
44. *beat* The blacksmith——the hot metal into shape.
45. *see* We——him perform in the band concert.
46. *throw* The club has——its support behind the mayor.
47. *run* Sue Ann has——into this problem often.
48. *speak* They——to Carolyn about the scholarship.
49. *come* We have——to apologize for our rudeness.
50. *write* You or Beth should have——the new bylaws.

THREE TROUBLESOME PAIRS OF VERBS

Three pairs of verbs require special study and drill because they are more difficult to use correctly than any other verbs. These special verbs are *lie* and *lay*, *sit* and *set*, *rise* and *raise*. The most difficult to use correctly are the verbs *lie* and *lay*.

Lie and Lay

The verb *lie* means "to assume a lying position" or "to be in a lying position." Its principal parts are *lie*, *(is) lying*, *lay*, *(have) lain*.

The verb *lay* means "to put" or "to place something." Its principal parts are *lay, (is) laying, laid, (have) laid.*

The verb *lie* is intransitive (see page 13); that is, it never has an object. You never "lie" anything down.

The verb *lay* is transitive; that is, it may have an object or be in the passive voice. (See page 13.)

INTRANSITIVE The pattern **lies** on top of the fabric.
[no object]

TRANSITIVE You **lay** the fabric on a flat surface.
[object: *fabric*]

TRANSITIVE The fabric **is laid** on a hard, flat table.
[passive voice]

Memorize the principal parts of these verbs:

INFINITIVE	PRESENT PARTICIPLE	PAST	PAST PARTICIPLE
lie (to recline)	(is) lying	lay	(have) lain
lay (to put)	(is) laying	laid	(have) laid

If you do not habitually use these verbs correctly, you must begin your work on them slowly and thoughtfully. Only by taking time to think through each form you use can you eventually establish the habit of using the verbs correctly. When faced with a *lie-lay* problem, ask yourself two questions:

1. What is the meaning I intend? Is it "to be in a lying position," or is it "to put something down"?[1]

2. What is the time expressed by the verb and which principal part is required to express this time?

PROBLEM The heat was so unbearable that we (lay, laid) in the shade by the lake.

Question 1 Meaning? The meaning here is "to remain in a lying position." The verb which means "to remain in a lying position" is *lie.*

Question 2 Principal part? The time is past and requires the past form, which is *lay.* [lie, *lay,* lain]

SOLUTION The heat was so unbearable that we **lay** in the shade by the lake.

---

[1] You should be warned against two fairly common misconceptions about *lie* and *lay.* The first is that only people and animals *lie.* A moment's thought, however, will make clear that inanimate objects may also be in a lying position. The second misconception is that because an inanimate object in a lying position must have been put there, one should use *lay,* the verb meaning "to put," to say that the object is at rest. Regardless of its having once *been put down,* the object *lies* (not *lays*) there.

PROBLEM   Ginny (lay, laid) her new dress on the bed.

Question 1   Meaning? The meaning here is "to put." The verb which means "to put" is *lay*.

Question 2   Principal part? The time is past and therefore requires the past form, which is *laid*. [lay, *laid*, laid]

SOLUTION   Ginny **laid** her new dress on the bed.

PROBLEM   How long had it (lain, laid) there?

Question 1   Meaning? The meaning here is "to be in a lying position." The verb which means "to be in a lying position" is *lie*.

Question 2   Principal part? The time requires the past participle with *had*. The past participle of *lie* is *lain*. [lie, lay, *lain*]

SOLUTION   How long **had** it **lain** there?

PROBLEM   The cat is (lying, laying) on my good coat.

Question 1   Meaning? The meaning here is "to be in a lying position." The verb which means "to be in a lying position" is *lie*.

Question 2   Principal part? The time here requires the present participle, which is *lying*.

SOLUTION   The cat is **lying** on my good coat.

It will pay you to use this two-question formula each time you are in doubt about a problem in the use of *lie* and *lay*. Although slow at first, the process will speed up after a few trials, and you will be able to select the correct verb quickly. Of course, you must memorize the principal parts of the verbs before you can use the formula.

Two facts about the use of *lie* and *lay* may be of additional help.

1. Most errors in the use of these verbs are made when the speaker means "to assume or to be in a lying position." When this is the meaning you intend, be especially cautious.

2. When you wish to express the idea of "putting or placing something" in the past tense, always use *laid*.

EXERCISE 8. Using *Lie* and *Lay* Correctly.   Number your paper 1–10. After the proper number, write the correct one of the two words in parentheses. Use the two-question formula.

1. If you are sick, you should be (lying, laying) down.
2. They (lay, laid) the heavy crate on the handcart.
3. She had (lain, laid) a great deal of emphasis on usage.
4. Amy (lay, laid) down for a while.
5. I left my gloves (lying, laying) on the counter.
6. She had just (lain, laid) down when the doorbell rang.

7. They (lay, laid) their plans before the committee.
8. The calf (lay, laid) on a pile of straw.
9. She (lay, laid) her pen down and closed her notebook.
10. Don't leave your shoes (lying, laying) under the table.

EXERCISE 9. Using *Lie* and *Lay* Correctly. Choose the correct form of *lie* or *lay* to fill the blank in each sentence. Use the two-question formula.

EXAMPLE   1. I have ＿＿＿ the ribbons on the counter.
          1. *laid*

1. The letters are ＿＿＿ on the table for you to read.
2. Why don't you ＿＿＿ down for a few minutes?
3. Be careful when you are ＿＿＿ the new carpeting.
4. The mysterious package ＿＿＿ on the park bench.
5. Tomorrow we will ＿＿＿ new tiles in the hallway.
6. After an exhausting day, Carla ＿＿＿ on the sofa.
7. Danny ＿＿＿ the vase down and repaired the crack.
8. She ＿＿＿ on the track while the trainer taped her ankle.
9. The driftwood had ＿＿＿ on the beach for years.
10. Nina had not ＿＿＿ the keys by the telephone.

EXERCISE 10. Using *Lie* and *Lay* Correctly. Number your paper 1–20. After the proper number, write the correct one of the two verbs in parentheses. Use the two-question formula.

EXAMPLE   1. I want to (lie, lay) here a while longer.
          1. *lie*

1. The ancient relics had (lain, laid) in the desert.
2. Our dog always (lies, lays) in front of the fireplace.
3. This old diary was (lying, laying) in the attic.
4. They (lay, laid) their fishing gear in the boat.
5. I had just (lain, laid) down when the phone rang.
6. Sharlene was (lying, laying) her plans before the board.
7. The volcano that had (lain, laid) dormant erupted today.
8. We mixed the mortar, and Jan (lay, laid) the bricks.
9. The tourists were (lying, laying) on the sunny beach.
10. She was so depressed she (lay, laid) in bed all day.

11. Anita is (lying, laying) in the sleeping bag by the oak.
12. Until his fever breaks, Josh should (lie, lay) quietly.
13. Ivan and I (lay, laid) the planks across the sawhorses.
14. The cheetah (lies, lays) in the grass before pouncing.
15. Where did I (lie, lay) that library book?
16. The ungraded papers were (lying, laying) all over the desk.
17. Odelle knows she should not (lie, lay) her glasses there.
18. The detective saw the weapon was (lying, laying) nearby.
19. On Sunday, Mr. Evans (lies, lays) in bed reading the paper.
20. We (lay, laid) a fire but lost our matches.

Sit and Set

Sit usually means "to assume or to be in an upright, seated position."[1]
The principal parts of *sit* are *sit, (is) sitting, sat, (have) sat. Sit* is
almost always an intransitive verb; it rarely takes an object.

Set usually means "to put, to place something." The principal parts
of *set* are *set, (is) setting, set, (have) set.* Like *lay, set* is a transitive verb;
it may take an object.

Since all forms of *set* are made without changing the vowel, the
problem of using these two verbs is rather simple. You need only keep
in mind the fact that when you mean "to put something down," you use
set or *setting.* For all other meanings, use *sit* or *sat* or *sitting.*[2]

INFINITIVE	PRESENT PARTICIPLE	PAST	PAST PARTICIPLE
sit (to rest)	(is) sitting	sat	(have) sat
set (to put)	(is) setting	set	(have) set

EXERCISE 11. Using *Sit* and *Set* Correctly. Number your paper
1–10. After the proper number, write the correct one of the two verbs in
parentheses in each sentence.

EXAMPLE 1. Don't (sit, set) on the wet paint!
     1. *sit*

1. After he had struck out, Pete (sat, set) on the bench.
2. My little sister (sits, sets) quietly when we have company.

---

[1] Such expressions as "Sit the baby in the high chair" or "Sit him up" really mean "to put"
or "to place," and these expressions, which are acceptable, are exceptions to the general
rule.
[2] The expressions "The sun sets," "the setting hen," and "Wait for the cement to set" are
exceptions to the rule.

3. Where were the packages (sitting, setting) this morning?
4. We had (sat, set) our weary bones in the plush chairs.
5. I never (sit, set) in the balcony at the Bijou.
6. They were (sitting, setting) placemats on the table.
7. It makes no difference to me where you (sit, set).
8. We (sat, set) up folding chairs for the guests.
9. Mr. Han told me to (sit, set) the equipment on his desk.
10. I may never know who had (sat, set) on my glasses.

Rise and Raise

The verb *rise* means "to go up." Its principal parts are *rise, (is) rising, rose, (have) risen*. In other words, when the subject of the verb is itself moving upward, use *rise*. Like *lie, rise* is intransitive; it never takes an object.

The verb *raise* means "to force something to move upward." Its principal parts are *raise, (is) raising, raised, (have) raised*. When the subject of the verb is acting on something, forcing it upward, use *raise*. Like *lay* and *set, raise* is transitive; it may take an object.

Memorize the principal parts of these verbs:

INFINITIVE	PRESENT PARTICIPLE	PAST	PAST PARTICIPLE
rise (to go up)	(is) rising	rose	(have) risen
raise (to force up or be forced up)	(is) raising	raised	(have) raised

EXERCISE 12. Using *Rise* and *Raise* Correctly. Number your paper 1–10. After the proper number, write the correct one of the two verbs in parentheses in each sentence.

1. Air bubbles have been (rising, raising) to the surface.
2. Increasing the import duty will (rise, raise) retail prices.
3. The speaker (rose, raised) from her chair and approached the microphone.
4. This month, the star has been (rising, raising) in the east.
5. The rooster (rises, raises) early.
6. During the Revolutionary War, many American colonists decided to (rise, raise) up against King George III.
7. Balloons can (rise, raise) because they contain heated air, which is less dense than the surrounding air.
8. The Wilsons (rose, raised) six adopted children.

9. Mist was (rising, raising) from the ground.

10. The dough has been (rising, raising) for the past hour.

EXERCISE 13. Using *Lie-Lay, Sit-Set,* and *Rise-Raise* Correctly.
For each of the following verbs, write a brief sentence in which the verb is correctly used.

1. lie	6. raised	11. rising
2. raising	7. rises	12. rose
3. laying	8. have lain	13. setting
4. set	9. lay (past tense)	14. risen
5. lying	10. has laid	15. sat

EXERCISE 14. Using *Lie-Lay, Sit-Set,* and *Rise-Raise* Correctly.
Number your paper 1–25. After the proper number, write the correct one of the two words in parentheses in the sentence. Work slowly. Try for 100 percent.

EXAMPLE   1. Please (sit, set) wherever you like.
   1. *sit*

1. All week that box has (lain, laid) unopened on the desk.
2. We (rose, raised) our hats to salute the astronauts.
3. The phoenix (rose, raised) from the ashes.
4. The injured deer (lay, laid) motionless in the road.
5. I've been running errands all day and look forward to (sitting, setting) with my feet up.
6. Our applications were (lying, laying) in front of the file.
7. Would you please (sit, set) with us?
8. I always (lie, lay) the phone book on this table.
9. We arrived late and had to (sit, set) in the top row of the bleacher seats.
10. Kathy hummed as she (lay, laid) the baby in the crib.
11. Clean up the mess that's (lying, laying) on your floor.
12. Last night's victory really (rose, raised) the team's spirit and confidence.
13. If you (sit, set) the pie on the ledge, it may vanish.
14. Fred should (lie, lay) on his side to stop snoring.
15. After the fire, the museum (lay, laid) in a heap.
16. Tempers (rose, raised) as the debate progressed.
17. The police are (lying, laying) in wait for the crooks.
18. We were (sitting, setting) down when the alarm rang.
19. Never (sit, set) anything on the seat next to you.

20. Our St. Bernard often (lies, lays) in my lap.
21. Billows of dust (rose, raised) up from the field.
22. Who was the last one to (lie, lay) in the hammock?
23. Food prices have (risen, raised) more than five percent.
24. Haven't they (sat, set) down the piano yet?
25. You must (lie, lay) on a padded surface to do exercises.

REVIEW EXERCISE A. Using Verb Forms Correctly. Number your paper 1–10. In each sentence, identify any verb used incorrectly. Write it on your paper, and next to it write the form of the verb needed to correct the sentence.

EXAMPLE   1. The helicopter raised from the airstrip and headed north toward Hartford.
1. *raised—rose*

1. As I watched the horror movie, I could feel fear rising in my throat; I knew I had chose the wrong way to relax.
2. Aretha had taken her younger sister to the circus; things went well until the little girl's balloon bursted.
3. When we woke, we saw that the pond was froze.
4. When their parents had went shopping, the twins decided to play some computer games.
5. The defendant, who had been found guilty, was brung before the judge for sentencing.
6. After we had donated blood, we laid down for a few minutes and were then given orange juice.
7. Before we knew what was happening, Marvin had dove through the ice to rescue the child who had fallen into the lake.
8. If I hadn't been careless, I wouldn't have broke that vase.
9. While Jessica was in surgery, her concerned parents set in the waiting room and kept their hopes high.
10. Jorge walked up to the door and rung the bell, waiting nervously for the girl he had driven two hours to see.

TENSE

Verbs change in form to show the time of their action or of the idea they express. The time expressed by a verb (present, past, future) is its tense. There are six tenses. As the following conjugations of the verbs *go* and *be* will show you, the six tenses are formed from the principal parts of the verb. Study these conjugations and use them for reference in your work on tense.

9b. Learn the names of the six tenses and how the tenses are formed.

Conjugation of the Verb Go

Present infinitive: *to go*   Perfect infinitive: *to have gone*

Principal Parts

INFINITIVE	PRESENT PARTICIPLE	PAST	PAST PARTICIPLE
go	going	went	gone

Present Tense

Singular	Plural
I go	we go
you go	you go
he, she, it goes	they go

Present progressive: *I am going*, etc.

Past Tense

Singular	Plural
I went	we went
you went	you went
he, she, it went	they went

Past progressive: *I was going*, etc.

Future Tense

(*will* or *shall* + the infinitive[1])

Singular	Plural
I will (shall) go	we will (shall) go
you will go	you will go
he, she, it will go	they will go

Future progressive: *I will (shall) be going*, etc.

---

[1] For a discussion of the use of *shall* and *will*, see page 254.

Present Perfect Tense

(*have* or *has* + the past participle)

Singular	Plural
I have gone	we have gone
you have gone	you have gone
he, she, it has gone	they have gone

Present perfect progressive: *I have been going*, etc.

Past Perfect Tense

(*had* + the past participle)

Singular	Plural
I had gone	we had gone
you had gone	you had gone
he, she, it had gone	they had gone

Past perfect progressive: *I had been going*, etc.

Future Perfect Tense

(*will have* or *shall have* + the past participle)

Singular	Plural
I will (shall) have gone	we will (shall) have gone
you will have gone	you will have gone
he, she, it will have gone	they will have gone

Future perfect progressive: *I will have (shall have) been going*, etc.

Conjugation of the Verb Be

Present infinitive: *to be*   Perfect infinitive: *to have been*

Principal Parts

INFINITIVE	PRESENT PARTICIPLE	PAST	PAST PARTICIPLE
be	being	was, were	been

Present Tense

Singular	Plural
I am	we are
you are	you are
he, she, it is	they are

Present progressive: *I am being*, etc.

Past Tense

Singular	Plural
I was	we were
you were	you were
he, she, it was	they were

Past progressive: *I was being*, etc.

Future Tense

(*will* or *shall* + the infinitive)

Singular	Plural
I will (shall) be	we will (shall) be
you will be	you will be
he, she, it will be	they will be

Present Perfect Tense

(*have* or *has* + the past participle)

Singular	Plural
I have been	we have been
you have been	you have been
he, she, it has been	they have been

Past Perfect Tense

(*had* + the past participle)

Singular	Plural
I had been	we had been
you had been	you had been
he, she, it had been	they had been

Future Perfect Tense

(*will have* or *shall have* + the past participle)

Singular	Plural
I will (shall) have been	we will (shall) have been
you will have been	you will have been
he, she, it will have been	they will have been

9c. Learn the uses of each of the six tenses.

Each of the six tenses has its own particular uses, some of which require explanation. Study the following explanations of these uses; learn rules for the uses of the tenses; do the exercises. Use these pages for reference when you are confronted by a problem in tense in your own writing.

(1) The *present tense* is used to express action (or to help make a statement about something) occurring now, at the present time.

EXAMPLES   We **wait** patiently.
We **are waiting** patiently. [progressive form]
We **do wait** patiently. [The verb with *do* or *did* is called the emphatic form.]

> ☞ NOTE   In all tenses, as in the second example, continuing action may be shown by the use of the progressive form, which ends in *–ing*. The third example illustrates the emphatic form, consisting of a form of *do* plus the first principal part of a verb. The normal way of making a sentence emphatic is to pronounce the helping verb with stress. When there is no helping verb, *do* or *did* is added to carry this stress. These emphatic forms can be used in the present and past tenses only. The present tense is also used to indicate habitual action.

EXAMPLE   We **wait** for the bus every morning.

The present tense is often used to express a general truth, something which is true at all times.

EXAMPLES   Amy agreed that honesty **is** [instead of *was*] the best policy.
I have read that Alaska **is** [instead of *was*] the only state without an official nickname.

The present tense is also used occasionally to achieve vividness in writing about past events. This use of the present tense is known as the *historical present.*

EXAMPLE   Queen Elizabeth I **strengthens** England's power and **leads** it through its greatest era.

(2) The *past tense* is used to express action (or to help make a statement about something) that occurred in the past but did not continue into the present. The past tense is formed regularly by adding *–d* or *–ed* to the verb.

EXAMPLES   We **waited** for you yesterday.
We **were waiting** for you yesterday.

> ☞ NOTE   Past action may be shown in other ways.

EXAMPLES　We **used to wait** for the bus.
　　　　　　We **did wait** for the bus. [emphatic form]

(3) The *future tense* **is used to express action (or to help make a statement about something) occurring at some time in the future. The future tense is formed with** *will* **or** *shall*.

EXAMPLES　We **will wait** for you tonight.
　　　　　　We **will be waiting** for you tonight.

☞ **NOTE**　The future may also be indicated in other ways.

EXAMPLES　We **are going to wait** outside.
　　　　　　We **are about to wait** outside.
　　　　　　We **wait** outside **later**. [present with another word indicating future time]

(4) The *present perfect tense* **is used to express action (or to help make a statement about something) occurring at no definite time in the past. It is formed with** *have* **or** *has*.

EXAMPLE　Ted **has waited** for us often.

The present perfect tense is also used to express action (or to help make a statement about something) occurring in the past and continuing into the present.

EXAMPLES　We **have waited** for an hour. [We are still waiting.]
　　　　　　We **have been waiting** for an hour. [We are still waiting.]

(5) The *past perfect tense* **is used to express action (or to help make a statement about something) completed in the past before some other past action or event. It is formed with** *had*.

EXAMPLES　After we **had waited** for an hour, we **left**. [The waiting preceded the leaving.]
　　　　　　After we **had been waiting** for an hour, we **left**.

(6) The *future perfect tense* **is used to express action (or to help make a statement about something) that will be completed in the future before some other future action or event. It is formed with** *will have* **or** *shall have*.

EXAMPLES   By the time the bus **arrives**, we **will have waited** for at least an hour.
[The waiting precedes the arriving of the bus.]
By the time the bus **arrives**, we **will have been waiting** for at least an hour.

EXERCISE 15. **Understanding the Uses of the Six Tenses.**
Explain the difference in meaning between the sentences in the following pairs. The sentences are correct. Then name the tense used in each sentence.

EXAMPLE   1. I met you at 3:00.
I will have met you at 3:00.
1. *In the first sentence, the action occurred once and ended. In the second sentence, the action will be completed in the future before another action will be completed.*
past   future perfect

1. Marga lived in Brazil for eight years.
   Marga has lived in Brazil for eight years.
2. Why had she gone to the theater?
   Why has she been going to the theater?
3. How often have they been late?
   How often were they late?
4. Have the directions been explained clearly?
   Had the directions been explained clearly?
5. They discovered that Joe had been in the hospital.
   They discovered that Joe has been in the hospital.
6. We think that Anne will have sewn the quilt by her parents' anniversary.
   We think that Anne will sew the quilt by her parents' anniversary.
7. Was she driving?
   Had she been driving?
8. After June 30, they will have raised taxes twice this year.
   After June 30, they will be raising taxes twice this year.
9. I'll have spent my savings.
   I'll spend my savings.
10. Where had Julie gone on vacation?
    Where has Julie gone on vacation?

EXERCISE 16. Understanding the Uses of the Six Tenses. In each of the following items you are given the meaning of a sentence. Two sentences then follow. Only one of these sentences matches the given meaning. Number your paper 1–10. Next to the appropriate number, write the *letter* of the sentence that matches the *meaning*. Be prepared to name the tenses used in each sentence.

EXAMPLE   1. *Meaning:* It is not snowing now.
        a. It had been snowing all afternoon.
        b. It has been snowing all afternoon.
    1. a

1. *Meaning:* John still works for Mr. Porzio.
    a. John has worked for Mr. Porzio for a year.
    b. John had worked for Mr. Porzio for a year.
2. *Meaning:* Ann Rosine could be on her way to Worcester right now or could be going later.
    a. Ann Rosine is moving to Worcester, Massachusetts.
    b. Ann Rosine will be moving to Worcester, Massachusetts.
3. *Meaning:* Jaime is still in school.
    a. Jaime has been studying pharmacy since last summer.
    b. Jaime studied pharmacy last summer.
4. *Meaning:* Elena was born on Mary and David's wedding day.
    a. Barbara and Steven had had their first child, Elena, when Mary and David got married.
    b. Barbara and Steven had their first child, Elena, when Mary and David got married.
5. *Meaning:* Sabina will have finished working two jobs by the time she graduates.
    a. When she graduates from college, Sabina will have worked on a farm and in a department store.
    b. When she graduates from college, Sabina will have been working on a farm and in a department store.
6. *Meaning:* Lionel is not in law school yet.
    a. Lionel is going to attend Columbia University Law School in September.
    b. Lionel is attending Columbia University Law School.
7. *Meaning:* Alison takes a bus to work on a regular basis.
    a. Alison takes the bus to work.
    b. Alison is taking the bus to work.

8. *Meaning:* I don't know whether my work has paid off.
   a. After I had passed the test, I knew my work had paid off.
   b. After I pass the test, I know my work will have paid off.
9. *Meaning:* Rayae was a bank officer at the age of twenty-four.
   a. When Rayae turned twenty-five, she had been promoted to the position of bank officer.
   b. When Rayae turned twenty-five, she was promoted to the position of bank officer.
10. *Meaning:* The children will not miss the anniversary celebration.
    a. I'm sure Eva and Claude will celebrate their anniversary when their children come home from college.
    b. I'm sure that Eva and Claude will have celebrated their anniversary when their children come home from college.

WRITING APPLICATION A:
Making Writing Clear Through the Use of Correct Tenses

Time is extremely important in your daily life. You probably wear a wristwatch, and perhaps you set an alarm clock if you have to wake up at a particular time. When you write, the time your verbs express is equally important. Just as your wristwatch tells you the time, the tense of a verb signals the time for your reader. The incorrect tense can cause confusion.

Writing Assignment

As you near the end of high school, you are probably considering several different options for the future. You may be thinking about a vocational school, college, a job, or the military service. Jot down the steps you plan to take after graduation to reach a long-range goal. Use these notes to write a summary of your plans. Check your paper for correct use of tense.

SPECIAL PROBLEMS OF TENSE USAGE

The Past Perfect Tense

The past perfect tense requires special consideration because young writers frequently fail to employ it in expressing two actions that happened at different times in the past. The function of the past perfect tense is to make clear which of the actions preceded the other.

9d. Use the past perfect tense for the earlier of two past actions.

NONSTANDARD Sue mentioned (past) that she invited (past) the neighbors to her party. [The same tense has been incorrectly used for two actions that did not happen at the same time. Since the inviting preceded the mentioning, the past perfect form of *invite* should be used.]

STANDARD Sue **mentioned** (past) that she **had invited** (past perfect) the neighbors to her party.

NONSTANDARD The film Allan showed (past) us we viewed (past) last month. [The viewing preceded the showing.]

STANDARD The film Allan **showed** (past) us we **had viewed** (past perfect) last month.

NONSTANDARD There was (past) a parking lot where the brick house was (past). [Since the two verbs in this sentence are in the same tense, the sentence suggests that the lot and the house were there together.]

STANDARD There **was** (past) a parking lot where the brick house **had been** (past perfect). [The past perfect *had been* makes it clear that the house was there before the lot.]

STANDARD There **had been** (past perfect) a parking lot where the brick house **was** (past). [Making the other verb past perfect reverses the time order; the lot preceded the house.]

9e. Avoid the use of *would have* in "if clauses" expressing the earlier of two past actions. Use the past perfect.

NONSTANDARD If he would have taken more time, he'd have won the chess tournament.

STANDARD If he **had taken** more time, he'd have won the chess tournament.

NONSTANDARD If we would have stopped by, we'd have met your cousin.

STANDARD If we **had stopped** by, we'd have met your cousin.

EXERCISE 17. Using Tenses Correctly. Correct the following sentences, which contain errors in the use of tenses. Refer, if necessary, to the rules on pages 199–202 for the uses of the various tenses.

EXAMPLE   1. If I knew the last answer, I'd have had a perfect test.
          1. *had known*

1. The managers postponed the special sale after we distributed the posters around town.
2. Pam finally appreciated the old saying that every cloud had a silver lining.
3. By the time we graduate in June, Ms. O'Connell will be teaching Latin for twenty-four years.
4. Although Denny's skill was demonstrated during the season, he was not selected to play in the City All-Star game.
5. If they would have called sooner, I'd have given them a ride.
6. When I finally got to the dentist, my tooth already stopped hurting.
7. The company hired Ms. Littmann because she lived for many years in Japan.
8. I heard that Jeff saw the movie five times.
9. They were very impressed by Laura Montez, who wrote the story about the factory's safety hazards.
10. When I presented my speech before the committee, the members previously studied several reports on nuclear waste disposal.
11. Mr. Frey already complained to the neighbors many times before he called the police.
12. By then I will receive my first paycheck.
13. If she forgot the directions, we could have been lost.
14. The judges declared that we made the most interesting exhibit at the science fair.
15. If they had enough money, they could have taken a taxi.
16. As I thought about our argument, I was sure you lost your temper first.
17. By tomorrow we will be living in Los Angeles five years.
18. When we reviewed the videotapes of the game, we saw that the other team committed the foul.
19. If I would have known that my favorite rock group was in town, I'd have gone to the concert.
20. The clerk remembered that the manager has ordered the new shipment last Tuesday.
21. How could I have forgotten that Great Britain included England, Wales, and Scotland?

22. We estimate that when we're in our forties, we will be working more than twenty years.
23. If Gary would have read the advertisement, he could have saved a hundred dollars on that camera.
24. By this time tomorrow, my grandparents will be residing seven years in St. Petersburg.
25. Walt would have done much better on the exam if he was present at our study sessions.

Having with the Past Participle

9f. In participial phrases, use *having* with the past participle to express action completed before another action.

NONSTANDARD Being absent for the midterm exam, I was given a makeup test. [The present participle *being* is incorrectly used to express an action that has obviously been completed *before* the second action in the sentence.]

STANDARD **Having been** absent for the midterm exam, **I was** given a makeup test.

NONSTANDARD Choosing a college, Rosa sent her application. [The college had to be chosen *before* she could send an application.]

STANDARD **Having chosen** a college, Rosa **sent** her application. [This idea may also be properly expressed by using the word *after* before the present participle: **After** choosing a college, Rosa sent her application.]

The Present and the Perfect Infinitives

9g. Use the present infinitive (*to go, to see*, etc.) to express action following another action.

NONSTANDARD The dancers were upset because they had planned to have performed for us. [What had the dancers planned, *to have performed* or *to perform*? The present infinitive *to perform* should be used because the action it expresses follows the action of the verb *had planned*.]

STANDARD The dancers were upset because they **had planned to perform** for us.

NONSTANDARD He wanted to have invited all the seniors. [Did he want *to have invited* or *to invite*?]

STANDARD He **wanted to invite** all the seniors.

9h. Use the perfect infinitive (*to have gone, to have seen,* **etc.) to express action before another action.**

EXAMPLE   We **are** happy **to have met** you. [The action expressed by the perfect infinitive *to have met* came before the time of the other verb, *are.*]

EXERCISE 18. Using Verbs Correctly. The sentences in this exercise contain errors in the use of verbs. Correct the sentences according to the rules you have just studied. You will not need to change more than one verb or verbal for each sentence.

1. Spending three hours on a review of chemistry, we then worked on irregular French verbs.
2. I should have liked to have met them.
3. I reread the book review that I typed yesterday.
4. We gained two hours when we flew from Missouri to California because the sun rose in the east.
5. We wanted to have avoided any controversy.
6. Sometime before the bus leaves, I will finish packing.
7. They already ate dinner when I stopped by.
8. We were hoping to have had a short-answer test in history instead of an essay exam.
9. If you told me you were going shopping, I would have gone with you.
10. By the time dinner was ready, I did all my math homework.

EXERCISE 19. Using Tenses Correctly. The following sentences contain errors in the use of tense and in the use of the present participle and the infinitive. Correct the sentences.

EXAMPLE   1. I had hoped to have seen you there.
          1. *had hoped to see*

1. We had expected to have been among the top five teams.
2. Working after school for the whole year, Anita did not work during the summer.
3. We were surprised to learn that mushrooms were really spore-bearing fungi.
4. If the rain stopped, we would have eaten outdoors.
5. Making weekend plans before, I declined the invitation.
6. We wanted to have seen the Mayan temples in Mexico.

7. By July I will be taking piano lessons one full year.
8. They would have liked to have séen Ms. Steinem.
9. If we didn't stop at the gas station, we'd have seen the first act.
10. When Harold finally paid the fine, he already received the third overdue notice.

WRITING APPLICATION B:
Using Verb Tenses Consistently for Clarity

A time machine might be an intriguing idea. However, do not make your writing a time machine in which your readers are tossed from past to present to future without reason. Use verb tenses consistently and logically. Otherwise you may lose your readers in your confused world of time.

Writing Assignment

Choose an especially memorable event that has taken place in your senior year. Recreate the event in writing. You might use narration, description, or exposition. Read your writing carefully to make sure that all verb tenses are consistent.

ACTIVE AND PASSIVE VOICE

A verb is in the *active* voice when it expresses an action performed *by* its subject. A verb is in the *passive* voice when it expresses an action performed *upon* its subject or when the subject is the result of the action.

ACTIVE VOICE   The car hit a tree. [subject acting]

PASSIVE VOICE   The tree was hit by a car. [subject acted upon]

All transitive verbs (those that take objects) can be used in the passive voice. Instead of the usual situation in which the verb expresses an action performed by the subject and affecting the object, a passive construction has the subject receiving the action. Compare the following sentences.

ACTIVE VOICE | In the novel the spy stole the secrets.

S V O

PASSIVE VOICE | In the novel the secrets were stolen by the spy.

S V

In the novel the secrets were stolen.

S V

As you can see, to form the passive construction, the object of the active sentence is moved ahead of the verb and becomes the subject. A form of *be* is added to the verb, and the subject of the active sentence is either expressed in a prepositional phrase or dropped.

Notice that in the passive voice the main verb is always a past participle and that the tense is expressed by an appropriate form of *be*.

ACTIVE | The plumber **fixed** the leaky pipe.
PASSIVE | The leaky pipe **was fixed** by the plumber.
ACTIVE | The captain usually **reads** the lineup.
PASSIVE | The lineup **is** usually **read** by the captain.

The Retained Object

Active sentences that have direct objects often have indirect objects as well. When they do, either the direct or indirect object can become the subject in a passive construction:

S V IO DO

ACTIVE | The company sent us a letter.

S V

PASSIVE | We were sent a **letter** (by the company).

S V

PASSIVE | A letter was sent **us** (by the company).

In both of the passive sentences above, one of the objects has been made the subject and the other continues to function as a complement of the verb. In the first sentence the direct object is retained as a complement; in the second it is the indirect object that is retained. The object that continues to function as a complement in a passive construction is called a *retained object*.

Use of Passive Voice

The choice between the active or passive voice of any particular verb is usually a matter of taste, not of correctness. However, it is important to remember that a passive verb is usually less forceful than an active one and that a long succession of passive verbs usually produces an awkward and unpleasant effect.

AWKWARD PASSIVE　After graduation a trip to Louisiana was taken by Ed, and the bayou country was traveled through by him.

ACTIVE　After graduation Ed took a trip to Louisiana and traveled through the bayou country.

WEAK PASSIVE　The event was completed when a triple somersault was done by Mario.

ACTIVE　Mario completed the event by doing a triple somersault.

WEAK PASSIVE　Steady rains were hoped for by all of us, but a hurricane was wanted by none of us.

ACTIVE　All of us hoped for steady rains, but none of us wanted a hurricane.

SUCCESSION OF PASSIVES　I *was asked* by Ms. Long to visit her animal shelter for unwanted pets. Rows of cages *had been placed* along both sides of a room. A cloth by which a cage *was covered was removed* by Ms. Long, and a large parrot *was shown* to me by her. Elsewhere, a scrawny puppy *was being comforted* by an assistant. Ms. Long said that so many unwanted pets *had* recently *been brought* to her, it was difficult for all of them to *be housed* at her shelter. It *was agreed* by us that the responsibility of owning a pet *should be understood* by people before a pet *is bought* by them.

9i. Use the passive voice sparingly. Avoid weak and awkward passives. In the interest of variety, avoid long passages in which all the verbs are passive.

There are, however, some qualifications of this general rule which should be mentioned. The passive voice is particularly useful in two common situations.

(1) Use the passive voice to express an action in which the actor is unknown.

EXAMPLE　All the tickets **had been sold** many days ago.

(2) Use the passive voice to express an action in which it is desirable not to disclose the actor.

EXAMPLE　Poor judgment **was used** in making this decision.

In some instances the passive voice is more convenient and just as effective as the active voice. The following passive sentences are entirely acceptable.

The laser **was invented** by an American.
The space travelers **were cheered** by the crowds and **praised** by the press.
Ivy Swan, who **is known** by all for her songs, **has been emulated** by many young, hopeful singers.

Remember, however, that the active voice is generally stronger than the passive and less likely to get you into stylistic difficulties.

EXERCISE 20. Revising Sentences in the Passive Voice.
Revise the following sentences by changing the passive verbs to active verbs wherever you think the change is desirable. If you think the passive is preferable, copy the sentence unchanged.

1. After the computers had been installed by the service reps, a training session was held for us by them.
2. If the children had been enchanted by Mr. Wright's stories before, they would be even more enthralled by his new tale of a fantasy kingdom.
3. A community meeting was held by the area homeowners to discuss the landfill project, which had been proposed by the City Council.
4. The team's code of fair play was agreed to and observed by all the players.
5. While the decorations are being made by Calvin, the buffet will be prepared by Edna.
6. Potatoes had been cultivated by the Incas more than twenty centuries before they were grown by the Europeans.
7. Her ten-speed bike was ridden by her through the country.
8. The lesson on constitutional amendments, which had been assigned to us last week by the teacher, was reviewed by us before the test.
9. Shinae Chun is admired and respected by her colleagues.
10. If the practicality of home robots had been demonstrated by Mike Smith, his request for funding would not have been rejected by the committee.

THE SUBJUNCTIVE MOOD

Verbs may be in one of three moods: *indicative, imperative*, or *subjunctive*. Almost all the verbs you use are in the *indicative mood*. The *imperative mood* is used to express a request or a command.

IMPERATIVE **Draw** a circle around the verb phrase.
Turn off the radio immediately.

The only common uses of the subjunctive mood in modern English are to express a condition contrary to fact and to express a wish. These uses occur mainly in formal standard English and usually apply to only one verb form—*were*. The following partial conjugation of *be* will show how the subjunctive mood differs from the indicative.

Present Indicative		*Present Subjunctive*	
Singular	*Plural*	*Singular*	*Plural*
I am	we are	(if) I be	(if) we be
you are	you are	(if) you be	(if) you be
he is	they are	(if) he be	(if) they be

The present subjunctive is used only in certain rather formal situations.

EXAMPLES We recommended that she **be** invited to speak.
They urged that Thad **be** reinstated.
We move that Alma **be** nominated.

Past Indicative		*Past Subjunctive*	
Singular	*Plural*	*Singular*	*Plural*
I was	we were	(if) I were	(if) we were
you were	you were	(if) you were	(if) you were
he was	they were	(if) he were	(if) they were

9j. The subjunctive *were* is usually used in contrary-to-fact statements (after *if* or *as though*) and in statements expressing a wish.

CONTRARY TO FACT   If I **were** [not *was*] you, I would be very nervous. [I am not you.]
If Rex **were** [not *was*] thinner, he'd disappear. [He is not thinner.]
Doris teased me as though she **were** [not *was*] my sister. [She is not my sister.]

WISH   I wish I **were** [not *was*] fabulously rich.
I wish Ms. Perkins **were** [not *was*] our coach.

EXERCISE 21. Using the Subjunctive Mood Correctly. Some of the following sentences contain errors in the use of the subjunctive mood. Others are correct. Number your paper 1–10. If the verbs in the sentence are correct, write a + after the appropriate number. If a verb is incorrect, copy it and write the correct form of the verb next to it.

EXAMPLE 1. If I was you, I would apply for the scholarship.
        1. *was—were*

1. Willis insisted that every employee is invited to the company picnic.
2. I'd be a lobster fisherman if I was living on Cape Cod.
3. Gloria was confused all day because it seemed as though it was Friday, but it was only Thursday.
4. Striking out in each of her tries at bat, Katie moaned, "I wish I was a better hitter!"
5. Vernon lost many of his friends because he acted as if he were better than they.
6. If boxing was a less violent sport, many people would respect it more.
7. "I wish this book was shorter," sighed Sabrena as she turned to page 378.
8. We often complain about working too many hours; but if we were to work fewer, we would be complaining about paychecks with too few dollars.
9. I wish I was able to go to the concert, but I have to work.
10. "I wish it was next year already so that I would be in college," Takala said.

REVIEW EXERCISE B. Using Verbs Correctly. Some of the following sentences contain errors in the use of verbs. Others are correct. Number your paper 1–25. If the verbs in a sentence are correct, place a + after the corresponding number on your paper. If a verb is incorrect, write the correct form after the proper number.

EXAMPLE 1. I drunk more than a gallon of lemonade.
        1. *drank*

1. If I was Joan's coach, I'd tell her to relax more.
2. For the holidays they planned to have gone fishing.
3. We swum to shore when we spotted the shark.
4. If you would have written the report yesterday, you could have gone to the concert with us.
5. When the temperature rises, Sid becomes grouchy.

6. After he entered the ancient tomb, the archeologist tripped over a perfectly preserved mummy.

7. As the climbers ascended the mountain, they noticed a shiny object laying on the ledge beneath them.

8. If they weren't too proud to ask, I'd have been glad to help them paint the house.

9. Why don't you ask if they already seen that exhibit?

10. I should like to have read that best-selling novel.

11. They had forgotten that yesterday was my birthday.

12. As soon as we returned to the campsite, we discovered that someone took our food and gear.

13. If I had begun my chores this morning, I would have finished in time to go to the show.

14. Were they the ones who give you the videotape?

15. When the news of the explosion come over the radio, Dr. Trimble had already rushed to the site.

16. The fog was so dense I did not see the deer that run by me on the path.

17. Aunt Thelma found Grace's snapshots lying under the sofa.

18. He swept the floor and then lay the linoleum flooring.

19. If I was more confident, I could try out for the play.

20. If we would have had the engine tuned, I'm sure we would not be stranded on the highway now.

21. We have counted the money and have lain it in the safe.

22. As Ms. Hall interviewed the professor, she realized that the batteries went dead in the tape recorder.

23. In her report Clara explained that shock waves from earthquakes were recorded on seismographs.

24. They wished they were going to the music festival instead of the annual family reunion.

25. After we worked for six months, we asked for a raise.

CHAPTER 9 REVIEW: POSTTEST 1

Identifying the Correct Verb Form. Number your paper 1–25. After the proper number, write the correct form of the verb in parentheses.

EXAMPLE 1. When Greg was recuperating from surgery, his doctor said Greg should (lie, lay) down for an hour each afternoon.
   1. *lie*

1. It was only last year when Karl learned that the Great Lakes (are, were) bordered by eight states.
2. If I (was, were) a doctor, I would specialize in pediatrics.
3. Before she flew her first solo flight, Jeanne (took, had taken) many hours of instruction.
4. Everything was going smoothly until we (run, ran) into a bug in the program.
5. Without fail, the (rising, raising) and falling of the tide makes me feel calm and peaceful.
6. When I finish my electronics course, I hope (to learn, to have learned) the basics about all the electronic appliances we use at home.
7. As everyone cheered, Jennifer (blowed, blew) out all eighteen birthday candles with one breath!
8. The police are working hard to capture the person who has (stole, stolen) the money from Mr. Simmons' grocery store.
9. After she (tried, had tried) on the stylish shoes, Betty told the salesperson, "They feel fine; I'll take them."
10. Applause and cheers greeted the chorus after they had (sang, sung) their final song.
11. (Thinking, Having thought) that he was only an average writer, Tim was delighted when Mr. Fitzgerald, his new teacher, wrote, "This is an excellent essay!"
12. Coach Fonzo clocked the team as they (swam, swum) the relay.
13. Leaving the classroom, the seniors were happy (to finish, to have finished) their SAT's and ACT's.
14. We were amazed when the newscaster reported the Super Bowl score as though it (was, were) merely an ordinary statistic.
15. (Sitting, Setting) on the bench, Lois was anxious for the coach to send her into action.

16. As she stood in the middle of the crowd trying to see the stage, Teresa wished that she (was, were) an inch or two taller.

17. Steve (lay, laid) on the beach too long and got a sunburn.

18. Because they had failed (to solve, to have solved) the problem, the engineers were concerned.

19. We (seen, saw) the geyser, Old Faithful, when we visited Yellowstone National Park last summer.

20. Kieran would have been a better friend if he (would have been, had been) honest with Blaire.

21. Though most actors and actresses never win an Oscar, they are proud to be able to say they (did, done) their best.

22. Just as Kevin had made overseas contact on his shortwave radio, his aerial (breaks, broke).

23. After Alex (had been typing, was typing) for only two months, he developed a speed of forty words per minute.

24. Eleanor wished she (was, were) wealthy enough to take a trip around the world.

25. Now that you have completed this demanding exercise, you may (lie, lay) your pen down and take a well-deserved rest!

CHAPTER 9 REVIEW: POSTTEST 2

Using Verbs Correctly. Some of the following sentences contain errors in the use of verbs. Others are correct. Number your paper 1–25. If the verbs in a sentence are correct, write a + after the proper number. If a verb is incorrect, write the correct form after the proper number.

EXAMPLE 1. If she was he, she'd have spoken up.
1. *were*

1. The librarian set aside the damaged book.

2. She thought the runners had broke the world record.

3. If we would have checked, we'd have known the store was closed.

4. They were setting on the bench and feeding the ducks.

5. She laid a fire to ward off the cold.

6. We would have preferred to have eaten Chinese food.

7. As the officers followed the green van, it run a red light and almost hit the streetlight.

8. The shoppers laid down their purchases carefully.

9. Cindy retraced her steps and found the café at which she left her credit card.
10. If I was Luis, I would have argued with the umpire.
11. We cheered when the movie finally begun.
12. You should never have lain your radio near the edge.
13. They would have liked to interview the astronauts.
14. I had just laid down on the beach when it started to rain.
15. The ice cubes had not froze in time for the party.
16. Yesterday I swum in the Millers' new pool.
17. They were still living in the trailer they bought last year.
18. The rate of inflation has raised steadily.
19. When they returned to the scene, they discovered that the weapon was taken.
20. If your back aches, try lying on the floor.
21. When I enter college, my parents will be married thirty years.
22. Were you on the phone when he come to the door?
23. When we saw the group perform, Julia, the lead vocalist, just broke her contract with a big recording company.
24. If we had the chance, we would have stopped by your house.
25. They found the cat laying on the closet shelf.

CHAPTER 10

Correct Use of Modifiers

FORMS OF ADJECTIVES AND ADVERBS; COMPARISON

An adjective modifies a noun or a pronoun. An adverb may modify a verb, an adjective, or another adverb. These are familiar statements, but applying them to usage is sometimes difficult. Should you say "went quick" or "went quickly," "tastes strong" or "tastes strongly," "played good" or "played well"? These and other usage problems are discussed in this chapter.

DIAGNOSTIC TEST

Selecting the Correct Modifier. Number your paper 1–20. Select the correct one of the two words in parentheses in each sentence and write it after the proper number on your paper.

EXAMPLE 1. The hurricane hit the town very (sudden, suddenly).
　　　　　 1. *suddenly*

1. Some of these plums taste (bitter, bitterly) to me.
2. I didn't do as (good, well) on the test as I thought I had.
3. Have you seen a (friendlier, more friendlier) spaniel than mine?
4. Those imitation diamonds look (real, really) valuable.
5. The weather this afternoon is (pleasanter, more pleasant) than it was this morning.

6. Jan is younger than (anyone, anyone else) in her class.
7. Having tried both brands of glue, I found that Macrogrip is (stronger, strongest).
8. When you get to the sign for Route 8, turn (sharp, sharply) to the left.
9. This is the (baddest, worst) storm this town has ever seen.
10. The room won't look so (bad, badly) after it has been painted.
11. The close of the letter read, "With our (most sincerest, sincerest) thanks."
12. The coast road is more scenic, but Route 180 is (quicker, quickest).
13. The landscape looks (strange, strangely) in this eerie light.
14. The turbostream engine will give better gasoline mileage than (any, any other) engine ever made.
15. We build cars (sturdy, sturdily) enough to last one hundred thousand miles.
16. Rehearsals are going as (good, well) as can be expected.
17. Did you feel (sad, sadly) when you lost your watch?
18. Learning to dance (good, well) takes practice.
19. The lizard turned its head so (slow, slowly) that it looked as if it weren't moving at all.
20. Jeanne looked (casual, casually) in my direction.

ADJECTIVE AND ADVERB FORMS

Before reviewing the usage of adjectives and adverbs, you should make sure that you are able to tell which is the adjective form of a word and which is the adverb form. The fact that most adverbs end in –ly(*clearly, happily, eagerly*) will be helpful if you understand that not *all* adverbs end in –ly and that a few common adjectives do end in –ly. Some words have the same form whether used as an adjective or as an adverb.

The list that follows includes a number of common adjectives and adverbs with identical forms. It also includes some adjectives ending in –ly. Remember that the –ly ending is not always a sign that a word is an adverb.

ADJECTIVES	ADVERBS	ADJECTIVES ENDING IN –LY
a *short* race	She stopped *short*.	*nightly* walk
a *close* call	Stand *close* to me.	*bodily* harm
a *high* shelf	She jumped *high*.	*hourly* pay
a *right* answer	Do it *right*.	*unfriendly* man
a *first* time	She left *first*.	*lively* beat
a *hard* problem	He tried *hard*.	*seemly* choice
a *straight* path	Drive *straight*.	*early* class
a *last* chance	We play *last*.	*likely* area
a *fast* start	Walk *fast*.	*weekly* meeting

10a. Linking verbs, especially the verbs of sense (*taste, smell, feel,* etc.), are often followed by an adjective. Action verbs are often followed by an adverb.

EXAMPLES   The cider tasted **sweet**. [The adjective *sweet* is correct after the linking verb *tasted*. It modifies the subject *cider*.]
The voices sounded **angry**. [The adjective *angry* is correct after the linking verb *sounded*. It modifies the subject *voices*.]

Some verbs may be used as either linking or action verbs. When they are used as action verbs, the modifier that follows modifies the verb rather than the subject and is, therefore, an adverb; for example, *looked* may be used as a linking verb and as an action verb.

EXAMPLES   Chris looked **happy**. [After the linking verb *looked*, the adjective *happy* is correct. It modifies *Chris*.]
Chris looked **happily** out the window. [After the action verb *looked*, the adverb *happily* is correct. It modifies *looked*.]

When you are in doubt as to whether a verb is a linking verb or not, try substituting for it a form of *seem,* which is always a linking verb. If the substitution can be made without greatly changing the meaning of the sentence, the verb is a linking verb and should be followed by an adjective.

EXAMPLES   Chris looked happy. [*Chris seemed happy* has about the same meaning; hence *looked* is a linking verb.]
Chris looked happily out the window. [*Chris seemed happily out the window* does not make much sense; hence, *looked* is not a linking verb in this sentence.]

WRITING APPLICATION A:
Expressing Emotion Through the Use of Linking Verbs Followed by Adjectives

People often have a hard time expressing emotion, perhaps because they are shy or very private, perhaps because they have never had any practice. Emotions are real and important, however; they indicate that a person is human instead of mechanical, like a robot. The verb *feel* is usually used for expressing emotions. Linking verbs such as *feel* are often followed by adjectives instead of adverbs.

EXAMPLE   Incorrect: I feel *badly* about not making the varsity team my senior year. [The adverb *badly* is incorrect after the linking verb *feel*.]

Correct: I feel *bad* about not making the varsity team my senior year. [The adjective *bad* is correct after the linking verb *feel*.]

Writing Assignment

A writer named E. M. Forster once said about the English that they are "afraid to feel." He went on to say that he had been taught at school that the expression of feeling is bad form. How do you view the subject of feelings? Do you express them openly or "bottle" them up? Which feelings do you most often show? Write a paragraph on this subject. At some point, use the verb *feel* followed by an adjective or several adjectives.

10b. In making a choice between an adjective and an adverb, ask yourself what the word modifies. If it modifies a noun or pronoun, choose the adjective. If it modifies a verb, choose the adverb.

PROBLEM   They dug a hole (deep, deeply) enough to plant the tree.
SOLUTION   They dug a hole **deep** enough to plant the tree. [The adjective *deep* modifies the noun *hole*.]

PROBLEM   Has he been studying math (regular, regularly)?
SOLUTION   Has he been studying math **regularly**? [The adverb **regularly** modifies the action verb *has been studying*.]

EXERCISE 1. Selecting Adjectives and Adverbs.   Number your paper 1–20. Select the correct one of the two words in parentheses

in each sentence, and write it after the proper number. If the word modifies the subject, select the adjective; if it modifies the verb, select the adverb. Remember that a linking verb is followed by an adjective.

1. The sled's runners slid (smooth, smoothly) over the ice.
2. The weather outside looks (miserable, miserably).
3. Plan your outline as (careful, carefully) as possible.
4. The official explanation of the budget cut sounds (incredible, incredibly).
5. Why was she looking at me (suspicious, suspiciously)?
6. This apple tastes (peculiar, peculiarly) to me.
7. Don't feel (glum, glumly) about missing the game.
8. You can watch (contented, contentedly) from the sidelines.
9. Dawn goes jogging (regular, regularly).
10. He disappeared (quiet, quietly) behind the curtain.
11. The conference room smelled (stuffy, stuffily).
12. At the end of the first act, we all applauded (enthusiastic, enthusiastically).
13. The stage manager appeared (sudden, suddenly).
14. She spoke (serious, seriously) to the audience.
15. "The leading lady in the play," she said, "is feeling (sick, sickly)."
16. "She is resting (comfortable, comfortably) backstage."
17. "Her understudy will take over the lead (temporary, temporarily)."
18. The understudy seemed (nervous, nervously) to the audience.
19. After a while she was saying her lines (easy, easily).
20. The audience felt (happy, happily) for the understudy.

Bad and Badly

Bad is an adjective modifying nouns and pronouns. *Badly* is an adverb, modifying verbs, adjectives, and adverbs. Since the verbs of sense—*feel, smell, taste, sound*—are followed by an adjective (not an adverb) modifying their subjects, it is standard English to say *feel bad, smell bad*, etc.

Joan feels bad about the broken vase.

The warped record sounds bad.

The common expression *feel badly*, however, has, through usage, become acceptable English, although ungrammatical. Used with other verbs of sense, *badly* is not yet standard. Do not say *smell badly, taste badly*, etc.

Well and Good

Well may be used as either an adjective or an adverb. As an adjective, *well* has three meanings.

1. *To be in good health:*

   He feels **well**.[1] He seems **well**.

2. *To appear well-dressed or well-groomed:*

   She looks **well** in that dress.

3. *To be satisfactory:*

   All is **well**.

As an adverb, *well* means to perform an action capably.

   She wrote very **well**.

Good is always an adjective. It should never be used to modify a verb.

NONSTANDARD   The choir sang good at the concert.
  STANDARD   The choir sang **well** at the concert.
NONSTANDARD   We bowled very good as a team.
  STANDARD   We bowled very **well** as a team.

Slow and Slowly

Slow is used as both an adjective and an adverb. *Slowly* is an adverb. Except for the expressions *Drive slow* and *Go slow*, which have become acceptable because of their wide use on highway signs, *slow* should be used only as an adjective.

EXERCISE 2. Correcting Errors in the Use of Modifiers.
Number your paper 1–10. Some of the sentences contain errors in the use of *bad* and *badly*, *well* and *good*, and *slow* and *slowly*. If a sentence is correct, write + next to the appropriate number on your paper. If a word is used incorrectly, copy it on your paper and next to it write the correct form.

[1] *He feels* GOOD is also correct, though its meaning is not limited to health. Example: He feels GOOD about the new job offer.

EXAMPLE 1. After a long rehearsal, the dance troupe performed good.

 1. *good—well* [An adverb is needed here: *How* did the troupe dance? It danced *well*.]

1. After she had lost the election, Bernadette felt very bad.
2. Not knowing about the construction ahead, I couldn't understand why the bus moved so slowly down Commonwealth Avenue.
3. Ms. Stein is an unusually good teacher who prepares her lessons well.
4. Some shades of blue and green go good together.
5. Let's hope the rest of the day doesn't go this bad.
6. "I'm sure I did good on that test," Anzu confidently remarked.
7. Eating slowly aids digestion.
8. Aesop's fables end with such morals as "Look good before you leap."
9. "Please speak slow when you give your election speech," Mr. Schmidt advised the nervous candidates.
10. "Life can't be treating you all that bad," I told Walker.

EXERCISE 3. Analyzing the Use of Modifiers. Number your paper 1–25. If the *italicized* modifier in a sentence is correct, write a + after the proper number on your paper. If it is incorrect, write the correct form, and after the correct form write the word it modifies.

EXAMPLE 1. Something sounds *strangely* next door.
 1. *strange—something*

1. The players did *good* in the fourth quarter.
2. The bread dough rose too *quick*.
3. I am glad to see you looking *well* after the operation.
4. Limburger cheese smells very *bad*.
5. We walked *slow* on the icy sidewalk.
6. Liz seemed *sad* to hear the news.
7. The children sat *silent* during the ceremony.
8. Sam feels *bad* about forgetting your birthday.
9. Anita is afraid she did *poor* on the test.
10. She sounded very *angrily* on the phone.
11. These new jeans do not fit me *good* at all.
12. Rita answered the questions *precisely*.
13. Fortunately, no one was hurt *bad* in the accident.
14. The children waited *impatient* for dinnertime.

15. I could not see the game very *good* from my seat.
16. This old watch has been running fairly *good*.
17. Ms. Tate's company can do the job *efficiently*.
18. The judge rapped the gavel *sharp* to restore order.
19. The crowd stared *keenly* at the scoreboard.
20. We didn't win, but we played *well*.
21. My tennis shoes do not look *well* anymore.
22. Jen works *slow* but she is accurate.
23. Donna *nonchalantly* accepted the award.
24. The whole day has gone *bad* for me.
25. We felt *proudly* of your victory.

COMPARISON OF ADJECTIVES AND ADVERBS

10c. *Comparison* is the name given to the change in the form of adjectives and adverbs when they are used to compare the degree of the qualities they express. There are three degrees of comparison: *positive, comparative,* and *superlative.*

POSITIVE	COMPARATIVE	SUPERLATIVE
fat	fatter	fattest
eager	more eager	most eager
gladly	more gladly	most gladly
strong	stronger	strongest
loudly	more loudly	most loudly

Comparative and Superlative Forms

(1) Most adjectives and adverbs of one syllable form their comparative and superlative degrees by adding –er and –est.

POSITIVE	COMPARATIVE	SUPERLATIVE
neat	neater	neatest
warm	warmer	warmest
short	shorter	shortest

(2) Some adjectives of two syllables form their comparative and superlative degrees by adding –er or –est; other adjectives of two syllables form their comparative and superlative degrees by means of *more* and *most*.

When you are in doubt as to how a word is compared, consult an unabridged dictionary.

POSITIVE	COMPARATIVE	SUPERLATIVE
lively	livelier	liveliest
agile	more agile	most agile

(3) Adjectives of more than two syllables and adverbs ending in -ly usually form their comparative and superlative degrees by means of *more* and *most*.

POSITIVE	COMPARATIVE	SUPERLATIVE
delightful	more delightful	most delightful
quietly	more quietly	most quietly

(4) Comparison to indicate less or least of a quality is accomplished by using the words *less* and *least* before the adjective or adverb.

POSITIVE	COMPARATIVE	SUPERLATIVE
weak	less weak	least weak
contented	less contented	least contented
urgently	less urgently	least urgently

Irregular Comparison

Adjectives and adverbs that do not follow the regular methods of forming their comparative and superlative degrees are said to be compared irregularly.

POSITIVE	COMPARATIVE	SUPERLATIVE
bad	worse	worst
good well	better	best
many much	more	most

EXERCISE 4. Using Comparative and Superlative Forms.

Write the comparative and superlative forms of the following words. Use a dictionary.

EXAMPLE   1. flat
            1. *flatter, flattest*

1. tiny	6. expensive	11. bad	16. gently
2. magnificent	7. ill	12. abruptly	17. clear
3. few	8. modest	13. selfless	18. fishy
4. long	9. curious	14. wide	19. durable
5. wistful	10. proudly	15. good	20. thin

Use of Comparatives and Superlatives

10d. Use the comparative degree when comparing two things; use the superlative degree when comparing more than two.

COMPARISON OF TWO THINGS

Although both Laura and Ted wrote on the same topic, Laura's paper was **longer** [not *longest*].

The pitcher threw curveballs and sliders; the curveball was the **more** [not *most*] **successful** pitch.

Clara is the **more** helpful of the two tutors.

COMPARISON OF MORE THAN TWO THINGS

We went to the Crown Cinema because it was the **closest** [not *closer*] of the **three** theaters.

Of the **three** routes, the expressway is the **most** [not *more*] **congested** at rush hour.

Which of the **ten** photos is the **most** attractive?

☞ USAGE NOTE Rule 10d describes a practice generally observed by writers of formal English. In informal speech and writing, however, the superlative is often used for emphasis, even though only two things are being compared.

INFORMAL Which park did you like best, Yellowstone or Hot Springs? [formal: *better*]

Of the two operas, Mozart's *The Marriage of Figaro* is the most amusing to me. [formal: *more*]

10e. Include the word *other* or *else* when comparing one thing with a group of which it is a part.

NONSTANDARD	Diamond, a crystalline form of carbon, is harder than any mineral in the world. [Since diamond is also one of the minerals of the world, this sentence says illogically that diamond is harder than itself.]
STANDARD	Diamond, a crystalline form of carbon, is harder than any **other** mineral in the world.
NONSTANDARD	He ran more races than anyone in his club. [He is a member of the club; he cannot run more races than himself.]
STANDARD	He ran more races than anyone **else** in his club.

WRITING APPLICATION B:
Using Comparison to Express Critical Judgment

It is important for readers and viewers to develop critical skills before they attempt to make judgments. You are often asked to compare two or more people, places, or things. In order to express the comparison, you must use adjectives or adverbs in a comparative form. When you compare two things, you use the comparative degree; when you compare more than two, you use the superlative degree.

EXAMPLES   Of the three bird prints by Ray Harm, the one entitled *Cardinal* is the *richest* in bright color contrasts. [The superlative form is used because more than two things are being compared.]
Donatello's statue of David is *more realistic* than Michelangelo's *David*. [The comparative form is used because two things are being compared.]

Writing Assignment

Immature readers or viewers are often interested mainly in plot. They value violent action, dangerous missions, close escapes, and so on. More mature critics look for action that is significant. That is, they value action that reveals something meaningful about life or people and consider this action to be worthwhile. Write a comparison of several books or television shows. Judge whether the action is an end in itself or, rather, a means to reveal something significant. Use comparatives and superlatives correctly.

10f. Avoid double comparisons.

A double comparison is one in which the degree is formed incorrectly by adding –er or –est in addition to using *more* or *most*.

NONSTANDARD	Alice is a more faster swimmer than I.
STANDARD	Alice is a **faster** swimmer than I.
NONSTANDARD	She is the most friendliest girl in school.
STANDARD	She is the **friendliest** girl in school.

EXERCISE 5. Using Comparatives and Superlatives Correctly.

Number your paper 1–10. Some of the sentences contain errors in the use of the comparative and superlative degrees of adjectives. If a sentence is correct, write + next to the appropriate number on your paper. If a comparison is used incorrectly, copy it on your paper and next to it write the correct form.

EXAMPLE 1. That was the most highest grade Oscar ever earned on a Spanish test.

  1. *most highest—highest*

1. Colleen thought nothing could be as bad as the freezing temperatures; but when the ice storm arrived, she said, "This weather is even worser!"
2. Both twins, Holly and Julie, have brown eyes, but Holly's are darkest.
3. In each graduating class, the valedictorian is the student whose average is higher than that of any senior.
4. Because he wrote the Declaration of Independence, Thomas Jefferson is regarded as one of the most important Americans in United States history.
5. People need to develop a more clear sense of self-worth.
6. Sue made the mistake of buying a darker shade of paint than she needed for the small room.
7. Performing better than all the gymnasts, Mary Lou Retton was the first American to win an Olympic gold medal in her sport.
8. Myles is taking more classes than I.
9. Dividing the pie in two, Felicia took the least and gave me the larger portion.
10. According to my friend Juan, Houston, Texas, is more interesting and more exciting than any city in that state.

EXERCISE 6. Using Modifiers Correctly.

Number your paper 1–25. For each correct sentence, write a + after the proper number; revise each incorrect sentence and write the sentence correctly.

EXAMPLE   1. I am least prepared to take the test than you.
         1. *I am less prepared to take the test than you.*

1. She always listens intent.
2. I tried to sing as good as she sang.
3. Josh studied more than anyone in his physics class.
4. Marilyn jogged happily around the track.
5. I have narrowed my choices to two colleges, and I want to visit them to see which I like best.
6. If the volunteers continue to work slow, the decorations will not be ready for the dance.
7. The shoppers looked oddly at the street musicians.
8. If the dough smells badly, don't bake it.
9. Monica seems good enough to leave the hospital.
10. Mr. Brown is many pounds more heavier than I.
11. The pedestrian stared defiantly at the motorists.
12. He inched very gradual toward the doorway.
13. After a hot day, a cold glass of water tastes good.
14. The picture on this television set is much more clearer than the picture on that one.
15. How did you finish your assignment so prompt?
16. Thunderclouds loomed threateningly overhead.
17. We thought Patti was the most talented of all the actors in the community play.
18. Does she call you frequent?
19. They all did well on the test.
20. I read the shorter of the three books for my report.
21. You cheered more loudly than anyone at the concert.
22. She was less determined to win than her sister.
23. Gloria hesitated too longly before she answered.
24. He thought she seemed gracefuller than the other model.
25. Why is she walking so slow toward the house?

CHAPTER 10 REVIEW: POSTTEST 1

Selecting the Correct Modifier.   Number your paper 1–25. Select the correct one of the two words in parentheses in each sentence, and write it after the proper number on your paper.

EXAMPLE 1. Although Lillian Hellman wrote both plays and nonfiction, she is (better, best) known for her plays.
    1. *better*

1. In the twentieth century, American writers have produced a (more wide, wider) variety of fiction, nonfiction, drama, and poetry than has ever been seen in this country before.
2. In contrast, there was (less, least) variety among the writers of the nineteenth century.
3. Of this century's authors, such names as Hemingway and Faulkner sound (familiar, familiarly) even to casual readers.
4. However, some excellent writers, especially among women and minority groups, have come (slow, slowly) to public attention and appreciation.
5. Ironically, these writers have produced some of the (vividest, most vivid) characters and situations in literature.
6. As (good, well) as many of them wrote, it took a long time for their work to be recognized.
7. In his story "A Summer Tragedy," the black author Arna Bontemps makes the reader feel (sympathetic, sympathetically) toward a poor elderly couple.
8. You can argue for days about who is the (better, best) Harlem Renaissance poet, Langston Hughes or Countee Cullen.
9. Perhaps you have read Cullen's short poem "Incident," about a child who is hurt (bad, badly) by prejudice.
10. Both of these writers have appeal because their work looks (extensive, extensively) at human qualities.
11. In the past few years, greater attention has been given to writers who might have been largely ignored in (earlier, more early) times.
12. For example, the nonfiction work *Blue Highways* sold (good, well) when it was published in 1983.
13. The author, William Least Heat Moon, an American Indian college professor, decided to travel (slow, slowly) all over the United States on older roads.
14. Mr. Moon understands better than (anyone, anyone else) the great diversity of people in ordinary towns in America.
15. Probably the first American woman to produce as many novels, essays, and short stories as (any, any other) male writer is Joyce Carol Oates.

16. Readers and critics say her work is written (good, well), and her characters reflect many personalities.
17. Any author good enough to win a Pulitzer Prize feels (different, differently) after receiving it.
18. Publicity makes a prizewinner (famous, famously) overnight.
19. Alice Walker was considered better than (any, any other) novelist in 1983 when she won the Pulitzer Prize.
20. One of Walker's strengths is in depicting intelligent black women characters who can survive and grow, even when their lives are not going too (good, well).
21. Another woman, Joan Didion, has written books and essays on a wide variety of topics, from her trip to El Salvador to how (bad, badly) she feels when she has a migraine headache.
22. American literature has grown (richer, more richly) because of the presence of these and other "new" writers.
23. Millions of American readers look (hungry, hungrily) in bookstores for enjoyable books.
24. (Most likely, Most likeliest), they will choose a humorous paperback by someone like Erma Bombeck.
25. People who feel (sincere, sincerely) about the pleasures of reading welcome all writers of quality.

CHAPTER 10 REVIEW: POSTTEST 2

Identifying the Correct Use of Modifiers. Number your paper 1–25. Some of the following sentences contain errors in the use of modifiers. If a sentence is correct, write + next to the appropriate number on your paper. If the sentence is incorrect, write the incorrect word or words and then write the proper word(s).

EXAMPLE 1. Among my three brothers and sisters, my sister Giselle has the better sense of humor.
      1. *better—best*

1. "This is the most drab outfit I have ever had," said Louise. "Why did I buy it?"
2. Which is widest, the Mississippi River or the Colorado River?
3. My English teacher thinks that Shakespeare is better than any writer who ever lived.

4. My parents read both a morning and an evening newspaper, but I think the morning paper is best.
5. As Mr. Connolly explained the procedure for the experiment, Lisa said to me, "This is going to be real difficult."
6. When the temperature reached 103° F in August, the Board of Health issued a warning telling people to walk slowly when they were outdoors.
7. That paint is the most palest shade of blue I have ever seen.
8. Because the drummer played bad, the band's melody line was drowned out.
9. Pointing to two glasses partially filled with water, the magician asked, "Which glass has the least water?"
10. In preparing for a job interview, you should wear styles and colors of clothing that look attractively on you.
11. Mr. Martinez asked, "Is Donna still feeling badly?"
12. "If you pedal your bike that slow, you'll never get home," I told Mark.
13. Philadelphia and Atlantic City are the largest cities near my home, but Philadelphia is actually the closest of the two.
14. We found it hard to understand why Randy had spoken as rude as he did in response to a simple question.
15. Has Pete been saving money regular for that trip he wants to take to Alaska?
16. He can't play the guitar too good, but his records sell well.
17. Tommy Lee thinks a vacation in the mountains is peacefuller than any other kind of vacation.
18. The economist said that interest rates would be going up steady for the next five years.
19. Among the Tong triplets, Chi Wan has always been the more industrious one.
20. "Sharon has been working harder than anyone here," I said.
21. My sister's bedroom looked messily this morning.
22. The iced tea tasted too sweetly for me.
23. "Nurse Lopez, I feel remarkably well today, better than I have ever felt before," said Mr. Parker.
24. There is a control on the television set for making the picture a little less brighter.
25. Why do dogs smell badly when they get rained on?

CHAPTER 11

Glossary of Usage

COMMON USAGE PROBLEMS

Selecting Standard Words and Expressions. The sentences in this exercise contain usage problems discussed in this chapter. Number your paper 1–20. After the proper number, write the standard choice of the two given in parentheses.

EXAMPLE 1. We were (kind of, rather) disappointed with the results of the experiment.
1. *rather*

1. After Shirley had starred in our spring play, she acted (like, as if) she were an important and famous movie star.
2. Lionel gave a (credible, credulous) account of how he had spent so much money on his vacation.
3. Whenever we need the weed trimmer, we never know where (it's at, it is).
4. At the restaurant where I work, all four of us divide the tips evenly (between, among) ourselves.
5. Neither my parents (or, nor) their friends ever miss watching the Super Bowl game.
6. As I was about to pay for my new jeans, I suddenly realized I (had, hadn't) scarcely any money in my wallet.

7. Because it was (liable, likely) to rain, Lorraine canceled her plans to go swimming.
8. Will you please take your package (off, off of) the table?
9. (Accept, Except) for Carlos and Glenn, everyone went on the class trip.
10. The reason we are moving is (because, that) my parents have always wanted to live in Oregon.
11. Whenever I'm not doing (something, nothing) challenging, I grow easily bored.
12. Fairbanks, Alaska, is a long (way, ways) away from Orlando, Florida.
13. Although we do the same type of work, Hasina and I are (affected, effected) differently by it.
14. Whenever we go (anywhere, anywheres), Judy always seems to meet someone she knows.
15. (Bring, Take) the dog with you when you go out for a walk.
16. When I first went (in, into) the principal's office, I felt a little nervous.
17. Marie admitted that if she (had, would have) checked the oil, the engine wouldn't have given her a problem.
18. Looking at the crisp green beans, Rosa said, "(This, Those) kind of beans has always been my favorite."
19. It's an (allusion, illusion) to think you can become successful without hard work.
20. Emily's grandparents (immigrated, emigrated) to the United States from Poland.

Chapters 7 through 10 of this book describe the conventions of standard English usage observed by most careful users of the language. These conventions include subject-verb agreement, pronoun-antecedent agreement, the correct use of pronouns, the correct form and use of verbs, and the correct use of modifiers. In addition to vocabulary, these are the major areas in which standard English differs from nonstandard English.

There are, however, a number of special usage problems that require separate treatment. These are presented here in the glossary.

SUMMARY: LEVELS OF USAGE

Standard English

Informal The everyday language of people who observe the conventions of English usage, suitable for all but the most formal occasions.

Formal The language of most serious speakers when they take special pains to say the correct thing; appropriate for all serious writing and speaking, but suitable in any situation.

Nonstandard English

Idiomatic usages and dialects identifiably different from standard English; most often less appropriate than standard English for widespread communication; sometimes suitable for special, but not general, purposes.

If you are not sure of these terms after reading the brief summary, review Chapter 5, in which they are discussed in detail.

In doing the exercises in this chapter, as well as those in other parts of the book, follow the conventions of standard formal English.

The items in this glossary are arranged in alphabetical order, with exercises interspersed. Problems in spelling such as the difference between *already* and *all ready* and similar words often confused are taken up on pages 930–37, included in the chapter on spelling.

a, an These short words are called *indefinite articles*. They refer to one of a general group.

A woman bought the new car.
The pioneers came upon **a** herd of buffalo.
Maria was in **an** accident in her father's car.
Jonathan fished for **an** hour before he caught that bass.

Use *a* before words beginning with a consonant sound; use *an* before words beginning with a vowel sound. In the examples above, *a* is used before *herd* because *herd* begins with a consonant sound. *An* is used before *hour* because *hour* begins with a vowel sound.

Quiz wed,
Test Tues of next week

accept, except *Accept* is a verb; it means "to receive." *Except* as a verb means "to leave out"; as a preposition it means "excluding."

I **accepted** the gift gratefully.
Debbie has a perfect attendance record, if you **except** the day she stayed home with the flu.
We were busy every evening this week **except** Tuesday.

adapt, adopt *Adapt* means "to change in order to fit or be more suitable; to adjust." *Adopt* means "to take something and make it one's own."

When it rained on the day of the senior class picnic, we **adapted** our plans.
The Broadway play was **adapted** from a popular television miniseries.
The couple who **adopted** the baby read many books and **adopted** some suggestions for infant care.

affect, effect *Affect* is usually a verb; it means "to impress" or "to influence (frequently the mind or feelings)." *Effect* as a verb means "to accomplish, to bring about." *Effect* as a noun means "the result of some action."

Try not to let careless remarks **affect** you.
The school board **effected** [brought about] drastic changes in the budget for the coming year.
The **effects** [results] of the hurricane were shown on the evening news.

all the farther, all the faster Used informally in some parts of the country to mean "as far as, as fast as."

DIALECT   Thirty miles per hour was all the faster the first airplane could travel.
STANDARD Thirty miles per hour was **as fast as** the first airplane could travel.

allusion, illusion An *allusion* is a reference to something. An *illusion* is a mistaken idea.

In her essay she made many **allusions** to the American pioneers.

The behind-the-scenes report destroyed her **illusions** of Hollywood.

alumni, alumnae *Alumni* (pronounced ə·lum′nī) is the plural of *alumnus* (male graduate). *Alumnae* (pronounced ə·lum′nē) is the plural of *alumna* (female graduate). The graduates of a coeducational school are referred to (as a group) as *alumni*.

All of my sisters are **alumnae** of Adams High School.
Both men are **alumni** of Harvard.
My parents went to their college **alumni** reunion.

amount, number Use *amount* to refer to a singular word; use *number* to refer to a plural word.

The **amount** of research (singular) on stress **is** overwhelming.
A **number** of reports (plural) on stress **are** overwhelming.

and etc. Since *etc.* is an abbreviation of the Latin *et cetera*, which means "and other things," you are using *and* twice when you write "and etc." The *etc.* is sufficient.

The new store in the mall sells videotapes, audio cassettes, cameras, radios, electronic games, **etc.** [not *and etc.*]

and which, but which The expressions *and which, but which* (*and who, but who*) should be used only when a *which* (or *who*) clause precedes them in the sentence.

NONSTANDARD   Our jazz band was pleased with the audience's enthusiastic response and which we had not expected before the concert.
STANDARD   Our jazz band was pleased with the audience's response, **which** was enthusiastic **and which** we had not expected before the concert.
STANDARD   Our jazz band was pleased with the audience's enthusiastic response, **which** we had not expected before the concert.

anywheres, everywheres, nowheres Use these words and others like them *without* the final *s*.

I could not find my keys **anywhere;** I looked **everywhere,** but they were **nowhere** in the house.

at Do not use *at* after *where.*

> NONSTANDARD   Where are they living at now?
> STANDARD   **Where** are they living now?

EXERCISE 1. Selecting Standard Words and Expressions.
The sentences in this exercise contain usage problems presented on the preceding pages in the glossary. Number your paper 1–20. Write after the proper number on your paper the standard choice of the words in parentheses.

1. Some pets find it hard to (adapt, adopt) to city life.
2. This new product has had a harmful (affect, effect) on some people.
3. Does this poem contain any (allusions, illusions) to Homer's *Odyssey?*
4. Jane and Nina are (alumni, alumnae) of our school.
5. I own a large (number, amount) of campaign buttons.
6. During my travels in Europe, I met Americans (everywheres, everywhere).
7. Everyone likes peanut butter (accept, except) you.
8. One of the two lines looks longer because of an optical (allusion, illusion).
9. We all (adapted, adopted) the resolution to have a class picnic.
10. A fund-raising letter went out to all (alumni, alumnae) of the state university.
11. This is (all the farther, as far as) I can run.
12. How does humidity (affect, effect) the speed of sound?
13. Everyone (accept, except) Janet and me applied there.
14. I hope that at least one college will (accept, except) me for admission next year.
15. Ms. Benchley is an (alumna, alumnus) of Reed College.
16. Were any crops (affected, effected) by this year's dry spell?
17. The quiz-show contestant won a large (amount, number) of points by correctly answering questions about geography.
18. The expression "lock, stock, and barrel" is an (allusion, illusion) to the parts of a flintlock rifle.
19. Please (accept, except) my congratulations.
20. The ending of the movie had a great emotional (affect, effect) on the audience.

bad, badly   See pages 223–24.

because   The use of *because* after *reason is* ("The reason is because . . .") is common in informal English, but it is generally avoided in formal writing. In a sentence beginning "The reason is . . .," the clause following the verb is a noun clause used as a predicate nominative. A noun clause may begin with *that* but not with *because*, which usually introduces an adverb clause.

ACCEPTABLE   The reason she arrived late was **that** [not *because*] her car had a flat tire.

BETTER   She arrived late **because** her car had a flat tire.

WRITING APPLICATION A:
Learning to State Reasons Correctly

In both speaking and writing, you are often asked to defend a position. That is, you are to give the reasons behind a position or opinion you have. Sooner or later, you will be faced with the use of *because* after *reason is*. Is this correct or not? *The reason is because* may be acceptable in informal writing, but in formal writing it is not. Instead, you should think of the clause following the verb *is* as a predicate nominative.

EXAMPLE   The *reason* I object to capital punishment *is* **that it is cruel and unusual punishment.** (In this example, the noun clause following the verb *is* begins correctly with *that*, not *because*.)

Writing Assignment

Take a position on a controversial subject. Be prepared to defend your position with sound and logical reasons. In your topic sentence use either *the reason is* or *the reasons are*. Be sure to follow this construction with a noun clause or several noun clauses beginning with *that*.

being as, being that   Nonstandard English when used for *since* or *because*

NONSTANDARD	Being as Emily had lived in Montreal for five years, she could speak both French and English.
STANDARD	**Because** Emily had lived in Montreal for five years, she could speak both French and English.

beside, besides *Beside* means "by the side of" someone or something. *Besides* means "in addition to."

Who sits **beside** you in English class?
Besides my homework, I have an errand to run.

between, among The distinction in meaning between these words is usually observed in formal English. Use *between* when you are thinking of two items at a time, regardless of whether they are part of a group of more than two.

We have to choose **between** Anne and Lisa.
I cannot remember the difference **between** a polka, a two-step, and a mazurka. [*Between* is correct because the speaker is thinking of one dance and another dance—*two at a time.*]
They would know the difference **between** the four teams.

Use *among* when you are thinking of a group rather than of separate individuals.

She is respected **among** her peers.
We distributed brochures **among** the local fans.

bring, take Use *bring* when the meaning is to convey something *to the person speaking.* Use *take* when the meaning is to convey something *away from the person speaking. Bring* is related to *come; take* is related to *go.*

Remember to **bring** your new albums when you **come** to visit me this weekend.
Take [not *bring*] your warm jacket when you **go** to the game this afternoon.

can't hardly, can't scarcely See *Double Negative* (pages 255-56).

could of Sometimes carelessly written for *could have.* Do not write *of* for *have.* Similar expressions frequently written incorrectly are *ought to of, might of, must of.*

NONSTANDARD   Wanda could of told us it wasn't a costume party before we
rented these chicken suits.

STANDARD   Wanda could **have** told us it wasn't a costume party before
we rented these chicken suits.

credible, creditable, credulous   Sometimes confused because of their
similarity, these words have quite different meanings.

Credible means "believable."

The child gave a **credible** excuse for breaking the window in the kitchen.

Creditable means "praiseworthy."

Her quick thinking and competent action were **creditable.**

Credulous means "inclined to believe just about anything."

The **credulous** woman and her neighbors signed up for the trip to Mars.

WRITING APPLICATION B:
Using *Credible* and the Conjunction *As*

Whether you are reading or watching a movie or a television show, you
generally want characters who are *credible*. This means that they are
believable. A character who is thoroughly evil, for example, is not
believable if he suddenly does something kind and unselfish. When you
judge whether or not characters are *credible*, you are a literary critic. In
a topic sentence about a character's credibility, you might also use the
conjunction *as*. This construction, which introduces a subordinate
clause, arises as you tell *why* a character is or is not credible. (*Like* is
commonly substituted for *as* in this construction, but it is unacceptable
in formal English.)

EXAMPLE   In *The Red Badge of Courage*, Henry Fleming is *credible* because
he reacts *as* a young, new recruit would in his first battle. [The
word *credible* is used correctly. The conjunction *as* is used—not
like—to introduce the subordinate clause.]

Writing Assignment

Select a character from fiction, the movies, or television who has made an impression on you. Ask yourself if this character is *credible*. Why or why not? Frame a topic sentence similar to the example above. Then write at least one paragraph explaining why the character is or is not believable.

---

data The plural form of the Latin *datum*. In standard informal English, *data* is frequently used, like a collective noun, with a singular pronoun and verb.

INFORMAL The census data was finally published.

However, since *data* has only recently become acceptable as a singular word, you will be safer if, in your writing, you use the word as a plural. See **phenomena.**

FORMAL The census **data were** finally published.

discover, invent Do not use *invent* to mean "discover." *Invent* means "to make something not known before, to bring something into existence." *Discover* means "to find something that has been in existence but was unknown."

Elias Howe **invented** the sewing machine.
The engineers **discovered** new oil deposits in Michigan.

done Not the past form of *do*. *Done* always needs a helping verb: *has done, was done, will be done*, etc. The past form of *do* is *did*.

NONSTANDARD We done all our chores in an hour.
STANDARD We **did** all our chores in an hour.
STANDARD We **had done** all our chores in an hour.

don't A contraction of *do not, don't* should not be used with a singular noun or the third person of singular pronouns (*it, he, she*). Use *doesn't*. See page 143.

NONSTANDARD It don't worry us.
STANDARD It **doesn't** worry us.

effect, affect  See **affect, effect.**

emigrate, immigrate *Emigrate* means "to go from a country" to settle elsewhere. *Immigrate* means "to come into a country" to settle there.

The war has forced thousands of people to **emigrate** from their homeland to other, more peaceful countries.

Marie's grandparents **immigrated** to Israel in 1950.

etc. See **and etc.**

except, accept See **accept, except.**

famous, notorious Learn the specific meanings of these words. *Famous* means "well and widely known." *Notorious* means "widely known" but in an unfavorable sense.

Gloria Steinem and Betty Friedan are **famous** leaders of the women's movement in the United States.

Al Capone was a **notorious** gangster in the 1920's.

farther See **all the farther.**

fewer, less In standard formal English *fewer* (not *less*) is used before a plural noun. *Less* is used before a singular noun.

We printed **fewer** [not *less*] prom tickets this year.

I spent **less** time in the library this morning.

good, well See page 224.

EXERCISE 2. Identifying Correct Expressions. The sentences in this exercise contain usage problems explained on pages 241–45. Double negatives and the listed items explained elsewhere in this text are not covered. Number your paper 1–25. Write after the proper number the correct choice of the words in parentheses.

EXAMPLE   1. We could (of, have) taken the bus.
          1. *have*

1. (Being that, Because) Eric is shy, he doesn't say much.
2. (Fewer, Less) teen-agers were able to find summer jobs this year than last year.

3. When the car broke down, we had only five dollars (between, among) the six of us.

4. The science fiction story centered on two characters who (emigrated, immigrated) from their home planet to Earth.

5. I was glad that I had (brought, taken) a thermos of hot tea when we went hiking in the mountains.

6. (Beside, Besides) our volunteer work, our club sponsors an annual ski trip.

7. Please (bring, take) your guitar and sheet music when you come to my party.

8. Jon is so (credulous, credible) that he believed your crazy story.

9. They sold (fewer, less) new cars than used cars.

10. In what year was the transistor (invented, discovered)?

11. My reason for missing the rehearsal was not (credulous, credible).

12. Did you (bring, take) your gift back to the store?

13. Basketball is his favorite sport (beside, besides) tennis.

14. I had (fewer, less) cavities than my sister.

15. They (done, did) their best to win the play-offs.

16. Cold weather (don't, doesn't) bother him very much.

17. (Among, Between) the four of us, we can paint the house.

18. If I had known you weren't busy, I would (of, have) asked you to help me.

19. Many people (emigrated, immigrated) to the United States in the nineteenth century.

20. All the critics wrote about Gene Wilder's (creditable, credulous) performance in his most recent movie.

21. Alan Shepard, Jr., became (famous, notorious) as the first American in space.

22. I want to (invent, discover) a fabric that never gets dirty.

23. (Being that, Since) we were studying hard, we did not hear the news report about the school closings.

24. Shakespeare is a (famous, notorious) English dramatist.

25. Angie forgot to (bring, take) her homework assignment when she went to school this morning.

EXERCISE 3. Identifying Correct Expressions. This exercise covers all usage items explained in the glossary to this point.

Number your paper 1–25. If a sentence does not contain a usage error, write a + after the proper number on your paper. If it does contain a usage error, write the correct form.

EXAMPLE   1. We excepted the telegram nervously.
          1. *accepted*

1. Frank has less hobbies than his friend.
2. Dr. Nash stopped by to check on my progress, being as she was in the neighborhood anyway.
3. Will the thunderstorms affect the graduation ceremonies?
4. Would you please take this monstrosity out of here?
5. Anyone as credible as you would buy a refrigerator in the Antarctic.
6. Sue Ellen plays and enjoys many sports: baseball, tennis, bowling, field hockey, volleyball, and etc.
7. The reason for the widespread concern for eagles is because many are dying from lead poisoning.
8. Besides her full-time job, Mrs. Owens, who is a widow, is busy raising her three children.
9. She very graciously excepted our apologies.
10. I can't believe the amount of customers at our sale.
11. The story contains too many allusions to Marie Antoinette.
12. Margie couldn't find her bus pass anywheres.
13. Where will we be staying at on vacation?
14. Six laps of the pool is all the farther I can swim.
15. The manager divided the work evenly between the four of us.
16. We were grateful to our knowledgeable coach and who guided us patiently throughout the year.
17. My aunts, who are identical twins, are both alumnae of Smith.
18. The foreign exchange student has found it difficult to adapt to life in the United States.
19. If I had known you were ill, I could of let you read my notes from physics class.
20. The Russian ballet dancer immigrated from his homeland to find creative freedom.
21. Aileen became famous when she appeared in the documentary about outstanding young musicians.
22. The amount of push-ups that he can do is incredible.
23. We have discovered a new device for cleaning potatoes, and we call it our "Scrub-a-Spud."

24. To prepare her report, Judy used data that were published by the Department of the Treasury.
25. Even though Roy said it don't matter, I can see that my remark is bothering him.

√ **had of**   The *of* is superfluous.

| NONSTANDARD | If we had of asked permission, we could have used the auditorium for our meeting. |
| STANDARD | If we **had asked** permission, we could have used the auditorium for our meeting. |

had ought, hadn't ought   Do not use *had* with *ought*.

NONSTANDARD	They had ought to be more patient.
STANDARD	They **ought** to be more patient.
NONSTANDARD	I hadn't ought to go to the movies again.
STANDARD	I **ought not** to go to the movies again.

√ **he, she, they,** etc.   Do not use unnecessary pronouns after a noun. This error is sometimes called the *double subject.*

| NONSTANDARD | My cousin she designs her own clothes. |
| STANDARD | My cousin designs her own clothes. |

hisself, theirselves   These words are sometimes incorrectly used for *himself, themselves.*

| NONSTANDARD | Lou built the shed hisself. |
| STANDARD | Lou built the shed **himself.** |

illusion, allusion   See **allusion, illusion.**

immigrate, emigrate   See **emigrate, immigrate.**

 imply, infer   *Imply* means "to suggest something." *Infer* means "to interpret, to get a certain meaning from a remark or an action."

Mrs. Hanson **implied** during her lecture that we needed more practice. We **inferred** from her comments that we need to practice more than we have been practicing.

in, into In standard formal usage, observe the difference in meaning between these words. *In* means "within"; *into* suggests movement from the outside to the inside.

FORMAL Feeling nervous, I walked **into** [not *in*] the personnel department.

INFORMAL We threw some pennies **in** the well and made a wish.

FORMAL We threw some pennies **into** the well and made a wish.

invent, discover See **discover, invent.**

kind, sort, type In standard formal usage the adjectives *this, these, that, those* are made to agree in number with the words *kind, sort, type: this kind, these kinds; that sort, those sorts.*

We prefer **this kind** of magazine.
We prefer **these kinds** of magazines.

Rather

kind of, sort of In standard formal usage, avoid using these expressions to mean "rather" or "somewhat."

INFORMAL I feel kind of depressed today.

FORMAL I feel **rather** [somewhat] depressed today.

kind of a, sort of a The *a* is superfluous.

What **kind of** [not *kind of a*] sports car is this?

lay, lie See pages 189–91.

learn, teach *Learn* means "to acquire knowledge." *Teach* means "to dispense knowledge."

If Ms. Green **teaches** [not *learns*] us, we will **learn** more.

leave, let *Leave (left)* means "to go away." *Let* means "to allow, to permit."

NONSTANDARD Leave us finish our dinner.

STANDARD **Let** us finish our dinner.

NONSTANDARD He shouldn't have left us borrow his car.

STANDARD He shouldn't have **let** us borrow his car.

The expressions "Leave me alone" and "Let me alone" are both correct and are commonly used interchangeably. Strictly speaking, "Leave me alone" suggests that you want somebody to go away, leaving you by yourself. "Let me alone" suggests that you want somebody to stop bothering you.

less, fewer   See **fewer, less**.

liable   See **likely, liable**.

lie, lay   See pages 189–91.

like, as   *Like* is a preposition and introduces a prepositional phrase. *As* is usually a conjunction and introduces a subordinate clause.

Jo sings **like her sister**. [prepositional phrase]
Jo sings **as her sister does**. [subordinate clause]

Like as a conjunction is commonly heard in informal speech, but it is unacceptable in formal English.

INFORMAL   She plays golf like the pros do.
 FORMAL   She plays golf **as** the pros do.

like, as if   *Like* should not be used for *as if* or *as though*, which are conjunctions used to introduce clauses.

INFORMAL   She looks like she studied all night.
 FORMAL   She looks **as if** [as though] she studied all night.

likely, liable   These words are used interchangeably in standard English, but some writers of standard formal English prefer to observe the following distinctions: *Likely* is used to express simple probability.

Ginny is **likely** to arrive any minute.

Liable is used to express probability with a suggestion of harm or misfortune; it is also used to mean "responsible" or "answerable."

The children playing near the gravel pit are **liable** to get hurt.
Mrs. Lee is **liable** for the damages her daughter caused.

myself, ourselves Most careful writers of English avoid using pronouns ending in *–self, –selves* as subjects. See page 171.

Amy and **I** [not *myself*] are in charge of decorations.
Could you do a favor for Wanda and **me**? [not *myself*]

EXERCISE 4. Identifying Usage Errors. The sentences in this exercise cover usage problems explained in the part of the glossary that follows Exercise 3. Number your paper 1–20. If the usage is correct, write a + after the proper number; if it is incorrect, write a 0.

1. In his address to Congress, the President implied that an economic reversal might occur soon.
2. Without any warning, the cat jumped from the chair and leaped in my arms.
3. The children helped themselves to more turkey.
4. When you have time, will you learn me to sew?
5. Leave me figure this problem out by myself.
6. We had ought to have been more considerate.
7. Your room looks as if a tornado had been through it.
8. What am I to imply from your sarcastic remarks?
9. Ben did all the work himself.
10. If you had asked me, I would of told you.
11. What can you infer from the closing couplet of this sonnet?
12. You hadn't ought to complain so much.
13. Why doesn't he get his work done like he's supposed to?
14. Jane and myself are the editors of our yearbook.
15. We implied from the principal's announcement that our school's administration is becoming stricter.
16. I asked my boss if he would let me have Saturday afternoon off.
17. Some people they're always making a fuss about nothing.
18. Are you implying that I can't read music?
19. Leave them stay if they don't want to join us.
20. We cheered like we never cheered before.

nauseated, nauseous These words do not mean the same thing. *Nauseated* means "sick." *Nauseous* means "disgusting, sickening."

After riding on the roller coaster, the child became **nauseated**.
The chemical reaction gave off a **nauseous** odor.

none *None* may be either singular or plural. See pages 134–35.

notorious, famous See **famous, notorious**.

number The expression *the number of* takes a singular verb. The expression *a number of* takes a plural verb. (See page 144, Rule 7s.)

The number of candidates **was** surprising.
A number of candidates **were** nominated by the committee.

number, amount See **amount, number**.

of Do not use *of* unnecessarily. See **could of** and **had of**.

off of The *of* is unnecessary.

They pushed us **off** [not *off of*] the raft as a joke.

Do not use *off* or *off of* for *from*.

NONSTANDARD   I got some free advice off of the mechanic.
STANDARD   I got some free advice **from** the mechanic.

or, nor Use *or* with *either;* use *nor* with *neither.*

Either Gwen **or** Lily will lead the discussion.
Neither Gwen **nor** Lily will lead the discussion.

ought See **had ought, hadn't ought**.

persecute, prosecute Distinguish between these words, which have quite different meanings. *Persecute* means "to attack or annoy someone," often for a person's beliefs. *Prosecute* means "to bring legal action against someone for unlawful behavior."

The old regime **persecuted** the political prisoners.
The district attorney **will prosecute** anyone caught looting.

phenomena If you use this word, use it correctly. *Phenomena* is the plural form of the word *phenomenon*. Do not use it as a singular noun.

We studied **these** [not *this*] phenomena of nature, which **are** [not *is*] rare indeed.
We studied this **phenomenon** of nature, which **is** rare indeed.

politics, mathematics, athletics For the number of these words and other similar words, see page 142.

reason is because See **because.**

respectfully, respectively *Respectfully* means "with respect" or "full of respect." *Respectively* means "each in the order given."

Even though I disagreed, I listened **respectfully** to their side.
Jane Eyre, Emma, and *Adam Bede* were written by Charlotte Brontë, Jane Austen, and George Eliot, **respectively.**

Reverend, Honorable These titles should never be used with a person's last name alone. In addition, the word *the* commonly precedes the titles.

NONSTANDARD   Reverend Becker, the Reverend Becker, Honorable Hawkins

STANDARD   the Reverend Mark Becker, the Reverend M. L. Becker, the Reverend Mr. Becker, the Reverend Dr. Becker, the Honorable Paula Hawkins.

rise, raise See page 194.

same, said, such Avoid such artificial uses of these words as the following:

We worked hard on the homecoming float and had **same** guarded against pranksters.
Josie complains about taking care of her young cousin, but she is really fond of **said** cousin.
Steve suggested we skip classes and go to the beach, but I don't approve of **such.**

says Commonly used incorrectly for *said.*

NONSTANDARD   Doris argued and says, "We should have made reservations before we left."

STANDARD   Doris argued and **said,** "We should have made reservations before we left."

scarcely See *Double Negative* (pages 255–56).

shall, will   The old distinction between these words is no longer observed by most people. *Shall*, which was once considered the only correct form for the expression of the simple future in the first person, has been replaced by *will* in the speech and writing of most people.

> STANDARD   I **shall** be glad to mail your package.
> I **will** be glad to mail your package.

In a few expressions *shall* is the only form ever used and so presents no usage problem: *Shall we go? Shall I help you?* To use *will* in these expressions would change the meaning. With the exception of these special uses, *will* is as correct as *shall*.

sit, set   See page 193.

slow, slowly   See page 224.

so   Because this word is usually overworked, avoid it in your writing whenever you can.

> POOR   The car ran out of gas, so we walked two miles to the nearest service station.
> BETTER   When the car ran out of gas, we walked two miles to the nearest service station.
> BETTER   Because the car had run out of gas, we walked two miles to the nearest service station.

some, somewhat   Use *somewhat* rather than *some* as an adverb.

> FORMAL   The rate of inflation in Europe has slowed **somewhat** [not *some*].

take, bring   See **bring, take.**

this here, that there   The *here* and the *there* are unnecessary.

> NONSTANDARD   This here shop has the best bargains.
> STANDARD   **This** shop has the best bargains.

these kind, those kind   See **kind, sort, type.**

ways   Sometimes used informally for *way* in referring to distance.

> INFORMAL   They hiked for three hours, but they were still a long ways from the campsite.
> FORMAL   They hiked for three hours, but they were still a long **way** from the campsite.

well, good See page 224.

when, where Do not use *when* or *where* in writing a definition.

NONSTANDARD   A hurricane is when a tropical cyclone has winds faster than 75 miles per hour.
STANDARD   A hurricane is a tropical cyclone that has winds faster than 75 miles per hour.
NONSTANDARD   We read where the restaurant is going to close.
STANDARD   We read **that** the restaurant is going to close.

where . . . at See **at**.

which, that, who *Which* should be used to refer to things only. *That* may be used to refer to either things or people. *Who* should be used to refer to people only.

I like movies **which** [that] have happy endings.
Debra is an actress **who** [not *which*] inspires admiration.
Debra is an actress **that** inspires admiration.

The Double Negative

A double negative is a construction in which two negative words are used where one is sufficient. Formerly, double negatives were quite acceptable, but now they are considered nonstandard.

can't hardly, can't scarcely The words *hardly* and *scarcely* are negatives. They should never be used with negative *not*.

NONSTANDARD   It is so dark in here I can't hardly see where I'm going.
STANDARD   It is so dark in here I **can hardly** see where I'm going.

NONSTANDARD   There isn't scarcely enough time to eat lunch.
STANDARD   There **is scarcely** enough time to eat lunch.

can't help but In standard formal English, avoid this double negative.

FORMAL   We **can't help applauding** [not *can't help but applaud*] Ron's positive attitude.

haven't but, haven't only In certain uses *but* and *only* are negatives. Avoid using them with *not*.

FORMAL   They **had** [not *hadn't*] but two tickets left.
They **had** [not *hadn't*] only two tickets left.

no, nothing, none Not to be used with another negative word.

NONSTANDARD	Haven't you no money?
STANDARD	**Haven't** you **any** money?
STANDARD	**Have** you **no** money?

NONSTANDARD	Carol hasn't said nothing about the picnic.
STANDARD	Carol **has said nothing** about the picnic.
STANDARD	Carol **hasn't said anything** about the picnic.

NONSTANDARD	Joel didn't sell none today.
STANDARD	Joel **sold none** today.
STANDARD	Joel **didn't sell any** today.

EXERCISE 5. Identifying Correct Expressions. The sentences in this exercise cover usage problems explained in the section of the glossary that follows Exercise 4. Number your paper 1–20. Write after the proper number the correct one of the two words in parentheses.

EXAMPLE 1. I don't have (any, none) left.
  1. *any*

1. They only had a little (ways, way) to run before they could reach the finish line.
2. Neither the freshman class (or, nor) the sophomore class will have the problems we faced.
3. We were taught to treat our elders (respectively, respectfully).
4. Luis (can, can't) hardly keep from being proud of you.
5. We studied the Mayans, (who, which) had developed a system of writing, as well as an accurate calendar.
6. Ms. Peterson clearly explained the (phenomenon, phenomena) of a supernova.
7. Our enthusiasm has dampened (some, somewhat).
8. Many ancient rulers (persecuted, prosecuted) the people they conquered and made them slaves.
9. I was so sleepy after lunch that I (could, couldn't) hardly keep my eyes open.
10. The detectives (haven't, have) no clues in the case.
11. I (had, hadn't) no good reason for being late.
12. She (says, said) we were crazy to try skydiving.
13. We (had, hadn't) learned anything from the film.

14. The candidates (have, haven't) only three minutes each to state their platforms.
15. She would neither let me tell her the right answer (or, nor) let me give her any other help.
16. We (had, hadn't) but one choice to make.
17. The jazz band and the symphony orchestra will rehearse in rooms 115 and 135, (respectively, respectfully).
18. The manager insisted that there wasn't (any, no) reason for making the customers wait so long.
19. Now that we have moved, I live only a little (ways, way) from school.
20. I'm probably getting the flu, because I have felt (nauseous, nauseated) all day long.

REVIEW EXERCISE A. Selecting Appropriate Expressions.

The sentences in this exercise contain usage problems presented in the glossary. Number your paper 1–20. If a sentence does not contain a usage error, write a + on your paper after the proper number. If a sentence does contain a usage error, write a 0. Your teacher may ask you to write the correct form after each 0.

EXAMPLE   1. The amount of voters has grown.
        1. 0 (*number*)

1. Leave us explain our arguments.
2. Eugenia can't hardly wait for vacation to start.
3. Who first discovered the laser?
4. We worked hard to effect a change in the school's policy on flexible lunch hours.
5. Beside your loyalty as a friend, I appreciate your sense of humor.
6. I resent their allusions to my mistakes.
7. The library has a large amount of new books.
8. You would of had a bad time driving in the mountains without snow tires.
9. Being that I'm short, please let me stand in front.
10. Her talk implied that she favored the honor system.
11. The reason you are tired is because we watched the late show.
12. The principal has no patience with those type of behavior.
13. At the supermarket I bought kiwi fruit, papayas, mangoes, pineapples, coconuts, and etc.

14. Since Dan started his part-time job, he has had less chances to be with his friends.
15. My parents are members of the alumni association.
16. Bring your riding boots when you go to the stable.
17. Backlighting is when the main source of light is placed behind the subject you are photographing.
18. Jody dances as if his feet hurt.
19. Why don't you get some advice off of Rhoda?
20. Thirty feet is all the farther I can throw a football.

REVIEW EXERCISE B. Selecting Appropriate Expressions.
The sentences in this exercise contain usage problems presented in the glossary. Number your paper 1–20. If a sentence does not contain a usage error, write a + on your paper after the proper number. If a sentence does contain a usage error, write a 0.

1. We had to adapt the stage lighting for the rock concert.
2. The mayor made an illusion to the factory's outstanding safety record.
3. A large amount of nails are in the toolbox.
4. Where did you stay at over Thanksgiving?
5. Everyone except Tim has accepted the invitation.
6. Among the two choices, I like the first one better.
7. The data on acid rain are not complete.
8. My grandparents emigrated to the United States before my mother was born.
9. Do you know about Bluebeard, who was famous for his cruelty?
10. You are credulous enough to believe the fortune teller.
11. My sister she attends Iowa State University.
12. We inferred from Rudy's comments that the movie was dull.
13. The Whites grew all the vegetables theirselves.
14. I had ought to spend more time with my friends.
15. He has been the catcher for every game this year, and he is beginning to look kind of tired.
16. Ms. Robinson learned me all I know about public speaking.
17. What kind of a car is that?
18. We spoke respectfully to the Honorable Frank Murphy when he visited our class.

19. After two hours on the sailboat, I felt nauseous.
20. A number of suggestions have been submitted to the planning committee.

CHAPTER 11 REVIEW: POSTTEST 1

Identifying Standard Usage. Number your paper 1–25. After the proper number, write the standard choice of the two given in parentheses.

EXAMPLE   1. There are (fewer, less) people injured in plane crashes than in car accidents each year.
   1. *fewer*

1. (Being as, Because) my father has had several promotions, our family has moved several times.
2. Change brings with it a challenge to (adapt, adopt) to new circumstances.
3. Because Anna is a good driver with great patience, it was easy for her to (learn, teach) me to drive.
4. Having eaten pizza, chicken gumbo, and ice cream for dinner, Sidney felt (nauseated, nauseous) within an hour after the meal.
5. From his yawns and restlessness, I (implied, inferred) that Paul was very bored by the lecture.
6. We rose as the judge walked (in, into) the courtroom.
7. (Beside, Besides) the number listed on the program, the singer performed three additional songs in response to the audience's calls for "Encore!"
8. Each year, a large number of (alumni, alumnae) returned to Danbury High School for Homecoming Weekend.
9. A poem written in iambic pentameter is not (likely, liable) to be mistaken for prose.
10. "(This, This here) fruit salad is delicious!" said Kim.
11. We were so (affected, effected) by the movie that we actually cried during the wedding scene.

12. Business at Central Department Store this month had been (kind of, rather) slow.
13. Where would we be if no one had (discovered, invented) the microchip?
14. When he first began lifting weights, Bruno (could, couldn't) hardly lift twenty pounds.
15. The poodle (who, that) wore the red collar should have taken first place, in my opinion.
16. "I saw (that, where) your sister was elected," said Eve.
17. The (number, amount) of signatures on our petition comes to well over a thousand.
18. The district attorney stood and said, "I am ready to (persecute, prosecute) the case, Your Honor."
19. The number of visitors to the museum (averages, average) two thousand a day.
20. The reason for the flight's delay was (that, because) the electrical system needed to be checked.
21. In our automotives class the number of girls (is, are) equal to the number of boys.
22. "Glennette and (I, myself) have worked hard for the Red Cross this year," I said.
23. Will you please (leave, let) me make up my own mind about what I want to do?
24. It looks (like, as if) Greta will win this race.
25. All the data from standardized tests (indicates, indicate) that this year's class is working very well.

CHAPTER 11 REVIEW: POSTTEST 2

Revising Expressions by Correcting Errors in Usage. The sentences in this exercise cover problems explained in the entire glossary. Number your paper 1–25. If a sentence does not contain a usage error, write a + on your paper after the proper number. If a sentence does contain a usage error, revise correctly the portion of the sentence containing the error.

EXAMPLE 1. I was surprised to learn that Robert's parents are wealthy, because he doesn't act like he's rich.
    1. *doesn't act as if he's rich.*

1. The form said, "Please enclose a copy of your birth certificate, and we will return said document at a later date."
2. We couldn't help but admire the way the snow lay upon the hills.
3. You hadn't ought to be so careless about your new watch.
4. In a collision the guilty driver is liable for damage done to the other driver's car.
5. The weather was kind of muggy as we began to weed the garden.
6. The door scraped loudly because it was off of its hinges.
7. Members of the Student Council tried to effect the faculty's attitude toward the new dress code for school dances.
8. The picture of the notorious discoverer of the cure appeared on the front page of every major newspaper.
9. Theo don't care what others think; he has the courage to say what he believes.
10. Reverend Timothy Butler performed the wedding ceremony.
11. Esperanza and Patrick, respectfully valedictorian and salutatorian, delivered excellent commencement addresses.
12. When our teacher became ill and was replaced by a substitute, we found it difficult at first to adopt to a new routine.
13. Whenever I feel sad, I can't hardly wait to be with my friend Ines, because she always makes me laugh.
14. Arthur Fiedler he made the Boston Pops concerts popular with millions of people all over America.
15. The Honorable Cardiss Jackson will address the League of Women Voters on Wednesday evening.
16. Scientists are still unable to explain fully the phenomena referred to as UFO's.
17. Then Tom says, "Maybe I'll go and maybe I won't."
18. Because Eula made a mistake when she put the film into the camera, none of her pictures could be developed.
19. Three of the players came off of the bench and ran out onto the field.
20. Even when he is reading difficult material, Mato is very skillful in inferring the main idea of a passage.
21. Florence felt nauseous after eating too quickly.
22. I have never seen this kind of insect before.

23: Where was Beth at last night when everyone else went to the basketball game?
24. Neil is an expert on jazz trumpeters and who are famous.
25. My science teacher said, "You have done a credible job on your project."

USAGE
MASTERY REVIEW: Cumulative Test

A. AGREEMENT. Number your paper 1–10. Most of the following sentences contain verbs that do not agree with their subjects or pronouns that do not agree with their antecedents. If a sentence is correct, write + next to the proper number. If a sentence contains an error, write the correct form of the verb or pronoun next to the incorrect form used in the sentence.

EXAMPLES   1. Either the doctor or the nurses is going to lecture the medical students.
1. *is—are*
2. Which one of the workers forgot to punch out their time card?
2. *their—his*

1. My mother is one of those people who is very talented in many ways.
2. Because of the flu epidemic, the number of absentees have increased every day this week.
3. Before Greg had started working for his spending money, he thought twenty dollars weren't much to receive from his parents; now he knows the value of twenty dollars.
4. Since everyone turned in their essay on time, our teacher praised the class.
5. Behind by a score of four to three in the second half, the soccer team huddled to plan their strategy.
6. After we saw a film on auto safety, few if any of my friends now drives without first buckling their seatbelts.
7. Do you know whether anyone picked up their paycheck already?
8. I thought neither art nor physics were interesting until I took those courses; now I love them!
9. Often the whirring of the machines give me a headache at work.
10. Where are the five pounds of flour that I left sitting on the kitchen table?

B. PRONOUNS. Many of the following sentences contain errors in pronoun usage. Number your paper 11–20. If a sentence is correct, write + next to the proper number on your paper. If a sentence contains a pronoun error, write the pronoun on your paper and next to it write the correct form of the pronoun. Use standard format.

EXAMPLE   1. When the telephone rang, I hoped it would be Darren, and when I heard someone say, "Hi!" I knew it was him.
　　　　　1. *him—he*

11. As far as I'm concerned, no one sings better than him.

12. Robin said she would tell me what had really happened if I promised to keep the information a secret between her and I.

13. Is there anyone who thinks that him winning the design contest is unimportant?

14. After we graduate, Flora and myself plan to visit her cousin in Fargo, North Dakota.

15. Last week, we had a good time planning a surprise party for Bey and he.

16. When you entertain friends, courtesy requires you to consider the needs of those who you have invited to your home.

17. It seems to me that there ought to be someone else whom you can ask to do this work.

18. Could you give Bobbie and myself a minute of your time?

19. When Chico and me went downtown to buy concert tickets yesterday, who was in line but Claire!

20. After you have introduced yourself to the receptionist, give the name of the person who you wish to see.

C. IRREGULAR VERBS.

Number your paper 21–30. After the proper number, write either the past or the past participle of the verb given at the beginning of each sentence, whichever will correctly complete the sentence.

EXAMPLE   1. *break* When Cathy hit the ball into the stands, we cheered because she had——the school softball record.
　　　　　1. broken

21. *choose* At the beginning of her junior year, she——a more difficult English class because she wanted to prepare well for college.

22. *take* When we went to the laundromat, we——our own soap and bleach.

23. *lie* Because Gordon had sprained his knee, he——in bed and watched television programs for a while this afternoon.

24. *sing* After we had——the national anthem, we cheered as the team took the field.

25. *sit* Our dog Rusty——at the fence waiting for my brother Whitney to return from work.
26. *know* If I had —— that Alexis was such a good photographer, I would have asked her to take pictures for the yearbook.
27. *drink* After Rudy had —— four huge glasses of milk and eaten two apples, he said, "Great! Now I'll have some lunch!"
28. *write* When I saw that my history teacher had —— , "Very well done!" at the top of my research paper, I felt really happy.
29. *lay* Try as he might, Roger could not remember where he had —— the keys to the car.
30. *rise* According to news reports, the launch of the space shuttle occurred at 6:02 A.M., just after the sun had——.

D. VERB TENSES AND MOOD. Number your paper 31–35. The sentences that follow contain errors in the use of verb tenses or mood. Next to the proper number, write the incorrect form of the verb; then write the correct form next to it.

EXAMPLE 1. After I did the grocery shopping, I came home and unpacked my purchases.
  1. *did—had done*

31. Doris said that she wished we went swimming more often last summer.
32. I was amazed to learn that San Francisco had so many steep streets.
33. "If Gwen was with us on this boat ride, we would be having a better time," I said.
34. The seniors were excited because they were about to have gone on their class trip.
35. Working as a member of the voter registration team for three months, Scott felt satisfied at the rise in voter turnout reported after the election.

E. MODIFIERS. Number your paper 36–40. The following sentences present problems in the use of modifiers. If a modifier contains an error, copy it and the word modified on your paper; then write the correct form of the modifier on your paper.

EXAMPLE 1. When I opened the container, I knew immediately that the milk smelled badly.
  1. *smelled badly—bad*

36. Hearing the telephone ring, Elsie May ran real quickly to answer it.
37. Because the rowing team did bad in the race, the entire crew felt bad.
38. After we had compared carefully the prices of the two stereos, we decided to purchase the least expensive model.
39. She always does good on spelling tests.
40. When learning to ski, a person should start off slow until he has mastered basic techniques.

F. STANDARD USAGE. Number your paper 41–50. Each of the following sentences contains a blank for which two or three different completions are offered. Only *one* of the choices is correct. Next to the proper number on your answer paper, write the letter of the correct completion.

EXAMPLE   1. We agreed that we——listened to the comedian's jokes for another hour without losing interest.
    a. could have
    b. could of
  1. *a*

41. The girls divided their after-school time——part-time jobs, sports, and homework.
    a. among
    b. between
42. When the politician used jargon at the press conference, the reporters seemed——they were puzzled.
    a. as if
    b. like
43. Whether composed of feathers or of iron, the——of pounds in a ton is still 2,000.
    a. amount
    b. number
44. The Governor made it clear that she would not——the bill for her signature unless the legislature included her version of the tax increase.
    a. accept
    b. except

45. After we had seen the latest space-adventure film, I told Trulia that
    I don't like——of movie.
    a. that kind
    b. those kind
    c. that kinds

46. When you go camping next weekend, be sure to——all the food and
    equipment you will need.
    a. bring
    b. take

47. The reason I don't like to spend time with Ellis is——he talks too
    much and listens too little.
    a. because
    b. that

48. As she paged through the magazine, she couldn't find——articles
    that interested her.
    a. any
    b. hardly any
    c. scarcely any

49. Before the admission of women to West Point in the late 1970's, all
    of the——were men.
    a. alumnae
    b. alumni

50. ——opening a savings account, I am also beginning to purchase
    stocks.
    a. Beside
    b. Besides

PART THREE

COMPOSITION:
Writing and Revising
Sentences

CHAPTER 12

Sentence Completeness

FRAGMENTS AND RUN-ON SENTENCES

Two kinds of sentence errors sometimes persist even in the writing of high-school seniors. The first is the writing of part of a sentence, a *fragment,* as though it were a whole sentence, able to stand by itself, with a capital letter at the beginning and a period at the end. The second kind of error is the writing of two or more sentences as though they were one sentence. The writer makes the mistake of using a comma, or no punctuation at all, between the sentences. You may think of these two sentence errors as opposites. The fragment is not complete; the run-on sentence is more than complete.

SENTENCE FRAGMENTS

A group of words is a complete sentence when it has a subject and a verb and expresses a complete thought.

COMPLETE   After the flood the barn roof lay in the yard.
INCOMPLETE   After the flood the barn roof in the yard
INCOMPLETE   After the flood the barn roof lying in the yard

Because they lack a verb, the last two examples do not express a complete thought. Words ending in *–ing,* like *lying,* are not verbs when they are used alone. Such words may, of course, be used with a *helping* *verb* to form a verb phrase (see page 15). Unless a word ending in *–ing* does have a helping verb, it may not be used as the verb in a sentence.[1]

NO VERB   The barn roof lying in the front yard
VERB PHRASE   The barn roof **was lying** in the front yard.

NO VERB   Amy competing in the marathon
VERB PHRASE   Amy **will be competing** in the marathon.

12a. A *sentence fragment* is a group of words that does not express a complete thought. Since it is part of a sentence, it should not be allowed to stand by itself, but should be kept in the sentence of which it is a part.

The Phrase Fragment

A phrase is a group of words acting as a single part of speech and not containing a verb and its subject.

There are many kinds of phrases (participial, gerund, appositive, prepositional, infinitive), but regardless of their kind, they all have one important characteristic—they are parts of a sentence and must never be separated from the sentence in which they belong. When a phrase is incorrectly allowed to stand by itself, it is called a fragment.

Study the ways in which the unattached phrase fragments in the following examples are corrected.

FRAGMENT   Last Saturday I saw Gloria. Riding her new ten-speed bicycle. [This participial phrase fragment modifies the word *Gloria*. It should be included in the sentence with the word it modifies.]

FRAGMENT CORRECTED   Last Saturday I saw Gloria **riding her new ten-speed bicycle.**

FRAGMENT   The largest sailing ship afloat is the Soviet frigate *Kurstan.* Used by the Soviet Union as a training ship. [This participial phrase fragment modifies the word *frigate*. It should be included in the sentence with the word it modifies.]

FRAGMENT CORRECTED   The largest sailing ship afloat is the Soviet frigate *Kurstan,* **used by the Soviet Union as a training ship.**

[1] The following helping verbs may be used with words ending in *–ing* to form a verb phrase:

am	were	can (may) be
are	will (shall) be	could (would, should) be
is	has been	will (shall) have been
was	had been	might have been

FRAGMENT   We pitched our tent on the north side of the lake. At the edge of a grove of pine trees. [This prepositional phrase fragment modifies the verb *pitched*, telling where we pitched our tent. This sequence of phrases belongs in the sentence.]

FRAGMENT CORRECTED   We pitched our tent on the north side of the lake **at the edge of a grove of pine trees.**

FRAGMENT   My parents finally gave me permission. To go with Gail to the game at West Point. [Here, an infinitive phrase fragment has been separated from the word *permission*, which it explains. It should be included in the same sentence with the word it explains.]

FRAGMENT CORRECTED   My parents finally gave me permission **to go with Gail to the game at West Point.**

FRAGMENT   Aunt Deborah came bearing gifts. A wrist watch for Jean and a ring for me. [This appositive phrase fragment belongs in the sentence preceding it, separated by a comma from *gifts*, the word to which it refers.]

FRAGMENT CORRECTED   Aunt Deborah came bearing gifts**, a wrist watch for Jean and a ring for me.**

The Subordinate Clause Fragment

A second type of fragment is the subordinate clause that is incorrectly separated from the sentence to which it belongs. A clause is a group of words containing a subject and predicate and used as a part of a sentence. A subordinate clause does not express a complete thought and should not stand alone.

FRAGMENT   The orchestra played "A Night in the Tropics." Which Louis Gottschalk wrote in 1859.

FRAGMENT CORRECTED   The orchestra played "A Night in the Tropics," **which Louis Gottschalk wrote in 1859.**

12b. Do not separate a phrase or a subordinate clause from the sentence of which it is a part.

EXERCISE 1. Revising to Eliminate Fragments. Some of the items in this exercise consist of one or two completed sentences; others contain sentence fragments. Number your paper 1–20. If all the parts of an item are complete sentences, write *C* after the proper number. If an item contains a fragment, revise it to include the fragment in the sentence.

1. Elizabeth Blackwell was born in 1821. And died in 1910.
2. When, in 1832, her parents could no longer tolerate the social and political situation in Bristol, England, where Mr. Blackwell was a leading member of the business community. They immigrated with their eight children to New York.
3. After six years of adventures—some profitable, some unhappy—in the East, the family decided to move to Cincinnati. Where they hoped to prosper.
4. For a while things looked bright for the family. Despite the growing realization that some of them missed England.
5. But tragedy struck in 1832. Mr. Blackwell died.
6. Elizabeth established a school for girls. Feeling depressed by the economic plight of her family, which now consisted of her mother, four sisters, and four brothers.
7. By 1839 this school, staffed by several members of the family, had become quite successful. But Elizabeth was beginning to feel dissatisfied with teaching.
8. A woman friend, dying of cancer, suggested that Elizabeth, who loved to study, become a doctor. At first, Elizabeth totally rejected this suggestion.
9. In spite of herself, the idea of being a doctor plagued Elizabeth. Leading her to inquire into the possibility of a woman studying medicine.
10. When told that it would be impossible for a woman to become a doctor, she became determined to follow her dying friend's advice. Not certain how she should proceed against the forces of prejudice.
11. Elizabeth Blackwell's determination to study and practice medicine must be seen as courageous. Since matrimony was the only respectable career for a woman in the 1840's.
12. Her insistence on finding a place and a way to study medicine took Elizabeth Blackwell to North Carolina, where she received private instruction from two doctors. And taught music in boarding schools.
13. She then applied to and was rejected by medical schools in Philadelphia, the seat of medical education in America at that time. After which Elizabeth applied to schools around the country.

14. Finally, in 1847, the Medical Institution of Geneva College in northern New York State accepted Elizabeth Blackwell. Now known as Hobart College.

15. She graduated in 1849 at the head of her class. A young woman convinced that she was right and determined to change ideas about education.

16. She was not content with being the first woman in the United States to gain an M.D. degree from a medical school. Elizabeth Blackwell spent the next two years doing graduate work in Europe.

17. Once she was back in America, Elizabeth Blackwell led a life marked by an enthusiasm to encourage her sister Emily and a passion to practice medicine. Combined with an interest in helping the poor.

18. In 1857 Elizabeth Blackwell established the New York Infirmary for Indigent Women and Children, a hospital staffed by women. She decided to open the hospital on May 12, the birthday of her friend Florence Nightingale.

19. Because of Elizabeth's and Emily's breakthroughs in medicine and the social pioneering of the two other sisters, the Blackwell women are important in American history. Even though we may not hear their names very often.

20. Two women who married into the family, Antoinette Brown and Lucy Stone, also fought for women's rights and battled against social injustices. Besides the impressive women born into the Blackwell family.

RUN-ON SENTENCES

When a comma (instead of a period, a semicolon, or a conjunction) is used between two complete sentences, the result is referred to as a "run-on sentence." One sentence is permitted to "run on" into the next. In high-school writing, this type of sentence error is more common than the fragment error. Usually it results from carelessness in punctuation rather than from lack of understanding. Because the error involves the misuse of a comma—to separate sentences—it is sometimes referred to as the "comma fault." A worse, but less common, kind of run-on sentence results from omitting all punctuation between sentences.

12c. Avoid the run-on sentence. Do not use a comma between sentences. Do not omit punctuation at the end of a sentence.

RUN-ON SENTENCE   The choice of a camera is difficult, there are many good ones on the market.

These two sentences should be either separated by a period or joined into one sentence by a conjunction or a semicolon. There are four ways of correcting the error:

1. The choice of a camera is difficult. There are many good ones on the market.
2. The choice of a camera is difficult, **for** there are many good ones on the market.
3. The choice of a camera is difficult **because** there are many good ones on the market.
4. The choice of a camera is difficult; there are many good ones on the market.

As you grow older and do more and more writing, you develop a "sentence sense," which is the ability to recognize at once whether a group of words is or is not a complete sentence. Reading your compositions aloud, so that your ears as well as your eyes can detect completeness, will help you find any run-on sentences in your own writing.

> ☞ NOTE Do not be surprised, after being warned against sentence fragments and run-on sentences, if you find them being used occasionally by writers in the best newspapers and magazines. Professional writers (who have a strong sentence sense, or they would not be professionals) do at times write fragments and use the comma between sentences, especially when the ideas in the sentences are closely related. Leave this use of the comma and the use of the fragment to the experienced judgment of the professional.

EXERCISE 2. Revising Run-on Sentences.   The items in this exercise are run-on sentences. Write after the proper number on your paper the final word in the first sentence in each item and follow it with the first few words of the second sentence. Indicate how you would eliminate the faulty comma. You may use a semicolon, a comma and conjunction, a period and a capital letter, or other appropriate punctuation. Do not be satisfied with using a period and a capital letter in every case; to make clear the relationship between ideas, some of the items should be corrected in other ways.

EXAMPLE 1. Flo didn't hear about the party until Thursday, she had to change
her plans.
   1. *Thursday; therefore, she had . . .*

1. In social studies this year we are studying about ways to solve our
major national problems, so far we have covered poverty, unemployment, inflation, and pollution.
2. We have a pet lovebird at home, its call is as harsh and shrill as the
screech of chalk on the chalkboard.
3. Lovebirds are comical creatures, they are always busy rearranging
objects in their cage.
4. Ynes Mexia, the botanical explorer, discovered rare tropical plants
on her expeditions to Mexico and South America, these discoveries
were of great value to science.
5. Juan took an art elective and discovered he had talent, now he
spends his afternoons in the art room.
6. At an advanced age she began to write the story of her colorful life,
at least she thought her life had been colorful.
7. The astounding scientific developments of one generation are
accepted commonplaces in the next generation, the computer and
the cassette recorder, for instance, are taken for granted by
everyone today.
8. A new club is being formed for the study of social behavior, instead
of just reading, students will do research and conduct interviews
outside the school.
9. A large suggestion box has been placed in the hall just outside the
principal's office, students can, by this means, express their pet
peeves about the school, names should not be signed to the
suggestions.
10. First try to do the assignment by yourself, if you can't do it, ask your
teacher for help.

**EXERCISE 3. Revising to Eliminate Sentence Fragments and
Run-on Sentences.**   The following exercise contains sentence fragments and run-on sentences. Prepare to explain to the class how you
would eliminate the sentence errors.

1. I have never known anyone who was a better worker than Paula.
Who always did her homework in half the time I took, she usually
had done it twice as well, too.

2. Concentration was the secret of her success. Although she undoubtedly had a keen mind.

3. I asked Paula to help me with my math once. When I was particularly desperate, I hadn't been getting good grades for several weeks.

4. She could do the problems easily, and she could explain them to me. So that I could understand them, anyway, I didn't ask her again.

5. Mr. Rehman urges all musicians to continue to study their instruments in high school. Because he knows that as they get busier and busier, many students stop taking lessons, sports and other activities cut in on their practice time.

6. A mammoth crane was brought here to lift into place the steel girders. Huge orange-colored beams that were easily set into place. Almost as though they were matchsticks.

7. The time when a radio station may broadcast is determined by its license, some stations must go off the air at sundown.

8. Everyone was asking me about Stacey. Where she was and what she was doing, wild rumors had been circulating.

9. The city's water supply has been threatened. Very little rain or snow having fallen during the past weeks.

10. I learned to like poetry when I read Kipling, his poems appealed to me. Because of their strong rhythm and their rhyme.

11. I have learned to recognize several kinds of customers. Especially the kind that likes to argue about the merchandise, when I see one of these coming, I duck out of sight.

12. Some teen-agers spend an allowance foolishly, they don't know the value of money. Until they have to work for it.

13. Women's colleges were established in America in the nineteenth century. During the Victorian period. When girls were considered frail flowers to be kept safe and separate.

14. Audiences appeared to enjoy the play, the reviews in the papers, however, were unfavorable.

15. A back-to-school night for parents convinced the taxpayers of the inadequacy of our building, consequently the bond issue for a new building was passed by a large vote. When it was presented later in the year.

CHAPTER 13

Coordination and Subordination

RELATIONSHIPS BETWEEN IDEAS IN A SENTENCE

COORDINATE IDEAS

When a sentence contains more than one idea, the ideas may be equal in rank or unequal in rank. Ideas that are equal in rank are *coordinate*. (*Co–* means "equal"; *–ordinate* means "ordered" or "ranked"; hence, *coordinate* means "of equal order or rank.")

COORDINATE IDEAS   Mrs. Carter is an architect, **and** Mrs. Murphy is a contractor.

We tried everything that we could think of, **but** nothing worked.

The writer of the preceding sentences considered the two ideas in each sentence of equal rank; he gave them equal emphasis by expressing them in independent clauses. The clauses are coordinate clauses.

Clear Relationship Between Coordinate Ideas

The relationship between coordinate ideas (equal in rank) is made clear by means of the word used to connect the two ideas. Different connectives may be used to express different relationships. The common kinds of relationship between coordinate clauses are *addition*, *contrast*, *choice*, and *result*.

Addition

The following connectives are used to indicate that what follows is supplementary to what precedes.

EXAMPLE   I wrote to her, **and** she wrote to me.

also	furthermore
and	likewise
besides	moreover
both . . . and	then

Contrast

The following connectives are used to introduce an idea that in some way conflicts or contrasts with what has gone before.

EXAMPLE   I wrote to her, **but** she did not write to me.

but	still
however	yet
nevertheless	

Choice

The following connectives are used to introduce an alternate possibility.

EXAMPLE   You write to her, **or** I will write to her.

either . . . or	or, nor
neither . . . nor	otherwise

Result

The following connectives are used to state a result or consequence of the preceding statement.

EXAMPLE   I wrote to her; **therefore,** she wrote to me.

accordingly	hence
consequently	therefore

13a. Make clear the relationship between the ideas in coordinate clauses by using connectives that express the relationship exactly.

A good writer chooses connectives carefully, making certain that the connectives chosen will express exactly the relationship intended between the ideas in the sentence. In order to avoid a monotonous style you should always use a variety of connectives.

If the wrong connective is used, the relationship between the ideas will not be clear. The connectives in the following *not-clear* sentences were poorly chosen.

NOT CLEAR Mrs. Bothwell took a long vacation, and her health did not improve.

CLEAR Mrs. Bothwell took a long vacation, **but** her health did not improve. [contrast]

NOT CLEAR The veterans spent a year in the hospital, but they emerged entirely well.

CLEAR The veterans spent a year in the hospital; **consequently,** they emerged entirely well. [result]

☞ **NOTE** When used to join coordinate clauses, the words *and, but, yet, or,* and *nor* are usually preceded by a comma.

When used to join coordinate clauses, the words *besides, likewise, furthermore, moreover, however, nevertheless, otherwise, consequently, therefore,* and *accordingly* are usually preceded by a semicolon.

EXERCISE 1. Using Appropriate Connectives. Number your paper 1–20. Read each sentence thoughtfully. Determine the logical relationship between the two clauses and write after the proper number on your paper what this relationship is: *addition, contrast, choice,* or *result.* Then write an appropriate connective selected from the lists above—the word which will make unmistakably clear the relationship between clauses. Use a variety of connectives. Give the correct punctuation mark with each connective.

EXAMPLE 1. The demand exceeded the supply   prices remained the same.
　　　　　1. *contrast ; nevertheless*

1. The students were dismissed at one o'clock   nobody went home.
2. Bea was seriously injured in yesterday's practice   she will not be able to play in the game today.
3. Jimmy played right end   I played left end on the varsity.
4. Deliver the shipment by Friday   I will cancel my order!
5. Math has always been my hardest subject   I have never failed a math test.
6. In an auditorium of this size, you must speak louder   your audience will not be able to hear you.

7. This magazine publishes the best literary criticism   it is a financial failure.

8. Some of the best TV courses are offered at 6:30 A.M.   they reach only a small audience of early-rising intellectuals.

9. The American economy has long depended on a high level of military spending   some people fear the economic consequences of ending the arms race.

10. The oil burner had stopped during the night   the house was cold when we awoke.

11. We had heard the assignment   we hadn't understood it.

12. We were to be marked for neatness   we took greater pains than usual.

13. We returned late; the rented canoe was a wreck   the lifeguard said she'd like to see us after swim period.

14. We thought we were not to blame   we braved her wrath and didn't say a word.

15. We had planned on going to town that afternoon   we were slightly annoyed at being kept in camp.

16. The head counselor warned us to take better care of the property of others   she said she would send our parents a bill.

17. The bill which my parents received was quite unexpected   it took them some time to recover from the shock.

18. Sue's parents also received a bill   they were just as surprised as my parents.

19. They were all amazed at the high price of canoes   they paid the bills promptly.

20. Parents can be put to a great deal of trouble and expense by their children   they are usually patient and generous with us.

SUBORDINATE IDEAS

When ideas in a sentence are unequal in rank, the ideas of lower rank are subordinate. (*Sub–* means "under" or "lower.") If the idea of lower rank is expressed in a clause, the clause is a *subordinate* clause.[1] The main idea of the sentence is expressed in an *independent* clause.

EXAMPLES   The pilot, who was a veteran flyer, brought her crippled plane down safely. [Independent clause—greater emphasis: *The pilot brought her crippled plane down safely*; subordinate clause—lesser emphasis: *who was a veteran flyer.*]

[1] For a more detailed explanation of subordinate clauses, see pages 69–80.

Because each of them was politically ambitious, the council members rarely supported one another's proposals. [Main clause —greater emphasis: *the council members rarely supported one another's proposals*; subordinate clause—lesser emphasis: *Because each of them was politically ambitious.*]

Adverb Clauses

13b. **Make clear the relationship between subordinate adverb clauses and independent clauses by selecting subordinating conjunctions which express the relationship exactly.**

The relationship between the idea in a subordinate adverb clause and the idea in an independent clause is made clear by the subordinating conjunction that introduces the subordinate clause. The common kinds of relationships between subordinate adverb clauses and independent clauses are *time, cause* or *reason, purpose* or *result,* and *condition.*

Some of the conjunctions can be used in more than one way and therefore appear in more than one list.

Time

The following subordinating conjunctions introduce clauses expressing a time relationship between the idea in the subordinate clause and the idea in the independent clause.

EXAMPLE   Several guests arrived **before** *we were ready.*

after	before	until	whenever
as	since	when	while

Cause or Reason

The following subordinating conjunctions introduce clauses expressing the cause or reason for the idea expressed in the independent clause. The subordinate clause tells *why.*

EXAMPLE   We stopped **because** *the light was red.*

as	since	because	whereas

Purpose or Result

The following subordinating conjunctions introduce clauses expressing the purpose of the idea in the independent clause or the result of the idea in the independent clause.

EXAMPLES   Astronauts undergo the most rigorous training **so that** *they will be able to handle any emergency.* [The subordinate clause states the purpose of training described in the independent clause.]

Extreme differences of opinion developed in the committee **so that** *agreement seemed unlikely.* [The subordinate clause states a result of the committee's differences of opinion.]

that   in order that   so that

Condition

The following subordinating conjunctions state the condition or conditions under which the idea in the independent clause is true. Think of *although, even though, though*, and *while* as meaning "in spite of the fact that." They introduce a condition in spite of which the idea in the independent clause is true.

EXAMPLES   **Although** (in spite of the fact that) *it was raining*, we went to the game. [The clause states the *condition* under which we went to the game.]

If *you pass the examination*, you will pass the course. [The clause states under what condition you will pass the course.]

| although | though | provided that | if |
| even though | while | unless | |

EXERCISE 2. Using Appropriate Subordinating Conjunctions.

Number your paper 1–20. From the preceding lists, choose a subordinating conjunction to fill the blank in each sentence and write it after the proper number on your paper. Make sure the conjunction you choose fits the meaning of the sentence. After the conjunction, write the relationship it expresses: *cause* or *reason, condition, purpose* or *result, time*.

1. —— you buy a rare manuscript, make certain of its authenticity.
2. You may be swindled —— you fail to do this.
3. —— it is the oldest of rackets, all sorts of con men continue to forge works of the great masters.
4. It seems to work again and again, —— there are enough gullible people in the market.
5. William Henry Ireland was one of the most successful forgers, —— he was only a teen-ager at the height of his exploits.
6. Ireland began forging Shakespeare manuscripts —— his father had a keen interest in them.

7. —— his first efforts were difficult, he continued his questionable work with zeal.

8. There seemed to be no sort of forgery beyond his reach —— he had the necessary equipment.

9. —— many scholars greeted his work with enthusiasm, others were less easily persuaded.

10. —— he forged a document, Ireland had to do careful research on the proper details such a document would require.

11. Nothing he forged could be shown to others —— the ink had long since dried.

12. Special blends of ink were required —— the age would be properly deceptive.

13. —— his motives and methods were questionable, his work possesses a certain unique attractiveness.

14. Ireland's father published a collection of his son's forgeries —— he considered his son to be worthy of complete confidence.

15. The skepticism of scholars increased enormously, —— it became impossible to answer their objections.

16. Ireland published a truthful confession —— the documents were agreed to be fraudulent and his father's health became endangered.

17. —— he tried to ease his father's disappointment, the older man died in disgrace at the height of the furor.

18. His ill health was hardly surprising, —— real disgrace is a difficult burden to bear.

19. —— a love letter with a lock of hair enclosed was his masterpiece, Ireland also forged leases, contracts, notes, poems, and whole plays.

20. —— Ireland himself died in 1835, the art of forgery obviously did not die with him.

EXERCISE 3. Using Appropriate Subordinating Conjunctions.

Number your paper 1–20. From the lists of subordinating conjunctions on pages 283–84, choose an appropriate subordinating conjunction to fill the blank in each sentence and write it after the proper number on your paper. Notice that when an adverb clause begins a sentence, it is followed by a comma.

1. —— peace was declared, the citizens of the small country rejoiced in the streets.
2. —— the proper preparations are made, the children will be ready for the hike.
3. —— the doctor was at home, we decided to pay her a visit.
4. —— the barometer fell, weather warnings were sent out.
5. —— we had eaten a delicious meal, we sat around the fireplace and told ghost stories.
6. —— she had not slept well the night before, Melissa did not run as well as her coach had expected.
7. We waited for the hurricane —— we had closed the windows and bolted the door.
8. The players started scrimmage —— the coach blew her whistle.
9. Many people take courses in painting —— they want to express their creativity.
10. You will solve this math problem —— you take one step at a time.
11. —— Van Gogh is now considered a great painter, his work was not appreciated in his lifetime.
12. You are welcome to stay here —— you wish.
13. I bandaged my cut —— it would not become infected.
14. —— you arrived so late, you will have to sit at the back of the auditorium.
15. —— I had ordered two pairs of gloves, the mail-order company sent me two pairs of pants instead.
16. You may register to vote —— you are a legal resident.
17. —— the defense attorney made her final plea, the prisoner sat stiffly in a chair.
18. The doctor administered the new antibiotic —— no further complication would arise.
19. Many people fail to enjoy music —— they do not know how to listen properly.
20. —— the soldiers reached the clearing, they made camp.

EXERCISE 4. Revising Sentences by Inserting Subordinate Adverb Clauses. Revise each of the following sentences by adding a subordinate clause at the beginning or at the end of each sentence. Vary your choice of subordinating conjunctions.

EXAMPLE   1. The fans filed out of the stadium.
          1. *After the game was over, the fans filed out of the stadium.*

1. The heat became unbearable.
2. We started jogging in the afternoons.
3. Arturo agreed to come with us.
4. Lauren began clapping enthusiastically.
5. You will not have enough time to finish the composition.

Adjective Clauses

The subordinate clauses in the preceding exercises are *adverb* clauses. Subordinate *adjective* clauses are especially helpful in making clear the relationship between sentence ideas because they permit a writer to emphasize one idea above another.[1] A writer may, for instance, wish to express the following ideas in one sentence: *Sacajawea acted as interpreter for explorers of the West. She was a Lemhi Indian.* To emphasize that Sacajawea acted as interpreter, the writer places this information in an independent clause and subordinates the other idea by placing it in an adjective clause.

Sacajawea, who was a Lemhi Indian, **acted as interpreter for explorers of the West**.

On the other hand, for a different purpose, the writer may wish to change emphasis from one of these ideas to the other. This can be done by reversing the positions of the ideas.

Sacajawea, who acted as interpreter for explorers of the West, **was a Lemhi Indian**.

13c. Make clear the relative emphasis to be given ideas in a complex sentence by placing the idea you wish to emphasize in the independent clause and by placing subordinate ideas in subordinate clauses.

EXERCISE 5. Revising Complex Sentences with Adjective Clauses. Change the emphasis in each of the following sentences by placing in the independent clause the idea that is now in the subordinate clause and by placing in the subordinate clause the idea that is now in the independent clause.

---

[1] Adjective clauses may begin with *who, whom, whose, which, that,* and *where*.

1. Z, which is a voiced palatal fricative, is the last letter of the English alphabet.
2. Dictionary listings, which end with words beginning with z, proceed alphabetically.
3. *Zeal*, which comes from an ancient Greek word meaning "jealousy," is one of the more familiar words found there.
4. *Zero*, which can mean a symbol, a mark on a scale, a temperature, a gunsight setting, a location in space, or nothing at all, is also a verb.
5. Applying zinc to something, which sounds rather complicated, is called "zincifying."
6. Zinjanthropus, who is having a complicated time just being a two-million-year-old fossilized forerunner of modern human beings, is nicknamed "Nutcracker Man."
7. The word *zodiac*, which comes from an old adjective meaning "having to do with animals," is much younger than Zinjanthropus.
8. Human beings, who are not regarded as edible themselves, are nevertheless quite zoophagous in that they eat other animals.
9. Animal lovers, who may not welcome the name, can be called *zoophiles*.
10. *Zymurgy*, which means "the chemistry of fermentation," results in good wine and ends at least one dictionary.

CORRECTING FAULTY COORDINATION

Faulty coordination occurs when two unequal ideas are placed in coordinate clauses as though they deserved equal emphasis.

FAULTY COORDINATION   The Governor was a native of Ohio, and she was elected for a third term. [ideas of unequal rank]

The two ideas in this sentence are vastly different. It is unlikely that a writer would wish to give them equal rank. The faulty coordination can be corrected by placing one of the ideas in a subordinate position. Which idea the writer puts in the subordinate clause will depend on the purpose.

FAULTY COORDINATION CORRECTED   **The Governor**, who was a native of Ohio, **was elected for a third term**.

or   **The Governor**, who was elected for a third term, **was a native of Ohio**.

13d. Faulty coordination may be corrected by placing ideas of lesser emphasis in a subordinate position. An idea may be given less emphasis by being expressed in a subordinate clause or a modifying phrase or an appositive.[1]

(1) Subordination may be accomplished by means of a subordinate clause.

FAULTY COORDINATION   The books are on the new-book shelf, and they may be borrowed for a week.

CORRECTED BY AN ADJECTIVE CLAUSE   The books **that are on the new-book shelf** may be borrowed for a week.

CORRECTED BY AN ADVERB CLAUSE   **If the books are on the new-book shelf**, they may be borrowed for a week.

EXERCISE 6. Revising Sentences by Correcting Faulty Co-ordination.   Clarify the relationship between ideas in the following examples of faulty coordination by placing one of the ideas in a subordinate clause, either an adverb clause or an adjective clause. Choose carefully the subordinating conjunctions which introduce your adverb clauses.

1. I am taking a course in bookkeeping this year, and I will have a better chance of getting an office job this summer.
2. The material is tan with thin red stripes, and it will be used to make slipcovers for a couch and a chair.
3. Mr. and Mrs. Davis have donated a hundred books to our school's library, and they own a large bookstore in town.
4. The answer had to be a whole number, and so I knew that my answer of 6.33 was wrong.
5. Columbia College was originally named King's College, and it was established by King George III of England.
6. Mosquitoes and gnats buzzed around our heads, and we still had an enjoyable picnic in the park.

[1] For the use of subordination in achieving sentence variety, see pages 341–44. For the use of subordination in correcting stringy sentences and choppy sentences, see pages 352–53.

7. The rain had soaked the playing field, and it did not let up until the next day.
8. I am going to play baseball this Saturday, and the infield is still wet.
9. Nora and I heard that a course in photography would be given in the spring, and we signed up for it.
10. Our school marching band will be performing in the statewide semifinals in the middle of October, and it has a hundred members.

(2) Subordination may be accomplished by means of a modifying phrase.

FAULTY COORDINATION   The house is at the end of the street, and it is very modern in design.

CORRECTED BY A MODIFYING PHRASE   The house **at the end of the street** is very modern in design.

(3) Subordination may be accomplished by means of an appositive.

An appositive is a word, with or without modifiers, which follows a noun or pronoun and helps to explain it.

FAULTY COORDINATION   Ms. Fitch is the manager of the store, and she is tall and handsome.

CORRECTED BY AN APPOSITIVE   Ms. Fitch, **the manager of the store**, is tall and handsome.

EXERCISE 7. Revising Sentences by Correcting Faulty Co-ordination.   Revise the following sentences by correcting the faulty coordination in the ways prescribed.

Revise by inserting a subordinate clause:

1. Next Monday is a legal holiday, and my boss expects me to report for work.
2. Bessie Smith sang the blues in the 1920's and 1930's, and she had a strong influence on many younger jazz singers.
3. The hurricane was first spotted in the Caribbean, and it was heading northwest toward the Gulf Coast.
4. The department store had shoes in my size at a greatly reduced price, and I bought two pairs.

5. I saw myself on the six o'clock news, and I called all my friends to tell them to watch.

Revise by inserting a modifying phrase:

6. The call was to abandon ship, and it came from the captain.
7. I need to find a recent magazine article, and it should be about the process of digital recording.
8. The woman was playing the accordion, and she had a repertoire of hundreds of folk songs.
9. Neal hit a line drive to left field, and it happened with two out and runners on first and third.
10. The bottle was of household ammonia, and it fell onto the kitchen floor and spilled.

Revise by inserting an appositive:

11. Mr. Miller is the custodian of our building, and he came to this country only three years ago.
12. The new ruler is a woman of great experience in government, and she should be able to reconcile the factions in the country.
13. The violin was an instrument with a beautiful tone, and it belonged to my grandfather.
14. This passenger plane is the fastest one in the world, and it will take you to Europe in record time.
15. Her new book is a volume of poetry, and it received very favorable reviews.

SUMMARY

1. Make clear the relationship between ideas in a sentence by using connectives that express the relationship exactly.
2. Correct faulty coordination by placing ideas of lesser emphasis in subordinate position. Use a subordinate clause or a modifying phrase or an appositive.

EXERCISE 8. Revising Sentences. The relationship between ideas in the following sentences is not clear: the conjunctions used are not exact, or the sentences contain faulty coordination. Revise the sentences. Some may be revised in more than one way.

1. The Bay Challenge Cup represents the highest achievement in sailing, and it was first put up for competition in 1903.
2. The principle that government employees shall not strike has been recently challenged, and it applies to both federal and state employees.
3. High-school graduates are better educated today than ever before, and they have a hard time finding jobs.
4. The final chapters of this book outline a constructive program dealing with the problem, and they are the most important.
5. Every business has several ambitious competitors, and no business can afford to stand still.
6. The new regulations call for the opening of school at 7:30 every morning, and they are unpopular with both students and teachers.
7. Mr. Greenberg was a high-school coach for many years, and he is now coaching college teams in Ohio.
8. Representatives came from more than fifty countries, and they met in the United Nations Building in New York City.
9. The title of the book was very interesting, and the book itself was very dull.
10. Because their principal crop was potatoes and the potato season was poor, the farmers managed to avoid going into debt.
11. Miss Lang had not directed many plays, and she knew how to manage an inexperienced cast.
12. Helen may go to Wellesley next year, and she may go to Barnard.
13. Carl has taken piano lessons for only three years, and he is already a good pianist.
14. Mr. Stark has never paid back the money he borrowed, and he wants me to lend him more.
15. We waited on the corner for an hour, and the bus didn't come.
16. The Commercial High School is a large stone building on Market Street, and it is attended by students from all over the city.
17. Stewart Harrison was a famous detective, and he could not solve the arsenic murder case.
18. Miss Armstrong has been selling advertising for many years, and she has been made advertising director of the *Herald*.

19. I am going to the airport to meet a friend, and she is coming from Chicago.

20. Professor Drake had been head of the chemistry department for twenty years, and she died yesterday.

CHAPTER 14

Clear Reference

PRONOUNS AND ANTECEDENTS

The meaning of a pronoun is clear only when you know what it refers to. The word to which a pronoun refers is its antecedent. For example, the sentence, "He was talking with them," has little meaning unless you know to whom the pronouns *he* and *them* refer. Similarly, the pronoun *it* is meaningless in the sentence, "It chased me all the way home," unless you know to what *it* refers—a dog or a monster, for example.

In the following sentences, arrows connect the pronouns and their antecedents.

I asked Mr. Jordan for the answer, but he didn't know it.

The Potters have a new sailboat on which they intend to cruise.

Handing George the coat, the salesclerk said, "Try this on for size."

14a. A pronoun must refer clearly to the right antecedent. Avoid *ambiguous* reference, *general* reference, and *weak* reference.

Charlie is always thinking about cars. *It* [*cars?*] is his only interest. [The antecedent cannot be substituted; the reference is faulty.]

One simple way of testing pronoun reference is to substitute the antecedent for the pronoun.

Charlie is always thinking about cars. *They* [*cars*] are his only interest. [The antecedent fits.]

AMBIGUOUS REFERENCE

(1) Avoid *ambiguous reference.* **Ambiguous reference occurs when a pronoun refers confusingly to two antecedents so that the reader does not know at once which antecedent is meant.**

AMBIGUOUS   The President appointed Senator Moore as chairman because he was convinced of the importance of the committee's work.

Here the pronoun *he* can refer to either the President or Senator Moore. The context in which such a sentence appears will ordinarily provide readers with the clues they need to identify the antecedent. Occasionally, however, the use of a pronoun that can refer to more than one antecedent causes momentary confusion. Such ambiguous reference can usually be avoided by rephrasing the sentence.

CLEAR   The President, convinced of the importance of the committee's work, appointed Senator Moore as chairman.

CLEAR   Because Senator Moore was convinced of the importance of the committee's work, the President appointed him as chairman.

Occasionally, the only way to avoid ambiguity is to replace the pronoun with the appropriate noun:

AMBIGUOUS   The partnership between Jones and Potter ended when he drew the firm's money from the bank and flew to Brazil.

CLEAR   The partnership between Jones and Potter ended when Jones drew the firm's money from the bank and flew to Brazil.

EXERCISE 1. Revising Sentences by Correcting Ambiguous Pronouns. Find the ambiguous pronoun in each of the following sentences. Make the sentence clear either by revising it or by replacing the pronoun with a noun.

1. As soon as the students had left the classrooms, the custodians cleaned them.
2. Fay was arguing with Jane, and she looked unhappy.
3. One of the passengers told the bus driver that she didn't know the route very well.

4. We unpacked our dishes from the barrels and then returned them to the moving company.
5. Right after the accountant sent in a report to the treasurer, she became very much alarmed.
6. Pilar noticed that the principal was smiling in an odd way as she came into the office.
7. Raise the viewfinder to your eye, turning it slowly to the right until it is focused.
8. Our job was to remove the labels from the old bottles and wash them.
9. Mrs. Miller did a beautiful chalk drawing of our cat and then sprayed it with fixative.
10. International good will is essential to successful international trade. It will help to make a peaceful world.

GENERAL REFERENCE

(2) Avoid *general reference.* **General reference occurs when a pronoun refers confusingly to a general idea that is only vaguely expressed.**

The pronouns *which, this, that,* and *it* are commonly used in a general way.

GENERAL   The boys wore ski boots to their classes which the principal disapproved of.

In this sentence the pronoun *which* refers to the general idea, *the wearing of ski boots to class;* however, the pronoun is so placed that it appears to refer to *classes.* The writer did not mean that the principal disapproved of the classes. The sentence can be corrected by revision.

CLEAR   The principal disapproved of **the boys' wearing** ski boots to their classes.

In the following example, the pronoun *this* does not have a clear antecedent.

GENERAL   The trip to town was strenuous. The car broke down; a tire blew out; and Father sat on the basket of eggs. This put us in a poor frame of mind.

The pronoun *this* should be replaced with a definite noun, making clear the reference to a number of misfortunes.

CLEAR   These **misfortunes** put us in a poor frame of mind.

In the next example, the pronoun *it* does not have a clear antecedent. A definite noun makes the meaning clear.

GENERAL   Great ships were moving slowly up the harbor; tugs and ferryboats scurried in and out among them; here and there a white cabin cruiser sliced sharply through the blue water under the suspension bridge. It was thrilling to a young farmer.

CLEAR   The **sight** was thrilling to a young farmer.

Although you can sometimes correct general reference by merely substituting a noun for the unclear pronoun, you will often find it necessary to revise the entire sentence.

GENERAL   In her act Maria told jokes, did impersonations, and sang comic songs. This amused her audience.

CLEAR   Maria amused her audience by telling jokes, doing impersonations, and singing comic songs.

EXERCISE 2. Revising Sentences by Correcting General References. The following sentences contain examples of general, or vague, reference of pronouns. Revise the sentences or replace the unclear pronouns with nouns.

1. The Chinese were bitter when Russia withdrew its technical assistance; they said it would harm the Chinese economy.
2. Macbeth's mind was constantly imagining horrible things, and that frightened him.
3. He is a conscientious, hard-working man with an engaging personality, but it doesn't make him any richer.
4. A number of people gathered around the speaker and her microphone, which was due to curiosity.
5. I enjoyed the author's style and the type of characters she wrote about. It made me want to read her other books.
6. Rabbi Meyer came to the house daily, from which a sturdy friendship grew.
7. A great deal of effort went into planning the expedition, hiring the right sort of men, and anticipating every emergency, which accounts for the success of the undertaking.
8. Chicago stretches along the shore of Lake Michigan, which makes a beautiful shore drive possible.
9. School gymnasiums will be open every Saturday during the winter, and school playgrounds will be supervised during the summer

months. Other school facilities, such as the shops and the little theater, will be available to hobbyists. This will cost money, but the board of education thinks the public will be glad to meet the expense.

10. Even students with season tickets had to pay admission to the postseason games. We thought it wasn't fair.

WEAK REFERENCE

(3) Avoid *weak reference.* **Weak reference occurs when the antecedent has not been expressed but exists only in the writer's mind.**

WEAK   We spent the day aboard a fishing boat, but we didn't catch a single one.

In this sentence there is no antecedent of the pronoun *one.* The adjective *fishing* is not the antecedent, since it is fish, not fishing, that *one* refers to. The writer meant the pronoun to stand for the noun *fish.*

CLEAR   We spent the day aboard a fishing boat, but we didn't catch a single **fish.**

CLEAR   We spent the day aboard a fishing boat trying to catch some **fish,** but we didn't catch a single **one.**

In other words, the antecedent of a pronoun should be a noun. When the antecedent is "hidden" in a modifier or a verb form, the reference is weak.

WEAK   The people want honest public servants, but that has not always been a virtue of politicians.

In this sentence the antecedent should be the noun *honesty,* but the noun is "hidden" in the adjective *honest.* Correct the sentence by replacing the weak pronoun with a noun.

CLEAR   The people want honest public servants, but **honesty** has not always been a virtue of politicians.

In the next sentence, the antecedent of *it* should be the noun *writing,* which is "hidden" in the verb *wrote.*

WEAK   Lois wrote whenever she could find the time, but none of it was ever published.

CLEAR   Lois wrote whenever she could find the time, but none of **her writing** was ever published.

In the next sentence the pronoun *they* does not have an antecedent. The writer had *witches* in mind as the antecedent, but the word does not appear at all.

WEAK   She is a great believer in witchcraft, but she doubts that they ride on broomsticks.

CLEAR   She is a great believer in **witches,** but she doubts that **they** ride on broomsticks.

CLEAR   She is a great believer in witchcraft, but she doubts that **witches** ride on broomsticks.

Correct weak references by replacing the weak pronoun with a noun or by giving the pronoun a clear antecedent.

EXERCISE 3. Revising Sentences by Correcting Weak References.

The following sentences contain examples of weak references. Revise the sentences by correcting the weak references.

1. I take many pictures with my camera and consider it an enjoyable hobby.
2. Before you start painting the house, be sure to stir it thoroughly.
3. Being neighborly is important because you may need their help someday in an emergency.
4. The salesperson in the television store showed us some that cost thousands of dollars.
5. She was a virtuoso violinist, but she never owned a valuable one.
6. After reading about the private detective's exciting adventures, I decided that I too would someday be one.
7. She is highly intelligent, but she hides it from people she doesn't know well.
8. I telephoned him all day, but it was always busy.
9. She knows many Nigerian legends but has never visited it.
10. Our guide said the Pueblo village was well worth seeing, but it would take three hours.

INDEFINITE USE OF PRONOUNS

14b. In writing, avoid indefinite use of the pronouns *it, they,* and *you.*

The indefinite use of these pronouns in sentences like the following ones occurs in ordinary conversation but is not acceptable in writing.

INDEFINITE   In the final chapter it implies that the hero died a martyr's death.
BETTER   **The final chapter** implies that the hero died a martyr's death.

INDEFINITE   On this flight to California, they serve meals without charge.
BETTER   On this flight to California, **meals** are served without charge.

INDEFINITE   In some countries, you don't dare express political views openly.
BETTER   In some countries, **the people** don't dare express political views openly.

> ☞ **NOTE**   The expressions *it is raining, it seems, it is late* are, of course, entirely correct.

EXERCISE 4. **Revising Sentences by Correcting Faulty References.**   The sentences in this exercise contain examples of ambiguous, general, and weak reference. There are some examples of the indefinite use of *it, they,* and *you.* Revise the sentences either by replacing a faulty pronoun with a noun, or by revising the entire sentence. Make the meaning unmistakably clear.

1. Western farmers today can produce more because of machines and the many people working under them.
2. Nancy rode home from school with Suzie, but she didn't tell her anything.
3. We had a long assignment, an inadequate library, and insufficient time, which was very frustrating.
4. Golf wouldn't cost me so much if I didn't lose so many in the rough.
5. The radiator was leaking badly; it ran all over the garage floor.
6. In the cabin he checked the fuel. In those days this might mean the difference between life and death.
7. She overcame her hip injury which doctors had said was impossible.
8. Her spelling and sentence structure are not good, but most of it is due to carelessness.
9. Ruth saw Julie when she was in town last week.
10. In yesterday's editorial, it says the mayor has failed to live up to his campaign promises.

11. We talked with the other passengers as though we had had years of flying experience, but we had never been up in one before.
12. If the prospective buyer learns that the heating system in the house is unsatisfactory, he had better not buy it.
13. The witness testified that she had seen the accused when she was eating dinner in the dining car, which convinced the jury of her presence on the train.
14. The library does not have enough copies of some of the books in greatest demand by students writing research papers; which makes it hard for you.
15. In Washington they are skeptical about the success of the new farm program.

CHAPTER 15

Placement of Modifiers

MISPLACED AND DANGLING MODIFIERS

A sentence may be confusing for one of two quite different reasons. It may be confusing because the ideas, although clearly stated, are hard to understand. This kind of sentence does not represent faulty writing. But a sentence may also be confusing because of the clumsiness of the writer in arranging the modifiers in the sentence. A modifier should clarify or make more definite the meaning of the word it modifies. If the modifier is placed too far from this word, the effect of the modifier may be either lost or diverted to some other word.

MISPLACED MODIFIERS

15a. Place phrase and clause modifiers as near as possible to the words they modify.

A misplaced modifier may force the reader to reread the sentence in order to be sure of what it says. Sentences like the following examples may be clear on first reading; on the other hand, because of a misplaced word or group of words, they may mislead the reader or force a second look.

CONFUSING   Two meetings have been held to make arrangements for a return bout in the office of the State Athletic Commission.

Although most readers know that the return bout is not likely to be held *in the office of the State Athletic Commission,* they may be momentarily distracted by this interesting thought. Placing the phrase next to *held,* the word it modifies, makes the sentence clear.

CLEAR Two meetings have been held in the office of the State Athletic Commission to make arrangements for a return bout.

CONFUSING I bought a small computer for the accounting staff, which gave everyone a great deal of trouble.

The reader of this sentence will probably assume that the computer, not the staff, gave everyone trouble. Nevertheless, the clause *which gave everyone a great deal of trouble* should be next to *computer,* which it modifies.

CLEAR I bought the accounting staff a small computer, which gave everyone a great deal of trouble.

CONFUSING The thief decided to make a run for it when he saw the police officer, abandoning the stolen car and dashing into the woods.

This sentence would be clearer if, on first reading, it did not give the impression that the police officer was abandoning the stolen car and dashing into the woods. Moving the adverb clause *when he saw the police officer* to the beginning of the sentence makes it clear that the thief, not the police officer, ran away.

CLEAR When he saw the police officer, the thief decided to make a run for it, abandoning the stolen car and dashing into the woods.

The usual way to clarify a sentence containing a misplaced modifier is to move the modifier next to the word it modifies. Some sentences, however, cannot be clarified so easily. In the sentence above, for example, moving the participial phrases next to *thief,* the word they modify, changes the meaning of the sentence: *The thief, abandoning the car and dashing into the woods, decided to make a run for it when he saw the police officer.*

Often, you can improve a sentence by moving an adverbial modifier (in this instance *when he saw the police officer*) to the beginning of the sentence. Indeed, regardless of how it may fit elsewhere in the sentence, an adverbial modifier is often better placed at the beginning.

The point of this discussion of the placement of modifiers is that you recognize the importance of making yourself clear at first reading. Do not try to hide behind the weak explanation, "You know what I mean."

EXERCISE 1. Revising Sentences by Correcting Misplaced Modifiers. The following sentences may be confusing on first reading because of a misplaced phrase or clause. Revise the sentences by placing modifiers near the words they modify. You may find that placing an adverbial modifier first often improves the sentence. Doing the exercise orally in class will save time.

1. The students deserved the severe reprimand they received for their misbehavior in the cafeteria in the principal's office on Monday.
2. Commander Richardson was decorated for his action, but he was haunted by the memory of the men he had had to sacrifice for years after.
3. The company now runs a late bus for skiers leaving at 6:15.
4. The big schooner was steered through the channel by a daring skipper without running lights or motor about midnight.
5. One of our observers sighted a plane through binoculars that she could not identify.
6. The minister announced that next Sunday's sermon would be an explanation of the nature of sin, in which he hoped the congregation would take great interest.
7. The causeway has a drawbridge to permit the passage of fishing boats from which all fishing is prohibited.
8. The mystery has been solved after ten years of the missing portrait.
9. The community center was built by Mrs. Borden, who later became Mrs. Gruber, at a cost of $800,000.
10. The suspect tried to make the police believe that he had found the wallet in his car that didn't belong to him.
11. Detectives narrowed down the number of the houses where the robbers might strike by deduction.
12. Myra almost made the mistake one afternoon of running and diving when the pool was empty into the deep end.
13. I'll check the manuscript when you finish for accuracy.
14. He worked hard in his fields, raising crops that would bring in money without complaint.
15. At Tuesday's meeting, the mayor discussed the enormous cost of filling in the Buskill Swamp with city council members.
16. If what the directions say is true, this is a powerful insecticide on the package.

17. Father bought a gadget for his new car from a fast-talking salesclerk that was guaranteed to reduce gas consumption.
18. She wore a straw hat on the back of her head which was obviously too small.
19. Ms. Steinberg, the explorer, described her trips through the jungle in our social studies class.
20. Uncle Jim bought a new carriage for the baby that was named "Boodle Buggy."

DANGLING MODIFIERS

15b. A modifying phrase or clause must clearly and sensibly modify a word in the sentence. When there is no word that the phrase or clause can sensibly modify, the modifier is said to dangle.

DANGLING MODIFIER   Carrying a heavy pile of books, her foot caught on the step.

An introductory participial phrase modifies the noun or pronoun following it. In this example, the phrase *carrying a heavy pile of books* appears to modify *foot*. Since a foot could not carry a pile of books, the phrase cannot modify it sensibly. In fact, there is no word in this sentence that can be sensibly modified by the introductory phrase. The phrase, therefore, is a dangling modifier. The sentence may be corrected in two ways:

1. By adding a word that the phrase can sensibly modify.

   Carrying a heavy pile of books, **she** caught her foot on the step.

2. By changing the phrase to an adverb clause.

   While she was carrying a heavy pile of books, her foot caught on the step.

   Study the following examples of dangling modifiers and the ways in which they have been corrected.

DANGLING MODIFIER   Representing the conservative point of view, the liberals rebutted her.

CORRECTED   Representing the conservative point of view, she was rebutted by the liberals.

CORRECTED   Since she represented the conservative point of view, the liberals rebutted her.

DANGLING MODIFIER   After standing up well under the two-year exposure test, the manufacturers were convinced that the paint was sufficiently durable.

CORRECTED   After the paint had stood up well under the two-year exposure test, the manufacturers were convinced that it was sufficiently durable.

DANGLING MODIFIER   To win the baseball championship this year, Luis and Oscar should join our team.

CORRECTED   If we are to win the baseball championship this year, Luis and Oscar should join our team.

CORRECTED   To win the baseball championship this year, we should get Luis and Oscar to join our team.

It is only fair to point out that examples of dangling modifiers may sometimes be found in the works of the best authors. These examples, however, are either so idiomatic as to be entirely acceptable, or they are so clear that no possible confusion can result. The following examples are not objectionable:

> Relatively speaking, the cost of living has remained static for several years. To be perfectly frank, the rate of inflation is still too high.

It is important, however, that you realize the absurd meanings into which danglers can lead you so that you will avoid them in your own writing.

EXERCISE 2. **Revising Sentences by Correcting Dangling Modifiers.** Each of the following sentences contains a dangling modifier. Revise the sentences by correcting the danglers.

1. Coming up the front walk, the bouquet in the picture window looked beautiful.
2. Left alone in the house, the thunderstorm terrified him.
3. Enormous and architecturally striking, everyone is impressed by the new building.
4. When selecting a college, the social life seems to interest some students more than education.
5. After considering the proposal for several hours, it was rejected by the council.
6. While talking with friends, the topic of dentistry came up.

7. After spending Saturday morning working in the library, a feeling of righteousness possessed me.

8. After flying in darkness for two hours, the moon rose, and navigation became less difficult.

9. To keep the guacamole dip from turning brown, its surface should be covered with a thin layer of mayonnaise.

10. Living in this coastal town for many years, the fishing boats and their skippers were well known to him.

11. After working in the fields all day, little strength was left for social activities.

12. When only a youngster in grade school, my father instructed me in the art of boxing.

13. Yielding to the temptation to look at a classmate's paper, the proctor caught them cheating.

14. While working in California, her family was living in New York.

15. To understand many of the allusions in modern literature, a knowledge of Greek and Roman myths is essential.

16. Having promised to be home by midnight, the family was annoyed when I came in at two o'clock.

17. While playing in the highchair, I was afraid the baby would fall out.

18. Riding in the glass-bottomed boat, hundreds of beautiful tropical fish could be seen.

19. Being very shy, strangers frighten my little sister.

20. After being wheeled into the operating room, a nurse placed a mask over my nose.

TWO–WAY MODIFIERS

A third way in which a careless writer sometimes causes confusion is by placing a modifier in such a way that it may be taken to modify two words. As a result, the reader cannot be sure which of the two possible meanings is intended. Such a modifier is called a *two-way*, or a *squinting*, modifier.

EXAMPLE   Mary said *during the meeting* Jo acted like a fool.

Since the phrase *during the meeting* may be taken to modify either *said* or *acted,* this sentence is not clear. Did Mary say this during the meeting, or did Jo act like a fool during the meeting? The sentence should be revised to make it say one thing or the other.

CLEAR   **During the meeting** Mary said Jo acted like a fool.

CLEAR   Mary said Jo acted like a fool **during the meeting**.

Study the following examples of two-way modifiers:

NOT CLEAR   Mrs. Stewart asked us *before we left* to call on her.

CLEAR   **Before we left,** Mrs. Stewart asked us to call on her.

CLEAR   Mrs. Stewart asked us to call on her **before we left**.

NOT CLEAR   Tell Fred *when he comes home* I want to see him.

CLEAR   **When he comes home,** tell Fred I want to see him.

CLEAR   Tell Fred I want to see him **when he comes home**.

EXERCISE 3. Revising Sentences by Correcting Faulty Modifiers.
The sentences in this exercise contain misplaced, dangling, and squinting modifiers. Revise each sentence so that its meaning will be clear on first reading.

1. The Simpsons gave a toy robot to one of their children with a bullet-shaped glass head and flashing red eyes.
2. Pounding the piano keys with all her might, the chords of the prelude resounded through the concert hall.
3. The waiter brought us ice cream in glass bowls, which started melting almost immediately.
4. We saw a herd of sheep on the way to our hotel.
5. To succeed in college, a great deal of time must be spent studying.
6. When only five years old, my father took me to see my first baseball game.
7. Topped with yogurt, many people love fresh strawberries for dessert.
8. While trying to get ready for school, the doorbell suddenly rang.
9. Elaine told Joanne after the first act the drama gets more exciting.
10. By practicing a foreign language daily, great fluency can be gained.
11. While watching the football game, Sue's horse ran away.
12. A tarantula was shown to me by the museum's curator that had eight legs and a huge, hairy body.

13. Preferring the mountains to the seashore, the Great Smokies were chosen as our vacation spot.
14. After working in Washington for twenty years, the methods of lobbyists were familiar.
15. This bank approves loans to reliable individuals of any size.
16. Did you know when you were in Chicago I was living in Highland Park?
17. While tuning the radio, the car swerved dangerously toward a telephone pole.
18. Being completely untamed, Anita warned us that the animals were dangerous.
19. One can see more than a hundred lakes, flying at an altitude of several thousand feet.
20. Jack bought a book of shorthand lessons along with his new typewriter, which he read and studied diligently.
21. Living constantly under the eyes of the police, her nervousness increased.
22. Plans for a new road have finally been approved after three years of red tape to stretch across the valley.
23. Ramón wanted to know before the game began what the referees said to the two captains.
24. Believing that freedom was more important than security, homes, relatives, and countries were abandoned by these emigrants.
25. Rounding a sharp curve, a detour sign warned us of danger.

CHAPTER 16

Parallel Structure

STRUCTURES OF EQUAL RANK; FAULTY PARALLELISM

Parallelism in sentence structure exists when two or more sentence elements of equal rank are similarly expressed. Stating equal and closely related ideas in parallel constructions often adds clarity and smoothness to writing.

KINDS OF PARALLEL STRUCTURE

16a. Express parallel ideas in the same grammatical form.

There are three sentence elements that commonly require parallel treatment: coordinate ideas, compared and contrasted ideas, and correlative constructions. A sentence reads smoothly when the writer has taken the trouble to put parallel ideas in the same form.

Coordinate Ideas

Coordinate ideas are equal in rank. They are joined by coordinate connectives. The coordinate connectives most often used in parallel structure are *and, but, or,* and *nor.*

To express parallel ideas in the same grammatical form, pair one part of speech with the same part of speech, a verbal with the same kind of verbal, a phrase with a phrase, a clause with a clause. Do not pair unlike grammatical forms.

FAULTY   The committee studied all aspects of the problem—humane, political, and cost. [The adjectives *humane* and *political* are paired with the noun *cost*.]

PARALLEL   The committee studied all aspects of the problem—**humane, political,** and **financial.** [All three coordinate elements are adjectives.]

FAULTY   The math exam tested our knowledge of exponential functions, the quadratic formula, and solving linear equations. [two nouns paired with a phrase]

PARALLEL   The math exam tested our knowledge of exponential **functions,** the quadratic **formula,** and linear **equations.** [three nouns]

FAULTY   According to my teacher, my composition revealed exceptional creative ability but that I make too many spelling errors. [noun paired with clause]

PARALLEL   According to my teacher, my composition revealed exceptional creative **ability** but too many spelling **errors.** [noun paired with noun]

PARALLEL   According to my teacher, my composition revealed **that I have exceptional creative ability** but **that I make too many spelling errors.** [clause paired with clause]

Compared or Contrasted Ideas

FAULTY   Water-skiing no longer interests me as much as to go scuba diving. [gerund *water-skiing* paired with infinitive *to go*]

PARALLEL   **Water-skiing** no longer interests me as much as **scuba diving.** [gerund paired with gerund]

PARALLEL   **To water-ski** no longer interests me as much as **to scuba dive.** [infinitive paired with infinitive]

FAULTY   Her novel was praised more for its style than for what it had to say. [noun paired with clause]

PARALLEL   Her novel was praised more for its **style** than for its **ideas.** [noun paired with noun]

Correlative Constructions

Correlative constructions are formed with the correlative conjunctions *both . . . and, either . . . or, neither . . . nor, not only . . . but (also).*

FAULTY   At the gate they tried both persuasion and to force their way in. [noun paired with infinitive]

PARALLEL   At the gate they tried both **persuasion** and **force.** [noun paired with noun]

FAULTY The new clerk soon proved herself to be not only capable but also a woman who could be trusted. [adjective paired with noun]

PARALLEL The new clerk soon proved herself to be not only **capable** but also **trustworthy**. [adjective paired with adjective]

COMPLETED PARALLELISM

16b. **Place correlative conjunctions immediately before the parallel terms.**

NONSTANDARD Mrs. Sayers is not only president of the National Bank but also of the Chamber of Commerce. [*Not only . . . but also* should precede the parallel terms *of the National Bank* and *of the Chamber of Commerce*, not the word *president.*]

STANDARD Mrs. Sayers is president **not only** of the National Bank **but also** of the Chamber of Commerce.

NONSTANDARD The team both felt the satisfaction of victory and the disappointment of defeat.

STANDARD The team felt **both** the satisfaction of victory **and** the disappointment of defeat.

16c. **In parallel constructions repeat an article, a preposition, or a pronoun whenever necessary to make the meaning clear.**

Note that the omission or inclusion of a word in the paired sentences below changes the meaning.

Before the meeting I talked with the secretary and treasurer. [The sentence may mean that I talked with one person who holds the double office of secretary and treasurer.]
Before the meeting I talked with the secretary and **the** treasurer. [This sentence indicates that I talked with two persons.]

The weather was a greater handicap to the invading army than their enemy. [This sentence means that the invaders would rather fight the enemy than the weather.]
The weather was a greater handicap to the invading army than **to** their enemy. [This sentence means that the invaders had the harder job.]

We feel certain that she is capable, she will succeed, and you will be proud of her. [In a series of parallel *that* clauses, the meaning is usually clearer if the introductory word is repeated in each clause. Omission of the introductory *that* from the clauses may give the impression that this is a run-on sentence, the first sentence ending with *capable.*]

We feel certain **that** she is capable, **that** she will succeed, and **that** you will be proud of her.

EXERCISE 1. Revising Sentences by Correcting Faulty Parallelism. Revise the following sentences by putting parallel ideas into the same grammatical form. Correct any errors in the placement of correlatives and in the omission of a necessary article, preposition, or pronoun.

1. Its large size, simple structure, and how readily available it is, make the common cockroach convenient to study.
2. Cockroaches have smooth, leathery skin; long, thin antennae; and they have a body that is thick and flat.
3. They are not only found in urban areas but also in the tropics.
4. The Oriental cockroach is short-winged, while cockroaches from America have full wings.
5. North America boasts about sixty species, but only two in Great Britain.
6. Cockroaches may be dark brown, pale brown, or of a green color that is delicate.
7. Cockroach eggs are laid in small cases, carried on the female body, and then they deposit them in hidden crevices.
8. A typical cockroach lives as a nymph for about a year, and as an adult its life lasts about half a year.
9. The odors that attract cockroaches are sweet, but they emit disagreeable odors.
10. Cockroaches will eat anything, but they especially like sweet foods and foods that are starchy.
11. What a cockroach soils is far more than it consumes.
12. By day the average cockroach is quietly lazy, but busily energetic describes how it is by night.
13. We might not only view the cockroach with disgust but also interest.
14. The cockroach both is the most primitive living winged insect and the most ancient fossil insect.
15. We have as much to learn from the cockroach's evolution as there is to gain from extinguishing it.

16d. Include in the second part of a parallel construction all words necessary to make the construction complete.

Occasionally in your haste you may fail to include in one part of a parallel construction all the words necessary to make the construction complete.

INCOMPLETE   Linda always chose topics that were more difficult than the other students.

COMPLETE   Linda always chose topics that were more difficult than **those of** the other students.

In the first of these sentences you feel that something has been omitted because the sentence compares *topics* with *students*.

EXERCISE 2. Revising Sentences by Using Correct Parallelism.
Correct the parallelism in each of the following sentences by inserting the words that have been omitted.

1. Ms. Connor's lectures are easier to comprehend than Ms. Moore.
2. She is busy the entire day, since she gives half of each day to her work and to team practice.
3. A modern director's interpretation of *Hamlet* is very different from a nineteenth-century director.
4. A dog's ability to hear high-pitched sounds is much keener than humans.
5. How do your grades in English compare with science?
6. New cars this year are smaller than last year.
7. The biographical information in the encyclopedia is more detailed than the dictionary.
8. People have been more interested in reading the book than the movie version.
9. The view from the World Trade Center is even more spectacular than the Empire State Building.
10. The rate of interest paid by the Amalgamated Bank is higher than the Security Bank.
11. Radio reception on the top floor is usually clearer than the ground floor.
12. The strength in my left hand is greater than my right hand.
13. Some birds like to eat fruit as much as insects.
14. The damage caused by this year's natural disasters is greater than last year's.
15. For the past month the price of gold has risen more sharply than silver.

EXERCISE 3. Revising Sentences by Correcting Faulty Parallelism.
The following sentences contain faulty parallelism. Rephrase the sentences so that the parallelism will be correctly and logically expressed.

1. One of the accident victims suffered a broken arm, several broken ribs, and one of her lungs was punctured.
2. She not only was industrious, but she could be depended on.
3. As we were leaving the harbor, the radio weather report predicted gale-force winds, heavy rain, and that tides would be abnormally high.
4. A cloudy day is better for a game than sunshine.
5. She spoke about her experience in Australia and several predictions about the country's future.
6. To the unthinking person, war may be a romantic adventure, but a foolish and dirty business is the way the wise person regards it.
7. The unexpected cooperation of China was a greater surprise to Russia than the United States.
8. The skipper had a harsh voice, a weatherbeaten face, and was very stocky in build.
9. We were not sure that our request for a raise was fair or it would be granted.
10. The speech of cultivated Britishers is not so different as it used to be from Americans.
11. The public's attention has been centered on the need for more teachers, adequate classrooms, and there isn't enough new equipment.
12. This was a much harder assignment for me than Luis.
13. The ambassador did not know whether the President had sent for him or the Secretary of State.
14. Her friends not only were shocked by her failure but they felt a great disappointment.
15. The players were annoyed not so much by the decisions of the officials as the hostile crowd.
16. The company announced a bonus for all five-year employees and that deserving new employees would be given additional benefits.
17. The headmaster insisted that all of us return by ten o'clock and the housemasters must check us in.
18. High-school programs have been accused of being too closely tied in with college education and that they neglect the average teen-ager.
19. Pioneers came with hopes of being happy and free and to make their fortunes in the new world.
20. All delegates to the convention were advised that on their return they would both have to make a written and oral report.

CHAPTER 17

Unnecessary Shifts in Sentences

AWKWARD CHANGES IN SUBJECT AND VERB FORMS

Within a sentence a shift is a change from one subject to another or from one verb to another. Often shifts are acceptable because they are necessary to express the meaning the writer intends.

ACCEPTABLE SHIFT   The trials of peace are great, but the dangers of war are greater. [The shift in subject from *trials* to *dangers* is a natural one.]

The smoothness of a sentence is sometimes seriously affected, however, by an unnecessary and awkward shift.

AWKWARD   A student should choose books from the reading list so that you can be sure of their being acceptable to the teacher. [The unnecessary shift from *student* to *you* is awkward and confusing.]
ACCEPTABLE   A **student** should choose books from the reading list so that **he or she** can be sure of their being acceptable to the teacher.
AWKWARD   Pam did her math homework, and then her composition was written. [The shift from active to passive voice and the resulting shift in subject is unnecessary and awkward.]
ACCEPTABLE   Pam **did** her math homework, and then she **wrote** her composition.

17a. Avoid unnecessary shifts from one subject to another.

UNNECESSARY SHIFTS
   Fishers from many states visit the Ontario lake where *fish* are found in abundance and, in the cool, crisp air of the North woods, a welcome *relief* from summer heat is enjoyed. *Planes, trains,* or *automobiles* bring the

316

fishers to the edge of the wilderness. From there *boats* are used to penetrate the remoter waters where *trout, bass, pickerel, perch,* and freshwater *salmon* are caught.

SHIFTS AVOIDED

Fishers from many states visit the Ontario lakes where *they* find fish in abundance and, in the cool, crisp air of the North woods, enjoy a welcome relief from summer heat. After coming by plane, train, or automobile to the edge of the wilderness, the *fishers* use boats to penetrate the remoter waters, where *they* catch trout, bass, pickerel, perch, and freshwater salmon.

17b. Avoid unnecessary shifts from one verb form to another within one sentence.

(1) Avoid unnecessary shifts in the voice of verbs.

Unnecessary shifts from one subject to another are often the result of a shift from active to passive voice.

When the subject of a verb is acting, the verb is in the *active voice.* When the subject of a verb is acted upon, the verb is in the *passive voice.*[1]

S⟶V

ꓽIVE VOICE   Jane **won** both events. [subject acting]

S⟵V

PASSIVE VOICE   Both events **were won** by Jane. [subject acted upon]

Note that a shift in voice results in a shift in subject.

UNNECESSARY SHIFT   Volunteers made [active verb] the dangerous journey after dark, but no wolves were encountered [passive verb].

SHIFT AVOIDED   Volunteers **made** [active verb] the dangerous journey after dark but **encountered** [active verb] no wolves.

UNNECESSARY SHIFT   Since she knew the ability to speak well before a group is important, a course in public speaking was taken by her.

SHIFT AVOIDED   Since **she knew** the ability to speak well before a group is important, **she took** a course in public speaking.

(2) Avoid unnecessary shifts in the tense of verbs.

Changing without reason from one tense to another within a sentence creates an awkward and confusing effect. Stick to the tense you start with unless there is an excellent reason for changing.

---

[1] A fuller treatment of voice will be found on pages 209–12.

UNNECESSARY SHIFT   At this point the President reads [present tense] a prepared statement but refused [past tense] to answer any questions.

SHIFT AVOIDED   At this point the President **read** [past tense] a prepared statement but **refused** [past tense] to answer any questions.

SHIFT AVOIDED   At this point the President **reads** [present tense] a prepared statement but **refuses** [present tense] to answer any questions.

UNNECESSARY SHIFT   She caught [past tense] the puck and weaves [present tense] between two defenders.

SHIFT AVOIDED   She **caught** [past tense] the puck and **wove** [past tense] between two defenders.

SHIFT AVOIDED   She **catches** [present tense] the puck and **weaves** [present tense] between two defenders.

In correcting unnecessary shifts in subject and verb, you will often find the best method is to omit the second subject. This can usually be done by using the second verb in the same voice as the first and making the verb compound.

UNNECESSARY SHIFT   A good driver has complete control of the car at all times, and allowance is made for the carelessness of other drivers.

SHIFT AVOIDED   A good **driver has** complete control of the car at all times **and makes** allowances for the carelessness of other drivers. [The use of the compound active voice for both verbs corrects the awkward shift.]

EXERCISE 1. Revising Sentences to Eliminate Unnecessary Shifts in the Subject and in the Verb.

Most of the following sentences contain unnecessary shifts from one subject to another or from one verb form to another. By revising these sentences orally in class, show how these shifts may be avoided. Two of the sentences are acceptable. Identify them.

1. If one wants to try a delicious recipe from Puerto Rico, you should make rice with pigeon peas.
2. To start, sauté three tablespoons of diced salt pork until the fat has melted.
3. A chopped onion and two minced cloves of garlic should be added to the skillet, and then add two chopped green peppers.
4. After you have peeled two tomatoes, chopping them comes next.
5. The tomatoes, too, should be placed into the skillet, and you should cook the entire mixture for five minutes.
6. A tablespoon of capers goes in next, and you should follow this with a teaspoon of salt, two cups of uncooked long-grain rice, and three cups of water.

7. After you stir the rice, a pound of cooked pigeon peas needs to be added.
8. A tablespoon of achiote should not be forgotten to be included, since this spice imparts a lovely golden color to the food.
9. When the liquid comes to a boil, cover the skillet, the flame should be reduced, and simmer the mixture until the water has been absorbed.
10. Stir the mixture occasionally to keep the rice from sticking, and continue cooking until the rice is dry and fluffy.

EXERCISE 2. Revising Sentences to Eliminate Unnecessary Shifts in Tense. In the following passage the tense of the verbs is frequently shifted from past to present and from present to past. Decide in what tense (past or present) it should be written. Prepare to read aloud in class, changing the verb forms to remove the unnecessary shifts in tense.

1   Mr. Sampson, who had been for ten years the faculty adviser of
2 the high-school annual, sat calmly at his desk after school, watching
3 the autumn sun light the empty room, while he waited for the first
4 meeting of the new yearbook staff. A veteran like Mr. Sampson
5 could hardly be expected to show much emotion over the repetition
6 of an event he had taken part in so many times. He is not
7 particularly disturbed when the door opens and Jane Billings led a
8 noisy group of students into his room.
9   Following a general falling over desks and slumping into seats,
10 Jane called the meeting to order. This year, she explains, the staff
11 would produce the finest yearbook East High has ever had.
12 Someone wanted to know, first of all, what kind of cover the book
13 would have. A great preference is expressed for a thick and heavy
14 leather cover, suitably embossed, and bearing the seal and colors of
15 the school. Mr. Sampson smiles, for he had never yet known a new
16 staff that did not begin with a discussion of the cover.
17   Complete agreement about the cover having been so quickly
18 reached, Sue Thompson wants to know why last year's book was so
19 dull. Here Mr. Sampson smiles again. Everything's going to be just
20 fine, he thought, remembering that no staff in the past had ever had
21 a good word to say for its predecessors. "Let's have twice as many
22 pictures, a bigger sports section, not so much writing that nobody
23 ever reads." These weighty matters agreed upon, everyone wanted

24 to know whether the seniors aren't entitled to more space in the
25 book. "How about three or four instead of ten senior pictures to a
26 page? After all, it's our book."
27   Mr. Sampson listened and said nothing. He is quietly thinking
28 about next January, when the supply of snapshots will be disap-
29 pointingly small, when the budget will be alarmingly inadequate,
30 when compromise after compromise will be frantically made in
31 order to get a yearbook out at all. But he doesn't say much. He
32 knows it is better for the staff to find out for itself why last year's
33 book and all the books before it had been such complete "failures."

**EXERCISE 3. Revising Sentences to Eliminate Shifts in the
Subject and in the Verb.**   The sentences in this exercise are awkward because of unnecessary shifts in the subject and in the verb. Revise
the sentences to eliminate these shifts.

1. Adolescents naturally rebel against authority, but the authority of
   the law must be respected by them.
2. Lonely students might participate in an extracurricular activity so
   that new friendships can be made.
3. A senior must not only pass all courses and graduate, but also plans
   for your future must be made before the year is over.
4. My brother frequently procrastinates, and a tendency toward
   laziness is occasionally shown.
5. My father has some amusing peculiarities which are not recognized
   by him.
6. The union's demands were unacceptable even though some concessions were contained in them.
7. If a teacher wants to be liked, you must treat students impartially.
8. Coach Martin always insisted on long practice sessions and strict
   training, but her winning teams justify her methods.
9. The Vice-President flew to the Paris Conference, but few concrete
   results were accomplished by him.
10. A good student can win a college scholarship, and thus parents are
    relieved of part of the cost of a college education.
11. When you buy a car, a person should be sure he can afford the
    upkeep.
12. In the end Robert stays with his mother, and the girl he loves is lost
    to him forever.

13. The cement and sand are first mixed thoroughly; then add the water.
14. The experienced boat operator is aware of the danger of fire, and when filling the gas tank, great precautions are taken not to spill gasoline in the bottom of the boat.
15. As a young district attorney he handled the Tammany Hall case, and the backing of the Republican Party was won.
16. As the bus careens toward the edge of the road, we thought our time had come, and we grab our seats in desperation.
17. Many doctors recognize the value of health insurance, but the kind we should have is something they could not agree on.
18. Searching for the right words, Livia composed her closing sentence, and another essay was brought to its logical conclusion.
19. Sammy had just finished his bitter denunciation of all teachers and of one chemistry teacher in particular, when he turns around and Ms. Lerner was seen in the laboratory doorway.
20. An explorer must study maps very carefully so that you will be able to plan your trip efficiently.

CHAPTER 18

Sentence Conciseness

AVOIDING WORDINESS AND OVERWRITING

It is a mistake to believe that the more words a theme contains the better. Professional writers who are paid according to the number of words they write may find wordiness profitable, but they would never claim that it improves their articles. Most good writing is effective because it is not cluttered with unnecessary words.

Do not think, however, that wordiness appears only in long compositions. A long piece of writing may contain no superfluous words, whereas a short piece may be full of them. Studying the principles and doing the exercises in this section will make you aware of wordiness in writing and help you to avoid it in your own compositions.

SUPERFLUOUS WORDS AND UNNECESSARY REPETITION

The following example of wordiness was the opening paragraph of a high-school student's composition about an overnight hike. Lines have been drawn through the superfluous words.

When ~~in the course of human events, when~~ a woman finds it necessary to rest her weary bones, she packs up and goes on what is inappropriately called a vacation. Last summer I had the good fortune to go ~~during the summer~~ to a mountain camp in ~~the mountains of~~ eastern Pennsylvania. On the day that I arrived, ~~when I got to camp~~ I found that the camp had been quarantined because of the measles that one of the younger campers had brought in, ~~and no one who was in the camp could leave~~. After we had spent a week in camp, the prospect of an overnight hike in the mountainous wilds looked especially good to us campers who had been so long confined ~~to camp by the quarantine~~.

18a. Avoid wordiness by eliminating superfluous words and the unnecessary repetition of ideas.

WORDY   The game is played with tiny, little round balls which, in my opinion, I think are made of steel.

BETTER   The game is played with tiny balls which, I think, are made of steel.

WORDY   After descending down to the edge of the river, we boarded a small raft that was floating there on the surface of the water.

BETTER   After descending to the edge of the river, we boarded a small raft.

WORDY   The first story in the book is a masterpiece in itself and quite a story.

BETTER   The first story in the book is a masterpiece.

EXERCISE 1. Revising Sentences to Eliminate Superfluous Words. Revise the following sentences, eliminating superfluous words.

1. We watched the big, massive black cloud rising up from the level prairie and covering up the sun.
2. Far away in the distance, as far as anything was visible to the eye, the small, diminutive shapes of the campers' tents were outlined in silhouette against the dark sky.
3. Modern cars of today, unlike the old cars of yesterday, can be driven faster without danger than the old ones.
4. When what the speaker was saying was not audible to our ears, I asked her to repeat again what she had said.
5. It was in this mountain wilderness that the explorers found there the examples of wildlife for which they had been looking.
6. During this year's current baseball season, all home games and many away games in other cities may be watched at home on your television screen as they are brought to you over station WPIX.
7. The mediator said that if both parties would give in a little that a satisfactory settlement could be reached that would satisfy both parties.

8. In spite of the fact that the danger was neither tangible to the touch nor visible to the eye, it was very real to all the dwellers and inhabitants of the village in the foothills that circled around the base of Mt. Wilson.

9. The drive over to Cross Village follows and winds along the top of a great, huge bluff above the lake.

10. When at last the pounding finally began to stop, I stretched myself out prone upon the bed and attempted to try to go to sleep.

11. The world in its present state of affairs today is in great and dire need of great leaders who will work hard to prevent the recurrence again of a disastrously destructive world war.

12. During the hours in the morning before noon, there is a variety of radio programs of different kinds to which you may listen to.

13. As you continue on in the book a little further, you will be surprised and amazed by the clever skill of the writer of the book in weaving in together the many previously unrelated threads of his story.

14. At the final end of the picture, the villain abruptly and suddenly does an about-face and changes completely into a good person with admirable characteristics.

15. His mental thought processes puzzled his school teachers and made them despair of his future success in the years after his graduation from school.

16. I am always as a rule surprised to find out that a currently popular hit tune was also a popular number years ago in the past when my parents were both going to high school.

17. She was firmly determined to combine together both of the two divisions of the firm in order to achieve a stronger company eventually in the long run.

18. Circling around his adversary with a menacing look on his face, Broadhurst bided his time and waited for an opening through which he could connect up with his mighty right.

19. The President's struggle with Congress ended up in a victory for the President when the public voted at the November election to reelect him again to the Presidency for another term of four years.

20. The final conclusion of the novel on which she had been working on for more than five years was disappointing to everyone who read the manuscript, and she decided to revise and change the story.

EXERCISE 2. Revising Sentences by Eliminating Unnecessary Words. Revise the following wordy paragraphs. Eliminate all unnecessary words, but keep the ideas of the paragraphs clear.

1

When we were two hundred yards away from our objective, which was a small little grove of pine trees on the sloping side of a hill, we were confronted by a vast, wet swamp. I remembered that during the last two weeks we had had, out of fourteen days, ten days of rain, and decided in my own mind to send out a few scouts who might discover a way by means of which we could reach the grove without getting our feet wet. Then, when the scouts reported back that their efforts to try to find a dry path through the swamp had been unsuccessful, we gave up and resigned ourselves to sloshing knee-deep through the muddy water.

2

When, after eight years of education in school, the student enters the ninth grade and becomes a freshman, then he begins to find out what seniors are really like. Up until this point, seniors have been heroes to him, admired from a respectful distance away as though they were gods, unless he has happened to know one personally, of course. But now, however, his conception undergoes a change. The senior becomes an ogre whose one and only purpose in life seems to the freshman to be to make life as miserable as possible for each and every freshman. Every way the freshman turns in the school corridors, a senior hall cop, with a great big letter on his chest, grabs him with huge talons and tells him with hot and fiery breath that he cannot go down an up stairway. He is enticed into joining clubs which are ruled over and presided over by seniors who use him mainly for the performance of unpleasant errands beneath the dignity of a senior. Whenever the freshman cannot be of use, he is ignored. His former ambition to be a senior fades out and wanes until one day he begins to think thoughts of getting his revenge. In his frenzied brain the idea dawns on him if he is patient, he, too, will someday enjoy the privilege of molding the lives and characters of ninth-graders. This idea accounts for the fanatic, fixed stare which is to be seen in the eyes of so many freshmen.

CONCISENESS THROUGH REDUCTION

The opposite of wordiness is conciseness. In your effort to write well, you will profit from studying some ways to make your writing more concise. Of course, there is a danger in being too economical in your use of words; writing that is too concise will not be clear and will not achieve its intended effect. Nevertheless, the following rule will call to your attention some helpful methods of avoiding wordiness.

18b. Avoid wordiness by reducing clauses to phrases, and phrases to single words. This process is known as *reduction.*

1. *Clauses reduced to participial, gerund, or infinitive phrases*

CLAUSE **When they were trapped by a cave-in,** the miners waited for the rescue team.

PARTICIPIAL PHRASE **Trapped by a cave-in,** the miners waited for the rescue team.

CLAUSE **Because we had found no one home,** we left a note in the mailbox.

PARTICIPIAL PHRASE **Having found no one home,** we left a note in the mailbox.

CLAUSE **If you leave at noon,** you can get to Chicago at three o'clock.

GERUND PHRASE **Leaving at noon** will get you to Chicago at three o'clock.

CLAUSE We decided **that we would get an early start.**

INFINITIVE PHRASE We decided **to get an early start.**

2. *Clauses reduced to prepositional phrases*

CLAUSE The teams **that had come from Missouri** were not scheduled to play the first day of the tournament.

PHRASE The teams **from Missouri** were not scheduled to play the first day of the tournament.

CLAUSE **When the sun sets,** the streetlights come on.
PHRASE **At sunset** the streetlights come on.

CLAUSE **After you have graduated,** you will be looking for a job.
PHRASE **After graduation,** you will be looking for a job.

CLAUSE My cousin **who lives in Mexico** speaks Spanish fluently.
PHRASE My cousin **in Mexico** speaks Spanish fluently.

3. *Clauses reduced to appositives*

CLAUSE Dr. Brown, **who is the chief surgeon,** will operate.
APPOSITIVE Dr. Brown, **the chief surgeon,** will operate.

CLAUSE Her two dogs, **one of which is a collie and the other a spaniel,** perform different duties on the farm.

APPOSITIVE Her two dogs, **a collie and a spaniel,** perform different duties on the farm.

4. *Clauses and phrases reduced to single words*

CLAUSE　The dance classes **that have been canceled** will be rescheduled.
WORD　The **canceled** dance classes will be rescheduled.

CLAUSE　Laura is a runner **who never tires.**
WORD　Laura is a **tireless** runner.

CLAUSE　We met **a woman who dances in the ballet**.
WORD　We met a **ballerina**.

PHRASE　Her career **in the movies** was brief.
WORD　Her **movie** career was brief.

PHRASE　She greeted everyone **in a cordial manner**.
WORD　She greeted everyone **cordially.**

From these examples of reduction you can see how to make your own writing more concise. Usually the time for such reduction is during revision of your papers. Revising the sentences in the following exercises will give you practice in writing more concisely.

EXERCISE 3. Revising Sentences Through Reduction. The following sentences can be made more concise by reducing the italicized groups of words according to the directions given. Revise each sentence according to the directions.

1. (a) *Since she is an automobile dealer*, Mrs. Holmes has promised her children a car as a gift (b) *when they reach their seventeenth birthday.*
   [(a) Reduce clause to an appositive; (b) reduce clause to a prepositional phrase.]

2. After (a) *he had looked* everywhere for an old place (b) *that he could renovate*, Mr. Dayton bought the house (c) *that was deserted* on the edge of town.
   [(a) Reduce *he had looked* to a gerund (*–ing*); (b) reduce clause to an infinitive phrase (*to* + verb); (c) reduce *that was deserted* to an adjective.]

3. The orchard (a) *of apple trees* that stood (b) *in the area behind the house* yielded no fruit during his first year there, but it bore much fruit (c) *when the second season came.*
   [(a) Reduce phrase to an adjective; (b) reduce to one prepositional phrase; (c) reduce clause to a prepositional phrase.]

4. (a) *Since we were sitting in seats* (b) *that were near first base*, we were able to judge the accuracy of the decisions (c) *of the umpire.*
   [(a) Reduce clause to a participle (*–ing*), omitting *in seats*;

(b) reduce clause to a prepositional phrase; (c) reduce phrase to a possessive.]

5. (a) *Because it was necessary for her to be away from home* (b) *in the afternoon and in the evening* for many days, Mrs. Stein, (c) *who is the president of the Parent-Teacher Association*, hired a succession of baby sitters (d) *who were to take care of her children* (e) *while she was absent.*

[(a) Reduce clause to a participial phrase (*Having to be . . .*); (b) reduce two phrases to two words telling when; (c) reduce clause to an appositive; (d) reduce clause to an infinitive phrase (*to* + verb); (e) reduce clause to a prepositional phrase.]

EXERCISE 4. Revising Sentences Through Reduction.

Revise the following sentences by reducing the italicized clauses to phrases or appositives or single words, and the italicized phrases to single words. Omit unnecessary words, and occasionally change the word order.

1. We decided to wait for the bus *in order that we might save money.*
2. After I had finished the assigned reading, I read three novels *that were written by Virginia Woolfe.*
3. This small hotel, *which is situated in Connecticut*, is patronized mainly by *people from Boston.*
4. *After he lost a leg in an accident that occurred while he was hunting,* Monty Stratton, *who was a pitcher for the White Sox*, made a comeback in baseball *that was amazing.*
5. Our seats *in which we sat at the Army-Navy game* were almost on the forty-yard line, *and they were at the top of the stadium.*
6. The poetry *of Blake* had an influence *that is notable* on the poetry *of Yeats.*
7. *While he was inspecting his new house, which is in the suburbs*, Mr. Doyle stumbled over a piece of flooring and fell down the stairs *leading to the cellar.*
8. Our days *that we spent in the north woods* would have been perfect if it had not been for the mosquitoes *that were enormous and hungry.*
9. Inez, *who is an ambitious young actress*, found that the acting *that she did in a stock company in the summer* gave her the experience *that she needed.*
10. The most common complaint *that is made by students* is that every teacher chooses Friday *on which to give examinations.*

EXERCISE 5. Revising Paragraphs by Eliminating Unnecessary Words and by Using Reduction. Revise the following wordy paragraphs. Eliminate all unnecessary words and reduce clauses to phrases or appositives or single words. You may change the word order, but you must keep the ideas of the paragraphs clear.

1

As a result of the nation's energy shortage, the nation's government spends literally thousands of dollars in money each and every year making energy-saving improvements in selected homes in order to demonstrate to its citizens that energy-saving improvements can result in huge money savings on gas and electric bills. Despite such efforts, many people do not bother to take the advice of the government and to make the improvements to their own homes. According to a number of social scientists who are studying the problem of motivating people to conserve energy, homeowners do not always and everywhere respond to government planning and policy making in the way that government would like them to respond. As far as saving energy is concerned, many people wonder why they should make any improvements at all if they are able to afford the higher price of energy with the money they have. Furthermore, people desire convenience and comfort in the home, and this desire affects their decisions about their homes just as much as their desire to save energy or to save money. Therefore, if the government is to be more successful in convincing people to conserve energy, it must, by way of example, show people that a home with weatherstripping, for example, is or can be more enjoyable or more comfortable than a home without weatherstripping. According to social scientists, unless the government takes a different approach to the needs and wants of its citizens, its program to conserve energy in homes around the country may not succeed as well as could be expected.

2

Needless to say, I am not one of those who are members of the senior class who believe that the senior lounge should be closed during the week of exams. It goes without saying that seniors need a place that is quiet and relaxing in order for them to escape the pressures that accompany exam week. If the lounge is closed during this time, it would mean that seniors would be forced to use the cafeteria, which is crowded, or the auditorium, which is noisy, for the purpose of relaxation. Furthermore, the use of the senior lounge during exam week is by this time one of the few privileges that seniors are still able to enjoy here at East High; not long ago the right of seniors to park cars in the parking area reserved for members of the faculty was recently taken away by the Student-Teacher Council. If more privileges are taken away, the morale of seniors will weaken.

THE OVERWRITTEN STYLE

In their efforts to write impressively, high-school students sometimes produce writing that is so artificial, flowery, and cumbersome as to be absurd. Such a style results from the mistaken notion that big words, unusual words, and figures of speech, no matter how commonplace, are "literary." Unlike mistakes made through carelessness or laziness, a mistake of this kind is made by trying too hard to sound like a great writer. The resulting style is said to be "overwritten."

18c. Avoid an overwritten style. Write naturally without straining after a "literary" effect.

The following example of overwriting will make you aware of the fault. Doing the exercise that follows this will also help you correct overwritten passages in your own work.

HARBOR FOG

The fog slowly crept in and covered the metropolis with its sinister cloak of impressive quietude. An entire day of heavy rain had drenched the surrounding municipality, forming puddles in the thoroughfares which reflected the shimmering images of the gleaming street lights and the illumination emanating from multitudes of office windows.

As I stood on the magnificent span that arched above the swirling waters, the mournful warnings of the anchored ships pierced the dense fog. The constant beat of the harbor bell buoys and the gentle lapping of the murky water on the piling of this bridge combined to permeate the night air with a mystic tenseness.

The harbor boats moved tediously through the night, and their wakes left grotesque trails that slowly dissolved and enveloped themselves in the depths of the blackness.

Although it was late, the never-ceasing rumble of activity from the nearby city could still be apprehended. The penetrating night air was heavy with moisture and with each soft puff of breeze the salt of the sea could be detected.

During World War II, Representative Maury Maverick of Texas became impatient with the overwritten style of some government writing and branded this sort of writing with the descriptive term "gobbledygook." Here is an example of the gobbledygook that troubled Mr. Maverick: "Illumination is required to be extinguished upon vacating these premises." You can see how much more effective "Turn out the lights when you leave" would be.

EXERCISE 6. Revising Sentences to Correct an Overwritten Style. Each of the following sentences is an example of overwriting. Using simpler words, revise the idea that is here expressed in a forced and unnatural style.

1. In a vast explosion of frozen precipitation, Jan shot through the feathery drift, maintaining without apparent effort her equilibrium upon the fragile strips of ash strapped to the pedal extremities.

2. My exploration of the intriguing heights of the science of economics left me with the firm conviction that *Homo sapiens* is powerless when it comes to exerting any detectable influence on the fundamental operation of supply and demand.

3. The bitterest irony of our fevered time is the oft-repeated concept that only by creating more magnificent and more deadly instruments of explosive destruction can human beings bring to this whirling planet the era of tranquility for which it has longed since the beginning of time.

4. The sharp impact of wood upon the little white sphere was followed by a sudden emanation of sound, like an explosion, from the throats of the assembled multitude in the tiered stands as the soaring pellet arched over the greensward and came to rest beyond the masonry in left field.

5. Nothing so impresses one with the warm security and pleasing restfulness of one's native surroundings as extensive peregrinations into foreign realms and among the exotic areas on the surface of our world.

6. Following our educational endeavors of the day, several of us conscientious seekers after knowledge relaxed our weary cerebrums by lending our ears to the latest discs at Jacobsen's music emporium.

7. Laying aside for the nonce the tomes of wisdom, I selected from the periodical rack the current issue of my favorite pictorial publication and, elongated upon the resilient davenport, slowly perused the photographic narrative of the week's outstanding occurrences.

8. In order to forestall the embarrassment of a refusal, I preceded my request for Helen's company upon an excursion to the local cinema by inquiring of her nearest kin as to what Helen's social calendar held for the Friday evening in question.

9. Bent upon a week's exploration of our nation's vast regions of tranquil pristine wilderness, I bade a fond farewell to my anxious mater and, with my earthly possessions ensconced in a commodious rucksack, embarked upon my great adventure via public interstate omnibus.

10. Lifting the pigskin from the water-soaked gridiron with his trusty toe, Harvey booted it with mathematical precision directly between the white uprights silhouetted against the setting sun.

CHAPTER 19

Sentence Combining and Revising

VARIETY, INTEREST, EMPHASIS

SENTENCE COMBINING

Good writers avoid the choppy style caused by using too many short, subject-first sentences. Study how the following paragraph, written in a choppy style, has been revised to achieve a more fluent, more mature style. The revised version uses subordination, coordination, apposition, and other devices to indicate clearly the relationship between ideas.

The sinking of the *Titanic* was a great disaster. The *Titanic* weighed 42,000 metric tons. It was the largest ship of its time. It was the most luxurious ship of its time. The sinking was one of the worst maritime disasters in history. The *Titanic* was on its maiden voyage. The ship struck an iceberg. The iceberg was off the Grand Banks of Newfoundland. The accident happened on the night of April 14, 1912. The night was clear. The night was cold. The captain had received iceberg warnings. He had chosen to pass through a perilous ice field. The rate of speed was 42 kilometers per hour. He wished to reach New York ahead of schedule. The *Titanic*'s hull had sixteen watertight compartments. The iceberg punctured five compartments. The ship's designers thought no accident could puncture more than four compartments. The ship sank in less than three hours. Over 1,500 of the 2,220 passengers and crew drowned. Another ship, the *Californian*, lay stopped in the water. It was less than eighteen kilometers away. It did not respond to the distress signal. The radio operator was off duty. The *Carpathia* was ninety kilometers away. It reversed course. It sped through the ice floes. It picked up survivors. By the time it arrived, many lives had been lost. The *Titanic* disaster quickly led to the reform of maritime safety laws.

The sinking of the 42,000-metric-ton *Titanic*, the largest and most luxurious ship of its time, was one of the worst maritime disasters in history. On the clear, cold night of April 14, 1912, the ship, on its maiden voyage, struck an iceberg off the Grand Banks of Newfoundland. Although the captain had received iceberg warnings, he had chosen to pass through a perilous ice field at 42 kilometers per hour in order to reach New York ahead of schedule. The iceberg punctured five of sixteen watertight compartments in the ship's hull, one more than the ship's designers had thought possible in any accident, and the ship sank in less than three hours, with the loss of over 1,500 of the 2,220 passengers and crew. Another ship, the *Californian*, lay stopped in the water less than eighteen kilometers away, but it did not respond to the distress signal because its radio operator was off duty. The *Carpathia*, which was ninety kilometers away, reversed course, sped through the ice floes, and picked up the survivors, but by then many lives had been lost. The *Titanic* disaster quickly led to the reform of maritime safety laws.

Sentence-combining exercises provide useful practice in improving your writing style. As you combine short, choppy sentences in the exercises that follow, you will be making choices with regard to sentence structure and emphasis. This experience will enable you to achieve a more fluent style, richer in variety and interest.

19a. Combine short, related sentences by inserting adjectives, adverbs, and prepositional phrases.

Note how the following three sentences have been rewritten as one sentence by eliminating unnecessary words.

THREE SENTENCES The Prime Minister closed the session.
                    The Prime Minister felt weary.
                    He closed the session with the Cabinet.

ONE SENTENCE The **weary** Prime Minister closed the session **with the Cabinet.**

There may be more than one correct way to combine short sentences. Look at the examples that follow.

THREE SENTENCES The plane moved slowly.
                    The plane moved along the runway.
                    The plane moved toward the hangar.

ONE SENTENCE   **Slowly** the plane moved **along the runway toward the hangar**.

or

Along the runway, the plane moved **slowly toward the hangar**.

There are other correct ways in which these sentences could have been combined. Although you often have some degree of choice in combining short, related sentences, you may find that some combinations do not read smoothly, such as, *Along the runway toward the hangar slowly the plane moved.* You should avoid these combinations as well as those that change the meaning of the original short sentences.

EXERCISE 1. **Combining Sentences by Inserting Adjectives, Adverbs, or Prepositional Phrases.** Combine each group of short, related sentences by inserting adjectives, adverbs, or prepositional phrases into the first sentence and by eliminating unnecessary words. Add commas and conjunctions where they are necessary.

EXAMPLE   1. Peregrine falcons soar.
They soar gracefully.
They soar in the air.
1. *Peregrine falcons soar gracefully in the air.*

1. The peregrine falcon adapts to varying climates.
It adapts quickly.
It adapts easily.
2. The falcon dives on its victims and kills them.
The falcon is bluish gray.
It kills its victims by the force of the impact.
3. Peregrine falcons inhabit areas where birds are often plentiful.
The areas are open.
The areas are rocky.
The areas are near water.
4. Peregrines nest on the sides of cliffs.
They usually nest there.
They nest high on the cliffs.
They nest in small ledges.
5. Peregrine falcons became scarce.
They became extremely scarce.
They became scarce in the United States.
They became scarce because of the pesticide DDT.

6. No breeding pairs remained.
No pairs remained east of the Mississippi.
No pairs remained by 1970.
No pairs of falcons remained.
7. Scientists are reintroducing falcons.
The scientists are from Cornell University.
The falcons are wild.
The scientists reintroduce falcons under controlled conditions.
The scientists reintroduce falcons to the eastern United States.
8. The ban on DDT has helped the falcons.
The ban was effective.
The ban has helped considerably.
The falcons have been endangered.
9. Peregrines are hatching eggs.
These peregrines are in the Eastern wilderness.
They are hatching eggs for the first time.
It is the first time since the 1950's.
10. Peregrine falcons prefer nesting in cities.
They prefer nesting in large cities.
Some peregrines prefer this.
They prefer nesting on high skyscrapers.
They prefer the cities because of a supply of pigeons.
The supply of pigeons is abundant.

19b. Combine closely related sentences by using participial phrases.

Participial phrases—phrases containing a participle with its complements or modifiers—help you add concrete details to nouns and
pronouns in sentences. In the following example, the participial phrases
describe the subject of the sentence, the noun *ship*.

> **Badly damaged by high winds** and **deserted by half its crew**, the ship finally
> reached a safe harbor.

Participial phrases are a useful way to combine sentences. The following
example illustrates this.

TWO SENTENCES   The colors were orange, red, and blue.
                The colors were painted on the ceiling.
ONE SENTENCE   The colors **painted on the ceiling** were orange, red, and blue.

The second sentence has been turned into a participial phrase, *painted on the ceiling,* and attached to the first sentence. Unnecessary words have been deleted.

A participle or participial phrase must always be placed close to the noun or pronoun it modifies. Otherwise the sentence may confuse the reader.

MISPLACED   Wrapped in silver paper, the bride accepted the wedding present.
IMPROVED   The bride accepted the wedding present **wrapped in silver paper**.

EXERCISE 2. Combining Sentences by Using Participial Phrases.
Combine each of the following pairs of sentences into one sentence by turning either the first sentence or the second sentence of each pair into a participial phrase and inserting it into the remaining sentence. Punctuate the combined sentences correctly.

EXAMPLE   1. The employee asked for a raise.
                      The employee found out about the boss's temper.
              1. *Asking for a raise, the employee found out about the boss's temper.*

1. Tomb robbers searched inside a crypt.
   Tomb robbers found gold.
2. The pitcher concentrated on the batter.
   The pitcher forgot about the base runner.
3. The index in this book is very long.
   It contains every topic found on every page.
4. The student did not hand in her paper.
   The student realized that two pages were missing.
5. We held back our cheers.
   We waited for the speech to end.
6. The van failed to stop at the red light.
   It narrowly missed another car.
7. I left the bread in the oven too long.
   I burned the crust.
8. Our counselor was stung by a bee.
   Our counselor yelled angrily.
9. The teacher was pleased with the test results.
   The teacher congratulated the class.
10. The hurricane swept across the ocean.
    The hurricane demolished every boat in its path.

19c. Combine short, related sentences by using appositives or appositive phrases.

Appositives and appositive phrases add definitive detail to nouns and pronouns in sentences by helping to identify or explain them. Note how the appositive phrase in the following sentence helps identify the noun *captain.*

> The captain of the swim team, **holder of six school records**, won a full athletic scholarship.

Two sentences can often be combined through the use of an appositive or an appositive phrase.

TWO SENTENCES   Many students in the school play lacrosse.
Lacrosse is the national summer sport of Canada.

ONE SENTENCE   Many students in the school play lacrosse, **the national summer sport of Canada.**

EXERCISE 3. Combining Sentences by Using Appositives or Appositive Phrases.

Combine the following pairs of sentences by turning one of the sentences into an appositive or an appositive phrase. Punctuate the combined sentence correctly. Answers may vary.

EXAMPLE   1. Elizabeth Bowen was born in Ireland. She is one of the leading fiction writers in England since World War I.

1. *Elizabeth Bowen, one of the leading fiction writers in England since World War I, was born in Ireland.*

1. In *The Death of the Heart* the protagonist is a sensitive person, ill at ease with the world.
The Death of the Heart is one of Bowen's best-known novels.

2. Bowen was a nurse and an air-raid warden during World War II.
Bowen wrote about the psychological effects of war on civilians.

3. Nadine Gordimer is a South African writer.
She published her first stories at the age of fifteen.

4. Many of Gordimer's stories are set in South Africa.
Many of Gordimer's stories are accounts of modern-day social tensions.

5. In *Going Home,* Doris Lessing writes about a return visit to Rhodesia.
Going Home is an autobiographical narrative.

6. Doris Lessing is a sensitive observer of social and political struggles.
She describes people attempting to find meaning in life.

7. Katherine Mansfield is a modern master of the short story.
   She died of tuberculosis at the age of thirty-four.
8. Revealing the influence of Anton Chekhov, her stories focus more on character, atmosphere, and language than on plot.
   Chekhov was a great Russian writer.
9. *A Room of One's Own* is a book of essays by Virginia Woolf.
   A Room of One's Own is a short defense of women's rights.
10. Virginia Woolf was a member of the Bloomsbury Group.
    This group was a circle of British intellectuals.

19d. Combine short, related sentences by using compound subjects or verbs or by writing a compound sentence.

Compound subjects and verbs and compound sentences are common in writing. Writers, however, often overuse compound constructions by loosely stringing together ideas that belong in separate sentences (see page 352). You should not only learn the appropriate function of various connectives but should also avoid the overuse of *and* or *so* in your writing.

Compound subjects and verbs are joined by coordinating conjunctions such as *and, but,* and *or* and by correlative conjunctions such as *either—or, neither—nor,* and *both—and.*

EXAMPLES **Either** Mr. Sanderson **or** one of his students will bring the slide projector.
We watched the game this afternoon **and** cheered our team to victory.

Independent clauses are joined into a compound sentence by conjunctions such as *and, but,* and *for* or by other connectives such as *furthermore, yet, however, therefore, either—or,* and *neither—nor.* The relationship of the independent clauses determines which connective works best.

EXAMPLES Two cats were stranded in the tree, **and** no one could rescue them.
The police officer questioned him; **however,** he refused to answer. [Note the use of the semicolon.]

Ideas in separate sentences can be combined by using the appropriate connecting words. See pages 280–84 for a complete list of connecting words.

TWO SENTENCES   Rain had soaked the playing field.
Practice was canceled.

ONE SENTENCE   Rain had soaked the playing field; **therefore,** practice was canceled.

EXERCISE 4. **Combining Simple Sentences into a Compound Sentence.**

Most of the following items consist of two closely related ideas. Combine these ideas into a single sentence, using the appropriate connectives. (Consult the list of connectives on pages 280–84 if necessary.) Certain items contain unrelated ideas. In such instances, write *Unrelated* on your paper to show that the ideas are better expressed in two separate sentences.

EXAMPLE   1. The Congress will approve this bill.
The President will veto it.

      1. *The Congress will approve this bill, but the President will veto it.*

1. The basketball team has played well all season.
It will probably win the championship.
2. Frank worked hard on his homework.
His friend had given him the wrong assignment.
3. America must learn to use less energy.
There will be a more severe energy shortage in a few years.
4. Acid rain is a problem in the Northeast.
It has damaged many northern lakes.
5. The student account is empty.
We shall have to raise some money.
6. The prospects are bleak for new gym equipment.
The student council will continue to recommend this important purchase.
7. The atmosphere on Mars is very thin.
The planet is smaller than Earth.
8. School spirit sometimes wanes during the winter months.
The seniors have organized a carnival in December.
9. The class elections are in three weeks.
Everyone voted last year.
10. Sue is a well-qualified candidate.
Most of her class support her.

19e. Combine short, related sentences into a complex sentence by putting one idea into a subordinate clause.

Subordination allows you to express the relationship between two unequal ideas within a single sentence. Methods for subordinating ideas include the use of an adjective clause, an adverb clause, or a noun clause. Mastering these methods of subordination will improve the variety and clarity of your writing.

(1) Use an adjective clause to combine sentences.

Adjective clauses, like adjectives, modify nouns or pronouns. In the following sentence, the adjective clause is printed in boldfaced type.

> The detective **who solved the case** was a master at logical thinking.

To combine sentences by using an adjective clause, you must first decide which idea to emphasize (see page 287). Then you must choose the correct relative pronoun to join the sentences.

RELATIVE PRONOUNS   who, whom, whose, which, that

The adjective clause must always be placed close to the word or words it modifies.

TWO SENTENCES   The story has an intricate plot.
                I found the plot hard to follow.
ONE SENTENCE   The story has an intricate plot **that I found hard to follow**.
TWO SENTENCES   The woman heads the delegation.
                I met her yesterday.
ONE SENTENCE   The woman **whom I met yesterday** heads the delegation.

EXERCISE 5. Using Adjective Clauses to Combine Sentences.

Combine the following pairs of sentences by subordinating one idea in an adjective clause. Punctuate your sentences correctly.

EXAMPLE   1. Martin Luther King, Jr., married Coretta Scott.
             He met her while studying at Boston University.

> 1. *Martin Luther King, Jr., married Coretta Scott, whom he met while studying at Boston University.*

1. My uncle is an experienced traveler.
   He has recently returned from the Grand Canyon.
2. Richard prefers trout fishing.
   It requires more patience than deep-sea fishing.
3. This blanket is too heavy for the summer.
   It should be kept in the closet.

4. Pedro drove the truck.
   Pedro has just received his driver's license.
5. He gave me the rest of the money.
   He owed the money.
6. Melissa is about to begin her project.
   You can reach her after eight this evening.
7. Mr. Partridge coaches our basketball team.
   I introduced him to you.
8. Antique chairs lined the corridor.
   Each of them had a price tag on the arm.
9. I forgot the notebook.
   It was lying on the sofa.
10. The elephant sprayed water on passers-by.
    The elephant was standing near the fence.

(2) Use an adverb clause to combine sentences.

Adverb clauses can express a relationship of time, cause, purpose, or condition between two ideas within a single sentence.[1]

EXAMPLE **Although you present a convincing argument**, I will not change my mind.

To combine sentences by using an adverb clause, you must first decide which idea should become subordinate. You must then decide which subordinating conjunction best expresses the relationship between the two ideas.

TWO SENTENCES Elsie received the reply in the mail.
                She tore open the envelope impatiently.
ONE SENTENCE **When Elsie received the reply in the mail**, she tore open the envelope impatiently.

EXERCISE 6. Using Adverb Clauses to Combine Sentences.

Combine each pair of sentences by subordinating one idea in an adverb clause. (Consult the list of subordinating conjunctions on pages 283–84 if you need to.) Punctuate the combined sentences correctly.

EXAMPLE 1. Sally did her best.
              She was unable to win the prize.
          1. *Although Sally did her best, she was unable to win the prize.*

1. It is true that you learn to do by doing.
   It is obvious that you learn to write by writing.

[1] See pages 283–84 for a list of common subordinating conjunctions.

2. You should not make up your mind.
   You have studied all the evidence.
3. Money is undoubtedly important.
   It has never made anyone happy.
4. All students should learn standard English.
   They will never be embarrassed by their usage.
5. This critic recommends a new book.
   The book becomes a best seller.
6. She will invest her money with you.
   You can prove that the investment is safe.
7. We raised our prices.
   Our business increased.
8. She wanted to graduate in January.
   She could join the Navy.
9. You train rigorously.
   You will be able to do well in cross-country.
10. She was ill.
    She insisted on going ahead with the show.
11. The committee members could not agree.
    The whole matter was referred to the president.
12. The president took the responsibility.
    She wanted to settle the matter herself.
13. She decided to bring the issue before the entire club.
    Everyone could express an opinion.
14. There was a great deal of talk.
    Nothing was decided.
15. A decision is reached today.
    The donors will not give us the money.
16. The city council offered to give us money for a clubhouse.
    We would let the public use it.
17. We had never admitted the public to our meetings.
    We didn't want to admit them to our clubhouse.
18. We would not lose the chance for a new clubhouse.
    Some of us favored admitting the public.
19. I agreed with those in favor of admitting the public.
    I sympathized with the others.
20. No agreement was reached.
    The money went to another club.

(3) Use a noun clause to combine sentences.

A noun clause is a subordinate clause used as a noun. Read the following examples of noun clauses and note where they appear in the sentences.

> **Whoever buys that car** will be sorry. [noun clause as subject]
> Yesterday we learned **what Napoleon had accomplished**. [noun clause as direct object]
> We can spend the money for **whatever we like**. [noun clause as object of preposition]

A noun clause can also be used as a predicate nominative and as an indirect object. Noun clauses are usually introduced by *that, what, whatever, why, whether, how, who, whom, whoever*, or *whomever*.

Noun clauses are sometimes used without the introductory word *that*.

EXAMPLE   My sister said the trip would take three days.

EXERCISE 7. Using Noun Clauses to Combine Sentences.
Combine each of the following pairs of sentences by turning the italicized sentence in each pair into a noun clause. Use one of the introductory words listed above.

EXAMPLE   1. *They thought that they did not need help.*
This was a very foolish idea.
1. *That they did not need help was a very foolish idea.*

1. The new senator promised.
   The state would get more aid.
2. *Could they endure the debate?*
   That was uncertain.
3. *They might succeed.*
   This was the incentive that kept them working.
4. The odor of smoke convinced the family.
   They should call the fire department.
5. The attorney asked a question.
   He asked how the defendant had found the money.

REVIEW EXERCISE A. Using Sentence-Combining Methods.
Using the sentence-combining methods you have practiced thus far, combine each group of sentences into one smooth, well-written sentence. You may omit unnecessary words and change the word order, but

you may not change the meaning of the original sentences. Punctuate your combined sentences correctly.

EXAMPLE 1. Hugo Gernsback began publishing *Amazing Stories.*
He began in 1926.
Amazing Stories was the first science-fiction magazine.
1. *In 1926 Hugo Gernsback began publishing* Amazing Stories, *the first science-fiction magazine.*

1. Science fiction ranges.
   It ranges from projection to speculation.
   The projection is careful.
   The speculation is outlandish.
   Science fiction usually requires the appearance of credibility.
2. *Frankenstein* is an early example of science fiction.
   Frankenstein is a novel by Mary Shelley.
   Frankenstein describes the scientific creation of human life.
3. There is another early example of science fiction.
   The example is H. G. Wells's *The Time Machine.*
   The Time Machine entertains.
   The Time Machine offers social criticism.
   The Time Machine predicts the future.
4. Some critics did not accept science fiction as serious literature.
   These critics did not accept it easily.
   Writers often included science fiction in their works.
   These writers were major twentieth-century authors.
5. Today science fiction has supporters.
   Science fiction has many active supporters.
   They hold annual conventions.
   They present Hugo and Nebula awards.
   These awards are for the year's best writing.

REVIEW EXERCISE B. Combining Sentences to Add Variety to a Paragraph.   Combine the short, choppy sentences in the following paragraph into longer, smoother sentences. Be sure that the sentences you write add variety to the paragraph. Punctuate the paragraph correctly.

Mount St. Helens erupted in May 1980. It is near Vancouver, Washington. The eruption was sudden. The force was over five hundred times that of an atomic bomb. The explosion was caused by pressure from gas and molten rock. It tore the top off the mountain. It threw ash high into the air. The explosion and subsequent mudslides caused many deaths. More than thirty people died. The destruction left many homeless. The force of the blast leveled huge trees. The area was wide. The mud killed hundreds of deer and elk. The mud turned Spirit Lake into a mudhole. The lake was formerly picturesque. Much of the ash fell to earth within a few days. A cloud of dust remained in the stratosphere. This cloud was over much of the Northern Hemisphere. People saw spectacular sunrises and sunsets. This continued for two years. The sunrises and sunsets were rose-colored. The sunsets were due to solar rays. They struck microscopic particles of ash. Scientists suspect that intermittent showers will continue. The showers will consist of volcanic ash. They will continue for the next two decades.

REVIEW EXERCISE C. Combining Sentences to Add Variety to a Paragraph. Follow directions for Review Exercise B.

Several reported incidents indicate that extrasensory perception, or ESP, may exist. Several controlled laboratory experiments indicate that extrasensory perception, or ESP, may exist. ESP is usually divided into three kinds. These kinds are telepathy, precognition, and clairvoyance. Telepathy supposedly allows people to communicate by "reading minds." Telepathy is also known as thought transference. No conclusive scientific evidence for telepathy exists. Many people are convinced it works. For example, a retail store manager hired a man. This man was paid to identify shoplifters by reading their minds. He read their minds as they entered the store.

Another kind of ESP is precognition. Precognition is the ability to perceive things. These are things that are about to happen. For example, a mother had a dream. In the dream a heavy light fixture fell on her child's crib. She awakened from the dream. She immediately removed the child from the crib. Minutes later a storm developed. High winds shook the house. A chandelier fell on the crib.

The third kind of ESP is clairvoyance. Clairvoyance is the ability to see objects or events. These objects or events are distant or hidden. For example, a clairvoyant person is given the latitude and longitude of any spot on earth. Then this person can supposedly describe the features of that place accurately. No scientific theory adequately explains ESP. No scientific proof of it has been universally accepted. Many dedicated people are studying the subject.

AVOIDING MONOTONY

19f. Experiment with the length and structure of your sentences to achieve greater interest and variety.

Sentences in English—both spoken and written—begin with the subject. Any piece of writing in which most of the sentences needlessly depart from this normal order will strike a reader as artificial. However, an unbroken sequence of subject-predicate sentences may result in another stylistic fault—monotony. Such a sequence of sentences is monotonous because it lacks the logical connections and special emphasis that variations in sentence structure can provide. For example, the following sentences are perfectly clear:

> The two friends quarreled violently over a matter of slight importance.
> They never spoke from that time on.

But a closer connection can be made between these two sentences by moving the adverb phrase, which refers to the quarrel, up to the beginning of the second sentence:

> The two friends quarreled violently over a matter of slight importance.
> **From that time on** they never spoke.

Similarly, an important idea expressed by a modifier can be emphasized:

> Sue was not impressive in the classroom.
> **On the tennis court**, however, she came into her own.

The contrast is less striking when the second sentence begins with its subject:

> Sue was not impressive in the classroom.
> She came into her own, however, on the tennis court.

The normal order of sentences should not be shunned merely for the sake of variety. However, it is a good idea to remember that beginning a sentence with an important modifier may sometimes increase the force and clarity of your thought as well as provide a pleasing variation.

The exercises that follow are intended to give you practice in using different kinds of sentence openers. Used sparingly, these devices will improve your writing.

(1) Begin some of your sentences with a transposed appositive or with one of these modifiers: single-word modifier; phrase modifier; clause modifier.

Appositives

> The human brain, an enormously complex mechanism, contains about ten billion nerve cells. [subject first]
> **An enormously complex mechanism,** the human brain contains about ten billion nerve cells. [transposed appositive first]

Single-Word Modifiers

The book is long and badly written, and it failed to hold my interest. [subject first]
Long and badly written, the book failed to hold my interest. [single-word modifiers first]
A number of changes have been made here recently. [subject first]
Recently, a number of changes have been made here. [single-word modifier first]
The house was deserted and dilapidated and made a depressing picture. [subject first]
Deserted and dilapidated, the house made a depressing picture. [single-word modifiers first]

Phrase Modifiers

She was almost unbeatable on the tennis court. [subject first]
On the tennis court, she was almost unbeatable. [prepositional phrase first]
Joe tired rapidly during the second set and decided to save his strength for the third set. [subject first]
Tiring rapidly during the second set, Joe decided to save his strength for the third set. [participial phrase first]
Wendy Hsi worked late every night to win the essay prize. [subject first]
To win the essay prize, Wendy Hsi worked late every night. [infinitive phrase first]

Clause Modifiers

Investigators of the cause of the crash had to depend on evidence found in the wreckage because there were no survivors or witnesses. [subject first]
Because there were no survivors or witnesses, investigators of the crash had to depend on evidence found in the wreckage. [clause first]
Our leading lady, when she heard the orchestra playing the overture, suffered a severe attack of stage fright. [subject first]
When she heard the orchestra playing the overture, our leading lady suffered a severe attack of stage fright. [clause first]

EXERCISE 8. Revising Sentences by Varying Sentence Beginnings. This exercise will give you practice in beginning sentences in a variety of ways. Revise each sentence according to the instructions.

1. The Marine Historical Society has re-created a nineteenth-century coastal village at Mystic, Connecticut. [Begin with a prepositional phrase.]

2. Traveling, eating, and shopping with credit cards seems wonderfully easy until you receive your bill at the end of the month. [Begin with a subordinate clause.]

3. Some people are selfish and materialistic and are never happy with what they have. [Begin with single-word adjective modifiers.]

4. José worked part time at a gas station during his senior year in high school and managed to save a thousand dollars toward his college expenses. [Begin with a participial phrase: *Working . . .*]

5. The most glamorous of all the new professions created by the space age is that of the astronaut. [Begin with a prepositional phrase.]

6. Belmer, one of the oldest players in professional football, makes up in experience what he lacks in speed. [Begin with a transposed appositive.]

7. The college president stated at the alumni luncheon the immediate financial needs of the college. [Begin with a prepositional phrase.]

8. A university's primary responsibility is to its resident students, although it should encourage educational programs for its alumni. [Begin with a subordinate clause.]

9. This seems to be a highly technical book, to the casual reader. [Begin with a prepositional phrase.]

10. The first ships of the expedition will sail in October, if present plans are approved. [Begin with a subordinate clause.]

11. Navy divers expertly and rapidly repaired the damaged hull. [Begin with single-word adverb modifiers.]

12. The firm lacked funds for expansion and so attempted to borrow money. [Begin with a participial phrase: *Lacking . . .*]

13. The skin on the average adult weighs 8.8 pounds and occupies an area of 20 square feet. [Begin with a participial phrase.]

14. The expedition was led by Colonel Walter H. Wood of New York and spent several weeks at its camp on Seward Glacier. [Begin with a participial phrase.]

15. One can see at first glance that modern office furniture uses more metal than wood. [Begin with a prepositional phrase.]

EXERCISE 9. Revising Sentences by Varying Sentence Beginnings. Revise each sentence so that it will begin with a single-word, phrase, or clause modifier or an appositive.

1. A bowling team was formed this winter for the first time in the history of the school.
2. A sinister figure stepped cautiously into the dark room.
3. Candidates for a driver's license must take a written examination to prove their knowledge of traffic regulations.
4. The children, when both parents are working, are cared for in nursery schools.
5. The audience, tired and hot, soon became impatient.
6. We were frightened by the explosion and dared not move.
7. More than half of the 90,000 acres under cultivation had been ruined by the recent drought.
8. Jim, a merchant sailor for ten years, knew every important port in the world.
9. The new houses, although they look exactly alike from the outside, have very different interiors.
10. Competition has been growing more and more intense in the transportation industry.
11. A small boy, sobbing bitterly, ran toward me.
12. Music is to me an excellent tranquilizer when it is soft and rhythmic.
13. A person, when striving for the highest spiritual goals, will frequently become discouraged.
14. More and more people are rushing to local gymnasiums and health clubs either to reduce their weight or to improve their physical fitness.
15. Nothing is more satisfying than producing your own music, even if you cannot play an instrument well and are not musically inclined.

(2) Vary the structure of your sentences by means of subordination. Avoid the exclusive use of simple and compound sentences.[1] Skillful use of the complex sentence is an indication of maturity in style.

REVIEW EXERCISE D. Using Subordination to Combine Sentences. Using subordination, combine the short sentences in each group into one long, smooth sentence.

1. Alma Mahler Gropius Werfel, the "widow who married the arts," first married Gustav Mahler, the composer.

---

[1] For a review of subordination, see pages 282–91. For an explanation of the kinds of sentences, see pages 81–83.

Then she married Walter Gropius, the architect.

Then she married Franz Werfel, the novelist.

2. Amelia Earhart made her first solo crossing of the Atlantic in 1932.

   Five years later she attempted a round-the-world flight.

   She became a major figure of concern when her plane lost radio contact on the second of July.

3. Gwendolyn Brooks is a poet, the author of *A Street in Bronzeville.*

   She has won the Pulitzer Prize.

   She has taught poetry in several Chicago colleges.

4. A year after Simon and Garfunkel first recorded "Sounds of Silence," a studio engineer dubbed in additional background.

   Newly edited, the song became a national hit.

   It launched their successful career.

5. Time is an odd thing.

   It does not exist all by itself.

   It is a name we give to one of our ways of experiencing our lives.

6. Eleanor Roosevelt was both versatile and talented.

   She wrote some very important books.

   One of them was *On My Own.*

   She was twice a delegate to the United Nations.

7. The Pulaski Highway in Maryland and the Pulaski Skyway in New Jersey were named after General Casimir Pulaski.

   He was an exiled Polish count.

   He served under Washington in the Revolution.

8. The Shakespeare Memorial at Stratford-on-Avon houses a theater.

   Stratford-on-Avon is the birthplace of Shakespeare.

   The Memorial also contains a gallery and a library.

9. When spirits are distilled, the parts of the solution are separated by heating.

   The part of the solution that escapes first when heated is called the distillate.

   Cognac is the distillate of grape wines from the Charente region in France.

10. On March 10, 1876, Alexander Graham Bell spoke through the first electromagnetic telephone.

    He spoke to Watson, his assistant.

    He said, "Mr. Watson, come here; I want you."

AVOIDING "STRINGY" STYLE

19g. Give variety to your writing by avoiding the "stringy" style which results from the overuse of *and* and *so.*

In everyday conversation we tend to string our ideas out, one after another, by means of the simple conjunctions *and* and *so.* In writing, however, this sort of thing appears childish and monotonous. As you can see from the following examples, "stringiness" is an obvious fault which can be easily corrected. There are two ways to correct it.

(1) Correct a stringy sentence by subordination of ideas.

STRINGY SENTENCE   College admission standards continue to rise, *and* tension and anxiety build to a ridiculous point in college-preparatory seniors, *and* this spoils their final year in high school.

IMPROVED   As college admission standards continue to rise, tension and anxiety build to a ridiculous point in college-preparatory seniors, spoiling their final year in high school. [One *and* has been removed by means of the beginning subordinate clause. The other has been removed by means of the participial phrase, *spoiling their final year in high school.*]

The use of *so* as a conjunction is considered poor form. Its use can almost always be avoided by using a subordinate clause or a phrase expressing cause or reason.

POOR USE OF *SO*   Maria Martinez believed in tradition, *so* she experimented with ancient Pueblo pottery techniques.

IMPROVED   Believing in tradition, Maria Martinez experimented with ancient Pueblo pottery techniques.   *or*
Because she believed in tradition, Maria Martinez experimented with ancient Pueblo pottery techniques.

STRINGY USE OF *SO*   We heard the static on the radio, *so* we were afraid of a thunderstorm, *so* we decided not to go out in the boat.

IMPROVED   Fearing a thunderstorm when we heard the static on the radio, we decided not to go out in the boat.

(2) Correct a stringy sentence by dividing it into two sentences.

STRINGY SENTENCE   I am very fond of foreign films, and so I go to the Celtic Theater more than to the other theaters, and we get only the best foreign films in this country, so I not only learn a lot, but I see better pictures.

IMPROVED   Being very fond of foreign films, I go to the Celtic Theater more than to the other theaters. Since we get only the best foreign films in this country, I not only learn a lot, but I see better pictures. [stringiness corrected by subordination and by division into two sentences]

EXERCISE 10. Revising Sentences.   Revise the sentences by one or more of the following methods: subordination, division into more than one sentence, and reduction. Get rid of the monotonous use of *and* and *so.* You may add a few words of your own if the words will help you to improve the sentences.

1. Tom Sawyer made Becky Thatcher jealous by talking to Amy Lawrence, and then Becky became very upset, so she invited everyone except Tom and Amy to her picnic, and then spent recess with Alfred, and she pretended not to notice Tom.

2. Tom and Becky continued to be angry with each other for a while, and then eventually they made up, and Tom looked forward to going to Becky's picnic.

3. Mrs. Thatcher set the day for the picnic and Tom and Becky visited the cave called "McDougal's Cave" with the rest of the company, and played hide-and-seek after exploring the more familiar wonders of the cave.

4. They followed a little stream of water, and Tom played the role of a discoverer, and Becky thought that was fun and followed him.

5. They wound down through the cave this way and that and crept from cavern to cavern and found a spring-fed pool.

6. In one cavern the ceiling was completely lined with bats, and the bats swarmed down when Tom and Becky entered the cavern with their candles, and one of them almost snuffed Becky's candle out with its wings.

7. Soon the stillness of the cave dampened Tom and Becky's spirits, and they realized that they had gone some distance from the others, and suddenly they were afraid that they might be unable to get back.

8. They started back, and indeed they had become lost, and there was no way Tom could remember which route they had followed, and they had only one piece of cake and a few candle-stumps.

9. After several false starts through the various tunnels their candles gave out, and they were left in total darkness, and Becky wept, and they both thought they were certain to die in the pitch-black cave.

10. Leaving Becky alone, Tom took a length of rope and traced his way through the tunnels looking for an exit and soon saw a candle, so he shouted at the top of his voice, and the next thing he knew a familiar face was there in front of him.

CHAPTER 20

Sentence Revision

PRACTICE EXERCISES

This chapter contains exercises only. The exercises will help you in two ways: (1) they will test your understanding of sentence correctness, clearness, and smoothness; (2) they will give you practice in revising faulty sentence structure. The theory behind the inclusion of exercises in any textbook is that if you learn to criticize and revise the awkward sentences in the book, most of which have been taken from student compositions, you will be able to criticize and revise your own awkward sentences.

Use the exercises in this chapter to "keep your hand in" the skills of good writing. The exercises are of various kinds, and every exercise is devoted to more than one kind of skill.

Revising Sentences by Correcting Errors in Sentence Structure

EXERCISE 1. **Revising Sentences by Correcting Errors in Sentence Structure.** Immediately following the directions you will find a list of errors in sentence structure. Each faulty sentence in the exercise illustrates one of these errors. Some of the sentences are correct. You are to do two things: (1) write *before* the number of the sentence on your paper the letter of the error illustrated in the sentence; (2) write *after* the number of the sentence a revision that eliminates the error. How you correct the error is not important, provided your sentence is correct, clear, and smooth. If the sentence is correct as it stands, write a + before its number.

A   Lack of agreement (subject and verb, or pronoun and antecedent)
B   Incorrect case of pronoun
C   Dangling modifier
D   Lack of parallelism or faulty parallelism
E   Unclear reference of pronoun (ambiguous, general, weak)

EXAMPLE   1. Do you know whom it was?
       B   1. *Do you know who it was?*

1. People may disapprove of laws, but that doesn't prove they are good or bad.
2. Human behavior is complicated and difficult, not only to analyze but for evaluation.
3. The law is society's tested system of behavior, and they would have even worse problems without it.
4. Unless two individuals observe the same laws, the more powerful can always take advantage of the weaker.
5. Any wise judge, as well as the more experienced citizens, can appreciate that.
6. The fundamental principle behind all laws are the same.
7. It is that the rights of others limit the rights of any individual.
8. The law has many arms touching all of us, and to prescribe the limits proper to us in all our different roles.
9. It governs you as a student and I as a writer.
10. Hoping for order in our social dealings with one another, the fact that legality requires judicial decision often makes us impatient.
11. The complexity of judicial decisions reflects how complex is law itself.
12. When a law is carelessly formulated or improperly applied, a judge can cut them down to size.
13. The presiding judge in an American court of law is a person whom scholars agree has no counterpart in other nations.
14. Making every effort to avoid the "tyranny" of politics, the Constitution was written by men who knew how the law can be twisted to the selfish interests of those in power.

15. In the Constitution, legislative and executive power is restricted to a greater degree than they are in other national systems of government.

16. Facing one practical question after another, this restriction was less a matter of design than it was the result of many difficult decisions individually reached.

17. If the writers of the Constitution had not given the powers they did to the courts, they would have been subject to one of the other branches of government.

18. The mood of an executive and the whim of a legislator consequently does not determine one's fate in a court of law.

19. Instead, the acts of executives and the laws of legislatures all become subject, when necessary, to the judgment of a judge.

20. Abuse and violation of the existing law was the last resort of the colonists.

EXERCISE 2. Revising Sentences by Correcting Errors in Sentence Structure. Follow the directions for Exercise 1.

A Sentence fragment
B Run-on sentence
C Incorrect tense or verb form
D Misplaced modifier
E Unclear relationship between sentence ideas (lack of subordination, faulty coordination)

1. Our camp, which lays at the north end of the lake, is overshadowed by the cliffs that raise steeply above it.

2. Team teaching offers teachers at least one important advantage, it enables each teacher on the team to teach his specialty.

3. Since it has a full squad of seasoned players, this year's football team should win the championship.

4. The car was driven by a stunning girl with whitewall tires.

5. The band in its new uniforms and the high-stepping majorette with her twirling baton as well as the stirring music.

6. A compromise is a settlement of differences reached by mutual concessions between two parties.

7. Secret police with hidden cameras that were trying to take pictures at the meeting were physically ejected by angry students.

8. She had intended to have gone to the dance with her brother.

9. At home we suffer the constant interference of our parents, at college we will be free to make our own decisions.

10. Tickets for matinees will cost $3.50, and matinees will be given on Wednesdays and Saturdays.

11. These experiences will be valuable in my career as a social worker, and it is a career in which I shall work with people from all walks of life.

12. At the beginning of my junior-level Spanish course, the teacher reviewed the material I had the year before.

13. During negotiations between labor and management, work in the factory continued as usual.

14. The five junior-high-school buildings will cost eight million dollars, and they were approved by the taxpayers in yesterday's balloting.

15. We found several of the students in the shop very busy. Learning how to take a motor apart and put it together again.

16. The senator denied the many charges that had been made against her briefly and categorically.

17. In high school I have been unable to take some courses I wanted and have been required to take others I did not want.

18. Twenty percent of the students said they were satisfied with their own study habits, fifty-four percent said they wished they knew how to study more effectively.

19. If you would have come earlier, you could have seen the first act.

20. The demand for good television material exceeds the supply, and some of the best material, important news events, is not being fully used, and the reason is that news telecasts are not profitable.

Revising Sentences by Selecting the Best Expressions

EXERCISE 3. **Revising Sentences by Selecting the Best Expressions.** Number your paper 1–25. After each of the following sentences, the italicized part of the sentence is revised in two ways. If you consider one of these revisions an improvement, write the letter of the better one (*a* or *b*) after the proper number on your paper. If you consider the sentence correct as it stands, write +.

1. Behind one of the doors waits a tiger, *and the other has a beautiful lady behind it.*

   a. . . . and behind the other waits a beautiful lady.

   b. . . . and a beautiful lady waits behind the other.

2. If you go on a trip, *it will give you an excellent chance to practice your camera technique.*

   a. . . . you will have an excellent chance to practice your camera technique.

   b. . . . an excellent chance to practice your camera technique will be yours.

3. When developing films, *a darkroom will be needed.*

   a. . . . one thing you will need is a darkroom.

   b. . . . you will need a darkroom.

4. A deep-sea fisher needs an outboard motor much larger *than a fisher who fishes in sheltered waters.*

   a. . . . than that used by a fisher who fishes in sheltered waters.

   b. . . . than one fishing in sheltered waters.

5. This discovery had a bad effect on the mind of Usher, *he thought he had buried his sister alive.*

   a. . . . Usher, for he thought he had buried his sister alive.

   b. . . . Usher. He thought he had buried his sister alive.

6. Although they listen to several news broadcasts each day, *most people continue to buy a daily paper.*

   a. . . . a daily paper continues to be bought by most people.

   b. . . . the buying of a daily paper by most people continues.

7. It had been stated earlier in the press that representatives of union and management *would either meet around the clock until they reached an agreement or accepted government arbitration.*

   a. . . . would meet around the clock until either they reached an agreement or government arbitration was accepted by them.

   b. . . . would meet around the clock until they either reached an agreement or accepted government arbitration.

8. During the winter *Angela both developed her skill in skiing and ice-skating.*

   a. . . . Angela developed her skill in both skiing and ice-skating.

   b. . . . Angela developed both her skill in skiing and in ice-skating.

9. *Pat and him told Mike and I* the answers to the homework problems.
   a. . . . Pat and him told Mike and me . . .
   b. . . . Pat and he told Mike and me . . .

10. Ever since the accident, *driving past that spot*, the whole experience has returned.
    a. . . . while driving past that spot, . . .
    b. . . . as I have driven past that spot, . . .

11. The Governor sent her budget message to the legislature yesterday, conferred with the director of the budget this morning, *and a conference with the press was held this afternoon.*
    a. . . . and held a conference with the press this afternoon.
    b. . . . and this afternoon held a conference with the press.

12. *Was it he who* you thought stole the money?
    a. Was it he whom . . .
    b. Was it him whom . . .

13. When one of the girls *have completed their report, ask them* to bring it to me.
    a. . . . has completed their report, ask them . . .
    b. . . . has completed her report, ask her . . .

14. Don't expect *Jane and I to be as good as her* in English.
    a. . . . Jane and me to be as good as she . . .
    b. . . . Jane and I to be as good as she . . .

15. Plans for the P.T.A. party *include not only dancing but also* a floor show and a buffet supper.
    a. . . . not only include dancing but also . . .
    b. . . . include not only dancing, but also the guests will enjoy . . .

16. Jim had been in jail for safecracking *but because of good behavior was paroled.*
    a. . . . but because of good behavior had been paroled.
    b. . . . but had been paroled for good behavior.

17. To my complete surprise the students *acc ted the new type of examination which the teachers had prepared without a complaint.*
    a. . . . accepted the new type of examination without a complaint, which the teachers had prepared.
    b. . . . accepted without a complaint the new type of examination which the teachers had prepared.

18. The mayor's economy committee *has been investigating street-cleaning costs, and it has published a report on its findings.*
    a. . . . , which has been investigating street-cleaning costs, has published a report on its findings.
    b. . . . has been investigating street-cleaning costs, and a report has been published on its findings.

19. The two causes of "college neurosis" are trying to get into college *and then you try to stay there.*
    a. . . . and then to try to stay there.
    b. . . . and then trying to stay there.

20. *The students received the new yearbook,* which came out on the last day of school, *with enthusiasm.*
    a. The students received with enthusiasm the new yearbook . . .
    b. The students with enthusiasm received the new yearbook . . .

21. *The telegram reached me too late advising against going to Washington.*
    a. Too late the telegram advising against going to Washington reached me.
    b. The telegram advising against going to Washington reached me too late.

22. *It is not the cost of a gift but its appropriateness that matters.*
    a. The cost of a gift does not matter, but the appropriateness of it does.
    b. It is not the cost that matters of a gift, but its appropriateness.

23. After being reprimanded twice, *the teacher for further punishment, sent Ann to the principal.*
    a. . . . by the teacher, Ann was sent to the principal for further punishment.
    b. . . . the teacher sent Ann to the principal for further punishment.

24. Public figures must learn to take *the reporters' questions and the jostling of photographers calmly.*
    a. . . . the questions of reporters and the jostling of photographers calmly.
    b. . . . calmly the questioning of reporters and the jostling of photographers.

25. *Driving through the mountains, we were impressed by the engineering achievements of road builders.*
    a. We were impressed by the engineering achievements of road builders, driving through the mountains.
    b. We were impressed by the engineering achievements, driving through the mountains, of road builders.

Revising Awkward Sentences

EXERCISE 4. Revising Awkward Sentences. This exercise is composed of awkward sentences which you are to revise. The sentences may be revised in any way that will make them clearer and smoother. Your purpose is to express the same idea in a better way. The faults in a sentence may not always be specific errors; they may be generally clumsy constructions. You may add words or omit words wherever you wish, provided you do not alter the meaning. Revise wordy passages. Eliminate errors in usage. Each problem can be handled in a single sentence, but your teacher may allow you to divide some of the problems into two sentences.

1. She tried to find out the boy's name that she was to invite.
2. Featherbedding is one result of automation, which is the practice of keeping workers on the job, which is unnecessary, because the job has been made obsolete by machines.
3. The dean was more impressed by the candidate's scholastic record than his athletic record impressed him.
4. There are many persons who have jobs part of the year, and a job is not held by them the rest of the year, being among the unemployed.
5. There is a great deal of Franklin's philosophy which certainly everyone who reads it can benefit from in his *Autobiography*.
6. Soon families will have helicopters just like cars today and will be able to go from place to place much more easier than by car since there will be a direct route and the traffic will be much less.
7. Since we hadn't no tire repair kit, the motorcycle was pushed to the nearest gas station where we had a patch put on it.
8. Tammy was an optimist, easygoing, and nothing ever seemed to trouble her no matter what happened.
9. Opening the curtain, an empty stage was revealed, but the stage crew arrived a moment later and, busily working and talking, the set was soon up for the first act.

10. In a child a negative attitude may come from the natural desire for recognition and independence, but when an adult shows a negative attitude, it may be a symptom of neurosis.

EXERCISE 5. Revising Awkward Sentences. Follow the directions for Exercise 4.

1. Mrs. Turnbull is a good author and through experience has found out what a reader wants and has given them it in this book.
2. From my own standpoint, gardening, whether flowers or vegetables, is a lot of fun, good exercise, and the experience it provides is valuable.
3. There are many ways to show loyalty to a friend that you can use, and one of these is not to talk about them behind their back.
4. In some countries the biggest problem of the people is getting enough food, but the biggest problem of some people in America is dieting which is when you keep yourself from eating too much food.
5. Psychologists have proved that a child's mind is often more active than an adult, and they are usually eager to learn.
6. The mechanic working for the airline that failed to check the landing gear was not only guilty of negligence, but, in effect, he was a murderer as well.
7. After the dances in the gymnasium, of which we have a reasonable amount, many couples go to some eating place which is not too far away to have a bite to eat.
8. I found out that shopping quickly weakens a friend's patience when I went to a department store with Dolores one day.
9. The clash between East and West of ideals were blocking world unity at a time when war might be led to if unity could not be achieved.
10. By the time you have got the children into bed, you are so exhausted that all ambition to study has been lost by you, and television is all that is left as the only entertainment until the return of the parents is made.
11. A single goal may dominate an individual so that it is the only thing they live for and they work so hard that they miss the fun in life and are never satisfied.
12. Being the first author to make a strong case for complete independence from England, Paine's book was a big seller, and it was about American independence.

13. Going even further into the effects of not having any more petroleum would have on the world is the realization that the thousands of factories in the world which use oil would have to close down.

14. After graduating from high school the learning we have attained may be lost or become hazy in a year of military training and it also adds another year to the time we will graduate from college to get a job.

15. There should be required by the school a pre-season physical examination, and there should be enforced a law to prevent anyone from playing football with a history of heart abnormalities.

PART FOUR

COMPOSITION:
The Writing Process

CHAPTER 21

Writing and Thinking

THE WRITING PROCESS

Whenever you write a paragraph or a composition, you are involved in a process that involves thinking, making decisions, and rethinking. A piece of writing is not something that you can or should do in a single sitting. Many steps are required from the time you first think about a piece of writing until the time you consider your work finished. In this chapter, you will learn about five stages in the writing process and the many steps that make up each stage.

THE WRITING PROCESS

PREWRITING—Identifying your purpose and audience; choosing a subject; considering attitude and tone; limiting a subject; gathering information; classifying and ordering information

WRITING A FIRST DRAFT—Expressing your ideas in sentences and paragraphs

REVISING—Improving the content, word choice, and sentence structure in a draft

PROOFREADING— Checking the revised version to correct inaccuracies in grammar, usage, and mechanics

WRITING THE FINAL VERSION—Preparing a final version and proofreading it

PREWRITING

The first stage in the writing process is called prewriting. During this stage you make decisions about four important questions: Why am I writing? For whom am I writing? What will I write about? What will I say?

THE WRITER'S PURPOSE

21a. Have in mind a clear purpose for writing.

Every piece of writing has a purpose—sometimes more than one purpose. If you write a composition about the origin of the game of basketball, your purpose is to give information or explain. If you write a paragraph about what happened when you took your driving test, your purpose would be to tell about a series of events.

Most writing has one of the following four purposes:

(1) Narrative writing tells a story or relates a series of events.

EXAMPLES   A composition about your first job interview
           A letter to a friend about your first day on a new job

(2) Expository writing gives information or explains.

EXAMPLES   A paragraph answering an essay question about what a water table
           is and why it is important
           A composition about the discovery of King Tut's tomb in Egypt

(3) Descriptive writing describes a person, place, or thing.

EXAMPLES   A composition describing the Grand Canyon
           A letter to a friend describing a new boyfriend or girlfriend

(4) Persuasive writing attempts to persuade or convince.

EXAMPLES   A letter to the editor about suggestions for improving lunch hour in
           the cafeteria
           A brochure encouraging 18-year-olds to register to vote

EXERCISE 1. Identifying Purposes for Writing.   Decide what the writer's purpose is in each of the following paragraphs.

1   *Discriptive*

David Gordon's new ballet *Field, Chair, and Mountain* uses ordinary folding chairs in a unique way. The dancers enter the stage carrying their own chairs. In the first section of the "chair" part of this ballet, the chair is each dancer's partner, giving support and balance as the dancers move in unison in a long series of graceful, intricate ballet movements. A romantic duo between the lead male and female dancers is played also with the chair as central to the movements. In the final part of the "chair" section of this ballet, the whole troupe of dancers dance in pairs, each pair with a chair. The graceful, innovative, sometimes humorous movements are danced to the music of a nineteenth-century piano concerto by the Irish composer John Field.

2   *Expository*

Haleakala National Park, established in 1916 on the island of Maui, Hawaii, is the eroded peak of a 10,000-foot dormant volcano. The volcano last erupted sometime around 1790. The crater of Haleakala is so large that all of Manhattan could fit into it with room left over for part of the borough of Queens. Visitors may view the crater by paying about $200 for a helicopter ride or renting a horse (about $110) for an eight-hour tour of the crater. By car, visitors can drive to the lookout point at the western edge of the summit, stopping to watch the spectacular sunrise. The cheapest way to see the crater, and the most "personal," is to hike the four-mile trail that descends almost 3,000 feet to the crater's bottom.

EXERCISE 2. Identifying Purposes for Writing. Identify the purpose you would have in writing about each of the following topics. Number your paper 1–10. After each number, write the letter of the appropriate purpose. Some items may have more than one purpose.

   a. To describe a person, place, or object
   b. To tell a story or relate a series of events
   c. To explain or give information
   d. To persuade someone that an opinion is right

1. What a penguin looks like   *discriptive*
2. The history of the founding of the state of Pennsylvania   *Expository*
3. Something funny that happened to you on a shopping trip   *narrative*
4. How to replace a door   *Expository*
5. How to plant a rose bush   *Expository*
6. Why high-school students should volunteer to help elderly people in the community   *persuasive*

7. Who Sam Houston was ~~clause~~ *discriptive - Expository*
8. What your brother's car looks like *discriptive*
9. What the difference is between a psychiatrist and a psychologist *Expository*
10. Why children and adults should visit a dentist every six months for a checkup *pursasive Expository*

CRITICAL THINKING:
Analyzing How Purpose Affects Writing

For test only

Synthesis is- to creat a greater whole. smaller to greater

Analysis is the critical thinking skill that you use when you think about how a whole can be broken into its smaller parts. You use analysis in writing when you narrow a broad, general subject into a limited, more specific topic. Analysis is also the skill that you use when you think about how the parts of a whole are related to each other and how each part affects the whole. During the prewriting stage, you will analyze how audience and purpose will affect your finished piece of writing.

The purpose that you choose will affect both the content of your writing and the words you choose to express your ideas. If your purpose is to inform, you will include many specific details and write in fairly formal language.

> Natural sunlight and some artificial sources of illumination can cause a host of visual difficulties. Ultraviolet light from the sun and from lamps can cause cataracts and retinal damage. Even during winter, when the amount of ultraviolet radiation reaching the earth's surface is greatly reduced, those such as skiers and skaters exposed to intense direct or reflected light can suffer harm. Dr. Morris Waxler of the Food and Drug Administration says that they should wear sunglasses that filter out ultraviolet light during exposure to the midday sun and to other strong sources.
>
> JANE E. BRODY

However, if you are writing to tell a story, you will use less formal language and choose details or events that will interest your reader.

> When I was seven and my brother thirteen, my parents took us for a vacation to Florida. We drove from the freezing January of Cleveland, Ohio, to the tropical sunshine of sunny Miami, making the trip in three days. The warmth and the ocean were unbelievable to us, straight from the gray cold of Cleveland's winter. My brother

and I hurried to the beach and spent all of our first afternoon swimming, building sand castles, and—worst of all—lying on our stomachs at the shoreline while the waves washed delightfully over our legs. Of course, I didn't realize it at the time, but I was absorbing enough ultraviolet rays to burn my legs badly. By evening, I was in considerable pain; by morning I could not walk. I spent the next three days in bed, recovering from that painful sunburn. And that's the last bad sunburn I've ever had. Since then, I've used sun screen liberally to cover my fair, freckled skin, and I always limit my time in the sun. Nothing is worth the pain of a bad sunburn, as I still remember it.

If your purpose is to persuade, you will use formal language to express specific opinions, reasons, and evidence. Your writing style will be concise, and you will concentrate on expressing your ideas as clearly as you can.

Descriptive writing uses less formal language and a looser, freer writing style. Your description will include specific concrete and sensory details as you try to create a vivid image for your reader.

EXERCISE 3. Analyzing How Purpose Affects Writing. Each of the numbered items identifies a topic and an audience plus two purposes for writing. Consider how each purpose would affect the piece of writing. For example, for each purpose think about what specific aspect of the topic you might choose to write about. Decide also what kinds of details you might include in your writing. Be prepared to discuss your answers.

1. *Topic:* Choosing wood for a bookcase
   Audience: Class of adults taking a woodworking class
   Purpose: a. To inform   b. To describe

2. *Topic:* How to read a checking account statement
   Audience: A group of high-school seniors
   Purpose: a. To inform   b. To tell a story

3. *Topic:* Using a word processor
   Audience: Students in a word-processing class
   Purpose: a. To tell a story   b. To inform

4. *Topic:* Volunteering to tutor elementary-school students who need help in learning to read
   Audience: Group of high-school students
   Purpose: a. To persuade   b. To inform

THE WRITER'S AUDIENCE

21b. Identify the audience for whom you are writing.

Before you actually begin writing, it is helpful to determine who your audience will be. For example, a composition about donating blood to the blood bank in your community might be written for any of the following audiences: a group of senior citizens, a group of fourth-graders, a group of medical students, or a group of high-school chemistry students. For each of these audiences, your essay will be somewhat different.

EXERCISE 4. Identifying Purpose and Audience. Go to the library and find six different samples of writing. You may include magazine and newspaper articles, novels, and short stories. For each piece of writing, be prepared to tell what you think is the writer's main purpose and who you think is the intended audience.

CRITICAL THINKING:
Analyzing How Audience Affects Writing

The following paragraphs were written for an audience of adults who share a knowledge of, and interest in, wildlife:

> Until recently most students of migration focused on its mechanics, such as energetics, or navigation and orientation. Little was known about what happens to "our" birds during the months they are away from their breeding grounds. Where do they go? What dangers do they face? How do they live in their winter homes? Nature's grandest theatrical event remained largely mysterious.
>
> Now ornithologists who followed the birds into the tropics are able to answer some of those questions. One point, though it may ruffle our proprietary instincts, ought to be cleared up at once. A good many of the most familiar birds in our gardens and forests are not "ours" at all. Families such as the wood warblers, vireos, flycatchers, and tanagers are, for the most part, not northern birds that happen to fly south for a while to escape the wintry blasts. They are tropical birds that come north for a few months every year to raise a family and then return to their ancestral homes.
>
> FRANK GRAHAM, JR.

Imagine that you were writing this same information for a class of fifth-graders. What changes would you make? You would have to explain or omit some unfamiliar terms, such as *energetics, navigation,* and *orientation.* You would surely have to tell students that ornithologists are the scientists who specialize in the study of birds. If it were possible, you might pick the names of more familiar species of birds to list in the second paragraph. In addition, you might generally simplify the vocabulary and shorten the sentence length to make the information easier to understand. You might also replace the rather flowery phrases *grandest theatrical event, ruffle our proprietary instincts,* and *ancestral homes.*

Because audiences vary widely in age, background, interests, and knowledge, you need to adjust your writing to your particular audience's needs. You need also to be aware of any *biases* (prejudices) the audience might have either in favor of a topic or against it. This is particularly important in persuasive writing. To understand how your audience affects your writing, consider each of the following questions. You will use the answers to these questions to adapt your writing to a specific audience.

1. Is the audience made up of friends, acquaintances, or strangers? Is the audience made up of some combination of these groups?
2. What background information does the audience already have about the topic? What background information will you need to supply? Will you, for example, need to explain the history of a situation or explain references to unfamiliar people or places?
3. What terms will be unfamiliar to the audience? Which of these terms will you need to define? Which ones can be replaced by easier words or expressions that will not need to be defined?
4. Does the audience have any bias (strong feelings either for or against) toward the topic? If so, what is the bias—violently opposed, moderately opposed, or in favor?

EXERCISE 5. Analyzing an Essay. Read the following paragraphs carefully, and then answer the questions that follow.

One series of experiments has shown that the activity of certain immune defense cells called natural killer cells can be greatly enhanced by the brain's trained response to a totally extraneous stimulus from the outside world—a strong odor. The killer cells are part of the body's surveillance system that protects against invasion and probably against cancer.

The research was designed by Dr. Novera Herbert Spector of the National Institute of Neurological and Communicative Disorders and Stroke, a unit of the National Institutes of Health. The experiments were done mainly at the University of Alabama medical school in Birmingham by Brent Solvason, Dr. Vithal Ghanta, and Dr. Raymond Hirahito.

Mice were exposed for three hours at a time to the odor of camphor. The scientists showed that exposure to this odor, by itself, had no detectable effect on the immune system. But in the experiments, some of the mice were also given injections of a synthetic chemical called poly I:C (for polyinosinic-polycytidilic acid), which is known to enhance the activity of natural killer cells. The exposures were repeated nine times in a strategy similar to that of the Pavlovian conditioning in which dogs were given food every time a bell rang. In each session of the immunity experiments, the mice were exposed to the odor and given injections of the chemical.

Then, in the tenth session, the mice were exposed only to the odor of camphor. They received no injections at all. Nevertheless, every mouse showed a large increase in natural killer cell activity.

1. Who would you say is the intended audience for this article?
2. What is the writer's purpose?
3. Make a list of at least four words that you would have to define or replace if you were writing this information for a group of fifth-graders.
4. Which of the following do you think you would have to give background information about if your audience did not know much about science?
   a. immunological defense system
   b. University of Alabama medical school
   c. Pavlovian conditioning
   d. synthetic chemicals
5. If your audience were any one of the following, would you keep or drop the second paragraph containing the information about who designed the research and who did the experiments?
   a. a group of doctors
   b. a group of fifth-graders
   c. a group of average adult readers
   d. a group of high-school biology students

EXERCISE 6. Rewriting Paragraphs for a Different Audience.
Bring to class several paragraphs (at least three) from a high-school or college textbook or an adult reference book. You might choose a topic

that interests you—one for which you already have some background knowledge or experience. Rewrite the paragraphs for two of the following audiences. At the beginning of each version, identify the audience for whom you are writing.
a. A group of fourth-grade students
b. A group of specialists or experts in the field you are writing about
c. A group of high-school students who have no previous knowledge of your topic
d. A group of adults who have no previous knowledge of your topic
e. A group of exchange students from the Soviet Union

EXERCISE 7. Analyzing How Audience Affects Writing. For each numbered item, answer the following questions. Be prepared to discuss your answers.
a. Which audience would have the most knowledge of the topic? Which would have the least knowledge?
b. For which audiences would technical terms need to be defined?
c. For which audiences would background information be necessary?
d. Which audiences might be biased in favor of the topic? Which might be biased against the topic?
e. Which of the audiences listed would you choose to write for? Why?
1. *Topic:* Why all high-school students should be required to take four years of mathematics in high school
   Purpose: To persuade
   Audience: (a) Members of a nine-grade math class, (b) group of high-school mathematics teachers, (c) members of the local board of education, (d) parents of a group of third-graders
2. *Topic:* How to repair an electric plug
   Purpose: To inform
   Audience: (a) A group of licensed electricians, (b) a group of high-school students, (c) a group of men and women who know nothing about electrical repairs, (d) a group of second-grade students
3. *Topic:* Why you should write to your Congressional representative to make your views known on important issues
   Purpose: To persuade
   Audience: (a) A group of newspaper writers, (b) a group of high-school students in an English class, (c) a group of business and banking executives, (d) a group of sixth-graders

4. *Topic:* The dangers of eating wild plants that might be poisonous
   Purpose: To inform
   Audience: (a) A group of campers in a national park, (b) a group of young children (ages seven to nine), (c) a group of botanists, (d) a group of people who eat only "natural foods"

5. *Topic:* Why the zoning should be changed in a residential area to allow factories to be built in that area
   Purpose: To persuade
   Audience: (a) A group of homeowners who do not want the zoning laws changed, (b) members of the city council who have to approve all changes in zoning laws, (c) owners of the land on which the proposed factories will be built, (d) members of the general public (readers of the local newspaper)

CHOOSING A SUBJECT

21c. Choose a subject that is appropriate to your audience.

If you are willing to take the time to provide background information and define terms, you can probably write about any subject for any audience. You could, for example, explain the concept of probability to an audience of third-graders. You would, however, have to know your subject well in order to be able to simplify it enough for a very young audience. Whenever the choice of topic is up to you, avoid choosing a subject that is too difficult for your audience.

Your subject should also be appropriate to the audience's interests and concerns. For instance, people who rent apartments will not be interested in tax laws that involve homeowners, but the topic may have great appeal to a group of homeowners. Similarly, a discussion of the latest fashions in work clothing probably would not interest anyone required to wear a uniform at work.

EXERCISE 8. Choosing a Topic Appropriate for an Audience.
For each of the following topics, suggest two audiences for which the topic would be appropriate. Suggest one audience for which the topic would not be appropriate. Be prepared to explain your choices.

1. How to make money on the stock market
2. How to improve your scores on the Graduate Record Exam (given to college graduates applying to graduate school)

3. The latest bargains in air fares to Europe
4. What to look for on a hiking trip along the Appalachian Trail
5. How to get along with teen-agers
6. Benefits of owning term life insurance as opposed to straight life
7. The most valuable postage stamps in the world
8. Planning a Thanksgiving dinner for thirty
9. The history of the amendment to the U.S. Constitution that gave women the right to vote
10. How to do batik (a method of dying cloth)

EXERCISE 9. Choosing Subjects for Writing. Read the following list of broad subjects. Choose five that you would be interested in learning more about, or choose five subjects of your own.

1. Politics today
2. How to make a movie
3. Ideas for making money
4. American folk songs
5. The history of jazz
6. Great American novels
7. Learning to fly a plane
8. Oil painting
9. Raising healthy children
10. Ancient Greek civilization
11. Coin collecting
12. The American theater today
13. History of football
14. Household repairs
15. Car repairs
16. World War I
17. Cross-country skiing
18. Photography
19. Spy novels
20. The Civil War

TONE

21d. Identify your attitude toward your subject, which will be expressed through the tone of your writing.

Before you begin writing, you need to determine your attitude, or point of view, toward your subject. Your *attitude* may be favorable (positive) or unfavorable (negative), humorous or serious, angry or enthusiastic. Attitude influences the kinds of details you include in your writing. For example, if you had a humorous attitude toward your topic of an overnight camping trip, you would choose humorous incidents to relate. If your attitude were serious, you might include advice about necessary equipment and safety precautions.

Your attitude affects not only the details that you include in your writing, but also the language that you use to express your ideas. Your choice of language will help to create a *tone* that is serious or humorous, formal or informal, personal or objective.

Consider, for example, the following paragraph from *Travels with Charley: In Search of America*. In it, the writer John Steinbeck explains the reasons for his journey across America. What would you say is the tone of the paragraph?

> My plan was clear, concise, and reasonable, I think. For many years I have traveled in many parts of the world. In America I live in New York or dip into Chicago or San Francisco. But New York is no more America than Paris is France or London is England. Thus I discovered that I did not know my own country. I, an American writer, writing about America, was working from memory, and the memory is at best a faulty, warpy reservoir. I had not heard the speech of America, smelled the grass and trees and sewage, seen its hills and water, its color and quality of light. I knew the changes only from books and newspapers. But more than this, I had not felt the country for twenty-five years. In short, I was writing of something I did not know about, and it seems to me that in a so-called writer this is criminal. My memories were distorted by twenty-five intervening years.
>
> JOHN STEINBECK

The tone of the writing is serious and fairly formal (Steinbeck does not, for example, use contractions or slang words). The writer's attitude toward his topic seems positive, even respectful.

Contrast the tone of Steinbeck's paragraph with the tone of the following excerpt from a movie review.

> "Cross Creek," an account of a woman's struggle to become a writer, is given a supernal glow by the director Martin Ritt. The picture seems to be suffering from earthshine: everything is lighted to look holy, and whenever the score isn't shimmering and burnishing, nature is twittering. It's all pearly and languid, and more than a little twerpy—it's one long cue for "Oh, What a Beautiful Mornin'." Loosely based on Marjorie Kinnan Rawlings' semi-autobiographical tales about what she learned during her years in an orange grove in the Florida swamps, the movie opens in 1928. We're meant to admire Mrs. Rawlings (Mary Steenburgen), a Northerner, for her courage in leaving her home and husband and going down to Florida to write. But the script doesn't give even a hint of why she bought the grove (sight unseen), or why she thinks she'll find more propitious conditions for writing gothic romances in the subtropical marshland than she had in her bedroom or her study in New York. The filmmakers view her as a feminist ahead of her time—a heroine who gives up a social life and goes out on her own to face

hardships. Yet the way they tell the story, she's almost immediately equipped with everything she has cast aside. When her jalopy gives out before she arrives at her property, it's said to be in hopeless condition, but the courtly and handsome hotelkeeper Norton Baskin (Peter Coyote), who drives her to her tumbledown shack, shows up again a day or two later bringing the car, which has been repaired so that it looks sparkling and new. Meanwhile, friendly neighbors have been dropping in, and Mrs. Rawlings has hired a young black woman, Geechee (Alfre Woodard), to clean and cook, and field hands to take care of the crops. The house is already transformed; it's gracious and orderly, and she's at her typewriter, with a potted gloxinia blooming nearby. She's ladylike, and the local people do everything for her. So what's so heroic about her—beyond her managerial skills?

PAULINE KAEL—THE NEW YORKER

The tone of Pauline Kael's paragraph is informal (note the contractions and colloquial words, such as *twerpy* and *jalopy*) and negative. She clearly does not like the movie, and her tone is appropriately sarcastic.

EXERCISE 10. Identifying Tone. Bring to class five different samples of paragraphs from a variety of sources, such as magazines, short stories, novels, and nonfiction books. Identify the tone of each paragraph and the author's attitude toward the subject.

LIMITING THE SUBJECT

21e. Limit your subject so that it can be adequately covered in the form of writing you have chosen.

A *subject* is a broad, general area of knowledge, such as "Robots" or "Art." A *topic*, on the other hand, is a limited subject—one that is specific enough so that it can serve as the basis for a paragraph or a composition. "The Use of Robots in the Home" and "Vincent Van Gogh's Landscapes at Arles" are limited subjects, or topics.

A topic for a paragraph is, of course, necessarily more limited than a composition topic because you have far less space in which to develop the main idea. Remember that a topic for writing must be adequately covered in the space that is available to you. You must provide readers with enough information so that they are not left with numerous questions about the topic.

EXERCISE 11. Distinguishing Between Subjects and Topics.
Number your paper 1–10, and identify each item as either a broad, general subject (*S*) or a topic (*T*). The topics should be limited enough so that they can be adequately covered in a short composition.

1. How to prepare tacos
2. The history of automobiles
3. William Shakespeare
4. The juvenile justice system
5. Efforts to save the endangered manatee
6. Better television programs
7. How to create a crossword puzzle
8. The care and feeding of African violets
9. Dieting and exercise
10. Major league baseball

CRITICAL THINKING:
Analyzing the Elements of a Subject

A broad, general subject may be analyzed (divided and subdivided) into smaller elements that may serve as the limited topic for writing. Depending on the subject, the basis for the first set of divisions may be any of the following: time periods, examples, features, uses of, causes, types of.

EXAMPLES   1. *Subject divided into examples*
        Subject: Dogs that are bred for hunting

      Main divisions: Retrievers
                       Hounds
                       Setters
                       Pointers
                       Spaniels
    2. *Subject divided into features or aspects*
        Subject: Dreams
      Main divisions: Why people dream
                       Types of dreams
                       Interpreting dreams
                       How scientists study dreaming

EXERCISE 12. Analyzing Subjects to Develop Topics for Writing. From the following list of subjects, choose the five that most interest you. Analyze each of these subjects by dividing it into at least three smaller parts. (Note: There is no single "right" way to analyze a subject. For each subject many different analyses are possible.)

1. Congress
2. Tennis
3. Personality
4. The Southwest
5. American literature
6. Exploration
7. Pollution
8. Space travel
9. Oceans
10. Alcoholism
11. Mountains
12. Popular music
13. Medicine
14. Precious metals
15. Trees

EXERCISE 13. Limiting a Subject to Develop Topics Suitable for Paragraphs. Choose one of the subjects that you analyzed into smaller parts for Exercise 12. Could each of these smaller parts be covered adequately in a paragraph of about 150 words? If not, continue dividing the parts further until you have at least three topics that can be adequately covered in a paragraph. List these limited topics.

GATHERING INFORMATION

21f. Gather information appropriate to your purpose.

The kinds of details that you include in your writing are largely determined by your purpose. For example, in the following paragraph the writer includes specific facts and examples in order to inform the reader about how and where shark fins are processed for food.

> The Sharks' Fin Trade Merchants Association has a membership of sixty-four firms, all of which process shark fin for restaurants. Most of them are in a district called Sai Ying Poon in the western portion of Hong Kong island. These tiny shops, each of them employing a dozen workers, take the dried fins and laboriously scrape off the black skins, taking care not to remove meat as they do so. They carefully split the dorsal fins and remove the structural bones, again with great care so that the valuable meat is not lost.
>
> —————— EILEEN YIN-FEI LO

If, however, your purpose were to describe a room, you would give specific and concrete details that would help the reader to visualize the room, as in the following example.

> I went on down the hallway and out onto the back porch and finally into the kitchen that was built at the very rear of the house. The entire room was dominated by a huge black cast-iron stove with six eyes on its cooking surface. Directly across the room from the stove was the safe, a tall square cabinet with wide doors covered with screen wire that was used to keep biscuits and fried meat and rice or almost any other kind of food that had been recently cooked. Between the stove and the safe sat the table we ate off of, a table almost ten feet long, with benches on each side instead of chairs, so that when we put in tobacco, there would be enough room for the hired hands to eat.
>
> HARRY CREWS

On the following pages, you will learn about many different techniques for gathering information for writing. You may use a combination of several different methods, or you may decide to use only one technique. Practicing all of these techniques will help you decide which ones you find most useful and easiest to work with.

Direct and Indirect Observation

(1) Use your powers of observation to note specific details.

Whenever your observations are made directly through your senses of sight, smell, sound, taste, or touch, they are called *direct observations*. In the following paragraph, the writer records direct observations made at the opening ceremonies of the Maori art exhibit from New Zealand. The ceremonies began at the moment of dawn when a group of about a hundred Maori men, women, and children assembled on the steps of the Metropolitan Museum of Art in New York City.

> From the top of the steps, the women called out again to the group, and the calling, chanting, and wailing continued as the procession made its way into the museum, normally dark and deserted at such an hour, and through the Egyptian Wing. Arriving at the Sackler Exhibition Hall, where the Maori works were assembled, the Maoris were quiet for a moment, but they resumed chanting as they wove cautiously through the collection of intricately carved gateways, lintels, weapons, pendants, figureheads, clubs, and other objects of wood, stone, and bone—chanting now directed to the objects

themselves. The warriors darted along the walls, and the group finally stopped before the Fort, a large, totemlike doorway of red-ochre and muted-green wood on which is a large carved head with abalone-shell eyes of iridescent green. The chanting stopped, three elders sat down, and the group was addressed by some of the exhibition's sponsors. J. Richardson Dilworth, of the Metropolitan, and Donald Cox, of the American Federation of Arts (which had organized the show), assured the Maoris of the care and respect their art would be accorded; Sir James Henare, a *Kaumatua* (elder), spoke of his wish that the United States and New Zealand would be separated in the future only by the great Pacific Ocean; and R.J. McCool of Mobil spoke of Mobil's plans to convert natural gas into gasoline in New Zealand. At 7:30 A.M., the Honorable Mr. Koro Tainui Wetere, the Minister of Maori Affairs, first speaking in Maori and then smoothly switching to English, declared the exhibition officially open. As the elders and the Americans began shaking hands and touching noses—the traditional Maori greeting—several of the warriors broke jubilantly into a loud, energetic dance, which lasted only a minute or two.

THE NEW YORKER

If your observations are not made directly through your own senses, they are called *indirect observations*. When you listen to other people telling about their experiences or when you read about other people's observations, you are making an indirect observation. Much of the information that you gather for your writing will be indirect observations.

CRITICAL THINKING:
Observing Specific Details

The writer who described the opening ceremony of the Maori art exhibit (pages 382–83) carefully noted details of color, movement, and sound. Obviously, you cannot possibly notice every detail that your senses experience, but you can work toward improving your powers of observation. Concentrate on paying attention to as many specific details as possible.

EXERCISE 14. Improving Your Powers of Observation.
Choose one of the following experiences. Take a pencil and paper with you, and carefully list as many sensory details (details of sight, sound, smell, touch, and taste) as you can. Sit (or stand) in one place, and spend at least ten minutes observing specific details. Try to make your list as long as possible.

1. Visit a shopping mall.
2. Sit on a park bench near a playground.
3. Visit a crowded supermarket.
4. Sit in the school cafeteria during lunch hour.
5. Observe the street outside your home at 6 A.M.
6. Observe an empty field (or woods or vacant lot).
7. Go to a restaurant.
8. Stand in some kind of a line.
9. Wait for a bus or subway.
10. Observe a school hallway before (or after) school.

EXERCISE 15. Testing Your Powers of Observation. Arrange a test of observational skills for your classmates. You might, for example, assemble a group of twenty-five objects on a table and cover them with a cloth. Ask students to try to remember everything they see as you uncover the objects for thirty seconds, and then cover them again. Ask students to list all of the objects they remember. Another observation test would be to ask students to list all of the details they remember from a slide (a photograph of a busy scene, perhaps, or a city street) shown for twenty seconds.

A Writer's Journal

(2) Keep a writer's journal to record your thoughts and feelings about your experiences.
A writer's journal can be a source of ideas for writing topics. It can also help you to remember specific details about a particular experience. One coach for a professional football team recently asked all of his players to keep a journal about how they felt and what they thought after every game. The journal, the coach believed and the players agreed, helped them to understand their feelings and their experiences better.

In your journal, you can record any of the following kinds of things: your own experiences, ideas, and feelings; reactions to other people and the things they say and do; reactions to current events; opinions about movies, books, TV shows; things you want to remember or do someday. A writer's journal should contain only those ideas, experiences, and feelings that you want to share with others. You might also consider keeping a private journal for your own use.

EXERCISE 16. Using a Journal Entry to Gather Ideas for Writing. Read the following journal entries, and then answer the questions that follow.

January 22nd. Not too often that frost hits southern Florida—sometimes the central part of the state, but not here. Temperature going down to 30 degrees tonight after two days of "Arctic" weather. Rest of the country is having weird weather, too, with $-27°$ in Chicago combined with a wind-chill factor that makes it $-80°$. Wow! I'm glad I'm missing that. Poor Uncle Bernie in Chicago. Trying to save my vegetable garden. Draped all of the vegetables with black plastic. Mom helped me water the ground well without getting leaves wet. I feel sorry for the farmers with acres and acres to try to save. Can't use smudge pots here; don't even know where I'd find one. We've moved my two zebra finches to the kitchen, the warmest room in the house. They're so delicate they'd never survive the chill in the rest of the house. Hoping for the best tonight.

January 23rd. Temperature went down to 29! A record for Florida. Vegetable plants are all frozen, but I tried my best. When the weather warms, I'll start again with tomato seedlings, eggplant, peppers. Farmers here have lost most of their crops, and the upstate citrus crops are badly damaged.

1. On the basis of these entries, the writer decided that he could write a composition describing how to plant a small vegetable garden. Think of two other topics, suggested by the entry, that he might write about. List as many topic ideas as you can think of.
2. Suppose you decided to write a composition about how to care for zebra finches. Where would you look for information? What kinds of details would you look for?
3. Suppose you decided to write a paragraph about record temperatures (high and low) in Miami, Florida, during the last ten years. Where would you look for information?

4. If you had a chance to ask a Florida citrus farmer some questions about the freeze, what questions would you ask? Think of at least three questions.

Brainstorming and Clustering

(3) Use brainstorming and clustering to find writing ideas.

Both brainstorming and clustering are techniques used to generate a free flow of ideas. You may use these techniques either to think of topics for writing or to generate specific details to develop a topic you have already chosen.

Brainstorming

When you *brainstorm* you think of one specific subject or topic, and then write down every idea, word, or phrase that comes to mind as you concentrate on that subject or topic. The end result is a long list of words or phrases—the longer, the better—written under the subject or topic you started with. Work as quickly as possible, jotting down every idea that occurs to you, and keep going until you feel that you have absolutely run out of ideas.

As you brainstorm, do not stop to evaluate the ideas you are listing; that comes later. Your purpose is simply to write down everything that comes to mind. Only when you have finished brainstorming should you stop to evaluate the items you have listed.

The following list resulted from a five-minute brainstorming on the subject "Deer."

DEER

Hunting deer
Kinds of deer—tiny Keys deer; white-tailed deer
Deer endangered?
What happens to deer in winter—food supply?
Deer need salt
Bambi and other deer stories
Gentle, peaceful creatures
What do they harm? Eat gardens, crops
Relatives of antelopes? Many African species?
Sayings associated with deer—shy as a deer, run like a deer
Social structure of deer—travel in groups? Stay in families? How many born each year?
Where are most deer living—what parts of the U.S.?

Many road signs about deer crossing; urban areas?
Life cycle of deer
Males called bucks; females—does; babies—fawns

Clustering

Clustering, sometimes called *making connections*, is similar to brainstorming. The end result is a diagram (instead of a list, as in brainstorming) with ideas grouped together around the subject or topic you started with. Begin by writing a subject or a limited topic in the center of a piece of paper, and then draw a circle around that word or phrase. Think about the circled item, and write around it whatever related ideas come to mind—just as you did with brainstorming. As you add each new idea, circle it and draw a line connecting it either to the word or phrase in the center or to a related idea already on the paper. (In fact, it is a good idea to write down related ideas close to each other.) Continue to write down whatever new ideas occur to you, circling them and drawing lines (whenever it is possible to do so) to connect them to ideas already on your paper.

Here is a clustering diagram for the same subject, "Deer." Notice that not all of the ideas can be grouped together; some are related only to the subject "Deer."

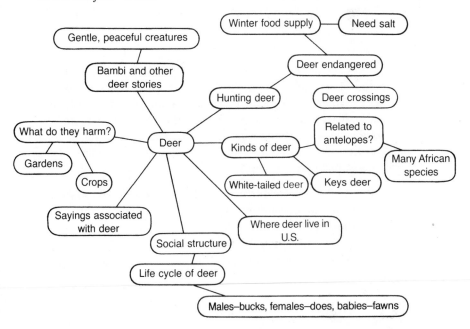

EXERCISE 17. Using Brainstorming or Clustering to Gather Information. Choose one of the topics that you developed in Exercise 13 on page 381, or choose another limited topic. In this exercise you will generate specific ideas and information to use in developing the limited topic. Use either brainstorming or clustering, whichever technique you prefer, to gather information about the topic you have chosen.

Asking the 5 W-How? Questions

(4) Gather information and ideas by asking the 5 W-How? questions.

The *5 W-How?* questions are *Who? What? Where? When? Why?* and *How?* These basic questions can help you gather specific details to use in your writing. Not every question will apply to every topic.

EXAMPLE   *Topic:* The founding of this city (community)
    Who?   Who founded this city?
    What?   What was here before the city was founded?
    Where? Where was the first settlement built?
            Where is the oldest part of the city?
    When?   When was the city founded?
    Why?   Why was the city founded founded at this particular place?
            Why did the first people come here?
    How?   How was the city founded?

EXERCISE 18. Gathering Information by Asking the 5 W-How? Questions. Use the *5 W-How?* questions (*Who? What? Where? When? Why? How?*) to gather information about one of the following topics or a topic of your own. Write the specific questions that you ask, as well as the answers to the questions. (You may need to do some research to find the answers to some of the questions.) Some of the *5 W-How?* questions may not apply to the topic you have chosen.

1. Something funny that happened to you or someone you know
2. The record-breaking achievement of an outstanding athlete
3. An important change in your life
4. An experience with a natural disaster
5. A solution to an important problem in your community (or city or state)

6. An important event in world history
7. The achievements of a great American
8. The major battle in the Civil War (or any other war)
9. An important election
10. An accident

Asking Point-of-View Questions

(5) Gather information and ideas by viewing the subject from different points of view.

Another questioning technique for gathering information requires that you consider your topic from three different points of view. Each point of view has a basic question that will generate other questions specific to a topic. The three basic questions are: (1) What is it? (2) How does it change or vary? (3) What are its relationships?[1]

1. *What is it?*

In this first point of view, you will focus on the topic itself. If your topic is a place, person, or object, you will ask questions that will elicit specific details about what the topic looks like, what it does, and how it is different from others of its kind.

EXAMPLE *Topic:* My favorite place to be alone and think
[Where is the place? What does it look like? Why have I chosen it as my favorite place? How does it make me feel when I am there?]

This point-of-view question (What is it?) can be useful even when your topic is an abstract idea. By analyzing what the topic is, you will be able to define it and to understand how it differs from other, similar ideas or topics.

EXAMPLE *Topic:* What is a democracy?
[How does a democracy work? What are its unique characteristics that make it different from other forms of government? What nations today have democratic forms of government?]

[1] This technique is based on ideas in *Rhetoric: Discovery and Change* by Richard E. Young, Alton L. Becker, and Kenneth E. Pike (New York: Harcourt Brace Jovanovich, 1971).

2. *How does it change or vary?*

This second point of view focuses on how a topic changes over a period of time. Questions related to this point of view enable you to discover information about a topic's history and about its future.

EXAMPLE   *Topic:* Being a passenger on a transcontinental railroad
[When was the first transcontinental railroad completed? What was railroad travel like in those days? How long did it take to travel across America? What is transcontinental railroad passenger service like now? How long does it take to go cross-country? What are passenger cars like? Is there more service for passengers today than fifty years ago, or less? What will passenger railroad service be like ten years from now? Will there be improvements, such as the high-speed bullet train?]

From this second point of view (How does it change or vary?), you can also consider how a topic keeps its identity even when it varies. The following example poses questions about the nature of the fourteen-line form of poetry called the sonnet.

EXAMPLE   *Topic:* What is a sonnet?
[What are the defining characteristics of a sonnet that distinguish it from other types of poems? What are the major types of sonnets? How do they differ? What are some examples of famous sonnets? What are some examples of modern sonnets?]

3. *What are its relationships?*

For the third point of view, you focus on the different elements or aspects of your topic, considering how the elements are related to each other and to the topic as a whole. This approach uses the critical thinking skill of analysis, which breaks a whole into its parts and determines how the parts are related.

EXAMPLE   *Topic:* Requirements for a successful speech
[What are the various elements that must be present if a speech is to be successful? What is the effect of each of the following elements: content, organization, humor, presentation? Which of these elements is most important? Least important? Or are they all equally important?]

When you consider a topic from the point of view of "What are its relationships?" you may also consider how the topic itself is related to similar topics.

EXAMPLE *Topic:* Reasons for lack of participation in school band
[Why are so few students joining the school band? What is happening to participation in other after-school activities? Are there common causes for the diminished participation in all after-school activities? What, if anything, can be done to increase student participation in these activities?]

EXERCISE 19. Gathering Information by Asking Point-of-View Questions. Use the three different point-of-view questions (What is it? How does it change or vary? What are its relationships?) to generate a series of specific questions for two writing topics. Choose two topics you have already worked with in this chapter, or choose two new topics from any of the exercises in this chapter. If you prefer, you may choose two writing topics of your own. (The topics should be sufficiently limited for a composition.) Write each of the three basic point-of-view questions on your paper. For each of the two topics, write as many specific questions as you can think of under each basic question. When you have finished writing all of the questions that come to mind, write the answers to each question. You may have to do some research to find some of the answers. Save this material to use in a writing assignment.

CLASSIFYING INFORMATION

21g. Classify your ideas and information by grouping related ideas together.

The next step in the writing process is to organize the long list of details you have collected. Note this information on sheets of paper or on note cards. Spend some time studying your collection of details to see what patterns you can find. In *classifying* your information, you will be grouping together related ideas under a heading that explains what they have in common. The result will be an informal outline.

CRITICAL THINKING:
Classifying Ideas and Details

What do the following details have in common?

EXAMPLE   Maps of the route
               Reservations at a hotel or motel or campsite
               Adequate cash or credit cards
               Car in good running order
               Food for snacks, games for children

All of these may be classified under the heading "Preparations for a long car trip or vacation."

It is, of course, much more difficult to "see" the several possible groupings when you are looking at a jumbled list of details or notes. The following questions should help you to classify ideas and information.

1. Among the items listed, are there any that can be grouped together under a larger heading? What do the items have in common?

2. Do some items seem more important than others? Which are the most important (or main) ideas?

3. Which items seem to be subdivisions (examples, parts, etc.) of the main ideas? If you have not listed any of these subdivisions for your main ideas, what do you think they might be?

4. Are there some items that do not seem to fall into any groupings? (You can expect to find these single items among your notes.) Do not hesitate to discard, at this point in the writing process, items that do not seem to fit into any of your groups or headings.

The following outline is based on the list of details about deer on pages 386–87. Notice that the writer has grouped the details under two main headings.

Types of deer in U.S.
    White-tailed deer of northeastern U.S.
    Keys deer of the Florida Keys
    Black-tailed deer of the Pacific coast
    Mule deer of the plains and western U.S.
Dangers to deer
    Natural dangers
        Lack of food (caused by flooding, winter)
        Animal predators
        Disease
    Dangers caused by people
        Hunters
        Cars

The act of classifying information can often suggest details that are missing. You may notice, for example, that the writer has included in this outline several details that were not in the original list of brainstormed ideas—information such as other types of American deer (black-tailed deer and mule deer). The writer also included disease and animal predators under the heading "Natural dangers." On the other hand, she chose to omit many details on the original list of brainstormed information because of the limited space of a short composition.

EXERCISE 20. Classifying Ideas and Information. Look carefully at the following list of ideas for a composition on cave-dwelling animals. First, decide which ideas can be grouped together because they are related. Then decide on the wording of main headings that will show what the ideas have in common. (Note: The headings are not included in this list.) On a separate sheet of paper, write the ideas you have grouped together under their main headings. You may omit any items that do not seem to fit.

a. Cave-dwelling animals called *troglodytes*: salamanders, fish, insects, and crustaceans (shrimps, crabs, crayfish)
b. Animals are blind—eyesight not useful in complete darkness
c. Scarcity of food, must be brought in (by stream, bird droppings) from outside
d. Animals have no pigment; consequently are white
e. No vegetation can grow in caves; no light
f. Weather not a threat—temperature fairly constant
g. Environment usually small with fewer predators than at surface and less competition for existing food
h. High humidity in caves, advantage for skin-breathing animals such as some salamanders
i. Slower metabolism (rate of body functions) than surface animals, allowing them to exist on less food
j. Cave-dwelling animals produce fewer and larger eggs; newborn animals have better chance to survive
k. Animals have longer legs than surface relatives—can search for food more easily
l. *Ursus spelaeus*—extinct species of cave bear; fossils found in caves

ARRANGING INFORMATION

21h. Arrange your ideas in order.

Once you have classified your ideas under main headings, consider the best order in which to present these ideas to your readers. Often, the order will be suggested by your purpose. Chronological order might be appropriate, for example, in a composition on how to prepare for a college-entrance examination, since you might treat the topic as a step-by-step process. If, on the other hand, you are trying to persuade your readers to volunteer to visit elderly residents in a nursing home, you would probably arrange your ideas in the order of importance —with the most important reason last.

In expository compositions background information is often necessary for the reader to understand what you have to say. Such background information, as well as technical terms that need to be defined for your audience, should be presented first. Then arrange your ideas in the order that you think will be clearest and most interesting for your audience. (You will learn more about different types of order in Chapter 22.)

REVIEW EXERCISE A. Following the Steps for Prewriting. Prepare to write a paragraph or short composition on a topic of your choice. If you wish, you may use any of the topics in this chapter that you have not already worked with. Choose a subject, and limit it to a topic that can be covered adequately in a single paragraph. Decide on your purpose and audience, and consider how each will affect your writing. Using at least one of the techniques for gathering information discussed on pages 381–91, make a list of specific details to include in your writing. Classify the details into related groups, make up the main headings, and arrange the information in an appropriate order. The end result of this exercise should be an informal outline for a paragraph or short composition.

WRITING THE FIRST DRAFT

You have completed all of the prewriting steps and are now ready to begin the actual writing of the first draft. A draft is a rough or preliminary version of a piece of writing. This second stage in the writing process is sometimes called *drafting*.

WRITING THE FIRST DRAFT

21i. Write a first draft, keeping your audience and purpose in mind.

Remember that the first draft is only a preliminary version—not the final version of your writing. Before you are finished, you will spend a good deal of time making changes to improve the content, the organization, and the wording. You will also spend time proofreading your revised version to correct errors in spelling, punctuation, capitalization, and usage.

The starting point for your first draft is the informal outline that resulted from all of your prewriting activities. Keep this outline before you as you write. As you are writing sentences and paragraphs, remember that your goal is to express your ideas as clearly as possible. Choose specific details and language that are appropriate to both your audience and purpose.

CRITICAL THINKING:
Synthesis

Analysis is the breaking down of a topic into smaller parts. *Synthesis*, the reverse of analysis, is the creating of a new whole from smaller parts. All writing is a kind of synthesis—the creation of a piece of writing from words and ideas. Architects are engaged in synthesis when they create new buildings; composers when they create new music; and artists when they create paintings and sculpture from basic raw materials. Synthesis is a creative activity.

As you write your first draft, you will be rethinking all of your earlier decisions about content and organization. Perhaps you will decide to omit material you had planned to include; perhaps you will find that you need additional specific information to support an idea or point. You may decide to define a term or change the order in which you had planned to present your ideas. At this stage of the writing process, everything is still flexible, and you should feel free to make whatever changes seem appropriate to you.

EXERCISE 21. Analyzing a First Draft. The following excerpt is from a first draft of a composition about cave animals. Read the excerpt carefully, and answer the questions that follow it.

Caves are dark, damp hollow places within the earth. Sometimes they are hollowed-out places in hillsides. Because no light can reach the inside of a cave and light is necessary for photosynthesis to take place, no plants grow inside of caves, and it is plants that we associate as a source of food for animals. You would expect that caves should be empty of animal life, but that is not true. Thousands of animal species live full-time in caves. They have a special name: troglodytes, or "cave dwellers." Many other species of animals live part-time in caves (bears, bats, some tropical birds), but this paper is about full-time cave-dwelling animals.

A cave isn't the easiest place in which to live, as you can probably imagine. It is dark all the time—*pitch* dark—because no light from the sun can enter the cave except at the cave entrance. There is also very little food in a cave—no plant food, as we have mentioned already. What little food there is must be "imported" from the outside. Usually, it comes into the cave from a stream or, if bats live in the cave, from droppings.

So why would any animal want to live in such a hostile environment? They do. One of the advantages to living in a cave, if you are a troglodyte, is that the weather poses no threat. Usually the temperature inside of a cave remains pretty much the same, unlike the surface world with its extremes of heat, cold, and storms. Life in a cave may be more peaceful than life on the surface, because there are usually fewer predators and less competition for the existing food supply. Some animals that require high humidity to breathe through their skins, like the salamander, are delighted by the high humidity inside of a cave; they never would make it in the outside world.

Troglodytes look different because of the adaptations they have made to living in total darkness. For one thing, most are blind or have no eyes at all and have lost the power to see because it has been unused for generations. Also, troglodytes are white because they have no pigment. Apparently, pigmentation has the purpose of protecting creatures from the effects of the sun. These cave-dwelling creatures have adapted to their environment in other ways. They have longer legs than their relatives on the surface, apparently to enable them to search more easily for food on the craggy surface of the cave walls. Also, their metabolism rate is slower; this slower rate enables the cave-dwellers to get by with less food. They have adapted to their environment in one more way, too, in the way in which they reproduce.

Compared to their surface relatives, they lay fewer eggs and the eggs are bigger. This means that the newborn creatures are bigger and more likely to survive in the challenging environment of the cave.

1. What would you say is the writer's purpose?
2. Who do you think is the intended audience for these paragraphs? How can you tell?
3. Which of the following words or terms do you think need to be defined or explained?
   a. photosynthesis   c. predators
   b. species   d. pigment, pigmentation
4. Suppose the audience for these paragraphs is a group of third-grade students. Would the writing have to be changed in any way? If so, how? Now suppose that the audience is a group of biology teachers. How appropriate is the writing for this audience? What needs to be changed or added?
5. What would you say is the topic of these paragraphs? Is the topic limited enough for a short composition?
6. What is the tone of these paragraphs? Is the tone consistent? Is the tone appropriate for the writer's apparent audience and purpose?
7. Suppose that you could ask a scientist who had done research on troglodytes three questions. What questions would you ask? If you had the answers to your three questions, would the information improve the paragraphs in the first draft?
8. What specific advice would you give the writer of this first draft about how to improve it?

EXERCISE 22. Writing a First Draft.   Use the prewriting notes you developed for Review Exercise A (page 394) to write a first draft of a paragraph. Refer to the Guidelines for Writing Effective Paragraphs (page 438) for some extra help before you begin.

REVISING

Many writers actually do some revising as they write the first draft. They may, for example, substitute precise words for vague ones, change sentence beginnings, or cross out entire sentences. Even if you do make changes as you write, you will still need to spend considerable time revising. Reread your first draft many times, concentrating on how to improve it.

REVISING YOUR FIRST DRAFT

21j. Revise your first draft.

Revising requires several rereadings of the first draft. First, consider each sentence in relation to the paragraph and to the writing as a whole. For a composition, you will need to judge how effectively each paragraph contributes to the total work. In all of these cases, the most important questions are: Is the main idea adequately developed or supported? Is the development or support clear and logical? Next, look closely at each sentence to see how well it expresses what you intended to say. Finally, concentrate on each word in each sentence. Which words, if any, are unnecessary and should therefore be deleted? Which words need to be more precise?

An important part of the revising process is rethinking your writing once more in terms of purpose, audience, and tone. Remember that purpose, audience, and tone affect both the content of your writing and the language you use.

At some point during the revising stage, many teachers ask students to exchange papers and comment on each other's first drafts. The purpose of responding to a classmate's writing is to make helpful suggestions, such as pointing out ideas that are not developed fully. If you are asked to respond to another writer's paper, be honest but tactful in your comments. A writer should not be so discouraged by others' negative comments that he or she sees no way to make a paper better. One good technique for commenting on another person's paper is to mention a strength for every weakness that you cite.

You can use the Guidelines for Revising on page 401 of this chapter with almost any form of writing. On pages 405–406 you will find a set of revising and proofreading symbols that will help you mark changes on your first draft. As your teacher directs, copy the Guidelines for

Revising and the Revising and Proofreading Symbols into your notebook, and use them whenever you revise your own work.

You will learn more about revising in the chapters on the paragraph
and on different types of compositions. Detailed guidelines are provided
for each form of writing (paragraph, composition, letter) and each type
of writing (expository, descriptive, narrative, and persuasive).

CRITICAL THINKING:
Evaluating Words and Ideas

The critical thinking skill that you use when you revise is called
evaluating, or judging. Your judgments should be made on the basis of
carefully developed *criteria*, or standards. Throughout the composition
chapters of this book, you will find guidelines that express the criteria
for the specific forms and kinds of writing. (See page 655, for example,
for Guidelines for Revising Stories.)

EXERCISE 23. Analyzing a Writer's Revisions.   In revising the
following paragraph, the writer used the Guidelines for Revising
Expository Paragraphs on page 450. Read the paragraph, noting the
changes made by the writer. (The changes are in handwriting.) Then,
using the guidelines on page 450, answer the questions that follow the
paragraph.

> Many high-school students ^seniors^ enroll in S.A.T. preparation courses. ~They~ ^in^
> hope to improve their ^the hope of improving^ S.A.T. (Scholastic Aptitude Test) test scores ~that~ ^the second^
> ^time around.^ most colleges require as part of an entrance application. Do these prepara-
> tion courses have ~any~ effect in ^actually improve,~ improving test scores? ~Course-givers~ say ^Those who give the courses^
> "yes"; the Educational Testing Service, which administers the S.A.T.
> exams, says "not ~really.~ ^much (or) A recent^ ~An~ independent study ~recently released~ ^done at the University of Michigan's^ analyzed a ^statistically^
> ^Center for Research on Learning and Teaching^
> large ~amount~ ^number^ of individual studies. The report concluded that "~reasonable~ ^and^
> gains could be made on S.A.T.'s through relatively ~small amounts of~
> coaching." The average improvement after a coaching course is 15 points on
> the verbal section and 20 points on the mathematics section. ~The word~

~of course~ have   *gains*
average ~infers~ that some students ~may make~ considerably higher, scores;
~others improve~ *senior*
~some~, less. One ~student~, Donna Sukenik of Shaker Heights, Ohio, ~complains~ *reported*
she thought coaching courses
that ~her verbal score actually was lower after a coaching course.~ "I think they
they help students review
can be very helpful in math, where ~you can refresh your memory about~
formulas.
~formulas and things like that," she said.~ "But I needed help in verbal—and   *try to line 6*
she complained.
my verbal score went down," According to ~the~ *an* Educational Testing Service
S.A.T. preparation course (many more hours of
study, ~it would take~ 40 hours of, class time and ~a lot of extra~ homework ~to~
might help a student)
additional
answer two or three, questions correctly in each section for an average gain of
the   section
13 points on, verbal, and 21 points on, math, *the* ~section~ *section*.

1. What do you think is the writer's purpose?
2. Who do you think is the writer's audience?
3. What is the writer's main idea? Is it adequately and clearly developed?
4. The writer crossed out parts of several sentences in revising the paragraph. Why do you think these changes were made?
5. What specific information did the writer add to the revised version?
6. Find three examples of sentences the writer combined. Why do you think she made these changes?
7. Find two examples of places where the writer moved information. Why do you think she did this?

EXERCISE 24. Revising a First Draft.   Revise the first draft in Exercise 21 for an audience of high-school students. Use the Guidelines for Revising on page 401 as you consider each word and each sentence. Reread your draft several times as you revise it.

REVIEW EXERCISE B. Revising a First Draft.   Revise the first draft that you wrote in Exercise 22, or revise another piece of your writing.

GUIDELINES FOR REVISING

Content

1. Is the content suited to the purpose and audience? Are unfamiliar terms explained and background information supplied when necessary? (See pages 368–72.)
2. Is the subject appropriate for the audience? Is the writer's tone appropriate to the topic and the purpose? (See pages 376–79.)
3. Is the subject suitably limited for the form? (See pages 379–81.)
4. Is the topic adequately developed with information and ideas suitable for the purpose and form? (See pages 381–91.)
5. Are the ideas clearly organized?
6. Have all ideas that do not directly relate to the main idea been omitted?

Word Choice and Sentence Structure

7. Does the writing contain precise, specific words rather than vague words? (See pages 734–36.)
8. Does the writing contain no unnecessary words? (See pages 322–32.)
9. Are the ideas smoothly joined with transitional words and phrases? (See pages 424–25.)
10. Do sentence beginnings vary, as appropriate to meaning? (See pages 347–48.)
11. Do sentence structures and lengths vary, as appropriate to meaning? (See pages 346–54.)

PROOFREADING

When you are satisfied that your revision is as good as you can make it, you turn to the next stage in the writing process: *proofreading*. In this stage you look for and correct inaccuracies in grammar, usage, and mechanics (spelling, capitalization, and punctuation).

PROOFREADING YOUR WRITING

21k. Proofread your revised version.

If possible, let some time elapse before you proofread your revised version. When you see it again after a short time, you will view it more objectively and will be more likely to spot inaccuracies. One technique that will help you to focus on each word and mark of punctuation separately is to cover all of your paper below the line you are proofreading with a plain sheet of paper. When you finish proofreading a line, lower the cover sheet one more line. This method keeps you from reading ahead and overlooking inaccuracies.

CRITICAL THINKING:
Applying the Standards of Written English

The purpose of proofreading is to apply the standards of written English to your writing. These standards, sometimes called *conventions*, are the rules of written English that are generally used in books, magazines, and newspapers. The main reason for applying these standards is to prevent your reader from being confused about what you mean or being distracted by inaccuracies. The Guidelines for Proofreading on page 403 summarize the standards of written English, which are explained in greater detail in Parts 1, 2, 3, 5, and 6 of this book. Refer to those parts whenever you are not sure whether you have applied the standards of written English correctly.

EXERCISE 25. Applying the Standards of Written English. Each of the following sentences has an error in grammar, usage, or mechanics. Rewrite each sentence, correcting the error. If you cannot correct an error, follow the instructions given in parentheses, using the index of this book to find the explanation of the standard. Then correct the error.

1. One of the girls know the answer. (See the rule on subject–verb agreement with indefinite pronouns.)
2. Please give me the loaf of bread, that is on the bottom of the front row. (See the rule on punctuating restrictive adjective clauses.)
3. Between you and I, we've just run out of time. (See the rule on using the objective case of pronouns for the object of a preposition.)
4. Where did you put the tickets. (See the rule for punctuating questions.)
5. Whenever I don't get enough sleep or feel really tense and nervous. (See the rule about sentence fragments.)

6. I wish you wouldn't be so late, you know how I like to get to places on time. (See the rule about run-ons.)
7. The boat had sank to the bottom of the lake. (See the rule on forming the past participles of irregular verbs.)
8. We've sure been waiting a long time. (See the rule on using adjectives and adverbs correctly.)
9. She had lain the box on the kitchen table, but it disappeared. (See the rule for the correct use of *lie* and *lay*.)
10. Elaine goes to John F. Kennedy junior high school in North Miami Beach. (See the rule for capitalizing names of specific buildings.)

EXERCISE 26. Proofreading a Revised Draft. Proofread the draft you revised for Review Exercise B (page 400) or another paper you have revised. Be sure to check each of the points in the Guidelines for Proofreading that follow.

GUIDELINES FOR PROOFREADING

1. Is every sentence a complete sentence, not a fragment or run-on? (See pages 271–78.)
2. Does every sentence end with a punctuation mark? Are other punctuation marks used correctly? (See Chapters 32–33.)
3. Does every sentence begin with a capital letter? Are all proper nouns and appropriate proper adjectives capitalized? (See pages 769–78.)
4. Does every verb agree in number with its subject? (See pages 132–44.)
5. Are verb forms and tenses used correctly? (See pages 179–209.)
6. Are subject and object forms of personal pronouns used correctly? (See pages 158–63.)
7. Does every pronoun agree with its antecedent in number and in gender? Are pronoun references clear? (See pages 147–49, 294–300.)
8. Are frequently confused words (such as *lie* and *lay, fewer* and *less*) used correctly? (See pages 237–56.)
9. Are all words spelled correctly? Have spellings been checked in a dictionary? (See Chapter 38.)
10. Is the paper neat and free from obvious crossed-out words and erasures? (See Chapter 30.)

WRITING THE FINAL VERSION

CORRECT MANUSCRIPT FORM

21l. Write the final version, following correct manuscript form.

The last step in the writing process is to prepare a clean copy of your carefully revised and proofread draft. There is no single correct way to prepare a manuscript, but the following standards are widely used and accepted.

1. Use lined composition paper or, if you type, white 8½ × 11-inch paper.

2. Write on only one side of a sheet of paper.

3. Write in blue, black, or blue-black ink, or use a typewriter or word processor. If you type, double-space the lines.

4. Leave a margin of about two inches at the top of a page and margins of about one inch at the sides and the bottom. The left-hand margin must be straight; the right-hand margin should be as straight as possible.

5. Indent the first line of each paragraph about one-half inch from the left margin.

6. Follow your teacher's instructions for placing your name, the class, the date, and the title on the manuscript.

7. If the paper is more than one page long, number the pages after the first one. Place the number in the upper right-hand corner, about one-half inch from the top.

8. Write legibly and neatly. If you are using unlined paper, try to keep the lines straight. Form your letters carefully, so that *n*'s do not look like *u*'s, *a*'s like *o*'s, and so on. Dot the *i*'s and cross the *t*'s. If you are typing, do not strike over letters or cross out words. If you have to erase, do it neatly.

9. Before handing in your final version, proofread it carefully to make certain that your recopying has been accurate.

EXERCISE 27. Writing the Final Version. Write the final version of the paper you proofread for Exercise 26. Use the rules for correct manuscript form or rules your teacher provides. Be sure to proofread this version carefully before you hand it in.

CHAPTER 21 WRITING REVIEW

Practicing the Writing Process. As directed by your teacher, write a paragraph on a topic of your choice. Complete each of the parts of the prewriting stage. Write a first draft. After you have written your first draft, let it sit for at least a few hours, preferably a whole day. Then look at the first draft carefully to see how you can improve it. As you revise the paragraph, keep your audience and purpose in mind. Consider how clearly the ideas are expressed and whether or not the sentences read smoothly. For help in revising the first draft, refer to the Guidelines for Revising on page 401. Proofread your revised version before you prepare a final copy, using the Guidelines for Proofreading on page 403. Be sure to proofread the final copy once again before turning it in.

REVISING AND PROOFREADING SYMBOLS

SYMBOL	EXAMPLE	MEANING OF SYMBOL
≡	Maple High school	Capitalize a lower-case letter.
⌿	the First person	Lower-case a capital letter.
∧	the first May	Insert a missing word, letter, or punctuation mark.
/	seperate	Change a letter.
ℐ	Tell me the the plan	Leave out a word, letter, or punctuation mark.
⌇	an unusual idea	Leave out and close up.
⌒	a water fall	Close up space.
∿	recieve	Change the order of the letters.
tr.	the last Saturday of September in the month	Transfer the circled words. (Write tr. in nearby margin.)
⁋	"Help!" someone cried	Begin a new paragraph.
⊙	Please don't go	Add a period.
⌄	Well what's new?	Add a comma.
#	birdcage	Add a space.

⊙	the following ideas ⊙	Add a colon.
∧ ;	Houston, Texas; St. Louis, Missouri; and Albany, New York	Add a semicolon.
=	two teenagers	Add a hyphen.
∨	Sally's new job	Add an apostrophe.
stet	An ~~extremely~~ urgent message	Keep the crossed-out material. (Write *stet* in nearby margin.)

CHAPTER 22

Writing Paragraphs

STRUCTURE AND DEVELOPMENT OF PARAGRAPHS

A paragraph is a unit of prose writing. Paragraphs may be short compositions, complete in themselves, or they may be part of a longer piece of writing. By practicing how to write effective paragraphs, you will improve your ability to present your ideas—whether it be in a short piece of writing or a longer composition or research paper.

The rules that govern the structure and development of paragraphs do not usually apply to paragraphs in novels, short stories, or newspaper articles. However, these paragraph rules do apply to most of the writing that you will do in school.

PREWRITING, WRITING, REVISING

22a. A paragraph is a series of sentences that develop one main idea.

In many ways a paragraph is a complete composition on a small scale. It deals with one topic, which it introduces, develops fully, and then concludes. The ideas in a paragraph, like those in a longer piece of writing, must be arranged according to a definite plan and should follow one another clearly and smoothly.

> I myself was always recognized, though quite kindly, as "the slow one" of the family. The reactions of my mother and my sister were unusually quick—I could never keep up. I was, too, very inarticulate. It was always difficult for me to assemble into words what I wanted to say. It was not until I

was over twenty that I realized that my home standard had been unusually high and that actually I was quite as quick or quicker than the average. Inarticulate I shall always be. It is probably one of the causes that have made me a writer.

AGATHA CHRISTIE

THE TOPIC SENTENCE

22b. The sentence that states the one main idea of a paragraph is called the topic sentence.

Most paragraphs contain a topic sentence that states the paragraph's main idea. Usually, the topic sentence is placed at or near the beginning of the paragraph. Placing the topic sentence at the beginning helps readers by giving them a clear idea of what is going to be discussed in the paragraph. Stating the main idea at the beginning of the paragraph also helps writers keep clearly in mind the main idea they are going to develop.

In the following paragraph the writer, a native American, develops the main idea by giving specific examples.

> **The widespread use of cloth brought on many new variations to women's dresses.** One popular style used a cape, decorated with beadwork and shells, which could be worn over any plain calico dress. Some capes were actually the decorated remnants of worn-out cloth dresses. Some cloth dresses were decorated with buckskin additions that were fringed. Some dresses were made of velvet, with decorations of ribbons and metal sequins. The most valuable dresses had their tops covered with elk teeth or cowrie shells.
>
> BEVERLY HUNGRY WOLF

Topic Sentence in the Middle of Paragraph

Occasionally, the topic sentence will appear in or near the middle of the paragraph, as in the following example:

> Over the years I have lost most of the things that have been important to me. I have a recurring dream in which all of these objects turn up again in a neat little pile: a leather-bound notebook, several watches, a stubby fountain pen with which I wrote a script full of flourishes, slips of paper on which I have scribbled crucial thoughts, a brown-and-white cashmere scarf that made me think of myself, briefly, as the mistress of an English country house. **Because of, or in spite of, my tendency to lose things, I am the most intractable of hoarders.** Every apartment I have lived in has become filled with magazines and slightly faulty appliances. It is a real effort of will for me to throw even used-up items out. I check the bottoms of cereal boxes for

malingering flakes and dribble out the reluctant drops in milk cartons. I watch myself at these routines and recognize that they are important to me, a way of stopping gaps. There is one tube of toothpaste that has been lying in my various medicine cabinets, untouched, for several years. The tube is cracked with age, and recently, when a friend volunteered to test it, the toothpaste squeezed out in a dried gob. "Throw it out," she said, not unreasonably.

DAPHNE MERKIN—*THE NEW YORKER*

Topic Sentence at the End of Paragraph

Sometimes the topic sentence comes at the end of a paragraph, where it serves as a climax to the series of details that lead up to it.

Convinced that he had identified "the African," about whom his grandmother had spoken, [Alex] Haley searched through shipping records in London and Annapolis to trace Kunta Kinte's arrival in America in 1767 and his sale to the Waller family of Spotsylvania County, Virginia. After that line was established, his job was largely a matter of working through census records to trace the family's migrations from Virginia to North Carolina and, after emancipation, to Tennessee. **Roots is Haley's account of his family, from Africa to America, from freedom to slavery and on to freedom again.**

DAVID HERBERT DONALD

The Implied Topic Sentence

In your reading you will find that not every paragraph has a topic sentence. Often the topic sentence is implied, or suggested. If the main idea is clearly developed in the paragraph, the reader knows what it is even though it is not directly stated in a topic sentence. Most narrative paragraphs have no topic sentence. Rather, they imply to the reader, "This is what happened, and this is what happened next."

The following paragraph has no topic sentence. In it the writer is describing a woman named Sylvia Beach, who was a patron of many writers during the 1920's. What is the paragraph's main idea?

When I first saw her, in the early spring of 1932, her hair was still the color of roasted chestnut shells, her light golden brown eyes with greenish glints in them were marvelously benign, acutely attentive, and they sparkled upon one rather than beamed, as gentle eyes are supposed to do. She was not pretty, never had been, never had tried to be; she was attractive, a center of interest, a delightful presence not accountable to any of the familiar attributes of charm. Her power was in the unconscious, natural radiation of her intense energy and concentration upon those beings and arts she loved.

KATHERINE ANNE PORTER

If the writer were to include a topic sentence, it might state, "Sylvia Beach was a vibrant, intensely energetic woman who was not beautiful by conventional standards." This main idea is definitely implied in the details the writer conveys; a topic sentence is not necessary.

Although many paragraphs written by professional writers have no topic sentences, you will be asked in this chapter to write paragraphs with topic sentences. Practice in creating effective topic sentences and in writing paragraphs that develop the main idea stated in a topic sentence is the best possible training for becoming a more effective writer.

Topic and Restriction Sentences

Sometimes a writer uses two sentences, not just one, to state a paragraph's main idea. The first sentence announces the paragraph's topic, and the second sentence restricts or limits the topic by telling what exactly the paragraph is about. These two sentences, called *topic and restriction sentences*, usually appear at the beginning of a paragraph.

In the following paragraph, for example, the topic and restriction sentences are boldfaced. The writer is talking about why people should use the word *crisp*, an adjective, instead of *crispy*, a made-up advertising word.

> **Crisp is a splendid word, blessed with a great etymological pedigree that runs parallel to its onomatopoeia: the word's sound helps evoke its meaning. Crispy is an itsypooism.** It's O.K. to say *crunchy,* because the imitative noun, *crunch,* needs a *y* to turn it into an adjective, but *crisp* is an adjective that later was used by English potato-chip makers as a noun. One of the senses of *crisp* is *short*; surely this adjective needs no lengthening. Stick with *crisp*; resist itsypooisms.

WILLIAM SAFIRE

introduce then limit.

WRITING EFFECTIVE TOPIC SENTENCES

To be effective, a topic sentence must meet all three of the following requirements:

(1) A topic sentence should be neither too limited nor too general.

A topic sentence must state an idea that can be further developed by succeeding sentences in a paragraph. For this reason, a single fact is usually too limited to serve as a topic sentence. Similarly, a sentence that states a general idea that it would take whole books to develop is too broad for a topic sentence. Remember that the topic sentence controls the paragraph's contents by stating the single main idea that the rest of the paragraph will develop.

TOO LIMITED Milk is a good source of Vitamin D.

TOO GENERAL Vitamins are good for you.

SUITABLE Vitamin D, one of the essential vitamins necessary for the healthy growth of teeth and bones, can be found in many foods.

(2) A topic sentence should state the paragraph's main idea precisely.

An effective topic sentence is neither vague nor wordy. Eliminate all unnecessary phrases, such as "This paragraph is about . . ." or "In this paragraph I am going to talk about . . ." State the paragraph's main idea as clearly as you can.

VAGUE There are some new devices to help deaf people.

WORDY A new invention recently invented helps deaf people to "hear" when they are using the telephone because the telephone tones are being converted into print that a deaf person can read, something like a teletype machine.

PRECISE A computer scientist has invented a device for hearing-impaired persons that can be attached to a telephone and uses the telephone's touch tones to print out messages.

VAGUE Some people are really annoying.

WORDY I am going to talk about those annoying people who always like to give advice on what should have been done or what might have been done long *after* something has already happened, when it's easy enough to give advice.

PRECISE A "Monday-morning quarterback" is someone who gives advice or criticizes others' decisions about past events.

(3) A topic sentence should arouse the reader's interest.

Whenever possible, word your topic sentence so that it catches the reader's interest. Sometimes this can be accomplished with a specific detail or a clever twist.

WEAK	Money can be many things.
IMPROVED	We tend to think of money as bills and coins, but this was not always the case.
WEAK	Everybody should know how to do the Heimlich maneuver.
IMPROVED	If you have ever choked on a piece of food and struggled for breath, you have some idea of how important the Heimlich maneuver can be.

EXERCISE 1. Improving Topic Sentences.

Some of the following topic sentences are too general for a paragraph; others are too limited. Other sentences need to be made more clear, more interesting, or both. Rewrite each topic sentence so that it is an effective topic sentence for a paragraph. You may make up any information you need or use reference books to find out more information.

1. Some people work too hard.
2. I'd like to tell you something about what it was like, according to my grandmother, growing up in the days before there was television.
3. An hourglass measures time.
4. Most birds fly, but not the ostrich.
5. There are four basic blood types: A, B, AB, and O.
6. I'm going to tell you some interesting information about penguins.
7. The human ear is very complicated.
8. A great many people are extremely afraid of every snake that they ever see, but everyone should be made aware of the fact that, indeed, not all snakes are dangerous and in fact most snakes are beneficial to people.
9. Have you ever tried to use a potter's wheel?
10. The sitar is a stringed instrument from India.

EXERCISE 2. Writing Topic Sentences.

For each of the following lists of details, write an effective topic sentence that will be the first sentence in the paragraph. You will not necessarily use all of the details in a paragraph.

1. *Details:*
   a. Plant life discovered 884 feet below sea level
   b. Previously unknown species of plant, a purple algae of seaweed family
   c. Found by two botanists, Dr. Mark Littler and wife Diana, in waters off the Bahamas
   d. They were in a research submarine.
   e. Before this discovery, sun's rays thought to be too weak for marine plants to grow beyond 700 feet below sea level
   f. Algae providing food for fish and other deep-sea animals
   g. Dr. Littler, chairman of the botany department at the Smithsonian Museum of Natural History

2. *Details:*
   a. Israeli scientists using inexpensive technique for measuring air pollution
   b. Using vegetable plants sensitive to different kinds of air pollution
   c. Alfalfa plants sensitive to sulfur dioxide
   d. Eggplant sensitive to ozone and nitrates
   e. Tomato, lettuce, and cucumber plants measuring amounts of nitrates in the air
   f. Research scientists at Technion Institute in Haifa and Hebrew University in Jerusalem
   g. Measure air quality by planting these plants at certain distances from industrial sites and measuring the damage to the plants

3. *Details:*
   a. According to a survey, less leisure time than in 1973
   b. 26.2 hours a week of leisure time for average American in 1973
   c. 18.1 hours a week of leisure time for average American in 1983
   d. Average American working 47.3 hours a week in 1983, compared to average of 40.6 hours a week in 1973
   e. Leisure time spent watching TV, attending sports events, participating in sports or other kinds of exercise, eating out, attending concerts and movies
   f. According to survey, women have 23 percent less leisure time than men: women have 15.6 hours per week, men average 20.3.

4. *Details:*
   a. Human beings' need for sunlight to manufacture Vitamin D

    b. Vitamin D necessary for body to absorb calcium and to maintain strong, healthy bones

    c. Can be manufactured by exposing skin to sunlight; approximately 15 minutes in midsummer to the skin of a young, light-skinned person; more time for elderly, for dark-skinned people, or for people using sun screens

    d. During winter, when sunlight is weaker and fewer people spend time outdoors, increased need for Vitamin D

    e. Doctors suggest people get outside during winter for half-hour walk or "sunbath," especially elderly persons

    f. Recent discovery that some types of depression triggered by lack of sunlight in winter

SUPPORTING SENTENCES

22c. The topic sentence must be supported with sufficient details.

Since a paragraph is the development of the main idea stated in the topic sentence, the other sentences in the paragraph must give enough details to make that idea clear and convincing. Inexperienced writers often fail to provide sufficient details. Although there is no strict rule about paragraph length, a one-paragraph composition of only two sentences or of less than 100 words is insufficiently developed.

    In the following example paragraphs, the topic sentences deal with the same idea. In the first version, the writer merely repeats in different words the idea in the topic sentence. No new information or specific details are given to support the topic sentence.

WEAK   **Every student should engage in some extracurricular activity.** A student needs experience in such activities. No student should leave school every day when the final bell rings and have no definite interest to follow in after-school hours. Everyone can benefit from extracurricular work. No one should think of school as solely a place to study school subjects.

    In the second version, the topic sentence is made more specific, and several reasons are given to support its main idea. Also, specific examples are mentioned of the benefits of extracurricular activities.

IMPROVED   **Every student should engage in some extracurricular activity, because from extracurricular work you learn a great many valuable things that you won't learn in a classroom.** School is not just a matter of learning the difference between *lie* and *lay* or the causes of the Civil War; it is learning to live and work with others. You learn to work and play harmoniously, to give and take, to win and lose. When, as a member of a club, you are given a job to do, you learn to assume responsibility and to work unselfishly for the good of the group. In a radio club or a photography club, you get additional knowledge that may prove more valuable to you in the long run than knowledge obtained through homework or classwork. Furthermore, if you work hard in dramatics or in musical organizations, you will develop talents that will be satisfying to you all your life, talents that might not otherwise have been discovered. Finally, extracurricular activities can broaden your circle of friends.

Here is another example of a paragraph that does not have sufficient details.

WEAK   Sled-dog racing is not a well-known sport. Many people come from all over when there are sled-dog races. Even the dogs seem eager to start.

IMPROVED   **Sled-dog racing has yet to gain the national recognition of some other sports—squash, for instance—but not because its enthusiasts are insufficiently enthusiastic.** Many of the mushers at Saranac Lake had driven across the continent from Alaska or British Columbia, or had come from Minnesota and other unheated places not quite so far away. As for the dogs, they lunged at their traces as they waited in the starting chute, insanely eager to be off and pulling the sleds on courses that stretched as far as sixteen miles.

THE NEW YORKER

EXERCISE 3. Adding Supporting Information.   For each of the topic sentences, one or two supporting details have been given. List as many other details as you can think of that can be used to support the topic sentence. Try to have at least four details for each topic sentence.

1. *Topic sentence:* Studying for a final exam need not be such a traumatic experience if you organize the task into a series of orderly steps.
   a. Learning the definitions of key words and terms

2. *Topic and restriction sentences:* At any given moment of free time, every individual has to make choices about how to spend his or her leisure time. The possibilities are almost endless and vary from individual to individual.
   a. Jogging, bicycling, and other solitary exercises
   b. Talking on the telephone

3. *Topic sentence:* The United States is so vast that its geographical regions are greatly different in appearance.
   a. New England with its mountains, hills, and heavily wooded areas
4. *Topic sentence:* For anyone who is interested in rock music, nothing can match the experience of being at a rock concert.
   a. Loud, insistent beat of greatly amplified sound

EXERCISE 4. Improving Weak Paragraphs by Adding Specific Information. Each of the following paragraphs is weak because it does not contain enough specific information to support the topic sentence. Rewrite each paragraph, adding additional supporting information. You may either do some research or make up any information that you need.

1

Learning to handle a checking account is one of the unsung and uncelebrated milestones on the way to becoming an adult. It is important to pay bills promptly. You need to be able to figure out how much money is in the checking account. Bouncing checks is not good.
(Hint: Tell why it is important to pay bills promptly. Tell how to balance a checkbook and what the disadvantages are of bouncing a check. Give other reasons why handling a checking account is a sign of maturity.)

2

Psychologists and interior decorators know that colors can influence people's moods. Yellow is supposed to stimulate mental activity. Blue is restful and relaxing.
(Hint: Tell about other colors, and give more information about each color's effects.)

3

Each of the sun's nine planets is vastly different in size, temperature, and terrain. The earth, our home, has a moderate climate and lots of water. Mars is very dry.
(Hint: Tell something about what is known about the size, temperature, and terrain of each of the planets.)

4

If it were possible to watch every single television show broadcast, you would probably find that all TV programming can be classified into various types. There is the situation comedy. There are dramas. There are soap operas and news or educational programs. There are children's shows. There are adventure programs.
(Hint: Vary the sentence structure, and give examples or more specific

information about each type of programming. Consider whether there are additional categories into which TV programs can be classified, and if there are, mention them also.)

THE CLINCHER, OR CONCLUDING, SENTENCE

22d. A paragraph may end with a clincher sentence.

At the end of a paragraph, particularly a long one, a writer will sometimes summarize the paragraph's main idea in a **clincher**, or **concluding, sentence.** Such a sentence may restate the topic sentence, summarize the paragraph's main points in support of the topic sentence, or add a general comment to the paragraph as a whole.

On page 410 in the paragraph about the words *crisp* and *crispy*, William Safire has a clincher sentence that restates the paragraph's main idea: "Stick with *crisp*; resist itsypooisms." This, of course, is a humorous clincher sentence because of its informal language ("Stick with") and the coined word *itsypooisms*. Clincher sentences are usually more serious, as in the following example.

> **The interpretation of words is a never-ending task for any citizen in modern society. We now have, as the result of modern means of communication, hundreds of thousands of words flung at us daily.** We are constantly being talked at, by teachers, preachers, salesmen, public officials, and moving-picture sound tracks. The cries of the hawkers of soft drinks, soap chips, and laxatives pursue us into our very homes, thanks to the radio—and in some houses the radio is never turned off from morning to night. Daily the newsboy brings us, in large cities, from thirty to fifty enormous pages of print, and almost three times that amount on Sundays. The mailman brings magazines and direct-mail advertising. We go out and get more words at bookstores and libraries. Billboards confront us on the highways, and we even take portable radios with us to the seashore. **Words fill our lives.**
>
> S. I. HAYAKAWA

The clincher sentence in this paragraph is a comment on all the examples of words that the paragraph mentions. (It is interesting to note that S. I. Hayakawa wrote this paragraph long before television came into use. What would he say now about how words overwhelm us?)

Do not overuse the clincher sentence; not every paragraph in a composition should have one. Avoid tacking a clincher sentence onto the end of a paragraph when it is not of any value. Avoid such weak and unnecessary concluding sentences as, "Those are the three reasons why baseball is my favorite sport," or "Now I have told you why baseball is my favorite sport."

EXERCISE 5. Writing Clincher Sentences. For each of the following paragraphs, try writing several different versions of a clincher sentence. Choose the version that you think is most effective, and write the paragraphs on a separate piece of paper. You may also, if you wish, make changes in the topic sentences and supporting sentences given below.

1

If your vision needs correcting, you now have several different options at your disposal. You may choose to wear eyeglasses, which are two pieces of plastic specially ground to suit your needs and held together by frames that sit on your nose and ears. If you prefer not to wear eyeglasses, you can choose from at least four different types of contact lenses, which are individually fitted to the wearer's eyes and vision needs. The oldest kind of contact lenses are the hard contacts. These are made of Plexiglas and are probably the least popular type of contacts sold today. Gas-permeable lenses are softer than hard contacts and allow oxygen to pass through to the eye, which causes them to be more comfortable than hard contacts. Soft contact lenses are cellophane-thin, flexible, porous pieces of plastic. The latest development in contact lenses is extended-wear lenses, which may be left on for as long as 30 days without removing them.

2

College students have many opportunities to participate in unusual short-term overseas study programs. Organizations such as Experiment in International Living offer students a chance to take seminars and travel around countries doing research and writing about their observations. For example, Margaret Offit, a senior at Wheaton College, participated in a study-research trip to Kenya. Some organizations, such as the American-Scandinavian Foundation, sponsor overseas programs that enable students to work at a wide variety of jobs. Earthwatch, which sponsors museum work and anthropological research, matches interested students with research projects. Other overseas programs are sponsored by the Future Farmers of America, the President's International Youth Exchange Initiative, and the International Association for the Exchange of Students for Technical Experience. *Many kinds of overseas study programs give opportunities to college students.*

REVIEW EXERCISE A. Writing Paragraphs with Clincher Sentences. Use the lists of details that you compiled in Exercise 3 to write four separate paragraphs. You may reword the topic sentences given in the exercise in any way that you wish. When you have finished a first draft of each paragraph, try writing several different versions of a clincher sentence. Decide which one is most effective and if the paragraph reads better with or without the clincher. Revise your four paragraphs, and write them on a separate sheet of paper.

REVIEW EXERCISE B. Writing Paragraphs with Clincher Sentences. Choose two of the numbered items in Exercise 2 on pages 412–14. Use the topic sentences that you wrote for the two paragraphs, and write supporting sentences and a clincher sentence for each paragraph. You do not have to use all of the details listed, and you may add additional information if you wish.

UNITY IN THE PARAGRAPH
ones

22e. Every sentence in a paragraph should be directly related to the main idea.

A paragraph, in which all of the sentences deal with the main idea stated in the topic sentence, is said to have *unity*. As you write, it is necessary to keep that main idea in mind so that you are not tempted to include in your paragraph details and information that are somewhat, but not really, related to your main idea. For example, in the following paragraph, the boldfaced sentences destroy the paragraph's unity and should be omitted.

> Because in most cities and towns all the water we need gushes forth at the mere touch of a faucet and because water is cheap, we Americans use it lavishly. New York City alone consumes one and a half billion gallons a day. Every day each of us uses about 83 gallons: 24 for flushing; 32 for bathing, laundry, and dishwashing; 25 for other uses, such as swimming pools, watering lawns, etc.; and the mere 2 gallons we use for drinking and cooking. These figures are surprising enough, but they do not cover the much greater daily consumption of water in agriculture and industry. **In 75 percent of the world, cities and towns lack any municipal supply of pure water. Citizens are forced to draw water from wells and streams, which are often contaminated.** These facts about our consumption of water should make us wonder how long our supply will last if we continue to drain it so recklessly.

The two boldfaced sentences destroy the paragraph's unity because they are about the water supply in other parts of the world. The paragraph, however, is about the water supply in America, as stated in the topic sentence.

EXERCISE 6. Identifying Sentences That Destroy Paragraph Unity. Examine each of the following paragraphs to test its unity. Each paragraph contains one or more sentences that are not directly related to the main idea as stated in the topic sentence. Find these sentences, copy them onto your paper, and be ready to explain how they destroy the paragraph's unity.

1

A dishonest newspaper may warp the day's news either by hiding a story or by slanting headlines. A paper with a strong political bias may hide a story favorable to the opposing party by placing it in an inconspicuous position. On the other hand, it may give large headlines and a front-page position to news favorable to its own party. Although newspapers do not change the facts in the stories which come to them, they may, if it serves their political purpose, change the total effect of a story by giving it a headline that is deliberately misleading or slanted. Headlines are written by those highly skilled in their jobs. Once the drudges of the newspaper office, these newswriters in recent years have been accorded greater respect as reflected in easier hours and higher pay. A headline may be made misleading simply by means of the kinds of words used. MAYOR JONES REPLIES TO CRITICS gives a quite different impression from MAYOR JONES CRACKS DOWN ON CRITICS.

[margin note: not in unity]

2

Restaurant work is the kind of work most likely to be available to teen-agers seeking employment at a summer resort. This kind of employment has one major disadvantage and several advantages. The disadvantage is that only the low-paying restaurant jobs are available to persons under eighteen: dishwashers, porters, and kitchen maids. These behind-the-scene jobs sometimes pay less than the minimum wage because members of the better-paid dining-room staff are expected to share their tips with those in the more menial jobs, but the generosity of waiters and waitresses is often uncertain. Other summer jobs, low-paying but pleasant, are the outdoor jobs of gardener, lifeguard, and camp counselor. It is possible sometimes to find a summer job as a salesperson, a stock clerk, or a bag packer in a supermarket. But even the menial restaurant jobs at a summer resort have some advantages. For instance, if you are lucky enough to work only evenings, you have the daytime for the beach and outdoor activities. Friendships with fellow workers frequently develop and add to your summer fun. There is, too, the daily fringe benefit of free meals and room.

3

The popularity of first names changes, with certain names in fashion for a generation or so. For example, the Top Ten names for girls in 1928 were Mary, Marie, Anne, Margaret, Catherine, Gloria, Helen, Teresa, Jean, and

Barbara. In 1983, none of these names made the Top Ten list for girls. The ten most popular girls' names in 1983 were Jennifer, Jessica, Melissa, Nicole, Stephanie, Christina, Tiffany, Michelle, Elizabeth, and Lauren. Unusual-sounding names can cause problems for children. One California lawyer, for example, named his son Shelter because he wanted him to have a truly unique first name. The most popular boys' names have changed also. John, William, Joseph, James, Richard, Edward, Robert, Thomas, George, and Louis were the most popular boys' names in 1928. In 1983, however, the ten most fashionable boys' names were Michael, Christopher, Jason, David, Daniel, Anthony, Joseph, John, Robert, and Jonathan.

4

The Seminole tribe is trying a new venture to cure the 47 percent unemployment rate on the Big Cypress reservation deep in the Everglades. With the help of an electronics company in Pompano Beach, Seminoles are being educated in the electronics field. The end result will be the opening of Seminole Electronics, Inc., on the Big Cypress reservation, which is 30 to 40 miles from the nearest town. Josephine North, 31, is typical of the Seminoles who are being trained for the electronics firm. She was a part-time artist before her training. Now, she will earn about $7 an hour as an employee at Seminole Electronics, Inc. The Seminoles are a 1,600-member tribe which is governed by a five-member tribal council. In the early 18th century, the Seminoles separated themselves (the name *Seminole* actually means "separatist") from the Creek tribe and moved to Florida. The educating of thirteen Seminoles was paid for by a government grant and supervised by Pocon, Inc., an electronics company that is helping the Seminole tribe start its new company.

EXERCISE 7. Writing a Unified Paragraph. Select one of the topic sentences that follow or a topic sentence of your own, and develop it into a paragraph of about 150 words. Be sure that every sentence you include relates directly to the topic sentence. You may reword the following topic sentences any way that you wish.

1. Our school's athletic program puts too much (too little) emphasis on competition.
2. People who grow up in a big city learn some valuable lessons early in their lives.
3. Judged by any standard, soccer (or any other sport of your choice) is an excellent team sport.
4. In order to linger in the reader's memory, in order to have been worth the time devoted to it, a good novel must have three important qualities.

5. For several reasons, spending my life working as a(n) _____ appeals to me more than any other career.
6. American citizens take for granted many freedoms that residents of other nations are not free to enjoy.
7. Preventive health care, like regular car maintenance, is something that people can do to help themselves avoid serious health problems.
8. One of the most important qualities of a good friendship is loyalty, which is evidenced in many different ways.
9. For visitors to get a sense of what this community is really like, they will need to visit certain places and sample certain experiences.
10. This is the way I envision my life ten years from now.

REVIEW EXERCISE C. Writing a Unified Paragraph. Look carefully at the list of details that follows, and choose sufficient details to write a unified paragraph. First, write a topic sentence that expresses the paragraph's main idea. Then select and arrange enough details to support that idea in five or six sentences. (You do not need to use all of the details.) Once you have written a first draft of your paragraph, go over it carefully to check on the logical flow of ideas. Make sure that every sentence supports the paragraph's main idea, and cross out or revise any sentence that destroys the paragraph's unity.

Details:
a. Spook Hill, a famed tourist attraction in Lake Wales, Florida
b. Strange phenomenon first noticed during the 1920's: Horses seemed to labor going downhill
c. Spook Hill actually a two-lane street called North Wales Drive
d. North Wales Drive slopes downward to a midway point, then slants uphill to a cross street
e. Lake Wales, Florida, incorporated in 1911; in central Florida
f. Known for its lumber mills and fruit-processing plants; also a lake resort
g. Sign at top of Spook Hill: Drive downhill to white line at lowest point of hill; take car out of gear; let it roll back *uphill*
h. Cars never fail to roll back uphill
i. Residents explain phenomenon as an optical illusion
j. Legend that a great warrior Indian chief, buried at Spook Hill, trying to protect his land from raids of a huge alligator, which he killed; or that the gator is seeking revenge

COHERENCE IN THE PARAGRAPH

22f. A paragraph should be coherent.

A paragraph is *coherent* when its sentences are logically and clearly related to one another. One way of achieving coherence is by linking ideas and sentences together by means of pronouns, references to ideas previously mentioned, and transitional expressions. A second means to achieve coherence in a paragraph is to arrange the details in a clear and logical order that the reader can easily follow. In this section you will practice both of these methods of achieving coherence.

Pronouns and Other References

(1) Keep the thought of a paragraph flowing smoothly by using pronouns and other references to words and ideas in preceding sentences.

Pronouns tie sentences together by referring to a noun or phrase in a preceding sentence. Also, synonyms are used to refer to a key word or phrase mentioned earlier in the paragraph. This kind of referring back to preceding ideas helps the reader to follow the writer's train of thought.

In the following paragraph, for example, pronouns and other expressions that refer to a preceding idea have been boldfaced. What does each boldfaced word or phrase refer to?

> One final effect of radio and TV on the language must be noted. There is no doubt that **these great media of information** have cut down considerably the time that used to be devoted to reading, both of newspapers and of books. **This** means in turn that while **radio and TV** may enhance the **spoken language** (if indeed **they** do), **they** also tend to make of us a nation of functional illiterates, absorbing our **language** through the ear rather than the eye. Some may view **this** as a return to **language** in **its** original form and function; others may consider **it** a reversal, pure and simple, to the semi-**literate** Middle Ages.
>
> MARIO PEI

Notice how many boldfaced words and expressions the paragraph contains. The writer is "weaving together" the sentences by referring many times to preceding ideas. Notice, also, that the references to preceding ideas are not mere repetition. Rather, the writer is *developing* the paragraph's main idea by adding new, specific information about the paragraph's topic. Several of the boldfaced words are *key words and phrases* that refer to the paragraph's main idea: *radio and TV, language, illiterates.*

Transitional Expressions

(2) Keep the thought of a paragraph flowing smoothly from sentence to sentence by using transitional expressions.

A *transitional expression* (sometimes also called a *linking expression* or a *connective*) is a word or phrase that makes a specific, logical connection between ideas. Notice in the following paragraph how the boldfaced transitional expressions tie the ideas together, show their relative importance, and generally help the reader to follow the writer's thought.

> Much is said and written about the number of deer reputedly slaughtered by wolves. Very little is said about the actual numbers of wolves slaughtered by men. **In one case** a general falsehood is widely and officially disseminated; **in the other** the truth seems to be suppressed. **Yet** one trapper operating along the boundary between Manitoba and Keewatin, in the winter of the first year of my study, collected bounty on a hundred and eighteen wolves of which one hundred and seven were young ones born the previous spring. According to law he should have killed those wolves by trapping or shooting them. **In fact** he did what everyone else was doing—and still does in the Far North, with the covert permission of Governments: he spread strychnine so indiscriminately over an immense area that almost the entire population of foxes, wolverines, and many lesser flesh-eaters was wiped out. That did not matter **since** foxes fetched no price that year. Wolves were worth twenty dollars each for bounty.
>
> FARLEY MOWAT

Transitional words and expressions may be grouped according to the kinds of ideas they express.

Transitional expressions may link similar ideas or add an idea to one already stated.

again	for example	likewise
also	for instance	moreover
and	further	nor
another	furthermore	of course
besides	in addition	similarly
equally important	in a like manner	too

Transitional expressions may link ideas that are dissimilar or apparently contradictory.

although	however	on the other hand
and yet	in spite of	otherwise
as if	instead	provided that
but	nevertheless	still
conversely	on the contrary	yet
even if		

Transitional expressions may indicate cause, purpose, or result.

as	for	so
as a result	for this reason	then
because	hence	therefore
consequently	since	thus

Transitional expressions may indicate time or position.

above	before	meanwhile
across	beyond	next
afterward	eventually	presently
around	finally	second, etc.
at once	first	thereafter
at the present time	here	thereupon

Transitional expressions may indicate an example or a summary of ideas.

as a result	in any event	in other words
as I have said	in brief	in short
for example	in conclusion	on the whole
for instance	in fact	to sum up
in any case		

EXERCISE 8. Analyzing a Paragraph for Coherence. In the following paragraph, identify the transitional expressions, pronouns, and key words and phrases that give the paragraph coherence. Be prepared to discuss your answers in class.

A crow's morning greeting is something that has to be experienced to be believed. I don't know whether it corresponds to some timeless ritual of the species, but it was always the same, and it was so strikingly, so emphatically a demonstration of pleasure at seeing us, that today, still, decades later, I smile inwardly when I think of it. I see him again, standing on the windowsill, the blue-black of his feathers glistening in the soft morning light, beginning to bow. With slow dignity he lowered his head, and the bluish eyelids came down over his bright little eyes. At the same time he spread his wings out and down, fanlike, until the long feathers touched the windowsill. When he was fully into his *réverénce*, he cooed in a gentle burble that was more like dove than crow. Two or three coos like this, raising and lowering the head with each one, and then it was time to get down to business again: inspection of the room, shoplifting, grabbing bits of food, disciplining us with a sharp blow of his beak if we got in his way.

RUDOLPH CHELMINSKI

EXERCISE 9. Revising Paragraphs for Coherence. Revise the following paragraphs so that the ideas and sentences are tied together more smoothly. Consider using pronouns, repetition of key words and phrases, and transitional expressions to improve the paragraph's coherence. You may reword sentences any way you wish, combining them or adding sentences of your own. Add a clincher sentence to your revised paragraphs.

1

You can reduce your chances of getting a cold. You can reduce the risk of suffering from other types of nasal congestion or nosebleeds. You can accomplish all of these goals by following certain suggestions. Keep the air in your home well moistened, and do not keep the air overheated. Do not keep windows shut airtight during the winter. Windows should let in some air, especially in the bedrooms. Avoid shaking hands with people who have colds. Doctors say that colds are spread by touching your hands to your eyes or nose after coming in contact with a cold virus. Do you have a lot of nosebleeds? If you have a lot of nosebleeds, avoid taking aspirin. Aspirin thins the blood and makes clotting more difficult. Use an aspirin-substitute.

2

It happened at a recent meeting of the Stepfamily Association of America. A group of teen-agers and young adults talked about what they disliked about their lives living with parents who had divorced and remarried. Now they were stepchildren. Some young people said that their natural parents made them feel guilty if they liked and enjoyed a stepparent. Some teen-agers said that they did not like to be forced into calling a stepparent "Mom" or "Dad." Some young people said that their natural parent would not speak up for them or spend time alone with them. The natural parent was afraid of antagonizing the stepparent. The young people felt this was unfair. Some teen-agers said that life in a household with a stepparent could be a lot of fun. There might be problems. The problems were the usual ones of teen-agers and parents.

3

Research scientists have completed a series of experiments. These experiments were designed to prove that the right and left hemispheres of the brain affect the human immune system differently. The immune system is the system the body uses to defend itself from infection from viruses, microbes, or other foreign particles. The experiments were conducted in the Medical School of Tours in France. The researchers removed a large portion of the left hemisphere of the brain from a breed of mice. The researchers found that when they did this, the number and activity of the mice's immune defense cells were reduced. They operated on another group of mice. They removed a large part of the right hemisphere of each mouse's brain. The immune defense cells did not decrease in number. Their activity was reduced. In left-handed humans the right side of the brain is dominant. In right-handed humans the left side of the brain is dominant. Dr. Norman Geshwind of Harvard University said that left-handed people are more likely to have an immune defense disorder than right-handed people.

A Logical Order

An important way to achieve coherence in a paragraph is to present your ideas in a logical order. In the following sections, you will study four different orders for arranging the details in a paragraph: chronological order, spatial order, order of importance, and comparison and contrast.

Chronological Order

(3) Details in a paragraph may be arranged in chronological order.

Chronological order is the order in which events happen in time. Chronological order is used both in narrative paragraphs, which describe a series of events, and in paragraphs that explain the steps in a process. In the following narrative paragraphs, the boldfaced words are transitional expressions, clauses, and phrases that make clear to the reader the order in which events happened.

The night was fast closing in **when he returned homeward**, laden with flowers which he had culled, with peculiar care, for the adornment of the sick chamber. **As he walked briskly along the road**, he heard behind him the noise of some vehicle approaching at a furious pace. Looking round, he saw that it was a post-chaise driven at great speed; and as the horses were galloping and the road was narrow, he stood leaning against a gate until it should have passed him.

As it dashed on, Oliver caught a glimpse of a man in a white nightcap, whose face seemed familiar to him, although his view was so brief that he could not identify the person. **In another second or two**, the nightcap was thrust out of the chaise-window, and a stentorian voice bellowed to the driver to stop, which he did, as soon as he could pull up his horses. **Then** the nightcap once again appeared: and the same voice called Oliver by his name.

CHARLES DICKENS

In the following paragraph, the writer describes a simple experiment to prove that sound waves travel through air. Each step in the experiment (the process) is described in the order in which it must be done.

Light a candle. Put a tin can on its side with the open end of the can about two inches from the lighted candle. The flame should be near the center of the open end of the can. Hold the can firmly and tap it hard on the bottom. Notice what happens to the flame each time the bottom of the can is struck. The bottom of the can vibrates and sets the air in the can to vibrating. The vibrating air causes the flame to flicker or go out.

ILLA PODENDORF

EXERCISE 10. Writing a Paragraph Using Chronological Order. Use the following information to write a paragraph in which details are arranged in chronological order. First, arrange the details in chronological order. Then write a first draft of your paragraph. When you revise the first draft, see if you can improve the paragraph by adding transitional expressions and phrases that make clear the order in which the events happened. You may reword the sentences in any way that you choose.

Topic sentence: The night of the Great Blackout, the night the power was out all over the city, turned out to be a lot of fun for our family.
a. We were all home by 7:00 P.M., when the power went off.
b. Dad had driven home from the plant by 6:00 P.M., and Mom had just come in from work when the lights went out.
c. We cooked hamburgers on a charcoal grill outdoors and made a big

salad for dinner.

d. The telephones weren't working either, so—except for a few visits from neighbors—the house was quiet.

e. Jim found a transistor radio, and we listened to the news of the blackout.

f. People were trapped for hours in elevators and crowded subways; we were lucky to be home.

g. After dinner we played a long game of Scrabble—all five of us.

h. By ten o'clock all of us were sitting around the fireplace telling funny stories about things we remembered when we were little.

i. The first thing we did was scramble to find candles and flashlights.

j. During the Scrabble game, Dad and Jim got a fire going in the fireplace.

EXERCISE 11. Writing a Paragraph That Explains a Process. In this assignment, you will write a paragraph telling how to do something. Choose one of the following processes or a process of your own. You should be familiar with the process, and it should be one that can be adequately explained in a single paragraph.

1. How to write a check
2. How to wash a dog (or take care of any other animal)
3. How to change a flat tire (on a car or on a bike)
4. How to study for a final exam
5. How to ask someone for a date
6. How to fly a kite
7. How to wash windows
8. How to write a letter of complaint
9. How to hit a home run
10. How to see a movie

PREWRITING Begin by listing all of the details in the process that you can think of, and then arrange them in the order in which they should be done. Be sure that you do not leave out any essential details. Ask yourself the following questions to elicit specific and concrete details for the paragraph you will write. What equipment is necessary in order to do the process? What is the end result of the process? In what order do I perform the steps in the process? Is this the necessary and essential order, or is some other order possible? What is the best way to do the process?

WRITING, REVISING, AND PROOFREADING   Write a topic sentence that will catch the reader's attention and tell what the paragraph is about. As you write, consider your audience and whether you will have to define unfamiliar terms or provide background information.

Reread the first draft several times to make sure that the process is clearly explained and that the steps in the process are easy to follow. Do the sentences read smoothly? Consider adding appropriate transitional expressions to clarify the order in which the steps must be done. Review the Guidelines for Revising Paragraphs on pages 450, 454, 457, and 459, and decide how your paragraph can be improved.

Use the Guidelines for Proofreading on page 403 to make sure that your paragraph is free from errors. Then prepare a final copy of the paragraph, and proofread that copy once more before you turn it in.

Spatial Order

(4) Details in a paragraph may be arranged in spatial order.

Spatial order, the order of position, is frequently followed in descriptive writing. A word picture is clear and coherent when the writer shows exactly where the various items in the scene are located. Usually this is done by following a logical plan that takes the reader smoothly and naturally from one part of the scene to another. The writer also may use phrases such as "in the foreground," "to the left," and "in the distance."

In describing the Van Tassel farmhouse, Washington Irving first gives a general impression of the house as an approaching visitor would see it. Next he describes the piazza (the porch), then the hall, the living room, and a view of the parlor as seen through a door beyond. The boldfaced transitional expressions locate the objects being described.

> It was one of those spacious farmhouses with high-ridged but low-sloping roofs, built in the style handed down from the first Dutch settlers, the low projecting eaves forming a piazza **along the front** capable of being closed up in bad weather. **Under this** were hung flails, harness, various utensils of husbandry, and nets for fishing in the neighboring river. Benches were built **along the sides** for summer use, and a great spinningwheel **at one end** and a churn **at the other** showed the various uses to which this important porch might be devoted. From this piazza the wondering Ichabod **entered the hall**, which formed the center of the mansion and the place of usual residence. **Here** rows of resplendent pewter, **ranged on a long dresser**, dazzled his eyes. **In one corner** stood a huge bag of wool ready to be spun; **in another** a

quantity of linsey-woolsey just from the loom; ears of Indian corn and strings of dried apples and peaches hung in gay festoons **along the walls**, mingled with the gaud of red peppers; and **a door left ajar gave him a peep into the best parlor**, where the clawfooted chairs and dark mahogany tables shone like mirrors; andirons, with their accompanying shovel and tongs, glistened from their covert of asparagus tops; mock-oranges and conch-shells decorated **the mantelpiece**; strings of various colored birds' eggs were suspended **above it**; a great ostrich egg was hung **from the center of the room**, and a corner cupboard, knowingly left open, displayed immense treasures of old silver and well-mended china.

WASHINGTON IRVING

EXERCISE 12. Writing a Paragraph Using Spatial Order. Use the following topic sentence and list of details to write a paragraph describing a room. Use transitional expressions and phrases that will help locate the objects you are describing. Plan an orderly progression, such as top to bottom or right to left. You may combine or reword sentences any way that you choose. Add specific information such as color, types of, contents, etc.

Details:
  a. Small table beside the bed—clock radio, pile of magazines, box of tissues, red metal lamp
  b. Bed against the wall—blue bedspread, newspaper on bed, jacket
  c. Socks on floor; dirty laundry overflowing from wicker hamper
  d. Three posters on the wall (tell what's on the posters)
  e. Concert ticket stubs on dark cork bulletin board
  f. Desk covered with books, papers, dirty clothes
  g. Blue director's chair
  h. Wooden dresser; trophies and books on shelves above dresser
  i. Stereo and two speakers; record collection in orange-crate
  j. Collection of caps and hats

EXERCISE 13. Writing a Paragraph Using Spatial Order. Use spatial order to organize the details in a paragraph that describes an imagined scene. You may write about the view from a mountain, from the top floor of a skyscraper, from an airplane, or from the roof of your house. You may, if you wish, write about what you imagine you see inside a cave, on the bottom of the ocean floor, on the moon, or on a space station. Make your details as specific as possible, and present them to the reader in an orderly way, using spatial order.

Order of Importance

(5) Details in a paragraph may be arranged in the order of their importance.

The order of importance is used when giving reasons in a paragraph that explains or in one that persuades. The *order of importance* usually means proceeding from the least important reason to the most important reason. Occasionally, however, especially when one reason is emphasized, the writer may proceed from the most important reason (stated first) to reasons of lesser importance. In the following paragraph, the actress Helen Hayes gives three reasons why she believes that elderly people should write an autobiography. Identify the three reasons and the order in which she has arranged them.

> I also like to see older folks write an "autobiography." Writing is very therapeutic. In fact, experts say it promotes self esteem and personal integration. Personally, I think it also clears away the cobwebs and stimulates a fresh way of thinking and looking back at your life. Most important, perhaps, it leaves a private history of yourself and your family. Don't you wish your grandmother and her grandmother before her had done that?
>
> HELEN HAYES

EXERCISE 14. **Writing a Paragraph Using Order of Importance.** Choose one of the following topic sentences (either *should* or *should not*).

Topic sentence: Elderly workers should (should not) be made to retire at age seventy.

Then decide which of the following reasons support your topic sentence. You may add other reasons of your own if you wish. List your reasons in the order of importance, from least important to most important. Then write a paragraph based on your list of reasons. As you write, try to develop each reason into a sentence that is interesting to read, and try to make the paragraph read smoothly.

Details:

    a. People who have been working all of their lives deserve to spend the last years of their lives relaxing and doing whatever they want to do.

    b. People who are older than seventy do not have the physical stamina to perform their jobs well.

    c. If people work past the age of seventy, they are taking away jobs from younger workers.

    d. People who are seventy and over have so much experience in their work that they are the most valuable of all workers.

    e. If people are willing and able to work past the age of seventy, they should have the freedom to do so; the choice should be left to the elderly worker to make—and not be made for him or her.

    f. Many people who are elderly (past the age of seventy) need money and need to work in order to survive.

    g. Working keeps people "young"; if you take away some people's work, they lose their reason to live.

    h. Some people past the age of seventy are less mentally alert than they once were and would be a danger to themselves and others in some kinds of work.

    i. People should prepare for retirement age so that they have plenty of things to do (besides work) to keep busy and happy.

EXERCISE 15. Writing a Paragraph Using Order of Importance. Write a paragraph in which you organize information by means of the order of importance. You may use one of the following topics or one of your own.

1. Reasons for joining an athletics team (name the sport)
2. Reasons for buying a used car instead of a new car
3. Reasons for not smoking cigarettes
4. Reasons for changing your eating habits if you are overweight
5. Reasons for writing a business letter
6. Reasons for being angry with a friend
7. Reasons for being late to work
8. Reasons for going shopping
9. Reasons for going to college
10. Reasons for not watching television

Comparison and Contrast

(6) Details in a paragraph may be given in order of comparison or contrast.

Paragraphs may be developed by means of *comparison* (showing how two objects, situations, or ideas are alike) or *contrast* (showing how they are different). Occasionally, a writer may use both comparison and contrast in a single paragraph. Facts, incidents, concrete details, or examples may be used to point out the similarities or differences in the two subjects.

A paragraph of comparison or contrast may use the *block method* of development, in which all of the ideas about one subject are presented first, followed by all of the ideas about the second subject. The following paragraphs use the block method of development. Notice that all of the features of northern buildings are discussed in a block, then the features of buildings farther south, then the features of buildings in the tropics.

If you travel over regions where the buildings were made in earlier times, you will notice great differences from North to South. In the North the roofs are steep to shed the snow, the windows small to keep out the cold, the building materials often easily worked soft woods provided by the abundant nearby forests. The ceilings are low to conserve heat, the chimneys numerous or large, the doors and windows arranged to baffle chilling drafts, and the hearth is the focus of the dwelling. As you move south, the roofs flatten, the windows grow larger, the ceilings rise, so that houses on the steamy James River, in Virginia, for example, have very high ceilings and also a through hall to permit easy cooling of the rooms. As you near the tropics, the woods become harder to work and more vulnerable to dampness and insects. The roofs may get still flatter unless the rainfall is torrential, in which

topic sentence

buildings in the North

buildings in the South

buildings in the tropics

case they steepen again as in Celebes. The patio usually replaces the hearth, and the walls of adobe or stone become thicker in order to preserve coolness; now the windows are small and deeply recessed to keep the hot sun from penetrating the interiors. All these practical arrangements were worked out empirically long ago.

JOHN BURCHARD

A second method of organizing information in a paragraph of comparison or contrast is the *alternating* or *point-by-point method.* In this method, each feature of both subjects is discussed one at a time. For example, the following paragraph discusses the aspects of outside work, building maintenance, ease of cleaning, and preparations for leaving a house or apartment. For each of these aspects, life in both an apartment and a house is discussed.

In several respects, living in an apartment building is easier than living in a house. **For one thing**, there is no outside work to do in an apartment building. Apartment dwellers can forget those chores that keep homeowners busy, like mowing the lawn, cleaning the sidewalk, and repairing the porch. A **second advantage** to living in an apartment building is that the responsiblity for heat, water, and electricity falls on the building superintendent, not on the occupants of the apartments. When a sink is stopped up or a short develops in an electrical circuit, house dwellers are responsible for repairs, and they usually try to solve such problems themselves to save the cost of a plumber or an electrician. An apartment is **also** easier to clean than a house because normally it has fewer and smaller rooms. **Finally**, when apartment dwellers leave home, whether for an hour or a month, they have only one door to lock. Home-

contrast 1

contrast 2

contrast 3

contrast 4

owners, on the other hand, have to take many more precautions in leaving a house empty for a period of time.

You can see that the boldfaced transitional expressions signal when each of the four different aspects or features is introduced. For each feature, both apartment life and life in a house are discussed.

EXERCISE 16. Writing a Paragraph of Comparison or Contrast. Each of the following topics can be developed by comparison or contrast or a combination of both. Select two of these topics, or two of your own, and develop each into a paragraph of about 150 words. Use the block method of development for one paragraph, and use the point-by-point, or alternating, method for the second paragraph.

1. A school you formerly attended and the one you attend now
2. A novel you have read and its movie or TV version
3. Women's gymnastics and men's gymnastics
4. Chinese cooking and Japanese cooking (or any other two types of cooking)
5. Two heroes (or heroines) in a novel or movie
6. Riding on a bicycle and riding on a motorcycle
7. Waking up on Monday morning and waking up on Saturday (or Sunday morning)
8. Going to the dentist and going to the doctor
9. Getting ready for a job interview and getting ready for a date
10. Playing tennis and playing racquetball (or any two other sports)

EXERCISE 17. Writing a Paragraph of Comparison or Contrast. Carefully observe two specific objects, places, or people. If possible, study the two subjects at the same time so that you can take notes about the ways in which they are alike and the ways they are different. You might, for example, carefully observe two apples or two dogs or two children. You might observe two different paintings by the same artist or listen to two different songs by the same musical group. You might observe the same place at different times of day. Take as many notes as you can about the ways in which the subjects are different and the ways in which they are alike. Then write a paragraph of comparison or contrast, or both. Before you begin your first draft, decide whether you will use the block method of organizing details or the point-by-point method.

REVIEW EXERCISE D. Choosing Methods of Paragraph Development. For each of the following limited topics, choose which kind of order you would use in developing a paragraph based on the topic. (For some topics, more than one order is possible.) Be prepared to discuss why you chose a particular order.

> a. chronological order   c. order of importance
> b. spatial order   d. comparison or contrast

1. Reasons why you need to watch your diet
2. An accident that you were involved in
3. Difference between a savings account and a checking account
4. Advertisements on television and advertisements in print media (newspapers and magazines)
5. The place where you would most like to live
6. Important safety tips for automobile drivers (or for pedestrians or bicyclists)
7. Your earliest memory
8. Why people go to scary movies
9. A promise that was broken
10. What your room looks like

REVIEW EXERCISE E. Writing Coherent Paragraphs. Choose three of the topics from Exercise D, or choose three topics of your own that you can develop using different orders. Write three different paragraphs of about 150 words each. In one, arrange the details in chronological order. In the second, use order of importance. In the third, use either comparison or contrast or spatial order.

PREWRITING First, decide whether or not the topics you have chosen are sufficiently limited for a paragraph or whether you wish to limit them even further. Work on one paragraph at a time. Try writing several different versions of a topic sentence, and make a list of the details you want to include. Arrange the details in the order you have chosen for the paragraph.

WRITING, REVISING, AND PROOFREADING   As you write the first draft of each paragraph, concentrate on presenting your information clearly and in a logical order. When you revise the first draft, make sure that the paragraph has unity—that is, all of the sentences are directly related to the paragraph's main idea. See if you can improve the paragraph's coherence by adding transitional expressions, pronouns, and other phrases that will help to connect the ideas clearly. Refer to the Guidelines for Writing Effective Paragraphs that follow and the Guidelines for Proofreading (page 403) before you write your finished version of each paragraph.

GUIDELINES FOR WRITING EFFECTIVE PARAGRAPHS

1. Does the paragraph have a topic sentence that clearly states the paragraph's main idea?
2. Does the topic sentence arouse the reader's interest?
3. Do supporting sentences develop the paragraph's main idea with sufficient detail?
4. Would the paragraph be improved by adding a clincher, or concluding, sentence that restates the main idea, summarizes specific details, or suggests a course of action?
5. Does every sentence in the paragraph directly relate to the main idea? Have all sentences that destroy the paragraph's unity been eliminated?
6. Are the ideas in the paragraph arranged logically according to a definite plan?
7. Does the paragraph contain pronouns and transitional expressions that link ideas clearly to one another and make the paragraph easy to follow?

THE PROCESS OF WRITING PARAGRAPHS

22g. Follow the steps in the writing process.

In Chapter 21 you studied the processes of writing, the many writing and thinking steps that are involved in producing a finished piece of writing. For your review, here is a list of the steps involved in writing a paragraph. The page references are to sections in this book that contain detailed information for each step.

1. Develop a topic that is suitable for a paragraph. (See pages 379–80.)

2. Determine your purpose for writing the paragraph. (See pages 368–71.)

3. Consider how the audience will affect your writing. (See pages 372–76.)

4. Gather information about the limited topic of your paragraph. (See pages 381–91.)

5. Choose an appropriate method of development for your paragraph. (See pages 427–36.)

6. Write an effective topic sentence. (See pages 411–12.)

7. Develop a working plan for your paragraph by classifying and arranging your details. (See pages 391–94.)

8. Write a first draft of your paragraph. (See pages 395–97.)

9. Revise the first draft of your paragraph. (See pages 398–401.)

10. Proofread your paragraph before writing the final version. (See pages 401–403.)

FOUR TYPES OF PARAGRAPHS

22h. Learn to write four types of paragraphs: expository, descriptive, narrative, and persuasive.

Like longer forms of writing, which you will study in later chapters, paragraphs can be classified into four types: the expository paragraph, the descriptive paragraph, the narrative paragraph, and the persuasive paragraph. The type of paragraph you write often depends upon your purpose for writing.

1. An *expository paragraph* informs or explains.

2. A *persuasive paragraph* attempts to convince the reader that an opinion is true or to persuade the reader to perform a specific action.

3. A *descriptive paragraph* describes a particular person, place, or object.

4. A *narrative paragraph* tells a series of events.

Sometimes a single paragraph may combine two purposes. Description, for example, is often combined with narration; persuasive paragraphs often contain some exposition. For each of these four types of paragraphs, however, certain types of order and certain methods of paragraph development are appropriate.

THE EXPOSITORY PARAGRAPH

An *expository paragraph* may give information, explain something, or define the meaning of something. The first of the expository paragraphs on page 441, for example, explains why the concept of freedom was unique to ancient Greek culture. The second paragraph explains how condensation trails are formed. The expository paragraph is by far the most common type of paragraph that you will write in school. Expository paragraphs may be developed with facts and statistics, examples, causes and effects, or definitions. In the following sections, you will study each of these methods for developing expository paragraphs.

As a rule, the tone of an expository paragraph is both factual and unemotional. This tone is achieved by using clear and precise language with few loaded words. An expository paragraph should also be objective rather than subjective, which means that the writer's personality (and the word *I*) should not intrude into the paragraph. The following examples show a subjective treatment of a topic and an objective treatment of the same topic. Notice also how the two examples vary in tone.

SUBJECTIVE   When I lost my book bag full of schoolbooks and notes, I really learned the hard way that people have got to have identification on their luggage, book bags, and other stuff they really care about.

OBJECTIVE   To insure that luggage, book bags, and other valuables can be properly identified and returned if they are lost, airline companies advise that all such valuables be tagged with name, address, and telephone number.

The subjective example is more appropriate for a personal narrative paragraph that tells a story about the narrator's losing his or her book bag. It is not, however, appropriate in tone or attitude for an expository paragraph.

Developing an Expository Paragraph with Facts and Statistics

(1) An expository paragraph may be developed with facts and statistics.

A *fact* is a statement that can be proved to be true; a *statistic* is a fact that describes large masses of numerical data. In the following paragraph, the purpose of which is to give the reader information, facts support the statement made in the topic sentence.

> **Basic to all the Greek achievement was freedom.** The Athenians were the only free people in the world. In the great empires of antiquity—Egypt, Babylon, Assyria, Persia—splendid though they were, with riches beyond reckoning and immense power, freedom was unknown. The idea of it never dawned in any of them. It was born in Greece, a poor little country, but with it able to remain unconquered no matter what manpower and what wealth were arrayed against her.
>
> EDITH HAMILTON

The following paragraph is also developed by a series of facts. Its purpose is to explain to the reader what condensation trails are and how they are formed.

> **Condensation trails, usually called contrails or vapor trails, are visible artificial clouds of water droplets or ice crystals that form in the wake of an airplane.** They form because the water in the exhaust of aircraft engines condenses in the cool air. For a contrail to form, the air around the plane must be colder than −60 degrees C. If the air is warmer, the warmth will prevent condensation of the moisture coming from the engines, and no contrail will form. Jets, which fly in the very cold upper layers of the atmosphere, are the planes most likely to produce contrails.

A paragraph based on facts and statistics must have sufficient details to support the topic sentence and to make the paragraph interesting. In the following revision, the writer improved the first draft by adding specific facts and by explaining the statistics. Notice, also, that the writer has substituted more precise words for vague words.

Educators
Many people concerned with education are beginning to *question* think about

properly
whether or not computers are being used right in the schools. In high

schools, computer literacy courses take up 64% of students' time according
of 1,082 schools made at Johns Hopkins University. Students of their computer time
to a recent study. They spend another 18% in drill and practice. Another 6%
and about

electronic games, word processing, and data retrieval.

in ~~recreational games~~. Many teachers complain that drill and practice on the computer, *for most* *high school* *students*, is a waste of time. ~~The computer is nothing~~ *software that uses the computer as* more than a workbook page, *does not make good use of computers.* ~~and it is cheaper and easier to use a workbook~~.

One way in which computers are being used well is in word processing, *which teaches* ~~teaching~~ students how to write and revise their writing on the computer. ~~And~~ teachers of learning disabled and handicapped students *also praise the computer's* ~~are crazy about the~~ *"infinite patience." Only rarely, however, do* ~~computer. But~~ computer programs ~~do not~~ utilize the computer's unique powers ~~except rarely~~. In one *simulation* ~~software~~ program, students can dissect a frog *on the screen* and then put it back together again. ~~When~~ *If* the parts are put back ~~in the right~~ *correctly* *reassembled* ~~place~~, the frog jumps ~~up and~~ off the screen. Another teacher uses a computer *to help high school* hooked up to a piano ~~to teach~~ students ~~to~~ compose their own music. *Students sit at a keyboard, make up a musical phrase, program it into a computer, and then improvise over it. The computer can even print out a student's original music in musical notation.*

CRITICAL THINKING:
Distinguishing Between Facts and Opinions

In order to write effective expository and persuasive paragraphs, you must be able to distinguish between facts and opinions. Remember that a *fact* is a statement that can be proved to be true. It is a fact, for example, that days are shorter in the winter in the United States and nights are longer. An *opinion*, on the other hand, states a judgment or a belief. In most cases, opinions cannot be proved either true or false. Both as a reader and as a listener, it is necessary for you to know when you are being given an accurate, true, verifiable fact and when you are listening to someone's opinions. As a writer, the ability to distinguish between a fact and an opinion is a thinking skill that you must master.

FACT Twenty-three students in this class have bought a particular brand of pocket calculator.

OPINION This is the best brand of pocket calculator.

FACT Public schools in this city are presently closed for two months during the summer.

OPINION The school year should be extended so that it lasts for eleven months, with only one month vacation in the summer.

Opinions often use words that indicate some kind of judgment, words such as *most, should, should not, greatest, best, worst,* etc. When you write, remember that opinions cannot prove anything; facts and statistics can.

EXERCISE 18. Distinguishing Facts from Opinions. Some of the following statements are facts; some are opinions. Write *F* for each fact and *O* for each opinion. (Assume that statements that are written as facts are true.)

1. The number of corporate mergers (corporations joining to become a single corporation) has increased during the past 15 years.
2. There should be more women executives in industry.
3. Local department stores report their highest sales this year were in the month of December.
4. People should wait until they are at least twenty-one to marry.
5. An average cup of tea contains less caffeine than an average cup of coffee.
6. Anne McCaffrey is the best writer of fantasy.
7. For many years automobile companies have been researching the possible use of air bags as a safety device for automobiles.
8. A bibliography is an alphabetical list of authors, titles, and page numbers used as references in a research paper.
9. Every high-school student should be required to take two years of a foreign language.
10. Driver's licenses are renewable every four years.

EXERCISE 19. Writing Paragraphs Based on Facts and Statistics. For this assignment you will write a separate paragraph based on the information given in each numbered item.

1

Survey Question: Here is a list of things that people sometimes say are problems in professional sports. For each, tell me what kind of problem you think it is.

	BIG PROBLEM	SMALL PROBLEM	NO PROBLEM
Drug abuse	74%	24%	2%
High player salaries	55%	27%	18%
High ticket prices	54%	34%	12%
Alcohol abuse	52%	38%	10%

	BIG PROBLEM	SMALL PROBLEM	NO PROBLEM
Unnecessary violence	41%	50%	9%
Team owners who meddle	34%	46%	20%
Too much TV pro sports	27%	25%	48%
Poor sportsmanship	24%	56%	20%
Fixed games	24%	35%	41%
Incompetent officials	23%	47%	30%
Too many pro teams	17%	27%	56%
Racial discrimination	11%	26%	63%

2

a. 1.8 million adults in United States enrolled in basic education courses
b. Federal government spending $75 million a year to support these programs; state and local governments spend about the same
c. Averages two dollars per year for each adult who is functionally illiterate (can't read or write)
d. Not enough space in programs for adults who want to learn basic reading and writing skills
e. More than 26 million Americans functionally illiterate—cannot read a notice, address an envelope, or write a check
 f. Lisette Quinones, age 20, waiting for two years to begin a basic education course at LaGuardia Community College in New York City
g. Critics say much more money needs to be spent for basic education courses for adults to eliminate long waiting periods for these classes

PREWRITING   Do not try to use all of the statistics or facts given in the numbered items. In paragraphs developed by facts and statistics, you do not want to overwhelm or confuse your reader with too many numbers. For each paragraph, decide first which four or five pieces of information you will use. Then write a topic sentence that expresses the paragraph's main idea. Your topic sentence will be supported and developed by the information you have chosen.

WRITING, REVISING, AND PROOFREADING   Concentrate on expressing your ideas clearly in fairly formal language as you write the first draft. Try to tie the sentences together with transitional expressions, pronouns, and repeated key words and phrases so that the ideas are clearly related to each other.

Ask someone else to read your first draft to tell you whether or not it is easy to understand. Such feedback will help you to make sure that you have expressed your ideas clearly. Follow the Guidelines for Revising

Expository Paragraphs on page 450, and refer to the Guidelines for Proofreading on page 403.

Developing an Expository Paragraph with Examples

(2) An expository paragraph may be developed with examples.

An *example* is a specific instance of a general statement. Often, several examples illustrate the point made in the topic sentence, as in the following paragraph:

> **Victoria was considerably more cultivated than some of her biographers allowed.** She spoke perfect German, excellent French, and adequate Italian; she was well-read in literature and history; she sketched charmingly, and she had a trained ear for music. Because as queen she was uncomfortable in the company of scientists of whose fields she was ignorant, it is sometimes assumed that she was less well-educated than she was. But few men of her era, let alone women, received any training at all in the sciences. Victoria was almost a bluestocking by modern standards.
>
> LOUIS AUCHINCLOSS

EXERCISE 20. Writing an Expository Paragraph Developed with Examples. Choose one of the following topic sentences or one of your own, and write a paragraph using examples to illustrate the paragraph's main idea. You may need to do some research to find information.

1. Several of the original thirteen colonies were founded as places where colonists could find religious tolerance.
2. Some of the most popular musical groups today rocketed to fame as a result of a single recording.
3. Every person born in a certain month shares a particular gemstone as his or her "birthstone."
4. Italian cooking (or any other type of ethnic cooking) has contributed some outstanding dishes to the American scene.
5. The United States can be justly proud of its many accomplishments in the space program.

PREWRITING Begin by listing examples and details that you might include in your paragraph. You may revise the topic sentence any way you wish to focus your paragraph more clearly on your main idea. Try to have at least two or three examples to support the topic sentence, and decide on the order in which you want to arrange them.

WRITING, REVISING, AND PROOFREADING   As you write your first draft, make sure that the examples are clear and have sufficient information for the reader to understand them. You may find that each example takes two or three sentences. When you have finished your first draft, go back over it several times, checking for content, style, and organization. Use the Guidelines for Revising Expository Paragraphs (page 450) and the Guidelines for Proofreading (page 403).

Developing an Expository Paragraph with Causes and Effects

(3) An expository paragraph may be developed by discussing cause and effect.

A *cause* is an event or situation that produces a result, and an *effect* is anything brought about by a cause. Basically, there are two types of cause-effect paragraphs. In one type, you begin by stating an effect and going on to mention the cause or causes. Such a paragraph answers the question "Why?" In the following paragraphs, Nora Ephron discusses the reasons why things go wrong whenever she tries to record on her video-cassette recorder (VCR).

> Sometimes things work out. Sometimes I return home, rewind the tape, and discover that the machine has recorded exactly what I'd hoped it would. But more often than not, what is on the tape is not at all what I'd intended; in fact, the moments leading up to the revelation of what is actually on my video cassettes are without doubt the most suspenseful of my humdrum existence. As I rewind the tape, I have no idea of what, if anything, will be on it; as I press the "play" button, I have not a clue as to what in particular has gone wrong. All I ever know for certain is that something has.
>
> Usually it's my fault. I admit it. I have mis-set the timer or channel selector or misread the newspaper listing. I have knelt at the foot of my machine and methodically, carefully, painstakingly set it—and set it wrong. This is extremely upsetting to me—I am normally quite competent when it comes to machines—but I can live with it. What is far more disturbing are the times when what has gone wrong is not my fault at all but the fault of outside forces over which I have no control whatsoever. The program listing in the newspaper lists the channel incorrectly. The cable guide inaccurately lists the length of the movie, lopping off the last 10 minutes. The evening's schedule of television programming is thrown off by an athletic event. The educational station is having a fund-raiser.
>
> NORA EPHRON

These paragraphs really combine narration with exposition in a humorous discussion of why a VCR fails to record properly. Nora Ephron, discussing her own experiences, uses the subjective *I* and a more informal tone than would be appropriate in a straight expository cause-effect analysis.

The second type of cause-effect paragraph does not answer the question "Why?" Rather, it states a particular cause and goes on to describe the effects or results of that cause. In the following paragraph, the writer discusses several different causes and their effects.

Strong gases and toxic fumes from such things
as paint solvents and industrial chemicals may be
absorbed in the soft-contact-lens plastic, causing
eye irritation if the concentration is strong enough.
Cosmetics, lotions, soaps and creams, hair sprays,
or any aerosol discharges that come in contact with
the lenses may also stick. Eye irritation may result,
and the lenses may get coated to a point where they
have to be replaced. Chemicals such as iron in
ordinary tap water can also damage soft lenses.
Hands should be washed and rinsed thoroughly,
and dried on a lint-free towel, before soft lenses are
handled.[1]

(marginal labels: cause 1, effect 1, cause 2, effect 2, cause 3, effect 3, cause 4)

EXERCISE 21. Writing a Cause-Effect Paragraph. Write an expository paragraph using cause and effect as the method of development. You may choose one of the following topics or one of your own.

1. Causes of shyness
2. Effects of a cold virus
3. Effects on teen-agers of their family's move to another state
4. Causes of hiccups
5. Effects of increasing the interest rate
6. Causes of the War of 1812 between the United States and Great Britain
7. Effects of being left-handed in a "right-handed world"
8. Effects of depression
9. Reasons why many young adults do not register to vote and consequently do not vote

[1] From "Soft Contact Lenses—How Good Are They?" by James H. Winchester in *Reader's Digest*, November 1975. Reprinted by permission of *Reader's Digest*.

10. Effects of sibling rivalry (rivalry between brothers and sisters for parents' attention and affection)

PREWRITING Begin by making a list of causes or effects for the topic you have chosen. You should have at least two, but your paragraph will be even stronger with three or four. Which of the causes or effects that you have listed do you think is the strongest? You may wish to put that one last. Write a topic sentence that states the paragraph's main idea. Then briefly outline your paragraph, listing the supporting details (causes or effects) in the order in which you plan to present them.

WRITING, REVISING, AND PROOFREADING Follow the paragraph outline that you have developed. As you write, try to express your ideas as clearly as possible. You may want to add specific information (facts, statistics, examples) to back up each of the causes or effects you include.

When you revise, check to see whether the ideas are arranged in the most effective order. Consider adding transitional expressions such as *as a result of, consequently, because, therefore,* and *effect* to help the reader distinguish between causes and effects. Refer to the Guidelines for Revising Expository Paragraphs (page 450) and the Guidelines for Proofreading (page 403).

EXERCISE 22. Revising Weak Cause-Effect Paragraphs. Read the following paragraphs carefully, and revise them on a separate sheet of paper. Make sure that you include an effective topic sentence and that causes and effects are clearly distinguished. Consider adding specific information, examples, statistics, etc., to support the causes and effects.

1

One reason for the high dropout rate among high-school students in some schools is that students are tired of going to school. Another reason is that many students want or need to work, and some decide to work full time at part-time jobs they already have.

2

Americans move a lot. The average American moves ten times in his or her lifetime, and about 16 percent of the American population moves each year. This means that children change schools a lot. They have to keep making new friends. Adults find new jobs and are separated from their families sometimes.

Developing an Expository Paragraph by Definition

(4) An expository paragraph may be developed by definition.

A paragraph of definition may occur by itself as a one-paragraph composition, or it may be part of a longer composition. In either case, the subject being defined must first be identified as part of a general class. This usually occurs in the paragraph's topic sentence. In succeeding sentences, specific information and details are given to show how the subject is different from the other members of that general class. In the following example the writers first define romantic fiction in a general way. Then they give many facts and examples to clarify the phrase "escape from reality."

> **Romantic fiction is primarily the kind which offers the reader an escape from reality**. It often deals with distant lands and times. The things that happen in it are more exciting or mysterious or adventurous or strange than the things that happen in real life. Often it deals with such things as tournaments and besieged castles and perilous journeys through hostile country. Sometimes its characters have long journeys to go alone through forests, . . . are besieged in lonely old houses, or are shut up on islands in the midst of faraway lakes, or lie in hushed hiding while a mortal foe treads close by. Sometimes there are pirates, hidden treasures, shipwrecks, thrilling flights from a close-pursuing enemy, last-minute rescues, ominous prophecies, missing heirs, disguised princes, intrigue, murder, breathless suspense. Again, romance is often pervaded by an atmosphere of strange things about to be revealed; often it deals with places and people now changed or forgotten or long since passed away. In short, romance shows life not just as it is, but as we like to imagine it to be.
>
> RALPH P. BOAS and EDWIN SMITH

You may write an extended definition of an even more abstract word or idea, such as *love, happiness,* or *success.*

In the following paragraph, the writer defines Braille by giving information that distinguishes it from all other types of alphabets.

> Many think that Braille is merely conventional letters, figures, and symbols raised so that they can be perceived by the fingers. It isn't; it is quite unlike any conventional alphabet, consisting rather of raised dots bearing no physical resemblance to actual letters or figures. When "written" by hand, the dots are punched out on stiff paper with the help of a template and a small tool resembling an awl. Because it would be virtually impossible to punch out the dots from underneath, Braille is written backwards so that for most European languages it can be "read" with the fingers in normal left-to-right order when the page is turned over.
>
> TOM BURNAM

EXERCISE 23. Writing a Paragraph Developed by Definition.
Write a paragraph that is an extended definition of one of the following
words, or choose a word of your own to define. To define your term
more precisely, you may need to include specific examples.

1. water
2. dolphin
3. marriage
4. the Renaissance
5. sculpture
6. success
7. terrorism
8. bald eagle
9. a democracy
10. a lyric poem

GUIDELINES FOR REVISING EXPOSITORY PARAGRAPHS

1. Is the topic of the paragraph limited to an idea or event that can be
adequately explained in a single paragraph?
2. Does the paragraph contain a topic sentence that clearly expresses the
paragraph's main idea?
3. Does the paragraph contain sufficient details to support the main idea in the
topic sentence?
4. Are the supporting ideas arranged in a logical and effective order?
5. Is the paragraph clear and easy to understand? Is the language appropriate for the intended audience?
6. Does the paragraph contain whatever background information is necessary
for the audience to understand the paragraph's ideas?
7. Does the paragraph contain transitional expressions that make the ideas
easy to follow? Do the sentences in the paragraph flow easily from one to
another?
8. If appropriate, does the paragraph contain a clincher sentence?

REVIEW EXERCISE F. Writing an Expository Paragraph.
Choose one of the following topics for an expository paragraph (or
select a topic of your own), and write a paragraph of approximately 150
words. You may need to do some research.

1. The significance of *honor* in modern life
2. A formula for writing a best-selling book
3. What you can learn from a person's body language
4. The benefits of having a part-time job
5. The influence of a peer group on teen-agers
6. How the human eye works
7. How to identify poison ivy or poison oak
8. Why houseplants die
9. The average life expectancy of a newborn American boy or girl compared to the average life expectancy of newborns in another nation
10. The best type of television advertisement

THE PERSUASIVE PARAGRAPH

A *persuasive paragraph* is one that is written in support of an opinion or in an effort to persuade the reader to follow a certain course of action. You will learn more about the techniques of persuasive writing in the chapter on persuasive composition (pages 574–625).

The basis of a persuasive paragraph should be a limited topic that states an opinion about a debatable issue. The topic must not only be debatable; it must also deal with an important and meaningful issue —not merely a personal preference.

NOT APPROPRIATE   Basketball is the best high-school sport.
NOT APPROPRIATE   Rye bread is better than white bread.

Both of these topics are debatable, but they are inappropriate as topics for a persuasive paragraph because they state personal preferences.

APPROPRIATE   One hour should be added to the school day.
APPROPRIATE   Every high-school student should be required to take a one-year computer course.

Both of these topics are appropriate because they are serious topics for which arguments can be presented either for or against the opinion as stated.

The topic sentence of a persuasive paragraph should clearly and concisely state the writer's opinion. Remember, however, that a topic sentence should not be so brief that it is uninteresting.

Developing a Paragraph with Reasons

(5) A persuasive paragraph is developed with reasons.

A *reason* is a statement that supports an opinion. An opinion that is not supported by reasons is not convincing; the reader needs to have some kind of "proof" that the opinion should be believed. Reasons may be facts, statistics, examples, or quotations from experts. You need to assemble adequate support for your opinion—usually at least two reasons in a persuasive paragraph. Reasons are most convincing when they, in turn, are supported by facts, as in the following example.

The United States' Electoral College system is outmoded, ineffective, and should be abolished; the President should be elected instead by direct popular vote. Three times in United States history (1824, 1876, 1888) and almost again in 1976, the loser in popular votes was actually sworn in as President. Under the present Electoral College system, the candidate who takes a plurality of votes in a state takes all the electoral college votes. Thus, millions of voters are in effect disenfranchised. Although 1.8 million Texans voted for Carter in 1980, Carter received none of Texas's votes, as specified in the Electoral College system. The United States should reform its election laws so that each person casts a vote of equal weight. In Alaska, for example, 95,000 voters cast three electoral votes; while in Texas, a single electoral vote requires 372,000 voters. Write to your Congressional representative, urging him or her to work to replace the present Electoral College system with a system by which the Presidency and Vice-Presidency are directly decided by popular vote.

[margin annotations: topic sentence; Reason 1; Reason 2; Reason 3; call to action]

One type of reason that you may use to support an opinion is a statement made by an *authority*, an expert in the field being discussed. In the following paragraph, a political science professor is cited (quoted). Because she is knowledgeable and experienced in the field of politics, her opinion offers strong support for the suggestion made in the previous paragraph.

> Dr. Elizabeth McElderry, political science professor at State University, supports the movement for direct popular election of the President. "Why should the Presidency and Vice Presidency be the only national offices that are not elected by direct popular vote? Surely each citizen of the United States should have an equal vote and a vote that, somehow, should be effective—not lost in the Electoral College system."

If you were writing to support the opposing viewpoint—the view that the Electoral College system should be retained—you could doubtless find an authority who agrees with you. That is what makes persuasive writing so challenging; you can create an argument in support of an opinion, and you can also create an equally effective argument in support of the opposite opinion.

The following model paragraph analyzes the pros (arguments for) and cons (arguments against) working part time while you are in school. This type of presentation of the arguments on both sides of an issue is another type of persuasive writing.

> **There are many advantages and some disadvantages involved in working part-time while you are in school. On the one hand**, part-time work can offer you an interesting experience that contributes to your education. It helps you to be more independent of your family. For many students, a job provides needed spending money and helps cover many of the hidden costs of a high school education. Thus part-time work helps many students to remain in school. The experience that you gain through part-time work may be of great help to you in making a decision as to the type of occupational career you would like to follow. **On the other hand**, you may gain temporary advantages at the expense of values that are more important from the long-range point of view. For example, you may lose time needed for sleep, rest, study, club activities, and play. As a result, you may find it hard to adjust to what the school expects from you as well as to what your employer has a right to expect. It is obvious that, if you work five hours a day in school and five or six hours a day on the job, you are carrying too much of a load. **Work experience is most desirable—but you have to strike a balance between school and the job.**
>
> HAROLD J. MAHONEY and T. L. ENGLE

Reasons in a persuasive paragraph are usually given in the order of importance with the most important reason given last. However, an effective paragraph may also be written by giving the most important reason first, followed by less important reasons. Make sure that the reader is able to distinguish important from less important reasons.

The tone of a persuasive paragraph should be reasonable, fair, and unemotional. The impression that you wish to give the reader, to be most convincing, is that you have researched the issue thoroughly and have come to a reasonable conclusion. In order to achieve this impression, avoid name calling or using words with extremely negative connotations when referring to the opposing point of view. The reasonable tone of your persuasive paragraph is a result of the logical presentation of reasons and facts to back up your opinion. You should try to be specific, accurate, clear, and forceful in presenting your ideas.

GUIDELINES FOR REVISING PERSUASIVE PARAGRAPHS

1. Is the topic of the paragraph one that is debatable and important?
2. Does the paragraph contain a topic sentence that states the writer's opinion clearly and succinctly? Is the topic sentence interesting?
3. Is the writer's opinion supported by at least two reasons?
4. Is each reason supported with facts, statistics, examples, quotations from an authority, or some other kind of specific information?
5. Are the reasons arranged in order of importance—usually with the most important reason given last?
6. Are the ideas in the paragraph easy to follow and understand? Is the language appropriate for the intended audience?
7. Is the tone of the paragraph reasonable and fair? Does the paragraph contain emotional language that might detract from the argument?

EXERCISE 24. Writing a Persuasive Paragraph. Each of the following can be used as a topic sentence for a persuasive paragraph. Choose one of the topics (or one of your own), and decide whether you are for or against the position stated in the topic sentence. You may reword the topic sentence so that it accurately reflects your opinion on the issue. Think of at least two reasons to support your opinion and, if possible, specific evidence to back up each reason. Then write a persuasive paragraph in which you present your opinion, the reasons why you hold that opinion, and the evidence to back up each reason.

1. Presidential elections should (should not) be held during a 24-hour period so that polls in all the time zones open and close at the same hours.
2. All restaurants should (should not) be required to have non-smoking sections.
3. Students who are caught cheating on a final examination should (should not) automatically fail the course.
4. The board of education should (should not) have one member who is a high-school student.
5. Everyone under the age of eighteen should (should not) have an eleven o'clock curfew on school nights.
6. The minimum wage should (should not) be raised.
7. In order to graduate from high school, every student should (should not) be required to pass a series of exams testing competency in major subject areas.
8. A driver-education course should (should not) be required of every tenth-grade student.

THE DESCRIPTIVE PARAGRAPH

Description is the means by which a writer helps the reader to share an experience fully. Description appears in all kinds of writing: expository, narrative, and persuasive. Since passages of description are usually woven into these other forms of discourse, whole paragraphs consisting solely of description are not common. Nevertheless, writing a paragraph-length description permits you to concentrate on improving the ability to convey sensory impressions in words.

Developing a Paragraph with Concrete and Sensory Details

(6) A descriptive paragraph is developed with concrete and sensory details.

In the following paragraph, the writer describes part of a German city as Italian workers saw it after World War II. Notice in this paragraph two important elements of description: (1) an abundance of specific concrete and sensory details, and (2) the use of figurative language (boldfaced examples in this paragraph).

Closer to the center of town a few dusty trees break the linear bleakness. Then on a boulevard, divided in the middle by a row of trees that meet overhead with trees on either curb to form two leafy tunnels, the traffic begins to swirl, dragging you mercilessly on, past a park into the unfinished glass and chrome and concrete world of the city. **Modest skyscrapers act as bookends** for lower structures, furniture showrooms and stores of electronic equipment. Vast windowless walls of concrete, some studded, some **quilted** for texture, loom over garages, amusement arcades, record shops, restaurants, and **potbellied trucks dribbling** their premixed concrete near the **hoardings** of a would-be skyscraper. At the end of a short street, drab with two-story buildings, rooming houses, and **dejected shops, squats** a miniature station, its newly painted **gingerbread eyebrows** giving it a **sullen expression. Half-defiant, half-apologetic**, a remnant of the past, it looks out on the wrong century.

ANN CORNELISEN

The details in a descriptive paragraph may be given in either spatial or chronological order. In the preceding example, the writer organizes her description spatially, starting with the "few dusty trees" near the center of the town, moving along the boulevard, and finally reaching the downtown part of the city. In the following example, which combines narration and description, N. Scott Momaday uses chronological order to describe a scene. Details are given in the order in which the woman comes upon them.

She went out into the soft yellow light that fell from the windows and that lay upon the ground and the pile of wood. She knelt down and picked up the cold, hard lengths of wood and laid them in the crook of her arm. They were sharp and seamed at the ends where the axe had shaped them like pencil points, and they smelled of resin. When again she stood, she inadvertently touched the handle of the axe; it was stiff and immovable in the block, and cold. She felt with the soles of her feet the chips of wood which lay all about on the ground, among the dark stones and weeds. The long black rim of the canyon wall lay sheer on the dark, silent sky. She stood, remembering the sacramental violence which had touched the wood. One of the low plateaus, now invisible above her, had been gutted long ago by fire, and in the day she had seen how the black spines of the dead trees stood out. She imagined the fire which had run upon them, burning out their sweet amber gum. Then they were flayed by the fire and their deep fibrous flesh cracked open, and among the cracks the wood was burned into charcoal and ash, and in the sun each facet of the dead wood shone low like velvet and felt like velvet to the touch, and left the soft death of itself on the hands that touched it.

N. SCOTT MOMADAY

The details in a descriptive paragraph may also reveal a main impression or mood. In the preceding paragraph the mood is somber and silent—but soft and peaceful, too. The details, as well as the writer's style, create a dominant impression of the description.

GUIDELINES FOR REVISING DESCRIPTIVE PARAGRAPHS

1. Is the paragraph's topic limited to a single person, place, object, or event?
2. Does the paragraph clearly identify the subject being described?
3. Does the paragraph contain enough specific and concrete details?
4. Does the paragraph contain sensory details that appeal to more than one of the senses—not just the sense of sight?
5. Are the details in the paragraph arranged in a logical order?
6. Does the paragraph present the reader with vivid images of the subject being described?

EXERCISE 25. Improving Weak Descriptive Paragraphs. The following descriptive paragraphs are weak because they do not contain sufficient concrete and sensory details. Use your imagination to add enough specific details to make each paragraph interesting. Write your revised paragraphs on a separate sheet of paper.

1

The sunset was beautiful. The light seemed to change every moment. A lot of colors lit up the clouds, and the different colors changed. Finally, it was dark.

2

The young man was standing at the stage door. He was obviously waiting. He looked nervous. He held a poster in his hand, and kept rolling it and unrolling it. We could see what was on the poster. Finally, the stage door opened, and the star came out. The young man asked for an autograph.

EXERCISE 26. Writing a Descriptive Paragraph.   Choose one of the following topics or a topic of your own, and write a paragraph-length description. When possible, select concrete and sensory details that will appeal to more than one sense. Arrange the details in either chronological or spatial order.

1. A football scrin:mage
2. Two people arguing
3. The inside of a telephone booth
4. A sunrise
5. A picnic that you remember
6. An alleyway
7. A cat (or dog) asleep in the sun
8. A garden
9. A dance
10. A crowded supermarket on a Saturday afternoon

THE NARRATIVE PARAGRAPH

A narrative paragraph tells a story or describes a series of events. Narrative paragraphs usually occur as part of a longer work, such as a novel or short story, and are almost always arranged in chronological order. You may write narrative paragraphs in a personal narrative, a composition that tells about something that you experienced.

Developing a Paragraph with an Incident

(7) A narrative paragraph is developed with an incident or an anecdote.

In a short story or a novel, a writer may include a number of sentences that deal with a particular event or *incident*. Usually, such paragraphs have no topic sentences. An *anecdote* is a brief story that illustrates some point. In the following paragraph the topic sentence makes a point that is developed by the events described in the rest of the paragraph.

Luck is sometimes the deciding factor in a game. In the eighth inning of the deciding game of the World Series of 1924, the Giants were leading the Senators by the fairly comfortable margin of 3–1. A hard-hit ground ball struck a pebble, bounded over the head of third baseman Fred Lindstrom, and two runs came in, tying up the game. The contest went into extra innings. In the last of the twelfth, the Giant catcher, about to dash for a pop fly behind the plate, caught his foot in his mask and, to free himself, missed an easy out. The batter, given another chance, then doubled. The next man up hit another grounder toward third base. The ball again struck a pebble, soared over the third baseman, and the game and series were won by the Senators.

Occasionally, narrative writing is combined with other kinds of writing. Narration and description are often combined, and sometimes an incident is used to illustrate a point made in what is otherwise an expository paragraph. The following paragraph, for example, begins with an abstract idea about the connection between a word and what it stands for. The idea is then illustrated by an incident.

In my sensory education I include my physical awareness of the *word*. Of a certain word, that is; the connection it has with what it stands for. At around age six, perhaps, I was standing by myself in our front yard waiting for supper, just at that hour in a late summer day when the sun is already below the horizon and the risen full moon in the visible sky stops being chalky and begins to take on light. There comes the moment, and I saw it then, when the moon goes from flat to round. For the first time it met my eyes as a globe. The word *moon* came into my mouth as though fed to me out of a silver spoon. Held in my mouth, the moon became a word. It had the roundness of a Concord grape Grandpa took off his vine and gave me to suck out of its skin and swallow whole, in Ohio.

EUDORA WELTY

Eudora Welty's paragraph is a good example of how several of the different modes of writing (expository, descriptive, narrative, and persuasive) can be combined in a single paragraph. Her paragraph contains description as well as narration and exposition.

GUIDELINES FOR REVISING NARRATIVE PARAGRAPHS

1. At the beginning of the paragraph, is all of the essential information (characters, setting, place) provided so that the reader will be able to understand the events being described?

2. Are events arranged in chronological order?
3. Does the paragraph contain specific details to make the story interesting?
4. Does the paragraph contain any details or incidents that distract the reader from the main point of the story?
5. Is the language appropriate for the intended audience?
6. Does the paragraph contain some concrete and sensory details to enhance the reader's understanding of an event?

EXERCISE 27. Writing a Narrative Paragraph. Choose one of the following topic sentences, or choose one of your own. Write a narrative paragraph of about 150 words in which you develop the topic sentence by means of an incident or anecdote. You may write about an incident that you experienced, or you may write about a fictional incident that an imaginary character experienced. (You may reword the suggested topic sentences any way you wish.) Use chronological order to arrange the details you include in your paragraph.

1. Some kinds of work can be a lot of fun, or some kinds of fun can be a lot of work.
2. It's very easy to misunderstand what a person means, so if you want to keep a friendship in good order, make sure you check that what you think your friend said is really what your friend meant to say.
3. One of the best feelings in the world is to set yourself a goal, to work hard to achieve it, and then to achieve it.
4. Being fearless isn't always a good idea; some fears are worth keeping.
5. In our house, we grew up with certain classic sayings that helped us understand what "real life" was going to be like.
6. Practicing may be dull, but it pays off.
7. I learned—the hard way—the importance of obeying traffic rules.
8. A week we spent without television taught our whole family a lot.
9. Sometimes we learn really to value something only when we don't have it any more.
10. I think it's a good idea to ask people for advice, but every once in a while their advice may be surprising.

PREWRITING   Make a list of details that will make clear to the reader where the event takes place and who was involved. Decide how you can describe the event briefly (after all, you are writing one paragraph), yet interestingly. You might consider how you (or the imaginary main character) feel about the incident or what you learned from the experience, and write a topic or clincher sentence that comments on the meaning of the incident.

WRITING, REVISING, AND PROOFREADING   As you write, concentrate on adding specific details that will make the story interesting. Read your first draft carefully, checking to see if the order of events is easy to understand. Refer to the Guidelines for Revising Narrative Paragraphs (pages 459–60) and to the proofreading guidelines (page 403) before you write your final version.

EXERCISE 28. Writing a Narrative Paragraph.   Imagine yourself in one of the following settings or situations. Write a paragraph telling what happens. You may add a topic sentence or a clincher sentence that tells how you feel about the experience. If you prefer, you may write about an imaginary character's experiences.

1. Receiving an Oscar for your performance in a movie
2. Arriving on the planet Mars to live there for a year
3. Making your first solo airplane flight
4. Swimming the English Channel
5. Winning an Olympic gold medal
6. Reaching the top of the world's highest mountain
7. Discovering a new chemical element
8. Taking a journey in a time machine (either into the past or into the future)
9. Rescuing someone from a fire
10. Being elected President of the United States

CHAPTER 22 WRITING REVIEW

Writing Different Types of Paragraphs. In this assignment you will write three different paragraphs: (1) an expository paragraph, (2) a descriptive paragraph, and (3) a narrative paragraph or a persuasive paragraph. For each paragraph, choose a topic or topic sentence that you have not already worked with, or choose a topic of your own. Identify the type of paragraph you have written and the method of paragraph development (facts, examples, incidents, reasons, etc.) that you have used.

Writing Expository Compositions

INFORMATIVE AND EXPLANATORY COMPOSITIONS

The literal meaning of *compose* is "to form by putting together." A composition is a piece of writing formed by putting together the ideas you have on a subject. This suggests two important points about writing a composition. The first is that you must have some ideas on the subject about which you are going to write. The second is that you must be able to put these ideas together in such a way that they will form an effective whole. A composition, like the paragraphs you have studied in earlier chapters, has a central, controlling idea that must be supported with more specific ideas. Since a composition is considerably longer than one paragraph, it is usually composed of three distinct parts—the introduction, the body, and the conclusion.

In this chapter the emphasis will be on expository writing. In general, the purpose of expository writing is not primarily to amuse or entertain (although it may do both), but to inform or explain. Keep in mind, however, that the four modes—exposition, persuasion, narration, and description—usually overlap and that an expository composition may well contain elements of persuasion, narration, and description. The essential quality of expository writing is clarity. Most of the writing you are required to do in school—tests, reports, essays—is expository, and most of the writing you will do after you leave school will be of this kind.

PREWRITING

SEARCHING FOR SUBJECTS

23a. Search for subjects for your expository composition.

Your Own Experiences

Unless your teacher specifies what you are to write about, your first step in writing is to search for possible subjects. That search begins in your own mind—with your own experiences, your own knowledge, your own interests.

Your first thought may be that you have no experiences, knowledge, or interests that other people would want to read about, but that is not true. All writers start with what they know. Like other writers, you have lived in a family, a community, and a nation; and you have formed ideas about people, places, and things. You have read books and watched television; you have participated in group activities; and you have obtained information that is of interest to other people.

You can begin your search for subjects by taking an inventory of your own personal experiences, knowledge, and interests. Questions such as the following are useful in taking such a personal inventory:

1. What am I really interested in? What do I care about?
2. What do I know how to do well?
3. What do I know a great deal about?
4. What experiences have I had that many other people may not have had?
5. What is the most enjoyable or satisfying part of my life?

Once you recognize that you have experiences, knowledge, and interests that can provide subjects for writing, you can make use of techniques that will help you tap into your own resources. Two of the most useful techniques are the writer's journal and brainstorming.

If you keep a writer's journal, a notebook of your thoughts and feelings recorded on a daily or an occasional basis, you have a ready source of information about your own experiences. You can at any time read through that journal, searching for subjects for your writing. Since your purpose in expository writing is to inform or explain, you will be looking for subjects that will lend themselves to that purpose. You might find a note about your frustrations the day you could not complete an experiment in your biology class. That note might lead to the following subjects: choosing a college major, science courses in high schools, the benefits of studying biology, and life in a drop of water.

A technique that you can use alone or with other students is brainstorming. You brainstorm when you allow your mind to flow freely from one thought to the next, generating as many ideas as possible without stopping to critique them. You can begin brainstorming with a question such as "What have I done this week?" or with a word or a phrase such as "television" or "leisure time." If you began brainstorming with the word *television*, you might develop the following list of subjects:

> television viewing habits
> selecting a new television
> using television wisely
> the effects of television on children
> television and advertising
> watching football on television
> playing video games
> computer games
> computer technology
> computers in movies
> computers in school

Such a list may be generated by an individual or by a group, one idea leading to another until a number of subjects have been generated.

EXERCISE 1. Searching for Subjects in Your Own Experience. Use your writer's journal or brainstorm by yourself or with other students to develop a list of possible subjects for expository writing. Remember that the purpose of expository writing is to inform or explain, and be sure to identify subjects that lend themselves to that purpose. Make a list of at least fifteen possible subjects.

The Experiences of Others

Your knowledge, experiences, and interests extend beyond what has happened in your own life. They include what you have read about, what you have seen on TV or in the movies, and what you have observed in the lives of those around you. When you search for subjects, use outside sources to expand your thinking beyond your own firsthand experience.

To search actively for subjects, observe closely. Keep a notebook and pencil with you as you walk through your neighborhood, down your street, or through a crowded shopping area. Look for subjects you could tell other people about: a new collection in the local museum, the activities sponsored by the parks and recreation department, how to use the city bus system.

You can also search for subjects as you read. Keep a notebook nearby as you read your daily newspaper or your favorite magazine. Perhaps a newspaper article on a politician will suggest an idea about voter registration. An article on current best-selling audio tapes might give you an idea about the care and handling of tapes and tape players.

EXERCISE 2. Searching for Subjects in the Experiences of Others. For two days, keep a notebook of your observations and of ideas suggested by your reading. Keep in mind the purpose of expository writing: to inform or explain. Make a list of at least fifteen possible subjects for expository writing.

SELECTING AND LIMITING SUBJECTS

23b. Select and limit a subject for expository writing.

Selecting a Subject

If you have kept your own knowledge and interests in mind as you searched for subjects, you may be able to write a good expository composition on any subject you have found. However, careful analysis of the subjects you have identified will probably reveal that you find some subjects more interesting than others and that you know more about some subjects than others. You can analyze your interest in and knowledge of each of the subjects you have identified by asking yourself questions such as the following ones:

1. In what way is this subject interesting to me? Is it more interesting to me than the other subjects I have identified?

2. What do I know about this subject? Do I know enough about it to explain it well or to be truly informative on the subject?

When you use these questions to analyze each subject on your list, you should be able to select the one subject that you can handle best. If you were to analyze the brainstorming list on page 465, you might discover that you are really interested in computer technology but do not know enough about it to be able to explain it or inform others about it. On the other hand, you might have a great deal of experience watching football on television but not find it interesting enough to write about. You might find that you are both knowledgeable about and interested in the subject "computers in school." You really enjoy computer classes and have been observing how computers are used in the various classrooms in your high school. This subject would be a good choice for you to write about.

EXERCISE 3. Selecting a Subject for an Expository Composition. Using the following list of possible subjects for expository compositions, analyze your interests. Select the three subjects in which you are most interested. For each of those subjects, analyze your knowledge by asking the following questions:

1. What do I know about this subject?
2. Do I know more about this subject than other people might know?
3. Do I know enough about the subject to explain it well?
4. Would I know where to go to get additional information?

After you have analyzed your own knowledge, choose the one subject which you have the most knowledge about and in which you have the greatest interest. Be prepared to discuss your choice of subjects with other members of your class.

Dieting	The art of photography
Physical fitness	How to use the library
Ice-skating	Magazines
Training pets	To write or phone?
Generic drugs	The world's food shortage
Job hunting	Colleges
High-school graduation	Modern architecture
Cars	Great American food(s)
Intuition	Junk food
Tennis	Collecting antiques

EXERCISE 4. Selecting a Subject for Your Expository Composition. Using the lists of subjects you developed for Exercises 1 and 2, analyze your interests and your knowledge. Use the questions on page 466 to make your analysis. Select one subject for an expository composition.

Limiting a Subject

The *subject* of your composition is the broad area of content, "dieting" or "physical fitness." The *topic* is the more specific content, the way that your composition will focus on the subject: "how to stop dieting and stay thin" or "twenty minutes a day for physical fitness."

The topic not only provides a focus or an approach to the subject, it also limits the subject to a manageable size. You should know before you limit your subject how long your composition is going to be. On that basis, you must limit your subject so that you will be able to cover it adequately in the space at your disposal. Most in-school expository compositions are about five pages or 500 words in length. Study the following examples of how a subject may be limited for treatment in compositions of different lengths.

Broad Subject	Energy
Slightly Limited Topic	The Energy Problem Today
More Limited Topic	Renewable Sources of Energy
Further Limitations	How a Solar-Energy Cell Works
	Growing Trees for Fuel
	Building a Backyard Windmill

Notice how each additional limitation narrows the previous subject or topic by focusing on specific parts or aspects. The first two limitations might be covered adequately in a book, while the last three topics are suitable for short compositions.

EXERCISE 5. Limiting Your Subject. Analyze the two subjects you have selected (one for Exercise 3 and one for Exercise 4) and make a list of at least ten topics related to each of the subjects. Remember that each topic should focus on a specific aspect or part of the subject, should lend itself to the explanatory or informative purpose of exposition, and should be narrow enough to be covered adequately in a brief composition. As you develop your list of topics, keep in mind the possibility that you might be asked to write a composition on one or more of the topics.

CONSIDERING PURPOSE, AUDIENCE, AND TONE

23c. Evaluate your topic: consider purpose, audience, and tone.

Usually the purpose, audience, and tone of a piece of writing are determined for the writer at the same time, or even before, the writer discovers a specific subject. Nevertheless, the writer must continue to think about purpose, audience, and tone throughout the writing process —as subjects are discovered and limited topics are formed, as information is gathered to support topics, as first drafts are written, and as revisions are made.

The journalist covering a city beat for a newspaper knows the writing purpose is to inform the newspaper's readers about city activities. The journalist is also aware of the interests and backgrounds of the newspaper's readers and recognizes that a serious tone is appropriate for most articles written about city activities. However, purpose, audience, and tone must be considered each time the journalist writes a report on a city-council meeting or interviews the mayor and writes a report about the mayor's views on downtown redevelopment. The writer thinks about purpose: What is the information the article should provide and what concepts or actions should be explained? The next thought may be about audience: What are the readers' biases about downtown redevelopment, and what do they already know about it? Will the readers expect the newspaper to approach this topic with a serious tone, or would they appreciate a light and humorous approach? The good journalist will continue to ask these questions as the article is planned, written, and revised.

In your own writing, you need to ask the same kinds of questions. When you are asked to write an expository composition, you know the purpose is to inform or explain; but you still need to consider that purpose as you plan, write, and revise. You may or may not be assigned a specific audience for your expository composition, but either way, you must consider both audience and tone throughout the writing process.

Considering Purpose

Since your purpose in writing an expository composition is to inform or explain, you need to consider whether the topic you have chosen lends itself to that purpose. A topic such as "why the United States should provide food to Third World nations" will direct the writer into a persuasive argument, rather than a presentation of information. A more appropriate topic for an expository composition would be "current efforts of the United States to provide food to Third World nations." The latter topic calls for information: What are the current efforts? When you consider the topic you have chosen for your own composition, ask yourself whether it clearly calls for information or explanation, and revise it if necessary.

EXERCISE 6. **Shaping a Topic for Purpose.** Some of the topics below are appropriate for an expository purpose and some are not. Identify the topics that are inappropriate for exposition and rewrite them as necessary to make them appropriate. Be prepared to explain your decisions.

1. How to create a square-foot garden
2. Why we need a student council
3. The importance of voting
4. How women won the right to vote
5. The use of standardized tests in secondary schools
6. Too many standardized tests
7. A physical-fitness regimen for busy people
8. Why you should learn to write an expository composition
9. The need to dress for success
10. How to study for an exam

Considering Audience

The audience of your expository composition may be your teacher, other members of your class, readers of a particular magazine or newspaper, or a group of parents. Since different audiences will have different backgrounds and interests, you must study the needs of your audience to determine how to develop your topic and write your composition. For example, if you are aware of the specific backgrounds and interests of your audience, you are able to select language and examples or details that the audience will understand and appreciate. When you know your readers, you know what terms you should define, and you know what they will find offensive or pleasing.

Suppose you were going to write a composition on a physical-fitness program. For a group of teen-agers, you would probably provide information on forms of exercise appropriate for physically active people. For a group of businessmen and -women, you would probably provide information on forms of exercise appropriate for people with more sedentary life styles. For either of these groups, you would want to present the information in a nontechnical manner and define any specialized terms you use. Conversely, if you were writing the paper for a group of physicians, you would need to provide a thorough, highly technical explanation of the fitness program and its physiological effects.

When you evaluate your audience for your own writing, use the following questions:

1. What is the background of this audience? What experiences have they had? What do they already know about this topic?

2. What are the interests of the people in this audience? What can I do to ensure their interest?

3. What is the attitude of the audience toward this topic? How will that attitude affect what I have to say?

4. Why will this audience be reading my composition? What does this audience want or need to know about the topic?

5. Will this audience need special help in order to understand my topic or anything I might want to say about it?

EXERCISE 7. Analyzing Audience. Read each of the following excerpts from expository essays. Analyze the intended audience of each essay by answering the questions that follow.

1

Collaborative practice beckons all of us. Some healthcare executives are responding; many are not. To be successful, this innovation requires both effort and commitment, but the benefits are enormous for patients, professionals, and cost containment. In a time of competition for patients and pressures for expense control, the benefits of initiating this concept more than justify the required effort and commitment.

LILLIAN M. SIMMS, JEPTHA DALSTON, and PETER W. ROBERTS

2

At this point, the expanding page takes over fully. There's no need to write from the outline; rather a word processor enables you to write on the outline. Ideas expressed in words or phrases on the outline are expanded and transformed into complete sentences and paragraphs. The cursor moves existing text to its right to accommodate the new words and sentences that precede it. The expandable page keeps it all right in front of you. This method for writing the first draft is the decisive advantage of a word processing system. The outline provides a direction for my writing; the expandable page provides the path.

MARTIN JAMES O'CONNELL

1. Does this paragraph contain any specialized language? If so, what?
2. What knowledge does the writer assume the reader has?
3. What interests does the writer assume the reader has?
4. What information does the writer assume the reader is seeking?
5. How would you describe the writer's intended audience?

EXERCISE 8. Evaluating Audience. Select three of the topics you developed for Exercise 5, or any three other topics of your choice, and use the questions on page 471 to evaluate the audience for your expository composition. Write your answers on a sheet of paper and be prepared to discuss them in class.

Considering Tone

After you have evaluated your audience, you can decide what the tone of your composition should be. The tone of a composition reflects the writer's attitude toward the topic, and an inappropriate attitude might offend the audience. For example, campaign workers for a particular political party might well be offended by an essay with a mocking or satirical tone on the importance of political parties in America. On the other hand, such an audience would probably be delighted with an essay mocking the weaknesses of the other political party. Remember that the purpose of an expository composition is to inform or explain, and that purpose cannot be achieved if your audience stops reading because the tone of the composition is offensive.

More often than not, the tone of an expository paper will be serious. Other tones may be taken, however—admiring, critical, satirical, mocking, light, humorous—as long as the tone does not interfere with the writer's ability to convey information. Notice how Russell Baker uses a light and humorous tone to explain punctuation in the following model. Baker's tone enhances, rather than interferes with, the expository purpose.

A colon is a tip-off to get ready for what's next: a list, a long quotation or an explanation. This article is riddled with colons. Too many, maybe, but the message is: "Stay on your toes; it's coming at you."

RUSSELL BAKER

Tone is communicated primarily through *diction*, the words that the writer uses and the way those words are arranged. The writer's diction may be *informal*, as in the above paragraph by Russell Baker. Notice Baker's use of words: *tip-off, what's,* and *Stay on your toes.* The informal *tip-off,* as opposed to more formal words such as *suggestion* or *intimation,* contributes to the light tone of the essay. The expression "Stay on your toes" is far more informal than a similar message such as "Scrutinize the forthcoming information." Contractions, such as *what's* in Baker's paragraph, are also informal; they are conversational in tone and suggest that the writer is approaching the subject in a light, almost casual way. Notice the difference between the following sentences, one with contractions and one without.

More than half of all students in the senior class cannot identify what they are going to do after graduation.
More than half of all students in the senior class can't identify what they're going to do after graduation.

More formal diction consists of generally more difficult or abstract vocabulary and more frequent use of very long or complicated sentences. Notice how the diction contributes to the formal tone of the following paragraph.

There exists a rock-solid consensus in urban-industrial society as to what is the proper measure of our progress beyond the primitive. It is the degree to which the environment we inhabit becomes more artificial, either by way of eliminating the original given by nature or by way of the predictive anticipation and control of natural forces. To be sure, the human environment must always have a touch of the artificial about it. One might almost say that the living space of human beings is destined to be "naturally artificial" to the extent that they spontaneously surround themselves with artifacts and institutions and with cautious, customary deliberations about their future. Human beings invent and plan and imaginatively embroider —and the result is culture, a buffer zone of the man-made and man-construed which it is as proper for humanity to inhabit as it is for plant and animal to reside in their sphere of tropisms and reflexes and instinctive responses. But in acknowledging the cultural capacity of human beings, we must not ignore the fact that there *is* a natural environment—the world of wind and wave, beast and flower, sun and stars—and that preindustrial people lived for millennia in close company with that world, striving to harmonize the things and thoughts of their own making with its non-human forces. Circadian and seasonal rhythms were the first clock people knew, and it was by co-ordinating these fluid organic cycles with their own physiological tempos that they timed their activities.

THEODORE ROSZAK

Compare the language and sentence structure of this paragraph to the one by Russell Baker. Roszak uses lengthy, complicated sentences and formal words and phrases such as *predictive anticipation, customary deliberations, man-construed, millennia, circadian rhythms,* and *physiological tempos.* Of course, this vocabulary reflects Roszak's assumptions about audience as well as his intended tone.

Tone also is affected by the *point of view* the writer takes. If the writer writes in first-person point of view, the tone is more friendly, more personal, than in a third-person point of view. The third-person point of view separates the reader from the writer, while the first-person point of view brings the reader and writer closer together. Notice the difference in tone between the following passages, the first written in first person and the second written in third person.

Before I begin building a bookcase, I generally spend a few hours looking over the plans and making sure that I have all the equipment and materials at hand.

Before amateur carpenters begin building bookcases, they generally spend a few hours looking over the plans and making sure that all needed equipment and materials are at hand.

Although little else is different between the two sentences, the switch from first person focuses the reader's attention on the subject and away from the writer, creating a more distant, more formal tone. Even greater distance and formality can be created by the use of the impersonal pronoun *one,* as in the following example.

Before one begins building a bookcase, one must generally spend a few hours looking over the plans and making sure that all needed equipment and materials are at hand.

When considering a choice of point of view for your own expository writing, you should be aware that contemporary formal writing is frequently in the first-person point of view. At one time the first-person point of view was considered embarrassingly familiar for most kinds of writing. Today, many writers consider the third-person point of view to be too artificial and avoid it whenever possible.

EXERCISE 9. Writing in a Formal Tone. Using what you have learned about how diction and point of view reflect a writer's tone or attitude toward a subject, rewrite the paragraph by Russell Baker (page 473) in a formal tone.

EXERCISE 10. Analyzing Tone for an Expository Composition. For each of the three topics you selected for Exercise 8, identify your own attitude and the tone you would use in an expository composition. Be prepared to discuss why you chose the tone and how that tone will affect the writing of your composition.

REVIEW EXERCISE A. Evaluating Your Own Topic for Purpose, Audience, and Tone. Choose one of the three topics you analyzed in Exercise 10. Use the following questions to evaluate that topic for purpose, audience, and tone.

1. Does this topic lend itself to an explanatory or informatory purpose?
2. Is this topic narrow enough that I can explain it thoroughly and effectively in a brief composition?
3. How will I ensure that my audience finds this topic interesting?
4. What does my audience want or need to know about this topic?
5. Is there anything about this topic that my audience will have difficulty understanding? Are there any terms that should be defined?
6. Does my audience have any biases toward or against any of the information I would be presenting on this topic?
7. What is my own attitude toward this topic?
8. What is the tone I intend to convey?
9. Will my audience feel that this tone is appropriate for the topic?
10. What techniques will I need to use to convey this tone?

CHOOSING A TITLE

23d. Choose a title that reflects your purpose and topic.

Once you have considered the purpose, audience, and tone of your composition, a title may also come to mind. Some writers use what is called a working title to guide their planning and writing much as a topic and a thesis statement serve as guides.

You should keep in mind that a good title reflects both topic and purpose, catches the reader's attention, and hints at what is to come in the composition itself. If you were to use one of the topics suggested earlier in this chapter, "growing trees for fuel," for example, you would begin with your purpose, to inform. Then you would consider how you could interest the audience (a general audience of somewhat educated adults who might be interested in this topic) and suggest what the composition is about. Finally, you would consider your attitude toward the topic and how you could reveal that tone in the title. The result might be "Seedlings Today: Energy for the Future." The title reflects the informative purpose, the needs of the relatively well-informed audience, and the serious tone you want to convey. Later in the writing process, perhaps after writing the first draft, you would reconsider this working title and revise it as needed.

EXERCISE 11. Writing Working Titles. The following topics have been developed for expository compositions with a serious tone. An audience is specified for each of the ten topics. For each topic, write a working title that reflects the informative purpose, the needs of the audience, and the intended tone. Try also to create a title that would capture the interest of the audience.

1. New attitudes toward marriage and the family   General adult
2. Choosing between a junior college and a four-year college   High-school seniors
3. Audience rating in the motion-picture industry   General adult
4. Characteristics of a good student   Parents
5. How to win the game (any game)   Amateur players
6. The benefits of a good attitude   High-school students
7. Choosing the right shoes   Any sports enthusiast
8. Reading spy novels   General adult
9. Robots in the home   General adult
10. Camping versus staying in a hotel   Parents

EXERCISE 12. Writing a Title for Your Expository Composition. Write a working title for each of the three topics you used in Exercise 10. Assume that you will eventually choose one of the three topics and corresponding titles for your own composition.

GATHERING INFORMATION

23e. Gather information on your topic.

If you have chosen a subject and a topic that are familiar to you, you probably already have a great deal of information for your composition. Now that you have evaluated your limited topic and chosen a working title, you are ready to pull that information together.

There are several techniques you can use to gather additional information on your topic. If your topic developed from some idea you had jotted down in your journal, you may find information by reading through your journal again. For example, if a note in your journal directed you to the topic, "preparing for the SAT's," you could go back to that journal entry and review everything you had written about the experience. You might find a note about how your teacher had suggested getting a good night's sleep the night before the test, as well as a note about the success rate of students who had enrolled in a special SAT review course offered by the school.

Questioning strategies are also helpful in the search for information. You can prod your own thinking process by asking yourself questions, and you can gather new information by asking other people questions. The standard journalist's questions, *Who? What? When? Where? Why?* and *How?,* are useful in gathering information for any kind of writing. The point-of-view questions can help you examine your topic from three different perspectives: What is it? How does it change or vary? What are its relationships?

Two techniques that work especially well when you are attempting to stimulate your own thinking about a topic are brainstorming and clustering. The purpose of brainstorming is to create a free, uninterrupted flow of thought. You jot down as many ideas as possible in a short period of time without stopping to judge the relative value of the ideas. Imagine, for example, that you have decided to write a composition about TV commercials. For a long time, the common commercials have bothered you, and so you will use this writing assignment to state why. After five minutes of brainstorming, during which you have recorded every idea and impression that occurred to you, you might arrive at a list of ideas and details such as the following one:

necessity for commercials
interrupts programs too
   often
irritating ads
too much repetition
singing commercials
romantic touch
sexist commercials
cure-all medicines
my favorite TV programs
meaningless terms
tiresome slogans
meaningless testimonials
insulting ads
dangerous ads
15-second ads
misleading
false impressions of life

no commercials in some other
   countries
some good commercials
emphasize luxuries
no reasons given why product
   is best
dramatic
banks and finance companies
cold cereals
detergents
cosmetics
pretty women and handsome
   men
keeping up with the Joneses
false scientific statements
magazine ads
applies to radio, too
children (box tops, etc.)

The purpose of clustering, like brainstorming, is to generate ideas quickly. Clustering, however, is a visual technique that involves the circling of words or phrases to show the relationships of the ideas being developed. By circling the initial topic and then circling and connecting each new word or phrase with the previous one, you create a kind of diagram of your thought process. One advantage of clustering is that the visual display of connections and relationships among ideas can give you a head start on organizing your ideas for your composition. After a few minutes of clustering on the topic of TV commercials, you might have a diagram similar to the one on the following page.

Any of these techniques can be helpful as you try to gather ideas to develop your topic into a complete composition. The important thing is to generate or collect as much information as possible so that you will have an adequate supply of details and ideas to use in your paper.

EXERCISE 13. Gathering Information on a Topic. Using the three topics you evaluated in Exercise 10, gather information for an expository composition. Use a different information-gathering technique—journal review, journalist's questions, point-of-view questions, or clustering—for each of the three topics. Be prepared to discuss which of the three techniques seemed most useful.

CLASSIFYING AND ARRANGING IDEAS

23f. Classify and arrange your ideas.

The next step in writing a composition is classifying and arranging the ideas you have gathered. Begin by analyzing the information to determine the major ideas under which the other information should be organized. These major ideas can be used as headings, and then you will be able to group the other ideas in lists under the appropriate heading. For the topic, "TV commercials," used in the example of brainstorming and clustering, you might classify your ideas according to your major objections to TV advertising. The resulting groupings might look something like the following ones:

Major Heading:	*Details/Examples:*
insulting	meaningless testimonials
	singing commercials
dangerous	keeping up with Joneses
	emphasizes luxuries
	cure-all medicines
irritating	interrupts programs too often
	too much repetition

Notice how similar these groupings are to the clusters that were formed during the clustering exercise. Notice also that some of the ideas that were generated are now being left by the wayside, and that the writer will probably look for additional supporting details for one or more of the major headings.

After the writer has discovered the major ideas and the relationships among the supporting ideas, the next step is to think about the order in which the ideas should be presented. Usually this organization becomes obvious as the writer thinks about the topic and the main ideas. If you were planning to compare or contrast two things, camping versus staying in a hotel, for example, you might begin with the ideas on camping and then go on to the ideas on staying in a hotel, or vice versa. If you were explaining how to win the game of *Scrabble*, you might list your ideas chronologically (what you should do first, next, and last) or you might list them by order of importance. For our example on TV commercials, the writer might want to proceed from the least to the most important objection. Consequently, the headings would be rearranged in the following order: (1) irritating, (2) insulting, and (3) dangerous.

As you begin classifying and arranging ideas for your own composition, do not hesitate to experiment. Try more than one kind of order and keep moving the details and examples around until you find the arrangement that seems most logical. Remember also that your list of major headings and supporting details and ideas may change during this process. You will find that some of the original material should be eliminated altogether, some of it should be rephrased or revised slightly, and some of it should be combined.

EXERCISE 14. Classifying and Arranging Ideas and Details. In Exercise 13 you gathered information on three different topics. For each of those three topics, classify and arrange the ideas and details you gathered. Remember that you may find it necessary to rephrase, combine, or eliminate some of the material you have gathered.

Preparing a Topic Outline

Many writers begin writing directly from a working plan similar to the one you created when you classified and arranged your ideas. Some writers use the working plan to develop a more formal plan known as a topic outline. In a topic outline, each item is merely a topic to be discussed in the paper; it is not a sentence. For most of the outlining that you will do, the topic outline will be adequate; it is easy to develop from the working plan and it is clear enough to serve the purpose of an outline. The following outline of the first part of an essay on TV commercials uses topics.

  I. Necessary
      A. To pay costs of a TV program
      B. To sell sponsors' products
 II. Irritating
      A. Repetitious
      B. Frequent

Preparing a Sentence Outline

There are some occasions, however, when you may prefer to use a sentence outline, which is always clearer because it gives more detail. A sentence outline is preferable if you are outlining for someone else who may not grasp the full meaning of the short headings in a topic outline. A comparison of the sentence outline below with the topic outline on the previous page will indicate the advantage of the sentence form.

    I. Commercials are necessary.
        A. The money a sponsor pays to a station to air commercials during a TV program pays for the production costs of that program.
        B. It is the commercials that sell the sponsors' products.
    II. Commercials are irritating.
        A. The constant repetition is irritating.
        B. The too-frequent interruption of programs is irritating.

You should observe the following rules of form when you are making either a topic outline or a sentence outline for your own expository composition.

1. Place the title above the outline. It is not one of the numbered or lettered topics.

2. The terms *Introduction, Body, Conclusion* should not be included in the outline. They are not topics to be discussed in the composition. They are merely organizational units in the author's mind.

3. Use Roman numerals for the main topics. Subtopics are given letters and numbers as follows: capital letters, Arabic numerals, small letters, Arabic numerals in parentheses, small letters in parentheses.

Correct Arrangement of Numbers and Letters

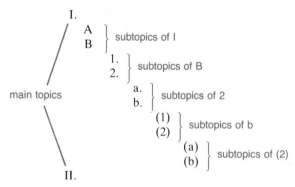

4. Indent subtopics so that all letters or numbers of the same kind will come directly under one another in a vertical line.

5. Begin each topic and subtopic with a capital letter; otherwise, capitalize only proper nouns and proper adjectives.

6. In a topic outline do not follow topics with a period.

7. There must never be, under any topic, a lone subtopic; there must be either two or more subtopics, or none at all. Subtopics are divisions of the topic above them. A topic cannot be divided into fewer than two parts.

8. As a rule, main topics should be parallel in form, and subtopics under the same topic should be parallel in form. If the first topic in a list of topics is a noun, the others should be nouns; if it is an adjective, the others should be adjectives, and so on. Topics in the form of phrases should not be mixed with topics in the form of nouns or a noun and its modifiers. Subtopics need not be parallel with main topics.

The second half of the outline for the composition on television commercials is given below to show parallelism of topics.

III. Insulting

parallel main topics— adjectives

    A. Implied virtues of product   ⎫
    B. Meaningless testimonials   ⎬ adjectives and nouns
    C. Catchy tunes   ⎭

IV. Dangerous

parallel subtopics— verb and object

    A. Create demand for luxuries
        1. Dissatisfied family   ⎤ adjective
        2. Debt-ridden parents ⎦ and noun
    B. Promote phony cure-alls

A violation of the parallelism of topics is illustrated by the following part of the outline, incorrectly phrased.

FAULTY PARALLELISM

IV. Dangerous
    A. Create demand for luxuries [verb and object with modifying phrase]
        1. Dissatisfied family [adjective and noun]
        2. Parents in debt [noun and phrase]
    B. Promotion of phony cure-alls [noun and phrase]

9. Do not mix the topic and sentence forms of outline.

MIXED FORMS

IV. Dangerous [topic]
    A. Commercials create a demand for luxuries. [sentence]
        1. The family becomes dissatisfied without all the advertised products. [sentence]
        2. Debt-ridden parents [topic]
    B. People are misled by phony cure-alls. [sentence]

10. For each number or letter in an outline there must be a topic. Never place an *a*, for instance, next to *1* like this: *1a*.

The complete outline for the composition on TV commercials is given below. Note that all ten points about correct outlining have been carefully observed.

Compare this outline with the original list of ideas and details in the brainstorming example on page 478, the clustered ideas and details on page 479, and the working outline on page 480. Notice that in this final outline, the writer has added a fourth topic. This additional topic allows the writer to develop a paper that acknowledges the reasons advertising exists, while it also discusses the objections to its existence. Notice also that some of the supporting ideas have changes in wording in order to make the outline clear and consistent in form.

TELEVISION COMMERCIALS

I. Necessary
   A. To pay costs of a TV program
   B. To sell sponsor's products

II. Irritating
   A. Repetitious
   B. Frequent

III. Insulting
   A. Unexplained virtues of the product
   B. Meaningless testimonials
   C. Catchy tunes

IV. Dangerous
   A. Create demand for luxuries
      1. Dissatisfied families
      2. Debt-ridden parents
   B. Promote phony cure-alls

EXERCISE 15. Revising a Faulty Outline. Demonstrate that you understand the rules on pages 482–84 by correcting the following faulty outline. Make parallel the main topics and subtopics under the same main topic. Change sentences to topics, and be sure there are no isolated subtopics. Omit topics if necessary. Write the outline with proper alignment and number-letter designations.

HOW TO STUDY

I. The conditions for studying must be right.
   1. You should allow enough time

2. Quiet Place
3. Proper Equipment
   a. textbooks
   b. reference books

II. The Techniques
  A. Assignments that are mainly reading
    a. How to take notes
    b. Memorizing
  B. Writing Assignments
    1. Term papers

III. Conclusion

EXERCISE 16. Developing a Topic Outline.   Arrange the items in the following list in a correct topic outline. Begin by placing the title, which is included in the list, at the top of your paper. Then group related topics and find a main topic for each group. The topics are correctly phrased so that if properly grouped, they will be parallel. Finally, place and letter the subtopics correctly and copy the outline neatly in perfect arrangement.

counselor at summer camp	shelf stocker in a supermarket
indoor work	requires an interest in children
from tips	waiter at a summer hotel
summer jobs	confines one to camp
heavy work	from baby-sitting for guests
assures an outdoor life	enjoying hotel's social life
making extra money	close to home

EXERCISE 17. Writing Your Own Topic Outlines.   For Exercise 14 you classified and arranged lists of ideas and details for three different topics. Create a topic outline for each of the three topics.

WRITING A THESIS STATEMENT

23g. Write a thesis statement for your expository composition.

After classifying and arranging your information and creating a topic outline, you should write a thesis statement for your composition. A thesis statement is the controlling idea of the composition. It states what the writer will cover in the essay, it reflects the writer's purpose, and it suggests the tone of the paper. Like the topic sentence of a paragraph, the thesis statement focuses both the writer's and the reader's attention on the direction of the composition. It is a generalization or an assertion that requires additional support or explanation in order to have meaning for the audience.

The thesis statement is usually included in the introductory section or introductory paragraph of the composition. Occasionally a writer will wait until the end of the paper to state the thesis, and some writers suggest the thesis without ever making a complete statement. You will find, however, that the use of the thesis statement in the beginning of your paper will serve as a helpful guide as you write the paper.

To develop a thesis statement, start with your topic and expand it to create a precise statement of what the paper will cover. Make it so direct that it can apply only to one paper, so direct that only one essay could be written to support it. Compare the following two thesis statements for the composition on TV commercials. The first one is vague and undirected while the second one provides an exact, clear direction for the paper.

1. TV commercials are objectionable in many ways.
2. Although TV commercials are necessary, most of them are irritating, insulting, or dangerous.

EXERCISE 18. Writing Thesis Statements. Write a thesis statement for each of the three topic outlines you developed in Exercise 17. Be sure that each thesis statement includes the purpose of the composition and provides precise direction for the content of the paper.

WRITING

WRITING THE FIRST DRAFT OF YOUR COMPOSITION

23h. Write the first draft of your composition.

If you have completed the planning stage carefully, you will have already solved many of the problems involved in the actual writing. You have a topic and an outline. You know your purpose, your audience, and your tone. Using the thesis statement as the controlling idea of your composition, you can now begin to write.

The Introduction

(1) The introduction makes clear the purpose of the composition and arouses the interest of the reader.

Before you present the first point in your composition, you will introduce the subject. Whether or not the introduction is a separate paragraph depends upon the length of the entire paper. In a short composition, the introduction might be only one sentence. In a long composition, it might be one paragraph or more.

A good introduction should make clear the purpose of the composition. It may give facts that will explain the choice of subject, and it may give information necessary to the understanding of the subject. In most cases the introduction should also contain the thesis statement or suggest the thesis of the paper. It should, if possible, arouse the interest of the readers so that they will want to read further.

The following are four ways of creating an introduction that attracts the reader's attention: (a) beginning with a story, (b) beginning with a startling statement, (c) beginning with a question, and (d) beginning with an example.

(a) Begin with a story.

Vilhjalmur Stefansson (1879–1962), the great arctic explorer, once wrote an article explaining that we can learn a great deal from the Eskimo about how to dress warmly in cold weather. He could have begun by stating this thesis and then gone on to explain how the

Eskimo's clothing, although much lighter than our winter clothing, is also much warmer. But Mr. Stefansson knew something about the interest value of narrative and began his article as follows.

During the winter of 1909, an elderly woman of Flaxman Island, northern Alaska, went out to gather driftwood half a mile from her house. She was wearing only one coat or shirt, hair side turned in. With a sudden onslaught rare in the Flaxman country, a gale descended. She could not find her way home; she had to wait the storm out.

Most Eskimos would have built themselves some sort of a shelter in such a blizzard, but our aged woman thought it too much bother. In the blinding storm, she felt around with her feet until she discovered a tiny knoll. Taking off her mittens, she placed them on the hillock and sat down, using them as insulation to keep her body heat from melting the snow beneath her. Like all good Eskimo garments, her jacket was so designed that she could slip her bare arms out of the sleeves to cross them within the coat upon her bare breast, thus warming them and using them as added radiators to warm the inside of her shirt. With her back to the wind, she settled herself to wait the gale out, leaning slightly forward with elbows on knees so as not to topple over when she fell asleep. Every now and then, stiffened from sitting, she would pick up her mittens and walk around in a small circle. When tired of this, she would sit down again on them and try to sleep. The gale lasted till late afternoon the next day.

When the weather cleared, the old lady came home. She was not very hungry, because she had slept or rested most of the time. It was during the first day that she had been most hungry. No one thought anything of her experience, except that some argued that she should have taken the trouble to build a shelter.

Had she known she was going to be caught out, she would have worn two coats, the entire costume weighing about ten pounds. What she wore weighed six or seven. A Minneapolis businessman going to his office in January would wear from twenty to thirty pounds, and he wouldn't be planning to sit out a two-day blizzard. The difference in their clothing systems explains largely why the average Minnesotan is more eager to move to California than the average Eskimo. In our time, the Eskimo has been the sole possessor of a clothing system adequate in the sense that it permits in January a degree of mobility, efficiency, and comfort similar to that of July. We have taken a long time to understand how it works, and we are still a long way from making full use of its principles.

VILHJALMUR STEFANSSON

(b) Begin with a startling statement—a fact or an opinion.

A good introduction attracts the reader's attention. One way to do this is to tell a story. A second way is to begin with such a startling statement that any reader will be intrigued or shocked enough to want to read further.

The following are the opening statements of five articles. It should be obvious that their authors were counting on their shock value to attract the reader's attention:

1. What we have to do, what at any rate it is our duty to do, is to revive this old art of lying.—OSCAR WILDE

2. In one comic book story, out of fifty-one pictures, no less than forty-five are scenes of violence and brutality.—FREDERIC WERTHAM

3. The past fifty years of what we call civilization have utterly ruined childhood.—PHILIP WYLIE

4. Europeans have made a cliché of saying that nothing is so sad as the sight of Americans having a good time.—BERNARD DE VOTO

5. Never was there a stranger purpose than that which brought us together that June night in Euston Railway Station.—VIRGINIA WOOLF

(c) Begin with a question.

Asking a question at the beginning of a composition offers two advantages. First, it is an easy way to make clear what the article is about. The reader assumes that in the article the author will answer the opening question. Second, a question stirs an immediate response in the reader. In wondering how to answer it, the reader is forced to think about the subject of the article, something that every author wants the reader to do. Here are examples of how two authors used a question in the introduction to an article.

> What is a tropical jungle like, not from distant generalities or sweeping surveys, but as seen by an ordinary human on a very usual walk?
>
> WILLIAM BEEBE

> What do college grades predict? Can you forecast from the record of a young man graduating from college now how successful he's likely to be a few decades from now?
>
> SYLVIA PORTER

The next example actually combines two kinds of openings—the startling statement and the question.

> According to the Nobel prize-winning chemist Dr. Wendell M. Stanley, the next century will find mankind able to control to a remarkable degree the hereditary traits of plants, animals, and humans. Hermann J. Muller, another Nobel laureate, has also predicted the guidance of human evolution. The notion that man may be able to manipulate his genetic endowment is at once exciting and troublesome: How accurate are such predictions likely to be, and how desirable is the prospect of their fulfillment?
>
> LOUIS LASAGNA

(d) Begin with an example.

Beginning an introduction with an example calls direct attention to evidence in support of the writer's thesis. It is a vivid and colorful way of attracting attention while leading the reader directly to the purpose of the essay. Notice how the introductory paragraph of the composition on TV commercials begins with examples of slogans from TV commercials.

> Restore happiness to your marriage by using Whiteshirt laundry detergent. Your husband will love you for it. End those lonely Saturday nights—use Bretheen mouthwash. Only Aloha Sealines Super-duper jets will fly you upside down to Hawaii! Thus the barrage of TV commercials continues day and night in almost every American home. I think most of the commercials are irritating or insulting or dangerous. I believe they can be improved so that they will be not only less offensive to the public but also more effective as advertisements.

EXERCISE 19. **Identifying Good Introductions.** Thumb through a number of magazines looking at the opening paragraphs of articles. Try to find an example of each of the four kinds of beginnings mentioned in this chapter. If you discover any other methods writers use to attract a reader's attention in an introduction, note them as well. Copy the introductions and be prepared to discuss them in class.

EXERCISE 20. **Writing Introductions for Your Own Composition.** Select one of the three topic outlines and thesis statements you developed for Exercises 17 and 18. Choose the one you find most interesting and feel most comfortable writing about. Assume you are going to use this outline and thesis to write a complete composition and then try your hand at writing introductions. Write three different introductions using three of the techniques discussed above. After you have finished writing, select the one that you feel is most effective and save it for your composition.

The Body

(2) The body develops the main ideas in the outline.

Paragraphing

1. *Using paragraphs to develop subtopics.* As you write the first draft, you must decide at what points new paragraphs begin. When you begin a paragraph, you notify the reader that you are taking up another phase of your subject. The amount of space you devote to an idea is an indication of the emphasis it receives in your explanation of the topic. In a brief composition you may find it advisable to devote one paragraph to each of the major (Roman numeral) topics in your outline. For example, if you have three main topics, you will have three main paragraphs. Add to these an introductory paragraph and a concluding paragraph, and you will have a five-paragraph composition. In the sample composition on pages 497–500, which is written from an outline with four major topics, there are eight paragraphs. Two of these are the introductory paragraph and the concluding paragraph. The six others are necessary because two of the four major topics require two paragraphs each for proper development.

In a longer paper—a research paper, for instance—you cannot follow a simple formula for paragraphing; indeed, you may wish to devote several paragraphs to a subtopic.

2. *Avoiding the overlong and the very short paragraph.* When paragraphing your writing, bear in mind that your reader will be able to follow you more easily if your paragraphs are not too long. Paragraphs of 300 words are probably too long for high-school writers to handle effectively. On the other hand, a number of paragraphs of less than 100 words may indicate poor planning. Such paragraphs show that the writer is not taking time to support the topic sentence, and they give the composition a broken-up appearance, which is confusing because it does not emphasize the major ideas.

Achieving Coherence

1. *Arranging your ideas to achieve coherence.* When you arranged topics and subtopics in your outline, you were designing a plan to achieve coherence. You should also consider how you can achieve coherence by arranging the paragraphs that form the body of your composition in a logical order. The order you choose will depend upon the topic of your composition. Compositions that explain opinions are frequently arranged in the order of importance, moving from the least important idea to the most important idea or from the most important to the least important. In compositions that explain how to do or to make something, chronological or spatial order may be the most appropriate method of arranging ideas. For many topics, some ideas need to be presented first because they help to explain later ideas. See pages 427–36 in Chapter 22 for a more thorough discussion of arranging ideas to achieve coherence.

2. *Using transitional expressions to make transitions between paragraphs.* Because the beginning of a paragraph signifies a shift to another phase of your subject, you should make your train of thought clear to the reader by showing the relationship between this new phase and the phase discussed in the preceding paragraph. There are several devices for accomplishing this transition between paragraphs:

(a) *Pronouns.* Using pronouns to refer to a person or idea mentioned in the preceding paragraph.

(b) *Repetition.* Repeating in the first sentence of a paragraph a key word or term used in the preceding paragraph.

(c) *Direct Reference.* Referring directly to a preceding idea, often by means of a summarizing phrase.

(d) *Connectives.* Using transitional expressions such as *accordingly, for example, similarly,* and *thus.*

You can use all four of these devices to keep thoughts flowing smoothly from paragraph to paragraph in the same way that linking words and connectives keep the thought flowing from sentence to sentence. For a more thorough discussion of transitions, see pages 424–25 in Chapter 22.

3. *Using transitional paragraphs to achieve coherence.* Sometimes, especially in a long paper, you may wish to let your reader know that you have completed your discussion of one phase of the subject and are now about to take up another. A brief paragraph will easily accomplish this purpose. Such a paragraph is called a transitional paragraph.

So much, then, by way of proof that the method of establishing laws in science is exactly the same as that pursued in common life. Let us now turn to another matter (though really it is but another phase of the same question), and that is, the method by which, from the relations of certain phenomena, we prove that some stand in the position of causes toward the others.

THOMAS HENRY HUXLEY

Study the model transitional paragraph above. Notice how Huxley has used the first sentence of the paragraph to summarize the preceding discussion. In the second sentence of the paragraph, he suggests the content of the discussion that is to follow. Such paragraphs are especially useful whenever there is a major shift in the content of your essay or composition.

EXERCISE 21. Identifying Transitional Devices. Regard each of the following sentences as the opening sentence of a paragraph. Point out the device or devices used in each sentence to effect a transition from what had been discussed in the preceding paragraph.

1. In this vast domain, obviously, the planet Earth is insignificantly small.
2. Wherever such networks have been established, systems which do not yet belong to the networks—even systems as large as solar systems—are regarded as primitive.
3. Easing the inevitable tensions, therefore, is not merely desirable: it is quite necessary for survival.
4. As a result, it is difficult to describe those microscopic forms of life with the unaided eye.
5. In sophisticated regions, too, the same conclusions apply.

EXERCISE 22. Identifying Transitional Expressions. Examine a daily newspaper or a current magazine to find further examples of transitional devices used by professional writers. Copy onto your paper five paragraph openings that contain such devices. Underline the transitional expressions.

EXERCISE 23. Analyzing Transitional Paragraphs. Study the paragraphs below. For each paragraph, determine the content of the discussion preceding the transition and the content to be discussed following the transition. Be prepared to discuss your analysis in class.

1

The entries in an unabridged dictionary such as the *Webster's Third New International Dictionary*, however, differ in some respects from the entries in a college dictionary. Let us consider these differences.

2

Whereas at the beginning of *Pride and Prejudice* the reader sees Elizabeth as confident, even headstrong, in her opinions, later in the novel her self-assurance begins to falter. Take, for example, her meeting with Darcy at Rosings.

EXERCISE 24. Writing the Body of Your Own Composition. Using the thesis statement and outline for which you wrote an introductory paragraph in Exercise 20, write the body of your composition. Use your thesis statement to guide your thinking and your outline to guide your organization. Try to write at least one paragraph for each main topic in your outline. To maintain unity of thought, try not to depart from your outline. Avoid paragraphs that are either too long or too short, and use transitional devices or paragraphs to achieve coherence.

The Conclusion

(3) The conclusion summarizes or reemphasizes the main points of the composition.

Once you have completed the body of your composition, you are ready to write the conclusion. The conclusion should bring the composition to a satisfactory close for the reader. Sometimes a conclusion will summarize all the main points made in the essay; at other times a conclusion may forecast or predict changes that might occur in the future. When you write your own conclusion, remember that you should create a definite closing and not leave your readers feeling that you simply ran out of something to say. Professional writers use many different techniques to create a satisfactory conclusion. Notice the variety in the following examples:

1

But as Mr. Backster and all other scientists know, his hypothesis could be wrong. The hypothesis will have to be tested by other scientists in other laboratories.

Suggests future course of action.

EDWIN STEINKAMP

2

You have now made a basic trout-fly. Tell someone to go catch a fish with it.

J. A. MAXTONE GRAHAM

Uses one sentence to summarize process explained in essay; concludes with light, catchy suggestion to reader.

3

Then, Sir, from these six capital sources—of descent, of form of government, of religion in the Northern Provinces, of manners in the Southern, of education, of the remoteness of situation from the first mover of government—from all these causes a fierce spirit of liberty has grown up. It has grown with the growth of the people in your Colonies, and increased with the increase of their wealth; a spirit that unhappily meeting with an exercise of power in England which, however lawful, is not reconcilable to any ideas of liberty, much less with theirs, has kindled this flame that is ready to consume us.

Summarizes main points of the composition: There are six sources of disobedience in the colonies.

EDMUND BURKE

4

In the case of some cities, no given advantage can be found to "explain" their existence in a specious way. All that Birmingham seems to have had, to begin with, was a good supply of drinking water —no novelty in Renaissance England. Alcaeus made the point in 600 B.C. when he wrote of the

Uses quotation to restate thesis that "cities simply cannot be 'explained' by their locations or other given resources."

cities of Greece, "Not houses finely roofed nor the stones of walls well built nor canals nor dockyards make the city, but men able to use their opportunity."

JANE JACOBS

5

There have been some estimates that human cloning will be a reality within the decade. Who will say where we draw the line?

Poses a question for the reader to think about.

CARYL RIVERS

Conclusions vary in length as well as in technique. They may be as brief as one or two sentences or as long as two or three paragraphs. The brief, one- or two-sentence conclusion may be in a separate final paragraph or may be included as the end of the final paragraph in the body of the paper.

EXERCISE 25. Analyzing Conclusions. Using newspapers, magazines, or collections of essays, analyze the conclusions of three different essays. Use the following questions to conduct your analysis.

1. How many sentences are included in this conclusion?
2. Is the conclusion composed of a separate paragraph or paragraphs, or is it a part of a paragraph within the body of the essay?
3. Does the conclusion summarize or refer to the main points in the body of the essay?
4. Does the conclusion suggest some alternative or possibility for the future?
5. What could the writer do to make this conclusion more effective?

EXERCISE 26. Writing a Conclusion for Your Own Composition. Write a conclusion for the composition you began in Exercises 20 and 24. Remember that the conclusion may summarize what is contained in the composition or it may point out possibilities for change in the future. Be sure the conclusion is a definite signal to the reader that the composition has been completed.

STUDYING A SAMPLE COMPOSITION

The following composition is a model developed from the outline you studied on page 484. Read the composition and examine its organization. Study how the introduction captures the audience's interest and states what the composition will be about. Notice how the body develops the headings in the sample outline and how the conclusion brings the composition to a satisfactory close for the reader.

TELEVISION COMMERCIALS — *title*

Restore happiness to your marriage by using Whiteshirt laundry detergent. Your husband will love you for it. End those lonely Saturday nights —use Bretheen mouthwash. Only Aloha Sealines Super-duper jets will fly you upside down to Hawaii! Thus the barrage of TV commercials continues day and night in almost every American home. Although TV commercials are necessary, most of them are irritating or insulting or dangerous. I believe they can be improved so that they will be not only less offensive to the public but also more effective as advertisements.

introduction

uses examples to create interest

thesis statement

Even while I am registering my objections to commercials, I recognize that commercials are necessary. Without them we would have no television programs, for it is the sponsor who pays the bill. Since the money which pays for a TV program comes from the sale of the sponsor's products, the sponsor must have air-time in which to advertise. Americans must put up with the hourly brainwashing, and they must buy the sponsor's products if they want to enjoy television. They should not, however, have to endure the kind of advertising that accompanies most of the programs.

transition— key words

topic sentence

(compare outline: I, A and B)

This advertising is objectionable—first, because it is irritating. The two sources of irritation are the endless repetition of the same commercial and the

transition—direct reference

topic sentence

too frequent interruption of programs. I suppose that once advertisers have a slogan that has proved effective, they are reluctant to give it up, but if they realized how meaningless the familiar words become after a thousand repetitions, maybe they would find that an occasional change would be effective. My parents say that some of the ads commonly heard today, like "a combination of medically proved and tested ingredients," were used in radio advertising in the forties. The truth is that no one pays any attention to the worn-out slogans, and everyone is irritated rather than interested when the familiar lines begin.

(compare outline: II, A)

I think, too, that advertisers lose more than they gain when they insist on interrupting a program every ten minutes to plug their wares. Irritation of the viewer-buyer is surely not the way to sell anything. Just as the bad guys are about to destroy the good guys—for the first time in television history—the picture stops, and you are taken into a sparkling kitchen to observe the wonders of a floor wax or a detergent or a hand lotion, wonders you have already heard proclaimed night after night. As you are poised deliciously on the brink of disaster in an adventure film or carried away by the immortal lines of Shakespeare, the illusion is shattered by the shouted advice that only by banking at National can you end up a millionaire. If sponsors would all agree to confine commercials to the beginning and end of programs, the public's appreciation would be reflected in its buying. If they would realize how weary we get of the same old commercials, they might find an occasional change to be surprisingly effective.

transitional word
topic sentence

(compare outline: II, B)

Another kind of objectionable commercial is the kind that insults our mentality with its meaningless claims. Analyze the claims made by many TV commercials, and you will find yourself asking, quite logically, "Well, so what?" In our simpleminded way, we are expected to accept blindly the word of a cowpuncher or a water-skier as sure proof of the quality of a soft drink. Every Little Leaguer knows that the leading hitter in the American League has not really achieved his enviable record because of the breakfast food he eats. And parents know that not all family problems will be solved by downing a couple of headache pills. Even shy and desperate Danny doubts that a change in deodorant, shaving lotion, or mouthwash will make him irresistible to the prettiest models on TV. Claims that are completely without reason are insulting to thinking people. The writers of commercials should give their viewers credit for some brains.

transitional expression
topic sentence

(compare outline: III, A, B)

Finally, TV commercials can be dangerous. They can endanger the finances of the American family. The goal of advertisers is to create a demand if none exists. You should have the latest dishwasher, the newest electric hair dryer, a second car, and such status symbols as a backyard swimming pool and a winter vacation. To listen to the honeyed pleas of the handsome, suntanned, obviously happy announcers, you wonder how any of us can possibly live another minute without all the luxuries of a millionaire. But, then, the solution is so easy. Just apply for a personal loan—fast, courteous, no questions asked—and let the Easy Loan Finance Company pay all your bills at once. "We'll even write the checks." This lure could be

transitional word
topic sentence

(compare outline: IV, A, 1 and 2)

irresistible to a young breadwinner trying to keep up with the standard of living fostered by the commercials the family watches every night as they try to catch a program in between.

Commercials endanger our health as well as our budgets. Although the writers are careful to advise us to see our doctors "if the pain persists," they do strongly suggest that we ailing viewers can get the relief we want just as well by following the do-it-yourself patent-medicine approach. Hypochondriacs must go crazy after a day of television. They are presented with a sure cure for every ailment. They can fill their medicine cabinets until they are bursting with cure-alls, fill their objecting stomachs with pills, and cover their bodies with creams until they are either dead or unrecognizable. Certainly the daily bombardment leads many people into a way of living that is dangerous to both pocketbook and health.

transition—direct
reference
topic sentence

(compare outline:
IV, B)

The irritations, insults, and dangerous misrepresentations in TV commercials have been accepted as inevitable for far too long. Perhaps in the near future the broadcasting industry will recognize its mistakes and make changes to accommodate the needs and intelligence of the viewers. If not, there will be no viewers in the living room watching those commericals. We will all be out in the kitchen getting fat!

conclusion—
summarizes main
points and suggests
direction for the
future

EXERCISE 27. Evaluating an Expository Composition. Study the composition above and answer the following questions. If you need help in evaluating the composition, review the information on the introduction, body, and conclusion of a composition, pages 487–96.

1. How effective is this introduction in arousing interest and stating the composition's main idea? How could it be improved?

2. Review the organization of the body. Is the supporting information presented in a logical order?

3. Study the paragraphs in the body. What other details, if any, do you think the writer could have added to support each topic sentence more effectively? Have any details been included that should be omitted? If so, what?

4. How effective is the composition's conclusion? Does it bring the composition to a close in a satisfactory manner? How could it be improved?

5. How might you rewrite the title to make it more interesting or indicative of the composition's content?

GUIDELINES FOR WRITING EXPOSITORY COMPOSITIONS

Prewriting

1. Choose a topic you understand well. If you do not understand the topic, you will have difficulty in explaining it to others.

2. Limit your topic so that it is manageable in a relatively short composition. It is better to develop a specific topic thoroughly than to skim the surface of a broader topic.

3. Take time to gather ample information to support your topic. Depending on your topic and audience, gather facts, statistics, specific details, examples, or incidents.

4. Keep your audience in mind. Determine whether any technical terms or unusual vocabulary will have to be defined in your composition.

5. Organize the information in a logical manner. No matter how valuable the information, your audience will not be able to understand it if the organization of your ideas is difficult to follow. Use an informal plan or outline to establish the basic organization for your paper.

Writing

1. Write an interesting introduction that clearly indicates what the composition is about.

2. Use your informal plan or topic outline as a guide when you draft the body of your composition. If your composition is to be brief, write one paragraph for each main topic. If your composition is to be longer than a couple of pages, consider devoting one paragraph to each subtopic in your outline. See the sample composition on pages 497–500 as a model for paragraph-

ing. Remember that a topic or subtopic may be emphasized by the quantity of information included in the composition. Use transitions (expressions and paragraphs) to show how ideas are related to one another.

4. Consider the tone you wish to convey and try to choose words and create sentence structures that are appropriate to that tone. Remember also that the language you choose should be appropriate for your audience.

5. When you write your concluding paragraph, attempt to bring a satisfying end to the thoughts in your composition. You may wish to restate your thesis, summarize your main points, or project possible future occurrences.

Revising and Proofreading

1. Check to see if you have included appropriate and sufficient information for your audience and purpose.

2. Study your organization to determine whether it is logical and appropriate for your content.

3. Reevaluate your choice of words by considering how appropriate your language is for your audience and the tone you wish to convey.

4. Proofread carefully and make any needed changes in grammar, mechanics, and usage.

CRITICAL THINKING:
Synthesizing Ideas

Synthesis is the critical thinking skill that involves the bringing together of a number of parts or elements to create a whole. In order to write an expository composition, you must use the critical thinking skill of *synthesis.* You bring together the thesis statement, the outline, the supportive details you have generated, and your knowledge of organization to create a whole—the complete composition.

EXERCISE 28. Synthesizing Ideas for an Expository Composition. Select a topic that is appropriate for an expository composition. Gather information for your topic, develop a thesis statement and an outline, and write an expository composition. Use the Guidelines for Writing Expository Compositions on pages 501–502 as an aid in the writing process.

REVISING

REVISING EXPOSITORY COMPOSITIONS

23i. Revise your composition by evaluating content, organization, and style.

The good writer is a good self-critic. Such a writer is willing to look at a first or second or third draft and say, "This sentence is ridiculous . . . throw it out!" Most professional writers go through at least three or four drafts of everything they write, and many have been known to rewrite a single passage dozens of times.

When you have finished the first draft of your paper, you must, in a sense, stop being the writer and become the reader, the editor, the critic. You must be able to distance yourself from your own words and ask questions about them. What did I intend to say here? Did I say it? What can be done to say it better? There are some techniques you can use to become a better self-critic. You can put the paper away for a few days and then come back to it with a fresh eye, more like a person who is reading the material for the first time. You can also read the paper aloud. Sometimes you can hear problems that your eyes skip over. And finally, remember that professional writers always have an editor who reads and criticizes their work. Ask someone else to be an editor for you.

Revising for Content

Begin the revision of your composition by studying the content. Remember that the purpose of your expository composition is to inform or explain, so you must be sure that the purpose is being met. Have you said what should be said? Have you said it thoroughly? Think about your thesis statement. Have you adequately supported the assertion you made in that statement? Check to see if the content of the introduction is adequate. Does it create interest and identify the thesis of the paper? Read each paragraph to determine whether you have adequately explained each topic and subtopic in your outline. Determine whether the composition has unity of content. Does all of the supporting information relate to the thesis?

Revising for Organization

After you have carefully analyzed the content of your paper, examine the organization of the paper. Are all of the topics and supporting ideas arranged logically and coherently? Will the arrangement of information make sense to the reader? Would another arrangement be more effective? Check to see if you have used transitional expressions or paragraphs to demonstrate relationships among the various topics and subtopics. Review each paragraph to determine whether you have arranged ideas logically within the paragraphs themselves.

Revising for Style

The style of your composition is primarily dictated by the language you use and the manner in which you structure your sentences. More than anything else, the language and the sentence structure should be clear; they should not get in the way of the understanding of the audience. The words you have chosen, the sentence structures you have created, and the point of view you have chosen should all reflect the tone you intend to convey. At the same time, the language and sentence structure should be appropriate for the audience, neither too difficult nor too simple.

GUIDELINES FOR REVISING EXPOSITORY COMPOSITIONS

Content

1. Does the introduction include a statement of the thesis and attract the attention of the audience?
2. Does each paragraph in the body discuss only one main idea?
3. Does the composition have unity; i.e., does every paragraph relate to and support the thesis of the paper?
4. Is the thesis adequately developed; that is, are enough points included to support thoroughly the assertions made in the introduction?
5. Does the conclusion bring the composition to a satisfactory close?

Organization

1. Does the composition follow a logical order of development—chronological, spatial, order of importance, or any other order dictated by the content itself?
2. Are transitions used to link ideas within each paragraph?

3. Are transitions used to show the relationships among ideas in various paragraphs?

4. Are the paragraphs of a length that will be easy for the audience to read?

5. Is the amount of information provided on any given topic in proportion to the emphasis that should be placed on that topic?

Style

1. Are the word choice, sentence structure, and point of view appropriate for the audience?

2. Are technical terms and words that would be unfamiliar to the audience defined or explained?

3. Are the word choice, sentence structure, and point of view appropriate for the intended tone?

4. Is the tone appropriate for the intended audience and for the informational purpose of the composition?

5. Is the tone consistent throughout the composition?

6. Is the point of view consistent throughout the composition?

7. Is the title interesting and does it suggest the composition's thesis and purpose?

EXERCISE 29. Analyzing Revisions. The following paragraph is an earlier draft of a paragraph from the sample composition on page 499. Analyze the writer's revisions and then answer the questions following the paragraph.

Another kind of objectionable commercial
~~There~~ is also the kind that insults our mentality with its meaningless
Analyze the claims made by many T.V. Commercials, and you
claims. ~~If one studies the claims, one~~ will find ~~him- or~~ herself asking, quite
try our
logically, "Well, so what?" In a simple-minded way, ~~people~~ are expected to
the *of a cowpuncher or a water-skier*
accept ~~blindly~~ someone's word as sure proof of the quality of a soft drink.
Every child knows that a .500 batting average is not the result of eating special cereals ⊙
And parents know that not all family problems will be solved by ~~swallowing~~
a couple of *pills* *downing*
~~two~~ headache ~~tablets.~~ Claims that are completely without reason are
insulting to thinking people. Even shy and desperate Danny doubts that a
change in deodorant, shaving lotion, or mouthwash will make him irresist-
ible to the prettiest models on TV. *The writers of commercials should give their viewers credit for some brains ⊙*

1. The writer revised the beginning of the first sentence. What was accomplished by this change?
2. In the second sentence, why has the writer added the phrase "made by many TV commercials" after "the claims"?
3. Why has the writer changed the pronouns "one" and "him- or herself" to "you," "yourself," and "our"?
4. Why has the writer changed "someone's word" to "the word of a cowpuncher or a water-skier"?
5. Why has the writer added the new sentence in the middle of the paragraph?
6. What is the effect of the change from "swallowing two headache tablets" to "downing a couple of headache pills"?
7. Why has the writer moved the sentence, "Claims that are completely without reason are insulting to thinking people," to the end of the paragraph?
8. Why has the writer added the new sentence at the end of the paragraph?

EXERCISE 30. Analyzing Someone Else's Writing. By critically evaluating someone else's writing, you not only are helping that person but also are learning something about the writing process. In turn, you can develop your sense of audience by studying the critical comments someone else makes about your own work. Exchange compositions with a classmate and use the Guidelines for Revising Expository Compositions on pages 504–505 to analyze the effectiveness of your classmate's writing. After you have each completed the analysis of the other's paper, sit down together and ask each other the following questions. Note the similarities and differences in organization and style between your two compositions.

1. Do you feel that your composition fulfills the expository purpose? Why or why not?
2. Is your paper interestingly written? Does it engage the audience?
3. Which part of the writing process was the most difficult for you? Which part was the easiest? Why? Is this generally true of all the writing you do, or is it true only of this assignment?
4. Which part of your composition do you feel is particularly well-written? Why do you think so?
5. Which part of your composition are you least satisfied with? Why is that part particularly unsatisfactory?

6. Which of my comments about your paper do you feel were most helpful? Why?
7. Which of my comments do you feel were inaccurate or misguided? Why?
8. Has exchanging papers with me been at all helpful to you in determining how to revise your composition effectively? Why or why not?

EXERCISE 31. **Revising Your Own Composition.** Revise an expository composition you wrote for this chapter. Refer to the Guidelines for Revising Expository Compositions to ensure that you examine your paper thoroughly. Be prepared to write two or three additional drafts of your composition before you have finished the revising stage.

REVIEW EXERCISE B. **Revising a School Composition.** Select an expository paper, one that informs or explains, that you have written for another class. It may have been written for a government, history, science, or literature class. Find a private spot and read the composition aloud. Use the Guidelines for Revising Expository Compositions on pages 504–505, and revise it carefully. At your English teacher's suggestion, show the revised composition to the teacher who originally assigned it. Ask the latter teacher to determine whether the revised version is better than the original.

PROOFREADING

PROOFREADING EXPOSITORY COMPOSITIONS

23j. Proofread your composition for problems in spelling, grammar, usage, and mechanics.

Expository writing, if it is to fulfill its informational purpose, must be clear and precise. Errors in spelling, punctuation, capitalization, grammar, or usage may confuse or irritate your audience and thus interfere with the attempt to convey information. By proofreading carefully, you will be able to identify and correct any errors that might have slipped by unnoticed as you were revising. Use the proofreading guidelines on page 403 to proofread any expository composition you write.

EXERCISE 32. Proofreading Your Expository Composition. Proofread an expository composition you have written in this chapter. Make notations on your paper indicating the corrections that should be made on your final copy. Be sure to refer to the Guidelines for Proofreading on page 403.

WRITING THE FINAL VERSION

PREPARING THE FINAL DRAFT OF YOUR EXPOSITORY COMPOSITION

23k. Prepare the final draft of your composition.

After you have proofread your revised draft, you are ready for the final stage of the writing process: preparing a final copy of your composition. Your main concern at this stage is to implement the revisions you have made in various drafts and the corrections you have made in the proofreading stage. You need to create a neat, attractive final copy that will reflect the thought and care you have devoted to the whole process. Your efforts to create a clean, clearly legible, final copy will be greatly appreciated by those who read your paper. Follow correct manuscript form (see Chapter 30) or your teacher's specific instructions for this assignment. After writing the final copy, proofread again to identify any inadvertent errors that might have occurred in the retyping or rewriting of your composition.

EXERCISE 33. Preparing Your Final Draft. Prepare a final draft of the expository composition you proofread for Exercise 32.

CHAPTER 23 WRITING REVIEW

Writing an Expository Composition. Write a three- to five-page expository composition. Remember the purpose of an expository composition is to inform or explain.

Audience: The members of the school board
or
An admissions committee at a university
    Tone: Formal

PREWRITING   Write the word *education* at the top of a sheet of paper and brainstorm for ten minutes for subjects for an expository composition. After you have completed the brainstorming activity, select a subject and narrow it to a topic that is appropriate for an expository composition. Consider your purpose, audience, and tone, and gather information to support your topic. Develop a working title, a thesis statement, and an informal outline for the paper.

WRITING AND REVISING   When you write your first draft, use your outline as a guide but allow yourself to make changes that seem appropriate at the time. If possible, write without stopping to correct or edit your work. After you have finished the first draft, put it aside for two or three days. Then ask someone you know to read and react to your paper. Revise your paper as many times as necessary to create an effective composition, proofread carefully, and create a clean final copy. You may wish to refer to the revision guidelines in this chapter, the Guidelines for Revising on page 401, the Guidelines for Proofreading on page 403, and the standards for manuscript form on page 404.

CHAPTER 24

Writing Expository Compositions

SPECIFIC EXPOSITORY WRITING ASSIGNMENTS

The general principles of writing exposition discussed in Chapter 23 apply to most of the writing you are likely to do in school. Nevertheless, certain kinds of expository writing come up often enough to merit special treatment. These types include: exposition that informs, exposition that explains, informal (personal) essays, explaining cause and effect, essays of classification, essays of definition, critical reviews, and essays of literary analysis. These specific forms of exposition may play a significant part in your school writing assignments from now on. As your teacher directs, concentrate on one type at a time, always applying the general ideas about the writing process (see Chapters 21 and 23) to each specific expository type.

EXPOSITION THAT INFORMS

A common purpose of expository writing is to inform. The essay questions that you answer on an examination and the reports that you write for your teachers are two examples of informational writing.

When you write a paper whose purpose is to inform, you take a subject and open it up to your audience. Your purpose is not to argue or to persuade but to convey information clearly and accurately. The hints, model, and guidelines that follow provide a blueprint for conveying information with clarity and accuracy.

Prewriting Hints For Exposition That Informs

1. *Select a subject on which you either have or can find adequate information.* When you write about something known to you, you will not be at a loss for ideas. Of equal importance, you will be better able to convey to your audience an interest in the subject.

2. *Identify the audience for whom you are writing.* Be sure to consider the kind of audience you are writing for as you determine the complexity of ideas and the language you will include in your explanation.

3. *Limit your subject by analyzing it into its categories or logical divisions.* Arrive at a manageable topic by taking a careful look at your subject to determine exactly what it consists of. For example, if you are writing to inform an audience about a relatively unknown country, your analysis may focus on such categories as comparative size or comparative resources or may yield such divisions as political character, cultural aspects, sociological makeup, and so on. Similarly, an analysis of the subject "pets" might lead to the limited topic "pets as therapy."

4. *Gather information on your topic.* Using the information-gathering techniques on pages 381–91, collect information which you can use to explain this topic to your audience.

5. *Explain your purpose in a thesis statement.* In a paper on "pets as therapy," for example, the following thesis statement will give your audience an indication of the direction that your paper will take: "Researchers are learning how pets can help cheer the depressed, reform delinquents, and even lower blood pressure."

6. *Organize your information in an informal outline.* Write your thesis statement at the top of a sheet of paper. Then list the facts that you have gathered about your subject. Review your list, looking for main ideas and for specific details that support each main idea. Arrange these in the most logical order for your particular topic. Add any further details related to the topic. Discard details that do not support a main idea.

Writing Exposition That Informs

Following is an informational composition about skiing. Note that the first sentence in the introduction states what direction the exposition will take: the beginnings of the sport. The body provides information that focuses on the development of skiing as a sport. Note (1) how each main idea is supported with specific details and (2) how each detail is related to the main idea. In the conclusion, the audience is left with a sense of the present-day popularity of skiing as a sport.

SKIING—THEN AND NOW

<u>We can't be sure just *where* skiing began.</u>
<u>However, there is no doubt about *how* it began.</u> In
northern Europe and Asia, deep snow blanketed
the land most of the year. Ancient peoples moving
from place to place are known to have experimented with crude footwear for easier going in the
snow. Those primitive efforts probably resulted in
history's first snowshoe. This was a help, but not
the answer.

introduction
thesis statement

We can guess that one day someone walking
down a steep, icy hill started to slide. Amazingly,
the trip to the bottom was accomplished in record
time. And it was much easier than legging it one
step at a time through the snow.

body
main idea: probable
circumstances of
invention

History's first skier was probably quite pleased
with the discovery and set about to improve his or
her sliding shoes. Smooth wooden slats attached to
the shoes were the result. We know this because
the word *ski* comes from a northern European
word meaning "a splinter cut from a log."

How old is skiing? Well, a pair of skis in a
Swedish museum is thought to be at least five
thousand years old. Stone carvings in a Norwegian
cave, said to date back at least four thousand years,
show skiing. And by the seventh century A.D. the
Chinese were writing about it.

details
main idea:
chronology

Skis helped people travel and hunt in the frigid
Scandinavian countries for centuries before anyone
thought about using them for sport. Then, in the
eighteenth century, Norwegian soldiers on skis
took part in a sporting contest in what is now the
city of Oslo. Zigzagging between bushes and trees
on their way down the slope, they accidentally hit

details
main idea: early uses

on the idea of the slalom. The slalom today is one of skiing's most popular and demanding events.

In the 1850's, the Norwegians began holding annual competitions in the valley of Telemark. They developed a means of holding the heel in place on the ski, thereby making the first ski jump possible. It took place on Norway's Huseby Hill, in 1879. In 1883, two main kinds of skiing —cross-country racing and jumping—were separated out for competition purposes.

> details
> main idea: beginnings of annual competition

During the next few decades, the new and exciting sport from Norway spread to almost every country that had snow, including England. It was in England that standards and rules for the modern slalom were officially set down, even though slalom is a Scandinavian word (*sla* means "slope" and *lom* means "track left in the snow").

> details
> main idea: spread of skiing

Skiing has grown to be extremely popular in the United States. The first U.S. ski club was organized in 1867 in, believe it or not, Laporte, California!

Today, wherever you can find a mountain and some snow, you are likely to see cars with ski racks on their roofs heading for the slopes and bumpers on the cars displaying stickers saying, "Think snow!"

> details
> conclusion

DON SMITH with DR. ANNE MARIE MUESER

EXERCISE 1. Writing Your First Draft. From the following list, select a subject on which you can write an informational paper. Analyze the subject and divide it into a number of logical divisions or main topics that can be developed in no more than seven paragraphs. As you write your first draft, refer to the Prewriting Hints for Exposition That Informs on page 511 and to the model.

1. Characteristics of the kangaroo (or of another undomesticated animal)
2. Talking books for the blind (or a similar subject related to the handicapped)
3. A United States President as a reflection of the times in which he held office
4. Sports spectators and violence
5. White House news conferences
6. A historical event of the present century
7. The city in which you live
8. A person you admire
9. Common American place names
10. Computerized cars

GUIDELINES FOR REVISING EXPOSITION THAT INFORMS

Refer to the following guidelines as you reread the first draft that you prepared for Exercise 1. Make any necessary notes for revision.

1. Is the subject suitably limited to a manageable topic, that is, to its categories or logical divisions?
2. Does the thesis statement give the audience a clear indication of the direction that the paper will take?
3. Is each main idea supported with specific details?
4. Do all details contribute to the unity of the exposition?
5. Are details arranged in a way that contributes to the coherence of the exposition?
6. Is adequate information included to inform the audience about the topic?
7. Are word choice and sentence variety appropriate for the particular audience?
8. Is there a concluding paragraph or sentence that leaves the audience with a sense of completeness?

EXERCISE 2. Preparing Your Final Draft. Use the following suggestions to prepare a final draft of the informational exposition that you wrote for Exercise 1.

1. Use the Guidelines for Revising Exposition That Informs to revise your first draft for content, organization, and style.

2. Use the Guidelines for Proofreading (page 403) to proofread your revised draft for any inaccuracies in spelling, punctuation, grammar, and usage.
3. As you write the final draft, follow correct manuscript form (see Chapter 30) or your teacher's instructions for this assignment.
4. Proofread your final draft for any recopying or retyping inaccuracies.

EXPOSITION THAT EXPLAINS

While exposition that informs is relatively common, the kind of exposition that you use most often is exposition that explains. For example, you may frequently find yourself telling someone (1) how to get somewhere, (2) how to make or do something, or (3) how something works.

Items 2 and 3 are examples of process explanations. When you write a process explanation, it is especially important to arrange your ideas in logical order so that your explanation is clear to your audience. The hints, model, and guidelines that follow will help you write explanations that are clearly and logically developed.

Prewriting Hints for Exposition That Explains

1. *Select a subject that can be adequately explained within the limits of your exposition.* In a seven-paragraph paper on "how to study," the subject might be limited to a single aspect of studying: conditions or techniques, for example.

2. *Identify the audience for whom you are writing.* Consider your audience when you decide on the complexity of the ideas and of the language that you will use in your explanation.

3. *Gather information on your subject.* Determine exactly which steps you must describe in the process you are explaining. Then make a list of the ideas you might include in your explanation. (For help in finding information on a subject that requires library research and in taking notes, see pages 672–86.)

4. *Organize your information.* Break down the steps of the process that you are explaining into those details that support each step. For example, if one of the steps toward the establishment of successful study habits is assembling proper equipment, include details related to that step (suitable chair, adequate lighting, etc.). An informal plan or a topic

outline (pages 481–85) in which you begin with a statement of your purpose will help you to organize your list and to put details where they belong.

5. *Arrange the steps in the process coherently, that is, in an order that will be easy for your audience to follow.* In a process explanation, the most natural order is chronological order—the time order or sequence in which each step is taken.

6. *Determine beforehand which parts of the process require thorough explanation.* Keep the needs of your audience in mind. Be prepared to define technical terms in words that the audience will understand. If necessary, include a simple diagram to make a complicated step in a process easier to comprehend. If the process involves amounts, measurements, or distances, be as precise as possible. Think of examples and comparisons that relate your explanation to something your audience already may understand. For example, in an explanation of how a navigator tells where a ship lies on the ocean, you might relate the terms *parallel* and *meridian* to the street name and street number in one's address.

Writing Exposition That Explains

The example that follows explains in part the process for making electricity from a mountain stream. As you read the explanation, note how the process has been broken down into three main steps with a series of supporting details (or in this instance, substeps). Note also that the writer includes a diagram (not shown) and makes use of definitions, examples, and transitional words. (This example is an excerpt from a longer explanation and, consequently, has no conclusion.)

MAKING ELECTRICITY FROM A MOUNTAIN STREAM

If you live in a mountainous area and a brook flows swiftly through your property, you can tap its energy with the miniature equivalent of a hydro-electric power station. A relatively small and simple system based on a water-driven turbine and a small electric generator can supplement current from your local utility. With a larger turbine and generator, you can free yourself from commercial power sources altogether. Large systems are costly, but where utility-supplied power is not available and the only alternative is a gasoline- or diesel-

introduction
thesis statement

powered generator, a home system can prove competitive.

The ability of a stream to produce electric power depends on two factors: flow, the technical term for the volume of water the stream carries; and head, the drop in elevation along the portion of the watercourse where the system will be built. Where little head is available—as in a river flowing through flatlands—an expensive, complex dam is essential to back up the stream and create an artificial difference in water level. A mountain stream, on the other hand, often supplies sufficient head for a home hydroelectric system and needs only to be dammed with a few boulders or logs to channel sufficient flow into the system's inlet pipe, called the penstock.

body

definition of technical term

definition of technical term

definition of technical term

Before planning a water-powered generating system, you must calculate both the head and the flow available from your stream. (Remember, however, that even streams running through private property are subject to laws regarding conservation and water rights; check with the local water resources agency before undertaking a hydroelectric project.) The easiest way to measure the flow of a stream no more than 7 feet wide is to interrupt it with a temporary plywood weir (*opposite*). The flow of a larger stream may be listed at a local U.S. Geological Survey office or, in Canada, at the municipal or district office responsible for natural resources. If not, you can hire a civil engineer to take flow readings. In any case, you will need monthly flow figures for an entire year to be sure that the water level does not drop too low for the generating purposes during the dry season. Also check to see that the stream is not subject to destructive flooding.

transition
first step

detail supporting
step 1

reference to diagram
of weir (not shown
here)

detail supporting
step 1

detail supporting
step 1

To measure the head that your stream can provide, you will need a long measuring pole marked off in 6-inch increments, a second pole exactly 5 feet long, a 50-foot steel tape, a hand-held sighting level and a helper. In general, you will need at least 50 feet of head to make home electrical generating practical.

detail supporting step 1

materials needed and exact measurements

Once you have exact figures for the flow and the head, a simple formula allows you to calculate the amount of power available in the stream. Multiply the head measurement, in feet, by the flow, in cubic feet per minute; then divide the result by 708 to get the theoretical yield, in kilowatts, of electric power. Because no system, no matter how efficient, will enable you to tap completely the theoretical potential of a stream, the calculated yield should be at least twice the number of kilowatts you need for your household.

transition

second step

detail supporting step 2

transition

detail supporting step 2

You will need the head and flow figures—as well as your kilowatt requirements and a detailed description of the topography surrounding your stream—when you begin shopping for a turbine and generator. Turbine manufacturers—most of them small firms in the western United States— generally sell their equipment in complete systems, each tailored to the customer's site and needs. The system will include the turbine and either an alternating- or a direct-current generator. For systems that are to be interconnected with public utility lines, the supplier will also include hardware and electric-safety devices to ensure that the electricity produced is compatible with that delivered by the utility.

transition; third step

ENERGY ALTERNATIVES—TIME-LIFE BOOKS INC.

EXERCISE 3. Writing Your First Draft. A. Plan and write a composition that explains one of the following subjects. Limit the subject to one that can be developed in no more than seven paragraphs. As you write your first draft, refer to the Prewriting Hints for Exposition That Explains and to the model.

1. How to design an efficient kitchen (or other room)
2. How to stop smoking
3. How a telephone call travels
4. How Polaroid pictures develop
5. How to prepare a résumé
6. How sweat glands work
7. How to make miniature furniture
8. How to build a bicycle from spare parts
9. How to avoid gridlocks
10. How eyeglasses correct nearsightedness or farsightedness

B. Under your teacher's direction, select, limit, and develop a subject of your own that clearly involves exposition that explains.

GUIDELINES FOR REVISING EXPOSITION THAT EXPLAINS

As you reread the first draft that you prepared for Exercise 3, keep the following guidelines in mind. Make any necessary notes for revision.

1. Is the topic limited so that it can be adequately explained in the space allowed?
2. Are the ideas developed in language appropriate to the audience?
3. Are ideas arranged in chronological order?
4. Are transitional words used to link the ideas?
5. Are any terms that might be unfamiliar to the audience explained?
6. Are examples, comparisons, specific measurements, and other explanatory details used as needed?
7. Are clear, varied sentences appropriate to the audience included?
8. Do all sentences contribute to the unity of the explanation?

EXERCISE 4. Preparing Your Final Draft. Use the following suggestions to prepare a final draft of the exposition that you wrote for Exercise 3.

1. Use the Guidelines for Revising Exposition That Explains to revise your first draft for content, organization, and style.
2. Use the Guidelines for Proofreading (page 403) to proofread your revised draft for any inaccuracies in spelling, punctuation, grammar, and usage.
3. As you write the final draft, follow correct manuscript form (see Chapter 30) or your teacher's instructions for this assignment.
4. Proofread your final draft for any recopying or retyping inaccuracies.

INFORMAL (PERSONAL) ESSAYS

The informal essay presents the writer's personal view(s) on a subject. Almost any subject can be suitable, as long as the writer can develop it in a discussion that will hold the audience's interest. Generally, the writer creates and sustains this interest by taking a fresh, unique approach to the subject and then developing it in an entertaining and enlightening discussion.

Because of its emphasis on personal expression, the informal essay may appear to be more loosely organized than the formal essay. However, like all effective compositions, the informal essay develops one main idea (the thesis) according to a systematic plan worked out during the prewriting stage. Without such organization the essay would have no unifying main point and would merely ramble through a jumble of personal statements and details that would hold little meaning or interest for the audience.

As you can see, the key to writing a successful informal essay is to make it interesting—both for yourself and for your audience. Accomplishing this will require careful attention to prewriting, writing, and revising skills. These will help you identify and express your own interest so that your audience can understand and share it.

Prewriting Hints for Informal Essays

1. *Select and limit your subject.* In the informal essay much of the information that you give to support your thesis will be drawn from your

personal knowledge and experience, so be certain to choose a subject that you know well. Take time to stop and think about your subject. Jot down ideas about it. Then, look over your list. Which ideas suggest a new slant on your subject—an unusual insight that you can develop in a stimulating discussion that will interest your audience? State this idea in a single sentence, which will become your thesis. For instance, if you have been hunting for a job, you probably have learned and experienced a number of things in your search. List these things, then cross off commonplace items, like advice to be neatly dressed for job interviews, stories of how you were nervous at an interview, and instructions on how to create a résumé, to name a few. Limit your subject to a fresh topic that will be interesting and informative. For example, you could focus on how you failed to get a job (such as in construction or kitchen work) because you were too neat, or how you enjoy job interviews.

2. *Gather sufficient information on your topic.* Exploring your subject likely brought to mind a great many specific facts, examples, and other information about it. Again, make another list. Under the topic of how you enjoy job interviews, for example, you might list your discomfort before going to your first interview, your experiences at the interview that changed your mind, and your various reasons for enjoying interviews now. At this point in your prewriting, do not worry about categorizing your information. Let your ideas and information flow out on the paper.

3. *Organize your information in a logical plan.* Identify the main ideas that you will use to develop your thesis. Many, if not all, of these ideas will become the topics of your paragraphs. Order your ideas in a sequence that will catch and hold your audience's attention. You could introduce your thesis in the first paragraph with an amusing anecdote, a question, a surprising statement, or some other engaging opening. You could then go on to develop your topic with supporting facts, specific details, or examples. Generally, you will want to present your most striking information at the beginning and at the end of your essay in order to attract your audience's attention and to leave the audience with a memorable idea or instance. As you organize your essay, be certain that you do not omit any logical connections, explanatory definitions, or other points that your audience will need in order to follow your discussion.

4. *Decide upon an appropriate tone and use it consistently.* Humor, irony, fear, sorrow, and other emotional points of view are often well

suited to the tone of an informal essay. Since most subjects can be approached from several points of view, you will want to identify your tone early in your planning so that you can maintain it consistently. If you open with an amusing incident, for example, you will want to bring in touches of humor throughout your essay. Keep in mind that humor, like all emotional tones, must be handled carefully. Too much humor can make an essay seem frivolous or juvenile; too little can create a weak or halfhearted effect. Too many surprising or unorthodox statements can alienate the audience and make the writer appear rash or unstable. Do not place emphasis on your tone. Instead, focus on your ideas and information and the relationships between them. Express these elements and relationships with words and details that carry, not broadcast, your tone.

5. *Strive to keep your audience interested.* Setting out with a unique thesis and a well-ordered plan for developing it will give you a necessary head start toward earning your audience's interest. While you are generating and organizing your information, striking words and images will probably occur to you. Note these down so that later, as you are writing your essay, you can use them to maintain and heighten interest in your discussion. Your familiarity with your subject and your views may mislead you to assume that your audience knows and feels what you do. Before you begin writing, try to set your plan aside and come back to it later. Examine it critically. For each idea and for the overall presentation of your ideas, ask yourself: (1) Have I provided everything that someone else would need in order to understand what I am saying and to feel as I do about it? (2) Would I find this essay interesting if these views and examples were being presented by someone else? If you cannot answer yes to these questions, reorganize your ideas and information, decide upon new examples, limit your subject further or in a different area—in short, change your plan until you are confident that your essay will attract and hold your audience's interest.

Writing Informal Essays

In the following informal essay the author, William Safire, gives his view on automobile telephones. The first paragraph begins the essay with an amusing anecdote, which is followed by four paragraphs of specific information about mobile telephones and their growing acceptance in society. The writer then asserts his differing position on mobile telephones and in the sixth paragraph states his thesis that "the invasion" of mobile phones "is an abomination and a horror show." The rest of the essay goes on to detail several of the writer's personal reasons for not wanting a telephone in his car.

Notice how the author attracts and holds his audience's interest in the following ways:

1. *He uses specific words and examples.* He does not simply say that he enjoys driving alone; he pits himself against "social engineers who want all worker-ants to march onto mass transportation." He gives specific examples of who can reach him on the telephone, even when he "cannot be reached." He gives the specific year, model, and idiosyncrasies of his car. Every paragraph contains specific references. Even the two-line seventh paragraph does not simply state "I drive to work alone" but, instead, that "I am one of the millions who drive to work alone."

2. *The author supports his views with specific incidents that are personal, yet likely shared by his audience.* In the last example cited above, the author identifies himself as "one of the millions" who may read his essay. He mentions taking messages for his daughter. He listens to his favorite music as he drives. He values his undisturbed privacy.

3. *The author creates a humorous tone by overstating his individualism.* He is a "perpetrator" of opposition to bureaucratic traffic planners. His home phone number "is unlisted, like the Beverly Hills Fire Department." He enjoys his music, which would make his "colleagues and family members sick." His time alone driving is "blessed," even though his car trembles so violently that it aids his back "better than any lounge chair with built-in vibrator-massager."

You may have noticed in this discussion of William Safire's essay that being specific, being personal, and being humorous all overlap. When you write your informal essay, state your personal ideas and examples with specific words and phrases that convey the emotional tone you want to achieve. Carefully analyze additional ways that this is done in "Calling All Cars."

CALLING ALL CARS

A generation ago, working on a story for the *New York Herald Tribune* about the radio pioneer David Sarnoff, I was told that I could reach him on the telephone in his car. That sounded exciting. As instructed, I dialed zero and asked for the mobile operator—and wound up connected to a woman in Mobile, Ala., who thought I had gone bananas.

specific, personal incident used to introduce subject

That would not happen in today's era of the cellular mobile phone. In an editorial, the New York Times gave warm support this week to a proposal to auction channels on the radio spectrum to car-phone companies.

That idea was first propounded on another subject by the conservative economist Milton Friedman, whose notion—much derided by liberals 20 years ago—was to get the Federal Communications Commission to stop giving away licenses to use the public airwaves for broadcasting, and instead to sell those licenses to the highest bidders, letting the free market rather than the regulators decide who gets to be heard.

transition

It is gratifying to see The Times embrace the Friedman no-free-lunch philosophy, but one sentence in that editorial cries out for rebuttal.

summary of introduction leading up to statement of thesis

"For example," went this encomium to the pace of change in communications technology, "everyone agrees that cellular mobile telephones are a boon."

Hold on. I'm part of "everyone," and I think the invasion of the sanctity of the personal automobile by the most intrusive instrument yet invented is an abomination and a horror show.

thesis

Why? Because I am one of the millions who drive to work alone.

supporting reason begins here

That makes me an elitist in the eyes of social

engineers who want all worker-ants to march onto mass transportation, ride together in a delivery-efficient mode, and march to their jobs in an uncongested stream.

That makes me a perpetrator of a highway-clogging "single-occupant vehicle" to traffic planners who reserve fast lanes to bureaucratically acceptable "high-occupancy vehicles."

But I enjoy driving to and from work alone. That half-hour each way is the only time I am unreachable by telephone.

Oh, lots of times at work I rev up my word-processing terminal and say imperiously to my assistant, "I cannot be reached," but she knows that if the President calls, I can be reached. Or the Vice President. Or the publisher. Or "Mr. Good-fellow," the White House speaker.

My house number is unlisted, like the Beverly Hills Fire Department, to give me a chance to think—but the office is open late and on weekends and has the home number, so I'm reachable. I take a great many messages on my home phone for my daughter, who has worked out her own way to be unreachable to some guys and I'm it.

That leaves my blessed "drive time." My car is a 1969 Cougar, and its violent trembling when in neutral soothes my back better than any lounge chair with built-in vibrator-massager now being featured in the catalogues. A modern cassette stereo radio sits in the dashboard, playing the old Sinatra-Garland-Jolson songs that—if I tried playing them at work or home—would make my colleagues and family members sick. (My "Prince" remains Machiavelli.)

I am all alone, not by the telephone, and I can sing along with Frank or daydream about the budget deficit without having to account, even

Margin notes:

use of specific jargon to poke fun at traffic planners

specific examples

use of personal examples to present information and establish identity with audience

specific words and images

reference to one of the "old songs" author enjoys

subconsciously, for the time. I'm driving; I'm getting someplace; I'll be right there; not guilty.

Comes the telephone in the car, and all that freedom is finished. We will all become always-reachables, under the tyranny of the telephone in the dominion of the dialed. Why do you think they call the mobile phones "cellular"? Because each geographical area is considered a cell, a word previously most often associated with prisoners and Communists.

transition linking information about mobile phones with personal information about author
examination of key term

Ah, the cellmasters say, it's all voluntary. You don't want a telephone in your car, you don't have to have one.

transition from previous paragraph

That's what they said about bathtubs. And telephones, and color televisions sets, and video-corders, and boiling-water faucets. You don't have to have them, but if you don't, you're a pariah. The day is coming when your boss will say "Whaddya mean, he's in his car—get him on the cellular phone!" And you better be there in your cell.

"Everyone agrees," says the editorialist, "that cellular mobile telephones are a boon." Some boon. When Reachability Day closes in on you, call him with your complaints; I'll be out of touch.

author's conclusion

WILLIAM SAFIRE

EXERCISE 5. Writing Your First Draft. Choose one of the following topics and develop it into an informal essay. If none of these topics appeals to you, choose a subject of your own, making sure to get approval from your teacher. Before you begin writing, review the Prewriting Hints for Informal Essays and the model above.

1. After-school jobs
2. On being a joiner
3. On being an individual
4. Music and moods
5. Exercise and keeping fit
6. Popular superstitions
7. Decisions I must make
8. How to be unpopular
9. On being "well-dressed"
10. Traits I wish I didn't have

GUIDELINES FOR REVISING INFORMAL ESSAYS

As in revising any composition, you will need to reread your informal essay several times. Do not try to revise all aspects of your essay at once. Instead, read through one time to evaluate your overall organization. Then, read each paragraph closely to make sure that it is organized within itself. Next, examine your sentences and, last, your words. Naturally, as you are revising each area you will probably notice improvements that you can make in other areas. For example, as you are examining a paragraph, you may notice words that you wish to replace with more colorful, more specific words. Do so, of course. Always be on the lookout for ways to improve your composition and your writing.

Following are several guidelines that you can use to revise the informal essay you wrote for Exercise 5.

1. Are all paragraphs related to the thesis statement, which is stated or clearly implied in the essay?

2. Is a topic sentence given in each paragraph, and do all sentences in that paragraph support that topic sentence?

3. Is the tone established within the first few paragraphs of the essay, and is the tone consistent throughout the essay? If the tone does change, is it for a good reason, and is the change signaled to the reader by a transitional expression and a change in content?

4. Is the tone appropriate to the content under discussion? Is the tone properly proportioned so that it does not dominate the essay? (For example, using a humorous tone does not mean cracking a series of jokes but, rather, using humorous incidents and words to express thematic ideas.)

5. Are specific words and examples used to discuss and illustrate general ideas? Have wordy constructions and inexact terms been replaced by concise, exact phrasing?

6. Have clear transitions been used to connect ideas and information within sentences, within paragraphs, and within the essay as a whole?

7. Have ideas and any special terms been sufficiently defined so that the audience can easily follow the discussion?

8. Can any examples, incidents, and other supporting details be changed or replaced to make them more informative or interesting?

9. Is the title attention-getting and suitable to the content of the essay?

EXERCISE 6. Preparing Your Final Draft. Refer to the following suggestions to prepare a final draft of the informal essay that you wrote for Exercise 5.

1. Use the Guidelines for Revising Informal Essays to revise your first draft for content, organization, and style. Pay particularly close attention to tone and specific wording as ways of maintaining your audience's interest.
2. Refer to the Guidelines for Proofreading (page 403) to proofread your revised draft for inaccuracies in spelling, punctuation, grammar, or usage.
3. Adhere to correct manuscript form (see Chapter 30) or your teacher's specific instructions to prepare the final draft of your informal essay.
4. Before submitting your final draft to your audience, proofread it one last time to catch any recopying inaccuracies.

EXPLAINING CAUSE AND EFFECT

When you explain a process, you explore a subject by finding out how something happens or how it works. When you explain cause and effect, you explore a subject by investigating the conditions (causes) that bring about a result (effect). For example, garbage, ashes, and abandoned cars may be cited as three causes of land pollution. Land pollution is the effect, or result, of the three cited causes.

Explaining a process is called *process analysis*. Process analysis focuses on *how* something is done or *how* something happens. Explaining cause and effect is called *causal analysis*. Causal analysis focuses on *why* something happens. Causal analysis is a useful device in developing a topic for a research paper in which you begin with an effect and investigate its causes or in which you support your thesis statement by investigating a series of cause-effect relationships. Causal analysis is also useful in less formal expository writing in which you explain the "why" of such topics as losing friends or winning arguments. The hints, models, and guidelines that follow will help you use causal analysis in both kinds of assignments.

Prewriting Hints for Cause-Effect Explanations

1. *Select and limit your subject.* Choose a subject that can be limited to a topic that you can explain adequately in the assigned space. In a research paper, for example, you will be able to explain in detail the causes of environmental pollution. In a five- to seven-paragraph expla-

nation, however, it would be better to limit your topic to the causes of a single kind of pollution: air, land, or water.

2. *Identify the audience for whom you are writing.* Consider your audience when you decide on the complexity of the ideas and of the language that you will use in your explanation.

3. *Make a list of cause-effect relationships related to your topic.* Then decide which would make the most effective cause-effect explanation.

4. *Further limit your topic by writing a one-sentence cause-effect statement.* For example, *Convenience packaging has led to extensive land pollution.*

5. *Develop a detailed list of causes that are directly related to your cause-effect statement.* Arrange your list in two columns, showing the likely causes that bring about a specified effect.

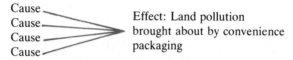

★For a research paper on environmental pollution, your list might include the causes related to several kinds of pollution. Each set of causes should be grouped so that they show a specific effect. For example, list likely causes related to land pollution; then list likely causes related to air pollution, and so on.

6. *Review your list carefully.* Omit causes that are unrelated to your statement. Add causes that should have been included. ★For a research paper, study your list of causes to determine if any are related to one another. For example, if *sewage* and *increased temperature*—two major causes of air pollution—appear on your list, check for other listed causes related to sewage (*organic wastes*, for example) and to increased temperature (*industrial use of water as a coolant*, for example).

7. *Organize your list in a logical way.* Write your cause-effect statement at the top of a sheet of paper. Then write the causes in a sensible order. The causes in a cause-effect explanation may be arranged in either of two ways: in chronological order (pages 427–28) or in the order of importance (page 432). In the latter arrangement, it is usually more effective to begin with the least important or least significant cause and to end with the most important or most significant cause. ★Refer to Chapter 27 for specific suggestions on gathering information for a research paper, organizing a research paper, and developing a formal outline from note cards.

Note: The starred hints will be of special interest to you if you are planning to write a cause-effect research paper.

Writing Cause–Effect Explanations

The following model has been excerpted from a research paper in which the writer has used causal analysis to develop her thesis statement. (Note: For purposes of this excerpt, footnotes have been omitted.)

Although it generates fewer headlines than a flood or an earthquake, the pollution of the environment is potentially one of the greatest dangers to human life. An understanding of what has caused the poisons being pumped into our air, water, and land may lead to measures that will guarantee a habitable world in the next several decades.

introduction

*thesis statement
signals cause-effect
relationships to be
traced in paper*

The paper goes on to define three different types of environmental pollution (air, land, and water). The three paragraphs that follow discuss the two different kinds of pollutants found in the air (solids and gases). Note how the writer uses words and expressions such as *is due to*, *may be caused by*, and *is created by* to signal a cause-effect relationship. Note also that the writer has at times put a cause-effect chain reaction into motion, in which the effect of one cause becomes the cause of other effects.

Solid pollutants are called "particulates." The three major particulates found suspended in air are soot, dust (from soil), and plant pollens. The presence of soot in the air is due mainly to the smoke from oil-burning and coal-burning furnaces in power plants, factories, and homes. Additional soot may be caused by the burning of garbage in incinerators located in municipal dumps and in apartment houses as well as by the burning of leaves and trash. Someone has said that attempts to get rid of waste by burning have resulted in changing one kind of garbage into another—air pollution.

*cause of soot signals
cause-effect*

signals cause-effect

*cause of soot
cause of soot*

Most of the dust that appears in homes is a mixture of soot and of dust that is blown into the

cause of dust

air from the soil. Because soot is greasy and smudges easily, it is by far a more annoying pollutant than dust. However, both dust and plant pollens, the third major particulate, are disturbing to people who suffer from allergies.

The principal gas pollutants in the air are sulfur dioxide, carbon monoxide, oxides of nitrogen, and hydrocarbons. Sulfur dioxide is created mainly by the burning of coal and of fuel oil. Sulfur dioxide is a poisonous gas that can produce irritants in the nose and throat. When combined with droplets of water in the air, it forms corrosive acids that attack human lungs. The remaining gas pollutants result mainly from the burning of gasoline in automobile engines. All of the gasoline exhaust gases are poisonous; in a closed space, they can cause death. The nitrogen oxides and the hydrocarbon gases cause smog and are largely responsible for the recurrent smog in Los Angeles.

cause of sulfur-dioxide signals cause-effect

cause-effect chain reaction signals cause-effect

cause of carbon monoxide, oxides of nitrogen, and hydrocarbons

cause-effect chain reaction

The rest of the paper goes on to discuss why water and land have become polluted and how knowing the causes can lead to at least a partial cure.

The following composition is an example of a less formal cause-effect explanation. In it the writer gives several causes for lost friendships. Note that the writer has arranged the causes in order of importance, beginning with the least important and ending with the most significant cause. Note also that the causes are not merely presented; they have been fleshed out with examples and illustrations.

WHY FRIENDSHIPS ARE LOST

Some of us make friends easily enough but find that keeping them is another matter. If you have difficulty holding on to your friendships, it may be time to look at yourself as a friend in order to discover the reasons for your inability to retain friends.

introduction

thesis statement

You may be losing friends because of a need

signals cause-effect explanation

always to be right; therefore, anyone who disagrees with you is wrong. Without being aware of it, you may be suggesting to your friends that you are better informed than they are. Thus in your need to be right, you may be sabotaging your friendships by coming across as a know-it-all.

cause(s): reason(s)
for losing friends

effect: inability to
retain friends

Another cause of sabotaged friendships is neglect. Instead of occasionally initiating suggestions for spending time together, perhaps you regularly wait for your friends to call you and to plan activities. Consequently, you give the appearance of expecting your friends to do all the giving while you sit back and do all the taking.

transition
cause

illustrations

In a somewhat different way, you may not be as sharing with your friends as they are with you. If, for example, you refuse to share your feelings with them while expecting them to share their feelings with you, they may assume that you do not want them as friends.

cause

examples

Not too surprisingly, a major cause of lost friendships is disloyalty. At times you may have criticized a friend in order to build up your own ego, or you may have allowed someone else to attack a friend unjustly without coming to your friend's defense. The ultimate disloyalty—dropping a friend at the first sign of trouble—does not bode well for present or future friendships.

signals cause-effect
cause

illustrations

A hard look at yourself as a friend and at certain actions and attitudes that may have caused you to lose friends in the past may help you to keep friends in the future. As Emerson put it, "The only way to have a friend is to be one."

conclusion

EXERCISE 7. Writing Your First Draft.   Choose one of the following topics and develop it in a cause-effect explanation. As you write your first draft, refer to the Prewriting Hints for Cause-Effect Explanations on pages 528–29 and to the appropriate model.

1. *For an explanation of no more than seven paragraphs*: why you failed (or succeeded) at something; why a candidate for public office lost (or won) a recent election; why some teen-agers have financial problems; why your favorite team had a winning (or losing) season; why fast-food franchises have succeeded.
2. *For a research report whose thesis statement is developed by causal analysis*: why certain animals become extinct; why most accidents occur at home; what made the 1960's a decade of protest; why newspapers lose readers; why media advertising can manipulate some consumers; why people exercise.
3. *A topic of your own*: Under your teacher's direction, select, limit, and develop a subject of your own that clearly lends itself to a cause-effect explanation. Decide beforehand whether you will develop a research paper or a less formal explanation.

GUIDELINES FOR REVISING CAUSE–EFFECT EXPLANATIONS

As you reread the first draft that you prepared for Exercise 7, keep the following guidelines in mind. Make any necessary notes for revision.

1. Is the topic limited to a cause-effect relationship that can be explained adequately in the space allowed?
2. Does the thesis statement introduce the cause-effect relationship(s) that the explanation will trace?
3. Are the causes explained either in order of importance or in chronological order?
4. Is the relationship between each cause and effect indicated by using such words and expressions as *cause, result, create, the reason for*, etc.?
5. Are the cause-effect explanations fleshed out with illustrations and examples that are appropriate to the audience?
6. Do all sentences contribute to the unity of the paragraphs in the explanation?
7. Are sentences or details arranged to make the explanation coherent?
8. Does the explanation end with a concluding paragraph or sentence?

EXERCISE 8. Preparing Your Final Draft. Use the following suggestions to prepare a final draft of the cause-effect explanation that you wrote for Exercise 7.

1. Using the Guidelines for Revising Cause-Effect Explanations, revise your first draft for content, organization, and style. If you developed a research paper, refer also to the Guidelines for Revising Research Papers (pages 696–97).
2. Referring to the Guidelines for Proofreading (page 403), proofread your revised draft for any inaccuracies in spelling, punctuation, grammar, and usage.
3. As you write the final draft of your cause-effect explanation, follow correct manuscript form (see Chapter 30) or your teacher's specific instructions for this assignment. If you wrote a research paper, refer also to the appropriate sections in Chapter 27.

ESSAYS OF CLASSIFICATION

Dividing information into classes is a way of organizing ideas. Items placed in each class must share common characteristics. For example, many colleges divide applicants into classes, or categories, according to ratings in the areas of high-school grades, standardized test scores, and quality of recommendations. Students in Class A might be those with the highest ratings in each of the areas, students in Class B with the next highest, and so on.

Classification is more than simply dividing information into groups, however. It is also a way of understanding and using the information. For example, most colleges believe that students in Class A described above will perform better in college than students in the other groups, that students in Class B will be next highest in performance, and so on. Many colleges, therefore, use this information as the basis for admitting and counseling students.

In papers that explain classifications, a limited topic is divided into classes. The writer defines each class and sometimes divides the classes into subclasses. The writer describes in some detail the classes and subclasses and provides examples. In addition, relationships among the classes are analyzed. (Does the student in Class A really succeed better in college than the student in Class B?)

Prewriting Hints for Essays of Classification

1. *Select a subject that suits your purpose and audience.* The basic purpose for a classification paper is to divide information into classes —smaller parts or related groups—to understand it better. Consider your audience in selecting your subject. If your audience is a general one, for example, avoid subjects whose classes are too technical or too removed from the knowledge and interests of your readers (such as classes of economic indicators: electricity output, raw steel production, money supply).

2. *Limit the subject to a suitable topic.* Whole books are devoted to classifying such subjects as political parties, military aircraft, and movies. Obviously, these subjects are too broad for a short paper. Remember that you want to define, describe, and give examples of each class involved. Limit the subject, therefore, to a topic with fewer classes.

EXAMPLES   Characteristics of major American political parties
        Republican party
        Democratic party
    Severe mental illnesses
        schizophrenia
        depression
        manic-depressive psychosis
        anxiety
    Successful movies of the 1980's
        adventure
        horror
        science fiction

3. *Gather information about your topic.* Clustering is one highly effective way to generate information about classes. Write your limited topic in the middle of a sheet of paper. Then, around the topic, write the names of its major classes. (Circle each class and draw connecting lines.) Continue dividing into classes and subclasses as appropriate.

EXAMPLE

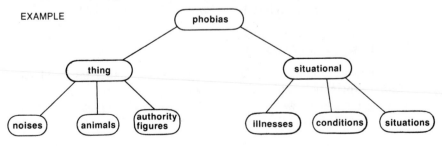

To gather additional detail about the classes and subclasses, use any of the methods for gathering information described on pages 381–91.

4. *Organize your information in a logical way.* An informal outline (pages 480–85) is often a useful tool for organizing material for a classification paper. In this outline each major class is a heading; subclasses become subheadings. (If you divide a class or subclass, remember to divide it into at least two parts.) Depending upon the length of your outline, you might also include details describing classes and subclasses.

EXAMPLE   Understanding Phobias

                Natural fears versus phobias

                Thing phobias
                    Categories
                        Noises
                        Animals
                        Authorities
                    Cause
                    Treatment

                Situational phobias
                    Categories
                        Illnesses
                        Conditions
                        Activities
                    Cause
                    Treatment
                  Future

In a classification paper, major classes are equally important; therefore, use some reason other than importance as a rationale for organization. In the sample classification paper on pages 537–41, for example, "thing" phobias are described first because they are the easier of the two major classes of phobias to understand. Once a class is defined and described, its subclasses are usually discussed before the next major class is introduced.

Writing Essays of Classification

The following example, "Understanding Phobias," illustrates the classification explanation paper. In this paper the writer explains phobias by dividing them into two large classes. Each class is defined and then broken into three subclasses as a further explanation. For each class the writer provides examples, traces a possible cause, and describes treatment.

UNDERSTANDING PHOBIAS

Everyone has fears. Young children are often terrified of being left alone in the dark, trembling in their beds at night. With a slightly queasy stomach, a passenger momentarily grips the seat arms as the huge jet lumbers up the runway for a takeoff. A high-school student faced with a three-minute speech in front of classmates feels weak-kneed and dry-mouthed as the moment approaches. These fears are normal; everyone has them, or fears like them, at some time. For most people, however, the moment passes and so does the fear and its accompanying physical reactions. The child grows older and becomes less afraid of the dark; the traveler continues to fly; the student survives the speech.

first paragraph of introduction; introduces topic and captures audience's interest

For some people, however, the fears do not leave. The fears remain, so severely sometimes that lives are permanently affected. These people —almost ten percent of the population of the United States—with what might be called permanent fears are *phobics*. The fears they have are called *phobias*. Unlike normal fears, phobias defy logic and are long lasting. They do not go away when someone points out the unlikeliness of finding a snake loose in downtown Manhattan, nor do they disappear when the phobic becomes older or changes jobs or moves to a new place. In fact, for some unfortunate people, living a normal life is possible only after years of professional treatment.

second paragraph of introduction; defines phobia by distinguishing from normal fear

Generally, phobias can be divided into two large categories: fears of things and fears of situations. Most phobics in the first category have a specific fear of one or two things—things that can be seen, touched, smelled, tasted, or heard. Thing phobias may themselves be divided into smaller groups. The largest and best known of these subgroups are noises (thunder, fireworks, wind, and so on), animals (especially rats, mice, worms, snakes, spiders, dogs, and cats), and people in authority (including police and fire officers, teachers, doctors, and nurses). Not all thing phobias, however, can be so easily classified. The list, in fact, is almost endless. There are scientific names for fears of the northern lights, mushrooms, money, fish, numbers (especially the number thirteen), taxis, almost any existing color, and any number of other items.

thesis statement; gives topic and purpose

statement and definition of first class; subclasses of first class

details

Many psychologists believe that most thing phobias begin in childhood with a frightening experience, followed by a slowly developing behavior pattern. A child, for example, may be frightened by an unexpected encounter with a large snake. Upon seeing the next snake (of any size), the child gives it a wide berth until, gradually over the years, a phobia about snakes develops. Even forgetting the early physical experience, the phobic may learn to tremble at the sight of a snake in a magazine or on television or even at the mention of the word "snake."

discussion of origins of phobias in first class

details

Most phobics of particular things learn to cope with their phobias simply by avoiding them. A snake phobic, for example, does not visit a reptile farm or spend much time in a biology room near brightly colored snakes curled in jars of formalde-

discussion of treatment of phobias in first class

details

hyde. Because thing phobias may be easily controlled in this way, most people in this first category do not find their lives seriously affected, beyond perhaps becoming intensely uncomfortable when confronted with the objects of their phobias.

The second large category of phobias—fears of situations—is perhaps the more complex of the two. Rather than fearing a specific object such as a cat or dog, a situational phobic fears any number of situations or conditions, often in combinations called "clusters." This type of phobic, for example, might live in terror at the thought of performing an activity (or activities) in public—such as eating, drinking, speaking, writing, or even being looked at by others.

statement and definition of second class
analysis of relationship between two major classes

Common types of situational phobias include fears of illnesses (such as cancer, diabetes, heart attack), fears of conditions (being in enclosed spaces or at heights, for example), and fears of activities (including riding a bicycle, flying on an airplane, or driving a car). What is perhaps the most common phobia of all in the United States, agoraphobia, belongs in the class of situational phobias. Agoraphobics fear being in public places. When the phobia is severe enough, agoraphobics may refuse even to step outside the house. Some therapists, in fact, specialize in home visits for the treatment of agoraphobia.

subclasses of second class

details

Like thing phobias, the class of situational phobias includes some rather bizarre examples. There are situational phobics, for example, who fear walking, being happy, thinking, having objects placed on their left, fear itself, and, quite simply, everything. Because of the famous Edgar Allan

examples

Poe stories, one of the better known unusual situational phobias is taphephobia—the fear of being buried alive.

Although their origins seem more complex than those of thing phobias, some situational phobias also begin, psychologists believe, with early experiences. The famous movie director Alfred Hitchcock, for example, had an irrational fear of being put into jail. Hitchcock once explained that when he was a child, his father had him placed in a cell for a few minutes to frighten him into good behavior.

discussion of origins of phobias in second class

details

While therapists might debate the origins of situational phobias, they do know that situational phobias develop over a period of years. For example, someone with agoraphobia (fear of being in public) might seem nothing more than a shy teenager. By middle age, however, that same phobic might faint at the thought of having to leave the house for a simple errand.

discussion of treatment of phobias in second class

For many situational phobics, simply avoiding the situation causing the fear is difficult. An urbanite who fears enclosed places, for example, might have a problem walking to an office forty floors up rather than riding an elevator; consequently, situational phobics often require years of professional treatment. Also, psychologists have found that situational phobics often have additional emotional problems—such as severe anxiety and depression —that make their illness difficult and costly to treat.

For both classes of phobics, the future looks brighter. Results of recent research about the brain's role in the emotion of fear might soon make

conclusion

the lives of phobics easier. Also, the public is gradually learning that victims of these dreadful fears are more than immature cowards. Finally, phobics may get the treatment and understanding they so desperately need.

EXERCISE 9. Writing Your First Draft. Using one of the topics listed below or a topic of your own, draft a classification paper. In writing your first draft, refer to the Prewriting Hints for Essays of Classification Explanations on pages 535–36 of this chapter and to the sample paper above. Refer also to the Guidelines for Writing Expository Compositions on pages 501–02. (If the topic listed below is not suitably limited, adapt it as you begin.)

1. Suitable toys for children
2. Raising money for school activities
3. Gift-giving made simple
4. Characteristics of voters
5. Bad television commercials
6. Telephones of the future
7. Careers for the year 2000
8. Movie ratings
9. Computer crimes
10. Compositions for English classes

GUIDELINES FOR REVISING ESSAYS OF CLASSIFICATION

As you revise your first draft, consider the general guidelines for revising expository compositions. Think about purpose, audience, organization, and style. Consider especially whether you have suitably divided and discussed the classes of your topic. In addition, use the following specific guidelines for revising classification explanations.

1. Is the subject limited to a topic with enough classes for a short paper?
2. Is the topic divided into two or more classes (and possibly subclasses)?
3. Do the items in each class and subclass share common characteristics?
4. Is the information about classes and subclasses organized in a logical way?

5. Are details and examples of each class and subclass provided?

6. Are relationships among the classes explained?

EXERCISE 10. Preparing Your Final Draft. As your teacher directs, revise the first draft of your classification paper and prepare your final draft. Use the following suggestions:

1. Before you begin, review the guidelines described above. Use the standard manuscript form recommended in Chapter 30 of this textbook.

2. Following the Guidelines for Proofreading on page 403, proofread your paper for inaccuracies in usage, spelling, grammar, and mechanics.

3. As your teacher directs, recopy your paper for submission, incorporating proofreading changes. Before submitting the paper, proofread it once again. If your teacher approves, make neat and clear corrections on this final copy.

ESSAYS OF DEFINITION

The essay of definition develops a topic by answering the question "What is it?" The purpose of a definition is to specify the individual identity of an object, idea, emotion, or any other subject. To arrive at a specific definition, a two-step process is used. The first step is classification, in which the subject being defined is assigned to a larger class, or category; for example, *tiger* can be assigned to the larger category of "cat." The second step is differentiation, in which specific features of the subject are presented to show how the subject differs from other members of the larger category; for example, a tiger is a *large Asian* cat *having a tawny coat with black stripes.*

The definition of *tiger* given above is a *limited* definition (sometimes called a *dictionary* definition), which presents a brief statement of the characteristic features of the subject being defined. An *extended* definition goes into greater detail about the subject by giving a chain of defining characteristics that specify various aspects of the subject. Extended definitions are often useful when dealing with complex terms, such as *happiness, life, democracy*, and other subjects that have many meanings. Extended definitions are also well suited to detailed discussions of subjects that have many features, such as a gasoline engine, Great Britain, or the American Revolution.

In addition to the two-step process of classification-differentiation, other methods for identifying the characteristic features of a subject are commonly used to create informative definitions. One method is comparison, in which the subject is said to be *like* something else based on shared features, as in the case of a particular housecat that is said to be *like* a tiger in having striped fur. Another method is to identify the use(s) of the subject; for example, a tiger is a large cat that plays an important role in maintaining the ecological balance of Asian jungles. In some cases, discussing how a subject develops can help define it; for example, a tiger is a large cat that can become a threat to native villagers when it is injured or becomes old and must seek easier prey than wild game. Other methods of exposition, such as narration, description, and analysis, can also be helpful in defining features of a subject. When giving a definition, particularly an extended definition, you will often find that using a combination of methods will provide the best approach to specifying the characteristic features of your subject.

Prewriting Hints for Essays of Definition

1. *Select and limit your subject.* A definition may be as short as a few words or as long as an entire book. Limit your subject to a topic that can be categorized and then differentiated within the length and time limits of your essay. Generally, you will do this by focusing on particular circumstances or conditions that apply to your subject. For example, rather than try to define fully what a tiger is, you could focus on particular characteristic features, such as a physical description of the tiger, the tiger's place in its environment, and a history of the decline in the number of wild tigers.

To decide which features of your subject to develop, review your own knowledge, and, when possible, examine source materials. Determine what you can discuss in sufficient detail to present an informative examination of characteristic features of your subject. Make sure that the features you discuss specifically characterize your subject. For example, if you were discussing a tiger's hunting skills, you would want to focus on skills that belong only to the tiger and are not also shared by other large cats.

2. *Consider the interests and knowledge of your audience.* Another major consideration in deciding upon a topic is your audience's interest

in it. If you were writing an essay on tigers for a science class, you would want to focus on physical features of the tiger and its environment, such as average measurements of the tiger, the tiger's place in its food chain, and the methods used to study tigers in the wild. If your essay were for a history class, you might examine how tigers have affected the development of a particular region or country, what tigers symbolize to native communities, and why tigers are now being protected in game reserves and national parks. Notice in this last group of examples that the *5 W-How?* questions (see page 388 for further discussion of the *5 W-How?* questions) can provide an effective means for discovering specific features of your topic.

Determine your audience's familiarity with your subject so that you do not give insufficient or unnecessary information in your essay. Define terms and ideas that your audience is not likely to know, and do not include facts, details, and other points of discussion that are already known or are not of interest to your audience. However, in many cases, you will still want to present at least part of the basic specific definition of your subject. If you were discussing tigers, you could probably assume that your audience knows that a tiger is a large Asian cat with tawny, black-striped fur. Nevertheless, you would probably present one or more of these characteristic features in your essay. The point here is that you should not dwell on these commonly known features but, instead, should use them to relate additional information about your subject that will interest your audience.

3. *Gather and organize information about your subject.* Examine your subject in detail. Explore its significant features by asking questions: What are your subject's uses? What are its parts? Does it vary? When and where does or did it exist? When or where is it used? Notice that here again the *5 W-How?* questions are helpful in generating ideas. The particular questions that you ask will depend upon the characteristic features of your subject.

To organize your information for a definition, begin by introducing your topic; then, use several of its distinctive features to classify the topic within at least one category. Next, differentiate your topic from other members of the category by discussing specific features that it does not share with them. Conclude with a further insight about your topic, perhaps an advantage, use, or ability, or a disadvantage, misuse, or inability revealed in your definition.

To help your audience progress smoothly through your paragraphs, begin with commonly known ideas and details and use transitional words and phrases to introduce less familiar information. For example, you would begin defining *tiger* by describing the animal's well-known appearance and then move into less familiar features, such as its lifespan, swimming ability, and eating habits.

4. *Make sure that your definition is useful.* Avoid common fallacies that will weaken your definition. One such fallacy is making the definition circular, which means using the topic of the definition within the definition itself, as in defining *freedom* as "the state of being free." A circular definition obviously fails to specify the identity of a topic and contributes nothing to your audience's knowledge of or interest in it.

A second fallacy is making the definition too inclusive, which means defining the topic too loosely, so that the definition does not specify the topic. For example, a definition that states only that "a tiger is a large cat that sometimes attacks humans" is too inclusive because lions and panthers are also large cats that sometimes attack humans.

Related to the fallacy of inclusiveness is the fallacy of exclusiveness, which means defining the topic too narrowly, so that important features of it are not included. An example of a definition that is too exclusive would be "a tiger is a large cat that lives in India." This definition is correct as far as it goes, but it does not go far enough because it excludes tigers that live elsewhere in Asia. You could, of course, make the true statement that "a tiger is a large cat that lives in India"; however, you would not want to give this statement as a definition unless you were going to develop it further in an extended definition. As you can see, you will need to examine your topic closely and word your definition carefully.

5. *Make your definition both precise and interesting.* Avoid making your definition too simple or too obscure. Tailor your discussion to your audience's level of understanding by using appropriate diction and sentence structure. Sometimes, you will need to use terms in your definition that are more complex than the topic you are discussing, as in defining a tiger as a "carnivorous predator." In other cases, the terms you use will be simpler, as in a tiger is a "large cat."

Your primary concern in defining a topic is to make your definition precise and accurate; however, always strive to make your essay interesting as well. Vary your wording and sentence beginnings by using synonyms and by subordinating clauses and phrases. Try to offer unique information in your essay and to present it in a manner that will catch your audience's attention.

Writing Essays of Definition

In the following essay, "The Wood Stove," the author presents a number of characteristic features that define wood-burning stoves. As you can see, this is an extended definition, which gives a lengthy discussion of features that are defined by various methods.

Immediately following the thesis statement, similarities between wood stoves and fireplaces are discussed. In this way wood stoves are classified with fireplaces as wood-burning cooking devices. In the third paragraph, several physical similarities between wood stoves and fireplaces are given; then, in the fourth paragraph, the author begins to present characteristic features that distinguish wood stoves.

Notice how detailed descriptions of specific features of a wood stove are accompanied by discussions of how these features are used. Such descriptions and discussions provide two informative methods for defining important aspects of a wood stove so that the audience can both see what a wood stove looks like and see how it works. Because the main purpose of a wood stove is to cook food, detailed discussion of how this is done offers significant insight into one of the key characteristic aspects of the topic being defined. When you write your extended definition, be alert for the most important characteristic features of your topic so that you can explore these key features in detail through additional methods of definition.

After discussing a number of characteristic features that define wood stoves, the author concludes with three paragraphs that offer insights into the advantages and disadvantages of using wood stoves. In this way the conclusion projects the definition into specific circumstances that the audience would encounter due to the wood stove's characteristic features discussed in the essay. Although informal usage is generally out of place in a composition, the colloquial quotation given in the closing paragraphs helps to leave the audience with a folksy impression that is well suited to a discussion of a rustic topic like a wood stove.

THE WOOD STOVE

Wood stoves were considered to be an improvement over fireplaces for cooking, but they still required a lot of attention. As with the fireplace, dry kindling and green wood had to be cut to fit the firebox and kept on hand, and the fire had to be watched so that it didn't go out or get too hot.

The fire was built in the firebox located on the left-hand side of the stove right under the cooking surface. To save time, people often used coals right from the fireplace to start the fire.

title

introduction
thesis statement
specific features that
classify wood stoves
with fireplaces

body

At the bottom of the firebox is a coarse iron grate through which the ashes fall into the ash box. The soot which rises into the flue later falls back down into the soot tray which is directly underneath the oven. Both the ash box and soot tray are drawers that must be cleaned out once a week if the stove is used regularly.

specific description that relates wood stoves to fireplaces

The cooking surface of a wood stove usually has six eyes (round openings with iron lids). Sometimes they are all the same size, sometimes of varying sizes. The one at the center in the back of the stove is the hottest, the two over the woodbox are middling, and the other three are the cooler ones. The heat under the eyes cannot be regulated individually, so pots have to be moved from one to the other according to how much heat is required. Sometimes, when people wanted to heat something in a hurry, they would remove an eye and place the pot directly over the flames in the firebox.

specific features that differentiate wood stoves from fireplaces

note that discussion of how wood stoves are used aids in specifying characteristic features

Most of the stoves were fairly simple, though some of them got quite elaborate. One larger variety even had a flat griddle on top for frying things like pancakes, eggs, and bacon.

description of additional special features

The oven is usually located on the right hand side of the stove and is heated from the left and top by the circulation of heat from the firebox. The heat flows from the firebox through a four-inch high air space directly under the cooking surface to the other side. It heats more evenly than one might imagine, but if something tends to cook more on one side than the other, it has to be turned around at regular intervals. The main problem with the oven is that it is difficult to keep the temperature constant. Many varieties have a temperature gauge on the door, but this acts as a warning signal

discussion of characteristic feature of wood stoves—again, note that discussion of how oven works adds defining details

rather than as a regulator. If the oven gets too cool, more wood has be added; and if it gets too hot, the only thing that can be done is to open the door slightly or put a pan of cold water on one of the racks. For something that takes an hour to bake, the fire has to be tended three or four times to maintain the temperature.

When cooking biscuits and cornbread, early cooks often started them on the lower rack of the oven to brown the bottom and then placed them on the higher rack to brown the top. Cakes, pies and roasts were usually kept on the bottom rack all the time. When broiling meat or toasting bread, the top rack was used.

specific details on cooking aid in identifying characteristic feature of oven

About two feet above the cooking surface, most wood stoves have two warming closets. These are metal boxes about six inches deep with a door on each, and they are used to keep food warm until it is ready to be served. The stoves also have a damper that seals off the right side of the firebox and greatly cuts the circulation of heat. It doesn't put out the fire, but it cools the rest of the stove so that it can be left unattended fairly safely. When the damper is closed, the coals will remain hot for several hours. It has to be left open when the stove is in use.

characteristic feature of wood stoves and details about use

characteristic feature of wood stoves and details about use

We asked Margaret Norton, a real chef on a wood stove, what some of the advantages and disadvantages of using one are. Here's what she told us—"I've always used a wood stove because we live up here in the woods and there's always plenty of wood. They're good in the wintertime because they sure do warm up the kitchen. In the summer it gets uncomfortable hot in here; 'course we can go out on the porch every few minutes. But

conclusion

advantage and disadvantage of wood stoves

we're used to it. With this you have to build a fire
and wait till it's ready, but by the time you make up
your cornbread or peel your potatoes, it's hot.

"Sometimes wind'll blow down the pipe hard additional
and smoke the house, and the soot flies out all over disadvantages of
wood stoves
the place and you have to wipe off everything. And
you have to clean it out every so often and watch
that sparks don't fall out on the floor.

"And of course you have to gather your wood, another disadvantage,
and that's a disadvantage when you're out of it. But followed by an
advantage of wood
if the electricity goes off or the gas gives out, you're stoves
all right if you've got wood."

ELIOT WIGGINTON

EXERCISE 11. Writing Your First Draft. Choose one of the
following topics and develop it in an essay of definition. Before you
begin writing, review the Prewriting Hints for Essays of Definition and
the model above.

1. Select five of the words listed below and write a limited definition of
   each in two or three sentences. Begin by classifying the subject;
   then, differentiate it from other members of the class. Write your
   definitions before looking them up in the dictionary. Compare your
   definitions with those in the dictionary. What differences do you
   notice?

   a. mansion   f. surgeon
   b. chapel   g. canoe
   c. vase   h. dictionary
   d. dog   i. radar
   e. optimist   j. golf

2. Select one of the following subjects and develop it into an essay-
   length extended definition. Begin by using the two-step classification-differentiation method to create a specific definition; then,
   use additional methods of definition to discuss key characteristic
   features of your subject in more detail. Draw your information from
   your personal experience, from reference books, and from any
   other sources you wish.

a. a natural athlete
b. a friend
c. a poem
d. a funny joke
e. a snob

f. a good (or poor) student
g. a natural leader
h. a worthwhile goal
i. good manners
j. success

3. Following the same instructions given in 2, write an essay-length extended definition of a subject of your own choice. Be sure to get your teacher's approval of your subject before you begin writing.

GUIDELINES FOR REVISING ESSAYS OF DEFINITION

Reread your essay of definition several times. Look for ways to make your definition more precise and informative. As you review the first draft you prepared for Exercise 11, refer to the following guidelines to give you tips on where and how to make your revisions.

1. Has the subject been limited sufficiently to a topic that can be defined within the space and time restrictions of the essay?

2. Has the topic been specifically defined through classification and differentiation of its characteristic features?

3. Does the definition accurately identify the topic so that the definition could not also fit another topic and so that it does not omit any important characteristic features of the topic being defined?

4. Does the discussion of each characteristic feature contain all necessary descriptive and supporting information, and has no unnecessary or repetitive information been included?

5. Has the audience's knowledge and interest in the topic been considered so that unfamiliar terms have been defined and information already known to the audience has been omitted?

6. Are ideas, details, and structural elements (phrases, clauses, sentences, and paragraphs) tied together with transitions?

7. Have precise terms been used to specify the elements of the definition?

8. Have word choice, sentence structure, and other elements of the essay been varied to keep the audience's interest?

9. Does the conclusion employ key characteristic features presented in the definition to suggest further insights or implications about the topic?

10. Does the title state the topic that is being defined?

EXERCISE 12. Preparing Your Final Draft. Use the following suggestions to prepare a final draft of the essay of definition that you wrote for Exercise 11.

1. Using the Guidelines for Revising Essays of Definition, revise your first draft for content, organization, and style. Pay particular attention to the specific words that are used to define key features of your topic and relationships between them.
2. Referring to the Guidelines for Proofreading (page 403), proofread your revised draft for inaccuracies in spelling, punctuation, grammar, and usage.
3. Follow correct manuscript form (see Chapter 30) or your teacher's instructions to write the final draft of your essay of definition.
4. Before submitting your final version to your audience, proofread it one more time to catch any inaccuracies in recopying. Read slowly, backward and forward across each line several times. Examine each word and mark of punctuation. Make sure that any corrections you make are neat and are clearly marked.

CRITICAL REVIEWS

The critical review examines the content and evaluates the effectiveness of a creative work (such as a book, film, painting, or recording) so that the review's audience can determine whether the work would appeal to them. The critical review provides (1) a summary of the work's subject and main theme or story line, (2) a discussion of major points and elements in the work, and (3) the reviewer's assessment of the work's strengths and weaknesses. The critical review may either praise or find fault with a work; usually, a mixed evaluation is given, citing strengths in some areas and weaknesses in others.

While the examination of the work in a critical review should rest upon objective analysis, evaluation of the work entails subjective analysis as well. The reviewer should always use objective information to support and express subjective evaluations so that the audience may judge whether the reviewer's assessment is well founded. Nevertheless, a short statement of the reviewer's personal tastes and opinions is definitely appropriate in the critical review and, in fact, is often enjoyed and appreciated by the audience.

Prewriting Hints for Critical Reviews

1. *Identify and limit your subject.* The first step in identifying your subject, which is the work you are reviewing, is to classify it according to categories that define various features and aspects of it, such as *subject matter* (fiction, nonfiction, opera), *medium* (novel, film, record album), *genre* (science fiction, documentary, still life), or *audience* (teen-agers, tennis players, farmers). Next, in one or two sentences state the work's subject and unifying idea—its theme, thesis, or main story line. Under this statement note the work's main sections or scenes that present the unifying idea. You will use these notes in composing your summary, which should take up not more than a third of your review, so focus closely on only those elements of the unifying idea that are necessary for understanding the main purpose and meaning of the work.

2. *Gather sufficient information on your topic.* Thoroughly know the work that you are reviewing. If it is a film, see it more than once. If it is a recording, listen to it a number of times. As you repeatedly experience the work, note specific quotes, incidents, background scenery or melodies, and other details that you can use to illustrate important characteristics of the work. Gain further knowledge by reading reviews and discussions about the work, about its creator, about its sources, or about other aspects of it. Identify major points and elements of the work. In fiction, for example, these might include characters, setting, symbols, themes, significant phrases or images, and other literary devices. In the case of a recording, you might note the instrumentation, variations in volume or melody, themes, or similarities to and variations from other musical works. To recognize what is important in a work, look for elements that (1) are repeated, (2) are given the most space or time, (3) are emphasized by the characters or the creator of the work, (4) are necessary to present the work's unifying idea, and (5) are necessary to an appreciation of the work. Besides being important to your summary and your examination of the work, these major points and elements will serve as objective bases for your evaluation.

3. *Organize your information in a logical plan.* Organize the information in your summary, using the same pattern or order in which it appears in the work. Next, examine the work's major points or elements according to their order of importance, their order of appearance, their relationships to one another, or according to one of the other organizational methods discussed in Chapters 21–23. Using the objective information in your summary and your examination of major elements,

evaluate the strengths and weaknesses of the work. In many cases some parts of the work—such as characterization, composition, or orchestration—may be weak, while other parts are well executed and effective. Discuss how the parts, singly and in combination, affect the overall effectiveness or enjoyment of the work. To gain insight into the work for your evaluation, ask yourself:

a. Has experiencing this work made me aware of something I did not know or feel before?
b. Have any of the arguments, dramatizations, or other elements in this work changed or confirmed my views?
c. What can an audience expect or hope to gain from this work?
d. To whom would I recommend or not recommend this work?

Make sure that your views and evaluations are supported by specific details from the work.

4. *Give your audience an accurate representation of the work.* Remember that your review of a work will likely influence your audience's interest or disinterest in it. Make sure that you cover all important elements of the work and that you give them proper emphasis, so that you do not misrepresent the work's content, style, or theme. Base your evaluations on the work's own criteria; for example, do not find fault with a surrealistic painting because it contains distorted or incongruous images. The surest ways to make your review accurate are to maintain an objective approach, and to use specific details and quotations from the work to present information and to express your opinions.

5. *Describe any special features of the work.* Special features and distinctive methods of presentation can enhance or diminish a work. For example, a book might have an interesting variety of typefaces or especially large type for those with poor eyesight, or it might have uncomfortably small type, which could also be blurred or in some other way difficult to read. Illustrations, maps, photographs, indexes, footnotes, and other special features can be helpful or intrusive, depending upon the context and characteristics of the particular work. Special effects, costuming, sound tracks, camera techniques, and other distinctive features affect the enjoyment and understanding of films, television programs, and other video productions. Be sure to let your readers know of any special or distinctive features that play a significant role in the work you are reviewing.

6. *Give your individual response to the work.* Do not merely claim that a work is "good" or "bad" or that you liked or disliked it. Give specific reasons and examples, explaining why the work was or was not enjoyable or worthwhile. Your response to the work is prompted by specific elements within it. Determine which elements led you to respond favorably or unfavorably; then, explain in your review why or how these elements influenced your opinion. Avoid overstatements, snide comments, and other inappropriate evaluations. For instance, you cannot truly claim that "this is the greatest movie ever made" because (1) you have not seen all the movies ever made, (2) there are many criteria for judging the greatness of movies, and (3) a number of these criteria are subjective, preventing any one film from being universally considered "the greatest." Offer a well-considered appraisal of the work, either at appropriate points in your review or in a short, reasoned discussion in the concluding paragraph.

Writing Critical Reviews

Following are three critical reviews: the first of a novel, the second of a film, and the third of a recording. There is no set form for the heading of critical reviews. In many cases the review, like an essay, is titled, and the name of the work being reviewed, its creator, and other information about it are given in the discussion or in a listing below the title. In other cases, the review is titled by the name of the work being reviewed and is accompanied by the creator's name, the producer's or publisher's name, and additional information. The reviewer's name is given either below the review's title or at the end of the review. Sometimes, only the reviewer's initials appear at the end of the review, and the reviewer's name is listed elsewhere, usually in the masthead of a magazine or index in an anthology. For your critical review, use the heading format expected by your audience, usually your teacher.

In the following review of *Heretics of Dune*, the reviewer begins with his favorable evaluation of the book and its author, and relates this book to its predecessors in the *Dune* series. The second paragraph offers a summary of the book's main story line and mentions further links between *Heretics of Dune* and previous *Dune* books. Notice how the reviewer uses specific names and terms from the story, such as *Bene Gesserit* and *ghola*, to discuss the plot. By defining these names and terms, the reviewer also provides additional insights into the novel's science-fiction world. The review ends with a restatement of the reviewer's opinion, along with his recommendation of the book. In the review's first and last paragraphs, the reviewer directly addresses one of the book's special features—that it is part of the *Dune* series. In the first paragraph, those familiar with the series are told that this new install-ment is in the same vein as previous ones; in the last paragraph, readers new to the series are assured that they need not have read the other installments to enjoy this one. In both cases the reviewer makes a natural link between this special feature and his favorable opinion of the novel.

HERETICS OF DUNE
By: Frank Herbert. G. P.
Putnam's Sons. $16.95

Despite occasional disappointments, the *Dune* series remains one of science fiction's landmark achievements. The writer's complex canvas of cul-tural, social and political analysis, combined with his incisive understanding of character, rivals the best works in the so-called mainstream. This fifth volume of the series, taking place many centuries after the events of the last book (*God Emperor of Dune*), shows the slowly evolving plan of the Bene Gesserit Sisterhood nearing its completion.

reviewer's evaluation

Modeled after Catholicism's Jesuits, the Bene Gesserit make use of special social, physical and mental techniques to pursue a plan known in detail only to the innermost circle of its leaders. To help bring it to fruition, the Sisterhood calls one of its best military people out of retirement. Miles Teg must protect and see to the education of a special protege—Duncan Idaho. Idaho made his appear-ance in the first book of this series, as swordmaster and teacher to the revered mystic and leader Paul Atreides. Killed in battle protecting Paul, he re-

summary of the story line

discussion of important characters

turns again and again as *ghola,* a genetic replica of the original. Miles must use not only his military skills, but also those special skills that make him a *mentat,* a human computer, to protect Idaho from enemies both within and without the Sisterhood. Slowly he begins to understand his true role in the Sisterhood's plan, a plan that involves all of the major groups from earlier groups, a new group returning from a centuries-long exile in deep space, and a young girl capable of commanding the giant sandworms of Rakis, once called Arrakis, or Dune.

specific terms from work used to present information

Herbert has few equals in his ability to tell a tale at once complex and suspenseful. The interplay of ideas merges gracefully with the plot, and even newcomers to the series should have no trouble following the book's various threads.

reviewer's evaluation and advice to audience

N.C. [Neil K. Citrin]

reviewer's initials

The next review deals with the film *Dune.* The short introductory paragraph states the reviewer's evaluative thesis that the film's director was not primarily interested in making *Dune* entertaining. The reviewer briefly mentions in the next paragraph two of the director's previous films, and then goes on in the next four paragraphs to discuss in more detail the relationship between the director and the film. Through this discussion a number of specific facts about special features of the film, about the book upon which the film is based, and about the director's background are all interrelated to support the reviewer's initial evaluation. The two paragraphs that follow summarize the main plot and offer an evaluation of some of the characters. The next two paragraphs go into detail about special effects, which play a major part in the film, and the final paragraph gives the reviewer's overall appraisal of the film and his personal response to it. As in the book review above, take note of how the reviewer uses specific details from the work to support his opinions and evaluations.

'DUNE' PLOT LOSES OUT TO WEIRDNESS

By Jay Boyar

Entertainment, as we ordinarily understand the word, is only an incidental consideration in the movies of David Lynch.

introductory statement of reviewer's thesis

His first feature, an outrageous cult film called *Eraserhead*, is an avant-garde masterpiece but only marginally enjoyable. And although *The Elephant Man*, his next movie, is a terrific horror picture, the considerable amusement it provides seems to emerge almost accidentally.

background of director

Now along comes *Dune*, which Lynch wrote and directed, making it quite clear that all this time he has been less the showman than the *freak* showman. Lynch is mainly interested in discovering weirdness. His attitude appears to be that if what he's exploring happens to interest moviegoers, fine. If not, fine too.

reviewer's opinion

I'll be surprised if his latest film catches on big with audiences; it's sophisticated in ways that turn in on themselves and risk shutting the viewer out. Like a freak show, *Dune* is fascinating without actually being engrossing.

David Lynch was an odd choice to adapt Frank Herbert's popular 1965 science-fiction novel. What's best about the book is the intricacy of Herbert's plotting. The multi-layered narrative pulls you in completely, and you're delighted to remain in Herbert's world for as long as he will have you.

discussion of book upon which film is based

But Lynch, who was trained as a painter and sculptor, seems to have little interest in—or talent for—storytelling. Perverse pageantry is more his style.

People who loved the book might like the movie for the striking visualizations it offers of characters and settings. (Herbert himself is said to have enjoyed the film.) But considered on its own merits, the movie seems only partially formed. And if you are new to the *Dune* mythos, you won't be confused by the film as much as you'll feel a bit stranded. Lynch's stripped-down plot seems to lack a crucial dimension.

more of reviewer's opinion and evaluation

Much of the story is set on Dune, a world where water is so scarce that its inhabitants wear outfits called stillsuits that trap and recycle the moisture of their bodies. This parched planet is important because it's the only place in the known universe where a miraculous spice known as melange is found. The spice is in great demand because it expands life and consciousness. Opposing super-powers—the good Atreides and the evil Harkonnens—battle for control of Dune.

summary of story line

At the center of the story is a handsome young man named Paul Atreides (Kyle MacLachlan), who may or may not be Dune's messiah. The chief villain is the disgusting Baron Vladimir Harkonnen (Kenneth McMillan). Many characters drift in and out of the saga, most of whom speak in the measured tones common to science-fiction epics. (To me, such characters have always sounded like Tonto with a Ph.D., but it's a convention of the form you can learn to live with.) In the cast are many well-known actors, including Sting, the rock star, who, despite the hype about his appearance in the movie, gets only about five minutes of screen time.

discussion of leading characters

reviewer's response to minor characters

David Lynch doesn't approach moviemaking like any other director, so it follows that when he makes a film with special effects, those effects are really special. In the sword fight scenes, the partici-

discussion of special effects

pants seem to become panes of Plexiglas to do battle. And a Rube Goldberg contraption that Paul uses to test his reflexes may remind you of a videogame with the dangers made real and three-dimensional.

One reason the effects seem so original is that Lynch has manufactured arresting sounds to accompany the images. This is particularly true when it comes to the giant sandworms of Dune. Their 1,000-foot bodies are commanding creations in themselves, but the thunder they make as they race across the planet's surface and their bleak, raspy cries further the illusion. In fact, Lynch's use of sound and music (by Toto and Brian Eno) throughout the film is experimental and uncommonly expressive.

Dune doesn't hold together, but it's not negligible either. Watching the film, the overall impression is of seeing an underwater parade. The floats seem really to float and everything appears to move in slow motion. Some of what's on view is startling, possibly unique. But always there's the risk that an unforeseen current will sweep across the screen, carrying everything away.

discussion of soundtrack

reviewer's evaluation of special features

reviewer's evaluation and personal response

The final example is a review of Bruce Springsteen's record album *Born in the U.S.A.* The introductory paragraph offers a discussion of Bruce Springsteen's previous work and an evaluation of it by the reviewer. The reviewer's evaluation carries over as a transition into the second paragraph, which examines and evaluates individual songs on the album. Note how the reviewer cites specific songs and lines from one particular song to express and support his discussion. In the third paragraph, the reviewer draws analogies between the work of Bruce Springsteen and two other recording artists. The reviewer concludes with a reflection on whether Springsteen can perform as well in an upcoming tour.

RETURN OF THE ROCK HEROES

[Bruce] Springsteen has aspired to be a rock-and-roll hero—an ambition that has sometimes seemed a curse. In the past he has strained to give his songs a mythic stature by writing about romantic stereotypes—"tramps like us"—and then by singing the lyrics as if he were trying to belt each word out of the ballpark.

introduction and discussion of work's creator

In the better part of "Born in the U.S.A.," however —and in the album's anthem, "Dancing in the Dark"—his writing and singing have a welcome air of restraint. The single exists in two radically different versions. The original version (which is also in the album) is relatively unadorned; but this week Columbia will issue an exciting dance remix created by Arthur Baker, who recasts the song as a rock-and-roll symphony in the spirit of "Born to Run." In either version, it's a breathtaking record. Keyed to a synthesizer line that sounds like a French horn, the music is sunny and spacious. The relentless, battering beat recalls Martha and the Vandellas' "Dancing in the Street." The record celebrates the romance of rock, but it's also about the claustrophobia and despair behind that romance. When Springsteen sings "I'm just tired and bored with myself," he captures in a line the listlessness and lack of self-esteem that has led more than one lonely teen-ager to lose himself in the vicarious excitement of rock and roll.

statement of reviewer's thesis

specific supporting example

discussion of distinct special feature

discussion of work's theme
specific supporting example

Springsteen's new-found austerity first became apparent two years ago on "Nebraska," an album of downbeat songs he recorded solo, recasting rock in the image of Woody Guthrie's dust-bowl ballads. But this time he evokes the American dream running on empty through music that is brash, clotted, electrifyingly direct. There's never been an Eddie Cochran-style rave-up quite like "Working on the Highway," with its chain-gang lyrics cutting against its good-times jangle. And when Spring-

further development of reviewer's thesis
specific reference

specific reference

steen's voice arches into a falsetto at the close of "I'm on Fire," his eeriest new song, it's one of the purest, most affecting moments on record this year. It will be interesting to see whether Spring-   reviewer's evaluation
steen, in his long-awaited tour that starts June 29, can bring moments like this to life in the context of the larger arenas he will be playing.

JIM MILLER

EXERCISE 13. Writing the First Draft.   Write a critical review on any work of your choice. Because critical reviews can be written on any creative work, you have a wide range of selections: novels, nonfiction books, collections of short stories or poems, dramas, television programs, films, record albums, paintings, sculpture, live performances, and more. You might want to choose a work you have read, heard, or seen in another class or on your own, or you might want to take this opportunity to experience a new work. In making your selection, of course, be sure that it is acceptable to your teacher. Before you begin writing your review, closely reexamine the Prewriting Hints for Critical Reviews on pages 552–54 and the three models above.

GUIDELINES FOR REVISING CRITICAL REVIEWS

After you have written your critical review, set it aside for a few hours or longer. Then, reread it carefully, using the following guidelines to improve and correct it.

1. Does the summary of the work's subject and unifying thesis, theme, or story line accurately convey the content of the work?

2. Are specific citations from the work used to express and support the summary, examinations of elements, and evaluations?

3. Does the review discuss strong and weak elements or features of the work?

4. Does the reviewer present well-supported evaluations of the work's parts and of the work's overall effectiveness or worth?

5. Is the audience given sufficient, accurate information to determine whether the work will be of interest?

6. Are quotations from the work given verbatim and enclosed within quotation marks?

7. Does the review contain the work's title, creator's name, and other information that the audience would need to identify and, if possible, locate the work?

8. Are transitions used to provide coherence between ideas and information, sentences within each paragraph, and the separate paragraphs of the review?

9. Are any distinctive features of the work, such as illustrations or typeface variations in a book, or background music and costuming in dramatic productions, covered in the review?

10. Is the past or present tense (either is acceptable) used consistently in all verbs in the summary? Are all other verb tenses and pronoun references correct?

EXERCISE 14. Preparing the Final Draft. Use the following suggestions to prepare a final draft of the critical review you wrote for Exercise 13.

1. Reread your draft several times, making corrections and revisions with each reading until you are satisfied that your review gives your audience a complete, well-organized, clearly stated discussion and evaluation of the work being reviewed. To help you recognize problem areas, consult the Guidelines for Revising Critical Reviews.

2. Refer to the Guidelines for Proofreading (page 403) while you check your revised draft for inaccuracies in spelling, punctuation, grammar, and usage. Pay special attention to the rules concerning quotation marks and to the use of other marks of punctuation with quotation marks.

3. Adhere to correct manuscript form (see Chapter 30) or to your teacher's specific instructions when you write your final draft.

4. Before you submit your review to your audience, carefully proofread your final draft one last time to eliminate any possible recopying inaccuracies. Go over your paper line by line, from beginning to end and backwards from the end to the beginning. Look at each individual word and mark of punctuation to be certain that they are correct and the best choices you can make.

ESSAYS OF LITERARY ANALYSIS

Through the process of analyzing a literary work, you will discover much about its composition and meaning. When you organize your findings into an essay of literary analysis, you pass along a portion of your knowledge to your audience. In this way, both you and your audience can enjoy a greater appreciation of the work by gaining insight into its sources, themes, allusions, and other aspects that add dimension to it.

To conduct an analysis of a literary work, you must be familiar with the terms and concepts used to identify major elements within that genre of literature. Such elements include plot, setting, and dialogue in fiction (short stories, dramas, and novels), while the major elements of poems and songs include rhyme scheme, meter, and scansion. Several major elements—for example, symbolism, allusion, point of view, and imagery—are found in most literary works and should be examined in any literary analysis.

Adhere to the rules and conventions that apply to any expository composition when writing your essay of literary analysis. Begin your essay with an introduction that gives (1) the title of the work you will be analyzing, (2) its author's name, and (3) the thesis of your essay. After you have stated your thesis, develop your literary analysis in several paragraphs in the body of your essay. Following your analysis, your conclusion should sum up how your discussion supports your thesis and should close with a suggestion of further areas of study or further implications of your analysis.

Prewriting Hints for Essays of Literary Analysis

1. *Identify and limit your subject.* Limit your subject, which is the literary work you are analyzing, to a suitable topic by examining categories that apply to the work. Begin with categories of literary elements. If you were analyzing a drama, you could examine its characters, theme, dialogue, or setting, for example. You will likely find it helpful to approach each category with questions. For a drama, you could ask: Are the characters realistic or stereotyped? Does the drama's main theme provide a unique insight into human nature or a reaffirmation of common knowledge? How much do the dialogue and setting affect the plot or the theme(s) of the drama? Further specify your topic by applying categories from other fields of knowledge, such as history,

psychology, law, or physics, to the work you are analyzing. Some sample questions that you could ask of a drama would include: Do the characters or setting depict a particular historical place or era, and if so, what is revealed about the manners, customs, or society of that place or era? Does a character's speech or behavior provide any significant insight(s) into human motivation, learning, personality, or other psychological behavior? Is the fairness or unfairness of a legal standard explored through the action of the drama? Do any physical laws appear to govern the plot or a specific character's actions? Questions like these can be drawn from nearly any category of human activity to limit your topic. By asking questions from more than one category, you can quickly arrive at a specific topic for your literary analysis. For instance, you could examine how a dramatic protagonist's main conflict (two literary categories) is against an unjust law (legal category) that existed during a particular era (historical category). You can devise questions by using a variety of methods, such as the *5 W-How?* method and others discussed in Chapter 21 on pages 388–91. Specific topics are sometimes suggested by problems, such as those you encounter yourself while reading the work, or those presented in class discussions or exercises and study guides in your text(s). Use several methods to generate a choice of topics for your literary analysis. Before you select a particular topic, determine whether the literary work contains sufficient information for you to analyze that topic within the space and time restrictions of your essay.

2. *Gather sufficient information on your topic.* Reread the work that you will be analyzing. If it is a lengthy work, such as a novel, skim through it, spending extra time closely reading sections that particularly apply to your topic. If you are dealing with a poem or a short story, read it carefully several times. As you read, analyze the work. Study its characters, plot, theme(s), imagery, rhyme scheme, and other literary elements related to your topic. Make notes—write down ideas, quotations, and any details that you can use to develop your analysis. Include everything you can find. If you have a long passage to cite, jot down key ideas, images, or phrases, along with the page number of the passage. Be sure to place quotation marks around all citations taken verbatim from the work. When quoting two successive lines of poetry, separate them with a slash (/). When giving three or more lines of poetry, place a colon where you want to introduce them in your discussion; then, begin

the citation on the next line of your text and give the lines of poetry exactly as they appear in the work. After you have collected a few pages or a stack of index cards full of notes, begin organizing your information. However, keep in mind that you probably are not finished gathering information. Later, as you are developing your analysis, you will likely discover that you need additional details or a particular quotation that you recall, but that you did not note down. Remember that prewriting steps often carry over into one another and into the writing of your essay, so you will likely continue gathering information throughout the process of developing your essay.

3. *Organize your information in a logical plan.* Use the defining features of your topic as headings for organizing the details, quotations, and other information that you plan to use in your analysis. For example, if you were to analyze a dramatic protagonist's opposition to an injustice during a particular historical era, you would group your information under *the protagonist's opposition, the injustice,* and *the particular historical era.* As you organize your information, you will probably have some details and quotations that fall under more than one heading and others that do not seem to fit anywhere. Put those that belong in more than one group at the top or bottom of the list, because they may provide a good transition point between paragraphs later when you write your essay. By identifying the defining features of your topic and then listing details and quotations under them, you are creating the main points and supporting information that you will develop in the paragraphs of your essay. Do not discard any information that does not fit in your groupings; you may change your plan later and have a use for it. Examine your groupings of information to identify relationships between items within each group and between groups. One relationship that is commonly found in literary and other analyses is comparison-contrast, which you can use to analyze similarities and differences between specific details and between entire groups of information. (Further discussion of comparison-contrast is given in Chapter 22, pages 434–36.) Additional relationships that you could use to organize and analyze your information could include cause and effect, chronological order, and order of importance, for example. Before establishing a relationship between your topic and information, ask yourself: Will an analysis and discussion of this relationship enhance knowledge and appreciation of the work? If the relationship merely

summarizes some aspect of the work, it will provide little, if any, additional knowledge and is not worth developing. In such cases, you will need to reexamine your topic or reorganize your information in order to discover another relationship that you can analyze to provide insight into the work's meaning, significance, or composition. This insight, which is the result of your analysis of your topic and information, will be the thesis of your essay. If your topic were a dramatic protagonist's opposition to an injustice that was characteristic of a historical era, your analysis of your information might lead you to conclude that the protagonist's conflict against the injustice reflects the unrest that brought an end to that particular historical era. This conclusion could be stated as your thesis, perhaps this way: "In this drama the protagonist's conflict against the injustice of his times reflects the growing unrest of the populace, which eventually brought this era of history to an end." Then, this thesis would be stated in your introduction, perhaps with a change of wording to make it fit smoothly, and the groupings of information used in your analysis would become the paragraphs that form the body of your essay.

4. *Consider your audience's familiarity with the work.* If your audience is familiar with your work, avoid summarizing it Simply refer to specific passages and details at appropriate points in your discussion. If your audience is not familiar with the work, summarize the main elements, such as plot, theme, imagery, or dialogue, that define its distinctive form and content. Generally, summary information is best given in a short paragraph in the introduction or immediately following it, so that your audience has an overview of the work before you discuss it in your analysis. Whether your audience is familiar with the work or not, you will probably want to include short bits of summary at specific points in your essay to clarify the ideas or information you are discussing. Nevertheless, minimize summary information and devote the majority of your essay to your analysis. Always use a serious, factual tone, appropriate to all expository essays, throughout your summary and the rest of your analysis.

5. *Support your analysis with specific information from the work.* Use specific details and quotations to support the ideas that you present in your analysis. Make sure that all direct quotations are given exactly as they appear in the work and are enclosed in quotation marks. Clearly show the connections between ideas and supporting information by linking them with transitions, relative pronouns, and other devices that specify how they are related. Fit all quotations smoothly and correctly into your discussion. Make sure that verbs, pronouns, and other parts of speech within each quotation agree with the elements of your sentences

in the surrounding text. Whenever you change part of a quotation, that part is no longer exactly as it appeared in the work and, consequently, should not be enclosed along with the rest of the citation in quotation marks.

Writing Essays of Literary Analysis

Read the following poems:

OTHERS, I AM NOT THE FIRST

Others, I am not the first,
Have willed more mischief than they durst:
If in the breathless night I too
Shiver now, 'tis nothing new.

More than I, if truth were told,
Have stood and sweated hot and cold,
And through their reins in ice and fire
Fear contended with desire.

Agued once like me were they,
But I like them shall win my way
Lastly to the bed of mould
Where there's neither heat nor cold.

But from my grave across my brow
Plays no wind of healing now.
And fire and ice within me fight
Beneath the suffocating night.

A. E. HOUSMAN

FIRE AND ICE

Some say the world will end in fire,
Some say in ice.
From what I've tasted of desire
I hold with those who favor fire.
But if it had to perish twice,
I think I know enough of hate
To say that for destruction ice
Is also great
And would suffice.

ROBERT FROST

Look over the poems again. Read them, silently and aloud, several times. Your repeated readings of the poems may lead you to see similarities and differences between them. For example, both authors deal with harmful human emotions, and the words *fire* and *ice* appear as metaphors in both poems. You could relate these points of likeness and difference and develop them into a comparison-contrast between the two works.

Begin your examination by looking up the meanings of unfamiliar words, such as *reins* and *agued* in "Others, I Am Not the First." *Reins* refers to the region of the loins and kidneys, once believed to be the seat of the affections and emotions. *Ague* is an attack of fever and recurring chills; therefore, to be *agued* means to be subject to fits of fever and shivering. To organize your examination of the likenesses and differences between the two poems, you might find it helpful to devise a chart of significant elements of the poems and your thoughts about them, perhaps this way:

Points of Comparison and Contrast Between "Others, I Am Not the First" and "Fire and Ice"

"Others, I Am Not the First"	"Fire and Ice"
The words *fire* and *ice* appear in lines 7 and 15. In both stanzas there is the idea of strong conflict.	The words *fire* and *ice* have literal meanings. Some predict *the world will end in fire* (line 1); others predict *in ice* (line 2).
Fire is associated with desire, ice with fear (lines 6–7).	The words *fire* and *ice* take on symbolic meaning.
	Fire (line 4) stands for unbridled desire. Ice (line 7) stands for hate.
The speaker's desire calls for *more mischief* than he dares. He is restrained by fear (lines 2, 8, 15).	These forces are not antagonists, but alternatives.
The contest between the two emotions affects him physically. He is *agued* (line 9).	
He shivers although it is a calm (*breathless*) night. He sweats *hot and cold*. He relates his suffering to the suffering of others (lines 1, 5–8, 9).	He has known firsthand the destructive nature of fire and ice. He has *tasted of desire* and knows *enough of*
There is no relief for his suffering	

(lines 13–14).

The conflict within him will be resolved only in death (lines 10–12).

Housman emphasizes the personal
suffering caused by conflicting emotions.

hate to imagine their potential for
destruction.

Frost emphasizes the danger of destructive emotions.

You might conclude from this set of notes that Housman uses the words
fire and *ice* to create a metaphor for personal emotional conflict, while
Frost uses the words both literally and figuratively to project a vision of
the world's destruction. This could become the thesis of your essay, and
you could gather supporting ideas, details, and quotations under the
defining features of this thesis.

The main ideas that would be developed in each section of your
essay could be outlined this way:

INTRODUCTION

Paragraph 1   *Thesis*: Housman uses the words *fire* and *ice* to create a metaphor
for the personal conflict between desire and fear, while Frost
uses the words both literally and figuratively to present twin
visions of the world's destruction.

BODY

Paragraph 2   In Housman's poem *fire* stands for intense desire and *ice* for the
paralyzing fear that frustrates desire, thereby causing physical
and emotional anguish.

Paragraph 3   In Frost's poem *fire* and *ice* are not antagonists but alternatives,
either of which can annihilate the earth.

CONCLUSION

Paragraph 4   Housman explores a conflict of warring emotions; Frost, the
danger of destructive emotions.

You could relate the specific ideas in your chart to each main idea or
paragraph topics. Then, using the resulting outline, you could write a
theme, such as the one that follows:

The Emotions of "Fire" and "Ice" in A. E.   title
Housman's "Others, I Am Not the First" and
Robert Frost's "Fire and Ice"

A. E. Housman, in "Others, I Am Not the   introduction
First," and Robert Frost, in "Fire and Ice," ex-

plore different dimensions of harmful human emotions. Despite the differences in their investigations, both poets use the terms *fire* and *ice* to identify emotional states. Housman uses the words to create a metaphor for the personal conflict between desire and fear, while Frost uses the words both literally and figuratively to present twin visions of the world's destruction.

In Housman's poem, *fire* stands for intense desire and *ice* for the paralyzing fear that frustrates desire, thereby causing physical and emotional anguish. The speaker in the poem states that his desire calls for "more mischief" than he is willing to dare because he is restrained by fear, which makes him "shiver." As this physical reaction indicates, the contest between desire and fear affects him bodily. He suffers both heat and cold (line 6), and describes himself as "agued." Although the night is "breathless" and oppressively hot, he shivers as well as sweats, experiencing both chills and fever. There is no consolation, "no wind of healing," in the knowledge that he does not suffer alone and that many others have "sweated hot and cold." The conflict between desire ("fire") and fear ("ice") will have its resolution only in death—"the bed of mould."

In Frost's poem, *fire* and *ice* are not antagonists but alternatives, either of which can annihilate the earth. In the opening lines of the poem, the speaker alludes to predictions that "the world will

thesis statement

topic sentence

body

specific quotations and details used to analyze key words

topic sentence

specific details and quotations used to analyze key words

end in fire" or "in ice." The speaker reflects that these physical forms may not be the only kinds of "fire" and "ice" that could bring the earth to a cataclysmic end. Like Housman's speaker, he associates fire with desire. Based on what he has "tasted of desire," he agrees "with those who favor fire" as the force that will destroy the world. On the other hand, he states that he knows "enough of hate" to believe that ice "would suffice" as an equally devastating form of destruction. Through the images of "fire" and "ice," the poem suggests that emotional extremes of desire and hatred could bring about the destruction of the world.

analysis of poem's meaning

Both Housman and Frost deal with harmful human emotions. Housman explores a conflict of warring emotions; Frost the danger of destructive emotions. In Housman's poem, *fire* and *ice* are opposing forces in human nature, burdening the speaker with desires that he is afraid to pursue. In Frost's poem, *fire* and *ice* are not opposites but options in human nature, both equally powerful and destructive. The "fire" and "ice" discussed in these two poems can represent a number of specific destructive forces, but all of them share one quality, which may be the key to their harmfulness —they are all extremes.

conclusion

topic sentence

summary of thesis and analysis

suggestions of further meaning in the poem

EXERCISE 15. Writing Your First Draft.   Write an essay of literary analysis on a novel, short story, drama, or poem of your choice. Before you begin writing, review the Prewriting Hints for Essays of Literary Analysis on pages 563–67 and the model above. Be sure to get your teacher's approval of the literary work that you choose.

GUIDELINES FOR REVISING ESSAYS OF LITERARY ANALYSIS

Reread the first draft of your essay of literary analysis. Then refer to the following guidelines as you make revisions in your draft.

1. Is the thesis of the essay stated clearly in the introduction? Does the introduction also give the title and the name of the author of the work that will be analyzed?
2. Has the thesis been developed by a convincing literary analysis, presented in several paragraphs within the body of the essay?
3. Have a sufficient number of details and quotations from the work been given to support each point of the analysis?
4. Have all quotations been given verbatim as they appear in the work and been enclosed in quotation marks?
5. Have the relationships between ideas and supporting information been made clear through the use of transitions, techniques of sentence combining, and other methods?
6. Has sufficient summary and explanatory information been given to enable the audience to follow the literary analysis in the essay?
7. Does the conclusion summarize the main result(s) of the analysis and suggest additional meanings or implications of these results?
8. Have sentence structure, diction, pronoun usage, and other elements of the essay been varied in order to keep the audience's interest?
9. Have all repetitive and unnecessary words, references, and other material been deleted?
10. Does the title of the essay inform the audience of the essay's thesis?

EXERCISE 16. Preparing Your Final Draft. Use the following suggestions as you prepare the final draft of the essay of literary analysis that you wrote for Exercise 15.

1. As you revise your draft, consult the Guidelines for Revising Essays of Literary Analysis and the general guidelines for revision discussed in Chapter 21 on page 401. Closely examine the content, organization, and style of your essay.
2. Refer to the Guidelines for Proofreading (page 403) as you review the spelling, punctuation, grammar, and usage in your draft.

3. Follow correct manuscript form (see Chapter 30) or your teacher's specific instructions when you write the final draft of your essay of literary analysis.

4. Be sure to give your essay one final proofreading to correct any inaccuracies you have made in recopying it. Reread it more than once, and if possible, try to have someone else read it before you submit your essay to your audience.

CHAPTER 25

Writing Persuasive Compositions

LANGUAGE AND LOGIC

Argument is a familiar feature of your daily conversation. The word *argument* in this sense means "a debate or discussion," not "an angry disagreement." In class you argue about history, current events, and literature. Essay-type examination questions often ask your opinion and expect you to support it with knowledge. People in all kinds of work —scientists, teachers, sales representatives, journalists, politicians, lawyers—know the importance of being able to argue convincingly.

In argumentative, or persuasive, writing your purpose is to persuade the reader to accept your views on a debatable subject. You try to prove that your opinion is right. In its simplest form, persuasive writing is a statement of opinion, backed up by reasons and evidence. In its more elaborate form, persuasive writing is a skillfully planned, tightly reasoned kind of writing, designed not only to convince an audience of a certain opinion, but also to persuade the audience to take a specific action. Persuasive writing may appeal to the emotions as well as to reason.

DEVELOPING A PERSUASIVE COMPOSITION

As in any type of writing that you have studied so far, persuasive writing involves many thinking and writing steps. Perhaps more than with any other type of writing, the prewriting steps are of crucial importance in persuasive writing, for it is before you actually begin writing that you plan your logical presentation of ideas. The effectiveness of a piece of persuasive writing depends almost entirely on this logical presentation of opinion, reasons, and evidence.

PREWRITING

CHOOSING A FORM AND AN AUDIENCE

In this chapter, you will practice two forms of persuasive writing: the letter to the editor and the persuasive composition.

A *letter to the editor* is a brief essay that expresses the writer's views on a specific topic. Letters to the editor appear on the editorial page of a newspaper or magazine and are usually no more than a few paragraphs. The audience for a letter to the editor will be the readers of the newspaper or magazine.

A *persuasive composition* has at least five paragraphs (an introductory paragraph, three paragraphs in the body, and a concluding paragraph), but it is often much longer. Persuasive compositions may be written for a specific audience. For example, an essay about the selection of members of a jury may be directed to an audience of lawyers, an audience of the general public, or an audience of persons accused of committing a crime. You can guess that an audience might have a particular *bias* (already held opinion and ideas for or against a topic). Lawyers, for example, might want to keep the process of jury selection the same, while persons accused of committing a crime might want to change the makeup of juries so that the juries accurately reflect the population of the community in which they live.

It is important to identify your audience for yourself so that you can take into account the audience's biases as you prepare your argument. If your audience is predisposed to oppose your opinion, for example, you will have to provide additional evidence to try to convince them. If, however, your audience agrees wholeheartedly with your views, you might choose a more challenging topic for your composition—one for which there is some likelihood of disagreement.

As with any other type of writing, the audience will also affect the amount of background information you will need to provide. If your audience is very familiar with the topic, you can assume that they already know what you are talking about. An audience unfamiliar with a topic will need to have important terms defined and will need to know what the current situation is and what the history of the problem is.

EXERCISE 1. Identifying an Audience's Attitudes and Biases. Think carefully about what attitude or bias each of the following audiences is likely to have. Is the audience likely to be in favor of the opinion stated in the position statement, violently opposed to it, moderately opposed, or neutral (having no strong feelings either way)?

1. *Position statement*: As part of the requirement for graduation, all high-school students should be required to volunteer two hours every week for some community service project.
   a. A group of high-school seniors
   b. A group of high-school teachers
   c. A group of parents of high-school students
   d. A group of directors of community service projects
2. *Position statement*: People should not be able to obtain driver's licenses (even learner's permits) until they are 21 years old.
   a. A group of 16-year-olds
   b. A group of insurance company executives
   c. A group of 18-year-olds who hold full-time jobs
   d. A group of police officers
3. *Position statement*: High-school students should be able to help design their own curriculum. That is, they should have some say in what courses are offered and what the requirements are for graduation.
   a. A group of high-school principals and teachers
   b. A group of school-board members
   c. A group of high-school students
   d. A group of parents of high-school students
4. *Position statement*: Factories and other places of employment should provide free or low-cost day-care centers for employees who are parents of preschool children.
   a. A group of employees who have no children
   b. A group of employees who are mothers of preschool children
   c. A group of factory owners and other employers
   d. A group of owners of profit-making day-care centers

CHOOSING A TOPIC

25a. Choose a limited topic that is debatable.

When you choose a topic for a persuasive composition, you must choose a debatable issue. That is, the topic must be one for which there are arguments pro (for) and con (against). Also, the topic must state an opinion and not a fact, because facts are not debatable. By definition, a *fact* is a statement that can be proved to be true. An *opinion,* on the other hand, is a judgment or belief that cannot be proved true or false. Opinions can only be supported by means of evidence.

NOT SUITABLE   Polls on the East Coast close three hours before polls on the West Coast. (Fact)

SUITABLE   Polls should be open for a 24-hour period and close at the same time all over the United States. (Opinion)

NOT SUITABLE   Many special-interest groups have full-time paid lobbyists who try to influence members of Congress to vote in ways that will benefit their groups. (Fact)

SUITABLE   The conversations between all lobbyists and members of Congress should be made public so that the public can be aware of exactly how lobbyists are trying to influence elected officials. (Opinion)

A persuasive composition must also be about a significant issue. Like verifiable facts, personal tastes are completely unsuitable as topics for persuasive writing. A statement of personal preference is an expression of opinion, but it is not an arguable proposition.

NOT SUITABLE   Blue is a more beautiful color than red.

NOT SUITABLE   Tennis is more fun than golf.

Neither of these is a suitable topic for persuasive writing because matters of taste cannot be resolved by presenting evidence. To be sure, you could write an interesting composition in support of your taste, but no amount of arguing will ever establish an opinion of this kind as true or false. A statement of personal taste is an expression of opinion, but it is not an arguable proposition.

EXERCISE 2. Choosing a Suitable Topic for a Persuasive Composition.   Some of the following position statements are suitable as topics for persuasive writing; others are not. Write *S* for each numbered item that is a suitable topic; write *NS* if the topic is not suitable. Be prepared to explain your answers.

1. In 1973 Rosemary Casals won the Family Circle tennis tournament.
2. Laura Tanaka is the most qualified candidate for class president.
3. The school year should be extended to eleven months.
4. The starting salary for teachers should be significantly increased.
5. Jane Austen's novels are too old-fashioned to interest modern readers.
6. A Constitutional Amendment should be passed allowing the President of the United States to serve one six-year term instead of the two four-year terms now in force.
7. Students who hold after-school jobs should be excused from homework assignments.
8. The federal government should spend more money funding research for the cure of cancer.
9. Marian Anderson received the Presidential Medal of Freedom in 1963.
10. People who live in apartment buildings should not be allowed to keep dogs as pets.

WRITING A POSITION STATEMENT

25b. Express your opinion clearly in a single sentence.

The statement of the point to be argued is called the *position statement.* Sometimes it is also called a *thesis statement* or *proposition.* This statement expresses your opinion on the topic in a declarative sentence that often contains the words *should* or *should not.*

EXAMPLES My client is innocent and should be acquitted.
Money being spent on space exploration should be spent instead on solving domestic problems.

Sometimes issues are so complicated that you may have some doubts about what your opinion actually is. When this happens, spend some time doing research on the issue: read current magazine and newspaper articles; discuss the issue with friends, family members, and other adults whose opinions you respect. If you carefully try to understand the different viewpoints, you can decide what your own opinion is.

CRITICAL THINKING:
Making Position Statements Specific

A position statement should be so worded that its meaning is definite and its terms are not ambiguous. Which of the following three position statements is the most specific?

1. This community should do something about teen-age recreational facilities.

2. Recreational facilities for teen-agers need to be improved.

3. The city should sponsor a supervised recreation center for teen-agers in the old McDonald Center.

Of the three statements, the third is the most specific. It tells what should be done, who should do it, and where the recreation center should be. Both statements 1 and 2 are too vague.

Sometimes a position statement, even though it is specific, requires explanation or definition of some of its terms. These explanations and definitions can be given in the first paragraph of the composition.

EXERCISE 3. Making Position Statements Specific. Each of the following statements is too vague or general to serve as a position statement. Make up any information you need to rewrite each statement so that it is specific enough to serve as the position statement in a persuasive essay.

1. Something should be done about toxic waste sites.
2. We have to find a way to keep students from dropping out of high school.
3. There are too many highway accidents caused by drunk drivers.
4. What can we do about people who have no homes in the winter?
5. Vandalism on school property is a problem.
6. It would be a good idea to do something about acid rain.
7. Our school library needs improving.
8. Something should be done about the amount of cheating that goes on in school.
9. There are too many advertisements on television programs for young children.
10. Teen-agers need help in finding summer jobs.

EXERCISE 4. Writing Position Statements. Read each of the following news items carefully. Then, decide what your opinion is and write a clearly stated position statement that might serve as the basis of a letter to the editor. Remember that, whenever possible, a position statement should suggest a specific course of action to solve a problem.

1

Dr. Robert E. Gould, a New York psychiatrist, has stated that he believes that television sports are brutal and commercialized. Watching sports on TV, he believes, "instills viewers with a love of brutality. They hunger for blood." Other psychiatrists at an annual convention of the American Academy of Psychoanalysis have speculated that television sports harm children by teaching them the brutality of intimidation and "winning at any cost."

2

A heart transplant operation that involved transplanting a baboon heart into the body of a human infant has been widely criticized. Some critics say that the doctors involved in the transplant operation did not try hard enough to find a human heart to use because they were eager to experiment with an animal-to-human heart transplant. Other people criticize the whole procedure because they claim that the baboon was deliberately killed in order to obtain its heart for the transplant operation. These critics claim that it is wrong to take the life of an innocent animal in order to try to save a human life.

3

LIVERMORE, California—A 29-year-old woman has had to go to jail because she did not return 13 library books to the Alameda County Library.

"They are taking my fingerprints!" complained Constance Moore, after reporting to the Santa Rita jail last Friday.

Miss Moore was sentenced to report to the jail for booking and fingerprinting under a new Alameda County library policy. She did not have to stay in jail, however. The rest of her sentence was to perform one week's service in the public library.

4

WASHINGTON, D.C.—The National Council of Teachers of Mathematics has recommended that calculators be available for use in the classrooms from kindergarten through fourth grade. A report issued by this national organization has suggested that teachers in elementary schools reconsider their traditional emphasis on teaching students fractions, decimals, and percentages. According to this report, "Since computers and calculators can perform such operations more quickly and accurately . . . the traditional goals of elementary school mathematics must be re-examined." The report suggests that students be allowed to use calculators in classrooms, even during tests.

BUILDING AN ARGUMENT

Having written a position statement, you will now need to outline the argument you will use to support your opinion. Your argument must be as logical as you can make it. That is, you must present believable evidence in a clear and orderly manner.

Choosing Reasons

25c. Support your position statement with reasons and evidence.

Reasons are statements that explain why you hold your opinion and why the reader should also hold your opinion. A reason may be a fact, a statistic, an example, or an incident—anything that backs up your opinion.

The following outline for an argument gives three reasons to support the opinion in the position statement.

Position Statement: High-school seniors should be excused from final exams in courses in which they have maintained a B average.

Reasons: a. Students who have maintained a B average have already shown that they know the material of the course.

b. Students will work harder to get a B average if they know that this will excuse them from final exams.

c. Except in borderline cases, the final examination is not weighted heavily enough to raise or lower a student's final grade.

CRITICAL THINKING:
Evaluating Reasons

Look back at the argument outlined above. Are you convinced that students with B averages should be excused from final exams? The forcefulness of an argument—how convincing it is—depends almost entirely on the reasons that you choose to support the position statement.

(1) An argument must contain sufficient reasons.

The more sound reasons that you have to support your opinion, the more convincing your argument will be. Usually, a persuasive composition should contain at least three reasons.

(2) Each reason must be distinct.

The reasons given in an argument must be clearly different. They should not repeat or rephrase a previously stated reason.

WEAK   *Position statement*: This state should pass a mandatory seat belt law.
Reason 1: If you are in an automobile accident, chances of your being seriously injured are less if you are wearing a seat belt.
Reason 2: People who wear seat belts are safer than people who don't wear seat belts.
Reason 3: A mandatory seat belt law would protect drivers and their passengers.

Even though this outline looks like it has three reasons, they are not distinct reasons. All three repeat or rephrase the same idea: that wearing a seat belt protects people who ride in automobiles. Actually, of the three reasons given, only Reason 1 is clearly stated. Both Reasons 2 and 3 are vague and repeat Reason 1. The argument, therefore, is a weak one.

Consider the following reasons to support the same position statement.

IMPROVED   *Reason 1*: If you are in an automobile accident, the chances of your being seriously injured are less if you are wearing a seat belt.
Reason 2: Statistics show that only a small percentage of automobile drivers and passengers regularly use seat belts when it is left to them to decide whether or not to wear seat belts.
Reason 3: Statistics from states that already have mandatory seat belt laws show that the percentage of automobile drivers and passengers who use seat belts dramatically increases when there is a mandatory seat belt law.

Notice, first of all, that this argument outlines three entirely different points. The three reasons are distinct. Also, notice that these three reasons, in effect, present a logical argument. If you accept the truth of the three reasons, then there is only one logical conclusion: that a mandatory seat belt law should be passed (the statement made in the position statement).

(3) Each reason must be relevant to the position statement.

A *relevant* reason is one that is directly related to the position statement. Just as a paragraph must be unified, all of the reasons given in an argument must directly support the position statement. Irrelevant information that is only indirectly related to the position statement should not be used as a reason. Adding irrelevant reasons will weaken your argument and confuse your reader.

IRRELEVANT   *Reason*: Automobile manufacturers and legislators have been discussing for years the required use of air bags as automobile safety devices.

IRRELEVANT   *Reason*: Some automobiles have automatic shoulder belts that automatically lock into place.

Neither of these reasons is relevant to the argument about requiring a mandatory seat belt law; they should be omitted from the argument.

EXERCISE 5. Evaluating Reasons. Read the position statement and carefully consider each of the reasons that follows. Choose the reasons that you think would make the strongest case to support each position statement. Be prepared to discuss why each reason would strengthen or weaken the argument.

1. *Position statement*: High-school students should be allowed to work only on weekends and during vacations—not during the school week.
   a. Students who work during the school week are too tired to devote their energies to school work.
   b. Students who work during the school week do not have time to do homework assignments or study for tests. They cannot possibly keep up good grades.
   c. More than half of the senior class have after-school jobs.
   d. Many students need the money that they earn in after-school jobs.
   e. Students who have after-school jobs and also try to keep up with their school work and social activities endanger their health by not getting enough sleep.
   f. Schools do not have the right to infringe on students' freedom by preventing them from working after school.
   g. Too many freshmen and sophomores who begin with after-school jobs end up by dropping out of high school before they graduate.

   h. School is a student's work and should be the prime focus of a student's attention.

2. *Position statement*: Every U.S. citizen over the age of 18 should be required to serve on a jury.

   a. Some people may be excused from jury duty because of the nature of their occupations.

   b. Serving on a jury is an obligation of citizens—one of the duties they must perform in return for the benefits they enjoy as citizens of the United States.

   c. In order to have fair jury trials, juries must be made up of a representative cross-section of the adult population of the community.

   d. Names of possible jurors are derived from voter registration lists. Therefore, if an adult U.S. citizen does not register to vote, he or she is never called upon to become a juror.

   e. The Sixth and Seventh Amendments to the United States Constitution provide for trial by jury in criminal cases and in civil suits.

   f. Jurors listen to evidence in a trial of an accused person and decide whether the person is innocent or guilty.

EXERCISE 6. Thinking of Reasons. Choose one of the position statements that you wrote for Exercise 3 on page 579, or choose a different position statement. Write as many reasons as you can think of to support your opinion. Then, evaluate each reason on your list, eliminating those that are not distinct reasons (that repeat the position statement or another reason) and those that are not relevant to the argument. Write the position statement you have chosen, followed by all of the reasons you have created that strongly support your opinion.

EXERCISE 7. Thinking of Reasons. The following questions are arguable issues. Select one, and state your opinion in a clearly worded and specific position statement. Then, list at least three reasons to support your opinion.

1. Should all required courses be eliminated from high schools so that students may take whatever courses they choose?
2. Should high-school students be allowed to choose the teachers they want for the courses they will take?

3. Should students be given academic credits toward graduation for participating in athletics and other after-school activities?
4. Should all homework be eliminated for all high-school students?
5. Should the sale of cigarettes be prohibited by law?
6. Should state universities charge tuition fees for students who are residents of the state?
7. Should bicyclists be required to have bicycle licenses and to follow all traffic laws?
8. Should television network news programs be prohibited from predicting the winners in any election until after all of the polls are closed?
9. Should adult children be legally required to support their elderly parents?
10. Should the sale of candy, cookies, cakes, potato chips, and other junk foods be prohibited in all schools?

Refuting the Opposing Viewpoint

25d. Prepare to refute arguments that support the opposing viewpoint.

Remember that the topic for a persuasive composition must be debatable, which means that other people have views completely opposite from yours. Your success in persuasion may depend to a large extent on how well you refute the opposing arguments. Therefore, in planning a persuasive composition, take the time to think of the arguments against your views and prepare a strong reply.

For example, look back at the argument on page 581 for excusing seniors from finals in courses in which they have maintained a B average. If you were seriously trying to support this position statement, you would have to take into account the arguments of the opposing viewpoint, which might include the following reasons:

Reason 1: Taking final examinations reinforces learning because it forces students to review material that they may have forgotten.
Reason 2: Taking final examinations assures better learning because preparation for a final exam affords the student an overall view of the course.
Reason 3: If students with B averages are not required to take final examinations, they will not be motivated to do any work during the final weeks of the course.

How would you refute these reasons? First, state the opposing reason, and then tell why you believe it is not true. You might, for example, refute Reason 3 in this way:

> People who believe that all students should be required to take all final exams believe that even students with B averages and higher would not study if they did not have to take an exam for a grade. In a survey of thirty-two experienced teachers in our school, more than 90 percent of the teachers surveyed said that they did not believe that this would happen. "Students who do well throughout a semester," said Mrs. Abrams, head of the math department, "are students who really care about learning. They will study no matter what—even if they do not have to take a final."

You might make your refutation of Reason 3 even stronger by citing a survey of students with B averages or higher. If these students say that they will keep studying and doing their schoolwork even if they are excused from a final, you have an additional piece of evidence to refute the opposition's reason. In effect, you are telling the reader, "This is what my opponent says, but it is not true, and I will prove it to you."

EXERCISE 8. Refuting Opposing Arguments. Choose the position statement you worked with in Exercise 6 or Exercise 7. Spend some time thinking of all the arguments that the opposing viewpoint might use. (You may need to do some research by reading or discussing the issue with people who have opinions that differ from yours.) List all of the opposing reasons, and decide how you would refute each reason. Write a paragraph refuting each of the opposing reasons.

EXERCISE 9. Analyzing the Pros and Cons. The reasons given to support a position statement are the pro (reasons for) side, while the opposing reasons are called the con (reasons against) position. People talk about the pros and cons for every issue. Listed below is a chart of the pros and cons for a particular issue. Study the chart carefully, and answer the questions that follow it.

> *Position statement*: Air- and water-pollution controls for industries are too strict and should be drastically reduced.

> *PRO*

> *Reason 1*: The costs of meeting federal requirements are too high. These high costs must necessarily be passed on to the consumer when the industry prices its products. Lowering the pollution standards would lessen the cost of products to consumers.

> *Reason 2*: The pollution standards are too high. No one has proved that humans would be harmed if the standards were lessened so that there would be a little more air pollution and water pollution.

Reason 3: The costs of meeting federal pollution requirements are so high that many industries have gone out of business, and jobs have therefore been lost.

Reason 4: Each local community should have a right to decide how much air and water pollution it finds acceptable. The federal government should not interfere.

CON

Reason 1: Every industry has a moral and ethical obligation to clean up its garbage. We can no longer tolerate the dumping of wastes into the air and water, as has been done for centuries.

Reason 2: The standards set for tolerable levels of pollution in the environment were based on careful studies made by qualified scientists, who have proved that higher levels would not only endanger humans, but also all of the earth's plant and animal life.

Reason 3: Since air pollution and water pollution affect not just the immediate environment, but have far-reaching effects, the federal government must take control of setting pollution standards and enforcing them. We cannot leave these matters up to the individual communities or states.

Reason 4: If meeting pollution standards increases a product's cost, then that cost will have to be borne by the consumer. It is an integral part of manufacturing the product.

Reason 5: We cannot jeopardize the nation's health simply to keep manufacturers in business. If businesses fail because of the cost of meeting pollution standards, that is the fault of the businesses' managers for not making their operations cost effective. Pollution control is too important a matter to compromise because of jobs.

1. Which viewpoint do you agree with, the pro or the con? Explain why.
2. In the side that you have chosen, which do you think is the strongest reason? The weakest? Can you think of any additional reasons to support the side you have chosen? If so, list them.
3. Among the opposing arguments, which do you think is the strongest? The weakest? Can you think of any additional reasons to support the opposing viewpoint? If so, list them.
4. Look carefully at the reasons given for the opposing viewpoint. How would you refute each reason?
5. Look at Reason 2 in the *pro* argument and Reason 2 in the *con* argument. These two reasons seem to directly contradict each other. How can you tell which one is true?

Choosing Evidence

When you have formulated your position statement and listed the reasons to support it, the next step is to gather the evidence you will use to support each reason. *Evidence* is the specific information (facts, statistics, examples, incidents, and quotations from experts) that you use to back up a reason. Whenever possible, each reason in an argument should be supported by some kind of evidence.

25e. Gather sufficient evidence to support each reason and to refute opposing reasons.

The evidence that you use to support your reasons should come from a reliable source or should be the result of many personal observations. Facts and statistics offer strong support for a reason because these can be verified, or proved to be true. Consider, for example, Reason 2 in both the *pro* and *con* side of the argument in Exercise 9 on pages 586–87. Since these statements are directly contradictory, you might expect that one of the statements is probably true and the other necessarily false. Facts, statistics, and examples will show which one is true. Use *The Readers' Guide to Periodical Literature* and recent almanacs to gather facts and statistics to support your reasons. Encyclopedia articles and recent books on your topic will also provide evidence for you to use.

Another type of evidence often used in persuasive writing is discussing the opinion of an authority or expert in the field. To cite an authority is to quote the authority's opinion on the specific topic. Of course, an expert's opinion is not verifiable in the same way that facts are. However, if a person is respected in a field and if it cannot be demonstrated that the person is biased, an expert's opinion can lend powerful support to an argument.

EXERCISE 10. Providing Evidence to Support Reasons.
Look back at the argument you have outlined for Exercise 6 or Exercise 7. Choose one of these, and decide what kind of evidence you would look for to support each reason. You might mention the specific kind of facts or evidence, or you might cite a specific type of authority. Outline your argument again, this time including the evidence that you will use to support each reason.

CRITICAL THINKING:
Evaluating Evidence

Evidence that is given to support a reason must be *relevant* to that reason—that is, it must be directly and logically related to the reason. Any piece of evidence that is not directly related is irrelevant and should be eliminated from the argument. Remember that the overall effect of persuasive writing is that it is tightly knit and logical. Irrelevant information will weaken the argument and confuse the reader.

In the following example, two pieces of evidence are given to support a specific reason. Which evidence is relevant, and which is irrelevant?

> *Reason*: Since air and water pollution affect not just the immediate environment but have far-reaching effects, the federal government must take control of setting pollution standards and enforcing them. We cannot leave these matters up to the individual communities or states.
> *Evidence*: a. Acid rain is caused by air pollution from factories in industrial states, but it affects areas in states far from the factories. Airborne pollutants are carried by winds, combine with rain, and dump acid rain in communities that have not caused the pollution.
> b. Most communities and states already have their own regulations on tolerable levels of air pollution and water pollution.

The first piece of evidence is relevant to the reason because it gives an example of the kind of pollution that crosses community and state lines. The second piece of evidence, while it is true and related to the topic, is not directly related to the reason. It really offers no information at all on why the federal government must have the responsibility for maintaining pollution standards.

When you construct a persuasive argument, be very careful that the reasons are relevant to the position statement and that the evidence is relevant to the reason. Evaluating whether or not something is relevant is a critical thinking skill that can be improved with practice.

EXERCISE 11. Selecting Relevant Evidence.   Choose the items of evidence that are relevant to the reason given. There may be more than one piece of relevant evidence.

Reason: Industrial air pollution is a threat to the health of plants, animals, and humans.
Possible Evidence:
   a. Results of a four-year study on the causes and effects of acid rain on plants and animals

b. Quotation from a lung specialist on the effects of industrial air pollution on the lungs of animals and humans

c. Quotation from a factory owner on the amount of money spent to install safety devices

d. Results of a study made by the Clean-Air Commission on the effects of carbon monoxide (an industrial waste gas) on humans

e. A quotation from the president of an environmental group about the necessity for increased standards for water pollution control

f. A case study of an accident within a nuclear energy plant; no wastes were released into the air outside the plant

g. A quotation from the President of the United States on the need for increased cooperation by industry and government

EXERCISE 12. Analyzing a Letter to the Editor. Read the following letter to the editor, and then answer all of the questions that follow it. You will use these answers in Exercise 13.

To the Editor:

I am astonished every morning when I see the army of pre-school children, even infants, leaving their homes to be dropped off at day-care centers while their parents work. What ever happened to the traditional family values of raising young children at home with a loving mother? In a single generation, most young mothers have gone off to work.

Today, newborns are spending their waking hours cared for by strangers who have too many other children to take care of. Generally, the quality of day-care is poor. Workers are underpaid; sick children are regularly sent to day-care because no one is home to take care of them; little children are "warehoused" in front of a TV set all day.

Certainly there are some circumstances, as in a single-parent family, where it is necessary for the mother to work and someone else to care for a young child. More often, both parents are working not because they have to, but because they want a second car, a bigger house or apartment, a fancier vacation, and expensive video equipment. The little children suffer as a result.

Psychologists tell us that the quality of nurturing during the child's earliest months and years determines the emotional health of the child and the adult he or she will become. For children to be separated from their parents is an emotional trauma. I fear for what this day-care generation will be like as adults and even as teenagers. I hope that the parents of young children will reconsider their consumer desires and go back to the traditional American family values. Young children belong at home with the love, warmth, and security of a parent to care for them.

BILL OGILVIE

1. What is the writer's opinion about sending infants and young children to day-care centers? Where in the letter does he state that opinion?
2. Outline the writer's argument. What reasons, if any, does he give to support his opinion? What evidence does he give to support his reasons?
3. Which of the following pieces of evidence do you think would strengthen the writer's argument?
   a. Statistics on the reasons why mothers of preschoolers work
   b. Statistics on the average family income of working mothers of preschoolers
   c. Studies comparing the physical and emotional development of children cared for in day-care centers with the physical and emotional development of children cared for at home by non-working mothers
   d. Quotations from working mothers and fathers
   e. Quotations from child psychologists or psychiatrists on the effect on children of being cared for in day-care centers
   f. Quotations from day-care center owners and employees
4. Identify all the emotional appeals (see pages 622–24) in this letter. What, for example, is the emotional effect of the expression "warehoused" in the second paragraph? Identify other loaded words.
5. Who do you think is the writer's intended audience? How do you think the writer might change the letter if it were addressed to any of the following audiences?
   a. A group of working mothers
   b. A group of day-care center owners
   c. A group of ninth-graders
6. What generalizations does the writer make about children being raised at home and those being cared for in day-care centers? Do you think these generalizations are true in all cases? In most cases? In some cases? In few cases?
7. Do you agree with the writer's opinion, or do you disagree? Give reasons for your answer. If you were a working parent, under what circumstances would you want your infant or preschooler cared for by someone in a day-care center? Under what circumstances would you want to stay home to care for your child?

8. What is it that the writer wants the reader to do? Does he recommend a solution or solutions to the problem? If so, what are they?
9. Find out what kinds of day-care facilities exist in your community and how expensive they are.

EXERCISE 13. Writing a Letter to the Editor. Use the information that follows, along with the information you gathered in Exercise 12, to write a letter to the editor in response to the letter on day-care centers in Exercise 12. State your opinion, and support it with reasons and evidence. Then write your letter to the editor. If you wish, you may include any of the following information in your letter.

STATISTICS   a. Number of Two-Job Families—Both Parents Working (in millions)

1967—18.9	1970—20.5	1975—22.3
1980—25.6	1983—26.1	

    b. Number of Married Women in the Labor Force with Children Under 6 (in millions)

1960—2.5	1965—3.1	1970—3.9
1975—4.4	1980—5.2	1984—6.2

    c. Number of Divorced, Widowed, or Single Women in the Labor Force with Children Under 6 (in millions)

1960—.42	1965—.57	1970—.64
1975—.96	1980—1.3	1984—1.8

    d. By 1990, the number of children under 10 in the United States will reach 38 million.

QUOTATIONS   e. In 1979, Harvard psychologist Jerome Kagan compared infants cared for in day-care centers with infants cared for at home. He concluded: "There were essentially no differences in any of the gross measures—cognitive development, language, aggression, or attachment . . . We concluded that when you have good-quality day care, there are no big effects."

    f. In 1984, Dr. Burton White, Director of the Center for Parent Education in Boston, said: "A child needs large doses of custom-made love. You can't expect hired help to provide that. I see the trend toward increasing use of day care as a disaster . . . Both parents don't *have* to work—they both *want* to work to maintain a house or a lifestyle. They are putting their desires above the welfare of the baby."

EXAMPLES   g. Fel-Pro, Inc., manufacturer of automobile parts, maintains a day-care center for employees' children next to its factory.

h. Industry, labor, and local government share the cost of maintaining the Chinatown Garment Industry Day-Care Center in New York City, which cares for 75 preschool children whose parents pay according to their income.

PREWRITING   Write a position statement making clear your opinion on preschoolers and day-care centers. Then, outline your argument. You may refer to the original letter in Exercise 12 and reply directly to its arguments. Choose the statistics, quotations, and examples that you think will strengthen your argument. Propose a solution to the problem, telling what you think should be done or what you want the reader to do. End your letter with a concluding sentence that restates your opinion.

WRITING, REVISING, AND PROOFREADING   Check to see that the order in which you have arranged your reasons and evidence is effective. Eliminate any words or details that detract from the clear, logical effect of your letter. Check to see whether your first draft contains any emotional appeals and whether or not they are effective. Do you wish to keep them, improve them, or drop them? Try different wordings to see which sounds most effective.

REVIEW EXERCISE A. Collecting and Analyzing Letters to the Editor.
From recent magazines or newspapers (local newspaper or your school newspaper), clip two letters to the editor. Analyze each letter by answering all of the following questions:

1. What is the specific topic of the letter to the editor?
2. What is the writer's opinion about the topic? Is the opinion stated in a position statement? If so, write the sentence or sentences in which the opinion appears.
3. Outline the argument in the letter. Write each reason the writer gives to back up his or her opinion. Then write the specific evidence (facts, statistics, examples, quotations) the writer gives to back up each reason.
4. What does the writer want the reader to do? If this is stated in a specific sentence in the letter, write that sentence.

REVIEW EXERCISE B. Revising a Letter to the Editor.
Choose one of the letters to the editor that you analyzed in Review Exercise A.

Using your analysis, revise the letter. Improve it by adding a position statement (if there is not already one), more clearly stated reasons, and evidence to back up each reason. Consider adding a concluding sentence or paragraph to restate your position, summarize your reasons, or ask the reader to perform a specific action.

Outlining the Argument

25f. Outline your argument.

The final prewriting step in developing a persuasive composition is to outline your argument, which consists of your position statement, the supporting reasons, and the evidence. If you wish to end your composition with a "call to action" urging the reader to perform a specific action, that too should be included in the outline. The outline should be written in clearly stated sentences, following this format:

Position statement
Reason 1
Evidence
Evidence
Reason 2
Evidence
Evidence
Reason 3
Evidence
Evidence
Call to action

The number of reasons and the amount of evidence will vary. In general, a persuasive composition should have at least three reasons and, whenever possible, each reason should be supported by specific evidence. The more specific, factual evidence you can offer to support each reason, the more convincing your argument will be. Not all reasons, however, can be supported by evidence. If you have to choose among different reasons, it is a good idea to choose a reason that can be backed up by factual evidence. Such reasons offer the strongest support for your position statement.

EXERCISE 14. **Outlining an Argument for a Persuasive Composition.** Choose one of the position statements that you wrote for Exercise 3 (page 579), or choose another topic suitable for a persuasive composition. Outline your argument carefully, including reasons and evidence to support the position statement. Follow the outline format on page 594. Check to see whether you have arranged your reasons in the most effective order.

CRITICAL THINKING:
Evaluating an Argument

To write a convincing piece of persuasive writing, your argument must be as good as you can possibly make it. Before you begin to write, take the time to evaluate your argument. You will need to judge how effective each part of the argument is and also how well the parts work together as a whole. The following guidelines will help you to evaluate any argument that you outline for a persuasive composition. You may also apply these questions to persuasive writing that you read or to persuasive speeches that you hear.

GUIDELINES FOR EVALUATING A PERSUASIVE ARGUMENT

1. Is the opinion clearly stated? What is the position statement?
2. What are the reasons? Are the reasons clearly stated?
3. Is each reason relevant to the argument?
4. Is each reason distinct, or do the reasons merely rephrase the position statement or another reason?
5. How many reasons are there? A persuasive composition should have at least three relevant and distinct reasons.
6. Is each reason backed up by evidence? Is the evidence relevant to the reason?
7. Does the argument include any weak reasons or any irrelevant evidence?

EXERCISE 15. Evaluating a Persuasive Argument. Use the suggested guidelines given on the previous page to evaluate the argument you outlined for Exercise 14. Make any changes that you think are necessary to strengthen your argument.

EXERCISE 16. Evaluating Reasons. A student-faculty committee is discussing the question, "Should students trying out for varsity sports be excused from last-period study halls?" Reasons presented by both sides follow. Study the reasons and identify those which are irrelevant, or likely to lead the discussion off the subject.

Arguments in favor of excusing the students:
1. It will relieve locker room congestion after school.
2. Outdoor exercise is better for the students than studying in a stuffy classroom.
3. Recently, four students on a varsity team were sent to the office from last-period study because they created a discipline problem.
4. The students will have more time for practice. The more they practice, the better the varsity teams will be.
5. Study halls should be eliminated anyway so that the school day can be shortened.
6. Athletics are as important as studies.
7. Last year, our teams were the worst in years.

Arguments against excusing the students:
1. The students would waste the extra time because the coaches cannot join them until after school.
2. Those who are excused would have an unfair advantage over those who have a class the last period.
3. Sometimes the weather is bad, and the students could not go outdoors.
4. It is better for students to study in school before practice because they will be too tired after practice to study at home.
5. We don't excuse students for other outdoor activities, like fishing, or playing golf, or playing outdoors at home.

WRITING

WRITING THE FIRST DRAFT

25g. Write the first draft of your persuasive composition.

Use your outline of the argument as your working plan for the first draft.

The Introduction

Your composition should begin with an *introductory paragraph* that introduces the topic and includes your position statement. Often, the position statement is the last sentence of the introductory paragraph. The first paragraph of your composition also serves to arouse the reader's interest and to provide background information.

Sometimes more than one paragraph is needed as an introduction. The following example is the introduction from an essay by Tom Wicker entitled "Tambora's Lesson."

> On July 4, 1816, thick layers of ice formed in New England, New York, and Pennsylvania. In June, snow had fallen from 7 to 10 inches deep in Massachusetts, Vermont, and New York. But the worst was yet to come; in August, according to one account, "ice formed nearly an inch in thickness and killed every green thing in the United States."
>
> In Virginia, Thomas Jefferson applied for an emergency bank loan to tide him over his crop failures. Europe, too, was hard hit by the unseasonable cold and 1816 became known in England as "the year without a summer." Henry and Elizabeth Stommel argue in *Volcano Weather*, their book about the phenomenon, that a typhus epidemic that killed more than 65,000 people in the British Isles in 1816 was related to cold-induced famine.
>
> The cause of this global misery was the eruption of Mount Tambora, a volcano in the Dutch East Indies. In probably the most powerful volcanic outburst in 10,000 years, Tambora spewed 25 cubic miles of debris into the upper atmosphere. The heavier particles fell into the Pacific Ocean, forming a slush of pumice two feet thick; the lighter debris stayed aloft for months, circled the globe, and blanketed the skies over most of the Northern Hemisphere.
>
> But the eruption of Tambora was minor compared with the blast effect of a full-scale nuclear exchange between the United States and the Soviet

Union; and "the year without a summer" was mild and brief compared to the "nuclear winter" that would descend upon the Northern Hemisphere after a Soviet-American holocaust.

EXERCISE 17. Analyzing an Introduction. Refer to the introductory paragraphs of "Tambora's Lesson" by Tom Wicker as you answer the following questions.

1. The writer does not make clear the specific topic of the essay until the fourth paragraph. What is the specific topic?
2. What do you think is the purpose of all of the information about what happened in 1816 after the eruption of Mount Tambora? Can you tell at this point in the essay why the writer has included this information?
3. How effective do you think the beginning of the essay is? Do you want to read further? Explain your answer.
4. What specific details has the writer included about "the year without a summer"—1816?
5. Does the introduction contain a position statement? If not, try writing one. What do you think the writer's opinion is? Where would you place the position statement?

The Body

All of the paragraphs between the introduction and the conclusion constitute the *body* of the persuasive composition. In the body, every reason and its supporting evidence (as you have outlined them during the prewriting stages) should take up one paragraph. You may treat your refutation of the opposing viewpoint as one of your reasons, and you may present this refutation either before or after your other reasons.

The body of Mr. Wicker's essay "Tambora's Lesson" provides specific information to support the conclusion that he makes in the final paragraph of the essay (see Concluding Paragraph, page 600). As you read the body, notice the quantity of evidence and the sources that he cites for the evidence.

The theory that such a disastrous man-made winter—postulated in 1983 by a group of scientists working outside the Government—would follow nuclear war has now been given legitimacy by the National Academy of Scientists, in a study commissioned by the Department of Defense. The study was conducted by a committee headed by George F. Carrier of

Harvard, who termed its results "quite consistent" with earlier nuclear-winter studies.

The committee of specialists from Government laboratories, private industry, and academia found that exploding only about half the world's nuclear arsenals, equivalent to 6,500 megatons of TNT, together with the resulting fires, would propel at least 15 million tons of dust and 180 million tons of smoke into the atmosphere. That would blacken the skies for 6 to 20 weeks; and if it happened in spring or summer, temperatures throughout Eurasia and North America would drop by 18 to 55 degrees.

Within days, the pall of smoke and dust would block 99 percent of the sunlight normally falling on the Northern Hemisphere. Temperatures would drop catastrophically, destroying agriculture for at least a year, and many forests. The consequences—while not calculated by the academy study—are estimated in a new book, *The Cold and the Dark*, by four of the original nuclear-winter theorists, Paul Ehrlich, Carl Sagan, Donald Kennedy, and Walter Orr Roberts.

Together with crops, most farm animals would freeze and die, and plant photosynthesis and thus new crop growth would be all but impossible; famine would be an inevitable consequence. In the Arctic darkness of nuclear winter, blast survivors—many without shelter—would suffer from pollution, radiation, sub-freezing temperatures, hunger, the resulting disease, and hopelessly inadequate medical care and relief facilities. Resistant species such as rats and roaches, with their natural predators killed off, would proliferate to torment humans.

The academy committee did not estimate precisely how long the nuclear winter would last, since the rainfall that might wash the dust and soot back to earth could also be disrupted by the accumulation of the sun's heat in the upper atmosphere. But the authors of *The Cold and the Dark* suggest that even returning sunlight would bring a new danger—lethal ultraviolet radiation—because much of the upper atmosphere's protective ozone layer would have been burned away.

Taken with the incalculable destruction and loss of life that would be caused by nuclear blast, nuclear winter raises at least the possibility of human extinction following a Soviet-U.S. war. It certainly means that after such a war anything remotely like civilization would cease to exist in the Northern Hemisphere.

EXERCISE 18. Analyzing the Body of a Persuasive Essay.
Refer to the preceding paragraphs and to the essay's introductory paragraphs on page 597 as you answer the following questions.

1. The writer mentions a committee as the source of the information

that he gives about nuclear winter. Who was on the committee, and who commissioned their work?

2. What exactly did the committee say would happen if there were an explosion of about half the world's nuclear arsenals?

3. The writer cites four authors and a book entitled *The Cold and the Dark*. According to the authors of this book, what would happen to human life if the weather changed in the way that the committee predicted it would?

4. Because there is no way of testing that what the committee and the authors say will happen is true, whether or not you believe the information in this essay depends a great deal on how believable you think the sources of the information are. How believable would you say the committee commissioned by the Department of Defense is? How believable do you think the authors of *The Cold and the Dark* are? Explain your answers.

The Concluding Paragraph

The *concluding paragraph* may restate the writer's opinion or summarize the argument (the reasons supporting the position statement). Sometimes a concluding paragraph also asks the reader to perform a specific action, such as making a contribution or writing a letter to an elected official. Occasionally, the concluding paragraph will state the writer's conclusion, based on the evidence and reasons presented in the rest of the paper. In the following example, Mr. Wicker states the conclusion he has reached, based on the assumption that all of the information he has related is true.

> Therefore, the Academy of Sciences report can only speed the world's growing understanding that nuclear weapons *can never be used* except suicidally, and have no military or political value except to deter their use by others. That knowledge inevitably points toward fewer, not more, nuclear weapons—a conclusion that even Moscow and Washington must someday begin to act upon as well as talk about.

EXERCISE 19. **Analyzing a Writer's Argument.** Refer to the introduction (page 597), body (pages 598–99), and conclusion of Tom Wicker's article as you answer the following questions:

1. Restate the writer's conclusion in your own words.
2. Do you think this is a logical conclusion if the facts stated in the rest of the essay are true?

3. Do you agree or disagree with the writer's conclusion? Explain why.

4. What do you imagine would be the arguments of those who strongly disagree with Mr. Wicker? Outline the reasons and, if you can, the evidence the opposing viewpoint might use.

5. Consider once more the information in the introductory paragraphs about what happened on earth in the year 1816. How is this information related to the writer's argument? What exactly is Tambora's lesson?

6. Mr. Wicker supports his opinion about nuclear weapons with facts about the eruption of Mount Tambora, information stated by a committee of scientists commissioned by the U.S. Department of Defense, and information stated by a group of four scientist-authors. How believable do you think his argument is? Explain your answer.

EXERCISE 20. Writing a First Draft. Use one of the position statements or arguments you have worked with earlier in the chapter, or outline another argument on a topic of your choice. Write a persuasive composition. Include a precisely worded position statement in your introductory paragraph. If you have added a call to action in your outline, be sure to include it in the concluding paragraph.

REVISING AND PROOFREADING

REVISING

25h. Revise the first draft.

Revising a persuasive composition requires several careful rereadings of the first draft. Focus your attention entirely on just one aspect of the composition as you try to improve it.

(1) Focus first on the argument.

Your position statement, reason, and evidence should be so clearly stated that the reader can easily follow the logic of your argument. Transitional expressions such as *first, second, most important*, and *also* will help to highlight your reasoning.

As you focus carefully on your argument, make sure that you have included sufficient reasons (at least three) and that, whenever possible, each reason is supported by some kind of specific evidence. Refer to the Guidelines for Evaluating an Argument (pages 609–10 and 614), and make sure that each reason and piece of evidence is relevant to your argument. You may decide at this point to replace weak reasons or evidence or to rearrange your presentation of ideas. The whole point of this aspect of the revision is to make your argument as convincing as possible and to make sure that the reader can follow your argument easily.

(2) Make sure that the tone is formal and the style is concise.

Avoid slang, colloquialisms, or contractions in a persuasive composition; the tone should be both serious and formal. To give the reader the impression that you are being both logical and fair, avoid unacceptable emotional appeals, such as loaded words (see pages 622–24). You will also need to avoid logical fallacies, such as begging the question and attacking the person (see pages 620–21).

Eliminate any unnecessary, awkward, or elaborate words or phrases. Aim for expressing your ideas clearly, with no flowery phrases or unnecessary repetition. When you eliminate such "padding" from your composition, your argument will be easier to follow, and you will give the reader the impression that you know what you are writing about.

(3) Check the word choice.

Focus on each word, one at a time, to make sure that each word expresses the precise idea you wish to communicate. You may at this time choose a more exact word or insert clarifying words or phrases. Make sure that you are aware of the connotations (emotional associations) of every word and that you choose only those words that will help make your argument convincing.

The following paragraph shows part of a composition on student involvement in designing a curriculum. Notice how the writer has changed words and rearranged ideas.

It seems to me that students will be more interested in their classes and more

are consulted about *and if they are involved in making the school work*

likely to learn if they have some say over what courses are offered. They'll

They may

also be less likely to drop out of school maybe. It seems to me that all of the

fuss about making school harder and having students meet minimum

need

requirements is OK. But you've got to remember that students have to feel

they are *in school* *When students are self-motivated,*

that what they're learning is important in their life. I heard about a school

they will achieve more. For example, in

called Middle College High School in New York City. It has a program that

p

really gets students involved Peer counselors, who are trained by the faculty,

help students with problems. And a peer-faculty committee decides on

and another

disciplinary problems. Another group of students help to tutors other

peer

students who are having trouble in school. All of this type of involvement by

students has resulted in the consequence of a daily attendance of more than

b *nonexistent*

85 percent of the students. Behavior problems are almost not around, and

more than 80 percent

most of the students go on to college.

Use the following guidelines for revising your persuasive composition:

GUIDELINES FOR REVISING A PERSUASIVE COMPOSITION

1. Is the topic of the composition a debatable opinion about a serious issue?
2. Does the position statement clearly state the writer's opinion? Does the position statement appear in the introductory paragraph(s)?
3. Is the writer's opinion supported by at least three reasons?
4. Is each reason supported by some kind of evidence, such as facts, statistics, examples, or quotations?
5. Is necessary background information provided for the audience?
6. Is the tone consistently formal and serious?
7. Does the writer consider the opposing viewpoint and refute opposing arguments?
8. Does the concluding paragraph state the writer's conclusion, restate the writer's opinion, summarize the argument, or suggest a future course of action?
9. Does the essay avoid fallacies? (See pages 619–21.)
10. Do transitional expressions connect the writer's ideas and make the essay easy to understand?
11. Has the writer eliminated wordiness, vagueness, and unnecessary or distracting information?

EXERCISE 21. Revising a Persuasive Composition. Carefully revise the first draft of the composition that you wrote for Exercise 20. Refer to the preceding Guidelines for Revising a Persuasive Composition and check each item on the list.

PROOFREADING

25i. Proofread your revised version to make sure that it agrees with the conventions of written standard English.

The most effective way to proofread is to reread the revised version several times, focusing each time on a particular proofreading task, such as spelling, punctuation, usage, and capitalization. Use the Guidelines for Proofreading on page 403 to check all of the important aspects of mechanics and usage.

After you have proofread the revised version, write the final version on a separate sheet of paper. Follow the manuscript form required by your teacher. Be sure to proofread the final version once more to make sure that you have not made any mistakes in copying.

EXERCISE 22. Proofreading a Persuasive Composition.
Proofread the final version of the composition that you revised in Exercise 21. On a separate sheet of paper, write the finished version of your composition, and proofread it once again before turning it in to your teacher.

REVIEW EXERCISE C. Writing a Persuasive Composition.
Refer to the *Pro* and *Con* chart in Exercise 9 on pages 586–87. Write a persuasive composition based on your position (*pro* or *con*) and the reasons you choose to support the position statement. Provide evidence to back up each reason. You will have to do some research to find out actual information.

LOGICAL THINKING

You have seen that persuasive writing is based on an argument, a logical presentation of ideas. Logic, sometimes called clear thinking, is at the heart of persuasive writing. Learning to think more logically will help you become more effective as a writer, a speaker, and a listener. In this section you will study and practice two basic types of logical thinking: inductive reasoning and deductive reasoning. You will also learn to identify nine common fallacies, so that you can avoid these errors in reasoning as you plan your persuasive compositions.

INDUCTIVE REASONING

25j. Use inductive reasoning to make a generalization based on specific observations or evidence.

Inductive reasoning begins with a series of specific, concrete experiences or evidence. After carefully studying this evidence, you reach a conclusion based on the information you have gathered. This conclusion is often a *generalization*, a statement that explains all of the specific evidence and goes even further to make a general statement about a whole class of experiences.

Gathering Evidence

Suppose, for example, that you were investigating some of the reasons why students drop out of high school. You might begin by asking students who have left school what their reasons were.

EVIDENCE   Joe left school because he needed to earn money. Sarita left school because she got a good job. Tony dropped out of school to look for work. Dina left school for a full-time job.

Making a Generalization

On the basis of these four pieces of evidence, you might reach the following conclusion:

GENERALIZATION   Students drop out of high school to work.

You have made this generalization about all students on the basis of four pieces of evidence: your interviews with four students. Your *sampling* (the number of specific instances you studied) is far too small to make this a valid conclusion. The word *valid* means that you have correctly followed the rules of reasoning. In order to reach a valid conclusion about why some students drop out of high school, you would need to sample many, many more specific cases. Perhaps you would have to interview hundreds of students, perhaps thousands. Probably you would find that there are many reasons—not just one—why students drop out of high school.

Even if you were to interview several thousand drop-outs, you would still have to make what is known as "the inductive leap" in order to reach a conclusion. You know that there is no possible way for you to interview every high-school drop-out in the country or, for that matter, every student who has dropped out of school during the past sixty or so years. Your generalization about why students drop out of high school is based not on *all* of the evidence, but on a *sampling* of all of the evidence.

You may recognize inductive reasoning as the method that scientists use when they make conclusions based on a long series of experiments and measurements. The three basic steps in inductive reasoning may be summarized as follows:

1. Gather many specific pieces of evidence. Record your observations.
2. Look carefully at the evidence to see if you can explain it.

3. Make a generalization (conclusion) based on the evidence.

In order to make a sound (true) generalization, you must follow three rules for gathering evidence and wording your conclusion.

(1) A generalization must be based on sufficient evidence.

One, two, or three pieces of evidence cannot lead to a sound conclusion. A generalization based on only a few pieces of evidence is, in fact, a fallacy called a *hasty generalization*. (See page 619.) In an inductive argument, the evidence cannot *prove* that the generalization is true; rather, the evidence *supports* the generalization. The more evidence there is, the more likely it is that the generalization will be sound and believable.

(2) The evidence must be drawn from a random sampling of the population being studied.

Your evidence will be more reliable if it comes from a random sampling of the *population* (group being studied). For example, suppose that you are trying once again to make some conclusions about why high-school students drop out of high school. The answers you get from students that you interview are more likely to represent the whole population of drop-outs if you interview students at different schools across the country than if you interview only four friends at your own school.

(3) The generalization must explain all of the evidence.

Because generalizations make such broad statements, it is often a good idea to add a qualifying or limiting word or phrase, such as the following ones: *some, many, most, sometimes, often, usually, are likely to, probably, occasionally, may, among those studied,* etc. The generalization about high-school drop-outs and work would be more likely to be true if a limiting word were added, as in the following examples. Notice that the generalization no longer makes a statement about all high-school students who drop out of school.

EXAMPLES Some high-school students drop out of school to work.
Many high-school students drop out of school to work.
One of the reasons why some high-school students drop out of school is to find work.

EXERCISE 23. Making a Generalization. For each of the following situations, write a sound generalization based on the evidence presented. If no sound generalization is possible, tell why. (Hint: Many generalizations are possible for some items.)

1. The following figures show the median annual earnings for year-round full-time workers.

	WOMEN	MEN
1960	$3,293	$5,417
1970	$5,323	$8,966
1980	$11,197	$18,612
1983	$13,915	$21,881

2. Cholesterol is a fatty substance found in varying amounts in human blood. It is thought to be a cause of heart disease. Each person's cholesterol level can be tested by means of a simple blood test. The resulting figures measure the milligrams of cholesterol per 100 millimeters of blood serum. The National Institute of Health recently issued the following figures, which rate the risk of certain levels of cholesterol by the age of the person being tested.

AGE	MODERATE RISK	HIGH RISK
2–19	Greater than 170	Greater than 185
20–29	Greater than 200	Greater than 220
30–39	Greater than 220	Greater than 240
40 plus	Greater than 240	Greater than 260

Using Inductive Reasoning in Persuasive Writing

Whenever you write an argument in which you begin by presenting your evidence and end by making a logical conclusion based on the evidence, you are using inductive reasoning. Your logical conclusion must be true if all of the evidence you have given is true. This chapter contains two examples of persuasive writing that uses inductive reasoning.

Look at the argument outlined on page 582 for the passage of a mandatory seat belt law. The three reasons that are given are the equivalent of the evidence in an inductive argument. Each of these reasons can be proved to be true by means of facts, statistics, and examples. Now, assuming that you accept as true the three reasons and the evidence given to back up these reasons, only one logical conclusion is possible: This state should pass a mandatory seat belt law.

The second example of inductive reasoning at work in persuasive writing in this chapter is Tom Wicker's essay "Tambora's Lesson" on pages 597–600. Mr. Wicker builds to a conclusion by presenting three pieces of evidence: (1) facts about what happened on earth in 1816 when Mount Tambora erupted, (2) predictions made by a committee of scientists commissioned by the Department of Defense about what would happen to the earth's weather in the event of a nuclear war, and (3) predictions made by four scientists about what would happen to human, plant, and animal life on earth. If you accept that these three pieces of evidence are true, then Mr. Wicker's conclusion (see page 600) is a logical one.

EXERCISE 24. Outlining an Inductive Argument.   Each of the following statements is a generalization made as the conclusion of an inductive argument. For each generalization, tell what evidence you would need to support the generalization. If you disagree with the generalization, reword it to your satisfaction.

1. Students need to eat a nutritious breakfast in order to learn well.
2. Every person can learn to read.
3. Students who know how to use computers are more likely to be able to find jobs than students who do not know how to use computers.
4. Movies are better than they ever were.
5. Male drivers under twenty-five are involved in more automobile accidents than female drivers under twenty-five.
6. Lack of communication or bad communication can cause serious misunderstandings.

CRITICAL THINKING:
Evaluating an Inductive Argument

When you are writing or reading a persuasive paper, you may recognize that the argument is an inductive one. Use the following guidelines to evaluate an inductive argument:

GUIDELINES FOR EVALUATING AN INDUCTIVE ARGUMENT

1. What is the conclusion?
2. What is the evidence on which the conclusion is based?
3. Is the evidence sufficient to warrant the conclusion?

4. What is the source of the evidence? Is the source reliable?
5. Does the generalization explain or reflect all of the evidence? Is the generalization contradicted by some of the evidence?
6. Does the generalization make a universal statement?
7. Does the argument contain any fallacies? (See pages 619–21.)

EXERCISE 25. Analyzing an Argument. The following paragraphs are from an article entitled "Studies Weigh Hazard of Legal Drugs and Driving." Read the paragraphs carefully, and then answer the questions that follow.

While numerous studies have been done to establish exactly how alcohol affects drivers and how many crashes can be blamed on drinks, similar data do not exist about [legal] drugs and driving. The Food and Drug Administration requires warnings to drivers on all sedatives, but the requirement is based on an assumption that such drugs as tranquilizers, pain-killers and antihistamines affect driving skills, not on actual tests.

The information that does exist indicates that the problem of [legal] drugs and driving is far-reaching. Simulated road tests at the Southern California Research Institute showed that the drug diazepam, more commonly known as Valium, impaired drivers' abilities to stay in their lane, maintain an even speed and determine exits, and increased the time and distance needed to stop the car.

One study found that psychiatric patients taking one or more medications have two to three times as many accidents as psychiatric patients who are not taking drugs. Another determined that allergy sufferers have 50 to 100 percent more accidents and time lost from work because of accidents than nonallergy sufferers.

A study of accident victims admitted to Oslo hospitals indicated that 20 percent showed Valium in their blood. Eleven percent of those showed evidence of Valium alone, the rest showed a mixture of Valium and alcohol. A similar study in Dallas found Valium in the blood of 10 percent of drivers killed in car crashes.

"The weight of the circumstantial evidence in this case builds to an irrefutable conclusion," said J. F. O'Hanlon, a professor at the Traffic Research Center in the Netherlands.

LISA BELKIN

1. The paragraphs do not state the "irrefutable conclusion" J. F. O'Hanlon refers to in the last paragraph. On the basis of the evidence presented in the paragraphs, what do you think that conclusion is? State the logical conclusion in your own words.
2. How many different pieces of evidence does the writer cite? List each of the different studies mentioned in the article.
3. How reliable do you think the evidence is? Explain your answer.
4. In order to try to *prove* the conclusion (as stated in answer to Question 1), what kind of evidence would you need?
5. What do you think can be done to prevent car accidents that result from drivers having taken legal drugs?

DEDUCTIVE REASONING

25k. Use deductive reasoning to reach a logical conclusion based on a generalization.

Deductive reasoning is the opposite of inductive reasoning. Deductive reasoning begins with a generalization, applies that generalization to a particular example, and arrives at a logical conclusion. Inductive reasoning moves from the particular to the general; deductive reasoning, on the other hand, moves from the general to the particular.

GENERALIZATION	All animals need water.
SPECIFIC EXAMPLE	Camels are animals.
LOGICAL CONCLUSION	Camels need water.

The Syllogism

This three-part deductive argument is called a *syllogism*. The first part of a syllogism is a generalization, sometimes called the *major premise.* The second part, sometimes called the *minor premise,* applies that generalization to a particular example, leading to the third part of the syllogism: the *logical conclusion.*

GENERALIZATION	All human beings need oxygen to live.
SPECIFIC EXAMPLE	You are a human being.
LOGICAL CONCLUSION	You need oxygen to live.

Syllogisms do not have to deal only with facts. When deductive reasoning is used in persuasive writing, the generalization often states an opinion.

GENERALIZATION It is the duty of every American citizen eighteen or older to vote in every election.

SPECIFIC EXAMPLE Juan Rivera is an eighteen-year-old American citizen.

LOGICAL CONCLUSION It is Juan Rivera's duty to vote in every election.

Deductive reasoning is tricky because sometimes the reasoning seems to be logical, but the conclusion is false. In order to have a *valid* (logical) and true conclusion, you must follow three rules in deductive reasoning.

(1) Both premises in a syllogism must be true.

The conclusion cannot be true if either one of the premises is false. Consider the following examples.

FALSE SYLLOGISM All two-legged animals are human beings.
An ostrich is a two-legged animal.
An ostrich is a human being.

FALSE SYLLOGISM All tenth-graders must take physical education.
You are a tenth-grader.
You must take physical education.

In the first example, the major premise is false: there are many two-legged animals that are not human beings. The conclusion, therefore, is false even though the syllogism follows the correct rules of reasoning to reach the conclusion.

In the second example, the minor premise is false. You are not a tenth-grader if you are using this book; you are probably a high-school senior. Because the minor premise is false, the conclusion is false.

Remember that *both* the major and minor premise must be true if the conclusion is to be true.

(2) The generalization in a syllogism must make a universal statement.

A universal statement is one that applies to *all* instances of the population being discussed. Universal statements either contain or imply the word *All* or *Every*. A statement that contains a limiting word (such as *several, many, most, some, few*) is not a universal statement.

UNIVERSAL STATEMENT All butterflies are insects.
Butterflies are insects.
Every butterfly is an insect.

LIMITED STATEMENT Some seniors have applied to colleges.
Many seniors have applied to colleges.
Several seniors have applied to colleges.

If you try to use a limited statement as either the major or minor premise in a syllogism, you cannot make a valid conclusion.

EXAMPLE   Some seniors have applied to colleges.
           Jana is a senior.

No conclusion is possible because you have no way of knowing if Jana is one of those "some seniors" who have applied to colleges or if she belongs to the other group of seniors who have not applied to colleges.

(3) The minor premise must be a specific example of the group identified in the major premise.

This requirement in a syllogism is a little trickier than the other two requirements. You can understand it best by looking at an example of a false syllogism.

FALSE SYLLOGISM   Communists believe in government ownership of natural resources.
                   Mrs. Doe believes in government ownership of the coal mines.
                   (Therefore,) Mrs. Doe is a Communist.

The syllogism is false because it ignores a significant fact: People who believe in government ownership of coal mines are not necessarily Communists. Other people besides Communists may hold this opinion.

Look at another example, which may be even clearer.

FALSE SYLLOGISM   All people need love.
                   Rover, our dog, needs love.
                   Rover is a person.

In this syllogism both the major and minor premise are true. However, the second premise is not a specific example of the population being described in the first premise. Rover is not a person. If the second premise were changed to an example of the first, you could reach a valid and true conclusion.

EXAMPLE   All people need love.
           Donald is a person.
           Donald needs love.

Using Deductive Reasoning in Persuasive Writing

If you begin an argument with a generalization that you assume to be true and go on to consider a specific case of that generalization, you are probably using deductive reasoning. Of course, you do not include actual syllogisms in your composition, but sometimes the argument that you build is a development of ideas that could be stated in the form of a syllogism.

Consider, for example, the letter to the editor by Bill Ogilvie on page 590. One way of summarizing Mr. Ogilvie's ideas might be as follows:

SYLLOGISM   Preschool children should be cared for at home by their parents if they are to avoid the emotional trauma of separation.
Preschool children who are sent to day-care centers are not being cared for at home by their parents.
Therefore, the preschool children who are sent to day-care centers are suffering from the emotional trauma of being separated from their parents.

This is a fairly mild restatement of Mr. Ogilvie's argument. He says that besides suffering from the emotional trauma of separation from their parents, children in day-care centers are not being cared for properly.

CRITICAL THINKING:
Evaluating a Deductive Argument

In the preceding section you learned three rules that govern the logic of deductive reasoning. There are many more rules, and they are complicated. For now, concentrate on these three rules. As you write persuasive compositions and as you listen to persuasive speeches, you should be asking yourself whether the statements and conclusions are true.

To evaluate a deductive argument, use the following guidelines:

GUIDELINES FOR EVALUATING A DEDUCTIVE ARGUMENT

1. What are the writer's premises? (Sometimes the premises are not clearly stated; sometimes they are assumed.)
2. Are the premises true? How can I tell if they are true?
3. Does the generalization make a universal statement?
4. What is the writer's conclusion?
5. Does the conclusion follow logically from the premises? Is the conclusion true?
6. Does the argument contain any fallacies? (See pages 619–21.)

EXERCISE 26. Analyzing a Letter to the Editor. Read the following letter to the editor, and answer the questions following the letter. You should know that the writer is referring to an $800 million surplus in New York State funds and that an $800 million tax cut has been proposed.

To the Editor:

I disagree with those who think an $800 million tax cut for New York State is a good idea.

Present tax rates were not frivolously established simply to "spend." They are required to bring in the money to pay for public services, which all of us benefit from. Public schools, streets and highways, police protection, libraries, shelters for the homeless, hospitals, fire protection, all require tax dollars to exist.

Is there a presumption that these and other public services in New York State, and in its cities and towns, are in such great shape that no improvement is necessary?

We have overcrowded classrooms in our schools, mentally ill people wandering the streets confused and penniless, understaffed police forces in our cities, decent families paying 40 percent of their income for indecent housing, and citizens who would like to attend public college part-time but who can't afford the tuition. One might think of other problems. Why the big rush for a tax cut?

If we have a surplus in the state budget, after these years of austerity, let's use it to begin to address the many inadequacies in public services that New Yorkers have endured and are enduring.

And should we reach the level of adequacy, would it spoil some universal plan if we strove for excellence?

The public services that we purchase through our government are as much a part of the quality of our lives as the things we purchase individually.

We New Yorkers should stop apologizing for taxing ourselves to improve the society we commonly share.

EDWARD C. SULLIVAN
Assemblyman, 69th District

1. What would you say are the writer's premises? Are the premises true?
2. What do you think is the writer's conclusion? Do you agree or disagree with this conclusion?
3. Try writing the writer's argument as a syllogism.

ARGUMENT BY ANALOGY

Sometimes during a discussion, a person may use an analogy to clarify a point. An *analogy* is a comparison. To be effective, the two things or situations being compared must have many points in common. If there are too many dissimilarities, the analogy is a weak one and will not be effective.

WEAK ANALOGY   Being a student in school is like being a soldier in an army. Students must obey hall monitors, just as soldiers must obey their officers, so that the school can function effectively.

By drawing this analogy between a school and an army, the writer hopes to persuade readers to be more cooperative and obedient. However, the analogy is a weak one, even though both an army and a school must have discipline. Is military discipline the kind we want in a school? Is the job of an army officer like that of a school's hall monitor? Is winning a battle much like furthering an educational program? The analogy grows weaker the longer you study it, which is true of many analogies.

If you use an analogy in your writing, remember that an analogy can never *prove* anything. Nevertheless, analogies have their place in argument. If a good one occurs to you, use it for its clarifying effect. Almost invariably it will be interesting to your readers and will help them to understand your argument better.

EXERCISE 27. Identifying Inductive and Deductive Reasoning. This exercise is a series of examples of both inductive and deductive reasoning. Number your paper 1–5. After studying each item, tell whether the reasoning is inductive (*I*) or deductive (*D*). Be prepared also to discuss whether the conclusion is true.

1. Only Caribou Airlines flies nonstop between here and Atlanta. Carl said he was coming from Atlanta on a nonstop flight, so he must be flying on Caribou Airlines.
2. Based on the number of new cars in college parking lots, and the number of college students who spend their winter vacations at ski resorts and their summers abroad, I'd say that college students these days must be wealthy.
3. The per-pupil cost of education is greater in the high school than in the elementary school. In the future a greater proportion of pupils will be in high school than has been true in the past. The total cost of education, therefore, is sure to increase.

4. Statistics show that there has been an increasing number of muggings and violent crimes in the subways in the past two years. In a random survey of 1,600 subway riders, all complain that they feel unsafe on the subways. To protect riders, each subway train should have at least three police officers patrolling the cars.

5. On the basis of hundreds of tests with each make and model of automobile, government agency officials have concluded that small compact cars get more miles to a gallon of gas than large, heavy cars.

EXERCISE 28. Creating Syllogisms. Write five original syllogisms, following the three rules for creating syllogisms discussed on pages 612–13. Test your syllogisms by giving them to other students in your class to read. You might give them only your major and minor premises and see what conclusions they reach.

EXERCISE 29. Analyzing an Analogy. Read the following letter, and then answer the questions that follow it.

Imagine you were playing a game of checkers—playing to win.

Someone leans over your shoulder, puts a thumb on one checker and says, "Go ahead and play—just don't move this checker." Then someone else leans over your other shoulder and puts a thumb on another checker. Then a third person immobilizes still another checker, then another, then another . . . Soon all thumbs; no moves.

Could you ever expect to win a game like that?

Of course not!

Yet . . . most Americans expect their Senators and Congressmen in Washington to solve the monumental problems of recession, inflation, devastating unemployment, and a dangerous energy crisis while working under the same insurmountable conditions.

In the struggle to find solutions to these grave problems, the restricting thumbs are the high-pressure demands of special-interest groups—they do not really want to paralyze the nation's problem-solving efforts. Each just wants to immobilize one checker. Each is simply looking after its own special interest—making sure that their financial gains are not affected, insuring that certain tax advantages are not disturbed, guaranteeing the subsidies are maintained, etc. Collectively, they prevent *any* solution.

And in real life you can't see whose thumbs are coming down on the checkerboard. You don't know what forces are making the game impossible to win. That's why we the Citizens must step in and say, "THUMBS OFF!"

1. What situations are being compared in this analogy?
2. How effective do you think the analogy is?
3. What do you think the writer wants the reader to do?
4. In the last paragraph, the writer points out one important way in which the special-interest groups' lobbyists and the thumbs-on-checkers are different. What is that important difference?

EXERCISE 30. Creating an Analogy. Choose any one of the persuasive topics you have worked with so far in this chapter or any other persuasive topic. Think of at least one analogy that you might use in a persuasive composition discussing the topic. Your analogy should help to clarify a point. The two things or situations in the analogy should have more similarities than dissimilarities. Write a paragraph in which you present the analogy as part of your argument to support your opinion.

AVOIDING ERRORS IN REASONING

25l. Learn to recognize fallacies, and avoid them in your writing.

An error in reasoning is called a *fallacy.* Arguments that contain fallacies are not logical arguments, and their conclusions, therefore, are necessarily false. By learning to recognize some common fallacies, you will improve your ability to build logical arguments. You will also be able to detect errors in logic when you read or listen to others' attempts to persuade you.

CRITICAL THINKING:
Recognizing Fallacies

Hasty Generalization

When you make a generalization based on insufficient evidence, you are making a *hasty generalization*. A generalization must be based on a great deal of evidence or on many personal observations—not just one or two examples.

FAULTY   A month ago, I was forced off the highway by a car driven by a high-school student who insisted on passing, even though there was not enough room to pass. To avoid being sideswiped, I drove into the ditch. It is obvious to me that teen-age drivers are a menace and that the driving age in this state should be raised to twenty-one.

Stereotype

A *stereotype* is a belief that all members of a particular group share certain characteristics just because they are members of the group. Stereotypes lead to prejudice—prejudging individuals on the basis of their group identities rather than on their individual merits.

FAULTY   Foreigners can't be trusted.
          Englishmen have no sense of humor.

Cause-and-Effect Fallacy

The *cause-and-effect fallacy* makes the mistake of assuming that just because one event preceded another, the first event caused the second event. The Latin name for this fallacy is *post hoc, ergo propter hoc,* which means "After this, because of this."

FAULTY   The school's basketball team played in the state championship and had to travel a whole day to reach the city where the game would be played. They played the game the same day they traveled and lost badly. Obviously, they lost because they were tired from traveling. Championship games should not be played on the same day that a team travels.

Can you see the fallacy in this reasoning? The team may have lost because they were tired from traveling, but they may have lost for a number of other reasons as well. Maybe they lost because the team that defeated them was a better team. Their loss cannot be ascribed to the day of traveling.

Only Cause Fallacy

The example given for the cause-and-effect fallacy (the reason why the basketball team lost the championship game) is also an example of the only cause fallacy. In the *only cause fallacy* a complex situation is seen as the result of a single cause. Usually, a situation has many causes—not just a single cause. Being open-minded allows you to see that more than one cause is possible and that, similarly, more than one solution is possible to a problem.

FAULTY We can stop traffic fatalities if we make every instance of drunk driving punishable with a twenty-year prison sentence.
The drop-out rate for high-school students would decrease to almost nothing if classes were smaller.

False Analogy

You have already seen that an analogy is a comparison used in persuasive and expository writing to clarify a point. A *false analogy* is a weak or far-fetched comparison. The items being compared are dissimilar in so many ways that the comparison is not effective.

FAULTY Like the manager of a wild animal circus, the principal of a high school is engaged in the business of training animals. There is always the strain of having to keep the animals under control. A school can no more permit students complete freedom than a circus can release its wild animals. In both instances, the public would protest vigorously.

Attacking the Person

When you attempt to discredit an opponent's views by *attacking the opponent's character* or circumstances, you are guilty of the *ad hominem* fallacy, which means "to the person." In responding to an opponent's arguments, deal with the argument directly, rather than with the person.

FAULTY Lee Ann has proposed a series of reforms in the way the student government is run. Everyone knows that Lee Ann is never serious about anything. She is always joking and fooling around, so we shouldn't waste our time considering the reforms she has proposed. I'm sure it's all a big joke to her.

Either—Or Fallacy

Thinking of a problem or a solution as having only two possible extremes (causes, courses of action, etc.) is *either–or* thinking. A person guilty of the *either–or fallacy* sees situations as either good or bad, right or wrong, black or white, and ignores all possibilities between these extremes.

FAULTY   Either we will have to sell more tickets, or we will have to cancel the play completely.

          If we don't reelect Governor X, the state government will be ruined.

Non Sequitur

Non sequitur means "It does not follow" in Latin. When a conclusion does not logically follow from a premise (or premises), the writer has committed a *non sequitur fallacy*.

FAULTY   More than two thirds of the students participate in some after-school activity, such as sports, service groups, drama club, and newspaper. Because 100 percent of the student body does not participate in these activities, all of these activities should be canceled.

Circular Reasoning

Circular reasoning occurs when you give no distinct reasons to back up your opinion. Although it may look like you are providing reasons, you are really just restating and rephrasing the position statement.

FAULTY   My candidate is the best qualified of all. In character, experience, education, and intellectual ability, she is superior to everyone else who is running for this office. No one even remotely approaches her qualifications for the position. She stands head and shoulders above the other candidates. Therefore, she deserves your vote.

Begging the Question

If you assume that something is true in the course of an argument, you may be committing the fallacy of *begging the question*. You cannot, for example, assume that a judgment or an opinion is true and accepted by your reader.

FAULTY   Everyone agrees that this is an unfair tax.

          We all know that the senator's statement is ridiculous.

EXERCISE 31. Identifying Fallacies. For each of the numbered fallacies, make up one example. See if other students in the class can identify the fallacies.

1. Cause-and-effect fallacy
2. Only cause fallacy
3. Attacking the person
4. Begging the question
5. False analogy

6. Hasty generalization
7. Non sequitur
8. Circular reasoning
9. Either–Or Fallacy
10. Stereotype

EXERCISE 32. Detecting Fallacies in Writing. Read the editorials, letters to the editor, and advertisements in several issues of a daily newspaper. Bring to class any examples that you find of fallacies in reasoning.

PROPAGANDA: APPEALS TO EMOTION

When an organized group (government, institution, business) sets out to win over the public, the ideas and arguments it uses in its favor are called *propaganda*. The purpose of propaganda is to convince and persuade to action. Not all propaganda is bad, although the word has negative connotations. Most people would agree that a physician who tries to persuade an audience to stop smoking cigarettes is using "good propaganda."

In your persuasive writing, you will probably not use many appeals to the emotions. Persuasive writing, after all, is basically an appeal to logic and clear thinking. However, you may occasionally make use of some of these appeals to the emotions, and you should certainly learn to recognize them in others' attempts to persuade you to act or think in a certain way.

25m. Learn to recognize and evaluate propaganda techniques.

Loaded Words

Loaded words are words with strong emotional associations that may be either positive or negative. *Love* and *peace* are positively loaded words, for example; *cheat* and *war* have negative connotations. (See pages 737–40 for more about loaded words and connotations.)

Glittering Generalities

One type of loaded words is the *glittering generality*. These are words that are so strongly positive in emotional content that they can make you feel good just by hearing them.

EXAMPLE   A group of *clean-cut, all-American* volunteers will dance at the Inaugural Ball.

Propagandists often use slogans to oversimplify arguments and reduce them to a few words. Slogans are another form of glittering generalities.

EXAMPLES   The right is more precious than the peace.
          All that counts is liberty, equality, fraternity.

The Bandwagon

The *bandwagon appeal* asserts that you should do something because "everyone else" is doing it. The bandwagon approach appeals to the human need not to feel left out.

EXAMPLE   Don't be the last person to buy a yearbook. Almost five sixths of the senior class have already reserved their copies. Hurry—before the copies are all gone.

Plain-Folks Appeal

The *plain-folks appeal*, often used by advertisers, uses average, ordinary, everyday people to make you want to do what they are doing. If you see the "common man" or "average woman" using a product, you supposedly will be tempted to use it, too.

EXAMPLE   Ordinary working people are giving their support to Candidate X because he knows what their problems are and will work to help them.

Snob Appeal

Snob appeal is the opposite of the plain-folks appeal. Advertisers portray "beautiful people," the "jet set," wealthy and sophisticated men and women to help sell a product. The implied message is that if you use the product that these people use, your life will be more glamorous and exciting. Sometimes, the snob appeal approach tells you that you are unique, special, and extraordinary and should, therefore, use a certain product.

EXAMPLE   Only the elite wear Ultralovely watches—the timepiece of a select
society.

Testimonial

You have seen that to cite an authority, an expert in the field, is
acceptable evidence in an argument. However, the *testimonial* device
uses a famous person to recommend a product or candidate for office.
When that person is not an expert in the field, his or her preference or
opinion is an appeal to the emotions.

EXAMPLES   Kandy Kane, the beautiful singer, urges you to vote for Candidate
X for state senator.
Frank R., an actor who plays a doctor in a television series,
recommends this brand of cereal because he says it is the most
nutritious.

EXERCISE 33. Identifying Appeals to the Emotion.   Make up
an example of each of the following techniques for appealing to the
emotions. See if other members of the class can identify the technique
you have used.

1. Testimonial
2. Loaded words
3. Glittering generality

4. Snob appeal
5. Plain-folks appeal
6. Bandwagon appeal

**REVIEW EXERCISE D. Identifying Fallacies and Appeals to
Emotion.**   The type of persuasive writing that you experience most
often is advertising. Through pictures, music, and words, advertisers try
to get you to buy or use their products. Look through several magazines, and listen critically to advertisements you see and hear on
television and radio. Bring to class as many examples as you can of
logical fallacies and appeals to emotion in these advertisements.

Look also for examples of "good propaganda"—advertisements that
try to convince you to perform a specific action. You might find
advertisements from the American Heart Association, for example, or

letters from a charitable organization asking you to make a donation or to join a club. Bring examples of these to class also. Be prepared to discuss the appeals to emotion and logical fallacies, if any, in these examples.

Expressive and Imaginative Writing

PERSONAL NARRATIVES, STORIES, DRAMA, POETRY

Imaginative writing grows out of the writer's creative mind and imagination. Expressive writing may also be imaginative, but it has the additional characteristic of revealing the writer's own thoughts and feelings. You can find imaginative and expressive writing in popular magazines, literary anthologies, personal journals, and autobiographies. In this chapter, you will learn to write imaginatively and expressively through the personal narrative, the short story, the play, and poetry.

In a personal narrative, the writer relates a true story about an experience or event that is personally significant. In a short story or a play, the writer creates imaginary characters with an imaginary conflict. Like the personal narrative, the story and the play tell what happened. Unlike the personal narrative, which expresses the writer's feelings and thoughts about a personal experience, the story and the play are fictional works and do not necessarily express the writer's own feelings or thoughts. A highly personal form of writing, poetry is both imaginative and expressive. A writer may create a poem to transport the reader to imaginary places and times or to express deep personal feelings through movement, sound, and images.

WRITING A PERSONAL NARRATIVE

A personal narrative is a first-person account of an experience or event. When you write a personal narrative, you share your feelings about how an experience affected you or taught you something about yourself or life in general. Depending on the experience, you may include elements of suspense and action, vivid description, and dialogue, as though you were writing a story about yourself.

PREWRITING

Choosing a Personal Experience

26a. Choose a personal experience that is interesting or unusual.

Think about the events in your life that you remember because they were exceptionally moving, exciting, or humorous, or because they involved some kind of conflict or struggle. Perhaps you have had a once-in-a-lifetime experience, such as meeting a famous person or participating in a political convention or an athletic championship. All of these experiences are your personal sources for subjects. As you consider them, ask yourself if they would be interesting to other people. People enjoy reading about experiences that help them recall or appreciate similar personal experiences. People also enjoy reading about experiences that are unlike any they have had, that give them new insights or satisfy their curiosity about the lives of others. When you have selected a personal experience that would be interesting to others, be certain that it is one you feel comfortable sharing.

EXERCISE 1. Choosing a Personal Experience. Search for an interesting or unusual experience that would be suitable for a personal narrative. Consider significant events in your life that may fit one or more of these categories: (1) a turning point in your life, (2) a "first" time for doing something, (3) a best or worst experience, (4) a learning experience, (5) a meaningful day or holiday. An interesting experience will usually involve some conflict or struggle.

Read your journal for descriptions of interesting experiences and select one that you would like to share. You may also use the technique of clustering. To use clustering, begin by writing and circling one of the five categories in the center of a blank piece of paper. Focus on the category and write whatever experiences come to mind. As you write each idea, circle it and connect it with a line to the circle in the center or to other ideas. Do not judge what you are writing; make the connections freely, without being critical. Continue to write ideas, circling and connecting them to the ideas already on your paper. When you have finished, analyze what you have written and select the experience you think is most interesting or unusual.

EXAMPLE

Identifying Audience and Tone

26b. Identify your audience and choose an appropriate tone.

Once you have selected a subject, think about the people with whom you will be sharing it. If writing a narrative is an assignment, your audience may be your classmates. However, if you are writing for your school newspaper or magazine, your audience will include all the students, teachers, and administrators in the school, as well as their families and the local business people who support the school. For this broader audience, you may need to include background information or explanations of terms you use. You also must consider ways of writing about your experience that will interest people of different ages and backgrounds.

After you identify your audience, you must choose a tone. First, consider your attitude toward the experience and how you would like your audience to respond to it. This will help determine the tone, or feeling, you want to convey in your narrative. For example, if you were to write about the most exciting moment in your life, you might decide that you wanted your audience to feel the same eagerness and astonishment you had felt. You would choose a tone that would convey this feeling through the details you included and the language you used in writing your narrative.

EXERCISE 2. Considering Audience and Tone. Read the following groupings of subject and audience, and choose an appropriate tone for each. First, select an appropriate tone for audience *a*, and then choose one for audience *b*. Be prepared to explain your answers.

EXAMPLE   1. *Subject*: A practical joke that backfired
                 Audience: a. Close friends; b. Young children
           1. *Tone*: *a*. Humorous; *b*. Serious

1. *Subject*: The time I learned to swim
   Audience: a. Classmates; b. Readers of a sports magazine
2. *Subject*: The night I was lost in the woods
   Audience: a. Readers of the school newspaper; b. Young children
3. *Subject*: Meeting a famous movie star
   Audience: a. Readers of gossip magazines; b. People in your community
4. *Subject*: The day I learned how to lose gracefully
   Audience: a. Close friends; b. General audience
5. *Subject*: The most frightening moment of my life
   Audience: a. General audience; b. Young children

Gathering Information and Planning Your Personal Narrative

26c. Gather information and plan your personal narrative.

Gathering information for your narrative depends on your memory of an experience. Retrieving memories can be aided by reading your journal or diary for an account of an event. Also, the techniques of brainstorming and clustering are effective methods of recalling details, actions, and emotions.

Brainstorming is a technique in which you concentrate on one subject, such as "my canoe trip," and list words and phrases ("life jackets," "white-water rapids," and "leaky tent") that come to mind. As you write, do not stop to evaluate the entries in your list; continue to write everything that comes to mind. You may either set a time limit or simply continue until you have exhausted all your ideas. After your brainstorming session, review your list and select the most important details about your subject, filling in related descriptions and events.

Clustering, the technique you used in Exercise 1, helps you concentrate on making connections between your subject and specific details and actions. Again, do not judge what you are writing; keep your mind open to related ideas and words. For example, as you concentrate on the canoe trip, the memory of the white-water rapids might lead you to the memory of a friend falling out of the canoe. When you have finished clustering, you will be able to evaluate which of the related memories are most significant to you and will contribute the most to your narrative.

Once you have gathered sufficient information, plan your narrative by organizing your notes in the order in which you will write. The most frequently used order is *chronological order*, or the sequence in which the experience occurred. You may use an informal format such as the following to prepare your plan:

> *First:*   Three friends and I went to the Wolf River . . .
> *Then:*   We set up camp and . . .
> *Then:*   We climbed in the two canoes and . . .
> *Then:*   (and so forth)
> *Finally:*   We learned how resourceful we could be . . .

As you develop your informal plan, be sure to list all of the actions that contribute to the development of the incident or experience itself. For example, if you are going to write a personal narrative about playing basketball, do not include details about going to the game or details about what was happening elsewhere unless they have some direct bearing on your own experience.

Your plan should indicate where you will include your personal summary or commentary on the experience. The summary or commentary should come either at the beginning or the end, whichever you feel is more appropriate for your own personal narrative.

Read the following narrative by Russell Baker from his book *Growing Up*, in which he describes the change from childhood to adolescence, marked by his first pair of long pants. As you read, notice the organization and the tone of the narrative.

> The changeover from knickers to long pants was the ritual recognition that a boy had reached adolescence, or "the awkward age," as everybody called it. The "teenager," like the atomic bomb, was still uninvented, and there were few concessions to adolescence, but the change to long pants was

a ritual of recognition. There was no ceremony about it. You were taken downtown one day and your escort—my mother in my case—casually said to the suit salesman, "Let's see what you've got in long pants."

For me the ritual was performed in the glossy, mirrored splendor of Bond's clothing store on Liberty Street. She had taken me for a Sunday suit and, having decided I looked too gawky in knickers, said, "Let's see what you've got in long pants." My physique at this time was described by relatives and friends with such irritating words as "beanpole," "skinny," and "all bones." My mother, seeing me through eyes that loved, chose to call me "a tall man."

The suit salesman displayed a dazzling assortment of garments. Suit designers made no concessions to youth; suits for boys were just like suits for men, only smaller. My mother expressed a preference for something with the double-breasted cut. "A tall man looks good in a double-breasted suit," she said.

The salesman agreed. Gary Cooper, he said, looked especially good in double-breasted suits. He produced one. I tried it on. It was a hard fabric, built to endure. The color was green, not the green of new grass in spring, but the green of copper patina on old statues. The green was relieved by thin, light gray stripes, as though the designer had started to create cloth for a bunco artist,[1] then changed his mind and decided to appeal to bankers.

"Well, I just don't know," my mother said.

Her taste in clothes was sound rather than flamboyant, but I considered the suit smashing, and would have nothing else. The price was $20, which was expensive even though it came with two pairs of pants, and upon hearing it I said, "We can't afford it."

"That's what you think, mister," she said to me. "It's worth a little money to have the man of the house look like a gentleman."

In conference with the salesman, it was agreed that she would pay three dollars down and three dollars a month until the cost was amortized. On my attenuated physique, this magnificent, striped, green, double-breasted suit hung like window drapes on a scarecrow. My mother could imagine Gary Cooper's shoulders gradually filling out the jacket, but she insisted that Bond's do something about the voluminous excesses of the pants, which in the seat area could have accommodated both me and a watermelon. The salesman assured her that Bond's famous tailors would adjust the trousers without difficulty. They did so. When finally I had the suit home and put it on for its first trip to church, so much fabric had been removed from the seat that the two hip pockets were located with seams kissing right over my spine.

---

[1] *Bunco artist*: a swindler, in particular one who works as one of a group of swindlers in a card game or lottery.

My mother was dazzled. With visions of a budding Gary Cooper under her wing, she said, "Now you look like somebody I can be proud of," and off to church we went.

Baker begins this narrative with a commentary on the experience. Why do you think he placed the commentary at the beginning rather than at the end? When he begins telling about the experience itself, does he relate the actions in logical order? What comes first, second, and so forth? Many people find Baker's autobiography very interesting. Why might this particular experience be interesting to other people? What are some of the words, phrases, and details that reveal Baker's humorous tone?

EXERCISE 3. Gathering Information for Your Personal Narrative. Use the experience you identified in Exercise 1, or select a different one; then gather information about that experience by using the technique of brainstorming or clustering. Remember to write all the words and ideas as you think of them without judging what you are writing. After you have exhausted all ideas related to your subject, read your list or study your diagram, and determine the most important words and phrases.

EXERCISE 4. Planning Your Personal Narrative. Write an informal plan for your narrative using chronological order. Be sure to include only those details that are related to the experience and to include a personal commentary or reaction.

WRITING

Writing the First Draft

26d. Write a first draft of your personal narrative.

As you write your first draft, keep your narrative plan and notes in front of you. Fill in the important background information, sensory details, essential actions and dialogue, and personal commentary. Remember to write in the first person, using the pronoun *I*. Keep in mind your audience and tone as you select the details and language for your narrative.

EXERCISE 5. Writing a Draft of Your Personal Narrative. Before you begin writing, review your notes and narrative plan from Exercise 4. Write an opening paragraph that will capture your reader's attention and interest and establish your tone. Do not be concerned if you must alter your plan as you write; however, include all the narrative detail that is necessary for rounding out each phase of your narrative. Remember to write in the first person and to include a personal summary or commentary.

REVISING AND PROOFREADING

Revising and Proofreading Your Narrative

26e. Revise and proofread your personal narrative.

You can read and revise your draft more objectively if you have set it aside for two or three days and cleared your mind before you begin. Before you revise your first draft, you must read it several times, each time focusing on something different. First, read the draft as a whole to check the content and organization. Then read it for specifics, such as the use of sensory details and vivid description. Make revisions by cutting out unnecessary words and repetitive descriptive detail. When you are satisfied with your narrative, proofread your draft, correcting grammar, punctuation, and spelling. Finally, make a clean copy of your narrative.

The following model is an example of one writer's revisions. Note how the writer has made changes to strengthen the narrative, make the tone consistent, and correct inaccuracies.

By the time I reached the turn-off for Chicago, it started to get dark; all I

could see were endless pairs of red lights stringing ahead of me and endless

pairs of yellow lights behind. I felt like *the movie astronauts caught in a multicolored,* ~~a bead on a multicolored necklace~~ *streaked corridor of hyperspace with no exit. Where was Mission Control when you needed them?* ~~that glowed in the dark.~~ Should I stay in the center lane or move to the right?

If I moved to the right, could I stop in time in case a driver merged too fast, or was the road too slippery? Would I be caught in the world's longest chain collision on a Chicago highway? Why weren't these cars following the rules *[Come in, Mission Control!"]* they taught us in driver's education? [Every time I tried to allow enough space between me and the car ahead of me, someone cut in.] *tr.*

Again, ~~I felt~~ my fingers ~~cramping.~~ *ed and* The small of my back ~~began to~~ ache *d* because I was sitting bolt upright, as stiff as a steel rod. We never had this much traffic in Lansing, ~~even after the fireworks displays on the Fourth of July. A sign read "Hospital Trauma Center, Next Exit." I was convinced it was a center for hysterical, out-of-town drivers who panicked in traffic. Sometimes a car with a faulty muffler or a strange clanking sound would be in the lane beside me, and I wondered if the noise was coming from my little car.~~ *H* By the time I reached my exit, it was totally dark and I had ~~been~~ *to* squinting to read the *street* signs ~~as I passed by.~~ I had memorized my friends' instructions and followed them to the letter. When I finally pulled into their driveway, my head was pounding and my body hurt from the tension. But I took a deep breath, relieved that my panicked prayers had been answered and that none of the what-ifs had come true. I greeted my friends and ~~made a~~ call ~~home,~~ *ed Mission Control,* trying to sound nonchalant. Later that night as I was falling asleep, I thought, "If I could make it through that trip all right, I can make it through anything!" *I might even volunteer for the next moon shot!"* ~~And so far, that has been true.~~

As you analyze the writer's revisions, consider what has been added, deleted, or moved. Why do you think the writer made the changes in the second sentence of the first paragraph? Why did the writer change the position of the last sentence in that paragraph? In the second paragraph, the writer deleted three sentences. What is the effect of that deletion? It always is difficult to write an ending that is interesting, but not too cute or sentimental. Do you think the writer improved this narrative by changing the last sentence?

GUIDELINES FOR REVISING PERSONAL NARRATIVES

1. Does the beginning of the narrative arouse the interest of the reader and clearly establish the tone?
2. Is the organization appropriate and easy to understand?
3. Is the first-person point of view consistently maintained throughout the narrative?
4. Do the details contribute to the reader's understanding of the personal experience?
5. Are personal feelings about the experience conveyed through the tone of the narrative?
6. Has a personal commentary or summary been included?

CRITICAL THINKING:
Evaluation

When you judge the value of a piece of writing, you are *evaluating* it. This critical thinking skill enables you to assess your own writing and the writing of others. As you evaluate, you determine how well the writer has achieved his or her purpose through organization, content, and tone.

EXERCISE 6. Evaluating the Writing of Others. Either exchange drafts with other classmates or find an example of a personal narrative in a magazine or book. Evaluate the narrative, using the following set of criteria as a guide. Remember that you are evaluating the strengths as well as the weaknesses in the writing. Provide specific examples from the text to support your evaluation.

EVALUATION

Is the organization clear and easy to follow?
Has the writer included enough information?
Is the writer's tone consistent and appropriate?
Has the writer used descriptive details effectively?
Is the language interesting and specific?

EXERCISE 7. Revising and Proofreading Your Personal Narrative. Revise the draft of the personal narrative you wrote for Exercise 5. Use the Guidelines for Revising Personal Narratives. Also refer to the Guidelines for Revising on page 401 and the proofreading guidelines on page 403. Make a final, clean copy of your draft.

WRITING STORIES AND PLAYS

Short stories and plays are popular forms of entertainment—for the audience as well as the writer. In both forms of writing, you create a compact world of fiction, shaped from your imagination and experience. Although stories and plays differ in format, they share common elements: *conflict*, a problem or struggle; *plot*, the development and outcome of the action; *character*, the people who participate in the action; *dialogue*, the spoken words of the characters; and *setting*, the time and place of the actions.

PREWRITING

Choosing a Situation or Conflict

26f. Choose a situation or a conflict suitable for a story or a play.

Selecting a subject for a story or a play involves finding a situation or a problem in which a struggle occurs. This struggle is the conflict, or clash of opposing forces. Conflict, in this sense, does not mean violence. A character may be in conflict with the rules of authority or society, with the forces of nature, or with another character. A character may even experience the conflict of internal forces, such as honesty conflicting with loyalty.

You can find ideas for situations and conflicts by talking with other people, scanning the news for human interest stories, reading your journal, and closely observing the actions and lives of people around you. However, for a short story or short play, remember that the situation and conflict must be limited to actions that can take place in a short period of time, such as a day or, at most, a few weeks.

EXERCISE 8. Choosing a Situation and Conflict. Although ideas for situations and conflicts may come from outside sources, your imagination converts them into interesting subjects. Using your imagination, write one or more possible conflicts for each situation listed below. Finally, select a situation and a conflict that you could develop in a short story or a play.

EXAMPLE   1. Situation: A new video game has been installed at the neighborhood convenience store.
    1. *Conflict: A community group tries to force the store owner to remove the video game.*
    Conflict: A high-school student is worried that her younger brother is becoming obsessed with the video games.

1. Situation: A student must earn money in order to go to college.
2. Situation: The worst tornado in history has hit a small town.
3. Situation: The city council rules that High School No. 2 must be closed and torn down.
4. Situation: A person is a witness to a friend's dishonesty.
5. Situation: A student is accused of cheating on a test.

Considering a Theme

26g. Consider the theme of your story or play.

The theme of a story or play is an implied or stated insight about life or human nature revealed through the interaction of the characters, action, and conflict. Many writers do not actually state the theme; rather, the resolution of the conflict reveals some universal truth about life. Writers may have a theme in mind when they begin the search for a suitable situation and conflict, or they may discover a hidden theme as they develop the plot. In addition, writers sometimes create more than one theme, and readers sometimes discover themes that authors were not aware of. In contrast, some stories and plays, especially suspense thrillers and mysteries, do not have a dominant theme. Nevertheless, most memorable stories and plays embody some statement about life that readers can understand and relate to their own experiences.

When you consider how you might handle theme in your own short story or play, think about the memorable stories or plays you have read or seen and how theme was developed. Remember that the theme(s) and the conflict(s) should be interrelated; theme should grow naturally from the characters, their actions, and the resolution of the conflict.

EXERCISE 9. Considering a Theme. Identify one or more themes that might grow out of the conflict you chose in Exercise 8. Even though the meaning of your story or play may change as it is developed, thinking about possible themes at this time may help you focus your story or play.

EXAMPLE Conflict: A town is threatened by a flood, and the people must work together to save their homes.

Possible Themes: 1. In times of trouble, people display their best or worst qualities.

2. In times of crisis, some people discover what they really value in life.

Considering Purpose, Audience, and Tone

26h. Consider the purpose, audience, and tone of your story or play.

The general *purpose* of a short story or play is to entertain, but the specific purpose may be to evoke feelings of horror or fear, or to move the audience to laughter or tears. That specific purpose reflects your own attitude toward the conflict; for example, you want your audience to be moved to tears because you feel that the situation your characters face is sad.

You reveal your attitude, otherwise known as the *tone* of the story or play, through the details and language that you select. To convey horror, you describe the pitch-black night and the creaking sound of the floorboard just outside the door. To convey humor, you describe how the main character stumbles into the wall of the restaurant as he attempts to impress his date with his knowledge and sophistication. (For a review of tone, see pages 377–79.)

If you have a specific *audience*, you should consider what effect their backgrounds and interests will have on your story or play. If, for example, your audience is made up of students who live in a large city, how will you make them understand a teen-ager's conflict between helping to harvest the tomatoes before frost and marching with the band in the homecoming parade? If the members of your audience are from middle-income families, how will you help them understand the struggle to find enough money to stay in high school? Even if you do not have a specific audience for your story or play, you still must be aware that an audience exists. The members of the audience, whoever they may be, must understand the plot and the characters and find them interesting.

EXERCISE 10. Analyzing Purpose, Audience, and Tone.

Using the situation or conflict you identified in Exercise 8 or any other situation or conflict of your choice, analyze your purpose, audience, and tone by answering the following questions.

1. What will be the specific purpose of this story or play?
2. What is my own attitude toward this conflict and the characters who might be involved in it?
3. What details and what kind of language can I use to convey that tone?
4. What are the backgrounds and interests of the members of my audience?
5. What will I need to do to catch and hold my audience's interest in this story or play?

Selecting a Point of View

26i. Select a point of view that is appropriate for your story.

To determine a point of view for your story, consider the advantages and disadvantages of each point of view and decide which one is suitable. In first-person point of view, the story is told from the point of view of one person. That person may either participate directly in the conflict or witness the conflict. An advantage is that the story is narrated in the first person, *I*, which closely involves the audience. The disadvantage is that only the narrator's thoughts and observations are expressed; everything the reader learns is through the perception of one character.

In the third-person, or omniscient, point of view, the story is narrated by someone who is completely outside the story, but who knows all and can express each character's thoughts and actions. An advantage is the writer's freedom to reveal what any character thinks or does that relates to the conflict. The disadvantage is the distance created by this viewpoint; readers do not feel the urgency or immediacy of the actions.

Once you have selected a point of view, you must use it consistently throughout the story. Note the differences among the three points of view in the following examples:

First-person, directly involved in the conflict. I swallowed hard as I entered the manager's office. I had been dreading this moment for the past week.
First-person, a witness to the conflict. As Anita entered the office, I could tell

she was nervous, in spite of the determined glint in her eyes. Ms. Whiting also seemed determined. She looked, to me, like a general about to order an attack.

Third-person, omniscient. Anita squared her shoulders and tried to recall everything she had planned to say. But Ms. Whiting stared at her menacingly, waiting for her to make that first little mistake.

EXERCISE 11. Writing from Different Points of View. Read the following situation and write a few sentences from each point of view: (a) first-person, directly involved in the conflict; (2) first-person, a witness to the conflict; and (3) third-person, omniscient. Be prepared to discuss the point of view you think would be most appropriate for a story based on the situation and characters.

Situation: Two friends, who are walking through the park, find a wallet in the grass. When they open it, they discover one thousand dollars. One wants to keep the money, but the other wants to turn it in to the police.

Gathering Information and Planning a Short Story or a Play

26j. Gather information and develop a plot outline for your story or play.

As with any other form of writing, you cannot begin planning a story or a play until you have gathered information. Since a story or a play contains a fictional, or imaginary, situation and conflict, you will probably be inventing or creating information, as well as gathering it. You may use any of the typical information-gathering techniques —brainstorming, clustering, consulting your journal, questioning, and so forth. You may, in fact, need to use more than one of these techniques, continuing the gathering and inventing process until you have a thorough understanding of the action, the characters, the setting, and the conflict in your story or play.

Once you have gathered or invented the information, you are ready to develop a plan. The plan of a story or a play is an outline of the plot, the series of actions that builds to a climax and then a resolution of the conflict.

A basic plan for a story or play has three parts—the beginning, the middle, and the end. In the beginning section, you plan how you will present your main characters, establish the tone, suggest the nature of the conflict, and create interest. In the middle section, you plan a series of actions in which one or more characters are faced with problems. These actions build in intensity to the climax, or the point at which the characters are at the height of the struggle and the audience is most involved. In the last section of the outline, you show how the conflict will be resolved.

Study the following excerpts from a story by Hector Hugh Munro to see how he crafted the beginning, the climax, and the ending. Then review the outline on the right which shows how a plan might have been developed for this story.

"THE SCHARTZ-METTERKLUME METHOD"   Typical Plot Outline

Beginning:

Lady Carlotta stepped out onto the platform of the small wayside station and took a turn or two up and down its uninteresting length to kill time till the train should be pleased to proceed on its way. Then, in the roadway beyond, she saw a horse struggling with a more than ample load, and a carter of the sort that seems to bear a sullen hatred against the animal that helps him to earn a living. Lady Carlotta promptly betook her to the roadway, and put rather a different complexion on the struggle. Certain of her acquaintances were wont to give her plentiful admonition as to the undesirability of interfering on behalf of a distressed animal, such interference being "none of her business." Only once had she put the doctrine of noninterference into practice, when one of its most eloquent exponents had been besieged for nearly three hours in a small and extremely uncomfortable may tree by an angry boar-pig, while Lady Carlotta, on the other side of the fence, had proceeded with the water-color sketch she was

Beginning:
Introduce Lady Carlotta, a woman who takes what people say literally. Establish ironic tone. Suggest beginning of plot and conflict, Lady Carlotta's pretense of being the governess.

engaged on, and refused to interfere between the boar and his prisoner. It is to be feared that she lost the friendship of the ultimately rescued lady. On this occasion she merely lost the train, which gave way to the first sign of impatience it had shown throughout the journey, and steamed off without her. She bore the desertion with philosophical indifference; her friends and relations were thoroughly well used to the fact of her luggage arriving without her. She wired a vague noncommittal message to her destination to say that she was coming "by another train." Before she had time to think what her next move might be, she was confronted by an imposingly attired lady, who seemed to be taking a prolonged mental inventory of her clothes and looks.

"You must be Miss Hope, the governess I've come to meet," said the apparition, in a tone that admitted of very little argument.

"Very well, if I must I must,"said Lady Carlotta to herself with dangerous meekness.

. . .

Summary of Middle:

[Several paragraphs have been omitted in which Lady Carlotta goes to the Quabarl mansion, pretends to be the governess, shocks Mrs. Quabarl with her frank discussion of other people for whom she pretends to have worked, and takes Mr. and Mrs. Qualbarl literally when they say she should make history come to life. She has the children acting out the mythical story of the founding of Rome.]

Middle: Show how Lady Carlotta shocks Mrs. Quabarl with her responses to their upper-class style of living. Lead toward climax—Quabarls recommend making history come to life; Carlotta has children acting out the parts of **Romulus** and the she-wolf.

. . .

End:

End:

"Wilfrid! Claude! Let those children go at once. Miss Hope, what on earth is the meaning of this scene?"

"Early Roman history; the Sabine women, don't you know? It's the Schartz-Metterklume method to make children understand history by acting it themselves; fixes it in their memory, you know. Of course, if, thanks to your interference, your boys go through life thinking that the Sabine women ultimately escaped, I really cannot be held responsible."

"You may be very clever and modern, Miss Hope," said Mrs. Quabarl firmly, "but I should like you to leave here by the next train. Your luggage will be sent after you as soon as it arrives."

"I'm not certain exactly where I shall be for the next few days," said the dismissed instructress of youth; "you might keep my luggage till I wire my address. There are only a couple of trunks and some golf clubs and a leopard cub."

"A leopard cub!" gasped Mrs. Quabarl. Even in her departure this extraordinary person seemed destined to leave a trail of embarrassment behind her.

"Well, it's rather left off being a cub; it's more than half grown, you know. A fowl every day and a rabbit on Sundays is what it usually gets. Raw beef makes it too excitable. Don't trouble about getting the car for me, I'm rather inclined for a walk."

And Lady Carlotta strode out of the Quabarl horizon.

The advent of the genuine Miss Hope, who had made a mistake as to the day on which she was due to arrive, caused a turmoil which that good lady

End: Build to climax when Mrs. Quabarl fires Lady Carlotta and Lady Carlotta makes up an outrageous story about the contents of her luggage. End with real governess arriving at Quabarl mansion and Lady Carlotta arriving at her original destination.

was quite unused to inspiring. Obviously the Quabarl family had been woefully befooled, but a
certain amount of relief came with the knowledge.

"How tiresome for you, dear Carlotta," said
her hostess, when the overdue guest ultimately
arrived; "how very tiresome losing your train and
having to stop overnight in a strange place."

"Oh, dear, no," said Lady Carlotta; "not at all
tiresome—for me."

EXERCISE 12. Gathering Information. Using one of the information-gathering techniques explained in Chapter 21, gather information about the situation and conflict you selected in Exercise 8 or any
other situation and conflict you want to develop in a story or play.

EXERCISE 13. Developing a Plot Outline. Use the format explained and illustrated on pages 640–44 to develop a plot outline based
on the information you gathered in Exercise 12.

WRITING

Making Writing Interesting

**26k. Make your story or play interesting by using specific language
and vivid images.**

The content of a piece of writing is more important than its style. If what
you have to say is not interesting, your manner of saying it, no matter
how skillful, will probably not make it seem interesting to your reader.
Still, given the same content for a piece of writing, one writer may
produce an interesting story or play, while another writer may produce a
dull one. The difference may lie in their style of writing.

Interesting Writing Is Specific

Writing is said to be specific when it contains many precise details and
examples. The opposite of specific is vague or general. By comparing

the expressions in each of the following pairs, you will learn what is meant by specific writing.

VAGUE a beautiful day
SPECIFIC mountainous white clouds in a pale blue sky, crisp air, bright sunshine

VAGUE She bore a great burden.
SPECIFIC After her mother died, Sylvia helped raise her younger sisters and brothers and cared for her ill father.

As you compare the following three descriptions, note how, by means of additional details, the writing becomes less vague, more specific.

1. Some of the children on the outing seemed to be more interested than others in the planned activities.

2. The younger children at the Firefighters' Picnic could hardly wait for the games and races to begin. The older children, apparently indifferent toward sack races, the broad jump, and softball, stood around talking and watching the adults.

3. The younger children at the Firefighters' Picnic besieged Chief Barnard, jumping up and down as they circled him, clamoring for the games and races to begin. The older children, apparently indifferent toward sack races, the broad jump, and softball, stood in a group by themselves, talking and watching the adults, who were busily preparing food for everyone's lunch.

The second example is more specific than the first. Comparing the third example with the second, what details do you find that have been expressed more specifically in the third?

Specific writing is not only more interesting than vague writing; it is also clearer. It is clearer because every general statement, every abstraction, is followed by an example that clarifies what the writer means. Notice how the following excerpt from "Tears, Idle Tears," a short story by Elizabeth Bowen, includes specific examples to clarify how the doctor began to form his dreams of the future.

> Everybody had noticed how much courage she had; they said "How plucky Mrs. Dickinson is." It was five years since her tragedy and she had not remarried, so that her gallantness kept on coming into play. She helped a friend with a little hat shop ┤—general statement

called *Isobel* near where they lived in Surrey, bred | specific example
puppies for sale and gave the rest of her time to
making a man of Frederick. She smiled nicely and | specific example
carried her head high. Those two days while Toppy
had lain dying she had hardly turned a hair, for his
sake: no one knew when he might come conscious
again. When she was not by his bed she was waiting
about the hospital. The chaplain hanging about her
and the doctor had given thanks that there were | specific example
women like this; another officer's wife who had
been her friend had said she was braver than could
be good for anyone. When Toppy finally died the
other woman had put the unflinching widow into a
taxi and driven back with her to the Dickinsons'
bungalow. She kept saying: "Cry, dear, cry: you'd
feel better." She made tea and clattered about,
repeating: "Don't mind me, darling: just have a big
cry." The strain became so great that tears
streamed down her own face. Mrs. Dickinson | specific example
looked past her palely, with a polite smile.

Interesting Writing Is Rich in Images

An image is usually a word picture. "The law" is an abstraction; a police officer is an image. "Democracy" is an abstraction; a voter casting a ballot is an image. You cannot see the law or democracy, but you can see a police officer and you can see a voter casting a ballot. Abstract terms are necessary, but the interesting writer strives to give them specific equivalents as often as possible.

The more specific an image is, the more effective it is. "A police officer" is not as specific as "a heavy-set police captain, his gold badge glistening and his shoes highly polished."

Adjectives help you create specific images, but adjectives themselves may be specific in varying degrees. The phrase "pretty girl" is a vague image that is almost meaningless. "A slender redhead with startling blue eyes framed by long black lashes" is more meaningful and interesting.

Compare the following two descriptions of the same scene. Evaluate the images.

1. From our vantage point on the mountainside, we could see several small towns scattered about the valley.
2. From the narrow rock ledge on which we stood high on the precipitous mountainside, we could see the white church spires of five tiny villages scattered across the green floor of the valley.

Your writing also becomes more vivid and interesting when you use specific and active verbs. The forms of the verb *be—am, is, are, was, were, be, being, been*—are totally colorless. They do nothing to enliven style. Vague verbs like *walk, act*, and *move* are weak in their image-making ability. You can think offhand of half a dozen more interesting substitutes for each of them.

Like nouns, verbs—if they are specific enough—do not need modifiers. When a writer writes "The players *trotted* toward the sidelines," the verb *trotted* expresses the action so exactly that adverbs—*slowly, mechanically, dutifully*, for instance—would be unnecessary.

EXERCISE 14. Using Specific Language and Vivid Images. The following passage is an account of a high-school student and his father leaving their farmhouse home early on a very cold winter morning. As you read the passage, list at least ten examples of the writer's use of specific details and images that make the experience real to the reader.

With a faint rending noise the tires came loose from the frozen earth of the barn ramp. The resistance of the car's weight diminished; sluggishly we were gliding downhill. We both hopped in, the doors slammed, and the car picked up speed on the gravel road that turned and dipped sharply around the barn. The stones crackled like slowly breaking ice under our tires. With a dignified acceleration the car swallowed the steepest part of the incline, my father let the clutch in, the chassis jerked, the motor coughed. Caught, *caught*, and we were aloft, winging along the pink straightaway between a pale green meadow and a fallow flat field. Our road was so little travelled that in the center it had a mane of weeds. My father's grim lips half-relaxed. He poured shivering gasoline into the hungry motor. If we stalled now, we would be out of luck, for we were on the level and there would be no more coasting. He pushed the choke halfway in. Our motor purred in a higher key. Through the clear margins of the sheet of frost on our windshield I could see forward; we were approaching the edge of our land. Our meadow ended where the land lifted. Our gallant black hood sailed in the sharp little rise of road, gulped it down, stones and all, and spat it out behind us.

JOHN UPDIKE

Developing Interesting, Believable Characters

26I. Develop interesting, believable characters for your story or play.

The main character in a story or a play is always engaged in the conflict. This character is called the *protagonist*. Sometimes another character, called the *antagonist*, opposes the plans or wishes of the protagonist. A narrative may include other, secondary characters, depending on the writer's plan. Any character in a work of fiction must be believable and interesting or the audience will not care about the action and the conflict.

In developing characters for a short story or play, remember that believable characters are consistent in their behavior. Show a logical reason, a motivation, for any change in behavior. For example, if you created a character who suddenly stops being kind and generous and starts being cruel and heartless, you must explain why. Has the character been hurt or badly disappointed? Does the character feel cheated or betrayed?

You should also avoid stereotypes—the crotchety elderly person or the unintelligent beauty—in your story or play. Such characters are one-sided, trite, and predictable; they are neither interesting nor believable.

Using Description

Description is more obvious in a story than in a play. In a story, you often develop characters by describing their physical characteristics, their actions, and their personality traits. When you write a description of a character in a story, attempt to *show* rather than tell about the character. Select vivid, specific language (see pages 644–47) to create a word picture of the character's appearance, personality, and behavior. In a play, character description most often occurs in stage directions. These directions are intended to aid the director in casting the part and the actor or actress in playing the part. Occasionally, one character will describe another character through dialogue, but you would not want to use that technique often.

The excerpt that follows is from "Tears, Idle Tears." The narrator is describing a woman whose son has just created a scene in the park.

> Once she had got so far as taking her pen up to write to the Mother's Advice Column of a helpful woman's weekly about them. She began: "I am a widow; young, good-tempered, and my friends all tell me that I have great

control. But my little boy—" She intended to sign herself "Mrs. D., Surrey."
But then she had stopped and thought no, no: after all, he is Toppy's
son . . . She was a gallant-looking, correct woman, wearing today in London
a coat and skirt, a silver fox, white gloves and a dark-blue toque put on
exactly right—not the sort of woman you ought to see in a park with a great
blubbering boy belonging to her. She looked a mother of sons, but not of a
son of this kind, and should more properly, really, have been walking a dog.
"Come on!" she said, as though the bridge, the poplars, the people staring
were to be borne no longer. She began to walk on quickly, along the edge of
the lake, parallel with the park's girdle of trees and the dark, haughty
windows of Cornwall Terrace looking at her over the red may. They had
meant to go to the Zoo, but now she had changed her mind: Frederick did
not deserve the Zoo.

ELIZABETH BOWEN

Notice how the writer has combined vivid physical description with
descriptions of the woman's actions and thoughts to create a general
impression of the woman. What are the physical characteristics attribut-
ed to the woman? How do the woman's actions and thoughts contribute
to the general impression of her character? What is the general impression of the woman's character that is created by this description?

The following excerpt is from the descriptive notes for a character
who appears in *You Can't Take It with You.*

PENELOPE VANDERHOF SYCAMORE is a round little woman in her early fifties,
comfortable looking, gentle, homey. One would not suspect that under
that placid exterior there surges the Divine Urge—but it does, it does.
After a moment her fingers lag on the keys; a thoughtful expression comes
over her face. Abstractedly she takes a piece of candy out of the skull,
pops it into her mouth. As always, it furnishes the needed inspiration
—with a furious burst of speed she finishes a page and whips it out of the
machine. Quite mechanically, she picks up one of the kittens, adds the
sheet of paper to the pile underneath, replaces the kitten.

MOSS HART and GEORGE S. KAUFMAN

This description is part of the stage directions just before the character
appears onstage for the first time. The stage directions include a physical
description as well as a description of the behavior of the character as
the play begins. When you develop characters for your own play,
imagine how your characters look and sound and include a description
in your stage directions.

EXERCISE 15. Writing a Description of a Character for a Short Story or a Play. Either select a character from your notes and plot outline (Exercises 12 and 13) or choose a character from the list below. Gather or invent information about the person's physical appearance, actions, and personality traits; then write a one- or two-paragraph description for a short story or a one- or two-paragraph description to be included in the stage directions for a play.

1. A retired teacher who misses the students and classroom
2. A high-school student who desperately wants to be liked
3. An only child whose parents never say no
4. A college athlete whose grades are suffering
5. A job applicant who wants to make a good impression in an interview

Using Dialogue

The way a character speaks and the words a character uses can reveal significant details about the background, personality, and motivations of the character. In a short story or a play, therefore, the effective use of dialogue will help bring your characters to life.

Dialogue should be appropriate for the character's background and personality. For example, if a character is uneducated, the use of nonstandard language will demonstrate the lack of education. If a character is very shy, then halting, quiet speech will reveal that personality.

Study the following exchange between Tony and his father (Kirby) in *You Can't Take It with You.* Think about what the dialogue reveals about Tony's attitude toward his father and about his motivations.

KIRBY (*quietly*): That's enough, Tony. We'll discuss this later.

TONY: No. I want to talk about it *now.* I think Mr. Vanderhof is right—dead right. I'm never going back to that office. I've always hated it, and I'm not going on with it. And I'll tell you something else. (ED *starts down the stairs and crosses to* PENNY.) I didn't make a mistake last night. I knew it was the wrong night. I brought you here on purpose.

ALICE: Tony!

PENNY: Well, for heaven's—

TONY: Because I wanted to wake you up. I wanted you to see a real family—as they really *were.* A family that loved and understood each other. You don't understand *me.* You've never had time. Well, I'm not going to make *your* mistake. I'm clearing out.

KIRBY: Clearing out? What do you mean?
TONY: I mean I'm not going to be pushed into the business just because I'm your son. I'm getting out while there's still time.
KIRBY: But, Tony, what are you going to do?
TONY: I don't know. Maybe I'll be a bricklayer, but at least I'll be doing something *I want to do*. (*Doorbell.*)

MOSS HART and GEORGE S. KAUFMAN

Through this dialogue, Tony is portrayed as a young man who is desperate to get out from under his father's domination. His father, on the other hand, is portrayed as a man who does not understand his son's needs. What does the first line spoken by Kirby tell the audience about Kirby's personality? What part of the dialogue shows the audience that Tony is voicing feelings he has never admitted before? What other personality traits and background information do we learn from this dialogue?

When writing dialogue for a short story, keep in mind that you will need to include explanatory details that let your audience know who is speaking and how he or she is speaking. In a short story, for example, part of the dialogue in the excerpt from *You Can't Take It with You* might be written as follows:

Tony stopped in the middle of the stairway and glared at his father. "Because I wanted to wake you up. I wanted you to see a real family—as they really *were*. A family that loved and understood each other. You don't understand *me*. You've never had time. Well, I'm not going to make *your* mistake. I'm clearing out."

Puzzled by Tony's behavior, Kirby approached his son. "Clearing out? What do you mean?"

"I mean I'm not going to be pushed into the business just because I'm your son. I'm getting out while there's still time."

EXERCISE 16. Revealing Character Through Dialogue. Using the character you described in Exercise 15, create a situation and write dialogue that reveals the character's personality and motivations. You will have to include at least one other character who listens to or disagrees with the main character.

Creating a Setting

26m. Create a setting that is appropriate for your story or play.

Using Stage Directions in a Play

The scenery and the lighting for a play create the setting, which often reveals the year, time of day, or location of the actions. You describe the setting for your play in stage directions at the beginning of the script.

In addition to creating a physical place in which the characters live, the setting establishes a tone for the play. Notice how the first paragraph of the stage directions for *You Can't Take It with You* establishes a mood of friendly chaos. In the second paragraph of the directions, note how the character Penny interacts with the setting.

> The home of MARTIN VANDERHOF—just around the corner from Columbia University, but don't go looking for it. The room we see is what is customarily described as a living room, but in this house the term is something of an understatement. The every-man-for-himself room would be more like it. For here meals are eaten, plays are written, snakes collected, ballet steps practiced, xylophones played, printing presses operated—if there were room enough there would probably be ice skating. In short, the brood presided over by MARTIN VANDERHOF goes on about the business of living in the fullest sense of the word. From GRANDPA VANDERHOF down, they are individualists. This is a house where you do as you like, and no questions asked.
>
> At the moment, GRANDPA VANDERHOF's daughter, MRS. PENELOPE SYCAMORE, is doing what she likes more than anything else in the world. She is writing a play—her eleventh. Comfortably ensconced in what is affectionately known as Mother's Corner, she is pounding away on a typewriter perched precariously on a rickety card table. Also on the table is one of those plaster of Paris skulls ordinarily used as an ash tray, but which serves PENELOPE as a candy jar. And, because PENNY likes companionship, there are two kittens on the table, busily lapping at a saucer of milk.
>
> MOSS HART and GEORGE S. KAUFMAN

EXERCISE 17. Writing Stage Directions. Using the situation, conflict, and characters you have developed in previous exercises, consider an appropriate setting for the story line. The following questions may help you decide which details should be described.

1. *Location*: Should the setting be indoors, in a specific room, or should it be outdoors, in a forest, desert, cave?
2. *Time*: Does the conflict occur in the past, present, or future? Is it morning, afternoon, or night? How can you show this in the setting?
3. *Tone*: What details of setting would establish the mood of your play? What objects on the stage might contribute to the tone?

Using the information you have gathered, write the stage directions for your play. Remember, the audience's first impression will be of what is on the stage as the curtain rises. If a character is present, describe what the character is doing before he or she speaks.

Using Description in a Short Story

A reader's mental picture of a story's setting is inspired by the writer's use of vivid, specific descriptive details. This description is often interwoven with character descriptions, actions, and dialogue to create a total effect—an active, fictional world.

Read the following excerpt from "Tears, Idle Tears" and note how the setting relates to the action of the story and the character development.

> Frederick burst into tears in the middle of Regent's Park. His mother, seeing what was about to happen, had cried: "Frederick, you *can't*—in the middle of Regent's Park!" Really, this was a corner, one of those lively corners just inside a big gate, where two walks meet and a bridge starts across the pretty winding lake. People were passing quickly; the bridge rang with feet. Poplars stood up like delicate green brooms; diaphanous willows whose weeping was not shocking quivered over the lake. May sun spattered gold through the breezy trees; the tulips though falling open were still gay; three girls in a long boat shot under the bridge. Frederick, knees trembling, butted towards his mother a crimson convulsed face, as though he had the idea of burying himself in her. She whipped out a handkerchief and dabbed at him with it under his gray felt hat, exclaiming meanwhile in fearful mortification: "You really haven't got to be such a *baby*!" Her tone attracted the notice of several people, who might otherwise have thought he was having something taken out of his eye.
>
> ELIZABETH BOWEN

In this paragraph Elizabeth Bowen has combined vivid, colorful images of the setting with the development of character and action. Where is this scene taking place? In what way does the setting relate to the action that is taking place? What are some examples of the vivid and colorful language Bowen has used to describe the setting?

EXERCISE 18. Writing a Description of Setting for a Story. Select a setting that would be appropriate for a scene in the plot outline you developed in Exercise 13. Gather information about the setting: sensory details, objects, how the characters interact with the setting. Write one or two paragraphs in which you weave the setting and characters together to create a mood. Select vivid, specific words that will make the scene come alive for the reader.

Writing a First Draft

26n. Write a first draft of your short story or play.

As you approach your first draft, think of your writing as a puzzle. Each element of the story line is a piece of the puzzle, distinctive in action and description, yet part of a unified whole. Begin by reviewing your plot outline and your notes on character development, setting, conflict, and actions.

As you write, focus on a beginning that will capture your audience's attention; then concentrate on developing a sequence of actions that builds in intensity, creating suspense that explodes in the climax. Finally, unite all the elements in your story in the outcome by resolving the conflict. Do not expect a first draft to be perfect; you will have the opportunity to revise later. Professional writers often make several drafts before they are satisfied.

EXERCISE 19. Writing a Draft of Your Short Story. Write a short story based either on the plot outline you have developed or a new conflict. If you choose a new conflict, be sure to repeat all the prewriting steps of gathering information, thinking about characters and setting, and planning the plot and action. Read newspapers, magazines, and your journal to find new ideas for a conflict.

If you encounter difficulties in writing your draft, examine stories by professional writers and note how they handle problems of transition, resolution of conflict, and character development.

EXERCISE 20. Writing a Draft of Your Play. Either use the plot outline you have developed or find a new situation and conflict, and write a first draft of your play. Look for new ideas of conflict by talking with other people, scanning human-interest features, and observing life around you. Remember to gather information on characters and setting and make a plot outline. Prepare your stage directions, and write your draft in play format, as shown on pages 650–52.

REVISING AND PROOFREADING

Revising and Proofreading Your Story or Play

26o. Revise and proofread your story or play.

Allow time between finishing your draft and beginning your revision. If you are away from it for a while, you will be able to read it critically and appreciatively. First, consider your work as a whole and judge whether all the actions contribute to the story line, move it along, or make it believable.

Read your draft again, eliminating unnecessary words and improving and tightening your language. Check for natural-sounding dialogue that reflects the characters and their actions. You may do what many professional writers do at this point—ask someone to evaluate the draft. Often a writer can become too close to the work to see it objectively, and an evaluation by someone else can help point out flaws and reinforce strong points the writer has overlooked. Use the Guidelines for Revising Stories or Plays, the general Guidelines for Revising on page 401, and the Guidelines for Proofreading on page 403 as you work.

When you have trimmed, sharpened, and enlivened your writing until you are satisfied, proofread your draft for accurate spelling, grammar, and punctuation. Make a final copy of your story or play.

GUIDELINES FOR REVISING STORIES

1. Does the beginning of the story capture the audience's interest, establish the tone, and suggest the conflict?
2. Do the actions of the story flow logically and build suspense?

3. Is the point of view consistent throughout the story?
4. Are the characters believable and interesting?
5. Is the main character developed convincingly through description, dialogue, and actions?
6. Does the dialogue sound natural?
7. Is the setting described in vivid, precise language that contributes to the tone and story line?
8. Is the outcome—resolution of the conflict and possible change or growth in the main character—believable and satisfying to the readers?
9. Is the conflict appropriately limited for a short story?

GUIDELINES FOR REVISING PLAYS

1. Do the stage directions establish the setting and tone of the play?
2. Are the first actions of the characters, as the curtain rises, described in the stage directions?
3. Are directions for characters' actions and reactions included with the dialogue?
4. Does the dialogue sound natural?
5. Does the dialogue reveal the personality, background, and feelings of the main character?
6. Is the conflict developed clearly through the dialogue?
7. Is the outcome convincing and satisfying?
8. Is the setting appropriate for the conflict?

EXERCISE 21. Revising and Proofreading Your Story.
Review the Guidelines for Revising Stories and the general guidelines for revising (page 401) and proofreading (page 403). Revise your first draft from Exercise 19 and consider all the points of story line, character development, specific details, and vivid language. Proofread

your revised story for spelling, punctuation, and grammar. Follow the standards for manuscript form on page 404 as you prepare your final copy.

EXERCISE 22. Revising and Proofreading Your Play. Revise the first draft you wrote in Exercise 20. As you work, refer to the Guidelines for Revising Plays, as well as the general guidelines for revising (page 401) and proofreading (page 403). Before you make any changes, read your play aloud from start to finish and note places where improvements are needed. Then read your play for character and conflict development, suspense leading to climax, and a believable, satisfying resolution. After you have made revisions, you may wish to have a classmate evaluate the play. Incorporate any changes that would improve the stage directions, dialogue, characters, or story line.

When you are completely satisfied, proofread your play and make a final copy. Follow the play format used in the excerpts in the text. Leave a wide margin around the page and double-space or write on every other line on one side of the page only.

WRITING POETRY

Poetry has been part of human expression for centuries, since before the development of written language. A poem may be written for a variety of purposes—to express the poet's feelings about something, to share an experience, or simply to convey an unusual image. Some poetry follows definite patterns of meter and rhyme and other poetry does not. There are as many ways of writing a poem as there are people who write, but this section of your textbook will provide you with some techniques that may work for you.

PREWRITING

Selecting a Subject and Developing Ideas for Poetry

26p. Select an appropriate subject and develop ideas for your poem.

Your experience and imagination are unlimited sources for poetic subjects. You may write about rosebuds, parking lots, loneliness, or love. When you choose a subject for poetry, select a person, place, thing, or feeling that is significant to you. Some poetry is so personal it is not meant to be shared; therefore, as you select and develop your subject, be certain you feel comfortable sharing your poem with others.

Gathering ideas for a poem is similar to gathering information for a personal narrative. You can review your journal for descriptions based on close observation or for personal reactions to a significant experience. You may also gather ideas by talking with friends about a shared experience and recording their responses along with your own. Such experiences are not poetry, however, until they have been reshaped in your imagination.

An essential part of the poetic process is concentration. Since every word in a poem is loaded with meaning, you must focus your full attention on the subject so that you can become aware of all the possible images, impressions, and emotions related to your idea.

Exercises 23 and 24 will provide you with methods for selecting a subject and exploring that subject by concentrating on its different possibilities.

EXERCISE 23. Selecting a Subject for Poetry. One method of selecting a subject for a poem is to list the things in your life about which you feel strongly. Copy the following chart and then complete it to identify the extremes of your feelings.

	Most favorite	Least favorite
	(I like, love . . .)	(I dislike, hate . . .)
Season	*spring*	*winter*
Time of day		
Place		
Possession		
Holiday		
Animal		
Music		
Food		
Activity		
Person		
Other		

Review what you have written and evaluate your list by asking yourself why you feel strongly about each item. Identify the subjects that are most significant to you by writing an *X* next to them.

EXERCISE 24. Developing Ideas for Poetry. Using one of the subjects you identified in Exercise 23, write all the words and thoughts that come to mind when you concentrate on that subject. Do not stop to judge what you are writing; let your thoughts flow as quickly as you can write them.

EXAMPLE   *Spring*: melting snow
                lilacs
                soft rain
                blossoms on the trees
                lonely walks
                robins chirping
                new clothes
                wind blowing
                children playing, laughing
                mud splashing on my legs
                perfumed flowers
                cats meowing at night

After you have finished brainstorming, put a check beside the impressions or associations that most strongly reflect your feelings about the subject. Then, concentrate on those words and associations and write sensory details and descriptions for each. Use specific words as you elaborate.

EXAMPLES   *lilacs*: light lavender; deep, royal purple; fragile petals clustered together; soft, sweet scent . . .

     wind: cold sometimes, warm sometimes; whips kites around in the cloudy skies; blows hair, stings my face as one last touch of winter . . .

     mud: dark brown like coffee made of dirt; in the cold, dry flakes on my sneakers . . .

WRITING

Using Rhythm and Repeated Sounds to Develop the Meaning of Your Poem

26q. Use rhythm and repeated sounds to develop the meaning of your poem.

When poets express their personal feelings about a subject, their audience must be able to share and understand those feelings. Poets

communicate their feelings not only through the meaning of the words
they choose, but also through rhythms and repeated sounds.

Rhythm

Poets use rhythm, or meter, to convey both meaning and tone. The poet
combines words to take advantage of their natural accents, using the
meter to stress the words and create a movement that will most
effectively convey the meaning of the poem. Notice how the alternating
stressed and unstressed syllables contribute to the meaning of the
following lines by Donne and Longfellow. Both poets have controlled
the meter to place emphasis on the syllables that carry the meaning of
the poem.

> Ĭ lóng / tŏ tálk / wĭth sóme / ŏld ló / vĕr's ghóst
> Whŏ dĭed / bĕfóre / thĕ gód / ŏf lóve / wăs bórn.
>
> JOHN DONNE

> Téll me / nŏt, ĭn / móurnfŭl / númbĕrs,
> Lífe ĭs / bŭt ăn / émptȳ / dréam.
>
> HENRY WADSWORTH LONGFELLOW

The poet uses meter to control the movement of the poem. For
instance, a series of unstressed syllables, each followed by a stressed
syllable, suggests a walking movement. When you are writing your own
poem, make certain that you use a rhythm that is appropriate to your
subject. If, for example, you are writing about the first fragile lilacs of
spring, a poem that thumps along with a drumbeat meter would be
neither suitable nor effective.

Most poetry written before the nineteenth century, as well as much
of the poetry written through this century, has a regular rhythmic
pattern. In some poems, the rhythm is consistent in every line. In other
poems, the rhythm, or pattern, changes from one line to another, but is
consistent within the whole poem. The poem may, for example, have
three accents in the first, second, and third lines, followed by four
accents in the fourth line. Read the following stanzas from a poem from
the seventeenth century and notice how the rhythm changes in the
fourth line of each stanza but remains constant from one stanza to the
next.

Sweet day, so cool, so calm, so bright,
The bridal of the earth and sky;
The dew shall weep thy fall tonight,
    For thou must die.

Sweet rose, whose hue angry and brave
Bids the rash gazer wipe his eye;
Thy root is ever in its grave,
    And thou must die.

                GEORGE HERBERT

Study the rhythmic pattern in this poem. What relationship do the accented syllables have to the meaning of the poem?

    The poem by George Herbert is an example of formal poetry, sometimes called traditional poetry because it was the established way of writing for hundreds of years. Free verse, poetry that does not have a regular rhythm or rhyme, is frequently used by contemporary writers.

    Although free verse does not depend on regular meter, it does have rhythm. The rhythm of free verse is a natural rhythm, much like the sounds of speech. Just as accented syllables of words stress meaning in everyday speech, as in "I want to go," the accented and unaccented syllables in free verse reinforce the meaning of a poem. Read the following stanza from *Song of Myself*, and then compare the natural rhythms in this poem to the regular rhythms in the poem by Herbert.

I believe a leaf of grass is no less than the journey-work of the
    stars,
And the pismire is equally perfect, and a grain of sand, and the
    egg of the wren,
And the tree toad is a chef-d'œuvre for the highest,
And the running blackberry would adorn the parlors of
    heaven,
And the narrowest hinge in my hand puts to scorn all machin-
    ery,
And the cow crunching with depressed head surpasses any
    statue,
And a mouse is miracle enough to stagger sextillions of in-
    fidels. . . .

                WALT WHITMAN

After you have compared the two poems, think about the use of rhythm in the stanza by Whitman. How does the language of the poem help you to understand the significance of the experience for the poet? How does the natural rhythm work to convey meaning? Do you think you would have enjoyed this poem more if it had been written in regular meter?

Repeated Sounds

In poetry, patterns of repeated sounds help to convey meaning in much the same way rhythm does. The repeated sounds may be regular or random, exact or inexact. They may occur at the end of lines, in the middle of lines, and at the beginning of lines. Read the following groups of words and note how repeated sounds are used to evoke an emotional response and convey meaning:

1. bring / sling / thing / fling
2. I climb sky high
3. hear the roar of snarling cars
4. the weary woman wondered why

Each group of words represents a pattern of sound. The first group shares a common vowel sound as well as a common sound at the end. These are called exact, or perfect, *rhymes*. The second group repeats a vowel sound, the long *i*. This kind of repeated sound is called *assonance*. The third group repeats the consonant sound of *r* within or at the end of words and is called *consonance*. The fourth group of words repeats identical or similar sounds at the beginning of words and is called *alliteration*.

Formal poetry contains regular rhyme as well as regular rhythm. Read the following poem by Christina Rossetti and notice the regular pattern of exact rhyme at the ends of the lines.

Remember me when I am gone away,	a
Gone far away into the silent land;	b
When you can no more hold me by the hand,	b
Nor I half turn to go, yet turning stay.	a
Remember me when no more day by day	a
You tell me of our future that you plann'd:	b
Only remember me; you understand	b
It will be late to counsel then or pray.	a
Yet if you should forget me for a while	c
And afterwards remember, do not grieve:	d
For if the darkness and corruption leave	d
A vestige of the thoughts that once I had,	e
Better by far you should forget and smile	c
Than that you should remember and be sad.	e

CHRISTINA GEORGINA ROSETTI

Notice that the first eight lines of the poem, which is a sonnet, have the rhyme scheme *abbaabba*; the next six lines have the rhyme scheme *cddece*.

In a poem, rhyme has three purposes: (1) It gives the audience the pleasure of hearing repeated sounds, usually at regular intervals; (2) it sets off the lines; and (3) it helps hold the poem together. As in music, rhyme in poetry can also be an emotional stimulus. In the following lines from a sonnet, for example, notice how the rhyme contributes to the poet's feelings about his love:

> For thy sweet love remember'd such wealth brings
> That then I scorn to change my state with kings.
> WILLIAM SHAKESPEARE

For a better understanding of the purpose of rhyme, compare your emotional response to these lines to your response when the same feeling is expressed without the rhyme: When I remember your love, I know I would not change places with kings.

When you write poems with regular rhythm and exact rhyme, you should be careful not to produce a monotonous or mechanical effect. Study their use by poets like Shakespeare and Rosetti, and be careful to rhyme words that are important to the meaning of the poem.

In free verse, the repeated sounds are much more likely to be irregular and inexact, unlike the perfect rhyme used by Christina Rosetti. Notice the lack of regularly repeated sounds in the following excerpt from "The Horses"[1] by Edwin Muir.

> And then, that evening
> Late in the summer the strange horses came.
> We heard a distant tapping on the road,
> A deepening drumming; it stopped, went on again
> And at the corner changed to hollow thunder.
> We saw the heads
> Like a wild wave charging and were afraid.
> We had sold our horses in our fathers' time
> To buy new tractors. Now they were strange to us
> As fabulous steeds set on an ancient shield
> Or illustrations in a book of knights.
> We did not dare go near them. Yet they waited,
> Stubborn and shy, as if they had been sent
> By an old command to find our whereabouts
> And that long-lost archaic companionship.

---

[1] In this poem, the world has been devastated by atomic war and tractors can no longer be used to till the soil.

In the first moment we had never a thought
That they were creatures to be owned and used.
Among them were some half-a-dozen colts
Dropped in some wilderness of the broken world,
Yet new as if they had come from their own Eden.
Since then they have pulled our ploughs and borne our loads.
But that free servitude still can pierce our hearts.
Our life is changed; their coming our beginning.

EDWIN MUIR

EXERCISE 25. Writing a Poem with Regular Rhyme and Rhythm. Using the ideas you developed in Exercise 24 or another set of images and ideas of your choice, write a poem of at least eight lines. Develop a regular rhythm and rhyme scheme that reflect the meaning and impression you want to convey. Consider, for example, whether you need a threatening, heavy beat, or a light, cheerful beat. Consider what words you should rhyme. What are the important words and images, and what words could you use to rhyme with them? After you have chosen an appropriate rhythm and rhyme scheme, write your poem.

EXERCISE 26. Writing a Free-Verse Poem. Using the ideas you developed in Exercise 24 or any other set of images and ideas of your choice, write a free-verse poem of at least twelve lines. Think about some of the phrases and words from the ideas you gathered. Read them aloud and listen to the natural patterns they create. Think about the important words on your list. Are there any sounds—beginning sounds, vowel sounds, consonant sounds—that you could repeat to reinforce meaning and the impression you want to create? After you have discovered the natural rhythm of your words and ideas and decided how you will use repeated sound to convey meaning, write your poem.

Using Sensory Details and Vivid Language

26r. Use sensory details and vivid language in your poem.

Everything you experience through your senses may be recalled in descriptive images. For example, as you sit at your desk, you may be able to recall the sound of a cicada at nightfall or a scene observed during a long-ago vacation. You may recall the taste of a juicy apple or the smell of turkey roasting in the oven. You may recall the bite of the winter wind or the feathery weight of a snowball in your hand. Such recall of sensory perceptions when evoked by memory or words is known as *imagery*.

As you write your poem, use sensory details to evoke images in the minds of your readers. The following poem contains a series of distinct images evoked by the poet's use of the underlined sensory details. As you read the poem, try to experience the sights, sounds, smells, and physical sensations that the poet presents.

MEETING AT NIGHT

The gray sea and the long black land;
And the yellow half-moon large and low;
And the startled little waves that leap
In fiery ringlets from their sleep,
As I gain the cove with pushing prow,
And quench its speed i' the slushy sand.

Then a mile of warm sea-scented beach;
Three fields to cross till a farm appears;
A tap at the pane, the quick sharp scratch
And blue spurt of a lighted match,
And a voice less loud, thro' its joys and fears,
Than the two hearts beating each to each!

ROBERT BROWNING

Reread "Meeting at Night." Notice the poet's use of *vivid language* —specific words that identify or describe the sights, sounds, smells, feelings, or physical sensations that he wishes his readers to experience. In line 1, for example, the adjectives *gray, long*, and *black* help us picture the sea and the coast. In line 2, the adjectives *yellow, half, large*, and *low* help us see the moon hanging in the sky. Note also the effective use of such specific verbs as *leap* (line 3) and *quench* (line 6) and of such specific nouns as *tap, scratch* (line 9), and *spurt* (line 10).

EXERCISE 27. **Writing a Poem with Sensory Details and Vivid Language.** The poem you write for this assignment will be one which, like "Meeting at Night" (above), includes sensory details and vivid language.

PREWRITING   In planning your poem, list nouns, verbs, adjectives, and adverbs that identify the sensations that you wish your audience to experience.

WRITING   Use a subject that you identified in Exercise 23, or select one from the list below. After you have written a first draft, give your poem a title.

rain	a siren in the night
a motorcycle ride	a nightmare
a summer sunset	a favorite meal
an empty classroom	an old toy

Using Figurative Language

26s. Use figurative language in your poetry.

As you have seen, appeals to the imagination can be accomplished by the use of sensory details and vivid language. Poets use another technique—*figurative language*—that you should not overlook as you write your poems. Figurative language makes use of *figures of speech*. Those figures of speech used most frequently in poetic expression are the simile, the metaphor, and personification.

A *simile* is a direct comparison of two things that are usually unlike in most respects. In similes, the comparison is introduced by *like* or *as* or by a similar word (*seem, appear,* for example). Read these examples of similes:

1. I am still as an autumn tree.—ANNE MORROW LINDBERGH
2. We have tomorrow
   Bright before us
   Like a flame.
   ───LANGSTON HUGHES

Notice the structure of the simile: (1) something is mentioned (*I* in example 1); (2) then a word such as *like* or *as* is used; (3) then something else is mentioned (*autumn tree* in example 1). Which two things are being compared in example 2?

A *metaphor* is an indirect comparison that implies a likeness between two unlike things without using *like* or *as*. Read these examples of metaphors:

1. Love is a clock and the works wear out.—CARL SANDBURG

2. Tears
   The crystal rags
   Viscous tatters
   of a worn-through soul. —MAYA ANGELOU

In example 2, instead of saying that "Tears are *like* crystal rags," Maya Angelou implies that tears *are* crystal rags. What are the implied comparisons in example 1?

Your daily language is filled with similes and metaphors that have been used so often that they have become clichés. Avoid such overused comparisons as "He's as neat as a pin," "She's a bump on a log," and "My love is like a rose."

Personification is a metaphor in which human qualities are given to nonliving things, abstractions, or animals. In the following metaphor, for example, the poet has personified the morning by dressing her in a russet mantle and having her walk over the dew.

> But look, the morn, in russet mantle clad,
> Walks o'er the dew of yon high eastward hill.
>
> WILLIAM SHAKESPEARE

EXERCISE 28. Writing a Poem with Figurative Language. The poem you write for this assignment will be one in which you use figurative language.

PREWRITING   Before writing your poem, it may be helpful to complete the following items by making an unusual or a fresh comparison.

1. A thunderstorm is like . . .
2. I'm as tired as . . .
3. The night is . . .
4. The river roams . . .

5. Friends are like . . .
6. My feet . . .
7. A tiny mouse . . .
8. The bus . . .

Select an appropriate poetic form for your subject, choosing a form that is different from the one you used in Exercise 27.

WRITING   Write a short poem of three to six lines in which you use a simile, a metaphor, or personification. Use a subject that you identified in Exercise 23 or another of your choice. After you have written a first draft, give your poem a title.

REVISING AND PROOFREADING

Revising and Proofreading Your Poem

26t. Revise and proofread your poetry.

Set your poem aside for a while, so that when you begin to revise it, you can experience the sensory details and picture the images as your readers might. Poetry should please the ear as well as the eye, and one of the best ways to begin your revision is to read your poem aloud several times.

Read your poem first for *content*. Think about the impression you are trying to convey and examine whether you have been successful. Think about whether you have included enough details and specific images to share your impressions and ideas with your audience. Consider any figurative language you may have used. Will the figures of speech help your readers to see things in new ways, in ways that will support the general impression in your poem?

You must also examine the *form* of your poem. If you have used repeated sounds—rhyme, alliteration, consonance, assonance—think about the effectiveness of those sounds. Do the repeated sounds enhance the meaning of your poem without overpowering the reader or becoming mechanical? If you have used a regular rhythm, does the beat create a mood or a tone that is appropriate for the content of your poem? If you have used free verse, do the natural rhythms of the words you have chosen enhance the meaning of your poem?

Finally, think about *spelling, punctuation,* and *capitalization.* Note that each line of a poem usually begins with a capital letter. Some poets, however, use capitalization, or the lack of it, to reflect their meaning; for instance, by writing everything in lower case, a poet could make important ideas seem trivial. Since punctuation in poetry will affect the rhythm—commas indicating slight pauses, colons and end punctuation indicating longer pauses—you will want to make sure that you have used punctuation that supports the rhythm you have chosen. Review all of your punctuation and capitalization and determine how to use these mechanical devices to help express the meaning of your poem.

GUIDELINES FOR REVISING POETRY

1. Are the sounds of the poem—rhyme and alliteration—true to the meaning and imagery of the poem?
2. If there is rhyme, does it sound natural or is it forced or repetitive?
3. If there is alliteration, does it contribute to the meaning and the imagery?
4. Does the meter accurately control the desired movement of the poem?
5. Does the poem include sensory details and vivid language that will evoke the desired imagery?
6. If there is figurative language, is it clear and fresh?
7. Are the punctuation marks and capital letters appropriate for the rhythm and poetic form?

EXERCISE 29. Revising and Proofreading Your Poetry. Using the Guidelines for Revising Poetry, revise and proofread the poems you wrote in this chapter. When you are satisfied that your poems meet all the requirements of the Guidelines for Revising Poetry, make a clean copy of each. Be sure to give each poem a title.

CHAPTER 26 WRITING REVIEW 1

Writing About Conflict and Theme. Write a short story or a short play about an internal, nonviolent conflict in which the main character must make a choice between two possible actions. Consider the conflict and then determine the theme, as in the following:

CONFLICT A young woman is about to go away to college. She is excited, but she has been having nightmares about failing. Her fears have grown so strong, she is tempted to stay home.

THEME People fear most what they do not understand.

CONFLICT A young man who works part-time in a grocery store sees a poor, homeless old man shoplift food. He is torn between his compassion for the man and his duty to report the shoplifter.

THEME Sometimes you have to be cruel in order to be kind.

PREWRITING   Look through your journal to find human-interest features, brainstorm, cluster, or talk to other people to gather ideas and information on a conflict and theme. Think about how you can use description, dialogue, and actions to reveal the main character's personality and background. Consider the setting and the ways it can reflect your tone and the character's struggle. Develop a series of actions that lead to the character's resolution of the conflict and write a plot outline, specifying the beginning, middle (actions and climax), and outcome.

WRITING   Follow your plot outline as you write, but make changes if they improve the story line. Try to create an interesting beginning and then build suspense toward the climax. Show how the resolution causes a believable change in the main character. As you write, try to use interesting, specific language. If you are writing a story, remember to use a consistent point of view. If you are writing a play, include directions for the characters' movements on the stage.

REVISING AND PROOFREADING   Put aside your first draft for a day or two before you begin to revise. When you do revise, read your draft as a whole and evaluate the content, organization, and effectiveness of your writing. Use either the Guidelines for Revising Stories on pages 655–56 or the Guidelines for Revising Plays on page 656. When you are satisfied with your revision, proofread it, using the guidelines on page 403. Make a clean, final copy of your story or play.

CHAPTER 26 WRITING REVIEW 2

Writing a Sonnet.   Write a sonnet about a person or an experience that has affected you deeply. For example, you may have been inspired by someone who showed great courage in overcoming a disability or who taught you something about yourself or life in general. You may have hiked through the mountains and felt overpowering awe or seen a painting that made you feel joyful or sad. Use a rhythm that is appropriate for the meaning of your poem, and choose one of the following rhyme schemes: *abbaabbacddcee* or *ababcdcdefefgg*.

PREWRITING   Read your journal entries, observe people and things around you, brainstorm, or use clustering to identify a subject. Gather information on the sensory impressions, vivid words, and fresh comparisons your subject evokes. Determine how you want readers to respond and select a tone that will evoke that response. Also think about the ways rhyme and meter can enhance your subject.

WRITING   Using your notes, synthesize your ideas. Begin with a line and build your poem, making changes as you write. Try to vary the rhythm occasionally to avoid a singsong meter. Remember that exact rhyme, assonance, and consonance are alternatives for your rhymes. Include sensory details and figurative language that heighten the effect of your poem and create interest. Choose a title for your poem.

REVISING AND PROOFREADING   Wait a day or two before you begin your revision. Use the Guidelines for Revising Poetry on page 669 as you work. Read your poem aloud several times and evaluate the rhyme and meter, as well as the meaning and tone of the sonnet. Eliminate weak or unnecessary words and determine if the details and figurative language express exactly what you intended.

After you revise, check your punctuation, capitalization, spelling, and grammar. Refer to the general proofreading guidelines on page 403. Finally, prepare a clean copy of your sonnet.

CHAPTER 27

Writing a Research Paper

RESEARCH, WRITING, DOCUMENTATION

A research paper is an extended expository composition based on information gathered from a variety of sources to support the writer's ideas. In this chapter you will learn to use the writing process to prepare a research paper. You will also learn certain special procedures that apply primarily to papers based on research.

Like any extensive undertaking requiring sustained concentration over a period of several weeks, the preparation of a research paper requires self-discipline. It is more than likely that writing a research paper will do more to sharpen your study techniques and strengthen your self-discipline than any other assignment.

Plan to devote enough time to your research paper to ensure that your work will be thorough and unhurried. Research work is careful work. Do not be satisfied with a paper that will merely "get by"; take pride in the accuracy and completeness of your work.

PREWRITING

SELECTING A SUBJECT

27a. Select a subject that interests you and that can be researched in the sources available to you.

Since you are to do a large amount of reading, you owe it to yourself to choose a subject you really want to know more about. In a small way, the research paper requires you to become an authority on a subject; choose one that will hold your interest.

The subject must also lend itself to research in the sources available to you. For this reason, the life of a famous person is not a good subject for a research paper; a complete biography of the person has probably already been published, and you would tend to rely too much on just that one source. Subjects about which very little has been published may also be unsuitable. You may not be able to find information on highly technical subjects or subjects that have only recently been developed. No matter how interested you are in a subject, it will not be usable unless you have access to source material on it.

The library is not the only source of material, of course. You may be able to find some excellent books on your subject in inexpensive paperback editions. Government publications are also inexpensive. Other possible sources of information are personal interviews and correspondence with authorities on the subject. If you were writing a history of your community, for example, you could arrange to interview one of the long-time residents. For a paper on conservation efforts in your state, you could interview a local conservation officer or write to the state commissioner.

Another consideration to keep in mind is that the subject you decide to research should be a significant one. Subjects that are not of lasting importance, such as a current fad at your school, are not worth hours of research (although an examination of American fads in the last decade might be).

Finally, be certain that the subject you select can be presented objectively. The purpose of research is to discover the facts; if you choose a potentially controversial subject, you will need to examine the evidence on both sides of the issue.

EXERCISE 1. Selecting a Subject. Using one of the techniques that you learned in Chapter 21, such as brainstorming or clustering, list at least five subjects you would like to research. Evaluate the subjects in terms of the considerations discussed above, and choose one of the subjects to research.

Limiting Your Subject

27b. Limit your subject to a topic that you can cover adequately within the assigned length of the paper.

If you try to write a research paper on a broad subject, you will either spend far too much time on the paper and exceed the assigned length or simply skim the surface of the subject. Taking the time to limit the scope of the subject now will save you time and energy later and will result in a better paper.

Limiting a subject involves analyzing the subject to determine what it consists of—what its logical divisions are. Suppose you think you want to write a research paper on the broad subject of space, for example. You could analyze the subject as follows:

1. Space
2. Space travel
3. The U.S. space program

This topic is still too broad for a research paper of approximately 2,000 words; entire books have been written about the U.S. space program. Notice how the scope of the subject narrows and the paper becomes more manageable as you continue to analyze the subject:

4. The space shuttle
5. Materials and equipment developed for the shuttle
6. The development of the shuttle's protective ceramic tiles

As this example shows, it is possible to carry the limiting process too far; for item 6, for example, you would probably need access to NASA's files. Depending on the resources available to you, either item 4 or item 5 would probably be limited enough for your research paper.

As another example, suppose that you are interested in parapsychology, the study of mental phenomena. Your analysis of the subject might produce the following divisions:

1. Parapsychology
2. Extrasensory perception
3. Clairvoyance

At this point you have focused on one category of extrasensory perception, clairvoyance, but the topic is still too broad; a great deal could be written about clairvoyance. To further limit the topic, you must focus on one particular aspect of clairvoyance, such as "scientific studies of clairvoyance." This topic is limited enough to be manageable within the length of a research paper, yet not so limited that finding information on it will be difficult.

EXERCISE 2. Recognizing Suitable Topics. Decide which of the following topics are suitable for research papers and which are too broad, too limited, or otherwise unsuitable. Be prepared to explain your answers and to suggest how each unsuitable topic might be improved.

1. The novels of Virginia Woolf
2. Careers in medicine
3. The renovation of the Statue of Liberty
4. The contributions of Hispanics
5. The life of Sacajawea
6. The Common Market
7. Nuclear energy for industrial power
8. The Ferraro-Bush vice-presidential debate
9. Anthropomorphism in children's literature
10. Brain cell abnormalities in victims of Alzheimer's disease

EXERCISE 3. Limiting Your Subject. Analyze the subject you selected in Exercise 1 or another subject to develop several topics that would be suitable for a research paper. Make sure that the topics are neither too broad nor too narrow and that adequate resources on them are available.

CONSIDERING PURPOSE, AUDIENCE, AND TONE

27c. Evaluate your topic in terms of purpose, audience, and tone.

Before you begin your research, consider your topic in terms of the purpose, audience, and tone of a research paper.

CRITICAL THINKING:
Evaluating Your Topic in Terms of Purpose, Audience, and Tone

The critical thinking skill of evaluation requires a set of criteria, or standards, against which you can judge an idea or practice. The criteria for evaluating the topic of a research paper in terms of purpose, audience, and tone have been established through long usage by scholars.

Purpose

The purpose of a research paper is the same as that of other expository papers: to inform or to explain. The basis on which you limit your original subject will largely determine whether your topic is suitable for exposition. Suppose, for example, that your original subject was "Impressionism," and after analyzing it on the basis of features, you developed a topic such as "Line and pattern in the work of Mary Cassatt." Although such a topic might result in a good descriptive composition, it is not appropriate for a research paper. Evaluate your topic carefully to make sure that it will result in exposition. If not, you will need to select another basis on which to limit your original subject.

Audience

Your audience for a research paper (unless your teacher specifies otherwise) is a general one: educated people from many different backgrounds, who are interested in almost any topic that is written about clearly and in nontechnical terms. Such an audience would, for example, be interested in reading a nontechnical explanation of the formation of the Great Lakes by glaciers. This topic would not be suitable for an audience of professional geographers, however; it would offer them no new information. To avoid topics that are too technical for readers other than specialists, keep in mind that your audience is a general one.

Tone

As a serious assignment, the research paper requires a serious tone. For a general audience, try to achieve a tone that is formal and impersonal. Avoid informal expressions and first-person pronouns. The topic "my reactions to the outlandish threads women wore in the old days," for example, is inappropriate; it uses the first-person pronoun *my*, and "outlandish," "threads," and "the old days" are informal expressions more appropriate for use with people you know well. Recasting the topic as "women's fashions in the post-World War II era" solves these problems and conveys a serious attitude.

EXERCISE 4. Evaluating Topics. Evaluate the following topics for research papers in terms of purpose, audience, and tone. Be prepared to suggest how the topics might be improved.

1. Errors of calculation in Beethoven's symphonic orchestration
2. Hispanic voting patterns in the 1984 U.S. Senate elections
3. My super trip to a whale of a cave in Kentucky
4. Ethnic distribution of visitors to the 1984 New Orleans World Fair
5. Philosophical issues in the art of M. C. Escher

REVIEW EXERCISE A. Evaluating Your Topic. Evaluate each of the topics you developed in Exercise 3 in terms of purpose, audience, and tone. Decide which topic you will write your paper on and, if necessary, revise it so that it is appropriate for a research paper. Your teacher may ask you to submit the topic for approval before you begin your research.

PREPARING A WORKING BIBLIOGRAPHY

27d. Prepare a working bibliography.

The first step in researching your topic is to compile a working bibliography—a list of potential sources of information. Before checking the *Readers' Guide to Periodical Literature*, a vertical file, and specialized reference books, however, turn first to a good encyclopedia.

If you have limited your subject sufficiently, you will not find an entire encyclopedia article on your topic. You will, however, find an article on the broader subject of which your topic is a division. This article may suggest related ideas for you to keep in mind as you do your research. It may even lead you to revise your topic or to replace it with another topic. Be sure to consult your teacher if you make any major changes in your topic at this stage.

Research Aids

To find sources of information on your specific topic, you will need to use a number of the research aids explained in Chapters 34 and 35. Review those chapters before you continue your research, making sure that you are thoroughly familiar with the information in them. Whatever your topic, you will probably use the following research aids:

1. **The library catalog**. Do not confine your search to those materials cataloged under your specific topic. The listings for the broad subjects of which your topic is a part will also yield useful resources. If your topic is "clairvoyance," for example, you will probably find useful materials under more general headings, such as "Parapsychology" and "Extrasensory Perception."

2. **The *Readers' Guide*.** Past volumes of this index to periodicals will be just as useful as recent issues for most topics.

3. **Specialized reference books**. The specialized reference books listed in Chapter 35 can provide you with useful material and titles of additional books that may be worth investigating.

You can get an idea of whether a book or article is potentially useful by asking the following questions:

1. *Is the author an authority on the subject?* Authors who have written several books or articles on a subject may be especially knowledgeable in their fields. One indication that an author is recognized as an authority is the inclusion of his or her works in other works on the same subject.

2. *Is the book or article listed in any of the bibliographies you have examined?* Materials that appear repeatedly in bibliographies may be useful sources of information.

3. *What kind of magazine published a particular article?* Mass-circulation magazines, such as most of those sold at newsstands, generally do not treat topics in enough detail to be suitable sources for research papers. You will find more authoritative and in-depth treatments in specialized magazines and scholarly journals.

4. *What audience is a particular book intended for?* In general, books written for younger readers are too simple to be useful as resources for research papers. Books for specialists, on the other hand, may be too complex for a general audience.

EXERCISE 5. Evaluating Potential Sources.   Suppose that you were writing a research paper on scientific studies of clairvoyance. From their titles, which of the following sources sound as if they would be very helpful? Which ones would you not be sure about without more information? Which ones would probably be of little help?

1. Aune, David E. *Prophecy in Early Christianity and the Ancient Mediterranean.*
2. Bowles, Norma, and Fran Hynds. *PsiSearch.*
3. Christopher, Melbourne. *ESP, Seers, and Psychics.*
4. Cohen, Daniel. *ESP: The Search Beyond the Senses.*
5. Forman, Joan. *The Mystery Factor in Timeslips, Precognition, and Hindsight.*
6. Gattey, Charles Neilson. *They Saw Tomorrow: Seers and Sorcerers from Delphi Till Today.*
7. Grim, Patrick, ed. *Philosophy of Science and the Occult.*
8. Hansel, D.E.M. *ESP: A Scientific Evaluation.*
9. Tart, Charles T. *The Application of Learning Theory to ESP Performance.*
10. Taylor, John. *Science and the Supernatural.*

Bibliography Cards

As you compile your working bibliography, record each source on a card—one source to a card. Include *all* of the information in the following list; you will need it later, when you prepare the bibliography. For books, you can obtain this information from the library catalog; for articles, from the *Readers' Guide.* For pamphlets and newspapers, you must check the source itself to find the necessary information.

BOOKS

1. Call numbers in upper right-hand corner of the card
2. Author's (or editor's) full name, last name first for alphabetizing later (Indicate editor by placing *ed.* after the name.) If a book has two or more authors, only the name of the first author is written last name first; the names of the others are written first name first. For three or more authors, write only the first and add *et al.*
3. Title and subtitle, underlined (and editions, if second or later; and number of volumes, if more than one). Pamphlets only: series and number, if any
4. City of publication
5. Publisher's name (shortened, if clear)
6. Most recent copyright year (or date, for some pamphlets)

MAGAZINE, SCHOLARLY JOURNAL, NEWSPAPER,
AND ENCYCLOPEDIA ARTICLES

1. Author's full name (unless article is unsigned)
2. Title of article, in quotation marks
3. Name of magazine, journal, newspaper, or encyclopedia, underlined

4. For popular press magazines: date and page numbers. For newspapers: date, edition, section, page numbers. For scholarly journals: volume, year of publication (in parentheses), page numbers. For encyclopedias arranged alphabetically: edition (if given) and year of publication.

Although the card catalog will give you, for a book, all the information you need for your working bibliography card, it will not tell you much about the book's contents. One way to examine quickly a number of possibly useful books is to go to the shelf in the library where, according to its call number, a potential source is located. Since nonfiction books are classified by subject, you will find this source and on the neighboring shelves most of the books the library has on the subject. A glance at the table of contents and index will tell you how useful each book might be.

If you were writing on Shakespeare's Globe Theatre, for example, and you found listed in a book's table of contents a chapter on the Globe or a chapter on Elizabethan theaters including the Globe, you would list the book in your working bibliography. Even if the table of contents does not reveal information on your subject, such information may still be in the book. Look in the index and judge the usefulness of the book by the number of pages devoted to your subject. A listing such as "Globe Theatre, 250–75," for instance, would suggest that the book would be worth including in your working bibliography.

Assign each card in your working bibliography a number, and write the number clearly in the upper left-hand corner. Using these numbers when you take notes will save you the task of identifying the source of each note in detail. Notice the arrangement and punctuation of the information on the sample cards shown on page 681. Unless your teacher instructs you otherwise, follow this format exactly.

EXERCISE 6. **Preparing Bibliography Cards.** Prepare bibliography cards for the following five items. Add italics and quotation marks where necessary.

1. A book entitled The Soul of a New Machine by Tracy Kidder, published in Boston in 1981 by Atlantic-Little.
2. An unsigned article entitled Personal Computers, published in the December 1983 issue of Consumer Reports on pages 73 through 88.
3. An article written by Michael Rogers, entitled Computer Culture Made Easy, published in the November 19, 1984, issue of Newsweek on page 102.
4. A book entitled Whole Earth Software Catalog, edited by Stewart Brand, published in New York in 1984 by Doubleday.
5. A book entitled Digital Deli, edited by Steve Ditlea, published in New York in 1984 by Workman.

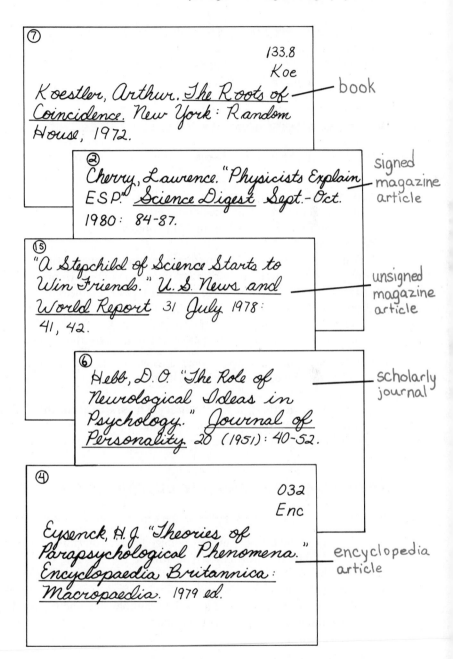

⑦

133.8
Koe

Koestler, Arthur. The Roots of — book
Coincidence. New York: Random
House, 1972.

②

Cherry, Laurence. "Physicists Explain — signed
ESP." Science Digest Sept.-Oct. — magazine
1980: 84-87. — article

⑮

"A Stepchild of Science Starts to
Win Friends." U.S. News and — unsigned
World Report 31 July 1978: — magazine
41, 42. — article

⑥

Hebb, D.O. "The Role of
Neurological Ideas in — scholarly
Psychology." Journal of — journal
Personality 20 (1951): 40-52.

④

032
Enc

Eysenck, H.J. "Theories of
Parapsychological Phenomena." — encyclopedia
Encyclopaedia Britannica: — article
Macropaedia. 1979 ed.

Cards in a Working Bibliography

EXERCISE 7. Preparing Your Working Bibliography. Prepare a working bibliography for the topic you have chosen to write on or for another topic. Your teacher may require you to prepare a minimum number of bibliography cards.

WRITING A PRELIMINARY THESIS STATEMENT

27e. State the preliminary thesis of your paper in one sentence.

To bring your topic into sharper focus before you research your potential sources, state the paper's thesis, or main idea, in one declarative sentence. This preliminary thesis statement serves as a further limitation of the scope of your topic and provides a guide for your research.

You may well revise this preliminary thesis several times as you continue your research and write and revise the paper. Expressing it as clearly as possible at this stage, however, will enable you to avoid gathering material that is not at all useful for supporting your ideas.

The writer of the research paper on scientific studies of clairvoyance mentioned earlier drew up the following preliminary thesis statement:

> According to the findings of some research, people with clairvoyance can "see" things without the use of the senses.

EXERCISE 8. Writing a Preliminary Thesis Statement. Keeping in mind your purpose and audience and the tone appropriate for a research paper, write a preliminary thesis statement for your paper.

PREPARING A PRELIMINARY OUTLINE

27f. Prepare a preliminary outline as a guide to your research.

Before you can take notes in an organized way, you must have some idea of the kinds of information you will be looking for. One way to approach this task is to formulate a series of *questions about the topic*, anticipating the questions the paper should answer for your audience. Your tentative answers to these questions can then become the headings and subheadings of a preliminary outline.

At this point, you do not need to concern yourself with matters of style or with the final organization of the headings. As you read and take notes, you may decide that some of the headings are irrelevant or are not covered well enough in the resources available to you. In addition, you will undoubtedly find other information that you will want to include. Like the preliminary thesis statement, the preliminary outline may be revised several times before you complete the paper.

Follow these suggestions in drawing up your preliminary outline:

1. Put the title of your paper at the top of a sheet of paper.
2. Below the title, write the word *Thesis* and your thesis statement.
3. Do not make the preliminary outline too detailed; you will add to it as you read and take notes.

The writer of the paper on scientific studies of clairvoyance formulated the following questions about the topic.

What is clairvoyance?
How do researchers conduct experiments on clairvoyance?
What kinds of experiments into clairvoyance have been conducted?
Do all scientists agree on the existence of clairvoyance?
What lies ahead for clairvoyance studies?

Using these questions, the writer drew up the following preliminary outline.

Title: Scientific Studies of Clairvoyance
Thesis: According to the findings of some research, the clairvoyant mind
         can "see" objects or events without the use of the senses.

1. Definition of clairvoyance
2. Scientific approach to clairvoyance
3. Experiments with clairvoyance
   —studies by J. B. Rhine
   —studies by Rhine's followers
4. Objections to experiments
5. Future of clairvoyance studies

☞ **NOTE** You may want to compare this preliminary outline with the final outline on page 702.

EXERCISE 9. Preparing a Preliminary Outline. Develop questions about your topic and use them to draw up a preliminary outline.

GATHERING INFORMATION ON YOUR TOPIC

27g. Take notes on cards classified by the headings and subheadings on your preliminary outline.

Your working bibliography and preliminary thesis statement and outline will provide you with a plan of action for your research. Always take notes *as you read*; the human memory is not a reliable guide for detailed information and quotations. Without a complete and accurate record of your research, you will find it impossible to reconstruct the information when you write the paper. With a package of 4-by-6-inch index cards, you are ready to read your sources. The note cards should be larger than the working-bibliography cards for two reasons: First, the cards will accommodate more notes; and second, you will be able to distinguish them from your smaller bibliography cards. Since you will be working with both kinds of cards at the same time, it is important that you be able to distinguish between them at a glance.

The following numbered items explain the entries on the sample card on page 685. Each explanation is numbered to correspond to the appropriate key number in the illustration.

1. *The "slug."* At the upper left-hand corner of a card, write a point from your preliminary outline, called a "slug." Include only information related to that point on the note card. Since your outline is a preliminary one, it is unlikely that every note you take will fall naturally under one of the outline's headings or subheadings. If you find that the notes you are taking do not fit any of the points in your outline, take the time to revise the outline accordingly and enter the new slugs on cards. You also may delete points if you cannot find enough usable information on them in your sources. If you decide to combine two headings, be sure to change your outline as well as the slugs on the appropriate cards.

2. *The bibliographical reference.* Enter the number of the source from your working bibliography at the upper right-hand corner of each note card. This will save you from having to recopy the publication information onto the note cards. You will often find that several of your sources provide information on the same point; thus you will have

several cards with the same slug, each card representing a different source.

3. *The note*. Most of your notes should be in your own words. A research paper should not be just a string of quotations strung together. Nor should it be written in a *derived* style, one that sounds like the style of your sources rather than like your own style. When you have read a paragraph carefully, *paraphrase* it by restating the ideas in your own words. When you do want to use an author's exact words, you must enclose them in quotation marks. Quote verbatim (word-for-word) only when the author's words are especially pertinent to your thesis and especially well expressed.

Whether you paraphrase or quote, you must give credit to your sources. *Plagiarism*—the use of another person's words or ideas without an acknowledgment of the source—is a serious, punishable offense, one that teachers are quick to detect.

Develop your own shorthand to save time in note-taking. Common ways of getting ideas down quickly are to (1) abbreviate as many words as you can without affecting the clarity of your notes; (2) use symbols for short words—*&* for *and*, for example; and (3) write phrases rather than whole sentences. Always write legibly, or you may not be able to read your notes later.

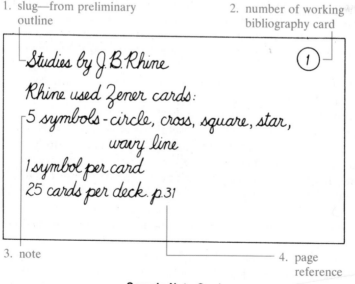

1. slug—from preliminary outline

2. number of working bibliography card

> Studies by J. B. Rhine (1)
> Rhine used Zener cards:
> 5 symbols - circle, cross, square, star, wavy line
> 1 symbol per card
> 25 cards per deck. p. 31

3. note

4. page reference

Sample Note Card

4. *The page reference.* At the end of each note, write the page or pages on which you found the information. You may need to return to the specific page later to clarify a point, and you must include page numbers when you prepare the citations for your paper. If the information runs over from one page to the next, place a slash mark at the point in the note where the page break occurs.

EXERCISE 10. Gathering Information on Your Topic. Read and take notes on your topic, using the preliminary outline you prepared in Exercise 9 as a guide. Remember to identify each note card with a slug and with the number of the source from your working bibliography. Take accurate and complete notes, being careful to use quotation marks for any material you copy verbatim. Revise your preliminary outline as you find additional points you want to include or as you decide to delete certain points.

CLASSIFYING AND ORGANIZING INFORMATION

27h. Classify and organize your notes, and prepare a revised outline.

When you are satisfied that you have enough notes to treat your topic adequately, your next job is to classify the notes and arrange them in the order in which you will use them. Since each note card has a slug, you can classify the notes easily by grouping all of the cards bearing the same slug into one pile. This simple mechanical task actually carries you a long way toward the organization of your paper. You will have before you a number of piles of cards, each treating one division of your topic as represented in your developing outline.

You now have to consider the usefulness of your notes and the order in which you will present the information in your paper. Study the notes in each group to see how well they support your preliminary thesis and outline. If you have a large number of cards in one group, you will know that you have found a good deal of information on the corresponding point in your developing outline. If you have little or no information on a point, you will need to research the point further or eliminate it from your outline.

As you read through the notes, the relative importance of the points will become apparent. The more important ones will serve as the major divisions of your paper, and the less important ones as the subdivisions. At this point, reevaluate your thesis carefully to make sure that you can support it with the information you have gathered. If not, you will need to revise it so that it clearly sets forth the main idea that your paper will attempt to prove.

Next, revise your outline so that it shows how your main headings and subheadings are related. To do this, you will need to arrange the material in a clear and logical order. You may decide to move a heading and its supporting information to another place in the outline or to rearrange the order of the notes within a group of cards. Although you may revise the outline again once you have written the paper, structuring it as carefully as you can now will give you a plan to follow as you write the first draft.

Put the outline into standard form, using either a topic outline or a sentence outline as your teacher directs. (You may want to review the section on outlining on pages 481–85.) Usually, the material for a research paper can be organized under six or fewer main headings. If you have more than six, review the organization of the material and the material itself to make sure that you have not included too much information or mistaken minor points for major ones.

REVIEW EXERCISE B. Preparing a Revised Outline. Classify and organize your note cards, revise your thesis statement if necessary, and prepare a revised outline. Your teacher may want to check your note cards, thesis, and outline before you write the first draft of the paper.

WRITING

WRITING THE FIRST DRAFT

27i. Write the first draft from your revised outline.

With your revised outline to guide you and your notes and bibliography cards nearby, you are ready to write the first draft of your research paper. You may want to review the suggestions for writing a first draft in Chapter 21, pages 395–96. Remember that the first draft is for your use only. Do not delay your work by trying to think of a clever introduction. You may start anywhere you want to; the important thing is to make a start, to put your ideas in a form that you will be able to follow when you revise the paper.

CRITICAL THINKING:
Synthesizing

The first draft of any composition is a synthesis, or putting together, of separate elements to form a new whole. Writing the first draft of a research paper is particularly complex because you must bring together facts and details from many sources, digest them thoroughly, acknowledge your sources appropriately, and present your findings in a unified, coherent fashion.

As you write, keep in mind your purpose, audience, and tone. Use the information on your note cards to support your thesis clearly and effectively, and be sure to credit your sources for both ideas and quotations, using one of the methods explained on the following pages. Remember that ideas that become familiar to you during your research may not be as well known to your readers, who will be relying on transitions, definitions of technical terms, and logical sentence and paragraph structure to understand your paper.

Documentation

Three methods of documenting sources are used for research papers: footnotes, endnotes, or parenthetical citations. Determine which method your teacher prefers you to use before you write your first draft.

No matter which method you use, remembering that your audience is a general one will help you decide which information to document, or credit. Not every fact needs to be documented. The fact that *Science* is an authoritative journal, for example, is likely to be known to a general audience and thus would not need to be documented. Never assume too much knowledge on the part of your audience, however. If you do not know whether a particular fact is general or specialized knowledge, give its source.

Footnotes

To indicate a footnote, write or type a number slightly above and to the right of the final punctuation mark at the end of the quotation or idea taken from one of your sources. This number refers the reader to the footnote, which appears at the bottom of the page. You must plan each page so that there will be enough space at the bottom to accommodate the footnotes for that page. Number the footnotes consecutively throughout the body of your paper, unless your teacher instructs you to do otherwise.

Remember that you must document all the ideas you have taken from sources, even though they are written in your own words. Do not make the mistake of using footnotes only to give sources of quotations.

The footnote for a book or a pamphlet gives the name of the author (first name first); the title (underlined); the city of publication, publisher, and date; and the page number(s).

The footnote for a magazine or newspaper article gives the author (unless the article is anonymous); the title of the article (in quotation marks); the name of the magazine or newspaper (underlined); the volume number, if any (for scholarly journals only); the date; and the page number(s).

Pay special attention to the punctuation of the following sample footnotes, taken from a variety of research papers, which show the correct format for the *first* mention of a source. Note that months of the year—except May, June, and July—are abbreviated.

[1] Doris Lessing, A Small Personal Voice: Essays, Reviews, Interviews (New York: Knopf, 1974) 47. [book by one author]

[2] Cleanth Brooks and Robert Penn Warren, Modern Rhetoric. 4th ed. (New York: Harcourt Brace Jovanovich, 1979) 179. [book by two authors]

[3] Virginia Woolf, The Diary of Virginia Woolf, 5 vols. (New York: Harcourt Brace Jovanovich, 1978–84) 2: 115. [one volume in a multivolume work in which all have the same title]

[4] Robert Coles, Eskimos, Chicanos, Indians, vol. 4 of Children of Crisis (Boston: Atlantic–Little, 1978) 12. [one volume in multivolume work with different titles]

[5] Virgil, Aeneid, trans. Allen Mandelbaum (Berkeley: U of California P, 1971) 92. [translation]

[6] Maxwell Perkins, "Thomas Wolfe," Thomas Wolfe: A Collection of Critical Essays, ed. Louis Rubin, Jr. (Englewood Cliffs: Prentice, 1973) 80. [one article in a collection of articles by different authors]

[7] Timothy Ferris, "Einstein's Wonderful Year," Science 84 Nov. 1984: 61–63. [article in a monthly popular press magazine]

[8] Carol Beckwith, "Niger's Wodaabe: 'People of the Taboo,'" National Geographic 164 (1983): 502. [article in a magazine that numbers its pages continuously throughout each volume year]

[9] "Navahos Upheld on Land Claims," New York Times 30 June 1970, late ed.: A20. [unsigned newspaper article]

[10] Louis C. Faron, "American Indians," Encyclopedia Americana, 1984 ed. [signed article in an alphabetized encyclopedia]

[11] Florence Wright, personal interview, 4 May 1984. [interview]

[12] "Music in the Age of Shakespeare," PBS, WGBH, Boston, 17 Sept. 1980. [television program]

[13] MacWrite, computer software, Apple Computer, 1984.

The following example shows how to footnote a quotation or an idea that the author of a source has, in turn, taken from another author.

[1] Frederic McDowell, "Recent British Fiction: Some Established Writers," Contemporary Literature 2 (Summer 1970): 108 qtd. in Paul Schlueter, The Novels of Doris Lessing (Carbondale: Southern Illinois U P, 1973) 75–76.

Once you have provided complete documentation for a source the first time you refer to it, you may use a shortened form for later references to the same source. The author's last name and the page number are usually sufficient.

[1] Doris Lessing, A Small Personal Voice: Essays, Reviews, Interviews (New York: Knopf, 1974) 47.

[2] Lessing 52.

If you use two or more sources by the same author, however, you must include a shortened form of the specific title each time you cite either source.

[4] Lessing, Voice 70.

[5] Lessing, Stories 116.

If you mention the title of the specific work in your paper, you do not need to include the title in the footnote. Similarly, if you include the author's name in your paper, you may omit it from the footnote.

Neither name nor title mentioned in text:

⁸ Lessing, <u>Voice</u> 64.

Title mentioned in text:

⁸ Lessing 64.

Name mentioned in text:

⁸ <u>Voice</u> 64.

EXERCISE 11. Preparing Footnotes. Assign footnote numbers and write footnotes for the following five items, in the order given. Assume that neither the authors' names nor the titles are mentioned in the text. Add italics and quotation marks where necessary.

Footnotes on page 1 of text:

a. An article entitled Psychic Research, by W. Stuckey, published in Science Digest volume 80, October 1976. Reference to page 32.

b. The same article as above, same page.

c. A book by C.E.M. Hansel entitled ESP and Parapsychology: A Critical Reexamination, published in Buffalo in 1980 by Prometheus Books. Reference to page 280.

Footnotes on page 2 of text:

d. An unsigned article in *Discover* volume 5, February 1984. Reference to page 8. Title of article: A PSI Gap.

e. An article entitled Clairvoyance, by Rex Stanford, in Psychic Exploration: A Challenge for Science, edited by John White and published in 1974 in New York by G.P. Putnam's Sons. Reference to pages 133–34.

Endnotes

Endnotes appear at the end of a research paper, rather than at the bottoms of the pages. They contain the same information as footnotes and follow the same format, but they are collected on a separate page headed "Notes," just before the bibliography. Endnotes should always be numbered consecutively within the manuscript.

Parenthetical Citations

Since 1984, the Modern Language Association (MLA) has recommended citing sources in the paper, within parentheses, rather than in footnotes or endnotes. With parenthetical citations, numbered notes are used only for explanatory comments—additional information that is interesting but that is not directly related to the paper's thesis. These notes may appear either at the bottom of the pages on which they fall or on a separate page headed "Notes," just before the bibliography.

Parenthetical citations should be kept as brief and uncluttered as possible. They should provide only enough information for the reader to be able to locate the source in the bibliography at the end of the paper. The basic elements of parenthetical citations are the author's last name, a shortened form of the title, and the page number(s).

Whenever possible, place the citation just *before* the punctuation mark at the end of the sentence, phrase, or clause containing a quotation or a paraphrased idea. For extended quotations—those of four or more lines—place the citation after the final punctuation mark. (The indented quotation on page 704 is an example of an extended quotation.)

In citing sources, you need not repeat the author's name within the parentheses if you mention it in the paper. If you also mention the title of the source in the paper, you may omit it from the citation as well. Use the following examples and those in the sample research paper at the end of this chapter as guides to the content and format of parenthetical citations.

Note particularly the punctuation of the examples. A comma is used between the author's name and the title, but not between the author's name alone (or title alone) and the page number. Hyphens between page numbers indicate consecutive pages in the source; commas indicate separated pages.

(Cohen 76) [one author; only one work by author in bibliography]

(Durant and Durant, Lessons of History 31) [two authors; more than one work by these authors in bibliography]

(J.B. Rhine et al., Extrasensory Perception 108–10) [more than three authors; a work by another author with the same last name is included in the bibliography]

(Woolf 2: 115, 187) [the source is a multivolume work]

(McAllister) [the entire work, rather than a specific page, is cited]

(Bernstein 100; Strunk and White 81) [two sources are cited for the same information]

(qtd. in Bell 91) [original source not available; material quoted from an indirect source]

(2.1.48–53) [quoted from Act 2, Scene 1, lines 48–53 of a play]

The Bibliography

Sometimes labeled "Works Cited," the bibliography provides the support for your research paper. It should include only those materials that you actually quote or paraphrase in the paper, not all of those you compiled for your working bibliography.

If you prepared the cards in your working bibliography carefully, you will have on hand all the information you need for the bibliography. The following guidelines will help you arrange and style the bibliography entries.

1. Alphabetize the entries according to the last names of the authors (for an anonymous work, use the first important word in the title instead). Since you entered the authors' last names first on the working bibliography cards, this is simply a matter of arranging the cards for the sources you used in alphabetical order. Do not number the entries.

2. If you cite more than one work by the same author, do not repeat the author's name each time. Instead, alphabetize the works by title, and use three hyphens in place of the author's name for each work after the first one.

3. Indent all lines after the first one.

4. Place a period at the end of each entry.

The following examples illustrate the correct format for various kinds of listings. The entries are not in alphabetical order because most of them are drawn from different bibliographies. For a complete bibliography in alphabetical order, see page 708.

Lessing, Doris. A Small Personal Voice: Essays, Reviews, Interviews. New York: Knopf, 1974. [book with one author]

---. Stories. New York: Knopf, 1978. [book by the author of the previous entry]

Brooks, Cleanth, and Robert Penn Warren. Modern Rhetoric. 4th ed. New York: Harcourt Brace Jovanovich, 1979. [book with two authors; also the book's fourth edition]

Woolf, Virginia. The Diary of Virginia Woolf. 5 vols. New York: Harcourt Brace Jovanovich, 1978–84. Vol. 2. [one volume of a multivolume work used; reference to specific volume number appears in the text]

Coles, Robert. Eskimos, Chicanos, Indians. Vol. 4 of Children of
Crisis. 5 vols. Boston: Atlantic–Little, 1978. [only one volume in multivolume work with different titles used]

Virgil. Aeneid. Trans. Allen Mandelbaum. Berkeley: U of
California P, 1971. [translation: U stands for University and P for
Press]

Perkins, Maxwell. "Thomas Wolfe." Thomas Wolfe: A Collection of
Critical Essays. Ed. Louis Rubin, Jr. Englewood Cliffs:
Prentice, 1973. 87–102. [one article in a collection of articles by
different authors]

Ferris, Timothy. "Einstein's Wonderful Year." Science 84 Nov.
1984: 61–63. [article in a monthly popular press magazine]

Beckwith, Carol. "Niger's Wodaabe: 'People of the Taboo.'"
National Geographic 164 (1983): 483–509. [article, contin-
uous-pagination magazine or scholarly journal]

"Navahos Upheld on Land Claims." New York Times 30 June 1970,
late ed.: A20 [unsigned newspaper article]

Faron, Louis C. "American Indian." Encyclopedia Americana.
1984 ed. [signed article]

Wright, Florence. Personal interview. 4 May 1984. [interview]

"Music in the Age of Shakespeare." PBS. WGBH, Boston. 17
Sept. 1980. [television program]

EXERCISE 12. Preparing a Bibliography. Prepare bibliography
entries for the following items according to the format you have learned
in this section. Add italics and quotation marks where needed.

1. A magazine article by Charles Tart entitled Psychic Lessons in
   Human Behavior, volume 7, February 1978, page 51.
2. An unsigned magazine article entitled Science, the Media, and the
   Paranormal in Science News, volume 112, August 20, 1977, page
   118.
3. A book entitled The ESP Experience: A Psychiatric Validation by
   Jan Ehrenwald, published by Basic Books, in New York, in 1978.

4. A book by Naomi Hintze and J. Gaither Pratt, entitled The Psychic Realm: What Can You Believe?, published by Harper & Row, in New York, in 1975.
5. A book of articles edited by Patrick Grim, entitled Philosophy of Science and the Occult, published by the State University of New York Press in Albany in 1982.

Charts, Diagrams, and Illustrations

Charts and diagrams may be included in your paper where they are of real value. With each, always give the source from which you copied it. Never cut illustrations from library sources.

REVIEW EXERCISE C. Writing the First Draft. Write the first draft of your paper, incorporating your research findings and crediting your sources. Keep your audience and purpose in mind as you write, and remember that the tone of the paper should be serious, formal, and impersonal.

REVISING

REVISING YOUR RESEARCH PAPER

27j. Revise your research paper for content, organization, and style.

Once you have prepared a rough draft of your paper, reread it critically, rethinking the scope of your ideas and looking for irrelevant material, unclear transitions, illogical arrangement of information, and unsupported assertions. Remember that your objective is to prove your thesis, not simply to discuss or illustrate it.

CRITICAL THINKING:
Evaluating a Draft of a Research Paper

In order to evaluate a draft of a research paper, you need a set of criteria. The following Guidelines for Revising Research Papers on pages 696–97 provide standards against which you can judge your work. (You may also want to review the Guidelines for Revising Expository Compositions on pages 504–505.) Ask yourself the questions in the guidelines each time you revise the paper. Some students find it helpful to exchange papers with a classmate and evaluate each other's papers; check with your teacher to make sure that this practice is acceptable in your class. Even if you do exchange papers, you will want to evaluate your own paper as objectively as possible, since it will in turn be evaluated by your teacher according to these or similar criteria.

GUIDELINES FOR REVISING RESEARCH PAPERS

Content

1. Does the introduction lead logically into the thesis statement and prepare readers for it?
2. Does the thesis state the main idea clearly and directly and reveal the writer's purpose, attitude, and tone?
3. Does each paragraph develop one idea?
4. Is the topic sentence of each paragraph adequately supported by specific details and examples from the writer's research?
5. Has the writer provided enough information for readers to be able to understand the line of reasoning?
6. Has the writer left out irrelevant or unnecessary information?
7. Does the end of the paper clearly conclude the presentation?
8. Does the conclusion reinforce the thesis statement?

Organization

1. Is the thesis statement the final sentence in the introduction?
2. Are the paragraphs arranged in a logical order?
3. Are the sentences within each paragraph arranged in a logical order?
4. Are quotations and ideas from sources incorporated into the text in ways that effectively support the thesis statement?
5. Are there clear and logical transitions between the paragraphs? Between the major sections of the paper?
6. Is the emphasis on various ideas appropriately distributed by means of the wording, position, or proportion of the text devoted to them?

Style

1. Is the language appropriate for a general audience?
2. Are any technical terms explained?
3. Has the writer avoided wordiness and redundancies?

4. Does the writer's tone reveal the serious attitude appropriate for a research paper?
5. Do the sentences vary in length and structure?
6. Does the title clearly indicate the topic of the paper?

EXERCISE 13. Evaluating a Draft of a Research Paper. The following paragraph is from the first draft of the research paper that appears at the end of this chapter. Evaluate this paragraph carefully, noting anything that is unclear or that you think should be revised. You may want to compare your comments with those of your classmates.

> In one account of clairvoyant ability I read, a young woman was driving home at night. They came to a roadblock, where a police officer told them about an accident a half-mile ahead. They made a detour and had been driving for a while; the woman began to tremble and cry. She told her husband that her sister was lying dead on the road they had just left! Forty-five minutes later, the phone rang. A local doctor called to tell the woman that her sister was dead. She had been killed on the spot in a car accident, the same accident the couple heard of an hour before (Louisa E. Rhine, "Psychological Processes" 95–96).

EXERCISE 14. Evaluating and Revising Your Research Paper. Evaluate and revise your research paper, using the Guidelines for Revising Research Papers and the techniques you learned in Chapter 21. If you revise the paper more than once, be sure to check each revision against the guidelines. Your teacher may require you to save your early draft to submit along with the completed paper.

PROOFREADING

PROOFREADING YOUR RESEARCH PAPER

27k. Proofread your research paper for grammar, usage, and mechanics.

When your research paper meets the criteria in the Guidelines for Revising Research Papers and represents your best effort, proofread it carefully to correct the grammar, usage, and mechanics. Remember that you want your audience to focus on the ideas and information in your paper, not on proofreading faults. If necessary, review the Guidelines for Proofreading on page 403.

EXERCISE 15. Proofreading Your Revised Draft. Proofread your paper carefully to correct the grammar, usage, and mechanics.

PREPARING A FINAL VERSION

PREPARING THE FINAL VERSION OF YOUR RESEARCH PAPER

27l. Prepare a final version of your research paper, following correct manuscript form.

Your final step is to prepare a clean copy of your revised and proofread draft. To make sure that you have copied correctly, proofread this version as well. Then, assemble the parts of the paper, using the following MLA guidelines unless your teacher directs otherwise.

1. Type or write your paper neatly and legibly on one side of acceptable paper.
2. Leave one-inch margins at the top, bottom, and sides of your page.
3. Double-space throughout, including title, quotations, and bibliography.

You will also need to assemble the parts of the paper in the following order or the order your teacher requires:

1. *The cover.* Using staples, metal clasps, or other fasteners, bind your paper in a stiff cover. Give the title of the paper on the outside; make the cover simple but attractive.
2. *The title page.* Use a separate page as a title page. As your teacher directs, place your name, information about your class (name and number of the course), and the date one inch from the top of the first page, even with the left margin. Double-space between these lines. The title is centered, with double-spacing between the information described above and the title. Do not put quotation marks around your title.
3. *The final outline.* Insert your final revision of the topic outline directly after the title page. In this position, the outline will serve as a kind of table of contents.

4. *The paper itself.* Begin the page numbering with the first page of the text proper. Number consecutively all the pages of the paper, including the bibliography and those containing only charts or diagrams. Place page numbers in the upper right-hand corner of each page, one-half inch below the top of the page and fairly close to the right margin. Use a number with or without the words *page, pages,* or their abbreviations. Write your title at the top of the first page, and double-space between the title and the first line of your paper.

5. *The bibliography.* Use as many pages as you need for the bibliography, allowing the same margins as those on the pages of the paper itself.

REVIEW EXERCISE D. Preparing the Final Version of Your Research Paper. Prepare the final version of your paper, proofread it carefully, and assemble the parts of your paper as your teacher directs.

CHAPTER 27 WRITING REVIEW 1

Writing a Research Paper Based on Library Sources. Select another subject and, using the stages of the writing process and the special procedures you learned in this chapter, write a second research paper.

CHAPTER 27 WRITING REVIEW 2

Writing a Research Paper Based on Personal Observation. Select a subject and analyze it to develop a topic that you can research in your own community through personal observation, such as site visits and interviews. Prepare a research paper based on your findings.

Abbreviations Used in Sources

The list on the next page explains a number of scholarly abbreviations you will encounter in your research. For the most part, you should avoid using these abbreviations in your own paper; exceptions are those shown in the examples in this chapter, such as *ed.* and *trans.*

c or ©   *copyright*; used before a date (©1965) to indicate when copyright was obtained. (The circled *c* is the international copyright symbol.)

c., ca.   *about* (from the Latin *circa, circum*); used with dates—"c." or "ca. 1732" means "about 1732."

cf.   *compare* (from the Latin *confer*); "cf. the Atlantic Treaty" means "compare with the Atlantic Treaty."

ed.   *editor, edited, edition*

e.g.   *for example* (from the Latin *exempli gratia*)

et al.   *and others* (from the Latin *et alii*); also, *and elsewhere* (from the Latin *et alibi*)

f., ff.   *following page, pages*; "p. 25f." means "page 25 and the following page"; "p. 25ff." means "page 25 and the following pages."

ibid.   *in the same place* (from the Latin *ibidem*); no longer recommended by the MLA.

id.   *the same* (from the Latin *idem*)

i.e.   *that is* (from the Latin *id est*)

l., ll.   *line, lines*

loc. cit.   *in the place previously cited* (from the Latin *loco citato*)

ms., mss.   *manuscript, manuscripts*

N.B.   *note well* (from the Latin *note bene*)

n.d.   *no date*; publication date not given in book

op. cit.   *in the work previously cited* (from the Latin *opere citato*); no longer recommended by the MLA.

p., pp.   *page, pages*

q.v.   *which see, whom see* (from the Latin *quod vide* or *quem vide*)

sic   *thus* (from the Latin); used (in brackets) after an error in a passage, to make clear that the original was copied accurately.

vide   *see* (from the Latin)

Helpful Hints for Research Papers

1. Do not return any of the sources you may have used for your paper until your final draft is complete, including any additional revision your teacher may ask you to do. As you write, you will probably find information on your note cards that is incomplete or that needs additional checking.

2. As you prepare working bibliography cards, double-check the spelling of such items as authors' names, titles of books and magazines, and names of publishing companies against your original sources. Then, when you transfer the information to your final bibliography, you will need only to check the same information against your bibliography cards.

3. As you insert names of authors and page numbers into your rough draft, check the spelling of authors' names and page numbers against the original sources.

4. In preparing note cards, use special symbols, such as a star (*), to indicate notes you especially want to use. These may include particularly interesting quotations or important definitions.

5. Keep a good dictionary nearby, and use it for more than checking the spelling or definitions of words. For example, the writer of the sample research paper on pages 702–708 needed to understand the basic nature of clairvoyance. This information is concisely explained in a good dictionary under the entry for "clairvoyance."

6. Be especially careful in checking the spelling of foreign words and the meaning and spelling of technical terms. Remember that it is extremely easy to miscopy such items as numbers and dates. Check this carefully in your original sources.

7. Before you begin work on your paper, make a chart for yourself that outlines the steps involved (for example, choosing and limiting the subject, developing an overview of the topic, locating sources and gathering information, filling out bibliography cards). If your teacher has given you a deadline for each step, make a note of that date. Then check off each step as you complete it.

8. If possible, make a copy of your paper for yourself before handing it in. In this way, you not only protect yourself against loss of your paper, but also have a model to study for your next year's paper.

Michael Davis

Psychology

April 8, 1986

CLAIRVOYANCE: INVESTIGATING A "SIXTH SENSE"

[The following sample pages are from a high-school student's research paper. Use them as a model in preparing your own paper.]

OUTLINE

Thesis: According to the findings of some research, people with clairvoyance can "see" things without the use of the senses.

I. Definition of clairvoyance

   A. Comparison with other types of extrasensory perception

   B. Examples of clairvoyant ability

II. Scientific approach to clairvoyance

   A. Need for valid evidence

   B. Need for extensive evidence

III. Experiments with clairvoyance

   A. Studies by J. B. Rhine

      1. Method of card-guessing

      2. Interpretation of data

      3. Favorable results of studies

   B. Studies by Rhine's followers

      1. Use of separate rooms

      2. Use of categories for subjects

      3. Use of random-number generator

      4. Use of remote locations

      5. Use of hypnosis

IV. Objections to experiments

   A. Possibility of fraud

   B. Lower scores from tighter controls

   C. Variable results from repeated efforts

V. Future of clairvoyance studies

Clairvoyance: Investigating a "Sixth Sense"

Have you ever had a hunch or made a wild guess about an event

that proved correct? Your sudden insight, some scientists claim, may

have been a form of extrasensory perception called clairvoyance.

According to the findings of some research that this paper will

examine, the clairvoyant mind can "see" objects or events without the

use of the senses. [thesis]

Clairvoyance, say scientists, is one of four categories of

extrasensory perception: (1) telepathy--reading the thoughts of

another, (2) precognition--sensing future events, (3) psychokinesis--

affecting objects by thinking about them, and (4) clairvoyance--perceiving

objects or events that are impossible to perceive by the

normal senses (Cherry 84). The category of clairvoyance includes such

acts as guessing the unknown contents of a sealed envelope or

describing the location of a lost child.

· In one account of supposed clairvoyant ability, a young woman was

driving home at night with her husband. They came to a roadblock,

where a police officer told them about an accident a half-mile ahead.

After they had made a detour and had continued driving for a few

mintues, the woman began to tremble and cry. She told her husband

that her sister was lying dead on the road they had just left!

Forty-five minutes after they had arrived home, the phone rang. The

caller, a local doctor, told the woman that her sister was dead. She

had been killed instantly in a car accident, the same accident the couple

had heard of an hour before (Louisa E. Rhine, "Psychological

Processes" 95-96).

Was the woman's sudden knowledge an example of clairvoyance?

Montague Ullman, a leading researcher of extrasensory perception,

warns, "Scientifically, of course, such cases don't prove anything,

because they can be called coincidence, unconscious self-deception,

or deliberate hoaxes" (47). [direct quotation]

Ullman and other investigators insist that clairvoyance exists;

yet in order to prove their claim, they recognize the need for

reliable data. Accordingly, clairvoyance has been the focus of

experiments based upon careful controls. Following the scientific

method, scientists gather evidence from these experiments and use the

evidence as the basis of proof.

During experiments, subjects may guess at hidden cards,

locations, numbers, or a variety of other items. If enough of these

guesses are correct, then scientists can be certain that more than

mere luck is at work. However, as an added precaution against lucky

guesses, scientists require extensive evidence, drawn from thousands

of experiments. They may even repeat a particular experiment with one

person hundreds of times before accepting its results.

This experimental research is relatively new. It began during the

1930's, when Dr. J. B. Rhine conducted experiments for all four

categories of extrasensory perception (Bowles and Hynds 27). In his

earliest attempts, he found clairvoyance the most suitable for

research. He stated:

Clairvoyance experiments are the easiest of all to conduct . . . . Not only

is it easier to control against the more common experimental errors, but

it is also easier to eliminate any alternative hypothesis that might be

applied to the data (Rhine and Pratt 53). [extended quotation]

Enthusiastically, Dr. Rhine performed hundreds of experiments, testing the clairvoyant powers of ordinary people. His method was surprisingly simple; in fact, with patience and accurate record-keeping, anyone can imitate it.

Rhine used a pack of cards called Zener cards, which contained five symbols: a star, a circle, a cross, a square, and a wavy line. One of these symbols was printed on each card. In the deck there were twenty-five cards, five of each symbol.

After shuffling the cards, the experimenter placed the deck on a table. Behind an opaque screen, which concealed the experimenter and the cards at all times, the subject either wrote down or called out in order the symbols in the deck (Bowles and Hynds 31). By pure chance, one would expect five correct guesses out of twenty-five in a single run-through of cards. Any scoring consistently higher than five correct guesses, Rhine concluded, was evidence of clairvoyance (Cohen 76).

[*The paper goes on to discuss Dr. Rhine's interpretation of his data, the favorable results of his studies, and the experiments of Dr. Rhine's followers. The following paragraphs make a transition from this section of the paper to the objections against clairvoyance experiments.*]

One recent development in clairvoyance research involves hypnosis. In tests, two groups of people perform Dr. Rhine's card-guessing experiment. One group is awake, while the other group is under hypnosis. The group under hypnosis has scored a significantly greater number of correct guesses than the other group. Although researchers find these results encouraging, they are performing further tests to measure the effect of hypnosis (Sargent).

As research into clairvoyance continues, however, opponents
refuse to accept the findings. According to Bowles and Hynds, the
unfavorable publicity the Rhines' work received may still be
influencing the general public's attitudes toward psychical research
(27). Critics cite three overwhelming problems in the studies: first,
that researchers do not guard enough against fraud; second, that they
get lower scores as they improve their testing methods; and third,
that they cannot get the same results every time they repeat an
experiment. [transitional paragraph]

[*The next section of the paper discusses each objection. The paper concludes
as follows:*]

Defenders, meanwhile, claim that scientific standards, such as
requiring similar results each time an experiment is repeated, need
not apply to research into the human mind. Arthur Koestler writes,
"[The standard of] repeatability [is] valid in the physical sciences,
but less so in the frontiers of medicine and even less in those
branches of psychology which involve unconscious processes . . ."
(29).

Although Koestler and others claim that clairvoyance "is a hard
reality" (23), many disagree, and the future of clairvoyance studies
is uncertain. Philip H. Abelson, editor of the authoritative journal
Science, sums up the controversy when he states that "these
extraordinary claims require extraordinary evidence. Findings that
question the basic laws of nature must be subjected to rigorous
scientific scrutiny" ("A Stepchild of Science" 42). Many, like Abelson,
believe that statistical evidence charting an unknown power at work

gives insufficient reason for abandoning assumptions about the way the
mind works. Remarks D. O. Hebb, professor of psychology at McGill
University, "I do not accept ESP for a moment, because it does not
make sense" (45).

Skeptics like Abelson and Hebb may be unfairly dismissing the
positive results of clairvoyance studies, which, compared with many
other fields, are still very new. By demanding "extraordinary
evidence" that extrasensory perception exists, they may be
overlooking much of the evidence this paper has discussed.

On the other hand, scientists who claim that clairvoyance is a
fact of life are exaggerating, for many questions remain. H. J.
Eysenck, professor at the University of London, calmly states the
crux of the issue:

> . . . very intriguing demonstrations have been given that suggest
> the existence of something outside the purview of physics and
> psychology, but no one has yet succeeded in bringing this something
> under adequate experimental control (1004).

Until scientists can present a reasonable explanation for
clairvoyance, Eysenck contends, "it would be unwise to claim any
more" (1004).

BIBLIOGRAPHY

Bowles, Norma, and Fran Hynds. Psi Search. New York: Harper, 1978.

Cherry, Laurence. "Physicists Explain ESP." Science Digest Sept.–Oct. 1980: 84–87.

Cohen, Daniel. ESP: The Search Beyond the Senses. New York: Harcourt Brace Jovanovich, 1973.

Eysenck, H. J. "Theories of Parapsychological Phenonomena." Encyclopaedia Britannica: Macropaedia. 1979 ed.

Hansel, C. E. M. ESP: A Scientific Evaluation. New York: Scribner's, 1966.

Hebb, D. O. "The Role of Neurological Ideas in Psychology." Journal of Personality 20 (1951): 40–52.

Koestler, Arthur. The Roots of Coincidence. New York: Random House, 1972.

Puthoff, Harold E., and Russell Targ. "Remote Viewing: New Research Frontier." The Signet Handbook of Parapsychology. Ed. Martin Ebon. New York: New American Library, 1978. 78–90.

Rhine, J. B. The Reach of the Mind. New York: Smith, 1972.

Rhine, J. B., et al. Extrasensory Perception After Sixty Years: A Critical Appraisal of the Research in Extrasensory Perception. Boston: Humphries, 1966.

Rhine, J. B., and J. G. Pratt. Parapsychology: Frontier Science of the Mind. Springfield: Thomas, 1972.

Rhine, Louisa E. Hidden Channels of the Mind. New York: Sloane, 1961.

———. "Psychological Processes in ESP Experiences: Part 1, Waking Experiences." Journal of Parapsychology 26 (1962): 88–111.

Sargent, Carl L. "Hypnosis as a Psi–Conducive State." Journal of Parapsychology 42 (1978): 264–67.

"A Stepchild of Science Starts to Win Friends." U.S. News and World Report 31 July 1978: 41, 42.

Taylor, John. Science and the Supernatural. New York: Dutton, 1980.

Ullman, Montague. "Can You Communicate with Others in Your Dreams?" The Psychic Scene. Ed. John White. New York: New American Library, 1974. 42–52.

CHAPTER 28

Writing Business Letters

STANDARD PRACTICE IN
BUSINESS CORRESPONDENCE

When you wrote your first friendly letters in elementary school, you probably made use of the advice given to you by your teachers. You tried to make your letters to your friends interesting, and you probably followed the instructions given about details of form, standard practice regarding neatness, use of stationery, and so on. At this stage, however, there is little point in attempting to lay down rules for what is obviously a gesture of friendship, and essentially personal.

Formal business correspondence, however, has little to do with friendship, and is fairly conventionalized. The reasons for this are plain. It is not the purpose of a business letter to say hello and express concern for your correspondent's continued health and happiness. It is often the case that the mail brings business letters to a desk rather than a person and, as often as not, to a person who has replaced the person originally addressed. A business letter is always intended merely to convey the required amount of information as efficiently and clearly as possible, with as little delay and distraction as possible. Today there are many designed preprinted forms in use, precisely to avoid unnecessary detail and inaccuracy.

There is, therefore, a great deal of value in learning the conventional methods of business correspondence, since all of us need from time to time to engage in it. It is also helpful for those who will be engaged in secretarial duties to master the general conventions involved. This can save valuable time later, for example, and allow you to devote more attention to the other aspects of secretarial work, which become more and more complicated by the year.

This chapter considers the general form of a business letter and its different parts, concludes with a discussion of the different kinds of business letters, and supplies models of them.

PREWRITING

FORM IN BUSINESS LETTERS

Whether formal or informal in tone, the business letter is always written according to a standard form.

28a. Observe standard practice in the writing of business letters.

(1) Use appropriate stationery.

Standard business stationery comes in two sizes, either of which is subject to slight variations by individual firms. The larger of the standard sizes is 8½ × 11 inches; the smaller is 5½ × 8½ inches, used for very short letters.

(2) Make an attractive "letter picture."

The "letter picture" is the overall picture a letter presents to the reader at first glance. People in business insist that their letters make a favorable impression. To make the picture attractive, you must center the letter on the page, leaving equal margins on the sides and at the top and bottom—the margins are the frame around your "picture." Space the letter parts carefully; consistently follow a standard pattern of indentation and punctuation; and make the letter absolutely free of strikeovers, erasures, and other marks that mar its appearance.

On page 711 two business letters have been reproduced in miniature. Note that the text of the letters is carefully centered on the stationery. The side margins are equal, and the top and bottom margins are equal. Two popular styles are represented: the block style without paragraph indentations and the block style with paragraph indentations. Note also that the text of the letters is placed attractively in relation to the

FertiGlobe, Inc.
855 Third Avenue
New York, New York 10017
Telephone: 212-599-0336

Telex: WUI-668626 FER GLO
Telex: WUD-645475 FER GLO
TWX: 7105815213
Cable: FERTIGLOBE

FertiGlobe

March 22, 1980

Mr. Paul Bruno
Sales Manager
Balzac Bag Company
555 South Monroe Street
Baltimore, Maryland 21224

Dear Mr. Bruno:

Thank you for your letter of February 4, 1980, and enclosed pricelist. We would like to order the following items:

1. 5,000 woven polypropylene bags with polyethylene liners, 22½" x 35", delivered to Tampa latest April 20th, and marked "DAP - M/V Catherine P", @ $0.55 per bag: $2,750.00

2. 4,500 woven polypropylene bags with polyethylene liners, 23" x 39", delivered to Tampa latest May 10th, and marked "URA - M/V Miss Calvi", @ $0.62 per bag: $2,790.00

Total: $5,540.00

All bags should be delivered to the warehouses of Manley Stevedoring, Inc., 710 Kings Road, Port Authority Complex, Tampa, Florida.

As always, it is a pleasure to do business with Balzac.

Yours truly,

Jeanette Hudson

Jeanette Hudson
Operations

CABLE ADDRESS "ELMEH"   (212) 889-4400

JOHN M. RIEHLE & CO.

INCORPORATED

Complete Insurance Service

SINCE 1898

757 THIRD AVENUE
NEW YORK N Y 10017

February 4, 1981

Miss Margaret Scanlon
651 East 78th Street
New York, NY 10089

Re: Homeowner's Insurance
    Plymouth Insurance Company
    Policy No. 88HO4297721

Dear Miss Scanlon:

Enclosed please find your Homeowner's Insurance policy No. 88HO4297721 issued by Plymouth Insurance Company for the period March 1, 1981 through March 1, 1982.

The annual premium, as indicated on the enclosed invoice, is $150.00.

Please return payment at your earliest convenience. A self-addressed envelope has been provided. If you have any questions, please do not hesitate to call.

Sincerely,

M. A. Roberts

M. A. Roberts
Account Executive

MAR/dg

Enclosures

MT. KISCO, NEW YORK   •   NEW CANAAN, CONNECTICUT   •   MASSAPEQUA, NEW YORK

letterhead. In general, the overall appearance is important here, not exact measurement.

(3) Follow standard practice in continuing a letter on a second page.

A business letter should be as short as possible without being abrupt or confusing. However, if a letter must be continued on a second page, use a second sheet; never write on the reverse side of a page. If a letter is to run over, you must anticipate that fact and arrange the material so that at least three lines can be written on the second page. Never complete a letter on one page and put just the leave-taking and signature on the next.

The first line on the second page of a business letter on 8½ × 11-inch stationery should be about two inches from the top. The page number should be centered about four lines above the first line of writing.

PARTS OF A BUSINESS LETTER

(4) Make the six parts of the letter conform to standard practice.

While you are studying the following descriptions of the six parts of a business letter, refer frequently to the model letter on page 715.

The Heading

Business firms use stationery bearing their letterhead, so that the writer does not need to supply anything but the date in the heading. When you write a business letter without a letterhead, you must give a complete heading: street address on the first line; city, state, and ZIP code on the second line, with a comma between the city and state; date on the third line, with a comma between the day and the year. If you use abbreviations, use them consistently.

The Inside Address

In the inside address you must give the name of the person or the firm (or both) to whom you are writing and the address, with the usual comma between city and state. Business firms file copies of the letters they write. Since the copies are filed under the name of the person or firm to which they are written, it is necessary to have an inside address on each letter. Ordinarily the inside address is placed four typewriter spaces below the heading or date and flush with the left-hand margin. If you wish to include the title or position of the person to whom you are writing, you may give the person's title after the name on the same line or, if the title is too long, on a separate line below.

EXAMPLES   Mr. James Moore   Ms. Lucinda Green, Principal
           Plant Supervisor   Westbend High School
           King Products, Inc.   Westbend, Iowa 50597
           1420 Havens Blvd.
           Chicago, Illinois 60637

The Salutation

The salutation, or greeting, is placed below the inside address (two spaces on the typewriter) and flush with the left-hand margin. It is always followed by a colon. The salutation varies with the nature of the inside address as follows:

1. If you are writing to a firm or a group, not to any specific individual, the traditional salutation is *Gentlemen*: (*Ladies*: or, rarely, *Mesdames*: for an exclusively female concern).

EXAMPLE   Soundcraft Corporation
          10 East 52nd Street
          New York, New York 10022

          Gentlemen:

When you use the traditional salutation (*Gentlemen*:), it is understood that the group you are writing to may be composed of both men and women. (You may instead use an impersonal salutation such as *Editors*: or *Personnel Department*: if you are addressing a specific group within a firm.)

2. If you are writing to a specific person but know only the official position and not the name, the traditional salutation is *Dear Sir*: (or *Dear Madam*:).

EXAMPLE   Personnel Manager
Airborne Instruments Laboratories, Inc.
160 Old Country Road
Mineola, New York 11501

Dear Sir:
or
Dear Madam:

(You may instead use an impersonal salutation such as *Personnel Manager*: if you wish.)

3. If you are writing to a man and have included his name in the inside address, the proper salutation is *Dear Mr.* ——:

EXAMPLE   Mr. D. H. White, Manager
Eastern Oil Company
60 East 42nd Street
New York, New York 10017

Dear Mr. White:

When writing to a woman who does not identify herself as *Miss* or *Mrs.*, you may use *Ms.* in the salutation. You may also address a man or woman by using both first and last names in the salutation.

EXAMPLES   Dear Ms. Alvarez:
Dear Jane Alvarez:
Dear Philip Wright:

In an address, always use a title with a person's name. Permissible abbreviations are *Mr., Messrs., Mrs., Ms., Dr., Hon.* Others should be spelled out: *Professor* Grace Tamura, *Reverend* Thomas E. Haupt, etc.

4. High government officials may be addressed as follows:

THE PRESIDENT
The President
The White House
Washington, D.C. 20015

Dear Mr. President:

SENATOR
The Honorable Nancy Landon Kassebaum
United States Senate
Washington, D.C. 20015

Dear Senator Kassebaum:

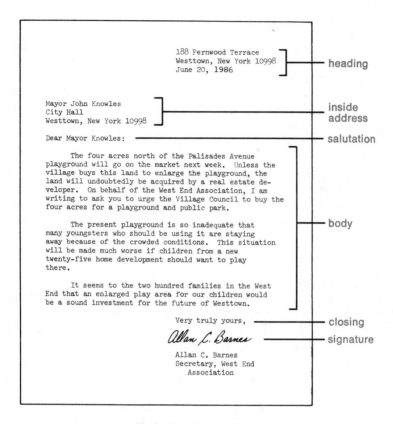

188 Fernwood Terrace
Westtown, New York 10998
June 20, 1986 — **heading**

Mayor John Knowles
City Hall
Westtown, New York 10998 — **inside address**

Dear Mayor Knowles: — **salutation**

The four acres north of the Palisades Avenue playground will go on the market next week. Unless the village buys this land to enlarge the playground, the land will undoubtedly be acquired by a real estate developer. On behalf of the West End Association, I am writing to ask you to urge the Village Council to buy the four acres for a playground and public park.

The present playground is so inadequate that many youngsters who should be using it are staying away because of the crowded conditions. This situation will be made much worse if children from a new twenty-five home development should want to play there. — **body**

It seems to the two hundred families in the West End that an enlarged play area for our children would be a sound investment for the future of Westtown.

Very truly yours, — **closing**

Allan C. Barnes — **signature**

Allan C. Barnes
Secretary, West End
Association

Model Business Letter

REPRESENTATIVE

The Honorable Charles Rangel
House of Representatives
Washington, D.C. 20015

Dear Mr. Rangel:

GOVERNOR

The Honorable William O'Neill
Governor of Connecticut
Hartford, Connecticut 06115

Dear Governor O'Neill:

MAYOR

The Honorable Edward Koch
Mayor, New York City
New York, New York 10007

Dear Mayor Koch:

The Body

There is no room for chat and discursiveness in business letters, but there is room for courtesy. Use simple language, clearly and directly phrased. The following trite phrasings, once in common use, are no longer considered good form: *Yours of the 5th inst. received and contents noted; beg to advise (remain, state, etc.); please be advised that; thanking you in advance*. For discussion of the contents of particular kinds of letters, see the treatment of the order letter, the letter of inquiry, the adjustment letter, and the letter of application on pages 719–25.

The first line of the body of a business letter is placed two typewriter spaces below the salutation. It may be indented either the usual five spaces of a typed manuscript or as far as the length of the salutation. In the pure block style, indentations are not used. Subsequent paragraph indentations will be uniform with the first one (see the letter pictures on page 711).

The Closing

In a business letter the standard form for the closing, or leave-taking, is *Yours truly* or *Very truly yours*. Less formal but frequently used is *Sincerely yours*. In writing to high government and church officials, you may use *Respectfully yours*, but avoid this in ordinary correspondence.

The closing is begun just to the right of the middle of the page in the block style with paragraph indentations and flush with the left margin in the block style without paragraph indentations. It is followed by a comma. Note that only the first word is capitalized.

The Signature

The signature is written in ink immediately below the closing and flush with it. The writer's name should be typewritten directly below the signature, a wise custom in light of the illegibility of many signatures. This typewritten repetition of the writer's name may be accompanied by his or her official position.

EXAMPLE   Very truly yours,
James MacPherson
James MacPherson
President

When writing to a stranger, a single woman may choose to place (*Miss*) in parentheses before her signature. A married woman may write her full married name in parentheses beneath her signature.

EXAMPLES   Very truly yours,
(Miss) Virginia Shaw

Very truly yours,
Elizabeth Blake
(Mrs. Henry G. Blake)

In general, however, do not put a title before a signature.

EXAMPLES   Very truly yours,
Thomas Strong [not *Mr.* Thomas Strong]

Very truly yours,
Sally Blake [not *Ms.* Sally Blake]

(5) Make the envelope conform to standard practice.

The addresses on the envelope should conform with the addresses used in the letter itself. Your own name and address are placed in the upper left-hand corner of the envelope. The name and address of the person to whom the letter is going are placed just below the middle of the envelope and slightly to the right, so that they occupy the lower right-hand quarter in a neat fashion with generous margins. Avoid crowding the edge of the envelope; if a particularly long line is necessary, as occasionally happens when you are writing the lengthy name of an organization, use a second line and indent it a few spaces from the left margin of the address. The name of the person you are addressing should be preceded by the proper title (*Mr., Dr., Ms.,* etc.). Always include the initial or the first name: *Ms. Georgia V. Bryce,* or *Ms. G. V. Bryce,* not *Georgia Bryce* or *Ms. Bryce.* Your own name in the return address need not be accompanied by a title. The stamp is always placed in the upper right-hand corner (see page 718).

(6) Fold the letter according to standard practice.

The folding of a letter is determined by the size of the envelope. If a letter written on standard 8½ × 11-inch stationery is to be placed in a long envelope, the letter is folded twice: up from the bottom about a third of the way, then down from the top so that when unfolded it will be right side up. If it is to be placed in a small envelope, the letter should be folded up from the bottom to within a quarter of an inch of the top; then the right side is folded over a third of the way and the left side folded over that fold. Insert the letter in the envelope with the fold at the bottom of the envelope (see page 718).

```
John Davis
1649 Muir Drive
Port Huron, Michigan   48060




              Ms. Stephanie Kinnery, President
              Kinnery Leathercraft, Inc.
              325 South Ames Street
              Marian, IN   46952
```

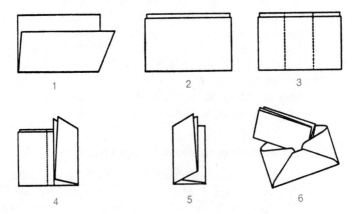

1   2   3

4   5   6

WRITING

KINDS OF BUSINESS LETTERS

28b. Learn the requirements for various types of business letters.

A busy office will turn out in a single day a dozen different kinds of business letters, but the average person, in carrying on private affairs, will have occasion to write only three or four types of letters. You will almost certainly have need at some time for the four types described on the following pages: the order letter, the letter of inquiry or request, the letter of adjustment or complaint, and the letter of application.

The Order Letter

The order letter is being outmoded by the prevalent use of printed order forms. However, there are occasions when it is necessary to write out an order in letter form. An effective order letter will fulfill the requirements that follow.

1. Set off the list of ordered items from the rest of the letter in a column arrangement.

2. Include all appropriate details as to quantity, catalog number, size, style, and price. The symbol @ means *each* or *apiece*: 3 boxes @ $1.25 = $3.75. It is usually wise to specify from what advertisement (magazine or paper and date) you have taken the information for your order.

3. Indicate how you are paying for the order: by check, money order, C.O.D., or charge account. Include money for postage if you think it is expected.

4. If you wish the merchandise sent to an address different from the address in the heading, give the address in the letter.

5. If you write the letter (instead of typing), print your name clearly under your signature. Sometimes a signature can be misread.

Study the following model order letter. Note how it conforms to the requirements listed on page 719.

```
                                        21 Cranberry Road
                                        Harmon, Illinois  61042
                                        November 20, 1986


New Fashions Shop
187 Main Street
Castleton, Illinois  61426

Gentlemen:

     Please send me the following articles advertised
in the Journal for November 19.

1 Heatherland tweed skirt, size 24 waist         $29.95
2 prs. Slimfit slacks, gray, size 10 long @ $22.95  45.90
1 Hemper blouse, white, Style A, size 34             19.95
                                        Total     $95.80

     I am enclosing a money order for $97.35 to cover
the order and parcel post charges of $1.55.

                              Very truly yours,

                              Judy Abbott

                              Judy Abbott
```

Model Order Letter

```
                          345 Graham Road
                          Bellmore, New York  11710
                          October 10, 1986


Box Office
Majestic Theater
245 West Forty-fourth Street
New York, New York  10018

Gentlemen:

        Please send me three tickets @ $16.00 for the
matinee performance of Hamlet on Saturday, November
28.  Acceptable alternate dates are November 21 and
December 5.

        I am enclosing a check for $48.00 and a self-
addressed, stamped envelope.

                          Very truly yours,


                          Albert Armstrong

                          Albert Armstrong
```

A simple kind of order letter is that in which only one type of thing is ordered—theater tickets, a book, or a pen, for example. Such a letter is illustrated above.

The Letter of Inquiry or Request

Occasionally you may require information that can be obtained only by writing a letter. Writing for material to use in a research paper, for facts about travel in a certain locality, for a college catalog, etc., are common situations of this kind. Be brief and direct. Make clear immediately what you wish; then stop.

Model Letter of Inquiry

348 Converse Avenue
Masonville, Iowa 50654
February 15, 1986

Bonar Plastics Corporation
1835 Washington Street
St. Louis, Missouri 63110

Gentlemen:

    For my Chemistry II class I am writing a re-
search paper on the manufacture of plastics. I should
appreciate very much your sending me any literature
on this subject that you may have for free distribution.

        Very truly yours,

        Mary Robinson

        Mary Robinson

118 Mountain Road
Kingston, New York 12401
April 17, 1986

School of Agriculture
Cornell University
Ithaca, New York 14850

Gentlemen:

    Please send me your general catalogue and any
additional literature you have on admission to the
School of Agriculture and courses in dairy farming.

        Very truly yours,

        Walter Owen

        Walter Owen

Model Letter of Request

The Letter of Adjustment or Complaint

When you write to a business firm to ask for correction of an error or to register a complaint of any kind, you will get better results if you restrain your annoyance and adopt a courteous tone. This is true also when you write to a government official complaining about poor service being given by municipal, state, or government employees.

```
                              14 Oklahoma Avenue
                              Tulsa, Oklahoma  74106
                              May 24, 1986

Guerber's Sports Company
85 Court Street
Maysville, Oklahoma  73057

Gentlemen:

        On May 14 I sent you an order which included two
white T-shirts, No. 86, size 36, @ $3.00.  When the
shipment arrived, I found that you had neglected to send
the shirts.  I assume that this was merely an oversight
in packing and will appreciate your sending me the
shirts.

                         Very truly yours,

                         Ralph Gray

                         Ralph Gray
```

Model Adjustment Letter

The Letter of Application

The letter of application is most important for you who are about to leave high school. Whether you seek a permanent job or temporary employment for the summer months, you will want to make a favorable

321 Fifth Street
Riverside, Missouri 64168
March 2, 1986

Personnel Director
Central Insurance Company
41 Bank Street
Riverside, Missouri 64168

Dear Sir:

Please consider me an applicant for the secretarial position advertised in Sunday's Herald.

I am eighteen years old and graduated last June from Riverside High School. Since then I have completed a six-months' course in secretarial training at the Clarkson Business Institute. In high school I completed two years of courses in shorthand and typing and worked as a student assistant for two years in the office. At Clarkson I studied office practice, business machines, business English, and bookkeeping.

For the past two summers I was employed as a fill-in stenographer by the Moore Trucking Company, where I did filing and billing as well as regular stenographic work. I feel at home in a business office and enjoy being given extra duties and responsibilities.

The following people have given me permission to use their names as references:

Miss Catherine Greenberg
Head of the Commercial Department
Riverside High School

Mr. Stanley Williams
Moore Trucking Company
Riverside, Missouri 64168

I shall be glad to come for a personal interview at your convenience. My telephone number is 592-3107.

Very truly yours,

Jane Parkman

Jane Parkman

Model Letter of Application

impression with your letter. Since the letter will undoubtedly be one of many received by your prospective employer, you must make sure that it is correct in every detail and sufficiently convincing to make the reader consider your application further. It should, if possible, be typewritten.

There are certain clearly definable requirements for a good letter of application.

1. Begin by naming the position for which you are applying. Mention how you learned about it.

2. State all the facts an employer would certainly want to know: your age, education, and experience.

3. Indicate, if you can do so naturally, that you are familiar with the requirements of the position, and explain why you believe you can meet them.

4. Give references (three, if possible) with addresses. If you have held other jobs, be sure to include among your references one of your former employers. Include also an older person who is acquainted with you and your family. Since you are still in school, a recommendation from a member of the faculty is appropriate. Before giving someone's name as a reference, ask permission.

5. Request an interview at the employer's convenience.

6. Be especially careful with all the details of letter form, neatness, spelling, grammar, etc. You would not wish to lose a good position simply because you were too lazy to look up the spelling of a word or to copy your letter a third or fourth time to ensure that it is perfect.

EXERCISE 1. **Making the Letter Picture.** Using the models on pages 711 and 715, lay out on a piece of typewriter paper a perfectly arranged business letter, using neatly drawn lines for the body of the letter. Use your own address and the present date in the heading. Make up an inside address. Be sure the salutation is proper.

EXERCISE 2. **Revising the Inside Address and Salutation.** The following inside addresses are mixed up. Rewrite them in correct block form. Beneath each, write the proper salutation.

1. Fred Emerson, a professor at Columbia University, West 116th Street, New York City 10027
2. Miami University, Dean of Admissions, Oxford, Ohio 45056
3. 10 East 53rd Street, Harper & Row, New York City 10022
4. Representative from your district in the House of Representatives

in Washington, D.C., Robert E. Thomas

5. Personnel Director of the Bradley Company, Cass City, 82–84 South Avenue, Illinois 61016, Carol T. Brooks

EXERCISE 3. Writing Order Letters.

1. Write a letter to the Board in Control of Intercollegiate Athletics, Yost Field House, Ann Arbor, Michigan 48103, ordering two tickets for the Michigan–Minnesota game on November 7. The tickets cost $6.00 each.
2. Write to any firm you wish, ordering at least three different articles advertised in a magazine or newspaper. Order more than one of some of the articles. Follow the model order letter on page 720.

EXERCISE 4. Writing a Request Letter.
Write a letter to the Dean of Admissions of any college or university stating that you wish to apply for admission at a certain date and requesting an application blank and other necessary forms.

EXERCISE 5. Writing an Adjustment Letter.
Write a letter to a business firm asking why you have received a bill for an order for which you have already paid C.O.D. Give all important details, dates, etc.

EXERCISE 6. Writing Letters of Application.

1. Using your local newspaper, select a help-wanted advertisement and answer it with a letter of application. Clip the advertisement to your letter when you hand it in.
2. Write to the manager of a summer camp, applying for a position as a counselor on the camp staff during the coming summer.
3. If you are going to work immediately upon graduation from high school, you probably have in mind the kind of position you intend to apply for. Write an imaginary letter of application for such a position.

☞ NOTE The United States Postal Service recommends the use of two-letter codes for states, the District of Columbia, and Puerto Rico. The service also recommends the use of nine-digit ZIP codes.

When you use two-letter codes for states and nine-digit ZIP codes, the address on business correspondence should look like this:

EXAMPLE Ms. Ann Washington
405 Vera Park Drive
Orlando, FL 32804-4335

The two-letter code is in capital letters and is never followed by a period. The following is a list of two-letter codes.

Alabama AL	Montana MT
Alaska AK	Nebraska NE
Arizona AZ	Nevada NV
Arkansas AR	New Hampshire NH
California CA	New Jersey NJ
Colorado CO	New Mexico NM
Connecticut CT	New York NY
Delaware DE	North Carolina NC
District of Columbia DC	North Dakota ND
Florida FL	Ohio OH
Georgia GA	Oklahoma OK
Hawaii HI	Oregon OR
Idaho ID	Pennsylvania PA
Illinois IL	Puerto Rico PR
Indiana IN	Rhode Island RI
Iowa IA	South Carolina SC
Kansas KS	South Dakota SD
Kentucky KY	Tennessee TN
Louisiana LA	Texas TX
Maine ME	Utah UT
Maryland MD	Vermont VT
Massachusetts MA	Virginia VA
Michigan MI	Washington WA
Minnesota MN	West Virginia WV
Mississippi MS	Wisconsin WI
Missouri MO	Wyoming WY

REVISING

Since your letter represents you, it is important that it represent you as favorably as possible. It is in the revising stage that you will attend to matters of accuracy, clarity and effectiveness of expression. The following guidelines will be helpful.

GUIDELINES FOR WRITING AND REVISING LETTERS

1. Is the letter attractive? Is the form correct, with each of the parts correctly placed?
2. Does the heading give the complete address and the full date? Are commas used to separate the city from the state and the day of the month from the year?
3. Is the inside address accurate, complete, and properly spaced?
4. Is the salutation appropriate? Is it followed by a colon?
5. In the body of the letter, are sentences grammatically correct and accurately punctuated? Are all words correctly spelled? Is paragraphing used properly?
6. Is the closing appropriate? Does the first word begin with a capital letter? Do the other words begin with a small letter? Does a comma follow the closing?
7. Is there consistent use of block or semiblock style in the letter? Is block style used on the envelope?
8. Is the address on the envelope accurate, complete, and attractively placed?
9. Has the letter been folded to fit the envelope?
10. Is the return address on the envelope?

CHAPTER 29

Effective Diction

APPROPRIATE CHOICE
OF WORDS

USING EFFECTIVE DICTION

When we refer to *diction*, we refer to two things: we refer to the *words* a writer uses and to the ways the writer puts those words to use. The word *diction* itself comes from a Latin word *dicere*, meaning "to point out in words." (This root word is also found in *dictionary, dictate, dictator*, and *dictaphone*.)

If you are writing a report on the causes of the Civil War for a history teacher, or if you are writing a report on DNA for a biology teacher, you will use formal diction. If you are writing a letter to a friend about the people in the old neighborhood, you will use informal diction, probably with some colloquialisms and, if slang is part of your own "voice," probably with some slang. If you are writing a profile of your neighborhood for a newspaper article, you will use formal diction, with perhaps a few colloquialisms, but no slang. If you are writing a book review of Isaac Asimov's *Foundation* series for a young-adult magazine, you will use diction that the magazine's young subscribers can understand. If you are writing a critique of the same series for an adult magazine, you are free to use more complex words and to discuss more complex ideas. Diction, then, is determined in large part by the audience you are writing for.

Diction, or word choice, can make all the difference between a vigorous, clear writing style and a weak or ambiguous style. Each of the following passages by professional writers is preceded by a passage written in diction that is vague and uninteresting:

a. About half way between West Egg and New York the motor road goes alongside the railroad to avoid an ash dump.
b. About half way between West Egg and New York the motor road hastily joins the railroad and runs beside it for a quarter of a mile, so as to shrink away from a certain desolate area of land. This is a valley of ashes—a fantastic farm where ashes grow like wheat into ridges and hills and grotesque gardens. . . .

F. SCOTT FITZGERALD

a. The San Bernadino Valley is very different from the moist coast of California because it is subject to the hot winds from the Mojave Desert.
b. The San Bernadino Valley . . . is in certain ways an alien place; not the coastal California of the subtropical twilights and the soft westerlies off the Pacific but a harsher California, haunted by the Mojave just beyond the mountains, devastated by the hot dry Santa Ana wind that comes down through the passage at 100 miles an hour and whines through the eucalyptus windbreaks and works on the nerves.

JOAN DIDION

a. You don't know me unless you have read a book entitled *The Adventures of Tom Sawyer*, but that doesn't make any difference. That book was written by Mark Twain. He chiefly told the truth in that book, but I never knew anyone who told the truth all of the time.
b. You don't know about me without you have read a book by the name of *The Adventures of Tom Sawyer*; but that ain't no matter. That book was made by Mr. Mark Twain, and he told the truth, mainly. There was things which he stretched, but mainly he told the truth. That is nothing. I never seen anybody but lied one time or another, without it was Aunt Polly . . .

MARK TWAIN

The differences between passage (a) and passage (b) are differences in diction—in word choice and in how the words are put together. Notice that the professional writers are much more specific in their diction. Instead of vaguely saying that "the road goes alongside" the railroad, Fitzgerald says "it hastily joins" the railroad; instead of saying vaguely that it "avoids" the dump, he says it "shrinks away" from it. The professional writers also often use figures of speech, in which they compare one thing to something else that seems quite different from it. Fitzgerald compares the valley of ashes to a farm that grows grotesque gardens (a figure of speech that ironically reminds us that ashes cannot grow anything). The professional writers also use sensory words that help us experience what they are describing. Didion tells us that the Santa Ana wind is "hot" and "dry" and that it "whines"; the westerlies, on the other hand, are "soft." Mark Twain's diction makes us hear a "real" voice—he tells his story using the lively diction of the American West in the late nineteenth century. Though Twain's diction would not be appropriate in a report to the chairman of the board, the genius of the novel is that Twain did decide to use the conversational diction of his hero, Huck Finn, and not the standard English of an impersonal narrator.

In this unit we will look at diction—first at correct word choice, and then at how different types of diction can affect your writing.

EXACT MEANINGS OF WORDS

29a. Know the exact meanings of words.

Some fine distinctions among word meanings are interesting chiefly to purists. This verse depends for its humor on the fine distinction between the reptile known as an alligator and the one known as a crocodile:

THE PURIST

I give you now Professor Twist,
A conscientious scientist.
Trustees exclaimed, "He never bungles!"
And sent him off to distant jungles.
Camped on a tropic riverside,
One day he missed his loving bride.
She had, the guide informed him later,
Been eaten by an alligator.
Professor Twist could not but smile.
"You mean," he said, "a crocodile."

OGDEN NASH

We laugh at Professor Twist, who is more concerned with diction than with the fate of his wife. Despite Nash's mockery of the pedantic professor, we all have an obligation to be certain we are using the correct word in our speaking as well as in our writing. Many words in the English language are spelled so similarly that they are often confused (*dessert* and *desert*, for example). Other English words have such subtle distinctions in meanings that a writer often carelessly chooses one word when he or she really intends the sense of another (*uninterested* and *disinterested* are examples).

EXERCISE 1. Distinguishing the Meanings of Words. Answer each question that follows. Use a dictionary if necessary.

1. Strictly speaking, if you are *livid* with anger, is your face reddish or grayish?
2. If you wear a diamond necklace to school, are you *flaunting* your wealth, or *flouting* it?
3. Is it a compliment to call a twenty-year-old man "*childish*," or is it an insult?
4. Are *oral* instructions written down or are they spoken? Or are they both?
5. When you read between the lines, are you *inferring* meaning or *implying* it?
6. If talking in corridors is forbidden, is it *prescribed* or *proscribed*?
7. If the sky suddenly darkens and you hear distant thunder, is a storm *immanent* or *imminent*?
8. Does the district attorney's office *prosecute* criminals or *persecute* them?
9. If you are looking for something to relieve your toothache, are you looking for an *anecdote* or an *antidote*?
10. If you give in to pressure to have your hair cut, have you *capitulated to* the pressure or *capitalized on* it?

EXERCISE 2. Choosing the Correct Words. Which word in parentheses best completes each sentence? Use a dictionary if necessary.

1. Denise makes a big point of (flouting, flaunting) the lunchroom rules.
2. "Scrambled" is a more (livid, vivid) verb than "went."
3. The old man looked at his first Christmas tree in (childish, childlike) wonder.

4. The spy received (oral, verbal) directions, rather than written ones.
5. Pulver (inferred, implied) that he would give up watching soap operas.
6. Cicero's name was on the (prescribed, proscribed) list, which meant he was a criminal who could be killed by anyone.
7. The Puritans believed that God was (immanent, imminent) in all of the natural world.
8. Ellsworth will (persecute, prosecute) his case against the fast-food chain.
9. Nora told yet another (anecdote, antidote) about her trip to Pikes Peak.
10. Which European leaders (capitalized, capitulated) to the Nazis?

MIXED IDIOMS AND METAPHORS

29b. Avoid mixed idioms and metaphors.

At times writers use not only the wrong words, but also the wrong idioms or metaphors.

An *idiom* is an expression that is peculiar to a certain language and that cannot be explained by definition of its individual words. For example, "to lose your head" is an idiom. The definitions of the individual words cannot tell us what the idiom means (they would give us an absurd meaning). "To make believe" is another idiom; defining the individual words "to make" and "believe" will not tell us what the idiom means. "To fall for" is another idiom that cannot be sensibly translated by examination of its individual words (a literal translation would give an absurd meaning to the sentence "Stephanie fell for Carl").

A *metaphor* is a comparison that shows a likeness between two otherwise dissimilar things. The "roof of the mouth," the "arm of the chair," the "foot of the table," the "nose of the plane" are all metaphors. William Shakespeare's "All the world's a stage," Psalm 23's "The Lord is my shepherd," and Emily Dickinson's "Hope is the thing with feathers" also are metaphors.

In some cases, we find people mixing idioms or metaphors. When this happens, the visual or logical aspects of what they are saying become absurd, sometimes comical. If you said "The ship of state went into a tailspin," you would be mixing two metaphors. What you are saying is that the nation or the state went into a decline, but the metaphors are so mixed that what we visualize is absurd: A ship, of course, cannot go into a tailspin. You are mixing the metaphor that compares the state to a ship ("the ship of state") and the metaphor that compares a depression or decline to the tailspin that an airplane goes into just before it crashes.

EXERCISE 3. Identifying Mixed Idioms or Metaphors. Write a sentence explaining what each of the following statements means in plain English. Then tell what idioms or metaphors the writer is mixing. (If you want a visual image of what is wrong, try to draw a picture of what you see.)

1. In 1969 the moon became another place where "the hand of man had set foot."
2. A senator speaking about the American spirit said: "It's vital to find out whether that spirit remains bright or whether we accept a little tarnish to keep the boat from rocking."
3. A memo from a corporate executive: "The President is sitting on a time bomb and he's running out of gas."
4. A legislator reports after a visit to constituents: "I've been keeping my ear to the grindstone recently."
5. An agency warns that "we're all going down the drain in a steamroller."

USING SPECIFIC WORDS

29c. Use specific words in your writing.

Our language is full of general nouns and verbs. The word *house* is a general noun that could refer to any number of specific dwellings: *a brick row house, an apartment house, a split level, a prefab, an adobe hut, a Cape Cod, a mobile home, a farmhouse.* Suppose you say you went to a *store*: Are you referring to *a 5 & 10, a hardware store, a grocery, a deli, a boutique*? You could even be more specific with that verb *went*. How did you go to the store? Did you *walk, run, dash, meander, fly*? Maybe you *rode the streetcar* or *drove*.

If there is anything that professional writers agree on, it is that the most effective writing is writing that is concrete and particular. Homer,

Shakespeare, Tolstoy, Twain—all wrote in terms of the particular. Thus, in *Julius Caesar,* Shakespeare did not merely say that "strange things were happening"; he wrote that "ghosts did shriek and squeal about the streets."

EXERCISE 4. Supplying Specific Nouns and Verbs. For each generalized noun or verb listed, supply at least three specific words or phrases and use them in sentences.

1. dog	6. run
2. desert	7. go
3. chair	8. talk
4. lunch	9. move
5. shoes	10. use

USING PRECISE WORDS

29d. Use precise words in your writing.

Many beginning writers tend to overuse certain vague words, words such as *say, go, have, do, nice, great, neat.* These words are perfectly correct, but they don't provide much content to your composition. When you find your writing is overloaded with such vague words, try to find some precise substitutes. Brainstorming with yourself can help. List words as they come to you. Eventually, a word or phrase will occur to you that will be much more precise than the vague one you chose at first. In fact, this is how professional writers work. A professional writer might spend as much time staring at the paper trying to think of "a better word" as he or she spends in actual composition.

You might use a thesaurus to help you find synonyms. Here, for example, are some of the synonyms listed by Roget's *International Thesaurus* for the verb *say*:

> utter, articulate, enunciate, pronounce, whisper, express, formulate, pour forth, chorus, chime, affirm, allege, proclaim, blurt, exclaim, murmur, mutter, mumble, sigh, yell, growl, snap, roar (and more)

Suppose you describe a story as "nice." Think for a moment and list all the adjectives or adjective phrases you could substitute for *nice.* Which one says what you really feel? *Exciting, sad, enjoyable, satisfying, puzzling, warm-hearted, true-to-life*? Perhaps in saying the story was "nice," you are really saying something negative about it. Do you really mean the story was *mediocre, so-so, easy to read but not memorable, unconvincing, lackluster?* Be precise; find the words that say what you really mean to say.

EXERCISE 5. Using Precise Words. The imprecise words in the following sentences are in italics. For each imprecise word, suggest at least three specific substitutes (words or phrases) and write sentences using them.

1. The mountain is *nice.*
2. Hilda is a *nice* girl.
3. That is a *great* boat.
4. *The Glass Menagerie* is a *great* play.
5. Lilly *said* goodnight to Antoine.
6. "Who's there?" *said* the stranger to the noise in the hall.
7. The dog *went* down the walk.
8. The car *went* down Route 1.
9. The skaters *went* into the woods.
10. Lucille *goes* to Philadelphia every Wednesday.

USING VIVID WORDS

29e. Use vivid words in your writing.

The three passages labeled (b) below are from Edward Abbey's essay "The First Morning," which is about his job as a park ranger in Arches National Monument in Utah. Each passage by Abbey is preceded by a passage which basically says the same thing but which uses vague, imprecise diction:

    a. It was snowing when I went to the park.
    b. "Snow was swirling through the air when I crossed the unfenced line and passed the boundary marker of the park."

    a. Some birds are near the rock, making noises.
    b. "Three ravens are wheeling near the balanced rock, squawking at each other and at the dawn."

a. The birds call and flap their wings. I smell breakfast cooking.
b. "The ravens cry out in husky voices, blue-black wings flapping against the golden sky. Over my shoulder comes the sizzle and smell of frying bacon."

You might have noticed by now that precise language is often language that creates mental pictures, or language that evokes sensations. For example, to say "it was snowing" does not create a very specific picture of what is going on with the weather, but to say "snow was swirling" does help us see how the snow was moving. To say the birds were "making noises" does not help us hear the specific *kind* of noise the birds were making; but to say "the ravens were squawking" gives a concrete auditory image. To say that you "smell breakfast" does not give the reader any specific sensory images, but to say that over your shoulder "comes the sizzle and smell of frying bacon" creates two specific sensory images (of sound and odor).

EXERCISE 6. Using Precise and Vivid Words. Rewrite each of the following sentences so that it expresses the ideas in more precise and vivid language. Use as many sentences as you want in your rewritten version.

1. Mickey's car is full of stuff.
2. I smelled breakfast cooking.
3. The weather was pretty bad.
4. A lot of noises came in the open windows.
5. We did lots of things on the eve of the holiday.

CONNOTATIONS AND LOADED WORDS

29f. Learn to recognize connotations and loaded words.

Semantics is the study of the meanings of words, changes in those meanings, and connotations of words. When you are selecting the right words, you must be aware of the words' connotations. *Connotations* are the various emotions and associations that are suggested by certain words. Connotations are distinct from a word's denotation, which is the word's strict dictionary definition. Not all words have connotations. The words *pen, paper, set, off*, and *listen* suggest no particular emotions or associations. But the words *skinny, slender, green, gray, intellectual*, and *egghead* do.

Connotations become attached to words through usage and common experience. The words *log cabin*, for example, refer literally to a dwelling made of logs. To many Americans, the words might suggest our pioneer past and Abraham Lincoln, and we might associate a log cabin with simplicity and strength.

Suppose several people see such a structure built of logs. One might describe the dwelling as a "log cabin" and would feel the suggestion of something rustic and simple. Another person might describe the same dwelling as a "shack." We would have feelings of poverty and unpleasantness. Yet another person might describe the dwelling as a "lodge," a word we associate with country retreats and with hunting. Yet another person might describe the same dwelling as a "chalet," which suggests Switzerland and perhaps a ski resort.

Suppose you want to write about someone who is not working. You might refer to that person as "unemployed," "out of work," "at leisure," "at loose ends," or "between jobs." None of those terms have strongly negative connotations. If you described the person as a "freeloader" or as a "moocher," your word choice would load your readers' feelings against the person.

Argument and persuasion will often use words with strong connotative associations. Persuasion is especially prone to search for words with powerful connotative pull, because the persuasive writer often appeals not so much to the reader's reason as to the *emotions*.

Here is semanticist S. I. Hayakawa on the power of connotative diction to affect the way we feel about a subject:

The parallel columns below illustrate how affective connotations can be changed while extensional meanings remain the same.

Finest quality filet mignon.	First-class piece of dead cow.
Cubs trounce Giants 15–3.	Score: Cubs 15, Giants 3.
French armies in rapid retreat!	The strategic withdrawal of the French forces to previously prepared positions in the rear was accomplished briskly and efficiently.
Urban Redevelopment Bill steam-rollered through Senate.	Senate passes Urban Redevelopment Bill over strong opposition.
She has her husband under her thumb.	She takes a deep interest in her husband's activities.

The governor appeared to be gravely concerned and said that a statement would be issued in a few days, after careful examination of the facts.

The governor was on the spot.

The story is told that, during the Boer War, the Boers were described in the British press as "sneaking and skulking behind rocks and bushes." The British forces, when they finally learned from the Boers how to employ tactics suitable to veldt warfare, were described as "cleverly taking advantage of cover."

EXERCISE 7. Recognizing Connotations. Each word in the following pairs has a similar denotation, or dictionary definition. Their connotations are different—some differences in meaning are subtle, some are obvious. Which word in each pair has a positive connotation? Which suggests negative feelings? In a sentence explain the distinctions between each word in the pair. In your sentence (or sentences), tell what emotions or associations are suggested by each word.

1. cautious / timorous
2. courageous / foolhardy
3. optimist / Pollyanna
4. hopeful / presumptive
5. lie / equivocate
6. concise / laconic
7. solemn / grim
8. guidance / manipulation
9. curious / nosey
10. freedom / license

EXERCISE 8. Defining Connotations. The names of animals frequently carry strong connotations, depending on the characteristics we associate with the animal (whether those associations are based on scientific evidence or not). Tell whether each of the following names would have positive or negative connotations if applied to a person. What mannerisms or habits do you associate with each animal that can account for the name's emotional effect?

1. snake	3. swine	5. worm	7. bat	9. skunk
2. owl	4. lamb	6. toad	8. whale	10. cat

Loaded Words

Words or phrases that are heavily connotative are often referred to as "loaded words." Because such words can be used to "slant" writing, they are often regarded with suspicion. Such loaded words, for example, are often used in commercials and advertisements, where the intelligent reader quickly recognizes them as examples of manipulation. Connotation is an important element in our use of language, particularly when we want to express our own attitude toward a subject, and when we want to influence the attitude of the readers as well. Here, for example, are the reports on a trial made by two newspapers. The newspapers had different points of view about the defendant in the trial. Their biases are clearly shown in the way they "slant" their descriptions of one day's testimony. One newspaper described the courtroom scene this way:

> Deathly silence prevailed this morning in the courtroom when in a monotone Halevy described in detail what he saw. The jurors listened transfixed to Halevy's story and the feeling among observers was that this was David Halevy's day.

The other newspaper described the very same testimony, saying:

> The atmosphere in the court was one of exhaustion when *Time* correspondent Halevy continued giving evidence and described the period of heavy bombing of Beirut. Three of the ten members of the jury fell asleep and even the judge, Abraham Sofaer, yawned just before the noon break.

EXERCISE 9. Recognizing Loaded Words. Each sentence in the following pairs has more or less the same denotative meaning, yet each sentence suggests different feelings toward the subject. Which words load the sentences positively? Which load them negatively? Can you explain the emotions or associations attached to the "loaded" words?

1. Lenahan dines every evening at 7.
2. Lenahan eats every night at 7.
3. The President has been obstinate as a negotiator.
4. The President has been firm as a negotiator.
5. Armand is fastidious about commas.
6. Armand is a nitpicker about commas.
7. The Nets squandered their ten-point lead.
8. The Nets lost their ten-point lead.

9. During rush-hour on Friday, the subway was filled with the aroma of perfume.
10. During rush-hour on Friday, the subway was filled with the stench of perfume.

EXERCISE 10. Using Connotative Meanings. Write two descriptions of a room, a meal, or a game. In one paragraph, use words that give your paragraph positive emotional weight; in the other paragraph, use words that will give your readers negative feelings about the subject.

COLLOQUIALISMS

29g. Avoid colloquialisms in formal writing.

One of the elements of a writer's style is the kind of diction he or she uses. A colloquial style is a style characterized by the use of *colloquialisms*—words, idioms, and expressions that are characteristic of informal spoken English, but which are not acceptable in formal written English.

Dictionaries usually label colloquial usage (Colloq.), and they note that this label does not indicate that the usage is nonstandard or slang. Though colloquialisms are never accepted in formal written English, many of them have acquired enough permanence in the language to be accepted in informal writing. In imaginative writing—in stories, dramas, personal essays, plays, and even in poems—colloquialisms are often used with great effectiveness to create realistic dialogue and a convincing "voice." In the following extracts, professional writers all use colloquialisms.

> The most useful thing I could do before this meeting today is to keel over. On the other hand, artists are keeling over by the thousands every day and nobody seems to pay the least attention.
>
> KURT VONNEGUT

> In the boondocks, we didn't wear shoes unless it was an absolute necessity.
>
> LEWIS GRIZZARD

There were lots and lots of houses available. We heard this from a lady named Mrs. Black. . . . She took us to visit a house which would have been perfect for us and our books and our children, if there had been any plumbing.

SHIRLEY JACKSON

I used to get all revved up.

PHILIP BOOTH—THE NEW YORKER

These writers have deliberately used colloquial language to give their language a contemporary, informal tone or, in some cases, to add humor. But if you were writing a report for your history teacher, you would not say that "President Lincoln *keeled over* after John Wilkes Booth fired his shot." You would say he "collapsed" or "slumped over."

If you were writing a report for a corporation, you would not propose expanding your business "into the *boondocks*." Notice in this case how imprecise the colloquialism is. This is a characteristic of colloquial language and one of the reasons it is not preferred in formal writing. In this report, you would have to say exactly where you were proposing the expansion. By "boondocks," do you mean the suburbs, the small towns nearby, or the farming area?

If you were writing a report on *The Glass Menagerie*, you would not say that Laura has "*lots and lots* of insecurities." You would say she has "several insecurities," or "many" or "two main insecurities."

If you were writing a letter to a prospective employer, you would not say you were "*all revved up* about this big deal job." You would say you were "very excited about this important job."

In formal writing then—in reports for school, in business letters, in office memos—you should avoid colloquial language. In your own informal writing, colloquialisms are acceptable as long as they express your meaning as precisely as possible.

EXERCISE 11. Replacing Colloquialisms with Formal Diction.
Rewrite each of the following sentences, replacing each colloquial expression with precise formal diction. If you have any questions about which words or phrases are colloquial, check the dictionary.

1. Lillian has gobs of energy.
2. Ernesto says he has the stuff to be class president.

3. The *News* has pegged McNaughton as a man of action.
4. As an actress, Tina can deliver the goods.
5. Ellsworth fell for the guy's phony sales pitch.
6. The famous miser Silas Marner salted away his money for years.
7. The plan to make Madeline a beauty didn't pan out.
8. The salesman racked up a large bonus.
9. At 10:00 P.M. the boss called it a day.
10. Fred wore a stupid hat to the movie.

SLANG

29h. Avoid slang in formal writing.

Slang consists of new words, or old words in new uses, that have made their way into the language because they are vivid or colorful. High-school and college students enjoy adopting the latest slang. Most slang is short-lived. It enjoys a brief popularity and then is forgotten. Therefore, it is always difficult to compile an illustrative list of slang terms which will be meaningful even a year later. The expressions in the following list were current a short while ago. How many of them do you recognize. Are any of them still in use?

SLANG

cool it	it's not my bag
groovy	heavy
uptight	nuts (crazy)
it's a drag	oddball
goof off	square
dig it	far out
cop out	bummer
off the wall	hang-up
bug off	weirdo
lousy	goofy

Occasionally a slang expression makes its way up the usage ladder and becomes acceptable even in formal writing, whereupon, of course, it is no longer slang. Slang should rarely be used in writing, and only when a special effect is being sought, as in reproducing dialogue.

Although dictionaries label words *informal* or *slang*, you cannot rely on their arbitrarily drawn distinctions as a means of deciding whether a word is appropriate to your composition. You need to understand the basic point that any word which is inappropriate to the general *tone* of your composition should not be used, regardless of its dictionary label. You should control your natural tendency to rely too much on informal English. The deciding factor is, of course, the degree of formality of your composition, which, in turn, determines the appropriateness of the words used. In a research paper, extremely informal English should be used very sparingly. In an informal essay, it may be used as frequently as in conversation.

Read the following sentences taken from formal compositions and note the inappropriateness of the italicized words.

In any eighth-grade classroom where *kids* of the same chronological age are grouped together, we expect to find a physiological age range of six or seven years.

There is a grave danger that we may expose far too many students of only medium ability to the long course of professional study in our universities. The employment situation in some professional areas, we must admit, is *not so hot.*

Dickens' *bag* was to reveal the social evils of the day so that they could be destroyed one by one.

EXERCISE 12. Identifying Slang or Informal Language. Point out the words and expressions in the following passage that are slang or so informal as to be inappropriate to the general tone.

While it is true that the students in the top 10 percent of any grade are capable of doing good work in the grade above them, to undertake a general upward transfer of these students would produce more socially maladjusted kids than you could shake a stick at. Efforts to meet the problem by cutting out the arbitrary division of a school into grades have been successful in small schools, where the need to classify and control has not been great and where parents couldn't care less what grade their children are in. Today the schools which allow children to go at their own speed, with a child doing sixth-grade work in one subject and third- or fourth-grade work in another, are considered pretty far out. Eventually this method of school organization may become general practice.

CLICHÉS

29i. Avoid clichés in formal writing.

A cliché is an expression that has been so overused that it has become dull and nearly meaningless. The term *cliché* comes from a French word for a kind of stereotyped plate used in printing. This plate would be used to make hundreds or thousands of impressions and all of them would be exactly alike—there would be no possibility of originality. In the same sense, clichés are expressions used over and over again, so that a person who speaks in clichés could be accused of having no originality.

There are thousands of clichés in the English language. Many of these expressions are figures of speech—metaphors, similes, or personifications. Many are hyperboles—exaggerations made for special effect. At one time, these expressions must have been considered original and forceful or amusing, but popular overuse has dulled their effect. Here are three popular clichés based on figurative language:

cold as ice
to fly off the handle
to miss the boat

"To fly off the handle" was once an original way of describing someone with an erratic temper who might lose control and cause an uproar, just as an axe-head might cause a disturbance when it loosens from the handle and flies off out of control. "To miss the boat" was once an original way of describing a person who missed out on something, just as a person who missed a boat would miss out on a journey (and stand watching the boat sail away without him or her).

When you revise your writing, be sure to examine your diction for the overuse of clichés. You will find that some clichés come to you so naturally that you use them automatically. Clichés offer us handy, ready-made comparisons and expressions; they help us avoid thinking for ourselves. You'll find, in fact, that clichés are so handy that it is often difficult to express their meaning in fresh, original ways. To do this, you have to stop and think about what you really mean to say.

EXERCISE 13. **Recognizing Clichés.** The following interview with a cliché expert mocks our overuse of clichés. Read it and answer the questions that follow.

Q: You mean you get a handsome salary?

A: I prefer to call it a princely stipend. You know what kind of coin I'm paid in?

Q: No. What?

A: Coin of the realm. Not that I give a hoot for money. You know how I refer to money?

Q: As the root of all evil?

A: No, but you have a talking point there. I call it lucre—filthy lucre.

Q: On the whole, you seem to have a pretty good time, Mr. Arbuthnot.

A: Oh, I'm not complaining. I'm as snug as a bug in a rug. I'm clear as crystal—when I'm not dull as dishwater. I'm cool as a cucumber, quick as a flash, fresh as a daisy, pleased as Punch, good as my word, regular as clockwork, and I suppose at the end of my declining years, when I'm gathered to my ancestors, I'll be dead as a doornail.

Q: *Eh bien! C'est la vie!*

A: *Mais oui, mon vieux.* I manage, I'm the glass of fashion and the mold of form. I have a finger in every pie, all except this finger. I use it for pointing with scorn. When I go in for malice, it is always malice aforethought. My nods are significant. My offers are standing. I am at cross-purposes and in dire straits. My motives are ulterior, my circles are vicious, my retainers are faithful, and my hopefuls are young. My suspicions are sneaking, my glee is fiendish, my stories are likely. I am drunk.

Q: Drunk?

A: Yes, with power ...

FRANK SULLIVAN

1. List at least five clichés that are based on figures of speech.
2. Rewrite a portion of this interview, without the clichés. Is it always clear what the cliché expert is saying?
3. Answer one of the interviewer's questions with a litany of clichés of your own.

EXERCISE 14. Replacing Clichés with Fresh Comparisons or Descriptions. Each of the following sentences contains a cliché that is based on a figure of speech. Rephrase each sentence so that you eliminate the cliché and replace it with a fresh comparison or description of your own. (The directions in parentheses might help you.)

1. Mildred is as straight as an arrow. (Describe Mildred's character without the cliché.)

2. The typist is as busy as a bee. (Describe the typist's movements without the cliché.)
3. Uncle Morty is as old as the hills. (Describe Uncle Morty so the reader gets a visual sense of his age, without the cliché.)
4. The goalie is as tough as nails. (Describe the goalie's abilities and character, to suggest toughness without the cliché.)
5. Uriah's hand feels as cold as ice. (Describe Uriah's handshake without the cliché.)

EXERCISE 15. Finding Fresh Comparisons. Write a paragraph in which you describe one of the following subjects. Tell how the subject looks, sounds, feels, smells, or tastes without using clichés.

1. A dog or cat eating
2. A meal you ordered in a restaurant or lunch room
3. A crowd you watched at a game
4. The players sitting on the bench
5. A tape deck you like or dislike

JARGON

29j. Avoid jargon in formal writing.

Jargon can have two meanings. (1) Jargon can refer to the specialized language of a particular group of people who do the same work or who have the same interests. Military personnel, computer users, editors, truck drivers, doctors, astronauts, and baseball players all have their own jargon. A waiter uses jargon when he calls into the kitchen, "Two eggs, wreck 'em!" An actress uses theater jargon when she says to a colleague going on stage: "Break a leg!" (In theater, this means "Good luck!") A sports writer uses jargon in writing, "Carl Furillo popped out to the shortstop."

In all these cases, jargon is perfectly acceptable. But jargon in a second sense is not acceptable in any kind of writing. (2) Jargon can also mean language that is incoherent and cumbersome, and which obscures meaning rather than clarifying it. This kind of jargon uses unnecessarily long and complicated words, often words of Latin origin. People who use this kind of jargon often say in twenty words what could be more clearly and precisely expressed in five. Such jargon often relies on clichés. Almost always, this kind of jargon says much less than it seems to say.

Here is a famous little proverb restated in jargon:

> A plethora of culinary specialists has a deleterious effect upon the quality of purees, consommés, and other soluble pabula.

In plain English this says:

> Too many cooks spoil the broth.

Can you translate this proverb from jargon into plain English?

> A mobile section of petrified matter agglomerates no bryophytes.

At times, a writer or speaker will use jargon deliberately to obscure an unpleasant meaning. People who steal computer programs are not called "robbers" or "cheats"; they are called by the more glamorous word "pirates." Government bureaucrats refer to increased taxes as "revenue enhancement." A nuclear power plant speaks of "energetic disassembly" instead of "explosion"; of "rapid oxidation" instead of "fire"; and of "normal aberration" instead of "a reactor accident." One state no longer has a "Death Row"; it has a "Capital Sentences Unit." A large corporation recently circulated a memo which referred to "eliminating redundancies in the human resource area," instead of "laying people off" or "firing people."

Such pompous use of language is often called *gobbledygook*, a word coined by a United States Representative who had heard enough of such "official talk" in Congress. The origin of the word *jargon* also points to the emptiness of such use of language. The word is ultimately of "echoic" origin, meaning it reproduces a particular sound in nature —*jargon* comes from a Middle French word for "a chattering of birds."

EXERCISE 16. Recognizing Jargon. In the following essay, Russell Baker mocks the popular tendency to use jargon instead of good, plain English.

AMERICAN FAT

Americans don't like plain talk anymore. Nowadays they like fat talk. Show them a lean, plain word that cuts to the bone and watch them lard it with thick greasy syllables front and back until it wheezes and gasps for breath as it comes lumbering down upon some poor threadbare sentence like a sack of iron on a swayback horse.

"Facilitate" is typical of the case. A generation ago only sissies and bureaucrats would have said "facilitate" in public. Nowadays we are a nation of "facilitate" utterers.

"Facilitate" is nothing more than a gout-ridden, overstuffed "ease." Why has "ease" fallen into disuse among us? It is a lovely little bright snake of a word which comes hissing quietly off the tongue and carries us on, without fuss and French horns, to the object which is being eased.

This is English at its very best. Easing is not one of the great events of life; it does not call for Beethoven; it is not an idea to get drunk on, to wallow in, to encase in multiple oleaginous syllabification until it becomes a pompous ass of a word like "facilitate."

A radio announcer was interviewing a doctor the other day. The doctor worked in a hospital in which he apparently—one never really hears more than 3 percent of anything said on radio—controlled the destinies of many social misfits. The announcer asked the purpose of his work.

The doctor said it was "to facilitate the reentry into society as functioning members"—the mind's Automatic Dither Cutoff went to work at this stage, and the rest of the doctor's answer was lost, but it was too late. Seeds of gloom had been planted.

The doctor's passion for fat English had told too much. One shuddered for the patients at his hospital—"institutional complex," he probably called it—for it must be a dreadful thing to find oneself at the mercy of a man whose tongue drips the fatty greases of "facilitate." He doubtless, almost surely, says "utilize" too, when he means "use," and "implement" when he means "do."

Getting his patients out of the hospital and back home has become for this doctor "the reentry into society," a technological chore of the sort performed in outer space. Having facilitated their reentry into society, he will be able to greet them as "functioning members."

How dreadful it must be, caged up and antisocial in a beautifully sterilized container for misfits, for a patient to find himself at the mercy of men whose English is fat, who see him as an exercise in engineering and who are determined to turn him into "a functioning member."

Peace, doctors! Of course it is merely a manner of speaking, although the "merely" may not be quite so mere as it sounds.

We are what we think, and very often we think what we say rather than what we say we think.

Long words, fat talk—they may tell us something about ourselves. Has the passion for fat in the language increased as self-confidence has waned?

We associate plain talk with the age of national confidence. It is the stranger telling the black hat, "When you call me that, smile." It is the campaign of 1948 when a President of the United States could open a speech by saying, "My name's Truman, I'm President of the United States and I'm trying to keep my job."

Since then campaign talk has become fatter and more pompous, as though we need sounds that seem weighty to conceal a thinness of the spirit from which they emanate. But politicians are not our corrupters here; we are all in love with the fat sound.

There is the radio disk jockey who cannot bring himself to say that the temperature at the studio is "now" forty-five degrees but must fatten it up, extend it, make more of it, score it for kettle drums, by declaring that the temperature at the studio is "currently" forty-five degrees, and often, carried into illiteracy in his passion for fat talk, "presently" forty-five degrees.

Newspapers seem to be the father and mother of fat. The bombing is never the stark, dramatic "intense," but always the drawled, overweight "intensive." Presidents are rarely allowed to "say" the weather is improving; the papers have them "declare" it, "state" it, "issue a challenge for the Weather Bureau to deny" it. . . .

Why do we like our words so fat but our women so skinny?

RUSSELL BAKER

1. What does Baker mean by "American fat"?
2. List the "fat" words Baker disapproves of, along with the "lean" equivalents he prefers.
3. What does Baker think our passion for "fat talk" reveals about us?
4. What people, according to Baker, are especially in love with the "fat sound"?

EXERCISE 17. **Identifying Examples of Poor Diction.** The following speech is a parody of the kind of speech a modern government official might write, if he or she were composing the Gettysburg Address today. The Gettysburg Address, of course, is one of the greatest of all American speeches, delivered by President Abraham Lincoln at the dedication of the Soldiers' National Cemetery on November 19, 1863. The parodist's intent is *not* to mock the Gettysburg Address; his purpose is to reveal the distinction between Lincoln's effective, eloquent diction, and the kind of "fat" talk that Baker so deplores. Find examples in this speech of the misuses of diction that have been pointed out in this chapter: vague imprecise words, mixed idioms and metaphors, colloquialisms that are out of place in a formal speech, clichés, and jargon. Next to each example, write out the simple eloquent words used by Lincoln.

I haven't checked these figures but 87 years ago, I think it was, a number of individuals organized a governmental set-up here in this country, I believe it covered certain Eastern areas, with this idea they were following up based on a sort of national independence arrangement and the program that every individual is just as good as every other individual. Well, now, of course, we are dealing with this big difference of opinion, civil disturbance you might say, although I don't like to appear to take sides or name any individuals, and the point is naturally to check up, by actual experience in the field, to see whether any governmental set-up with a basis like the one I was mentioning has any validity and find out whether that dedication by those early individuals will pay off in lasting values and things of that kind.

Well, here we are, at the scene where one of these disturbances between different sides got going. We want to pay our tribute to those loved ones, those departed individuals who made the supreme sacrifice here on the basis of their opinions about how this thing ought to be handled. And I would say this. It is absolutely in order to do this.

But if you look at the over-all picture of this, we can't pay any tribute—we can't sanctify this area, you might say—we can't hallow according to whatever individual creeds or faiths or sort of religious outlooks are involved like I said about this particular area. It was those individuals themselves, including the enlisted men, very brave individuals, who have given this religious character to the area. The way I see it, the rest of the world will not remember any statements issued here but it will never forget how these men put their shoulders to the wheel and carried this idea down the fairway.

Now frankly, our job, the living individuals' job here, is to pick up the burden and sink the putt they made these big efforts here for. It is our job to get on with the assignment—and from these deceased fine individuals to take extra inspiration, you could call it, for the same theories about the set-up for which they made such a big contribution. We have to make up our minds right here and now, as I see it, that they didn't put out all that blood, perspiration and—well—that they didn't just make a dry run here, and that all of us here, under God, that is, the God of our choice, shall beef up this idea about freedom and liberty and those kind of arrangements, and that government of all individuals, by all individuals and for the individuals, shall not pass out of the world-picture.

OLIVER JENSEN

PURPOSE, TONE, MOOD, AND DICTION

29k. Adjust your diction to control purpose , tone, and mood.

Writers choose diction not only to suit their audiences but also to suit their purposes. The most common purpose of writing is probably to give information (Chapter 23). Other purposes may be descriptive or narrative (Chapter 26) or persuasive (Chapter 25). Revealing a particular tone or mood may also be part of a writer's purpose.

Tone and Mood

Tone refers to the attitude the writer takes toward his subject. Tone can always be described by an adjective: *formal, informal, critical, approving, sarcastic, ironic, nostalgic, sad, angry, sentimental, bitter, strident, tongue-in-cheek, mocking, tender, horrific,* and so on. Mood is the atmosphere the writer creates. Mood is also described by adjectives.

Tone or Mood of Horror

Suppose you are describing a particular setting and you wish to convey a tone of horror. Paul Theroux does just that in this passage describing a tree in Malaysia called "The Midnight Horror." (The corolla are the petals of the tree's flowers.)

> During the day the tree looked comic, a tall simple pole like an enormous coatrack, with big leaves that looked like branches—but there were very few of them. It was covered with knobs, stark black things; and around the base of the trunk there were always fragments of leaves that looked like shattered bones, but not human bones.
>
> At night the tree was different, not comic at all. It was Ladysmith who showed me the underlined passage in his copy of Professor Corner's *Wayside Trees of Malaya.* Below the entry for *Oroxylum indicum* it read, "Botanically, it is the sole representative of its kind; aesthetically, it is monstrous. . . . The corolla begins to open about 10 P.M., when the tumid, wrinkled lips part and the harsh odor escapes from them. By midnight, the lurid mouth gapes widely and is filled with stink. . . . The flowers are pollinated by bats which are attracted by the smell and, holding to the fleshy corolla with the claws on their wings, thrust their noses into its throat; scratches, as of bats, can be seen on the fallen leaves the next morning . . . "
>
> PAUL THEROUX

Note the specific words that communicate the sense of horror: *stark black things; leaves that look like nonhuman bones; monstrous; tumid, wrinkled lips; harsh odor; lurid mouth; stink; bats.* This paragraph is from the opening of a horror story and it does, in fact, set the tone for the rest of the story's events.

EXERCISE 18. Using Diction to Control Tone. Write a paragraph describing Theroux's tree, but change the diction so that your tone is different. In your own paragraph, describe the tree in words that make it seem beautiful and mysterious—not disgusting. You may change any detail you wish; do not worry about being scientifically accurate.

Tone or Mood of Nostalgia

If you want to suggest a tone of nostalgia, you would choose words that suggest a fondness for things past. Eudora Welty does that in this passage describing a store she remembers from her childhood. Notice that she uses sensory diction, as Theroux does, but she uses words that evoke *pleasant* sensations. Find words that evoke these feelings.

Running in out of the sun, you met what seemed total obscurity inside. There were almost tangible smells—licorice recently sucked in a child's cheek, dill-pickle brine that had leaked through a paper sack in a fresh trail across the wooden floor, ammonia-loaded ice that had been hoisted from wet croker sacks and slammed into the icebox with its sweet butter at the door, and perhaps the smell of still-untrapped mice.

Then through the motes of cracker dust, cornmeal dust, the Gold Dust of the Gold Dust Twins that the floor had been swept out with, the realities emerged. Shelves climbed to high reach all the way around, set out with not too much of any one thing but a lot of things—lard, molasses, vinegar, starch, matches, kerosene, Octagon soap (about a year's worth of octagon-shaped coupons cut out and saved brought a signet ring addressed to you in the mail. Furthermore, when the postman arrived at your door, he blew a whistle). It was up to you to remember what you came for, while your eye traveled from cans of sardines to ice cream salt to harmonicas to flypaper (over your head, batting around on a thread beneath the blades of the ceiling fan, stuck with its testimonial catch).

Its confusion may have been in the eye of its beholder. Enchantment is cast upon you by all those things you weren't supposed to have need for, it lures you close to wooden tops you'd outgrown, boy's marbles and agates in little net pouches, small rubber balls that wouldn't bounce straight, frazzly kite-string, clay bubble-pipes that would snap off in your teeth, the stiffest scissors. You could contemplate those long narrow boxes of sparklers gathering dust while you waited for it to be the Fourth of July or Christmas, and noisemakers in the shape of tin frogs for somebody's birthday party you hadn't been invited to yet, and see that they were all marvelous.

EUDORA WELTY

EXERCISE 19. Using Diction to Control Tone. Write a paragraph describing Welty's little store, but change the diction so that your tone is not nostalgic, but frightened and uneasy.

Conveying Different Tones

Here are two writers, both of whom are writing about explorers. One uses an ironic, even sarcastic, tone to make us laugh at the incredible hardships explorers seem to bring on themselves. The other writer is serious and admiring. Which is which? Find words that help convey each writer's tone.

Above all others, the perseverance of La Salle in his search for the mouth of the Mississippi was unsurpassed. While preparing in Quebec, he mastered eight Indian languages. From then on he suffered accidents, betrayals, desertions, losses of men and provisions, fever and snow blindness, the hostility and intrigues of rivals who incited the Indians against him and plotted to ambush or poison him. He was truly pursued, as Francis Parkman wrote, by "a demon of havoc." Paddling through heavy waves in a storm over Lake Ontario, he waded through freezing surf to beach the canoes each night, and lost guns and baggage when a canoe was swamped and sank. To lay the foundations of a fort above Niagara, frozen ground had to be thawed by boiling water. When the fort was at last built, La Salle christened it Crèvecoeur—that is, Heartbreak. It earned the name when in his absence it was plundered and deserted by its half-starved mutinous garrison. Farther on, a friendly Indian village, intended as a destination, was found laid waste by the Iroquois with only charred stakes stuck with skulls standing among the ashes, while wolves and buzzards prowled through the remains.

When at last, after four months' hazardous journey down the Great River, La Salle reached the sea, he formally took possession in the name of Louis XIV of all the country from the river's mouth to its source and of its tributaries—that is, of the vast basin of the Mississippi from the Rockies to the Appalachians—and named it Louisiana. The validity of the claim, which seems so hollow to us (though successful in its own time), is not the point.

What counts is the conquest of fearful adversity by one man's extraordinary
exertions and inflexible will.

BARBARA TUCHMAN

Cherry-Garrard insists that one morning when he peeped out of the tent
his clothing froze instantly, trapping his head in that position. He claims that
for the next several hours he had to pull the sledge with his head screwed
around at an angle. Now this is ridiculous. This is the sort of thing you see in
a Hollywood cartoon, but our Oxford egg-collector is no humorist. Presumably it happened.

At last they got to the penguin rookery and after zoologist Wilson had
completed his research they stole five eggs and started home. En route
Cherry-Garrard broke two of these precious eggs. He was carrying them
inside his mittens and he explains simply that they "burst." Maybe. Maybe it
happened. But eggs seldom break unless they have been rudely handled.
Nevertheless, he tells us without further clarification, his eggs "burst." All
right, let it go. He emptied one mitten but kept the broken egg in the other
because he thought that when they stopped to eat he would pour it into the
cooker. For some reason he neglected to do this, "but on the return journey
I had my mitts far more easily thawed out . . . and I believe the grease in the
egg did them good.". . .

Two days after the tea vanished the weather improved enough for them
to prepare a meal—tea and pemmican flavored with burnt seal blubber,
penguin feathers, and hair from the sleeping bags. . . .

Three of the five eggs at last reached the Natural History Museum in
London where they were accepted and studied with no particular excitement. The value of this trip, therefore, depends on your interpretation. One
biographer commented that it had drawn Cherry-Garrard and his compan-
ions together in permanent spiritual bondage—which makes it sound almost
worthwhile. Another said that few men ever have absorbed so much
punishment for the sake of adding such an insignificant brick to the edifice of
knowledge. In other words the rookery had as much meaning, or as little, as
the Pole itself.

EVAN CONNELL

EXERCISE 20. Changing Diction to Change Tone. Rewrite
Connell's account of the explorers at the Pole who were searching for
the penguin eggs. This time, make the account admiring in tone. You
will have to change Connell's diction to diction that suggests the altered
tone.

CHAPTER 29 WRITING REVIEW

Using Effective Diction. This assignment calls for two paragraphs. In one paragraph, express your opinion on one of the following statements using formal diction and revealing a serious, formal tone. In another paragraph, explain your opinion on one of these statements using informal diction and revealing an informal tone: sarcastic, angry, mocking, light-hearted, comic, relaxed.

1. Education involves unlearning more than learning.
2. Discipline and creativity do not go hand in hand.
3. It is much easier to destroy something than to create it.

PART FIVE

MECHANICS

CHAPTER 30

Manuscript Form

STANDARDS FOR PREPARING
AND REVISING COMPOSITIONS

A neat, properly prepared manuscript is the mark of a careful writer. A messy, hard-to-read manuscript gives readers the impression that the writer does not care about the subject—or about the people who will read the paper. By following the simple procedures described in this chapter you can make sure that the final version of your manuscript is clear and that your ideas will be taken seriously.

THE MANUSCRIPT

Paper and ink. Write compositions on standard size (8 × 10½″) lined paper. Use black, blue, or blue-black ink. Write on only one side of the paper.

If you type, use standard size (8½ × 11″) white typewriter paper. Double-space, and use only one side of the paper.

Labeling and numbering pages. Follow your teacher's policy concerning labeling and numbering of pages. One common practice is to write your name, the subject (English IV), and the date in that order, one below the other, in the upper right-hand corner of the first page. Number all pages, except the first, with Arabic numerals in the upper right-hand corner. It is a good plan to write your name beneath the page number on each sheet.

Margin. Leave a margin of at least one and a quarter inches at the left and one inch at the right side of the paper. The left-hand margin must be even; the right-hand margin may be slightly uneven. In typewritten manuscripts, place the first line of all pages after the first at least one inch below the top of the paper and leave a one-inch margin at the bottom of all pages.

The title. Place the title of the composition in the center of the first line of a ruled page, and skip a line between the title and the first paragraph. The title of a typewritten composition should be placed about two inches below the top of the page. Composition titles should not be underlined or placed in quotation marks, except in rare instances when the title is itself a quotation.

Indentation. Indent the first line of every paragraph the same distance—about one inch in handwritten papers, five spaces in typewritten papers.

Long quoted passages may be set off by indenting the entire passage. In typescript such indented passages are single-spaced and written without quotation marks.

Neatness. Do not mar the appearance of a final version with cross-outs, insertions between lines, and afterthought additions in the margins. If you must make changes in the final version, make them neatly or rewrite the entire page. Strike-overs and messy erasures mar the neatness of typewritten work.

Never begin any line with a comma, dash, or other punctuation mark (with the exception of opening quotation marks).

REVISING THE FIRST DRAFT

All compositions should be written *at least* twice. The first draft of a composition is your own copy and need not conform to the manuscript standards noted above. Mark up this first draft with your revisions and corrections. When you are satisfied that you have made all necessary changes, write your final version.

Revision is an extremely important step in the writing process. You should look upon each theme, whether written for English or for any other class, as an opportunity to express your ideas about a subject in such a way that your audience will understand and appreciate those ideas.

For more information on specific techniques for revising your writing, refer to Chapter 21, "Writing and Thinking: The Writing Process," and to the Guidelines for Revising provided in the chapters on the various forms and purposes of writing.

Abbreviations

30a. Do not use abbreviations except in certain special instances in which abbreviations are customary.

NONSTANDARD   While jogging by the park one warm Tues. A.M., I saw a man slip from an alley across the st. and hop into a limousine bearing a Nev. license.

STANDARD   While jogging by the park one warm **Tuesday morning**, I saw a man slip from an alley across the **street** and hop into a limousine bearing a **Nevada** license.

(1) The following abbreviations are customary before a name: *Mr., Messrs., Mrs., Ms., Dr., Rev., St.* (Saint). The following are abbreviated after a name: *Jr., Sr.,* and the college degrees *A.B., Ph.D.,* etc. With the exception of the college degrees, these abbreviations are used only with a name.

NONSTANDARD   I called the dr. for the jr. varsity player.

STANDARD   I called **Dr.** Lee for the **junior** varsity player.

(2) The following abbreviations are customary when used with numbers: *A.D.* (*A.D.* 372); *B.C.* (271 *B.C.*); *A.M.* (before noon); *P.M.* (after noon). The following are acceptable in all writing: *etc.* (and so forth); *i.e.* (that is); *e.g.* (for example). Abbreviations for government agencies are customary after the full name has been given once: *EPA, OSHA.* Periods are not used with abbreviations of this kind.

(3) Do not use the symbol & or + for *and*.

Numbers

30b. Do not begin a sentence with a numeral.

NONSTANDARD   15 more people joined the line.

STANDARD   **Fifteen** more people joined the line.

30c. Numbers of more than two words should be written in numerals.

EXAMPLES   2,145,320; $214.35; 1985
                 four dollars; fifty cents; sixty-five
                 The new parking lots cost more than a million dollars.

Be consistent in your use of words and numerals.

NONSTANDARD   I make $90.00 a week, but my brother makes only seventy-five.
    STANDARD   I make **ninety** dollars a week, but my brother makes only **seventy-five**.

☞ NOTE   Rule 30c applies to ordinary writing. In mathematical, scientific, and statistical writing, most numbers are written as numerals, not spelled out.
    Never spell out the year or spell out page numbers following the word *page*.

30d. Hyphenate all compound numbers from *twenty-one* to *ninety-nine* and fractions used as adjectives.

EXAMPLES   She hiked for **twenty-two** days in the hills.
               one-third power, but **one third** of the power

30e. Write out numbers like *first, thirty-sixth*, etc., instead of writing them as numerals with letter endings: *1st, 36th*, etc.

EXAMPLES   My desk is the **fifth** (not 5th) one in the **fourth** (not 4th) row.
               She is **twenty-seventh** in her graduating class.
               We live in the **eleventh** house from the corner.

Dividing Words at the End of a Line

Try to avoid dividing words at the end of a line. If you must divide a word at the end of a line to maintain an even margin, use a hyphen between the parts of the word. Words should be divided between syllables. When you are not sure where one syllable ends and another begins, consult a dictionary. A few simple rules may help you to decide where to place the hyphen.

30f. Divide a word at the end of a line between pronounceable parts only. One-syllable words should never be divided.

NONSTANDARD   laugh-ed [one-syllable word]
STANDARD   **laughed**
NONSTANDARD   compreh-end [parts not pronounceable]
STANDARD   **compre-hend**

30g. A word having double consonants should be divided between the consonants.

EXAMPLES   sil-ly
com-mitment

Words like *filling* and *crossing* are exceptions. See rule 30i regarding prefixes and suffixes.

30h. Do not divide a word so that a single letter stands alone. Try to avoid dividing a word so that only two letters are carried over to the next line.

AWKWARD   e-vacuate, accesso-ry
IMPROVED   evac-uate, acces-sory

30i. Words having prefixes and suffixes should usually be divided between the prefix and the root of the word or between the root of the word and the suffix.

EXAMPLES   inter-act
leap-ing
fall-ing

CORRECTING COMPOSITIONS

Many teachers use a set of symbols like the one shown in this section to mark student compositions. What you are to do about each marking symbol is explained in the following list of symbols.

All changes that require rewriting of one sentence or more should be numbered (1, 2, etc.) in the margin where the symbol occurs and then rewritten, marked with the same number, on a separate "correction sheet" or, if there is space, on the final page of your composition. As the following instructions indicate, changes that do not require rewriting a whole sentence are to be made directly on the page involved.

Study the marked and corrected passages on pages 765–66.

Correction Symbols with Instructions

ms *manuscript form or neatness*
Rewrite the sentence or paragraph neatly on your correction sheet.

cap *use of capitalization*
Cross out the incorrect letter and write the correct form above it.

p *punctuation*
Insert punctuation, remove it, or change it as required.

sp *spelling*
Cross out the word; write the correct spelling above it; write the word
correctly spelled five times on your correction sheet.

frag *sentence fragment*
Correct it by changing punctuation and capital letter or by rewriting
on your correction sheet.

rs *run-on sentence*
Correct it by inserting the necessary end mark and capital letter.

ss *sentence structure*
Rewrite the sentence on your correction sheet.

k *coherence*
Rewrite the sentence or passage on your correction sheet.

nc *not clear*
Rewrite the sentence or sentences on your correction sheet.

ref *unclear pronoun reference*
Cross out the error and write the correction above it.

gr *grammar*
Cross out the error and write the correct form above it.

w *word choice*
Cross out the word and write a better one above it.

¶ *new paragraph*
This will not be corrected but should be carefully noted.

t *tense*
Cross out the error and write the correct form above it.

∧ *omission*
Insert omitted words above the line.

COMPOSITION PASSAGE MARKED BY TEACHER

cap/gr   A field producer in broadcast Journalism take
on a variety of tasks. He or she may assist on
k   the scene a news correspondent simply by handling
frag the technical details. The field producer getting
the film shot, back to the newsroom, and edited
into the final presentation. In other cases, the
nc   producer does the story research, making
arrangements and shooting film. Sometimes,
p   usually for in—depth stories the producer does
ref not work with a correspondent until it is being
edited. The producer develops the story, works in
the field with a camera crew, and edits the raw
rs   material, the correspondent helps write the final
sp/w report and narates it. The one thing a producer
rarely does is appearing before the camera.

PASSAGE CORRECTED BY STUDENT

cap/gr   A field producer in broadcast ~~J~~ournalism ~~take~~ *takes*
on a variety of tasks.⌐He or she may assist on
k   the scene a news correspondent simply by handling
frag ① the technical details.⌐The field producer ~~getting~~ *gets*
the film shot, back to the newsroom, and edited
into the final presentation.⌐In other cases, the
nc ② producer does the story research, making
arrangements and shooting film.⌐Sometimes,

p usually for in-depth stories, the producer does

ref not work with a correspondent until ~~it~~ *the film* is being

edited. The producer develops the story, works in

the field with a camera crew, and edits the raw

rs material the correspondent helps write the final

sp/w report and ~~narates~~ *narrates* it. ~~The one thing~~ a producer

w rarely ~~does is appearing~~ *appears* before the camera.

CORRECTION SHEET ATTACHED TO COMPOSITION

narrate, narrate, narrate, narrate, narrate

① He or she may assist a news correspondent on the scene by simply handling the technical details.

② In other cases, the producer also researches the story and makes all arrangements for the filming.

CHAPTER 31

Capitalization

STANDARD USES OF CAPITAL LETTERS

Capital letters serve many purposes. They indicate the beginnings of sentences, an important aid to the reader; they distinguish names, titles, etc., from the rest of the sentence; they show respect. Many uses of capital letters are conventions; i.e., they are generally used by educated people. Readers expect capital letters to be used according to these conventions, which are among the standards of written English.

DIAGNOSTIC TEST

Identifying Standard Uses of Capital Letters. Number your paper 1–20. Each of the following pairs of items presents two versions of capitalization. In most cases, either item a or b is correctly capitalized according to standard usage. After the proper number on your paper, write the letter of the version containing the standard usage. If neither version is correct, write *N*.

EXAMPLES
    1. a. a Movie starring Lena Horne
    1. b. a movie starring Lena Horne
    1. b.

    2. a. the diamond hardware Store
    2. b. The Diamond hardware store
    2. *N*

1. a. Resolved: That the dress code should be reinstated. ✓
   b. Resolved: that the dress code should be reinstated.
2. a. a nation in the middle east
   b. a nation in the Middle East
3. a. took courses in English, Spanish, and chemistry
   b. took courses in English, Spanish, and Chemistry
4. a. the crew of the Space Shuttle *Columbia*
   b. the crew of the space shuttle *Columbia*
5. a. at the intersection of Seventh avenue and Market street
   b. at the intersection of Seventh Avenue and Market Street
6. a. a letter of inquiry addressed to American airlines
   b. a letter of inquiry addressed to American Airlines
7. a. a trip to Yosemite National park
   b. a trip to Yosemite national park
8. a. chief justice Burger
   b. Chief Justice Burger
9. a. fought the Battle of Saratoga during the Revolutionary war
   b. fought the Battle of Saratoga during the Revolutionary War
10. a. enjoyed Hemingway's *the Sun also Rises*
    b. enjoyed Hemingway's *The Sun Also Rises*
11. a. made copies on the xerox machine
    b. made copies on the Xerox machine
12. a. a biography of the American novelist Edith Wharton
    b. a biography of the american novelist Edith Wharton
13. a. a visit to the West Coast of Oregon
    b. a visit to the west coast of Oregon
14. a. a birthday gift from Aunt Madge
    b. a birthday gift from aunt Madge
15. a. freedom to worship god according to personal beliefs
    b. freedom to worship God according to personal beliefs
16. a. Prime Minister Margaret Thatcher of England
    b. prime Minister Margaret Thatcher of England
17. a. a course in World History at Roosevelt high school
    b. a course in world history at Roosevelt high school
18. a. celebrating the fourth of July
    b. celebrating the Fourth of July
19. a. a delicious chinese dinner at Wong's Restaurant
    b. a delicious Chinese dinner at Wong's Restaurant

20. a. birds migrating across the strait of Gibraltar
    b. birds migrating across the Strait of Gibraltar

In the use of capital letters, as in all matters pertaining to language usage, variations are common. In standard usage, for instance, the names of the seasons are not capitalized, but some newspapers do capitalize them. Newspapers may also adopt what they call the "down style" of capitalization, in which words like *avenue, university,* and *library* are not capitalized as they are in standard usage when used with a particular name.

STANDARD USAGE	"DOWN STYLE"
Fifth Avenue	Fifth avenue
Brandeis University	Brandeis university
Detroit Library	Detroit library

The usage described in this book is standard ("up style") usage, which is generally followed in books and magazines.

31a. Capitalize the first word in a sentence.

If you do not always use a capital letter at the beginning of a sentence, review Chapter 12 to make sure that you can recognize the end of one sentence and the beginning of the next.

(1) Capitalize the first word of a formal statement following a colon.

EXAMPLE   The committee included the following statement: In light of these statistics, we recommend that city officials install four-way stop signs at that intersection.

(2) Capitalize the first word of a resolution following the word *Resolved.*

EXAMPLE   Resolved: That government support of space exploration be increased.

(3) Capitalize the first word of a direct quotation.

EXAMPLE   Ms. Simpson said, "Your sister is a born leader."

Do not capitalize the first word of a quoted sentence fragment.

EXAMPLE   I agree with Ms. Simpson's comment that my sister is a "born leader."

(4) Capitalize the first word of a statement or question inserted in a sentence without quotation marks.

EXAMPLE   My question is, Will this action solve the problem?

☞ NOTE   Traditionally, poets capitalize the first word in a line of poetry. This use of capitals, although by no means as common today as it once was, is still often found.

WRITING APPLICATION A:
Using Capitalization Correctly to Make Your Writing Clear

By now, you have probably begun to analyze and evaluate statements you encounter in the news media. Whether you agree or disagree with a statement, if you respond to it in writing you should be sure to use capitalization correctly to make your meaning clear. Notice in the following excerpt from a letter to the editor that the writer correctly capitalized the first word in her sentence as well as the first word of the statement she was responding to. These capital letters make clear which words are hers and which are those of the other letter writer.

EXAMPLE   A recent letter to the editor contained the following statement: The newspaper does not have the right to print subversive material under somebody's byline.

The writer of this letter went on to explain why she disagreed with the statement, arguing her case by citing facts as evidence.

Writing Assignment

Find a statement with which you strongly agree or disagree in an editorial or a letter to the editor. Write a letter to the editor responding to the statement, using capitalization correctly and arguing your case by citing facts.

31b. Capitalize the pronoun *I* and the interjection *O*.

You will probably have little use for the interjection *O*, which is used only in such rare expressions as "O happy day, come soon!" The common interjection *oh* ("Oh, what a beautiful morning!") is capitalized only when it appears at the beginning of a sentence. *Oh* is usually followed by a mark of punctuation, but *O* is rarely followed by punctuation.

EXAMPLES   Rejoice in the Lord, **O** ye righteous!
He was **oh**, so glad to see them.

31c. Capitalize proper nouns and proper adjectives.

A proper noun is the name of a particular person, place, or thing. A common noun names a kind or type. Words that name a kind or a type (*poodle, sloop, sonnet*) are not capitalized. Names given to individuals within the type are proper nouns and are capitalized (**Fifi, Wanderer,** "Sonnet on Chillon").

PROPER NOUNS	COMMON NOUNS
Denise Tseng	**woman**
Mexico	**country**
Suwannee River	**river**

A proper adjective is an adjective formed from a proper noun.

PROPER NOUNS	PROPER ADJECTIVES
France	French
Asia	Asian

Study the following classification of proper nouns.

(1) Capitalize the names of persons.

Before writing names beginning with *Mc* or *Mac* (meaning "son of"), find out whether or not the person spells the name with two capitals. Custom varies: **McDuff, MacNeill, Macdonald, Macmanus, Mackenzie,** etc. Names beginning with *O'* (meaning "of the family of") usually contain two capitals: **O'Casey, O'Conner.** Also ask about surnames of other origins: **LaCosta, LaCruz, Lafitte, LaFarge, La Guardia, Las Casas, de la Renta, De La Rey, de Kooning, De Kruif,** etc.

The abbreviations **Sr.** and **Jr.** following a name are capitalized: John D. Rockefeller, **Sr.**; Martin Luther King, **Jr.**

(2) Capitalize geographical names.

Cities, townships, counties, states, countries, continents   New York City, Concord Township, Dade County, New Mexico, United States of America, North America

Islands, peninsulas, straits, beaches   Coney Island, Keweenaw Peninsula, Straits of Florida, Turtle Beach

Bodies of water   Silver Lake, Lake Michigan, Delaware River, Pacific Ocean, Dead Sea, Willow Pond, Biscayne Bay

Mountains   Appalachian Mountains, Mount St. Helens

Streets   Park Avenue, Gulf Boulevard, Lincoln Parkway, Coast Highway, Interstate 80, Thirty-fourth Street [In a hyphenated street number, the second word begins with a small letter.]

Parks, forests, canyons, dams   Central Park, Redwood National Park, Palo Duro Canyon, Grand Coulee Dam

Recognized sections of the country or world   the South, the Northwest, the Far East

---

☞ **NOTE**   Do not capitalize *east, west, north*, and *south* when they indicate direction. Do capitalize them when they refer to recognized sections of the country.

EXAMPLES   At the corner, turn west, and you will see the museum on the south side of the street.
Is the Middle West the "heart" of the country?
I was turning north when a car going east hit my car.
The climate of the Southwest is dry.

The modern tendency is to write nouns and adjectives derived from *East, West, North*, and *South* without capital letters (a *southerner, southern* hospitality, *northern* cities, *middle-western* customs, *western* clothes), but in the light of conflicting authorities, the capitalization of such words is also correct.

Adjectives specifying direction are not capitalized unless they are part of the name of a country: northern Utah, western United States, but East Germany, Western Samoa.

☞ **NOTE**   Some nouns and adjectives derived from proper names are no longer capitalized: mackintosh, macadam, morocco leather, china dishes. Most such words may be written with or without capital letters, however: roman (Roman) numerals, plaster of paris (Paris), venetian (Venetian) blinds, turkish (Turkish) towel, gothic (Gothic) style, etc. When you are in doubt about the capitalization of words of this kind, refer to your dictionary.

EXERCISE 1. Identifying Standard Uses of Capitalization.
Number your paper 1–25. After the proper number, write the letter of
the standard form (*a* or *b*). In two of the items, both forms are correct;
write both *a* and *b*.

1. a. the Nile river
   b. the Nile River
2. a. She said, "Tell me, too."
   b. She said, "tell me, too."
3. a. Bering strait
   b. Bering Strait
4. a. Sunset boulevard
   b. Sunset Boulevard
5. a. We heard him say he was
      "pleased to be here."
   b. We heard him say he was
      "Pleased to be here."
6. a. Swedish immigrants
   b. Swedish Immigrants
7. a. Red sea
   b. Red Sea
8. a. an American Citizen
   b. an American citizen
9. a. Los Angeles County
      highways
   b. Los Angeles County
      Highways
10. a. east of the river
    b. East of the river
11. a. the Iberian peninsula
    b. the Iberian Peninsula
12. a. Fifty-Second Street
    b. Fifty-second Street
13. a. Hoover Dam
    b. Hoover dam

14. a. Charles Adams, Jr.
    b. Charles Adams, jr.
15. a. people of the Far East
    b. people of the far east
16. a. the Brooklyn Bridge
    b. the Brooklyn bridge
17. a. an Irish setter
    b. an Irish Setter
18. a. Palm Beach
    b. Palm beach
19. a. a westerner
    b. a Westerner
20. a. Crater Lake national
       Park
    b. Crater Lake National
       Park
21. a. Turn west after two
       miles.
    b. Turn West after two
       miles.
22. a. New Jersey Turnpike
    b. New Jersey turnpike
23. a. Eastern seaports
    b. eastern seaports
24. a. Georgia O'keeffe
    b. Georgia O'Keeffe
25. a. Sixty-sixth street
    b. Sixty-sixth Street

EXERCISE 2. Using Standard Capitalization. Write the following names, terms, and phrases, using capital letters wherever they are required in standard usage.

1. cook county
2. an african village
3. dallas, texas
4. latin america
5. four miles south
6. ranching in the south
7. forty-ninth street
8. lake of the woods
9. olympic national park
10. the arctic ocean
11. the pioneer mountains
12. a city like new orleans
13. a popular spanish singer
14. an arabian stallion
15. block island
16. russian dancer
17. washington boulevard
18. fulton county
19. the chinese frontier
20. james o'toole, jr.

(3) Capitalize names of organizations, business firms, institutions, and government bodies.

Organizations Spanish Club, League of Women Voters, National Geographic Society

Business firms Delta Airlines, Procter and Gamble Company, Control Data Corporation, International Business Machines, Grand Hotel, Fox Theater

Institutions Loyola University, Hocking Technical College, Plainview High School, National Science Foundation, First Baptist Church, Biology Department

Government bodies Congress, House of Representatives, Federal Aviation Administration, Department of Commerce, Internal Revenue Service

---

☞ **NOTE** The names of government bodies are capitalized when they are exact names. Do not capitalize such general names as the following: *the state legislature, the latest department meeting, commission agenda.*

☞ **NOTE** Do not capitalize words such as *hotel, theater, church, high school, college,* and *university* unless they are part of a proper name.

EXAMPLES   Chelsea Hotel   a hotel in New York
University of Hawaii   a university in Hawaii
Webster High School   a nearby high school
United States Postal Service   the local post office

(4) Capitalize the names of historical events and periods, special events, and calendar items.

Historical events   American Revolution, Renaissance, Civil War, Vietnam War

Special events   Special Olympics, Conference on World Hunger, Kentucky Derby, Senior Prom

Calendar items   Monday, June, Halloween, Memorial Day, Professional Secretaries' Week

> ☞ NOTE   The names of the seasons are not capitalized unless the seasons are personified.

EXAMPLES   an early winter
Summer's royal progress

(5) Capitalize the names of nationalities, races, and religions.

EXAMPLES   Caucasian, Semitic, Roman Catholic, Baptist, Congregationalist, Korean, Romanian, Afro-American

(6) Capitalize the brand names of business products.

EXAMPLES   Mazola, Xerox, Polaroid, Atari

> ☞ NOTE   A common noun that often follows a brand name is not capitalized except in advertising displays.

EXAMPLES   Phillips screwdriver, Campbell's soup, Waring blender

(7) Capitalize the names of ships, planes, monuments, awards, and any other particular places, things, or events.

EXAMPLES   the *Merrimac* (ship), Vietnam Memorial, Nobel Prize, Academy Award, Statue of Liberty

> ☞ NOTE   Do not capitalize the names of school subjects, except for languages and for course names followed by a number.

EXAMPLES   English, French, German, Latin, Italian, math, art, chemistry, home economics, Chemistry II, History III, Art 102

> ☞ NOTE   Schoolrooms and other nouns identified by a numeral or letter are usually capitalized.

EXAMPLES   Room 31, Parlor B, School District 18, Chapter 4

> ☞ NOTE   Names of school classes may or may not be capitalized, but the modern tendency is to capitalize them; however, the words *senior, junior, sophomore, freshman* are not capitalized when used to refer to a student.

EXAMPLES   The senior agreed to speak before the Sophomore Class.

EXERCISE 3. Using Standard Capitalization. Number your paper 1–25. After the proper number, write all items that are capitalized in standard usage. Write *C* after the number of a correct item.

1. itawamba junior college
2. section 5
3. a hotel across town
4. central high school
5. She is a junior.
6. the swiss people
7. a royal typewriter
8. winter blizzard
9. the barclay hotel
10. trigonometry
11. environmental protection agency
12. physics I
13. the bijou theater
14. labor day
15. history department
16. apple computer
17. two high-school seniors
18. bureau of the census
19. *zephyr* (train)

20. staff of the commission
21. the crusades
22. the great depression

23. the world series
24. newport athletic club
25. an italian restaurant

EXERCISE 4. Using Standard Capitalization. List in proper order the words that should be capitalized in each sentence. When the words make up a phrase, write them as a phrase: *Sunshine Skyway, National Gallery of Art.* Indicate the number of the sentence in which each word or word group appears.

EXAMPLE 1. When my family lived in mexico city, we often had picnics in chapultepec park.
    1. *Mexico City*
       Chapultepec Park

1. One of our science teachers, ms. stephens, took her biology II classes to winslow marsh to study snails and collect water samples for testing in the high-school laboratory.
2. The massachusetts institute of technology campus in cambridge extends for more than a mile along the charles river.
3. Iowa department of education planners agreed with franklin county leaders that the new community college should be built in an urban location to make it accessible to many residents.
4. The explorers' club from my high school in bond, kansas, visited the jones fire science training center, where they watched a demonstration of rappelling, the skill of descending a sheer wall with the aid of a double rope.
5. In 1754 columbia college, then called king's college, stood next to trinity college in lower manhattan, near the corner of broadway and wall street.
6. Mr. samuel reynolds, jr., my history teacher, captivated his audience of high school seniors as he vividly described the battle of britain during world war II.
7. Just west of fernandina beach, highway 1 crosses the amelia river and then curves by the entrance to fort clinch state park.
8. The denson hotel and the star theater, at the corner of river avenue and twenty-first street, are being renovated as part of the city's efforts to improve the area tourists first see when they enter the city from the barron bridge.
9. Kathleen o'brien, who still has her native irish accent, read some of william butler yeats's poems to our english class wednesday afternoon.

10. Sara turner, owner of turner's nutrition now, a chain of health food stores known for the development of ultravita yogurt, endowed memorial hospital's new wing, which was built this spring on the block between the hospital and finley mall.

31d. Capitalize titles.

(1) Capitalize the title of a person when it comes before a name.

EXAMPLES Superintendent Davis, Dean Williams, President Robinson, Prime Minister Shamir

(2) Capitalize a title used alone or following a person's name only if it refers to a high government official or someone else to whom you want to show special respect.

EXAMPLES Dr. Glenda Davis, superintendent of schools; Ms. Williams, dean of women; Marie Robinson, class president; *but* Victor Atiyeh, Governor of Oregon; Thurgood Marshall, Justice of the Supreme Court [titles of high government officials]
the Senator, *but* the work of a senator; the General's orders, *but* the insignia of a general; the Chief Justice, the Secretary of State, the Prince of Wales

---

☞ NOTE When used to refer to the head of a nation, the word *president* is usually capitalized. Two capitals are required in *vice-president* when it refers to the vice-president of a nation. The words *ex-* and *-elect* used with a title are not capitalized: *ex*-President, Governor-*elect*.

☞ NOTE When a title is used in place of a person's name, it is usually capitalized.

EXAMPLES Goodbye, Professor.
Yes, Senator, please ask about it.

(3) Capitalize a word showing family relationship when the word is used with a person's name but *not* when it is preceded by a possessive (unless the possessive is part of the name).

EXAMPLES   Uncle Juan, Cousin Nora, my cousin Nora, your mother, Ann's sister, *but* my Aunt Sandy (when "Aunt Sandy" is considered her name)

☞ NOTE Words of family relationship are usually, but not always, capitalized when used in place of a person's name.

EXAMPLE   I think someone told Grandma.

(4) Capitalize the first word and all important words in titles of books, periodicals, poems, stories, articles, documents, movies, paintings, and other works of art, etc. [The important words are the first and last words and all other words except articles (*a, an, the*), coordinating conjunctions, and prepositions of fewer than five letters.]

EXAMPLES   *Great Expectations, Fortune,* "The Force That Through the Green Fuse Drives the Flower," Bill of Rights, *Bird in Space* [sculpture]

☞ NOTE The words *a, an, the* written before a title are capitalized only when they are part of the title. Before the names of magazines and newspapers, they are not capitalized.

EXAMPLES   *The Count of Monte Cristo, A Farewell to Arms* [*The* and *A* are parts of the titles.]
Have you read the *Collected Stories* by Jean Stafford? [*The* is not part of the title.]
the *Science Digest,* the *St. Louis Dispatch*

(5) Capitalize words referring to the Deity.

EXAMPLES   God, the Almighty, Lord

Pronouns referring to God (*he, him,* and rarely, *who, whom*) are often capitalized.

EXAMPLE   Grace asked God to bring peace to His earth.

The word *god*, when used to refer to the gods of ancient mythology, is not capitalized.

EXAMPLE   Cassandra could foretell the future but was condemned by the god Apollo never to be believed.

EXERCISE 5. Using Standard Capitalization. Number your paper 1–25. After the proper number, write items capitalized in standard usage. Write *C* after the number of a correct item.

1. captain Ahab
2. discussed with the governor
3. Ms. Solomon, the center director
4. our class treasurer
5. the club president
6. the speaker of the House of Representatives
7. Rabbi Klein, a Navy chaplain
8. ex-president Carter
9. the leader of a brass band
10. a sergeant in an army
11. the lord in his wisdom
12. aunt Betty
13. senator Dole
14. mayor Fulton of Nashville
15. Irene Wilson, one of the deans

16. *down and out in paris and london* [book title]
17. the *tv guide* [magazine]
18. the magna carta
19. Harold Washington, mayor of Chicago
20. your aunt
21. the *Los Angeles times* [newspaper]
22. duties of a legislator
23. one nation, under god, indivisible
24. Mildred Zaharias, former national golf champion
25. "the world is too much with us" [poem]

WRITING APPLICATION B:
Using Capitalization Correctly to Make Your Writing Clear

Using capitalization correctly enables your reader to understand your meaning. Compare the following examples:

EXAMPLES   I concocted my formula for white peanut butter while I was living in west Virginia.
I concocted my formula for White peanut butter while I was living in West Virginia.

In the first example, the reader would naturally think that the writer had developed peanut butter that is white while living in the west part of the state of Virginia. The second example makes it clear that the writer is using a brand name and referring to a different state.

Writing Assignment

After an absence of ten years, you have returned to town to attend the tenth reunion of your graduating class. The organizers of the reunion have asked everyone in the class to write a composition for inclusion in a booklet to be distributed at the banquet. Write the composition, using capitalization correctly; tell where you have been during the last ten years and what you have done.

REVIEW EXERCISE. **Using Standard Capitalization.** This exercise covers all of the capitalization rules in the chapter. List in order the words that should be capitalized in each sentence.

1. The civitan club of midland township meets once a month in the restaurant next to the plaza theater.
2. As I started to laugh, aunt Dora and uncle John simultaneously asked, "you did what?"
3. In their english classes this term, the juniors have read *o pioneers!*, a novel by willa cather about swedish immigrants who settled in nebraska in the nineteenth century.
4. A recent report from the secretary of labor included the following statement: most of the new jobs in the next decade will be in service fields.
5. According to professor De La Rey, Tennyson's *idylls of the king* was published in 1859, the same year that saw the publication of Darwin's *origin of species*, FitzGerald's translation of omar khayyam's *the rubaiyat*, and Dickens' *a tale of two cities*.
6. In "canto I" the poet Ezra Pound describes an ominous sea voyage to the same mythical land of the dead visited by the hero Odysseus in the *Odyssey*, an epic by the greek poet Homer.
7. The president joined the secretary of state at Dulles international airport for their trip to south america for a conference on world economic problems.

8. Speaking to a reporter from the *County Clarion*, coach Sheila O'reilly explained the drafting of a team resolution, which read, in part, "Resolved: that we will win all of our games next year."

9. After graduating from high school, my cousin Jordan completed additional courses at Thompson vocational center and took a job with the Boone electronics company, which makes the electrowhiz circuit board.

10. When one student at Sunrise preschool woefully remarked that he was "tired of resting," the other children quickly echoed his comment.

11. My grandparents lived for many years in the middle west, but when they retired they moved to southern California, finally settling in mecca, a town between palm springs and the salton sea.

12. Last year, in american government I, we learned about our nation's system of checks and balances, which prevents a concentration of power in any one of the three branches of government.

13. In ancient egypt the people worshipped many gods equally until the sun god Ra became the principal deity.

14. The Raffles hotel in singapore, a base for many explorers' adventures in the far east, is named after sir Thomas Raffles, who founded the island country as a british colony in 1819.

15. Dr. Bruce Jackson, jr., principal of the high school, formerly taught mathematics I classes and an introductory class in computer science offered to freshmen and sophomores.

16. Representatives of fifty nations, including the United States, great britain, and the soviet union, met in san francisco, california, in 1945 to draft the charter of the united nations.

17. My favorite sport in the olympic games is the javelin throw, but I also like the swimming relays, and oh, the giant slalom is exciting to watch in the winter competitions.

18. From the St. Croix island national monument in Maine to the Huleia wildlife refuge in Hawaii, public lands managed by the federal government, including the military, equal a third of the nation's total acreage.

19. Susan McKay, president of the jogging club, has an exercise route that takes her three times a week through Myers park, down Carriage street, and then back west to Dean avenue.

20. The vice-president of the United States automatically takes over if the president dies in office.

21. I fed farm animals for the first time the summer I went to the regional YWCA camp with other junior high-school students from cities in the northeast.

22. One site proposed for the new high school is near refuge bay, just east of Eisenhower boulevard.

23. Shea stadium, which was built near the site of the New York world's fair, is the home of the mets, the national league baseball team in New York.

24. My aunt, who was stationed in the south when she was in the U.S. air force, likes spicy Texas chili.

25. The will of the swedish industrialist and inventor of dynamite, Alfred Nobel, established the Nobel prize to honor those who have benefited the world in the areas of literature, medicine, physics, chemistry, and peace; a prize in economics was added in 1969.

CHAPTER 31 REVIEW: POSTTEST 1

Identifying Standard Uses of Capital Letters. Number your paper 1–25. Each of the following pairs of items presents two versions of capitalization. In most cases, either item a or b is correctly capitalized according to standard usage. After the proper number on your paper, write the letter of the version containing the standard usage. If neither version is correct, write *N*.

EXAMPLES
  1. a. watched a program on the Public Broadcasting System.
      b. watched a program on the public broadcasting System.
    1. a
  2. a. They worked overtime at the Supermarket last weekend.
      b. They worked overtime at the Supermarket last Weekend.
    2. N

1. a. a copy of *sports Illustrated*
  b. a copy of *Sports Illustrated*
2. a. the prom attended by juniors and seniors
  b. the prom attended by Juniors and Seniors
3. a. conducted by Nancy Kassebaum, a senator from Kansas
  b. conducted by Nancy Kassebaum, a Senator from Kansas
4. a. took their Summer vacation in Minnesota
  b. took their summer vacation in Minnesota
5. a. a buyer for Smith's department store
  b. a buyer for Smith's Department Store

6. a. bought an Apple Computer
   b. bought an Apple computer
7. a. rafting on the Colorado River
   b. rafting on the Colorado river
8. a. a trip to mount Rushmore
   b. a trip to Mount Rushmore
9. a. the inventive people of the Stone Age
   b. the inventive people of the stone age
10. a. drove slowly along Beverly Hills boulevard
    b. drove slowly along Beverly Hills Boulevard
11. a. the states bordering the Gulf of Mexico
    b. the states bordering the gulf of Mexico
12. a. an official of the U.S. Department of State
    b. an official of the U.S. Department of state
13. a. the high school in Jefferson township
    b. the high school in Jefferson Township
14. a. a meeting in room 264
    b. a meeting in Room 264
15. a. mayor Wilson Goode of Philadelphia
    b. Mayor Wilson Goode of Philadelphia
16. a. Consuelo Rivera's office on Sixty-sixth Street
    b. Consuelo Rivera's office on Sixty-Sixth Street
17. a. visiting Yellowstone national park
    b. visiting Yellowstone National Park
18. a. married a Mexican-american woman
    b. married a Mexican-American woman
19. a. treated at County General hospital
    b. treated at County General Hospital
20. a. the largest Protestant church in town
    b. the largest Protestant Church in town
21. a. hope to finish high school
    b. hope to finish High School
22. a. prefers Hood's ice cream
    b. prefers Hood's Ice Cream
23. a. Nara's birthday next Thursday
    b. Nara's Birthday next Thursday
24. a. John Hancock's signature on the Declaration of Independence
    b. John Hancock's signature on the Declaration Of Independence
25. a. heard president Reagan's speech to the nation
    b. heard President Reagan's speech to the nation

CHAPTER 31 REVIEW: POSTTEST 2

Identifying Standard Uses of Capital Letters. Number your paper 1–25. Many of the following sentences contain errors in standard capitalization. If a sentence contains an error, write the corrected word, term, or phrase after the proper number. If the sentence is correct as written, write *C* after the proper number.

EXAMPLE 1. Manolo Cruz will be attending Stanford university in the Fall.
1. *University   fall*

1. The first woman appointed to the U.S. Supreme Court was justice Sandra Day O'connor.
2. I am studying russian, English, and Art this Semester.
3. The Cass county county seat is Cassopolis, Michigan.
4. Go north for two Streets and then turn east on Central Avenue.
5. The Mountain Ranges in the Western states offer a variety of hiking and hunting experiences for those who love the outdoors.
6. In October, the Veterans of Foreign Wars will hold their annual convention in Des Moines, Iowa.
7. For most Americans, Thanksgiving day is one for family gatherings.
8. Last summer I enjoyed reading *To Kill A Mockingbird* by Harper Lee, a southern writer.
9. HOMES is an acronym for the great lakes: Huron, Ontario, Michigan, Erie, and Superior.
10. Salt Lake City, Utah, is the headquarters of the Church of Jesus Christ of Latter-Day Saints, commonly called the mormon church.
11. Despite their political differences, my mother, a Democrat, and my father, a Republican, work together to increase voter registration.
12. Born in Mississippi, William Faulkner won the Nobel prize in 1949.
13. Auguste Rodin's bronze sculpture, *the thinker*, is one of the most famous Works of Art in the world.
14. In the History of the United States, only one person, Gerald R. Ford, has held the nation's highest office without being elected either president or Vice-President.
15. Among the items on display at the Smithsonian institution in Washington, D.C., is the armchair used by Archie Bunker in the comedy series *All in the Family.*
16. The senior class will hold its Prom on Friday, May 13.

17. George Strum, Mayor for two terms, has announced that he will be a candidate again next November.

18. The first American woman in space, Sally Ride, was a member of the crew aboard the space shuttle *challenger* launched from cape Canaveral, Florida, on June 18, 1983.

19. Aldous Huxley's novel *Brave new World*, published in the 1930's, foreshadowed many of the moral dilemmas that would accompany the development of Genetic Engineering in the 1970's and 1980's.

20. My sister Eartha attends Boston University, and my brother Bayard attends the university of Notre Dame.

21. Henry David Thoreau, the New England writer, immortalized a small Massachusetts Pond in *Walden*, an autobiographical account of his two years alone at Walden Pond.

22. Because Mike's letter was addressed to 730 Lexington Place instead of to 730 Lexington Court, it was delayed for six days.

23. America's political and economic interests are closely tied to those of its northern neighbor, Canada, and to those of its southern neighbors, the central American countries.

24. Because of a severe thunderstorm, the American Airlines Jet carrying passengers to Atlanta, Georgia, was detained at Chicago's O'Hare International airport.

25. When she came to Washington High School earlier this year, Ms. Morales, our new Principal, quickly earned a reputation as a good Administrator and a caring person.

SUMMARY STYLE SHEET

Kansas City	a city in Kansas
Frederick Douglass National Park	our national parks
Thirty-first Street	across the street
Shell Lake	a shallow lake
North America	northern Wisconsin
the Toastmasters' Club	a public-speaking club
Boeing Company	an aircraft company
Lakeland High School	a new high school
Black Hawk College	four years in college
the American Revolution	a successful revolution

the Chrysler Building	a New York City building
the Fourth of July	the fifth of July
the Senior Prom	a prom given by seniors
the Junior Class	junior classes
English, French, Latin	social studies, art, biology
History II	a course in world history
Fall's coat of many colors	spring, summer, winter, fall
Dean Marsh	Mrs. Marsh, the dean
the President (U.S.)	the president of our club
Mayor Smith	a mayor's duties
May God go with you.	tribal gods of the Cherokees
the South	a mile south (north, east, west)
Tell Mother (or mother).	Tell my mother.
Uncle Joe	my uncle
Prell shampoo	
a Methodist, an Arab	
The Pickwick Papers	
the *Saturday Evening Post*	

Punctuation

END MARKS AND COMMAS

Punctuation helps make the meaning of a sentence clear to the reader. Some marks of punctuation indicate in writing the pauses and stops that the voice makes in speaking. They indicate not only where a pause should come but also how long the pause should be—the comma standing for a slight hesitation, the period for a longer one. Other vocal inflections are conveyed by the question mark and the exclamation point.

DIAGNOSTIC TEST

Correcting Sentences by Adding or Deleting End Marks and Commas. Number your paper 1–20. After the proper number, write all words that are followed by incorrect punctuation, and add or delete end marks and commas in accordance with the standards of written English. Most of the following sentences contain errors in the use of end marks or commas. If a sentence is correct as written, write C after the sentence number.

EXAMPLES 1. We went to the mall, to the movies, and to our favorite restaurant, this afternoon.
     1. *restaurant*
     2. Well I think it's a good idea.
     2. *Well,*

1. Mr. Stanton will you please write a letter of recommendation for me?
2. Melody Jackson will be valedictorian, and John Gehrke will be salutatorian.
3. The students the teachers and the administrators are looking forward to the long Memorial Day weekend.
4. On the first day of the second semester of the school year Botow Okamoto drove up in a sleek red car.
5. When she took her first ride in a hot-air balloon. she experienced the amazing silence half a mile above the surface of the earth.
6. Students who do well in academic subjects should in my opinion be commended by their school administrators.
7. Lisa and Conrad arrived on time but everyone else was late.
8. No Sandy will not leave until the fifth of August.
9. Because I need exercise I ride my bicycle six miles each day.
10. Although Alan had worked very hard on his essay Mr. Burar felt it needed more revision.
11. Dolores Garcia a former Olympic swimmer is going to coach at our school next year.
12. Look at the size of the fish I caught.
13. On January 1 2000 my niece will celebrate her twenty-first birthday.
14. Mom or Dad or Uncle Paul will cook dinner tonight.
15. Tomorrow morning before school, the juniors will prepare juice, toast, and ham, and eggs for the seniors.
16. As I looked at the traffic which was backed up as far as I could see I decided to leave the highway and drive along local streets.
17. Please address all complaints to Joseph Redwing Jr Department of Consumer Affairs 4749 Cole Street Eugene OR 97401.
18. In San Francisco the summer temperatures often go no higher than sixty-eight degrees but in nearby San Jose the thermometer often climbs above eighty degrees in the summer.
19. Having suffered from headaches for ten days Mida decided to consult her family physician.
20. My grandmother a maid all her life saved her money and put both of her children through college.

This chapter and the one that follows describe the conventions for punctuating sentences according to the standards of written English and provide exercises to help you fix these uses in your mind. Punctuating exercises is at best an artificial activity, however, and you must be very careful to carry these punctuation principles over into your writing. Since punctuation is so closely related to meaning, many writers punctuate as they write, using punctuation to group certain ideas together and to separate other ideas from each other. Other writers prefer to concentrate first on getting their ideas onto paper; once they have revised what they have written, they proofread their writing, making certain that the grammar, usage, and mechanics follow the conventions of standard English.

Do not overpunctuate. Use a mark for punctuation for only two reasons: (1) because meaning demands it, or (2) because conventional usage requires it.

END MARKS

32a. A statement is followed by a period.

EXAMPLE   Spring break begins April 10.

32b. An abbreviation is followed by a period.[1]

EXAMPLES   Blvd.   Oct.
           B.C.   Messrs.

> ☞ NOTE   Abbreviations in the metric system are often written without periods.

32c. A question is followed by a question mark.

(1) Distinguish between a statement containing an indirect question and a sentence that asks a question directly.

EXAMPLES   Susan wants to know when the first match starts. [a statement containing an indirect question—followed by a period]
           Do you know when the first match starts? [a direct question —followed by a question mark]

[1] For a fuller discussion of abbreviations see page 761.

(2) Polite requests in question form (frequently used in business letters) may be followed by a period; a question mark is also correct.

EXAMPLES   Would you please correct my account in this amount.

Would you please correct my account in this amount?

(3) A question mark should be placed inside quotation marks when the quotation is a question. Otherwise, it should be placed outside the quotation marks.

EXAMPLES   Harold asked, "Have you heard from Dolores?" [The quotation is a question.]

Could I say, "I just don't want to go"? [The quotation is not a question. The whole sentence, however, is a question.]

32d. An exclamation is followed by an exclamation point.

EXAMPLES   What a wonderful idea!

How lovely!

You're joking!

Congratulations!

(1) Many exclamations begin with either "What a . . . " or "How . . . " as in the first two of the preceding examples. When you begin a sentence with these words, check the end mark carefully.

(2) An interjection at the beginning of a sentence is usually followed by a comma.

CUSTOMARY   Ah, there you are!

RARE   Ah! There you are!

(3) An exclamation point should be placed inside quotation marks when the quotation is an exclamation. Otherwise, it should be placed outside the quotation marks.

EXAMPLES   "What a good movie!" exclaimed Mary as she came through the doorway.

Don't say "It can't be done"!

32e. An imperative sentence may be followed by either a period or an exclamation point, depending upon the force intended.

EXAMPLES   Please write me a letter.

Hold that line!

EXERCISE 1. **Correcting a Passage by Adding End Marks.**
Many periods and all exclamation points and question marks have been omitted from the following passage. Copy in a column on your paper all words that should be followed by end marks. After each word, write the end mark required. If a new sentence should begin after the end mark, write the first word of the sentence, giving it a capital letter. Before each word, write the number of the line in which it appears.

EXAMPLE 1 How glad I was to see him alas, he seemed not so glad but did
           2 greet me with, "What a surprise" and asked, "How are you" it
           3 had been a long time . . .
           1. *him! Alas*
           2. *surprise!*
           2. *you?" It*

1   Lynn Block, Ph D, Director of Research for the Hubert F
2 Langston Soap Company, looked at her desk calendar. "Oh, no"
3 she groaned. Today she must conduct interviews to hire a new
4 secretary. "How nerve-racking it is when an applicant is unpre-
5 pared" Nonetheless, she was ready for the first interview, which
6 was set for 9:00 A.M. when 9:00 came, however, the applicant had
7 not arrived. "What a way to begin" she complained.
8   At 9:35 A.M., the receptionist ushered in the late arrival. "Oh,
9 dear" thought Dr Block. As the young man sat down, the depart-
10 ment head noticed his torn jeans, unironed tee shirt, and shaggy
11 hair that needed trimming. To questions about his qualifications,
12 the young man answered only yes or no, and he did not explain or
13 apologize for his lateness when asked about it, he mumbled
14 something about oversleeping. Dr Block closed the interview
15 shortly thereafter. "Gee," she puzzled, "this person has good
16 experience and typing skills, but he certainly doesn't seem to want
17 the job"
18   The next applicant, Ms Smith, was early, but the receptionist
19 didn't think that she was in the right place. "What does that mean"
20 wondered Dr. Block as she waited. In walked a young woman,
21 neatly dressed and wearing a professional tool belt with well-cared-
22 for carpentry tools around her waist. Ms Smith said, "I'm so sorry
23 to disturb you I must have taken a wrong turn when I got off the
24 elevator. I'm interested in the maintenance position being adver-
25 tised."

26   "I'll say" exclaimed Dr. Block. She gave the young woman
27   directions to the maintenance department on the Sixth St side of
28   the building and wished her luck. To herself, she mused, "Whew at
29   this rate, I may never get a new secretary." Then the receptionist
30   announced that the next interviewee had arrived—on time. "Now
31   what" wondered Dr. Block. Looking up to see a neatly dressed
32   young man approach, she asked, "Are *you* sure you're in the right
33   place it's been a highly unusual morning so far."
34   He replied, "Oh, yes I'm applying for the secretarial position.
35   I'm very much interested in it" Dr. Block smiled, and the interview
36   proceeded. He responded to her questions with brief, helpful
37   explanations and asked appropriate questions about the job duties.
38   About his future career plans, he said, "I would like to work up to a
39   position as office manager I like office work and believe good
40   management is vital to keeping any operation going smoothly."
41   "You're right about that" exclaimed Dr. Block. After the
42   interview ended, Dr. Block pondered her choices. She thought,
43   "Well, he doesn't have as much experience or quite as high a typing
44   rate as the first interviewee, but I know whom I'm going to hire"

THE COMMA

The comma—the most frequently used mark of punctuation—is used
mainly to group words that belong together and to separate those that
do not. Certain other uses have little to do with meaning but are
standard ways of punctuating sentences.

Items in a Series

32f. Use commas to separate items in a series.

EXAMPLES   She had been a correspondent for the wire service in London,
Paris, Rome, and Madrid.

There were books on the desk, posters on the wall, and clothing on
the floor.

☞ **NOTE** Do not place a comma before the first item or after the last item in a series.

INCORRECT   As part of the special short course, the students had learned, to replace the spark plugs, adjust the points, and change the oil, in three different makes of automobiles.

CORRECT   As part of the special short course, the students had learned to replace the spark plugs, adjust the points, and change the oil in three different makes of automobiles.

It is permissible to omit the comma before the *and* joining the last two items in a series if the comma is not needed to make the meaning clear. There are some constructions in which the inclusion or omission of this comma affects the meaning of the sentence.

Timepieces may be classified in the following categories: sundials, hourglasses, clocks, watches and chronometers. [four categories]

Timepieces may be classified in the following categories: sundials, hourglasses, clocks, watches, and chronometers. [five categories]

☞ **NOTE** Words customarily used in pairs are set off as one item in a series: *bag and baggage, pen and ink, hat and coat, pork and beans, bread and butter*, etc.

For supper they served a tossed salad, spaghetti and meatballs, garlic bread, milk, and fruit.

(1) If all items in a series are joined by *and* or *or*, do not use commas to separate them.

EXAMPLE   We can go under or over or around it.

(2) Independent clauses in a series are usually separated by a semicolon. Short independent clauses, however, may be separated by commas.

EXAMPLE   We talked, we walked, we laughed, and we sang.

32g. Use a comma to separate two or more adjectives preceding a noun.

EXAMPLES   She is a creative, intelligent executive.

Since that evening's schedule offered boring, silly, worthless programs, we turned off the television.

(1) Do not use a comma before the final adjective in a series if the adjective is thought of as part of the noun.

INCORRECT   It was a crisp, clear, invigorating, fall day.

CORRECT   It was a crisp, clear, invigorating fall day. [*Fall day* is considered one item. The adjectives modify *fall day*, not *day*.]

CORRECT   She hung small, round, delicate Chinese lanterns. [*Chinese lanterns* is thought of as one word.]

(2) If one of the words in a series modifies another word in the series, do not separate them by a comma.

EXAMPLE   Why did he wear a bright red cap?

Comma Between Independent Clauses

32h. Use a comma before *and, but, or, nor, for, so, yet* when they join independent clauses, unless the clauses are very short.

EXAMPLES   Monday's meeting had gone smoothly, yet I felt a controversy brewing.

The first chapter is slow-moving, but the rest of the story is full of action and suspense.

I'll go this way and you go that way. [independent clauses too short to require punctuation]

When the conjunction joins two verbs, not two main clauses, a comma is not used.

EXAMPLES   Geraldo gave me some good advice and got some from me in return. [The conjunction joins the verbs *gave* and *got*.]

Geraldo gave me some good advice, and I gave him some in return. [The conjunction joins two independent clauses.]

> ☞ **NOTE** Many writers use the comma before these conjunctions—as they use the comma before *and* between the last two items in a series—only when necessary to keep the meaning clear.

NOT CLEAR I carved the turkey and the family watched.
CLEAR I carved the turkey, and the family watched.
NOT CLEAR We didn't know whether to stay for the weather forecaster had predicted rain.
CLEAR We didn't know whether to stay, for the weather forecaster had predicted rain.

As you can see from the preceding examples, a reader may easily be confused if the comma is omitted. This is especially true of the comma before the conjunction *for*, which should always be preceded by a comma when it means *because*.

EXERCISE 2. Correcting Sentences by Adding Commas. The following sentences cover rules 32f–h. Number your paper 1–10. Write after the proper number the words in each sentence that should be followed by a comma, placing the comma after the word. Be prepared to explain the punctuation you use.

1. The police searched everywhere but there were no fingerprints to be found.
2. Albert Levin ordered salad juice and macaroni and cheese.
3. States along the Continental Divide include New Mexico Colorado Wyoming Idaho and Montana.
4. I played the melody on the guitar and the electric bass provided the rhythm.
5. She is a bright charming young woman.
6. We are learning more and more about space through our new and stronger telescopes our huge radar installations and our instrument-packed space probes.
7. When I missed the bus I lost my luggage hat and coat and briefcase.
8. They are responsible for the confusion arose because of statements issued by them.

9. Young children do not use capital letters consistently and their punctuation is frequently unconventional.
10. The smoke choked us the stench nauseated us and the wind chilled us.

Nonessential Elements

32i. Use commas to set off nonessential clauses and nonessential participial phrases.

A nonessential (nonrestrictive) clause is a subordinate clause that is not essential to the meaning of the sentence but merely adds an idea to the sentence.

NONESSENTIAL   Carla Harris**, who was offered scholarships to three colleges,** will go to Vassar in the fall.

The basic meaning of this sentence is *Carla Harris will go to Vassar in the fall.* The subordinate clause does not affect this basic meaning; it merely adds an idea to the sentence. It is a nonessential clause because it does not limit in any way the words it modifies—*Carla Harris.* Clauses that modify proper nouns are nearly always nonessential.

The opposite of a nonessential clause is an essential (restrictive) clause.

ESSENTIAL   Carla Harris is the only senior **who won scholarships to three colleges**.

Here the subordinate clause is essential to the sentence, for without it the sentence would mean something else: *Carla Harris is the only senior.* The subordinate clause limits the meaning of *senior—senior who won scholarships to three colleges.*

Study the following examples of essential and nonessential clauses until you understand the terms. Note the punctuation: *essential—no punctuation; nonessential—set off by commas.*

ESSENTIAL   New Orleans is the city **which interests me the most**.
NONESSENTIAL   Pierre**, which is the capital of South Dakota,** is on Lake Sharpe in the center of the state.

ESSENTIAL   The man **who said that** is my English teacher.
NONESSENTIAL   Mr. Gerz**, who is my English teacher,** said that.

> ☞ NOTE Many writers prefer to use *that* rather than *which* to introduce an essential clause that modifies a thing; *which* is acceptable, however.

Sometimes a clause may be interpreted as either essential or nonessential. In such instances the writer must decide which interpretation to give the clause and punctuate it accordingly.

EXAMPLES Dave took his problem to the librarian who is an authority on reference books. [interpreted as essential]

Dave took his problem to the librarian, who is an authority on reference books. [interpreted as nonessential]

Since the punctuation of the first sentence indicates that the clause is essential, the reader assumes that there is more than one librarian. Dave chose the one who is an authority on reference books. From the punctuation of the second sentence the reader assumes that there is only one librarian and that the librarian is an authority on reference books.

EXAMPLES My aunt who is an officer of a large bank lives in Rhode Island. [I have several aunts, and this is one of them.]

My aunt, who is an officer of a large bank, lives in Rhode Island. [I have only one aunt, no others.]

EXERCISE 3. Identifying Essential and Nonessential Clauses.

Some of the sentences in this exercise contain essential clauses; others contain nonessential clauses. Number your paper 1–20. If the italicized clause is essential, write *E* after the proper number; if it is nonessential, write *Commas* to indicate that you would use commas in the sentence.

1. Fellow employees *who always have a ready smile* make the job seem easier.
2. A neighborhood committee *whose members made us feel welcome* helped us settle into our new home.
3. My old Buick *which my parents helped me buy* is a big, four-door sedan.
4. The old Buick *which I drive* is like the one Mr. Chase drives.
5. She is wearing the shirt *which she received for her birthday.*

6. Her new shirt *which was a birthday gift* is in her favorite color.
7. People *who are overly nervous* may not make good drivers.
8. Adults *whose development has been studied and recorded* continue to mature, usually in predictable stages, after the age of eighteen.
9. Cities *which seem alike* bear a closer look.
10. School boards *which need to build new facilities* often ask voters to pass a bond issue.
11. The Suez Canal *which is 103 miles long* connects the Mediterranean Sea and the Red Sea.
12. I think people *who litter* are thoughtless.
13. That law *which may have met a real need one hundred years ago* should be repealed or rewritten to deal with today's situation.
14. Escape from tyranny was the impetus for many people *who settled America.*
15. The Federal Reserve System *which is the central bank of the United States* monitors money and credit growth.
16. Leontyne Price *who is well known for her performances as Cleopatra* is one of the world's leading sopranos.
17. The novel *which I just finished reading* is about politics.
18. My former boss *whom I had expected to see on my visit to the office* had left the company.
19. Peggy Moore *who grows her own vegetables* says she finds gardening relaxing.
20. The cars *which were built during that period* were recalled.

A participial phrase is a group of related words containing a participle (see page 52). Present participles end in *–ing*; past participles of regular verbs end in *–ed* or *–d*.

Like a nonessential clause, a nonessential participial phrase is set off by commas because it is not necessary to the meaning of the main clause.

NONESSENTIAL	Our dog**,** **howling at the moon,** was soon joined in song by other dogs.
ESSENTIAL	A dog **howling at the moon** may be joined in song by other dogs.
NONESSENTIAL	My baby brother**,** **frightened by thunder,** climbed into my lap for a hug.
ESSENTIAL	A child **frightened by thunder** often needs reassurance.

NONESSENTIAL The scattered band members came together suddenly, **quickly arranging themselves into the first formation.**

ESSENTIAL I watched the scattered band members **quickly arranging themselves into the first formation.**

EXERCISE 4. Correcting Sentences by Adding Commas. This exercise covers all comma rules given up to this point in the chapter. After the proper number, write all words in the sentence that should be followed by a comma. Add the comma after each word. Be prepared to explain your answers.

1. Any student who wishes to join the gymnastics team will have to excel in floor exercises on the balance beam and on the uneven parallel bars.
2. The sophomores decorated the gym and the juniors provided the refreshments.
3. Anyone taking the basic photography course will learn how to shoot close-ups portraits and still lifes.
4. The judge leaving her chambers stopped to talk to some court reporters who had gathered around her.
5. We got encouragement from everyone but our parents helped us most of all.
6. Careful writers distinguish between *uninterested* which means "indifferent" and *disinterested* which means "unbiased."
7. Any student wishing to sing act or perform on Class Day should sign up before tomorrow which is the deadline.
8. Governor Quigley whose speeches are filled with clichés appeared on television last night asking people to "tighten their belts bite the bullet pull their own weight and give till it hurts."
9. A sad-looking mongrel which had followed me halfway home suddenly trotted up to me and staring at me soulfully started to lick my hand.
10. A story which appeared in yesterday's newspaper was about the Toronto Maple Leafs which is my favorite hockey team.

Introductory Elements

32j. Use a comma after certain introductory elements.

(1) Use a comma after words such as *well, yes, no,* and *why* when they begin a sentence.

EXAMPLES   Well, what do you think?

Yes, you are welcome to join us.

Why, the whole story sounds suspicious!

(2) Use a comma after an introductory participial phrase.

EXAMPLE   **Giggling like a child,** he wrapped the last present.

☞ NOTE   Do not confuse a gerund ending in *–ing* and used as the subject of the sentence with an introductory participial phrase.

EXAMPLES   **Cleaning and painting my room** was hard but fun. [gerunds used as subjects—not followed by a comma]

Cleaning and painting my room, I ran across a favorite ring of mine. [introductory participial phrase—followed by a comma]

(3) Use a comma after a succession of introductory prepositional phrases.

EXAMPLE   **At the end of the block next to the old railroad station in Mill Heights,** my grandparents own a small house.

☞ NOTE   A single introductory prepositional phrase need not be followed by a comma unless it is parenthetical (*by the way, on the contrary,* etc.) or the comma is necessary to prevent confusion.

EXAMPLES   By the way, I heard from Grace Lee yesterday.

With athletes, injuries can end careers.

In the evening I like to visit friends.

(4) Use a comma after an introductory adverb clause.

EXAMPLES   **While Sal put on his tuxedo,** the flute player checked the sheet music.
Whenever the phone rings, my little sister is the one who answers it.
As soon as we left the house, we heard the phone ring.

EXERCISE 5. Correcting Sentences by Adding Commas. This exercise covers all comma rules to this point in the chapter. Number your paper 1–10. After the proper number, write the words in each sentence that should be followed by a comma, placing a comma after each word.

1. One draft is not enough for most writers can improve their work by revising it.
2. When they finished playing the drums were moved offstage to make room for the dancers.
3. By the end of the second day of school all students seemed to have found their correct classrooms teachers and lockers.
4. Oh if it's all right with you I'll ask Gloria and Agnes or Leo to help us.
5. In the second half Johnson evaded the defense caught a twenty-yard pass and raced into the end zone.
6. Speaking at the forum last night council candidate Kay Stone described her management experience as head of a household civic fund-raiser and business owner.
7. Having discussed at length the two themes proposed for the prom the committee whose members were not satisfied voted to reject both themes and seek fresh ideas.
8. Many of those in the long winding ticket line had arrived just within the past hour but we having arrived before dawn held places near the sales window.
9. Regional theaters are prospering in many American cities but the Broadway stage is still the goal of most young actors dancers and musicians.
10. As Phil began climbing the ladder began to slip out at the bottom and I immediately grabbed it to keep it in place.

WRITING APPLICATION A:
Using Commas Correctly to Make Your Writing Clear

Introductory participial phrases and adverb clauses lend variety to sentences, helping you avoid a monotonous tone. Unless these introductory elements are punctuated correctly, however, your reader may misread the sentence. Compare the following examples:

EXAMPLES   We finished eating. The table was cleared. We played *Monopoly*.
When we finished eating the table was cleared for a game of *Monopoly*.
When we finished eating, the table was cleared for a game of *Monopoly*.

Writing Assignment

You probably have read biographies and seen docudramas about famous people. Select a famous person who particularly interests you. Write an account of this person's life, including material that is lively and interesting as well as factual. Use introductory participial phrases and adverb clauses to add variety to your writing. Revise your paper and then proofread it to make sure you have used commas correctly.

Interrupters

32k. Use commas to set off an expression that interrupts a sentence.

Use two commas to set off an expression unless the expression comes first or last in the sentence.

(1) Appositives and appositive phrases are usually set off by commas.

An appositive is a word—with or without modifiers—that is set beside a noun or pronoun and identifies or explains it. An appositive phrase consists of an appositive and its modifiers.

EXAMPLE   An interview with Florence Cohen**, the noted landscape architect,** will appear Sunday in the *Herald* **, our local paper.**

When an appositive is so closely related to the word it modifies that it appears to be part of that word, no comma is necessary. An appositive of this kind is called a restrictive appositive. Usually it is one word.

EXAMPLES   Her cousin Rita
The novel *Arrowsmith*
My friend Jane
Catherine the Great
The preposition *with*

(2) Words used in direct address are set off by commas.

EXAMPLES   Do you know, **Lena,** where your brother is?

Jerry, please see about this.

You seem upset, **my friend.**

(3) Parenthetical expressions are set off by commas.

The following expressions are commonly used parenthetically: *I believe (think, know, hope,* etc.), *I am sure, on the contrary, on the other hand, after all, by the way, incidentally, in fact, indeed, naturally, of course, in my opinion, for example, however, nevertheless, to tell the truth.*

EXAMPLES   The train will, **I am sure,** be on time.
My insurance will, **of course,** cover the damage.
On the contrary, exercise is relaxing.
That clever Jameson was the first to solve the puzzle, **naturally.**.

Knowledge of this rule and of the expressions commonly used parenthetically is helpful in punctuating, but in many instances your intention is what determines the punctuation that you use. If you want the reader to pause, to regard an expression as parenthetical, set it off; if not, leave it unpunctuated. Sometimes, however, the placement of the expression in the sentence determines the punctuation. Study the following examples, noting in which ones the comma is a matter of choice and in which ones the placement of the expression governs the punctuation. All the examples given illustrate standard usage.

EXAMPLES   That is **indeed** startling news.
That is, **indeed,** startling news.
Indeed, that is startling news. [comma required by placement]

We **therefore** decided to table the issue.
We, **therefore,** decided to table the issue.
We decided, **therefore,** to table the issue. [comma required by placement]

I hope this report will help clarify the situation for you. [no comma because of placement]

This report will, **I hope,** help clarify the situation for you. [comma required by placement]

EXERCISE 6. Correcting Sentences by Adding Commas. The following exercise covers all comma rules to this point in the chapter. Number your paper 1–20. After the proper number, write the words in each sentence that should be followed by a comma, placing a comma after each word. Write *C* if the item is correct.

1. An absurd high-speed chase in the final scenes had the preview audience film critics from major newspapers rocking with laughter.
2. Indeed if I had known earlier my friend I would have been here sooner.
3. The plot of that book a murder mystery is in my opinion far too complicated.
4. This painting Betty is by Emilio Sanchez an artist born in Cuba.
5. Polish workers however did not seem to agree with government labor policies for many tried to organize their own trade unions.
6. Our plan I knew would have to succeed for there would be no second chance.
7. The nineteenth-century book *El Jíbaro* which was written by Manuel A. Alonso is by the way considered the first Puerto Rican classic.
8. Attacked without warning the villagers took no time as I vividly recall to sound an alarm secure their homes or save their personal belongings before fleeing the area.
9. If you quickly get your application in our office will be able to process it before the deadline which is this afternoon.
10. Please understand friends that as much as I would like to I cannot be at the picnic the game and the track meet at the same time.
11. The people riding in the front of the roller coaster were the ones who screamed the most loudly.
12. Our school composed largely of students from rural areas offers courses in agriculture and horticulture occupations that offer many local job opportunities.
13. Looking for economical transportation Harry who had never bought a car before nervously scouted the possibilities at Countryside Motor Sales which sells used sedans station wagons and pickup trucks.

14. Laura and John who buy sell and trade antiques are restoring an old townhouse which will serve as a display shop for the variety of items that they have to offer.

15. Napoleon's two brothers Joseph and Lucien tried to prevent him from selling Louisiana but Richard Livingston and James Monroe the American representatives succeeded in making the purchase.

16. Well having tried to reach you on the telephone I left a message with your sister and I told her it was very important which I hoped would help her remember to tell you.

17. In spite of an initial lack of support, Armanda and Julie who were very determined continued their campaign to clean up the vacant lots a task they admitted that would take some time.

18. Taken fishing at the municipal pier nine-year-old Tanya caught two croakers a small catfish and a good-sized butterfish which got away.

19. Before you start putting that jigsaw puzzle together Rosa I hope you are sure that it will when completed fit on the table.

20. When Jamie had finished the chicken and potatoes were all gone and left untouched were the beans carrots and salad.

WRITING APPLICATION B:
Using Commas to Make Your Writing Clear

Like blinking yellow lights at an intersection, the commas before and after certain parenthetical expressions signal the reader to prepare for a change—in this case, a change in the direction of the writer's presentation. Notice in the following example how the commas used to set off the parenthetical expression *however* prepare you for the information in the second sentence.

EXAMPLE   Leontyne Price's world-famous soprano voice was still powerful and still drew capacity crowds. In 1985, however, she decided to end her operatic career.

Writing Assignment

Write a composition discussing the advantages and disadvantages of the college you will attend or the job you will look for after you graduate from high school. Revise your paper, and proofread it carefully to make sure you have used commas correctly with parenthetical expressions.

Conventional Uses

32l. Use a comma in certain conventional situations.

(1) Use a comma to separate items in dates and addresses.

EXAMPLES   Hawaii achieved statehood on August 21, 1959, becoming the fiftieth state.

Write to me at 423 Twentieth Street, Salt Lake City, UT 84101, after the first of May. [*Two-letter postal abbreviation used with ZIP code*]

Their twins were born on Saturday, March 6, 1982, in Detroit, Michigan.

> ☞ NOTE   When only the month and day, or only the month and year, are given, no punctuation is necessary.

EXAMPLES   It was on June 20 that we began rehearsals.

A severe winter storm hit much of western Europe in January 1985.

When the items are joined by a preposition, do not use commas.

EXAMPLE   Joanna lives at 301 Green Street in San Diego, California.

(2) Use a comma after the salutation of a friendly letter and after the closing of any letter.

EXAMPLES   Dear Angela,   Sincerely yours,

(3) Use a comma after a name followed by *Jr., Sr., Ph.D., etc.*

EXAMPLES   Peter Grundel, Jr.   Lorraine Henson, Ph.D.

> ☞ NOTE   If these abbreviations are used within a sentence, they are also followed by a comma:
>
> Hazel Sellers, M.D., will be the guest speaker.

Unnecessary Commas

32m. Do not use unnecessary commas.

The tendency of modern writers is to use commas sparingly. You should be able to show either that the commas you use help the reader to understand what you have written or that they are required by standard usage—as in a date or address, for example. Unnecessary commas are just as confusing to the reader as the absence of necessary ones.

REVIEW EXERCISE. Correcting Sentences by Adding End Marks and Commas. This exercise covers end marks and all comma uses. Rewrite the sentences, inserting punctuation and capitalization where necessary.

1. Stalled in the traffic jam the motorcyclists Carl and Lou who were on their way home settled in to wait.
2. According to that book the history of fine arts is divided into the following periods: classical medieval renaissance baroque neoclassical and modern.
3. Our apartment at 310 Columbia Avenue Fort Wayne Indiana was cozy but I also enjoyed living at 2125 West Third Street in Omaha Nebraska.
4. Jay Carson Jr a senior with good organizational skills arranged for the benefit concert setting the date and ticket sales hiring the musical talent and handling the publicity.
5. In 1936 the library staff at the *Tribune* began recording the newspaper on microfilm and now the library has microfilm copies of every issue from October 14 1858 up to the most recent one.
6. When Jolene who was taking her road test got behind the steering wheel Mrs Ledbetter her mother smiling proudly looked on attentively.
7. On the spur of the moment Lilly who was known for her thoughtfulness decided against going to the party and went instead to see Jan her friend who had been hospitalized with appendicitis.
8. As the students watched Dr. Stanford an expert in distillation and a widely published author was demonstrating how to set up the special separation process explaining each step carefully.

9. Some neighbors were consoling the tornado victims some were directing traffic and the apartment manager was telephoning for the ambulance which had already been dispatched from the hospital.

10. Our company which we started as high-school seniors can provide all types of home office and factory cleaning services.

11. Lana had moved to Houston Texas in December 1984 and on June 1 1985 she was transferred to Louisville Kentucky.

12. How disappointed we were to find that our research papers on which we had worked for weeks were destroyed in the school fire, Ms Harper had not even had a chance to read them

13. When the doctor informed me that on the one hand only a very small percentage of people suffer a bad reaction to the vaccine and that on the other hand the disease it prevents is nearly always fatal what could I do but agree to have the shot

14. In an address delivered on Tuesday August 3 in Phoenix Arizona she said that the way to peace is through international economic cooperation political understanding and disarmament.

15. Although the ball was still rolling around the basket rim when the buzzer sounded it finally dropped through the hoop for the winning score.

16. In a pique my sister took the broom and began to sweep in the corners under the table and behind the couch.

17. Having found a good home the scrawny undernourished kitten had grown into a cat that was small but dark and beautiful.

18. At the edge of the deep woods along the shore of Goose Lake they made camp for the night.

19. Well if I had wanted to go I would have said so.

20. Surprisingly the secondhand clothes were not torn or dirty or out of style.

21. Use of the terms *self-service* and *cash-and-carry* can be traced to September 11 1916 and 79 Jefferson Ave Memphis Tennessee the day and place the first Piggly Wiggly grocery store opened.

22. Why I think it's remarkable that you have already completed the project for the others started before you did

23. The island of Tierra del Fuego named the Land of Fire by the explorer Ferdinand Magellan because of its many Indian bonfires lies off the southern tip of South America in a climate of high cold winds.

24. Benjamin Banneker a noted inventor astronomer and mathematician served on the commission that surveyed and laid out Washington DC

25. I beg your pardon sir but do I know you

CHAPTER 32 REVIEW: POSTTEST 1

Correcting Sentences by Adding or Deleting End Marks and Commas. Number your paper 1–25. Most of the following sentences contain errors in the use of end marks or commas. After the proper number, write all words that are followed by incorrect punctuation, adding or deleting end marks and commas in accordance with the standards of written English. If a sentence is correct, write *C* after the sentence number.

EXAMPLES 1. We spent several hours working in the hot muggy storeroom.
1. *hot,*
2. I wondered where you were?
2. *were.*

1. My parents were married on April 24 1965 in Butte Montana.

2. Here at Sachem High School, we take pride in our new computer lab our prize-winning debate team and our champion lacrosse team.

3. As far as I'm concerned you can do as you please!

4. Either you clean up your room today or you can sit in it all weekend.

5. Have I got a story to tell you.

6. Swimmers who pass the qualifying test today can move into a new category tomorrow.

7. Serving as President at the age of forty-two Theodore Roosevelt was the youngest person ever to hold the nation's highest office.

8. Oh don't throw out that newspaper; I haven't read the editorials yet.

9. Attaining success in engineering her chosen career is Nancy's highest goal.

10. Clear translucent water is one of the greatest attractions of the Caribbean beaches.

11. "Where are we going after work" asked Roberta.

12. Unless you can pay me cash right now I'm going to sell these tickets to someone else.
13. How wrong he had been to say after the fifth inning, "The game is won!"
14. Thoroughbred horses which have notoriously delicate leg bones seldom survive a serious break.
15. The great playwrights Socrates and Euripides lived in the fifth century BC in Greece.
16. The Falklands, a group of islands off the coast of Argentina are called the Malvinas by the Argentinians.
17. You go ahead, and I'll follow.
18. My opinion, Royale, is that you have a great deal of work still to do on this project.
19. Why I didn't know you were an expert at playing bridge!
20. Turning toward the group Brian paused and then began to speak.
21. After June 26 please forward my mail to 15 Platt Avenue, West Haven, CT 06516.
22. Sammy Davis Jr. is famous as an all-around entertainer.
23. The city government after all must tax residents in order to raise money for basic services.
24. Did Ms. Murphy really say, "The assignment is due Friday?"
25. For dessert, Billie Sue served strawberries, and cream.

CHAPTER 32 REVIEW: POSTTEST 2

Correcting Sentences by Adding or Deleting End Marks and Commas. Number your paper 1–25. Most of the following sentences contain errors in the use of end marks or commas. After the proper number, write all words that are followed by incorrect punctuation, adding or deleting end marks and commas in accordance with the standards of written English. If a sentence is correct, write *C* after the sentence number.

EXAMPLE   1. My best friend has moved to 9782, Revere Avenue, NY 10465.
          1. 9782

1. Marilyn and Antonio who work at a local child care center every afternoon thoroughly enjoy inventing, and playing games with the children.
2. Unfolding solar panels placing satellites into orbit and conducting medical experiments kept the space shuttle crew busy and interested throughout their recent space flight.
3. Because we had to rekindle the fire our cookout was delayed for an hour.
4. Well if you want to apply for admission to eight colleges you will surely have to pay a large sum in application fees.
5. On the beaches of Louisiana Florida and Georgia this has been a summer of boating fishing and swimming.
6. "It is my pleasure to introduce Cranston Fellows Jr. who has recently returned from a visit to Sydney Australia," said Adele Peters president of the Students' Foreign Exchange League.
7. The diplomats both educated at George Washington University in Washington DC were assigned to posts in Athens Greece and Nicosia Cyprus.
8. "The house is on fire" shouted my father. "Everyone out."
9. On the far wall to the right of the main entrance you will see a striking oil painting done in matte black, neutral gray and ash white.
10. "November 30 will be the deadline for submitting outlines note cards and thesis paragraphs for your research papers," said Ms. Walsh.
11. Coming home from the football game we were delighted to be greeted by the fragrant spicy aroma of Ned's spaghetti sauce.

12. Studying *Beowulf* for the first time the class enjoyed Grendel the grim gruesome monster.
13. The treasurer's report did I believe make it clear that the Senior Class has been very successful in its many fund-raising activities this year.
14. Interrupting his friends' conversation Philip asked, "Are you ready to leave"?
15. My aunt and uncle who have been married for twenty-five years plan to visit Egypt Kenya and Sierra Leone next October.
16. Joanne moaned, "Oh this weather is terrible"!
17. We spent the morning cleaning the basement and sorting boxes but in the afternoon we rode our bicycles along lovely country roads.
18. This is an emergency; I need to see a doctor immediately.
19. Naturally the seafood that I like best lobster is also the most expensive.
20. "Mr. President" said the Secretary of State "here is the preliminary draft of the treaty"
21. We have already decided to hold our class reunion on July 4 2006 at the Hyatt Regency Hotel in San Francisco California.
22. Professor Dimitri Pantermalis a Greek archaeologist recently announced the excavation of a rare mosaic dating from the second century AD when Greece was under Roman rule.
23. Much to my delight the festival offered jazz country rock and classical music.
24. Using hyperbole the city's largest department store took out a full-page newspaper ad reading "World's Most Spectacular Labor Day Sale"!
25. When they went to the prom Martha wore a white lace gown and George wore a light blue tuxedo.

SUMMARY OF USES OF END MARKS AND COMMAS

32a. Use a period at the end of a statement.
32b. Use periods with abbreviations.
32c. Use a question mark at the end of a question.
32d. Use an exclamation point at the end of an exclamatory sentence.

32e. Use either a period or an exclamation point at the end of an imperative sentence, depending on the force intended.

32f. Use commas to separate items in a series.

32g. Use a comma to separate two or more adjectives preceding a noun.

32h. Use a comma before *and, but, or, nor, for, yet* when they join independent clauses, unless the clauses are very short.

32i. Use commas to set off nonessential clauses and nonessential participial phrases.

32j. Use a comma after certain introductory elements.
(1) After words such as *well, yes, no, why*, etc., when they begin a sentence
(2) After an introductory participial phrase
(3) After a succession of introductory prepositional phrases
(4) After an introductory adverb clause

32k. Use commas to set off expressions that interrupt the sentence.
(1) Appositives
(2) Words in direct address
(3) Parenthetical expressions

32l. Use a comma in certain conventional situations.
(1) To separate items in dates and addresses
(2) After the salutation of a friendly letter
(3) After a name followed by *Jr., Sr., Ph.D.,* etc.

32m. Do not use unnecessary commas.

CHAPTER 33

Punctuation

OTHER MARKS OF PUNCTUATION

Although the marks of punctuation treated in this chapter are used less frequently than the period and comma, they are often important. Just as you have learned to follow certain conventions in grammar and usage and spelling, you should observe the conventional uses of the punctuation marks described in this chapter.

DIAGNOSTIC TEST

Correctly Using Punctuation Marks Other Than End Marks and Commas. Number your paper 1–20. Each of the following sentences contains an error in punctuation. Proofread each sentence, and, after the proper number, write as much of the sentence as is necessary to correct the punctuation.

EXAMPLE 1. Looking at Paulas pictures of our Senior Class trip, we felt as though we were back in Washington, D.C.
1. *Paula's*

1. Labor Day traffic was rerouted from the washed-out bridge consequently, a massive backup of cars developed.
2. Who is your favorite mystery writer on the following list, Agatha Christie, P. D. James, Wilkie Collins, or Edgar Allan Poe?

3. One of my favorite Biblical passages is the story of Jesus and the Samaritan woman in John 4–5.

4. Since Lydia visited Europe last summer, she has been using foreign expressions such as bon jour and ciao constantly.

5. The class judged the commercials to have little appeal for teenagers or adults, that is, they considered the ads suitable only for children younger than thirteen.

6. "How long will it take for the pictures to be developed?" I asked.

7. Our English class agreed that Richard Connell's short story The Most Dangerous Game is one of the best we have ever read because of its irony and suspense.

8. The confusion occurred because I thought the gift was your's instead of Dorothy's.

9. "Because we have recorded a twenty three percent increase in productivity," stated the factory owner to his employees, "each of you will receive a bonus in your next paycheck."

10. Its anyone's guess who will win the election.

11. Please turn down the radio I'm getting a headache.

12. Outstandingly successful people, whether they excel in politics, sports, or the arts, share a common trait: they are self-motivated.

13. We might and according to the tour schedule should have a free afternoon in Rome.

14. Juanita asked the librarian for the *Readers' Guide to Periodical Literature* and the latest *World Almanac*.

15. According to my sister, a college sophomore, her sociology professor expects his students to read "The New York Times" each day.

16. When we finish school at 2-15, I'll drive you home.

17. "You may not realize that auto mechanics are skilled specialists," said Mr. Busch on our first day in Auto Mechanics I.

18. Because I have spent so many happy times there, I love to visit my grandmother's and grandfather's house.

19. "The second string team will begin practice as soon as the varsity players have left the field," announced Coach Carberry.

20. Since I am on a tight budget, I was glad to see the ad announcing a special sale on mens' jeans.

THE SEMICOLON

33a. Use a semicolon between independent clauses not joined by *and, but, or, nor, for, yet, so.*

EXAMPLES Three candidates have filed for the new commission seat; none of them have any previous experience in public office.

Read all the choices; don't write the first answer that seems correct.

You must have some basis for deciding whether to use two independent clauses with a semicolon between them, or two sentences with a period (and capital letter). In most writing, the division into sentences is preferable. A semicolon is used only when the ideas in the two clauses are so closely related that a period would make too distinct a break between them.

33b. Use a semicolon between independent clauses joined by such words as *for example, for instance, that is, besides, accordingly, moreover, nevertheless, furthermore, otherwise, therefore, however, consequently, instead, hence.*

EXAMPLES Everyone in this area takes visitors to our local tourist attraction; **for instance,** I went there just last Sunday with my visiting aunt.

The speech was long and repetitious; **consequently,** listeners fidgeted in their seats and whispered among themselves.

The situation is intolerable; **therefore** we need to take immediate action.

When the connectives mentioned in this rule are placed at the beginning of a clause, the use of a comma after them is frequently a matter of taste. When they are clearly parenthetical (interrupters), they are followed by a comma. The words *for example, for instance,* and *that is* are always followed by a comma. The word *however* is almost always followed by a comma.

EXAMPLES Leaders of the two countries saw no hope for a settlement; **that is,** each claimed the other was stubborn and unwilling to compromise.

Leaders of the two countries saw no hope for a settlement; **however,** they were willing to meet again. [. . . they were willing, *however,* to meet again.]

Most of the words listed in this rule, however, are rarely used at the
beginning of a clause. They are usually placed later in the clause.

EXAMPLE   The situation is intolerable; we **therefore** need to take immediate
action.

33c. A semicolon (rather than a comma) may be needed to separate
independent clauses joined by a coordinating conjunction when there are
commas within the clauses.

EXAMPLE   Super Stop, the store on Falk Avenue, sells not only groceries but
also prescription drugs, cosmetics, hardware, garden supplies, and
sportswear; and its first shoppers, interviewed on the news last
week, seemed very pleased with the convenience the store offers.

☞ NOTE   As suggested in Rule 33c by the words "may be needed," you
are allowed considerable leeway in applying this rule. When there are only
one or two commas in the independent clauses, the semicolon is not
needed. It is required when there are so many commas, as in the example
above, that the sentence would be confusing without the semicolon because
the reader could not immediately see where the first clause ended.

33d. Use a semicolon between items in a series if the items contain
commas.

EXAMPLE   Winners in the competition were Alene Murphy, first place; Jeff
Bates, second place; Ed Davis, third place; and Nancy Green, who,
as a member of the Student Council, had proposed the contest.

WRITING APPLICATION A:
Using Semicolons to Make Your Writing Clear

Determining the amount of information to include in a single sentence is
an important part of writing clearly. You can help your reader understand that ideas are closely related by using semicolons to join independent clauses. Notice in the following example that the semicolon links
two independent clauses in one sentence, signaling the reader that the
ideas are closely related:

EXAMPLE   I am much more tolerant than I used to be; for example, my little
brother's teasing no longer bothers me, and I understand why my
mother is tired after a day at the office.

Writing Assignment

You have changed a great deal during your years in high school—not just physically, but intellectually and emotionally. Write a composition comparing and contrasting yourself as you are now and as you were three years ago. Revise your paper, and proofread it carefully to make sure that you have used semicolons correctly to join independent clauses that contain closely related ideas.

THE COLON

33e. Use a colon to mean "note what follows."

(1) Use a colon before a list of items, especially after expressions like *as follows* **and** *the following.*

EXAMPLES   Amazingly enough, the small bag held everything: shirts, pants, sweaters, a jacket, shoes, underwear, nightclothes, toiletries, and a present for my hosts.

Be prepared to answer the following questions: What was your last job? Why did you leave it? What other experience have you had? [list introduced by "the following"]

☞ NOTE   When a list comes immediately after a verb or a preposition, do not use a colon.

EXAMPLES   We **collected** blankets, canned goods, medical supplies, and clothing for the flood victims. [list follows the verb *collected*]

Dan has always been interested **in** snakes, frogs, lizards, and other reptiles. [list follows the preposition *in*]

(2) Use a colon before a long, formal statement or quotation.

EXAMPLE   Dr. Stafford made the following observation: Cooperation between the leading nations of the world is essential to the survival of the planet. [Note that a formal statement like this need not be enclosed in quotation marks.]

(3) Use a colon between independent clauses when the second clause explains or restates the idea in the first.

EXAMPLE   Those hanging lamps are the most popular kind: they are inexpensive, come in many colors, and are easy to install.

33f. Use a colon in certain conventional situations.

(1) Use a colon between the hour and the minute when you write the time.

EXAMPLE   8:00 A.M.

(2) Use a colon between chapter and verse in referring to passages from the Bible.

EXAMPLE   Proverbs 3:3

(3) Use a colon between volume and number or between volume and page number of a periodical.

EXAMPLES   *Harper's* 203: 16 [volume and number]

Harper's 203: 16–19 [volume and page numbers]

(4) Use a colon after the salutation of a business letter.

EXAMPLES   Dear Ms. Ayala: Gentlemen: Dear Sir or Madam:

WRITING APPLICATION B:
Using Colons Correctly to Make Your Writing Clear

Since the semicolon and the colon serve completely different purposes, it is important to distinguish between them in your writing. Your reader relies on your use of these marks to know whether to expect, for example, an independent clause closely related to the preceding one (after a semicolon) or a list (after a colon). Notice how misleading the misuse of a semicolon for a colon in the first of the following examples is:

EXAMPLES   Three committees were set up for the banquet; awards, decorations, and food.

Three committees were set up for the banquet: awards, decorations, and food.

Writing Assignment

You have been appointed to serve on the awards committee for a banquet honoring outstanding writers in the senior class. Decide what kind of awards to present and how many, and write a letter ordering the items. Revise the letter, and proofread it carefully to make sure that you have used colons correctly.

UNDERLINING (ITALICS)

33g. Use underlining (italics) for titles of books, films, plays, television programs, periodicals, works of art, ships, etc.   *Albums*

EXAMPLES   The Old Man and the Sea

the San Diego Tribune, or the San Diego Tribune

the Senior Scholastic

the View of Toledo, Appalachian Spring, The Thinker

the Norway, the Garden State Special, the Columbia

The use of quotation marks for titles is now generally limited to short compositions such as short stories and short poems and to parts of publications; the titles of the publications themselves are underlined. (Compare page 826.)

EXAMPLE   Read Chapter 39, "Americans in the Second World War (1941–1945)," from Rise of the American Nation.

> ☞ NOTE   When set in type, underlined words are italicized.
> *The Old Man and the Sea*   the *Senior Scholastic*

The words *a, an, the*, written before a title, are underlined only when they are part of the title of a book, article, etc. Before the names of magazines and newspapers, they are not underlined within a composition.

EXAMPLE   I found some good ideas for my paper in my text, The History of the Americas, and in several issues of the National Geographic Magazine.

33h. Use underlining (italics) for words, letters, and figures referred to as such and for foreign words not yet adopted into English.

EXAMPLES   The most common English word is <u>the</u>; the letters used most frequently are <u>e</u> and <u>t</u>; and numbers often confused are <u>7</u> and <u>9</u>.

I know the Latin phrase <u>ad initio</u>—it reminds me of all the setbacks I've ever had, but the saying <u>ad astra per aspera</u> gives me hope.

EXERCISE 1. Using Colons, Semicolons, and Italics Correctly. Number your paper 1–10. After the proper number, write the words and numbers that should be followed by a semicolon or a colon and write the appropriate punctuation after each. Write and underline all words that should be italicized.

1. From 1970 to 1981, one-parent families doubled in number; however, two-parent families in 1981 still comprised nearly 80 percent of families with children.

2. Performers in the show included the following band members playing two instruments apiece: Tony Fleming, trumpet and trombone; Donna Bryant, clarinet and saxophone; and Phyllis Ward, drums and steel guitar.

3. Our local paper, the <u>Morning Ledger</u>, always carries certain features: comics, advice columns, and a crossword puzzle.

4. Interesting stories are plentiful in the Bible; two of my favorites are the battle between David and Goliath in I Samuel 17:1–58 and the story of the good Samaritan in Luke 10:25–37.

5. Groups of students, all going to the museum to see Egyptian, Assyrian, and Greek exhibits, began boarding the buses at 8 30 but the buses did not leave until 9 00, when the parking lot was finally cleared, the last stragglers had boarded, and the drivers had verified directions.

6. Ms. Bell often assigns reading in current magazines; for instance, our latest one runs as follows: <u>The Atlantic</u>, 218:33–44; <u>U.S. News and World Report</u>, 26:5; <u>Changing Times</u>, 8:62–67.

7. According to historians, Michelangelo always thought of himself first as a sculptor his sculpture the Pietà is the only work he ever signed.

8. She revised her report three times: first, for content; second, for organization; third, for style.

9. Legislators were in a difficult position;they had to finance demand for increased services without calling for increased taxes.
10. While downtown, I bought several gifts;a cookbook for my father; a print of Rousseau's The Jungle for my mother and for my sister, the album featuring the soundtrack of Annie.

QUOTATION MARKS

33i. Use quotation marks to enclose a direct quotation—a person's exact words.

DIRECT QUOTATION   My sister said, **"**One of my favorite singers is Lena Horne.**"**

Do not use quotation marks to enclose an indirect quotation—one that does not give a person's exact words.

INDIRECT QUOTATION   My sister said one of her favorite singers is Lena Horne.

Enclose means to place quotation marks at both the beginning and the end of a quotation. Omission of quotation marks at the end of a quotation is a common error.

(1) A direct quotation begins with a capital letter.

EXAMPLE   She told me, "Finish this assignment first."

Exception: If the quotation is only a fragment of a sentence, do not begin it with a capital letter:

EXAMPLE   A reviewer called the movie "a futile attempt to trade on his reputation as a maker of blockbusters."

(2) When a quoted sentence is divided into two parts by an interrupting expression such as *he said* or *Mother asked*, the second part begins with a small letter.

EXAMPLES   "Take care," he warned, "that you don't spill anything out of the beaker."

"Did you," she asked, "make up the test that you missed?"

If the second part of a divided quotation is a new sentence, it begins with a capital letter.

EXAMPLE "Don't open the door," he pleaded. "We're still developing the film."

(3) A direct quotation is set off from the rest of the sentence by commas or by a question mark or an exclamation point.

EXAMPLES Flo said, **"**We could send them a telegram."

"What would you say to that**?"** she asked.

☞ NOTE If the quotation is only a phrase, do not set it off by commas.

EXAMPLE For him **"**one for all and all for one**"** is the key to having a successful club.

(4) Other marks of punctuation when used with quotation marks are placed according to the following rules:

1. *Commas and periods are always placed inside the closing quotation marks.*

EXAMPLE **"**I'm sure,**"** said Joe, **"**that we'll be done with this project by Friday.**"**

2. *Semicolons and colons are always placed outside the closing quotation marks.*

EXAMPLES **"**Eva,**"** my grandmother said, **"**you should keep up with your chores**"**; then she reminded me that it was my turn to wash the dishes.

Gail Sloan describes the following as **"**deserted-island reading**"**: *An Encyclopedia of World History*, the complete works of Shakespeare, and *Robinson Crusoe*.

3. *Question marks and exclamation points are placed inside the closing quotation marks if the quotation is a question or an exclamation; otherwise they are placed outside.*

EXAMPLES "Is everyone present?" asked the teacher.

"How perceptive you are sometimes!" she exclaimed.

Were you surprised when he said, "You win"?

Stop calling me a "little girl"!

No more than one comma or one end mark is used at the end of a quotation.

INCORRECT Did she find out who said, "No one can make you feel inferior without your consent."? [two end marks, period and question mark]

CORRECT Did she find out who said, "No one can make you feel inferior without your consent"?

INCORRECT Did you ever ask yourself, "Where will I be ten years from now?"?

CORRECT Did you ever ask yourself, "Where will I be ten years from now?"

(5) When you write dialogue, begin a new paragraph every time the speaker changes.

EXAMPLE "Hi, guys. Look what I just got!" said Jessie as she came up to her friends Mark and Sue. She was cradling a sophisticated new 35–mm camera in her hands.

"That's beautiful!" said Sue.

Raising his eyebrows, Mark said, "Yes, but where did you get it?"

"Oh, I got a great deal at the camera shop—and a loan from my mother."

"How," they both asked at once, "will you pay her back?"

"Well, I have my part-time job," said Jessie. "I'm also going to take pictures for people—at a modest price, of course. Say," she added, "wouldn't you two like to have your pictures taken?"

(6) When a quoted passage consists of more than one paragraph, place quotation marks at the beginning of each paragraph and at the end of the entire passage, not at the end of each paragraph.

> ☞ NOTE   Usually such a long quotation will be set off from the rest of the paper by indentation and single spacing. In such a case, no quotation marks will be necessary.

(7) Use single quotation marks to enclose a quotation within a quotation.

EXAMPLE   What she said was, "For Tuesday read Masefield's poem 'Sea Fever.'"

33j. Use quotation marks to enclose titles of chapters, articles, short stories, poems, songs, and other parts of books and periodicals.

EXAMPLE   Read Chapter 19, "The Progressive Movement."

> ☞ NOTE   Book titles and names of magazines are indicated by underlining (italics) (see page 821).

33k. Use quotation marks to enclose slang words, technical terms, and other expressions that are unusual in standard English.

Use this device sparingly.

EXAMPLES   I don't think he is a "nerd."

A coupling device used to transmit information from one computer to another is referred to as a "modem."

The names Kansas and Arkansas are derived from the Sioux Indian word for "downstream people."

EXERCISE 2. Using Punctuation Marks Correctly. Write the following sentences, inserting quotation marks, other required punctuation, and capitalization.

1. How many of you Mrs. Martinez asked have studied a foreign language for more than two years.
2. Nice try Donna was what the coach said.
3. We should have started our homework earlier said Beth we have answered only three questions so far.
4. Where have you been she asked.
5. Someone once asked George Bernard Shaw how old he was, and he answered I'm as old as my tongue and a few years older than my teeth.
6. To whom was Stendhal referring asked Mrs. Ross when he dedicated his novels to the happy few.
7. Was it Elizabeth Browning asked Sandra, who wrote the poem Shall I Compare Thee to a Summer's Day?
8. Cast off shouted the captain we're bound for Rio.
9. Would you let us hand in our research papers next week Ms. Lewis we asked none of the books we need are in the library.
10. Alice whispered thank you for lending me the article Is There Life on Other Planets? Barbara.

THE APOSTROPHE

33l. To form the possessive case of a singular noun, add an apostrophe and an *s*.

EXAMPLES   Dora's choice

Kelly's coat

Ross's sleeve

In words of more than one syllable that end in an *s*-sound, it is permissible to form the singular possessive by adding the apostrophe without the *s*. This is done to avoid too many *s*-sounds.

EXAMPLES   the Williams' apartment

the seamstress' work

Odysseus' travels

> ☞ NOTE   Since the use of the apostrophe varies among writers, it is not possible to make a hard and fast rule about the apostrophe in singular words ending in *s*. Thus *Hughes' poetry* and *Hughes's poetry* are equally acceptable. Punctuate according to pronunciation. If you say "Hugheses" or "McCullerses," write "Hughes's" and "McCullers's." If you say "Hughes" poems or "McCullers" novels, write "Hughes'" and "McCullers'."

(1) To form the possessive case of a plural noun ending in *s*, add only the apostrophe.

EXAMPLES   girls' team

the Millses' back yard

> ☞ NOTE   The few plural nouns that do not end in *s* form the possessive by adding the apostrophe and an *s* just as singular nouns do.

EXAMPLES   women's tournament

children's playground

(2) Personal pronouns in the possessive case (*his, hers, its, ours, yours, theirs*, and the relative pronoun *whose*) do not require an apostrophe.

INCORRECT   We thought the top score was her's.
  CORRECT   We thought the top score was **hers**.

INCORRECT   I have witnessed democracy at it's best.
  CORRECT   I have witnessed democracy at **its** best.

INCORRECT   Who's notebook is this?
  CORRECT   **Whose** notebook is this?

(3) Indefinite pronouns (*one, everyone, everybody*, etc.) in the possessive case require an apostrophe and an *s*.[1]

EXAMPLES   **Everyone's** vote counts equally.

She consented to **everybody's** request for a class meeting.

---

[1] Note the correct form of such words used with *else*: everyone *else's*; somebody *else's*. Note that there is no apostrophe in *oneself*.

EXERCISE 3. Using Apostrophes Correctly with Singular and Plural Possessives. Number your paper 1–10. After the proper number, write both the singular and plural possessive of the italicized word.

EXAMPLE   1. *citizen* rights
           1. *citizen's, citizens'*

1. *city* plans
2. *girl* clothes
3. *friend* emotions
4. *sheep* wool

5. *worker* wages
6. *man* shoes
7. *dog* dishes

8. *ox* horns
9. *student* grades
10. *doctor* fees

EXERCISE 4. Proofreading Possessives. Number your paper 1–20. If the possessive case for each item in the list has been correctly formed, write *C* after the proper number. If it has been incorrectly formed, write the correct form.

1. everyone's share
2. bus' windows
3. children's books
4. this school's reputation
5. pants' cuffs
6. Is this your's?
7. a girl's or a boy's bike
8. opened it's covers
9. flower's bud
10. The loss is our's.

11. a street of lawyer's offices
12. at the Gibb's home
13. that nation's debts
14. women's objections
15. found it's way home
16. travelers' briefcases
17. soldiers knapsacks
18. did its best
19. babie's toys
20. the poets' works

(4) In hyphenated words, names of organizations and business firms, and words showing joint possession, only the last word is possessive in form.

EXAMPLES   **father-in-law's** hobby
               commander-in-chief's order

ORGANIZATIONS   The **Economic and Social Council's** members
                   Black and Decker's tools
                   Johnson and Johnson's products

JOINT POSSESSION   **Dotty and Fay's** report
                     Paul and Brian's duet

Exception: When the second word is a possessive pronoun, the first word is also possessive.

INCORRECT Dotty and my report
  CORRECT **Dotty's and my** report

INCORRECT her classmate and her opinions
  CORRECT her **classmate's and her** opinions

(5) When two or more persons possess something individually, each of their names is possessive in form.

EXAMPLE **Tom's** and **Bill's** jackets

(6) The words *minute, hour, day, week, month, year,* **etc., when used as possessive adjectives, require an apostrophe. Words indicating an amount in cents or dollars, when used as possessive adjectives, require apostrophes.**

EXAMPLES a minute's work, five minutes' work

a day's rest, three days' rest[1]

one cent's worth, five cents' worth

EXERCISE 5. Revising Phrases by Forming Possessives. In the following list, the possessive relationship is expressed by means of a phrase. Revise each item so that the possessive case of the noun or pronoun is used to express the same relationship.

EXAMPLE 1. a vacation of two weeks
  1. *a two weeks' vacation*

1. hats of Carol and Pat
2. dressing room of the men
3. job of my sister-in-law
4. character of a person
5. business of Jorge and Ralph
6. speech of the governor-elect
7. worth of four dollars
8. catalog of Lord and Taylor
9. prize of Ralph Bunche
10. sides of it
11. remarks of the judges
12. a pause of a moment
13. worth of two cents
14. highlights of the film
15. shoes of the women
16. insignia of the sergeant-at-arms
17. trip of Maria and Alma
18. a wait of an hour
19. heat of the sun
20. albums of Simon and Garfunkel

---

[1] Also correct: a three-day rest, etc.

33m. Use an apostrophe to show where letters have been omitted in a contraction.

A contraction is a word made up of two words combined into one by the omission of one or more letters.

EXAMPLES For *do not* the contraction is **don't.** [the letter *o* omitted]

For *it is* the contraction is **it's.** [the letter *i* omitted]

For *they are* the contraction is **they're.** [the letter *a* omitted]

☞ NOTE The most common error in the use of the apostrophe in a contraction (except the failure to use it at all) comes from the confusion of *it's*, which means *it is*, with the possessive form *its* (*its* appearance), which has no apostrophe. Another common error, probably the result of carelessness, is the insertion of the apostrophe in the wrong place: *ca'nt* for *can't*, *does'nt* for *doesn't*, etc. Also note especially that *let's* in such an expression as "Let's go!" is a contraction of *let us* and requires an apostrophe for the omitted *u*.

33n. Use the apostrophe and *s* to form the plural of letters, numbers, and signs, and of words referred to as words.

EXAMPLES *Hawaii* is spelled with two **i's.**

He correctly placed the decimal before the two **6's.**

Don't you need **+'s** in that equation?

Try not to use so many **very's** in your writing.

EXERCISE 6. Proofreading Possessives and Contractions and Revising Phrases by Forming Possessives.

Number your paper 1–25. Write the following phrases and sentences, inserting apostrophes where they are needed and changing the phrases to possessive forms. If an item is correct, write *C*.

1. womens sports
2. statements of a mayor-elect
3. Its great, isn't it?
4. sand in its gears
5. Lets see whats going on.
6. I've found sulkings no help.
7. firm of Dun and Bradstreet
8. mens tennis
9. Whats its title?
10. on a minutes notice

11. locker of Frank and Henry
12. Whos on Vicky's bicycle?
13. this pianos keys
14. Its still early, Im sure.
15. If he lets us, well go too.
16. Her cousins' choices were the same as hers.
17. How many is are there in *Mississippi*?
18. girls playclothes
19. childrens magazine
20. Her scores were a 9.0 and two 8.5s in the freestyle event.
21. books of Woodward and Bernstein
22. It can be done by oneself.
23. office of the principal
24. dictionaries of Carlos and Rosa
25. Lets find out whos here.

THE HYPHEN

33o. Use a hyphen to divide a word at the end of a line.

Try to avoid dividing words at the end of a line in order to maintain an even margin unless it is necessary. For rules that will help you in deciding where to place the hyphen, see pages 762–63.

33p. Use a hyphen with compound numbers from *twenty-one* to *ninety-nine* and with fractions used as modifiers.

EXAMPLES   **forty-two** applicants
a **two-thirds** majority, *but*
two thirds of the voters

33q. Use a hyphen with the prefixes *ex–, self–, all–;* with the suffix *–elect;* and with all prefixes before a proper noun or proper adjective.

EXAMPLES   ex-mayor   non-European
self-controlled   anti-Fascist
all-star   pro-Canadian
president-elect   Pan-American

33r. Hyphenate a compound adjective when it precedes the word it modifies.

a third-floor office   an office on the third floor
an after-lunch speech   a speech after lunch

rain‑washed sidewalk   a sidewalk washed by rain
door‑to‑door canvassing   canvassing from door to door
well‑liked author   The author is well liked.

☞ **NOTE**   Do not use a hyphen if one of the modifiers is an adverb ending in –*ly*.

EXAMPLES   highly polished surface
quickly done task

33s. Use a hyphen to prevent confusion or awkwardness.

EXAMPLES   re‑collect [prevents confusion with **recollect**]
re‑form [prevents confusion with **reform**]
anti‑icer [avoids the awkwardness of **antiicer**]
semi‑invalid [avoids the awkwardness of **semiinvalid**]

THE DASH

33t. Use a dash to indicate an abrupt break in thought.

EXAMPLES   He might——if I have anything to say about it——change his mind.
The truth is——and you probably already know it——we can't do it without you.

33u. Use a dash to mean *namely, in other words,* or *that is* before an explanation.

EXAMPLE   It was a close call—the sudden gust of wind pushed the helicopter to within inches of the power line. [the dash means *that is*]

In this use, the colon and the dash are frequently interchangeable.

EXAMPLE   It was a close call: the sudden gust of wind pushed the helicopter to within inches of the power line.

PARENTHESES

33v. Use parentheses to enclose incidental explanatory matter that is added to a sentence but is not considered of major importance.

EXAMPLES Former Representative Jordan (Texas) was a member of that committee.

The population of the United States is shifting (see Chart B) to the South and the Southwest.

☞ NOTE For setting off incidental matter, commas, dashes, and parentheses are frequently interchangeable. Commas and dashes are more common than parentheses.

---

(1) Be sure that any material within parentheses can be omitted without changing the basic meaning or structure of the sentence.

IMPROPER USE OF PARENTHESES
Tina had been shopping (in that store) most of her life. [The idea in parentheses is too important to the meaning of the sentence to be placed in parentheses.]

(2) Punctuation marks are used within parentheses when they belong with the parenthetical matter. Punctuation marks that belong with the main part of the sentence are placed after a closing parenthesis.

EXAMPLES Fred Bates asked us (What a silly question!) if we really thought we could do it.

If the committee is headed by Alison (Is she here?), the student council will probably support it.

BRACKETS

You will seldom have a use for brackets. Commas, dashes, and parentheses are preferable as means of setting off parenthetical matter.

33w. Use brackets to enclose explanations within parentheses or in quoted material when the explanation is not part of the quotation.

EXAMPLES Ms. Gray was quoted as saying in her acceptance speech: "I am honored by it [the award], but I would like to share the recognition with those who made my work possible."

By a vote of 5–4, the Supreme Court overturned the lower court's ruling. (See page 149 [Diagram A] for a chronology of the case.)

REVIEW EXERCISE. Proofreading Passages for Punctuation and Capitalization. Most of the necessary punctuation and capitalization has been omitted from the following passages. When a passage is assigned, write it, proofreading it carefully and preparing a version that uses the conventions of standard English. The only changes you need to make in paragraphing are those required by dialogue. Some of the punctuation is incorrect, but in most instances you need only *add* punctuation and capitals. When you are in doubt as to a particular punctuation or capitalization problem, don't guess. Look up the rule.

1

No discussion of Americas outstanding sports figures would be complete without reference to Jim Thorpe who was voted in 1950 as the greatest athlete of the centurys first half. His feats in football track and baseball remain unique and his strength and speed are legendary born of irish french and indian heritage and reared in prague oklahoma Thorpe began earning honors early in his life he was an all american halfback for two years while playing for the local indian school and broke all previous records in winning the gold medals for the pentathlon and the decathlon at the 1912 olympic games where he was hailed as the greatest athlete in the world. Because hed already begun playing professional baseball however he was forced to return his medals a year later (they were restored posthumously in 1982) Thorpe spent six outstanding years in professional baseball but he became best known as a football player who could do everything well run pass catch punt and more. He played professional football for over ten years with great ability in 1969 sixteen years after his death and on the national football leagues fiftieth birthday Thorpe was named to footballs all time all professional team.

2

I was fast asleep at home on holly street three quarters of a mile from the scene when the event took place according to the police it was a rainy moonless night and the crime must have occurred after 1 30 AM those first on the scene the next morning were Jason Crawford a fellow senior and the principal. Jason told me later that he had been eager to get into the computer lab to finish his project when the lab door swung open both of them gasped. Jason said all he could get past the lump in his throat was oh no all five of the cherished hard won microcomputers were gone. Practically every student at newton high school had worked on the fund-raising efforts to acquire those computers including me Id been one of a dozen seniors whod participated in an all night rockathon wed spent twenty four hours in rocking chairs set up at the mall suddenly everyones opportunity to learn how to use them was gone too.

A week later the culprits were caught but they were caught without the machines which had already been sold I'm afraid at the next assembly the principal gave one of her most rousing speeches. If we can raise the money once we can do it again right

Okay okay count me in I said under my breath even if it means losing a good nights sleep.

3

Roger Morton sat back for a moment feeling slightly proud of himself. Have you finished those sample business letters yet asked Ms Zimsky the typing teacher. Yes Roger replied quickly. I think Ive improved on the format too. Look how much space is saved on each page Ms Zimsky glanced down These arent done the way they are in the book. Just do them that way for now though you need to finish this chapter today or youll be way behind. Theres no time to talk about format. Embarrassed and tired Roger later told his friend Annette about the incident. Your problem she mused isnt that you improved the letters its the same one I had once on my job at bartons shop. I learned that any time you want to change a procedure no matter how great an improvement it is you should first talk it over with the person who will need to approve it. Try discussing your idea again when Ms Zimsky has more time. Roger went back to the typing classroom after school and Ms Zimsky listened thoughtfully to all his suggestions Oh I see what youre doing here she said. Its really a very good idea in fact I think Ill share it with the whole class. See you tomorrow then Roger Yes said Roger with a smile and thanks for listening Ms Zimsky.

CHAPTER 33 REVIEW: POSTTEST 1

Correctly Using Punctuation Marks Other Than End Marks and Commas. Number your paper 1–25. Each of the following sentences contains an error in punctuation. Proofread each sentence, and, after the proper number, write as much of the sentence as is necessary to correct the punctuation.

EXAMPLES 1. Don's locker jammed we were late to class because we tried to open it.
1. *jammed;*
2. You're invited to Don and my party.
2. *Don's*

1. The face to face meeting of the diplomats improved communication and brought their nations' problems closer to a solution.
2. "When the air becomes seriously polluted by auto emissions," said Senator Angela Gardner, "isn't it time to make some changes"?
3. Pierre Franey and Craig Claiborne are two of the greatest chefs in America they have published several cookbooks.
4. In English, more words begin with the letter s than with any other letter.
5. "I made dinner reservations for 7:30 P.M.," said Roland.
6. The 1930's are called the Great Depression; they were years of poverty for many Americans.
7. "When I saw the bracelet, all I could say was, 'Oh, how beautiful!'" said Adrianne.
8. In our English class, we read several of Gerard Manley Hopkins poems, which I enjoyed very much.
9. "In order to use the computer, you do not have to understand its inner operations," read the user's manual.
10. According to a review I read in the paper, the film is one of the best antiwar documentaries ever made.
11. Last Sunday's newspaper included a feature on womens fall fashions.
12. Its time for the President's televised press conference.
13. Seventy five people were present at the statehouse when Governor Swensen signed the new bill.
14. The television commentator called the fumbled play an absolute disaster."
15. If you are interested in reading about the pain apartheid brings to a country, read the novel Cry, the Beloved Country by Alan Paton.
16. Did you read Shirley Jackson's short story The Lottery in your English class last year?
17. I had earned the money myself, naturally, I was careful to find out which bank offered the highest interest rate on a savings account.
18. Unfortunately, Susan B. Anthony, one of the leaders of the women's suffrage movement, did'nt live to see her goals realized.
19. Please pick up the following items when you go grocery shopping —milk, tuna fish, lettuce, pickles, peaches, and soap.

20. Senator Moynihan, D., New York addressed the graduates of Columbia University.
21. Ituha and Tala's bicycles are parked in front of the school.
22. I recently read that Dover Beach, by Matthew Arnold, is the most frequently anthologized poem in English.
23. Using an out-of-date slang word, Denise pronounced the performance "awesome".
24. My English teacher said that my revised essay is now acceptable, mutatis mutandis, which means "the changes having been made."
25. Martin Luther King, Jr., spent much of his life working to make the theory of, "liberty and justice for all" a reality.

CHAPTER 33 REVIEW: POSTTEST 2

Using Punctuation Correctly. Number your paper 1–25. Each of the following sentences contains at least one punctuation error. Proofread each sentence, and, after the proper number, write the sentence, punctuating it correctly.

EXAMPLE 1. Why did you let your work go until the last minute asked my friend Tanya when I told her my problem?
1. *"Why did you let your work go until the last minute?" asked my friend Tanya when I told her my problem.*

1. When I read The Hobbit, my favorite chapter was the one in which Bilbo meets Gollum.
2. Among the members of the Fine Arts Commission meeting in New York City were several talented people Diane Keaton actress Paul McCartney musician Paul Taylor choreographer and Lee Krasner artist.
3. My brothers and sisters and I have been encouraged to be self reliant since we were children.
4. The origin of the bacterial infection see note below and its cure posed a grave puzzle to the medical experts.
5. Shakespeares Hamlet is a popular play because it involves a ghost murder and romance.

6. I believe we will win this game, said the soccer coach to the newspaper sportswriter.
7. Paulette sent in my application before the deadline however she neglected to put a stamp on the envelope.
8. After we had returned from our class trip to Houston, our teacher Ms Ryan said "we were the most well behaved group she had ever chaperoned."
9. When a graduate of our high school appeared on television playing Scott Joplin's Maple Leaf Rag, a new interest in ragtime music blossomed at Franklin High School.
10. "These packages are your's arent they" asked Tamala.
11. Although the oil contract had not been renewed, the oil company made a delivery the customers complained when they received the bill.
12. The mayor elect met today with members of the Allentown Youth Council see picture on page 40.
13. When asked her opinion, the president of the brokerage firm said I favor purchasing blue chips those with a history of steady earnings and stable prices.
14. Monicas noisy muffler makes it impossible for her to drive down the street without attracting attention.
15. Suspending students from school for cutting classes creates a Catch-22 situation, said education consultant Cho Yin Lum.
16. In a stunning upset, said the radio announcer the Liberals have defeated the Conservatives!
17. At Book Lore the bookstore where I work sale's have increased twenty seven percent since last month.
18. Do you know that Europeans write their 7s differently from the way Americans do asked Estrella?
19. Ill never forget the first time I read Walt Whitmans poem When Lilacs Last in the Dooryard Bloomed it made me feel the tragedy of Abraham Lincolns death.
20. Have you read this months issue of Seventeen?
21. During the pep rally and even after it had ended the cheerleading captain, Teresa Suarez, led the students in enthusiastic cheering.
22. Within the next three weeks, new television stations will begin broadcasting from the following cities Salinas California Kalamazoo Michigan and Fairbanks Alaska.

23. George Gershwins Rhapsody in Blue is probably the best-known American composition in the world.

24. January 3 is the birthday shared by two world famous writers Cicero and J. R. R. Tolkien.

25. Helena knew it would be a less than perfect day when she heard herself saying Don't forget to dot your ts and cross your is.

MECHANICS
MASTERY REVIEW: Cumulative Test

A. CAPITALIZATION. The following sentences contain errors in capitalization. After the proper number, write the correct form of the word. If a sentence is correct, write *C* after the sentence number.

EXAMPLE 1. The american Pilots showed great skill in maneuvering the aircraft.
 1. *American pilots*

1. The first person to conquer the strenuous climb to the top of mount everest, the world's highest mountain, was Sir Edmund Hillary.
2. New York's empire state building was the world's tallest building for many years; today, Chicago's sears tower claims that title.
3. The police car traveled two miles north and then turned onto west dakota road.
4. One of the central aspects of american indian culture is a love of and respect for nature.
5. New York City's east river is really a part of Long Island sound.
6. For as long as anyone can remember, our town's two High Schools have had a friendly but intense rivalry.
7. Although the book itself is not very long, *a portrait of the artist as a young man* is one of the longest titles of a novel written in english.
8. My Doctor said that the excellent care I received at Jamestown Memorial hospital was responsible for my rapid recovery last year.
9. The members of the champion Soccer Team met the president last sunday while they were in Washington, D.C.
10. Jerusalem is a city held sacred by christians, jews, and moslems.

B. COMMAS. Most of the following sentences contain errors in the use of commas. After the proper number, write the word preceding the error, adding or deleting a comma. If a sentence is correct, write *C* after the sentence number.

EXAMPLE 1. Cawing noisily seagulls, and starlings clustered near the water's edge.
 1. *Cawing noisily, seagulls and starlings*

11. Drawn by the mysteries of life within the seas marine biologists study plant and animal life in the oceans' depths.
12. Only tall rugged trees silhouetted against an icy landscape faced the cross-country skiers, who reached the crest of the hill.
13. Preferring blue to all other colors, Richie always dressed in blue denim jackets and jeans.
14. Some of my friends thought the play was funny but I thought it was merely an example of outdated farce.
15. No I simply don't understand how to follow the instructions for assembling the bicycle!
16. The designer a woman of remarkable skill and cleverness is also a talented writer.
17. Well it seems to me Mr. Conlon that your bid is the best one we have received on this property.
18. Beside the brick walk at the side of the house the red geraniums provided an attractive decoration all summer long.
19. My youngest sister Marilyn was born on January 23 1977 in the midst of a blizzard.
20. For the third consecutive year the debate was held in Dover Delaware.

C. SEMICOLONS AND COLONS. The following sentences contain errors in the use of semicolons and colons. After the proper number, write the word preceding the error, adding, deleting, or changing a semicolon or a colon. If a sentence is correct, write *C* after the sentence number.

EXAMPLE   1. Today we will listen to some classical music, we will begin with Beethoven's "Ode to Joy."
  1. *music;*

21. That was my first encounter with an earthquake I hope it's my last!
22. When we got to the ballpark, it was already 3:30 P.M.
23. This year the penalty for cutting class is a two-hour detention consequently, fewer students are cutting classes than ever before.
24. The editor reads three newspapers every day the *Washington Post,* the *New York Times,* and the *San Francisco Examiner.*
25. The founder of the company created excellent working conditions the employees responded by setting records in every phase of the business.

26. This is my favorite kind of book it has fast-paced action, chilling suspense, and complex characters.

27. We received the decorator's ideas yesterday we are so excited about them that, despite our original plan to wait until spring, we will begin the renovation next week.

28. Last Tuesday, through an amazing coincidence, Elbert received letters from Washington, Connecticut, Washington, Oklahoma, and Washington, Nebraska!

29. On a dune overlooking the Gulf of Mexico, Billy Joe set up his materials; an easel, a partially completed canvas painting, a palette, brushes, and tubes of oil paints.

30. You are delaying now you'll regret your inaction later!

D. ITALICS AND QUOTATION MARKS. The following sentences contain errors in the use of underlining (italics) and quotation marks. After the proper number, write the words that should be underlined or enclosed in quotation marks, supplying the necessary punctuation.

EXAMPLE   1. The article is in this month's issue of Scientific American, the biology teacher said.
       1. <u>Scientific American</u>

31. The center of the low-pressure system, said the weather forecaster, is over Minnesota.

32. Millions of Americans have enjoyed reading Margaret Mitchell's famous novel, Gone with the Wind.

33. She subscribes to three magazines: <u>Sports Illustrated</u>, <u>Newsweek</u>, and <u>Consumer Reports</u>.

34. My parents are avid readers of the popular newspaper advice column Dear Abby. inside

35. Samuru bought the after-shave lotion the ads had termed Completely New, but the only difference he noted was in the color of the lotion.

36. T.S. Eliot's The Lovesong of J. Alfred Prufrock is one of the most important poems written in the twentieth century, noted Ms. Kerwin as she began her lecture.

37. I've made up my mind, said Carmen Alvarez, to return to Cleveland when I graduate from college.

38. "You won a free trip to Ireland? How wonderful! exclaimed Deirdre. I hope you'll have an exciting time."

39. One of the world's most famous anti-war paintings is Pablo Picasso's <u>Guernica</u>, which reveals the pain and suffering of the Spanish people during the Spanish Civil War of the 1930's.

40. "Now that you've finished all your work, are you ready for some fun?" asked Hannah.

E. APOSTROPHES. After the proper number, write both the singular and the plural possessive forms of the word.

EXAMPLE   1. frog
              1. *frog's, frogs'*

41. wall   43. child   45. deer

42. house   44. princess

F. THE HYPHEN, THE DASH, PARENTHESES, AND BRACKETS. Each of the following groups of sentences contains *one* sentence in which the punctuation is incorrect. After the proper number, write the letter of the incorrect item and write the sentence correctly, underlining your correction.

EXAMPLE   1. a. The passage was so difficult that I had to reread it four times before I understood the main idea.
              b. We enjoyed an afternoon walk through the well-planned gardens.
              c. "You will have time to re-vise your essay," said my English teacher.
           1. c. *"You will have time to revise your essay," said my English teacher.*

46. a. We did the job ourselves.
    b. The ex-President of the United States addressed the convention of the League of Women Voters.
    c. When the company developed a self-propelled robot, the price of its stocks rose on Wall Street.

47. a. "When the students return [to school], everything will be in order," said Superintendent Claudia Davies.
    b. If I pass the test [O happy day!], I will have enough credits to graduate.
    c. Finally, press the timer button. (See page 14 [Figure B] for correct location of the timer.)

48. a. Odessa Johnson—a drama student at Yale—has been cast for one of the leads in the movie version of William Faulkner's novel *The Sound and the Fury*.

   b. Just to change the topic for a minute—what are you doing after school?

   c. I'm going to clean my room today—no kidding!

49. a. This cabinet may be easily assembled in your own home (see instruction booklet).

   b. The trendy restaurant's menu items (sometimes more confusing than helpful) included salads entitled "Lettuce Eat" and "Yolked Together."

   c. My sister Sora (who is my identical twin) is also my best friend.

50. a. Because of the flu epidemic, one-fourth of the student body missed school during exam week.

   b. Dale's Department Store is having a twenty-five percent sale on small appliances.

   c. The third-party candidate received only one tenth of the total votes cast in the election.

PART SIX

AIDS TO GOOD ENGLISH

CHAPTER 34

Information in The Library

ARRANGEMENT AND RESOURCES OF THE LIBRARY

Libraries are sufficiently alike so that when you have become familiar with one library, you can easily find your way in others. You should understand the following:

1. The arrangement of books in the library
2. The uses of the card catalog
3. The names and functions of the parts of a book
4. The use of the *Readers' Guide*
5. The use of the vertical file
6. The location of items in your library

ARRANGEMENT OF BOOKS IN THE LIBRARY

34a. Learn the arrangement of books.

Fiction

Books of fiction (novels and stories) are usually arranged on the shelves alphabetically by authors. By this time you know where in your library the books of fiction are located. It is a simple matter, if you know the author of a book, to go directly to the book on the fiction shelves.

You can find out whether the library owns a certain book by looking it up in the card catalog (pages 851–54). If the book you want is listed in the catalog but is not on the shelf, ask the librarian about it. It may be "out" in circulation, or it may be "on reserve." Possibly, the librarian will reserve the book for you by placing your name on the waiting list. When your name comes up, the librarian will notify you.

Nonfiction: The Dewey Decimal System

The arrangement of nonfiction books is accomplished through an amazingly efficient system developed by Melvil Dewey, an American librarian.[1] Although only librarians need to know all the details of the Dewey system, every user of a library should understand the principle on which the system is based.

In the Dewey system, every nonfiction book receives a number. The number, which is written on the spine of the book, is determined by the particular classification of the book in the system. There are ten subject classifications, and any book can be fitted into one of them.

Within these broad divisions there can be an unlimited number of subdivisions. Since a decimal point plays an important part in the numbering of books, the plan is called the Dewey decimal system. A valuable feature of this system is that all books on the same subject are given the same number and may be placed together on the library shelves. Once you have learned the class number of the subject you are interested in, you can find most of the books in the library on this subject grouped in one place.

000–099	General Works (encyclopedias, periodicals, etc.)
100–199	Philosophy (includes psychology, conduct, etc.)
200–299	Religion (includes mythology)

---

[1] The Library of Congress system of cataloging, used in many public libraries but not commonly used in high-school libraries, classifies all books, both fiction and nonfiction. Each general subject category (Philosophy, Science, etc.) is assigned a code letter. For example, the letter *H* at the beginning of a call number designates Social Sciences. In addition, whole categories are often subdivided by adding a second code letter to the first. Thus, the letter *P* (which designates Literature) may be followed by the letter *S* to specify American literature. Call numbers include the letter codes, followed by a series of numbers that identify specific books within a category. For example, the book *Responses: Prose Pieces 1953–1976,* by Richard Wilbur, an American author, has the Library of Congress call number PS 3545. A complete schedule of Library of Congress categories and their letter code is usually available in the reference section of any library using this system.

300–399   Social Sciences (economics, government, law, etc.)

400–499   Language (dictionaries, grammars, etc.)

500–599   Science (mathematics, chemistry, physics, etc.)

600–699   Technology (agriculture, engineering, aviation, etc.)

700–799   The Arts and Recreation (sculpture, painting, music, photography, sports, etc.)

800–899   Literature (poetry, plays, orations, etc.)

900–909 ⎫
930–999 ⎭   History

910–919   Travel

920–929   Biography (arranged alphabetically by name of subject of biography)

Books having the same class number may be distinguished from one another by the author's name. For instance, all books on aviation are given the number 629.1. This number appears on the spine of the book. With the number appears the first letter of the author's name: if the author is Hood, the book's complete number is $\frac{629.1}{H}$. This number, including the first letter of the author's name, is known as the book's *call number*. To find the call number of a book, you look up the book in the card catalog.

LOCATING INFORMATION IN THE LIBRARY

The Card Catalog

Undoubtedly you have used the card catalog in your school or town library. You may not, however, know as much about it as you need to know in order to get the most help from it.

34b. Learn the uses of the card catalog.

The card catalog is a cabinet containing drawers filled with alphabetically arranged cards. In most libraries, the catalog holds at least three cards for each book in the library: at least one *author card*, the *title card*, and at least one *subject card*.

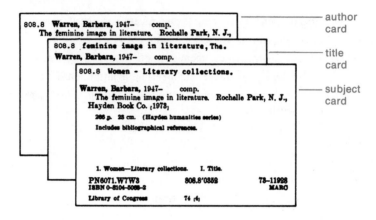

The Author Card

The *author card* has the name of the author at the top. When there is joint authorship, there is a card for each author. You may look up any book in the library by looking under the author's last name. Since the cards for all books by an author are placed together, you have the additional advantage of being able to find out what other books by the author the library owns. Cards for books *about* an author follow the cards for books *by* an author.

The Title Card

The *title card* has the book's title at the top. The quickest way to find a book in the catalog is to look it up under its title. Cards for books whose titles begin with *a, an*, or *the* are arranged alphabetically by the second word in the title. For example, the title card for a book entitled *The Writing of Fiction* would be found under *Writing of Fiction, The.*

The Subject Card

The *subject card* has at the top the subject with which the book deals. Subject cards are invaluable when you wish to find a number of books on a subject but do not know specific titles or authors.

Under the subject heading "Political parties—United States," for instance, you will find a card for every book in the library on this subject. In fact, you may find a card for every book that contains as little as one article or chapter on United States political parties, so thoroughly is the cataloging done.

Information Given on a Catalog Card

A brief study of the sample catalog cards reproduced on page 852 will show you that a complete card gives a great deal of information. In addition to giving the title, author, and call number of a book, the card may give the following information:

1. *Facts about authorship*: full name of the author; names of joint authors and illustrators, if any.
2. *Facts about publication*: the place of publication; the name of the publisher; the date of publication.
3. *Facts about the book*: number of pages; whether the book contains illustrations, diagrams, etc.; height of the book in centimeters.

"See" and "See Also" Cards

An important feature of a complete card catalog is the cross-reference cards which it contains. These are of two kinds—"see" cards and "see also" cards. The "see" card refers you to a subject heading under which you will find the material you wish. Suppose, for instance, that you wish to look up some books on World War I. You look under "World War I" in the card catalog. The card headed "World War I," however, says "see European War 1914–1918." This means that books on World War I are cataloged under the heading "European War 1914–1918." The "see" card tells you, in effect, "There is nothing here. You will find what you want under this other heading."

A second type of cross-reference card is the "see also" card, which refers you to places in the catalog where you may find additional titles on your subject. For instance, if you are looking for books about detectives and have found some listed under the subject heading "Detectives," you may find a "see also" card advising you to look also under the subject headings "Police" and "Secret Service." A "see also" card says, "There is more material in these places."

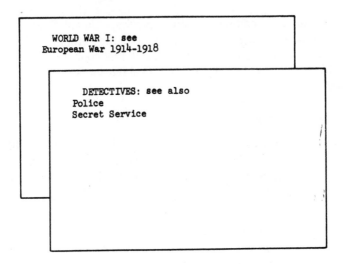

Sample Cross-Reference Cards

SUMMARY

The card catalog is a valuable library tool which may be used for the following purposes:

(1) To find the call number of a book

(2) To find out whether a certain book is owned by the library

(3) To find out what books by a certain author are in the library

(4) To find out what books on a certain subject are in the library

(5) To find out such facts about a book as may be given on a catalog card: facts about authorship, publication, number of pages, illustrations, etc.

EXERCISE 1. Using the Card Catalog. Using the card catalog in your library, find the title, author, and call number for each of the following books. Write them on your paper.

1. A history of American literature
2. A book about South America
3. A book by Edith Wharton

4. A book giving information about Edith Wharton
5. A book about baseball

Using the card catalog, find answers to the following questions. Write the answers.

6. Does the library own any books by Willa Cather? If so, give the title and call number of one of them.
7. Give the title, author, publisher, and publication date of a book about George Washington Carver.
8. Does the library own the complete plays of Shakespeare in one volume? If so, give the exact title and the publisher of the book.
9. Give the title, author, and date of publication of a book of American poetry.
10. Does the library own a copy of Charlotte Brontë's *Jane Eyre*? If so, give the publisher.

The Parts of a Book

Once you have found the right book, you should be able to take advantage of the various aids that the author and publisher have provided. To do so, you need to know the important parts of a book and the uses of each.

34c. Learn the names and functions of the parts of a book.

The Frontispiece

The frontispiece is a full-page illustration. If the book has a frontispiece, it faces the title page.

The Title Page

The first important page in a book, the title page gives the complete title, the subtitle (if there is one), the name of the author or editor (sometimes an affiliation, especially in a textbook), the name of the publisher, and the place of publication.

The Copyright Page

The reverse side of the title page is the copyright page. Here you find the year in which the book was copyrighted; i.e., registered in the government copyright office in Washington. Before publishers release a new book, they send two copies to the United States Copyright Office along with certain required information. The office then issues a copyright, which gives to the copyright owner exclusive right to print the book or any part of it during the lifetime of the author and for a period of fifty years after the author's death. Sometimes publishers secure a copyright in their own name, sometimes in the name of the author. The purpose of the copyright is to protect the author and the publisher, who have invested their work and money in the book. Reprinting copyrighted materials without the permission of the copyright owner is a criminal offense.

Often you will find more than one date listed on the copyright page: "Copyright 1946, 1949, 1955." This means that the first edition of the book was copyrighted in 1946. In 1949 and 1955 new material was added and a new copyright secured to cover the new material. In books published since September 1957, the international copyright symbol is used: © 1980. The date of copyright is very important when you wish to know whether the material in a book is sufficiently up-to-date to be reliable.

Publishers sometimes indicate on this page which printing of the book this particular volume represents. Note the distinction between a new copyright date and a new printing date. The former tells when the book was last revised; the latter, when it was merely reprinted.

The Preface, Foreword, Introduction

These terms are now used interchangeably to refer to matter at the beginning of a book in which the author, editor, or publisher explains the purpose and scope of the book, gives information that aids the reader in understanding the book, acknowledges indebtedness, etc.

The Table of Contents

The table of contents appears at the front of the book and consists of a list of the chapters and subdivisions with their page numbers. It provides a quick view of the content and organization of the entire book.

The table of contents may tell you how much information the book contains on a particular topic, but the index is a more reliable guide for this purpose. For example, a book on the history of aviation may or may not have a chapter title referring to fighter planes of World War I, but some mention of this topic is almost certain to be included in such a book. If it is, you will find it listed in the index.

List of Illustrations (Maps, Diagrams, Charts, etc.)

A list of illustrations with page numbers is sometimes included in books that give a prominent place to illustrations. Such a list would be of obvious value in an atlas, a history of art, or a book on fashions, for example.

The Appendix

The appendix contains additional material that the author did not wish to include in the body of the book. It may include long quotations from other works on the subject, lists, diagrams and tables, etc.

The Glossary

A glossary is usually a list of definitions of technical words used in the book. It is placed near the close of the book.

The Bibliography

The bibliography is a list of books consulted by the author in writing a book or recommended to the reader who wishes more information.

The Index

The index is an alphabetical list of topics treated in the book, given with page numbers. It is much more detailed than the table of contents. The index lists every reference to a topic and tells you exactly how many pages are devoted to it. When you have found a book that seems likely to provide information on your topic, the index will tell you how much information there is and exactly where to find it.

The End Papers

The pages pasted inside the front and back covers of the book are the end papers. Sometimes they are used for a map or an illustration or to give a kind of summary of the contents.

EXERCISE 2. Understanding the Functions of the Parts of a Book. Write answers to the following questions. You will notice that the last six items refer to this book.

1. List the parts of a book of nonfiction that you would not find in a book of fiction.
2. In a sentence or two, distinguish between printing date and copyright date.
3. Explain the purpose of a glossary.
4. Distinguish between a table of contents and an index.
5. Write the date when this book was copyrighted.
6. In which years was new material added?
7. By what firm was this book published?
8. Where is this firm located?
9. Skim the preface of this book and in a sentence or two state its primary purpose.
10. How many pages are there in the index of this book?

The Readers' Guide

A large part of the library reference work you will do in high school will deal with subjects of a contemporary rather than a historical nature. The best source of information, indeed very often the only source of information on truly current subjects, is the magazine. Without some sort of guide, you would have to spend hours hunting through magazines in search of articles on a subject. However, the *Readers' Guide to Periodical Literature* solves this problem for you.

34d. Learn how to use the *Readers' Guide to Periodical Literature*.

In the *Readers' Guide*, articles from some 170 magazines are indexed alphabetically by subjects and by authors. You may look up the subject in which you are interested and find the articles that have been written on it and the magazines in which they appeared.

Magazine stories are listed by title and by author; the complete entry is given with the author listing only. Poems and plays are listed by author.

Articles *about* moving pictures and plays are listed under the subject headings MOVING PICTURE PLAYS and DRAMAS, beneath the subheading **Criticisms, plots, etc.**

The Readers' Guide is published in paperbound pamphlets monthly six months a year and semi-monthly six months.

BALL, George Wildman
  Options on Iran. por Newsweek 95:43 Ap 7 '80
  Question of oil [interview by R. Christopher]
    por Macleans 93:50 Ja 7 '80

  about
  Mr. Ball's world. E. N. Luttwak. New Repub
    182:12-14 Ap 5 '80 •
BALL, Leslie D. See Waldron, D. jt auth
BALLANTINE, H. Thomas, Jr
  Role of government in health-care delivery in
    the 1980s [address, January 16, 1980] Vital
    Speeches 46:258-60 F 15 '80
BALLANTINE, Ian
  Uses and abuses of enchantment. D. Wein-
    berger. il Macleans 93:45-5 Ja 28 '80 •
BALLERINAS. See Dancers
BALLET
  See also
  Choreography
  Cleveland Ballet Company
  Dance Theatre of Harlem
  Houston Ballet Company
  Joffrey Ballet
  Maryland Ballet
  Merce Cunningham & Dance Company
  Metropolitan Opera Ballet
  Motion pictures—Dance films
  New York City Ballet
  Pittsburgh Ballet Theatre
  Television broadcasting—Dance programs
  Dance. J. Maskey. See issues of High fidelity
    and Musical America
  Domestic reports: news and views from across
    the country. See issues of Dance magazine
  Editor's log. W. Como. See issues of Dance
    magazine
  Opera ballet:
    Taming the two-headed monster. B. Laine.
      Dance Mag 54:51-3 F '80
  Presstime news. See issues of Dance magazine
  Reviews:
    Ballet Metropolitan of Columbus. A .Barzel.
      Dance Mag 54:51-3 F '80
    Dance Ring. A. Barzel. Dance Mag 54:44-6
      F '80
    Louisville Ballet. A. Barzel. Dance Mag 54:
      50-1 F '80
    Ohio Ballet. W. Salisbury. Dance Mag 54:
      116+ F '80
  Tulsa Ballet Theatre: old world-style for a
    new frontier. J. Pikula. il pors Dance Mag
    54:62-5 F '80
      Bibliography
  Dance, books. il Dance Mag 54:106+ Ja; 121 F;
    121 Mr '80

      Directories
  Dance directory. See issues of Dance magazine
    International aspects
  Foreign reports: news and views from around
    the world. See issues of Dance magazine

      Study and teaching
  Education briefs [ed by M. Pierpont] See is-
    sues of Dance magazine

      Australia
  Dance in Australia. A. Brissenden. il Dance
    Mag 54:12 F '80
      Canada
  See also
  National Ballet of Canada

Annotations (right column):
- author entry
- article by author
- article about author
- "see" cross reference to joint author
- title of article
- title and issue of magazine
- subject entry
- "see" cross reference
- volume number
- page reference
- date of issue
- illustration reference
- secondary subject heading
- "see also" cross reference

Occasionally during the year a cumulative issue is published including the articles listed in preceding months as well as those for the current month. At the end of a year, a large volume is published containing all entries for the year, and every two years a volume covering a two-year period is published.

You must remember, however, that the usefulness of the *Readers' Guide* is limited by the availability to you of the magazines to which it refers you. When you are taking down references from the *Readers' Guide*, you should know what magazines your library has. You should know, too, whether the library has kept back issues of all these magazines or only of certain ones and for how many years back it has the magazines.

A sample excerpt from the *Readers' Guide* is reproduced on page 859. You can probably understand the many abbreviations used, but if you cannot, you will find them explained in the front of the *Readers' Guide* itself.

EXERCISE 3. Using the *Readers' Guide*. Write answers to the following questions.

1. Is there in your library a list of the magazines to which the library subscribes? Does the list give the dates of back numbers on file? If so, for what years does the library have back numbers of either the *Atlantic* or *Harper's* magazine?
2. Where are the back numbers of magazines stored in your library? How do you get the particular number you want?
3. What is the date of the latest *Readers' Guide* in your library? What period does it cover?
4, 5, 6. Select one of the following subjects, look it up in the *Readers' Guide*, and list on your paper three articles *that you could get in your library* on the subject. Give the complete listing for each, as shown in the *Readers' Guide*. Show that you understand the abbreviations by spelling out all of them.

Housing	Aviation	Photography
Education	Taxation	Labor

7. Select a prominent person of today and look for an article about the person in the *Readers' Guide*. Give the complete listing.
8. Find and copy a "see" reference from the *Readers' Guide*.
9. Copy from the *Readers' Guide* the complete listing of a review of a motion picture.
10. Copy from the *Readers' Guide* the complete listing of a review of a play.

Information Files

34e. Learn the nature and proper use of the vertical file.

Useful information on current topics is often to be found in pamphlets, usually paperbound. They are published by government agencies, industrial concerns, museums, colleges and universities, radio stations, welfare organizations, etc. The librarian files pamphlets in a special cabinet, usually referred to as the vertical file, and can help you find material on your subject, especially if it is of contemporary interest.

In the vertical file the librarian also stores interesting pictures and significant clippings from newspapers.

34f. Use microfilm and microfiche to find information.

To save space, many libraries store some publications (newspapers, magazines, and books) or documents on microfilm or microfiche. *Microfilm* is a roll or reel of film containing photographically reduced publications. You view the film through a projector that enlarges each microscopic image to a size suitable for reading. *Microfiche* is a sheet of film, rather than a roll or reel, containing photographically reduced publications. To read the microfiche, you use a machine that, like the microfilm projector, enlarges the microscopic images to a readable size. The librarian in your library can tell you which publications are stored on microfilm or microfiche, where the microfilm or microfiche is located in the library, and how to use the microfilm and microfiche projectors.

34g. Use computers to find information.

Many libraries are replacing their present book lists, catalogs, and periodical lists with a computerized system. If this is the case, you will have to use the computer to find the lists of books and periodicals in the library. Instead of looking through the card catalog or the *Readers' Guide*, you type the information you need into the computer—for example, *subject: Geraldine Ferraro.* Then the computer searches for the titles and locations of the publications on that subject and prints a list. Depending on the type of computer, you might have to read the list from the screen, or you might be able to get a printout, or printed copy, of the list of books or periodicals. The librarian will be able to tell you what kinds of computer programs your library has, where the computers are located in the library, and how to use the computers.

34h. Learn the location of items in your library.

Your use of a library will be more efficient if you know the exact location of the principal items you may wish to use. If you will remember the information the following exercise calls for, you will save both the librarian and yourself a great deal of time.

EXERCISE 4. Locating Items in Your Library. Be prepared to state where each of the following items is located in your school or public library.

1. The desk where books are checked out
2. The card catalog
3. The *Readers' Guide*
4. The magazine rack and the newspaper rack
5. The pamphlet file
6. The fiction shelves
7. The encyclopedias
8. The biography shelves
9. The unabridged dictionaries
10. The reserved-book shelf or the new-book shelf
11. The computers
12. The microfilm and microfiche projectors

CHAPTER 35

Reference Books

SPECIAL SOURCES OF INFORMATION

Some libraries have bigger collections of reference books than others, but almost any library will have most of the standard reference books described here. It may surprise you to find how quickly and easily you can put a finger on needed facts, once you know that a reference book specifically made to supply them is in a nearby library. Familiarity with a library's reference books will increase your efficiency in looking up information.

Just reading the descriptions that follow here will not be enough. Familiarity comes from direct contact. Go to the library and spend a few minutes with each book. Look at the table of contents, locate the index, and sample enough text to see how it works.

Each of you might be asked to concentrate on one particular reference work listed here and to report on it later to the entire class.

All of you, however, should carefully study the descriptions of the books discussed here and do the exercises that end the chapter. Even though a reference work is not available here and now, you should know that it exists and you should know what to expect from it.

ENCYCLOPEDIAS

35a. Get acquainted with encyclopedias: their plan, content, and indexes.

You have probably been using an encyclopedia in your schoolwork for some time. You know that it is a collection of articles in alphabetical order on nearly all fields of knowledge. Articles are written by experts, and the level of factual accuracy is high.

When you were younger, you may have believed an encyclopedia article contained all anyone needed to know about a subject. By now, however, you realize that an encyclopedia article gives an overall view. It cannot go into detail or show evidence on debatable points. It is a useful introduction, but for study in depth fuller treatment is necessary. For example, an encyclopedia article of less than five pages on Franklin Delano Roosevelt cannot give you as much information as James MacGregor Burns does in his biography of more than twelve hundred pages.

The index is important. If you looked in the *Encyclopedia Americana* under the entry "Olympic Games," you would find an article several columns long. But in the index, you would find the volumes and page numbers of more than twenty other entries with information about the games. If you had not used the index, you would not have known about these other entries.

This has been the usual plan. In 1974, the *Encyclopædia Britannica* introduced a new plan. It expanded to thirty volumes. The first is an introduction to the rest of the encyclopedia. The remaining twenty-nine volumes are divided into a ten-volume *Micropædia* and a nineteen-volume *Macropædia.* The *Micropædia* contains shorter articles, and the *Macropædia* contains, in its smaller number of articles, extremely long, detailed, and in-depth treatments of the topics covered. Many of the *Macropædia* articles are much longer than full-length books. In using the new *Britannica,* you would usually turn first to the *Micropædia,* which includes complete cross-referencing, and then follow up the cross-referencing as far as you like. Whether this new approach to planning an encyclopedia will prove more popular or more helpful in dealing with today's vast amount of information remains to be seen.

Encyclopedias are kept up-to-date in three ways. First, a completely new edition may be prepared. Second, before a new printing some revisions may be made to keep up with new knowledge or developments. Third, encyclopedias publish yearbooks, which contain statistics, important events, and developments in every field pertaining to the year just preceding.

Encyclopedias in Many Volumes

Collier's Encyclopedia
24 volumes
Bibliography and Index in Volume 24
Publishes *Collier's Yearbook*

Encyclopedia Americana
30 volumes
Index in Volume 30
Publishes the *Americana Annual*

Encyclopœdia Britannica
30 volumes
Cross-referencing throughout *Micropœdia*
Publishes the *Britannica Book of the Year*

Encyclopedia International
20 volumes
Index in Volume 20
Publishes the *Encyclopedia International Yearbook*

World Book Encyclopedia
22 volumes
Research Guide and Index in Volume 22
Publishes an annual supplement

One- and Two-Volume Encyclopedias

Very often a brief, handy account of a subject is enough. For this purpose, a one- or two-volume "desk" encyclopedia is adequate. There are three well-known works of this kind. The *New Columbia Encyclopedia* and the *Random House Encyclopedia* are arranged alphabetically like dictionaries. The *Lincoln Library of Essential Information* has two volumes arranged in broad fields of knowledge with many subdivision articles and an index. Typical of the big fields covered are "The English Language," "Literature," and "History."

GENERAL REFERENCE BOOKS

Almanacs and Yearbooks

Although almanacs come out annually to cover a one-year period, many of their statistics include data for preceding years. Remember that an almanac tells about the year before its date: data for 1980 should be sought in the 1981 issue.

World Almanac and Book of Facts

Most popular of the handy annual reference books on the world today, the *World Almanac* gives facts and figures that are needed very often. Typical items are census tables, production quantities, export and import figures, election results, officeholders, sports records, Nobel and other prize-winners, and a summary of notable events. A full index is in the front.

Information Please Almanac

This almanac covers much of the same ground as the *World Almanac*, but in a different arrangement. Its full index is in the back. The *Information Please Almanac* covers fewer subjects, but its informal style is easy to follow and its articles are sometimes fuller.

The International Yearbook and Statesmen's Who's Who

The International Yearbook and Statesmen's Who's Who includes up-to-date information on international organizations and political, statistical, and directory information about each country of the world. A biographical section gives sketches of world leaders in government, religion, commerce, industry, and education.

Statesman's Year-book

The *Statesman's Year-book* calls itself a"statistical and historical annual of the states of the world," with information useful to diplomats, officials, journalists, and scholars dealing with international affairs. Starting with international organizations (such as the UN) it goes on to individual nations, giving facts about each under these heads: government, area and population, religion, education, welfare, justice, defense, finance, production, communications, currency and banking, and diplomatic representatives. The index is in the back.

Atlases

Don't think of an atlas as just a collection of maps. It contains information of many kinds: climate, rainfall, crops, topography, population, some history, etc.

There are many fine atlases. Find out which ones your library has and where they are kept. Because our day is marked by amazing numbers of new nations, new unions, and secessions, an atlas even a few years old may not show from ten to perhaps twenty or thirty nations as they now are. To find out how up-to-date an atlas is, check its copyright date in the opening pages.

A few of the atlases that are reliable (if you use a recent edition) are listed here.

General Atlases

Hammond Contemporary World Atlas
National Geographic Atlas of the World
New York Times Atlas of the World

Along with atlases showing the world as it is now are atlases showing it, or a region of it, as it was in one or more past periods. These historical atlases help us to visualize history.

Historical Atlases

The American Heritage Pictorial Atlas of United States History
Rand McNally Atlas of World History
Shepherd, William, *Historical Atlas*

BIOGRAPHICAL REFERENCE BOOKS

35b. Learn to use these handy biographical reference tools.

Many of the biographical reference works discussed here are likely to be on your library's shelves. Since their functions differ, be sure to find out what each can do for you.

General Biography

Biography Index **(1946 to date)**

This work, as its name implies, is not a collection of biographies, but an index that tells you where to find material on the life of nearly anyone about whom a book or an article has been published. It indexes current biographical books written in English and biographical material in more than 1,500 periodicals, in much the same manner as the *Readers' Guide to Periodical Literature*.

Like the *Readers' Guide*, the *Biography Index* is published regularly and in cumulative editions. It appears quarterly (in November, February, May, and August), with an annually published bound volume including all the year's listings. Arrangement is of two kinds: (1) straight alphabetical listing of persons written about, and (2) alphabetical listing of names under broad divisions by profession or occupation. Remember that this book is an *index* to biographical books and articles, not a book of biographies.

Dictionary of American Biography

This monumental work provides authoritative articles on the careers of hundreds of notable Americans no longer living, from the earliest historical times virtually to the present. Individual articles are more detailed than those in any encyclopedia, and there are more of them. The complete set of fifteen volumes includes a one-volume index, as well as separate supplementary volumes that keep the set up-to-date.

Dictionary of National Biography

From the long course of British civilization, this famous work selects notable Britishers no longer living, and covers their careers. It preceded our *Dictionary of American Biography* and was something of a model for it.

The New Century Cyclopedia of Names (3 volumes)

As the title may imply, this work deals with proper names of all sorts, including real, legendary, and mythological persons, places, and events, as well as literary works and characters and works of art—100,000 in all. Names hard to find elsewhere are often at hand in it, and historians commend its accuracy.

Webster's Biographical Dictionary

In this book, over 40,000 concise biographies appear in alphabetical order. Care has been taken to give the correct pronunciation of each name. Information given is somewhat fuller than that shown in a general dictionary. Though it offers some details, it is not intended to provide the complete life of any person. The biography of Abraham Lincoln, for example, occupies less than one column.

Who's Who, Who's Who in America, and The International Who's Who

These standard books, found in most libraries, give essential facts about notable *living* persons. Note that these are books of *facts*; they do not summarize the subject's life in any detail. Typical entries list parentage, place and date of birth, names of members of family, educational background, positions held, important achievements, writings and their dates, awards, clubs or societies, religious and political affiliations, and present address.

Who's Who gives information about notable British persons and some famous persons in other countries. It comes out yearly.

Who's Who in America gives facts about notable Americans. It comes out every two years. Although persons listed in *Who's Who in America* are dropped out after they die, entries for the most important persons thus dropped are preserved in a volume entitled *Who Was Who in America.*

The International Who's Who might prove useful to you in locating material on persons not listed in the above-mentioned sources. Well-known educators, artists, diplomats, etc., from various parts of the globe are included here. However, due to space limitations, many of the lesser-known figures do not appear.

Current Biography

Like the *Who's Who* books above, this monthly serial is concerned with *living* people. Each issue contains short, informal biographies of those currently prominent in the news. A picture of the person is often included. The scope is international.

Annually, articles in the twelve issues are put in alphabetical order in one bound volume. Currently, its cumulative index locates articles from 1971 on. A separate index covers those from 1940 through 1970. Biographies are also indexed by professions.

Books About Authors

Although the lives of authors are included in all biographical reference books and in the encyclopedias, the following books treat authors only. *The Writers Directory* briefly lists 18,000 of today's writers. It comes out every two years. Articles in the others are informal, longer, and include authors' pictures.

American Authors 1600–1900 by Kunitz and Haycraft

American Writers by Unger

British Authors Before 1800 by Kunitz and Haycraft

British Authors of the Nineteenth Century by Kunitz and Haycraft

Contemporary Authors: First Revision
Dictionary of Literary Biography, Gale Research Company
The Writers Directory, St. James Press, London/St. Martin's Press, N.Y.
Twentieth Century Authors by Kunitz and Haycraft
World Authors by Wakeman

Magill's *Cyclopedia of World Authors* is a popular reference that includes authors from all over the world. It gives biographical facts for each author and a critical sketch characterizing his or her works.

LITERATURE REFERENCE BOOKS

35c. Develop the habit of using reference books on literature.

You were just introduced to some standard reference books on authors. For information on literary works and their plots, characters, sources, quotations, etc., the following books are useful.

General

Benét's *The Reader's Encyclopedia*

This book describes itself aptly as "an encyclopedia of all the things you encounter in reading." It does have great variety: plots and characters, summaries of poems, allusions to myths and to the Bible, and descriptions of works of art, music, and so on. Though the Second Edition best meets today's interests, either is good.

Books of Quotations

At one time or another everybody wants to find the source or exact wording of a quotation. There are many books of quotations. Your library may have several. Because they differ in arrangement, you need to learn how to find what you want in the one you are using.

Bartlett's *Familiar Quotations*

Bartlett's is probably the best known. It provides four kinds of information: (1) the author of a quotation; (2) the book or speech which is its source; (3) its exact wording; (4) some famous lines by any author.

To find the author or source of a quotation, turn to the big index in the back of the book. This index lists important words alphabetically as keys to quotations. For example, *cat, gloves,* and *mice* are key index words to the quotation:

"The cat in gloves catches no mice."

Since quotations come under authors, who are listed in chronological order, you can find a number of quotations from a famous writer by looking in the author index for the page where quotations from the author's work begin, and turning to it.

Stevenson's *Home Book of Quotations* and *Home Book of Proverbs, Maxims, and Familiar Phrases*

Using a different type of arrangement, these books group quotations according to subject matter, not by author. This plan is convenient when you want quotations on a particular subject—success, love, duty, etc.

H. L. Mencken's *New Dictionary of Quotations*

The choice of numerous quotations marked by epigrammatic wit or satire makes this collection unusual.

Magill's *Quotations in Context*

This book of quotations includes the contexts of the quotations.

Indexes and Collections of Poetry

Stevenson's *Home Book of Verse* and *Home Book of Modern Verse*

When you want to find a popular poem, it is a good idea to look for it first in these two big anthologies. The poems are arranged by subjects: for example, Poems of Youth and Age; Love Poems; Poems of Nature; Familiar Verse; Poems, Humorous and Satiric; etc. Since the books are indexed in three ways—by author, by title, and by first line—you should have no trouble finding the poem you want if it is in either book.

Granger's Index to Poetry (sixth edition)

When you want to find a particular poem, *Granger's Index* can lead you quickly to a collection that includes it. It has three listings for each poem: by author, by title, and by first line. Whichever you use will give you the same information as the other two do.

Suppose you want to read "Casey at the Bat." Under that title you will find a number of abbreviations, each standing for an anthology containing the poem. A table in the front of the *Index* spells out the titles for which the abbreviations stand.

Now use the library's card catalog to find one of the books the *Index* lists for "Casey at the Bat." This is the whole process.

Remember that the *Index* does not print any whole poems, but its listings are quick poem-locators for almost any poem you want to find.

Other Indexes

Other useful indexes include the following ones: *Short Story Index, Play Index*, and *Essay and General Literature Index*.

OTHER REFERENCE BOOKS

Your teacher may ask members of your class to report on those of the following reference works that are in your library. A report should include author or editor, title, number of volumes or supplements, publication date, scope and arrangement of material, and principal uses.

Literature

> *American Authors and Books* by W. J. Burke and W. D. Howe, augmented and revised by Irving Weiss
> *Book Review Digest*
> *Bulfinch's Mythology*
> *Cambridge History of American Literature*
> *Cambridge History of English Literature*
> *Cyclopedia of Literary Characters*
> *Contemporary Literary Criticism*
> *Encyclopedia of World Literature in the Twentieth Century*
> *Guide to Great Plays* by J. T. Shipley
> *The New Century Classical Handbook*
> *Nineteenth Century Literary Criticism*
> *Oxford Companion to American Literature*
> *Oxford Companion to English Literature*
> *Oxford Companion to French Literature*
> *Oxford Companion to Classical Literature*
> *Oxford Companion to the Theatre*
> *Thirteen Hundred Critical Evaluations of Selected Novels and Plays*

Grammar and Usage

The Careful Writer: A Modern Guide to English Usage by Theodore M. Bernstein

A Dictionary of Contemporary American Usage by Bergen and Cornelia Evans

History and Social Studies

Cambridge Modern History

Dictionary of American History by J. T. Adams

The Dictionary of Dates by Helen R. Keller

Encyclopedia of American History by R. B. Morris

Encyclopedia of the Social Sciences

Encyclopedia of World History by W. L. Langer

Great Events from History

Statistical Abstract of the United States

Webster's New Geographical Dictionary

Science and Mathematics

Chambers Dictionary of Science and Technology

McGraw-Hill Encyclopedia of Science and Technology

Music and Art

Encyclopedia of World Art

Encyclopedia of the Arts, edited by Herbert Read

Grove's Dictionary of Music and Musicians

The Harvard Dictionary of Music, first edition, edited by Willi Apel. (The second edition contains additional and updated entries but abbreviates the first listings considerably. A paperback edition is also available, abridged: *The Harvard Brief Dictionary of Music*.)

The International Cyclopedia of Music and Musicians

The McGraw-Hill Encyclopedia of World Art

The New College Encyclopedia of Music, edited by J. A. Westrup and F. L. Harrison (the handiest and best one-volume popular work)

Vasari's Lives of the Painters, Sculptors, and Architects, new edition in four paperback volumes

Colleges and Universities

American Universities and Colleges, American Council on Education

Barron's Profiles of American Colleges

Comparative Guide to American Colleges, edited by James Cass and Max Birnbaum

Lovejoy's College Guide

EXERCISE 1. Explaining the Uses of Specific Reference Books. Be able to explain the principal uses of each of the following resource books, its advantages and its limitations.

1. An encyclopedia

2. Yearbooks

> *World Almanac and Book of Facts*
> *Information Please Almanac*
> *The International Yearbook and Statesmen's Who's Who*
> *Statesman's Year-book*
> *Americana Annual*
> *Britannica Book of the Year*
> *Collier's Yearbook*

3. An atlas

4. Biographical reference books

> *Biography Index*
> *Current Biography*
> *Dictionary of American Biography*
> *Dictionary of National Biography*
> *Webster's Biographical Dictionary*
> *New Century Cyclopedia of Names*
> *Who's Who, Who's Who in America, Who Was Who in America,* and *The International Who's Who*
> *British Authors Before 1800*
> *British Authors of the Nineteenth Century*
> *American Authors 1600–1900*
> *European Authors 1000–1900*
> *Contemporary Authors: First Revision*
> *Cyclopedia of World Authors*

5. Literature reference books

> Bartlett's *Familiar Quotations*
> Benét's *The Reader's Encyclopedia*
> Stevenson's *Home Book of Quotations*
> Stevenson's *Home Book of Proverbs, Maxims, and Familiar Phrases*
> Stevenson's *Home Book of Verse* and *Home Book of Modern Verse*
> *Granger's Index to Poetry*

EXERCISE 2. Distinguishing Between Specific Reference Books. Answer in writing the following questions.

1. Distinguish between *Who's Who* and *Who's Who in America*.
2. Explain the difference between the *Biography Index* and *Current Biography*.
3. Distinguish between a world atlas and a historical atlas.
4. Name three important differences between the *Dictionary of American Biography* and *Who's Who in America*.
5. List four books that contain information about events of the past year.
6. Which literature reference book would you use to find the author of a poem whose title you know?
7. Which literature reference book would you use to find the title of a book containing a poem you want?
8. Arrange the following titles in order according to the length of their biographical articles, listing the one with the longest articles first: the dictionary, *Dictionary of American Biography, Webster's Biographical Dictionary*.
9. Arrange the following titles in order according to the frequency of their publication, listing the most frequently published first: *Readers' Guide, Biography Index, Who's Who in America, Who's Who, Current Biography*.
10. Contrast the arrangements of Bartlett's *Familiar Quotations* and Stevenson's *Home Book of Quotations*.

EXERCISE 3. Selecting Reference Books to Find Specific Information. Number your paper 1–18. From the books and reference works given in brackets, select the one you would use to get the specified information. Write the title after the proper number on your paper. Be prepared to explain your choices.

1. Names of the senators in Congress from your state. [encyclopedia, *Who's Who in America, World Almanac*]
2. Quotations on the subject of love. [Bartlett's *Familiar Quotations*, Stevenson's *Home Book of Quotations*]
3. Books in your library about reptiles. [*Readers' Guide*, card catalog, vertical file]
4. A description of the present government of France. [encyclopedia, *Statesman's Year-book*]

5. The life of Abigail Adams. [*Biography Index, The Reader's Encyclopedia, Dictionary of American Biography*]
6. A list of magazine articles on education published during the past few months. [*World Almanac, Readers' Guide*, card catalog]
7. Life of the Secretary-General of the United Nations. [*Current Biography, Dictionary of American Biography, Webster's Biographical Dictionary*]
8. Which book would probably contain Lowell's poem "Patterns"? [*Granger's Index*, Bartlett's *Familiar Quotations*, Stevenson's *Home Book of Verse*]
9. A description and history of the rubber industry. [*Britannica Book of the Year, World Almanac*, encyclopedia]
10. International records in track events. [*Information Please Almanac, Statesman's Year-book, Readers' Guide*]
11. The source of the common expression "All the world's a stage." [Stevenson's *Home Book of Verse, Webster's Dictionary of Synonyms*, Bartlett's *Familiar Quotations*]
12. Titles and authors of biographies of the President. [*Biography Index, Who's Who in America, Webster's Biographical Dictionary*]
13. A quotation about youth. [Bartlett's *Familiar Quotations, World Almanac*, Stevenson's *Home Book of Quotations*]
14. The copyright date of any book in your library. [encyclopedia, card catalog, *Readers' Guide*]
15. The body of water into which the Suwannee River flows. [*Statesman's Year-book, World Almanac*, atlas]
16. A picture of an author who came into prominence during the past six months. [encyclopedia, *Current Biography, Who's Who*]
17. Leaflets recently published by the National Safety Council. [card catalog, *Readers' Guide*, vertical file]
18. Educational background of the president of an American university. [*Who's Who, Biography Index, Who's Who in America*]

EXERCISE 4. Using Library Tools or Reference Books to Find Specific Information. Which library tool or reference book, including the encyclopedia, would you use to find the following items of information?

1. Titles of recent magazine articles on the latest fashions in dress
2. The special power that the mythological character Clotho had
3. The title of a book, owned by your library, on conservation

4. An account of the climate of Tahiti
5. The life of the author of a best-selling first novel, recently published
6. The pronunciation of the name of the president of Kenya
7. Biographies (books and articles) of a famous person in today's world
8. The latest magazine articles about automobile accidents
9. An article on the life and work of a Latin American author
10. The native state of the Vice-President of the United States
11. The publisher and copyright date of a book in the library
12. The ten most populous cities in the United States
13. An illustrated article on the Navajo Indians
14. A history of the past year in sports
15. Pamphlets published by the Foreign Policy Association
16. Any books the library may have on stamp collecting
17. Officials of the present government of Pakistan
18. An illustrated article on Italian art
19. The name of the novel in which Eustacia Vye is a character
20. A picture of Lillian Hellman, modern dramatist

CHAPTER 36

The Dictionary

CONTENTS AND USES
OF DICTIONARIES

Dictionaries vary greatly in size, purpose, and reliability. From the unabridged dictionaries with upwards of 300,000 entries to the smallest pocket-sized ones, dictionaries offer a range of possibilities that calls for judgment on the part of the user.

Although dictionaries differ from one another in number of entries and method of presenting information, they all provide a report on the way language is used. Dictionary makers do not by themselves decide what words mean or how they should be pronounced and spelled. As a result of careful scientific research, dictionary makers are able to record the way the majority of educated people use the language: the meanings such people apply to words and the ways they pronounce and spell words.

To people who want to make themselves understood and who wish to understand what they read, such a reliable report on language practice is of obvious value. No speaker of English knows all the words. Everyone needs help sometimes with the meaning, spelling, pronunciation, and use of a particular word. The dictionary records the customary language practice of other literate speakers and writers.

KINDS OF DICTIONARIES

36a. Know the kinds of dictionaries.

Excluding the many special dictionaries—dictionaries of scientific terms, foreign-language dictionaries, etc.—there are two main kinds of dictionaries with which you should be familiar: the large *unabridged* dictionary, which you will probably use mainly in libraries; and the "college-size" dictionary, which you should have at hand when you study.

You should be warned against the small, often pocket-sized, dictionaries sold in book stores and drugstores for a few dollars. While these books may help you with common word meanings and spellings, they should be taken for what they are intended to be—inexpensive condensations for quick, general reference; they are not as dependable as scholarly, complete, up-to-date works.

College Dictionaries

The most practical dictionary for everyday use is the college dictionary, which usually has from about 100,000 to about 160,000 entries. Material in the front and the back often includes guides to punctuation, usage, and preparing research papers, and may contain other information useful to students. Because it is frequently revised, a college dictionary, when purchased, is likely to be more nearly up-to-date than an unabridged.

The four listed alphabetically below are well known and kept reasonably up-to-date.

The American Heritage Dictionary of the English Language, Houghton Mifflin Co., Boston

The Random House College Dictionary, Random House, New York, N.Y.

Webster's New Collegiate Dictionary, G. & C. Merriam Co., Springfield, Mass.

Webster's New World Dictionary of the American Language, Second College Edition, William Collins Publishing Co., Cleveland, Ohio

Unabridged Dictionaries

The largest dictionaries—containing over 300,000 entries—are called *unabridged* dictionaries. *Unabridged* in this context means only "not cut down from a bigger one." (The common idea that it means "containing the whole language" is mistaken, not to say impossible.) Out of the now small number presently available, three (two American and one British) are listed below:

The Random House Dictionary of the English Language, Random House, New York, N.Y.

Webster's Third New International Dictionary, G. & C. Merriam Co., Springfield, Mass.

The Oxford English Dictionary, Oxford University Press, New York, N.Y.

An unabridged dictionary has two or three times the number of entries in a college dictionary. Many entries are likely to be more detailed and to give more facts. An unabridged dictionary is more likely to contain a rare or very old word, a dialect or regional word. *Webster's* and the *Oxford* use many actual quotations from named writers to show words in certain senses. An unabridged dictionary, though unwieldy, does make available information a college dictionary cannot.

CONTENT AND ARRANGEMENT OF DICTIONARIES

36b. Familiarize yourself with the kinds of information in your dictionary and learn where and how each kind is given.

Although people most commonly use the dictionary to look up the spelling and meaning of words, to use it only for these purposes is to miss the many other kinds of information it has to offer.

Before making a detailed study of the treatment of individual words in the body of the dictionary, find out the other sources of information a good dictionary offers. The following study materials and exercises will help you discover the full resources of your dictionary and may lead you to refer to it more often and more efficiently.

Although all good dictionaries contain essentially the same facts, material may be arranged and handled quite differently. For example, some list items such as notable persons and places in the main alphabetical listing; others put them in separate sections. The location of abbreviations and foreign phrases may also differ. Get to know your dictionary.

EXERCISE 1. Understanding the Content and Arrangement of Your Dictionary. Using the dictionary with which you have been provided, write the answers to the following questions. Use the table of contents whenever it is helpful.

1. What is the full title of your dictionary?
2. Who is the publisher?
3. What is the latest copyright date? (Look on the back of the title page.)
4. Where does the complete key to pronunciation appear?

5. Is there a shorter key on each page? On every other page?
6. On what page do the explanatory notes on pronunciation begin?
7. On what page does the introductory article describing and explaining the dictionary begin?
8. What special articles are there on the history of the language, grammar, etc.?
9. On what page does your dictionary list the abbreviations used in the dictionary?
10. Are the other abbreviations, such as A.D., C.O.D., and UNESCO, explained in the body of your dictionary or in a separate section at the back?
11. Are guides to spelling, punctuation, and capitalization given? If so, list the page on which each begins.
12. Is there a section giving the meaning of commonly used signs and symbols? If so, give the page it begins on.
13. Are the names of important people and places listed in the body of your dictionary or in a separate section?
14. Does your dictionary provide derivations of words? If so, do they appear near the beginning or at the end of an entry?
15. Are the names of literary, mythological, and Biblical characters listed in the body of your dictionary or in a special section? To find out, look up Hamlet, Poseidon, and Deborah.

EXERCISE 2. Using Your Dictionary to Find Specific Information. Look up in your dictionary the answers to the following questions and write the answers in a column on your paper. *After each answer write the page number on which you found it.* If any of the items are not in your dictionary, write the number of the question and leave a blank space.

1. What does the abbreviation LL.D. mean? Give the English translation.
2. What is the population of Londonderry?
3. What was the occupation of Maria Mitchell?
4. Who was Europa?
5. Give the meaning of the French phrase *comme il faut*.
6. Give the spelling rule for retaining the silent final *e* on a word when you add a suffix.
7. Where should commas and periods be placed in relation to quotation marks—inside the quotation marks or outside?

8. Give the meaning of the sign R$_x$ used in medical prescriptions.
9. In what play is Iago the villain?
10. Where is Prince Edward Island?

A Dictionary's Information About a Word

Definitions

The main function of a dictionary is to give the meanings of words. Since a single word may have many meanings, an entry covering it must have a matching number of definitions. In some dictionaries, all definitions are simply numbered in sequence. In others, small subdivisions of meaning within a numbered definition are headed by letters in sequence.

Some dictionaries still put definitions in historical order, the earliest meaning first, the latest last. Others base order on frequency of use, the most common meaning first, the least common last. The first entry below shows historical order; the second, frequency of use.

> **mas·ter·piece** \'mas-tər-,pēs\ *n* (1605) **1** : a piece of work presented to a medieval guild as evidence of qualification for the rank of master **2** : a work done with extraordinary skill; *esp* : a supreme intellectual or artistic achievement

"From Webster's Ninth New Collegiate Dictionary. © 1984 by Merriam-Webster Inc., publishers of the Merriam-Webster® Dictionaries. Reprinted by permission of Merriam-Webster Inc."

> **mas·ter·piece** (mas′tər pēs′, mä′stər-), *n.* **1.** a person's most excellent production, as in an art. **2.** any production of masterly skill. **3.** a piece made by a journeyman or other craftsman aspiring to the rank of master in a guild or other craft organization as a proof of his competence. [MASTER + PIECE, modeled on D *meesterstuk*, G *Meisterstück*]

A label usually shows the part of speech of the word being defined. For example, *n.* stands for noun, *v.* for verb, and so on. (Abbreviations used are explained in a dictionary's front matter.) In older dictionaries, a word used as more than one part of speech was given a new entry for each one. Now these once-separate entries are usually gathered into one main entry, with definitions still grouped and labeled by part of speech—noun definitions together, verb definitions together, etc. Definition numbers commonly start over for each new part of speech. College-size and bigger dictionaries cling to these practices.

When you look up a word's meaning, read all its definitions. Unless you do, you can't be sure that the meaning you select best fits the context in which the word is used.

Even though you have looked up the meaning, you should be wary of using a word you have encountered only once. As any foreigner will tell you, a great many English words not only have more than one meaning, but they also have *implied* or *connotative* meanings, which are not given in a dictionary. Furthermore, there may be idiomatic uses of which a young student speaker or writer is not aware. Until you have had several contacts with a word and have had a chance to observe just how it is used, you will be wise not to try to use it solely on the basis of its dictionary definition.

For example, suppose you did not know the meaning of the verb *transpire*. Looking it up, you find that it has four meanings. The first two are technical meanings in the field of physiology. The third is "to become known," and the fourth, marked *informal*, is "to happen." Now suppose that you try to use this verb in place of "happen" in the sentence "The police happened along just in time to catch the thieves." You will not make any sense if you say, "The police transpired along just in time to catch the thieves."

Spelling

The bold-faced word at the very beginning of a dictionary entry tells you the accepted spelling. When there are two or more acceptable spellings, the various spellings are given. Any spelling given has enough standing to justify use of it if you prefer it.

EXAMPLE   **cat•a•log** *or* **cat•a•logue**

If grammatical change in the form of a word is likely to raise spelling problems, *inflectional* forms are given. (These are forms of a word resulting from its habitual usage, like the principal parts of verbs or the comparative and superlative forms of adjectives.) A dictionary is the best reference work to consult if you are uncertain about doubling a consonant, changing an *i* to a *y*, and so on.

The dictionary tells you that *bases* is the plural of *basis*, and *solos* is the plural of *solo*, although *heroes*, with the *e*, is the plural of *hero*. It also tells you that *refer* doubles its *r* when it is inflected (*referred, referring*) while *care* does not (*cared, caring*). Both the principal parts of irregular verbs you may have difficulty remembering and the spelling of frequently misspelled words (like *misspell*) can be found in any good dictionary. In general, you should think of the dictionary as the place to find the proper spelling (and forms) of

a. the plural of a word, if the plural is formed irregularly
b. the feminine form of a foreign word: **alumnus; alumna**, fem.
c. the principal parts of an irregular verb
d. comparative and superlative forms of irregular adjectives and adverbs
e. case forms of pronouns; **who;** *possessive* **whose;** *objective* **whom**

Syllable Division

When a word must be divided at the end of a line, it should be divided between syllables. Syllable division is indicated in the bold-faced entry word and often in inflectional forms. The break is usually shown by a centered dot **(bas•ket)**. In some dictionaries it is shown by a space **(bas ket)**. Look at the various sample entries throughout this chapter to see the different ways each dictionary shows syllable division.

Capitalization

Proper nouns and adjectives, commonly written with initial capital letters, are entered in most dictionaries with the usual capitals. *Webster's Third*, however, prints the entry word in small letters followed by a brief note such as: *usu cap* or *often cap*, short for *usually capitalized* or *often capitalized*.

Sometimes a word not capitalized in most of its meanings should be capitalized when used in one sense, or perhaps more than one. The abbreviation *cap.* following a definition number indicates that the word is capitalized when used in that sense.

EXAMPLE

> **cap·i·tol** \'kap-ət-ʾl, 'kap-t'l\ *n* [L *Capitolium,* temple of Jupiter at Rome
> on the Capitoline hill] (1699) **1 a :** a building in which a state legis-
> lative body meets **b :** a group of buildings in which the functions of
> state government are carried out **2** *cap* : the building in which the
> U.S. Congress meets at Washington

Pronunciation

Ordinary spelling cannot show the sounds of words precisely. Dictionary pronunciations respell each word, using one fixed symbol for each of the 42 or 43 common sounds of English. New, made-up symbols might have been used. Most of the symbols actually used look like ordinary letters of the alphabet, some with special marks added, but they work differently: each one stands exclusively and consistently for only one sound.

In different dictionaries symbols may differ, too. For the vowel in *burn* one may show /û/ and another /ə/. The sound is, of course, the same. Each dictionary explains its symbols in a key, usually in the front of the book, and also prints a shortened key at the foot of each pair of facing pages. The key shows each symbol tied to its sound *as heard in one or two familiar words*. To understand the respellings in a particular dictionary, you must familiarize yourself with what its symbols mean.

After each entry word, these symbols "spell" its sounds in order, divided into syllables as needed.

EXAMPLE   **cap•tain** /ˈkap-tən/

                  (kap′tən, kap′tin)

In long words, one syllable, or sometimes more than one, may be spoken with more stress or force than the others. This stress is shown by accent marks: heaviest stress by a heavier mark, lighter stress by a lighter mark. The marks may be either slanted or straight, either above or below the line of type, and either before or after the syllable involved.

EXAMPLES   **tax•i•cab:** tak′ se kab′

                 ˈtak se kab

                 tăk′ se kăb

When a word has more than one recognized pronunciation, all of the pronunciations are given. You will have to study your dictionary's way of giving pronunciations, since each of the most available dictionaries differs from the others in the system it uses.

Etymologies, or Word Histories

Most dictionaries indicate the history of a word. They show, by means of abbreviations and symbols, what language the word originally came from, and what its original meaning was. English is unusual among languages for the vast number of words it has taken from other languages. During their history, many words have undergone interesting changes in form or meaning. The source of recently coined words, such as *quark*, is explained in a dictionary. Knowing the source and original meaning of a word is often a great help in understanding the word's present meaning and correct use.

The abbreviations used to indicate the languages from which words derive are explained in the front of your dictionary. The examples in this chapter show how dictionaries vary in where they position an etymology within an entry. The symbol < means "from," like the abbreviation *fr.*

> ¹**book** \'bůk\ *n* [ME, fr. OE *boc;* akin to OHG *buoh* book; perh. akin to OE *bōc* beech (prob. fr. the early Germanic practice of carving runic characters on beech wood tablets) — more at BEECH] (bef. 12c)

"From Webster's Ninth New Collegiate Dictionary. © 1984 by Merriam-Webster Inc., publishers of the Merriam-Webster® Dictionaries. Reprinted by permission of Merriam-Webster Inc."

Restrictive Labels

Most of the words defined in a dictionary are part of the general vocabulary. Some, however, have to do with a special field or are used almost exclusively in a single region or are used at only one level of usage.

Dictionaries use restrictive labels—*subject labels* such as *Law, Med.* (medicine), *Chem.* (chemistry), etc.; *area labels* such as *southwest U.S.*; and *usage labels* such as *informal, slang,* or *dialect.*

Area label:

> **corn pone** *n, Southern & Midland* (1859) : corn bread often made without milk or eggs and baked or fried

"From Webster's Ninth New Collegiate Dictionary. © 1984 by Merriam-Webster Inc., publishers of the Merriam-Webster® Dictionaries. Reprinted by permission of Merriam-Webster Inc."

Usage label:

> **goon** (gōōn) *n.* **1.** *Informal.* A thug hired to commit acts of intimidation or violence. **2.** *Slang.* A stupid or oafish person. [From dialectal *gooney, gony†,* fool; popularized by the comic-strip character Alice the *Goon,* created by E.C. Segar (1894–1938).]

Usage note:

> **fi·nal·ize** (fī′nə-liz′) *tr.v.* **-ized, -izing, -izes.** To put into final form; to complete.
>   ***Usage:*** *Finalize* is closely associated with the language of bureaucracy, in the minds of many careful writers and speakers, and is consequently avoided by them. The example *finalize plans for a class reunion* is termed unacceptable by 90 per cent of the Usage Panel. In most such examples a preferable choice is possible from among *complete, conclude, make final,* and *put in final form.*

Usage labels provide a good general guide to usage, but all writers must learn to make judgments about these matters on the basis of their own observations. Assigning a label such as *slang* or *informal* is necessarily a subjective judgment on the part of a definer, and not all dictionaries agree about labeling the same word. Your knowledge of the connotations of a word and the situation in which you want to use it should be your guide in choosing or rejecting a particular word or meaning. If you are not sure of the appropriateness of a word without looking it up, you will do well not to use it until you know it better.

Synonyms and Antonyms

Dictionaries often list other words of similar meaning (synonyms) and sometimes also words of opposite meaning (antonyms) at the end of an entry. At times they also append a slightly longer note comparing two or more words with similar meanings, showing fine shades of differences as well as similarities.

In the following example, synonyms (SYN) are discussed in detail, and antonyms (ANT) are also given.

> **brave** (brāv) *adj.* [Fr. < It. *bravo,* brave, bold, orig., wild, savage < L. *barbarus,* BARBAROUS] **1.** willing to face danger, pain, or trouble; not afraid; having courage **2.** showing to good effect; having a fine appearance **3.** fine, grand, or splendid [a *brave* new world] —*n.* **1.** any brave man ✰**2.** [< 17th-c. NAmFr.] a North American Indian warrior **3.** [Archaic] a bully —*vt.* **braved, brav′ing 1.** to face with courage **2.** to defy; dare **3.** [Obs.] to make splendid, as in dress —*vi.* [Obs.] to boast —**brave′ly** *adv.* — **brave′ness** *n.*
>   **SYN.**—**brave** implies fearlessness in meeting danger or difficulty and has the broadest application of the words considered here; **courageous** suggests constant readiness to deal with things fearlessly by reason of a stout-hearted temperament or a resolute spirit; **bold** stresses a daring temperament, whether displayed courageously, presumptuously, or defiantly; **audacious** suggests an imprudent or reckless boldness; **valiant** emphasizes a heroic quality in the courage or fortitude shown; **intrepid** implies absolute fearlessness and esp. suggests dauntlessness in facing the new or unknown; **plucky** emphasizes gameness in fighting against something when one is at a decided disadvantage —**ANT.** craven, cowardly

Encyclopedia Entries

Besides giving information about words, the college dictionaries listed in this chapter (but not some unabridged dictionaries) give facts about many people and places. These may appear as entries in the body of the dictionary or in special sections at the back.

Important Persons

A dictionary usually covers these items about a person:

1. *Name*: spelling, pronunciation, and given names
2. *Date of birth* (*and death if deceased*)
3. *Nationality* (*and country of birth if different*)
4. *Why famous*

Note how a typical entry covers all four:

> **Er·ics·son** (er′ik sən) **1. Leif,** fl. 1000; Norw. explorer & adventurer: discovered VINLAND, believed to be part of N. America: son of ERIC THE RED: also sp. **Er′ic·son 2. John,** 1803–89; U.S. naval engineer & inventor, born in Sweden: builder of the *Monitor*

From *Webster's New World Dictionary*, Second College Edition, copyright © 1980 by the World Publishing Company. Reprinted by permission of Collins & World Publishing Company.

Dictionary information about contemporaries soon goes out of date. It may be safer to refer to *Who's Who* or *Who's Who in America* for up-to-date facts.

Important Places

In treating a geographical entry, a dictionary usually gives the following information:

1. *Name*: spelling, pronunciation
2. *Identification*: city, nation, lake, river, etc.
3. *Location*
4. *Size*: population, as of a city; area, as of a state, body of water, etc.; length, as of a river; height, as of a mountain
5. *Political importance*: If a city is capital of a state or nation, the fact will be noted, and the city may be named in the entry for the state or nation.

6. *Historical or other interest:* as in Yorktown, site of surrender of the British

7. *Controlling country:* as in Guam, a United States possession

Be sure that a dictionary uses the latest census for its (undated) population figures before you trust them. Old data can be seriously misleading.

SPECIAL DICTIONARIES

36c. Learn the use of special dictionaries.

Along with general dictionaries, there are dictionaries of the special vocabularies of law, medicine, slang, and so on.

Books of synonyms are useful to people who do much writing. They help you to vary your choice of words and to find the exact word needed. Their use is opposite to that of a dictionary. Instead of looking up a word you *mean to use*, you look up one you *mean to avoid* in order to find a substitute for it.

Roget's Thesaurus of English Words and Phrases

This is the classic book of synonyms, over a century old. Originally, its words were grouped by classes and subclasses of meaning, with a huge index attached. Some recent editions (including new words) retain this ingenious format. Others (at least one in paperback) put the material in dictionary form—straight alphabetical order.

Funk and Wagnalls Standard Handbook of Synonyms, Antonyms, and Prepositions

This is also a standard book, listing in alphabetical order most of the words you might want to use and giving synonyms and antonyms for them.

Webster's Dictionary of Synonyms

This is valued especially for its able discussion of distinctions between words of similar meaning.

EXERCISE 3. Using Your Dictionary to Find Information About Words. This exercise is designed to test your knowledge of the information given about a word in the dictionary. With your dictionary before you, begin work at the teacher's signal. Look up the answers to the following questions. While your speed indicates to some degree your efficiency in using the dictionary, accuracy is the more important consideration.

1. Which is the more usual spelling: *judgment* or *judgement*?
2. In the first pronunciation for *research*, is the accent on the first or second syllable?
3. Copy the correct pronunciation of the word *comely*, using the respelling and symbols.
4. Are the comparative and superlative forms of *comely* shown to be *more comely* and *most comely*, or *comelier* and *comeliest*?
5. Copy the word *automatic*, dividing it correctly into syllables.
6. How many different meanings are given in your dictionary for the word *run* as an intransitive (*v.i.*) verb?
7. What restrictive label, if any, is given to the word *swell* when used to mean "first-rate"?
8. What restrictive label is given the word *shank* when used in the expression "the shank of the evening"?
9. What are the past and past participle forms of the irregular verb *burst*?
10. Distinguish between the meaning of *councilor* and *counselor*.
11. What restrictive label is given to the adverb *erstwhile*? What does the label mean?
12. What restrictive label is given to the verb *gyp*?
13. What is the origin of the word *candidate*?
14. In what literary work does the character Mrs. Malaprop appear? For what was she noted?
15. Tell the story of Hero and Leander as given in your dictionary.

EXERCISE 4. Using Your Dictionary to Find Information About Words. Like the preceding exercise, this exercise will test your knowledge of the information given in a dictionary and your familiarity with the location of this information in the dictionary. At the teacher's signal look up the answers to the following questions. Accuracy is more important than speed, but speed is important.

1. Find two synonyms for the word *cowardly*.

2. Write the plural of *analysis*.
3. Write the comparative and superlative forms of *ill*.
4. What city is the capital of Burma?
5. What is the population of Dallas, Texas?
6. When did Queen Victoria reign?
7. For what is Johann Gutenberg famous?
8. What was George Eliot's real name?
9. What is the meaning of the abbreviation RSVP?
10. In the first pronunciation for *hospitable*, is the accent on the first or second syllable?
11. What is the meaning of the symbol $\bar{A}\bar{A}$ used by a doctor in writing a prescription?
12. Write two acceptable plurals of *octopus*.
13. Should you or should you not use a comma before the *and* joining the last two items of a series?
14. Give the rule for the formation of the plural of nouns ending in *o* preceded by a vowel. Give two examples.
15. What is the meaning of the Latin phrase *caveat emptor*?

CHAPTER 37

Vocabulary

MEANING THROUGH CONTEXT AND WORD ANALYSIS

Although it is likely that this may be your last year of systematic vocabulary study, the number of English words you know and are able to use will continue to be important throughout your life. Most immediately, you will see that a good vocabulary will help you to succeed in college or at a job. More important, however, your general knowledge or your knowledge of a specific field cannot be very deep or impressive unless you have a considerable stock of words at your command. The number of words you know is one indication of the pride you take in your mind. You owe it to yourself to have a vocabulary that fairly reflects your interests and abilities.

DIAGNOSTIC TEST

Selecting the Closest Meaning. Number your paper 1–25. After the proper number, write the letter of the word or expression that comes closest to the meaning of the italicized word.

1. to *augment* the budget
   a) increase
   b) examine closely
   c) reduce
   d) disapprove of

2. to *ascertain* the facts
   a) cover up
   b) review
   c) find out
   d) testify to

3. a king known for his *avarice*
   a) wisdom
   b) vanity
   c) deceitfulness
   d) greed

4. a *biennial* event
   a) twice yearly
   b) every two weeks
   c) every two years
   d) twice daily

5. a *blithe* mood
   a) bitter
   b) proud
   c) angry
   d) carefree

6. an offer to *capitulate*
   a) confer
   b) mediate
   c) compromise
   d) surrender

7. a suspicion of *collusion*
   a) robbery
   b) foolishness
   c) mistrustfulness
   d) agreement to deceive

8. to *conjecture* about the facts
   a) talk
   b) lie
   c) guess
   d) conceal the truth

9. to *corroborate* testimony
   a) testify about
   b) confirm
   c) deny
   d) question

10. to act under *duress*
    a) compulsion
    b) misunderstanding
    c) difficulties
    d) bribery

11. an imposing *edifice*
    a) natural wonder
    b) manner
    c) speech
    d) building

12. wholesome *environment*
    a) nourishment
    b) outlook
    c) surroundings
    d) diet

13. a leader's *foible*
    a) weakness
    b) habit
    c) example
    d) follower

14. an *interminable* show
    a) worthless
    b) endless
    c) tedious
    d) difficult to describe

15. to *intimidate* a witness
    a) make disappear
    b) make fearful
    c) bribe
    d) coach

16. to *nurture* a child
    a) neglect
    b) give medicine to
    c) scold
    d) feed and bring up

17. A sign of *opulence*
    a) poverty
    b) health
    c) wealth
    d) generosity

18. a *prosaic* sight
    a) commonplace
    b) solemn
    c) stirring
    d) peaceful

19. a *prudent* action
    a) unexpected
    b) ill-mannered
    c) sensible
    d) foolish

20. good-natured *raillery*
    a) scuffling
    b) boisterousness
    c) competition
    d) banter

21. a well-deserved *reproof*
    a) promotion
    b) reprimand
    c) apology
    d) recognition

22. an act showing *sagacity*
    a) experience
    b) feebleness
    c) good judgment
    d) old age

23. a *sanguine* outlook
    a) hopeful
    b) pessimistic
    c) quarrelsome
    d) depressing

24. the *travail* of the artist
    a) illness
    b) oppression
    c) bad luck
    d) toil

25. a *volatile* temperament
    a) changeable
    b) disagreeable
    c) sluggish
    d) easygoing

CONTEXT CLUES

37a. Find clues to meaning in context.

Occasionally we encounter all words in isolation—mainly in crossword puzzles and other word games—but most of the time a word that we read or hear is closely connected with other words that help to make its meaning clear. The words that surround a particular word in a sentence or paragraph are called the *verbal context* of that word. Consider this sentence, for example:

> Although she continued to predict victory, Captain Winters was really not *sanguine* about her team's prospects.

If you are not sure of the meaning of *sanguine*, the rest of this sentence provides some important clues. The first part suggests that there is something contradictory about the captain's predicting victory when she is not sanguine about her team's chances. From the whole sentence, you may reasonably conclude that *sanguine* must mean "hopeful" or "optimistic." Sometimes, of course, such reasoning will lead you into a wrong guess; but more often than not you will be right.

In addition to the other words, the situation itself often provides clues to the meaning of a word. In the example above, you would expect a captain to be concerned about her team's success. Thus, you would not suppose that *sanguine* meant "bored" or "disinterested." Clues provided by the situation being discussed often help in deciding between two very different meanings of the same word or of words that have the same spelling. For example, if you are reading about an argument, *retort* is likely to mean "a ready and effective reply." In a description of a scientific experiment, on the other hand, *retort* would probably mean "a vessel used in distilling."

EXERCISE 1. Using Context Clues to Determine Meanings of Words. Number your paper 1–10. After each number, write the italicized word in the sentence and write a short definition based on the clues you find in context. You may check your definitions with the dictionary later.

1. After listening to a good deal of coaxing, the mother finally *acceded* to her children's request.
2. After a *hectic* year in the city, George was glad enough to return to the peace and quiet of the country.
3. Although the risks were great, the dissatisfied officers met and formed a *cabal* against the commander-in-chief.
4. The last two lines of the poem are so *cryptic* that no two readers can agree about what they mean.
5. Any person who was not entirely *devoid* of honor would have been outraged at the suggestion.
6. A person on a reducing diet is expected to *eschew* most fatty or greasy foods.
7. A large constrictor grabs its prey in its mouth and quickly coils itself around the victim to *immobilize* it. The harder the animal struggles, the tighter the snake constricts.
8. Eventually, the criminal *expiated* this murder and many other crimes on the gallows.
9. According to Bacon, scientists should learn about nature through *empirical* observations based on experiments and on careful study of the greatest possible amount of evidence.
10. Despite the awesome *fecundity* of certain species of fish, the balance of nature limits the population.

EXERCISE 2. Using Context Clues to Determine Meanings of Words. Number your paper 1–10 and write the corresponding italicized word after each number. After each word write a short definition based on your understanding of the context. When you have completed the exercise, check your definitions against your dictionary.

Science gets most of its information by the process of (1) *reductionism*, exploring the details, then the details of the details, until all the smallest bits of the structure, or the smallest parts of the mechanism, are laid out for counting and (2) *scrutiny*. Only when this is done can the investigation be extended to (3) *encompass* the whole organism or the entire system. So we say.

Sometimes it seems that we take a loss, working this way. Much of today's public anxiety about science is the (4) *apprehension* that we may forever be overlooking the whole by an endless, obsessive (5) *preoccupation* with the parts. I had a brief, personal experience of this (6) *misgiving* one afternoon in Tucson, where I had time on my hands and visited the zoo, just outside the city. The designers there have cut a deep pathway between two small artificial ponds, walled by clear glass, so when you stand in the center of the path you can look into the depths of each pool, and at the same time you can regard the surface. In one pool, on the right side of the path, is a family of otters; on the other side, a family of beavers. Within just a few feet from your face, on either side, beavers and otters are at play, underwater and on the surface, swimming toward your face and then away, more filled with life than any creatures I have ever seen before, in all my days. Except for the glass, you could reach across and touch them.

I was (7) *transfixed*. As I now recall it, there was only one sensation in my head: pure (8) *elation* mixed with amazement at such perfection. Swept off my feet, I floated from one side to the other, swiveling my brain, staring astounded at the beavers, then at the otters. I could hear shouts across my (9) *corpus callosum*, from one hemisphere to the other. I remember thinking, with what was left in charge of my consciousness, that I wanted no part of the science of beavers and otters; I wanted never to know how they performed their marvels; I wished for no news about the (10) *physiology* of their breathing, the coordination of their muscles, their vision, their endocrine systems, their digestive tracts. I hoped never to have to think of them as collections of cells. All I asked for was the full hairy complexity, then in front of my eyes, of whole, intact beavers and otters in motion.

LEWIS THOMAS

Common Clues to Meaning

Although a sentence may provide clues to the meaning of a word in a variety of ways, there are three kinds of context clues that are particularly helpful.

Words Similar in Meaning

In the sentence, "The loud, *raucous* laughter of the troop irritated the lieutenant," you can guess at the meaning of *raucous* because you know the word *loud*. (*Raucous* means "harsh of voice, coarse.")

Words Used in Contrast

Contrasts often supply clues to meaning by pairing an unfamiliar word against a known one. In such a situation, you can usually assume that the unfamiliar word is more or less the opposite of the one you know.

EXAMPLES This accidental development did not *vitiate* the theory; it strengthened it. [*Vitiate* is contrasted with *strengthened*. It probably means "weakened" or "robbed of force."] The defendant claims he had no intention of breaking into the apartment, but the state contends that in his possession were found burglar tools and a floor plan of the apartment, indicating *premeditation*. [The prosecutor must mean that the defendant had previously planned to commit the crime; *premeditation* must mean "planning beforehand."]

Contrasts are often signaled by such words as *but, although,* and *however.* Sometimes *or* indicates a contrast, but you cannot assume that it always does. In the first sentence below, two antonyms are joined and contrasted. In the second example, however, two synonyms are joined by *or,* and no contrast is indicated.

CONTRAST *Rich* or *poor*, the people resented the tax.
NO CONTRAST No one thought her behavior *servile* or *subservient*.

In the second example, *servile* and *subservient* mean essentially the same thing: "slavish, overly submissive." Contrasts offer many helps to meaning, but for certainty you had better find other clues that confirm your guess or look the word up.

Supplied Definition

When writers anticipate that their readers may not know the meaning of an important word, they often provide a definition. They may introduce the definition with an expression such as *in other words,* or *that is,* or they may slip it in without calling attention to it. The definitions or explanations in the following examples are italicized, and the words defined are in boldfaced type.

The painting clearly shows the **aegis**, or *shield*, of Athena.

A word is often defined by a **synonym**—that is, *a word of similar meaning*.

His *observation* was *too obvious to mention*—a **truism**. [Notice that the explanation comes before the word defined in this example.]

Since the days of the early Greek philosophers, the word **atom** has designated *the smallest and last unit of matter that would be reached if a given body were divided into smaller and smaller parts*.

People do not go to the trouble of explaining things unless they want to be understood. Be on the lookout for definitions of difficult words.

EXERCISE 3. Using Context Clues to Determine Meanings of Words.

Number your paper 1–10 and after each number write the italicized word. Give a brief definition in your own words, based on the context.

1. Along with the discovery of the properties of poisons came the discovery of substances that had properties of combating the effects of poisons. These early *antidotes* were strange mixtures.
2. The border rebellion, *quiescent* during the winter months, broke out in renewed violence in the spring.
3. To the rest of us, the outlook just then seemed more ominous than *propitious*.
4. Most snakes are meat eaters, or *carnivores*.
5. The *salutary* effect of the new drug was shown by the rapid improvement in the patient's condition.
6. *Subterranean* temperatures are frequently higher than those above the surface of the earth.
7. Because the official could not attend the meeting herself, she had to send a *surrogate*, or deputy.
8. The method of reasoning from the particular to the general—the *inductive* method—has played an important role in science since the time of Francis Bacon.
9. If the leaders felt any *compunction* about planning and carrying out unprovoked attacks on neighboring countries, they showed no sign of it.

10. Formerly, a doctor who found a successful cure often regarded it as a trade secret and refused to *divulge* it to others.

EXERCISE 4. Using Context Clues to Determine Meanings of Words. Read the following passage and then write your own definitions for the italicized words. Consult your dictionary only after you have written your own definitions from context.

Most of the doctors who had treated cases of the peculiar disease were almost certain by then that the characteristic initial (1) *lesion* was the bite of some (2) *minute* creature, but they had little reason to suspect mites of being the guilty parties. At the time, it was generally believed that mites could transmit only two serious (3) *febrile* diseases—Japanese river fever and endemic typhus. Both of these are rarely found in the United States, and anyway both had been eliminated from consideration in this instance by laboratory tests. Moreover, the mouse, unlike the rat, had never been proved to be a reservoir for disease-bearing parasites. Mr. Pomerantz admits that hitting upon the mouse as the probable (4) *host* was largely intuitive. He is persuaded, however, that in singling out mites as the carriers—or (5) *vectors*, as such agents are known—of the disease he was guided entirely by (6) *deduction*.

Mites are insectlike organisms, closely related to ticks. Both are members of the Arachnida, a class that also includes spiders and scorpions. Compared to a tick, a mite is a minute animal. A mite, when fully (7) *engorged*, is about the size of a strawberry seed. In that state, it is approximately ten times its usual, or unfed, size. So far, science has classified at least thirty families of mites, most of which are vegetarian and indifferent to man and all other animals. The majority of the (8) *parasitic*, blood-sucking mites have to feed once in every four or five days in order to live. Most mites of this type attach themselves to a host only long enough to engorge, and drop off, (9) *replete*, after fifteen or twenty minutes. No one ever feels the bite of a mite—or of a tick, either, for that matter—until the animal has dropped off. Entomologists believe that both creatures, at the instant they bite, (10) *excrete* a fluid that anesthetizes a small surrounding area of the body of the host. Mites are only infrequently found in this country and until recently were practically unknown in New York City. Consequently, very few Americans, even physicians and exterminators, have ever seen a mite. Mr.

Pomerantz is one of those who have. He came across some in line of duty on three occasions in 1945.

BERTON ROUECHÉ

37b. Look up unfamiliar words in your dictionary.

For those words that context does not make sufficiently clear, the dictionary will provide you with the help you need. But here, too, context is important. Most words have a number of different meanings. To find the one you want, you will need to keep in mind the context in which you originally encountered the word. Once you have found the meaning you want, you will do well to read on through the whole definition. Most words have a range of different meanings; to know the word well, you should know more than one of its meanings. Moreover, learning the pronunciation, the derivation, and related forms of the word will help you to remember it. Once you take the trouble to go to the dictionary, you may as well get as much information as possible from it.

37c. Keep a vocabulary notebook.

Having learned a new word, you should not stop there. To ensure that the word will become a permanent part of your vocabulary, write it in your notebook. Follow it with its pronunciation, the sentence in which you first found it, and its definition. Whenever you learn a new word, enter it in your notebook in this way, and review your list from time to time. You will find that keeping a special section of your notebook for new words will result in noticeable vocabulary growth.

WORD ANALYSIS

37d. Use your knowledge of prefixes, suffixes, and roots.

In general, English words are of two kinds: those that can be analyzed into smaller parts (*unworkable, impolitely*) and those that cannot (*stone, money, winter*). The words of the first kind, those that can be divided, are made up of parts called prefixes, roots, and suffixes. Because these parts have broad, general meanings that remain essentially the same in different words, knowing something about word analysis can help you figure out the meaning of an unfamiliar word. However, there are some difficulties that make it unwise to depend entirely on word analysis for clues to meaning. It is not always easy to tell whether a particular group of letters is really the prefix or suffix it appears to be. The *–er* in *painter* is a suffix, but the *–er* in *winter* is not. To be certain, you have to know something about the origin of the word. Moreover, the original force of a combination of word parts may no longer have much to do with the modern meaning of a word. For these and other reasons, absolute dependence on word analysis would lead you to make as many bad guesses as good ones.

There are, however, some good reasons for having a general knowledge of the way English words are formed. Word analysis helps you to understand the peculiarities of English spelling and the connection between the related forms of a particular word. (Knowing about related forms often enables you to learn four or five new words as easily as one.) Also, word analysis gives you useful practice in taking a close look at words. In reading, you pass very quickly over words, hardly noticing more than their general shape. This is all very well for words you know well, but close examination is called for with unfamiliar ones. Most important of all, word analysis offers the key to the origin of English words. The fact that many different cultures have contributed to the vocabulary of English is one of its particular strengths. Educated people should know something about the history as well as the use of their words. After all, building a vocabulary is a kind of collecting, differing from the collection of stamps or coins in being less expensive and more useful. No collector worthy of the name is content to possess a specimen and know nothing about it. Word analysis will tell you a great deal about the words you add to your collection.

How Words Are Divided

Words that can be divided have two or more parts: a core called a *root* and one or more parts added to it. The parts that are added are called *affixes*—literally, "something fixed or attached to something else." An affix added before the root is called a *prefix*; one added after the root is called a *suffix*. A word may have one or more affixes of either kind, or several of both kinds. A root with no affixes at all is incapable of being divided. A word consisting of a root only is one like *stone* or *money*, to which word analysis does not apply.

The following table shows some typical combinations of affixes (prefixes and suffixes) and roots.

PREFIX[ES]	ROOT	SUFFIX[ES]	EXAMPLE
un–	work	–able	unworkable
post–	–pone		postpone
	friend	–ly	friendly
	fright	–en, –ing	frightening
il–	–leg–	–al	illegal
under–	take	–er	undertaker
	truth	–ful	truthful
	child	–like	childlike

Some of the affixes and roots in English are recognizable as complete words in themselves (*fright* in *frighten; child* and *like* in *childlike*). Most other affixes and roots were also once separate words, though the original words may no longer exist in our modern language. For example, *post* in *postpone* was a Latin word meaning *after*, and *pone* (*pono, ponere*) was the Latin word for *put*.

The Origins of English Words

In the lists that appear later in this chapter, prefixes and roots are grouped according to the language in which they originated: Old English, Latin (or Latin-French), and Greek. Although it is not possible here to give a detailed account of the contribution of these three sources to modern English, a brief discussion of word borrowing will make the lists more useful.

Old English

Old English, or Anglo-Saxon, is the earliest recorded form of the English language. It was spoken from about A.D. 600 until about A.D. 1100, and most of its words had been part of a still earlier form of the language. Many of the common words of modern English, like *home, stone*, and *meat* are native, or Old English, words. Most of the irregular verbs in English derive from Old English (*speak, swim, drive, ride, sing*), as do most of our shorter numerals (*two, three, six, ten*) and most of our pronouns (*I, you, we, who*). Many Old English words can be traced back to Indo-European, a prehistoric language that was the common ancestor of Greek and Latin as well. Others came into Old English as it was becoming a separate language.

As the speakers of Old English became acquainted with Latin, chiefly through contact with Christianity, they began to borrow Latin words for things for which no native word existed. Some common words borrowed at this time were *abbot, altar, candle, temple, fever,* and *lettuce.*

Many other Latin words came into English through French. In 1066, toward the end of the Old English period, the French under William the Conqueror invaded England and defeated the Anglo-Saxons under King Harold. For the next three hundred years, French was the language of the ruling classes in England. During this period, thousands of new words came into English, many of them words relating to upper-class pursuits: *baron, attorney, ermine, luxury.* English has continued to borrow words from French right down to the present, with the result that over a third of our modern English vocabulary derives from French.

Many words from Greek, the other major source of English words, came into English by way of French and Latin. Others were borrowed directly in the sixteenth century when interest in classic culture was at its height. Directly or indirectly, Greek contributed *athlete, acrobat, elastic, magic, rhythm,* and many others.

In the modern period, English has borrowed from every important language in the world. The etymologies in your dictionary trace the origins of words, often providing insights into their present meanings and into history as well.

EXERCISE 5. **Finding the Etymologies of Words.** Find out from your dictionary the origins of each of the following words. (For help in interpreting the etymology, see pages 885–86 of this book.)

abscond	demon	quart
air	legal	tyrant
chase	loyal	votary

Prefixes

English borrowed not only independent words from Greek, Latin, and French, but also a number of word parts from these languages for use as affixes and roots. These sources are indicated in the following list of prefixes and in the list of roots on pages 910–13.

Prefixes have broad general meanings like *not, under,* and *against,* and a particular one of them may appear in hundreds of different words.

In general, a knowledge of prefixes will help you to know when to double consonants in such words as *misspell* and *overrun*. Many prefixes have several different spellings in order to fit with various roots.

PREFIX	MEANING	EXAMPLES
Old English		
a–	in, on, of, up, to	afoot, awake
be–	around, about, away	beset, behead
for–	away, off, from	forsake, forget
mis–	badly, poorly, not	mismatch, misspell
over–	above, excessively	oversee, overdo
un–	not, reverse of	untrue, unfold
Latin and Latin-French		
ab–, a–, abs–	from, off, away	abduct, absent
ante–	before	antedate
bi–	two	bimonthly, bisect
circum–	around	circumnavigate
com–, co–, col–, con–, cor–	with, together	compare, coexist, collide, convene, correspond
contra–	against	contradict
de–	away, from, off, down	defect, desert
dis–, dif–	away, off, opposing	dissent, differ
ex–, e–, ef–	away from, out	excise, efface
in–, im–	in, into, within	induct, impose
in–, im–, il–, ir–	not	incapable, impious, illegal, irregular
inter–	among, between	intercede, intersperse
intro–, intra–	inward, to the inside, within	introduce, intravenous, intramural
non–	not	nonentity, nonessential
post–	after, following	postpone, postscript
pre–	before	prevent, preclude
pro–	forward, in place of, favoring	produce, pronoun, pro-American
re–	back, backward, again	revoke, recede, recur
retro–	back, backward	retroactive, retrospect

PREFIX	MEANING	EXAMPLES
Latin and *Latin-French* (continued)		
semi–	half	semiannual, semicircular
sub–, suf–, sum–, sup–, sus–	under, beneath	subjugate, suffuse, summon, suppose, suspect
super–	over, above, extra	supersede, supervise
trans–	across, beyond	transfuse, transport
ultra–	beyond, excessively	ultramodern, ultraviolet
Greek		
a–	lacking, without	amorphous, atheistic
anti–	against, opposing	antipathy, antithesis
apo–	from, away	apology, apocrypha
cata–	down, away, thoroughly	cataclysm, catastrophe
dia–	through, across, apart	diameter, diagnose
eu–	good, pleasant	eulogy, euphemism
hemi–	half	hemisphere, hemiplegic
hyper–	excessive, over	hypercritical, hypertension
hypo–	under, beneath	hypodermic, hypothesis
para–	beside, beyond	parallel, paradox
peri–	around	periscope, perimeter
pro–	before	prognosis, program
syn–, sym–, syl–, sys–	together, with	synchronize, sympathy, syllable, system

EXERCISE 6. Understanding Prefixes in Words. Divide the following words into prefix and root, putting a slant line (/) at the point of division. Then give the meaning of the English word. Be ready to explain the connection between the meaning of the prefix and the present meaning of the word.

EXAMPLE   1. amnesia
          1. a / mnesia (*loss of memory*)

1. absolve
2. amorphous
3. antipodes
4. biennial
5. circumspect
6. compunction
7. excise
8. hypodermic
9. impolite
10. subordinate

EXERCISE 7. Writing Words with Specific Prefixes. Find and write on your paper two words that contain each of the following prefixes: *ad–, de–, dia–, dis–, eu–, im–, ir–, mis–, post–, pro–, re–, sub–, trans–, syn–, ultra–*.

Suffixes

Suffixes, you will recall, are affixes added after the root, or at the end of a word. There are two main kinds of suffixes: those that provide a grammatical signal of some kind but do not greatly alter the basic meaning of the word and those that, by being added, create new words. The endings *–s, –ed,* and *–ing* are suffixes of the first kind; by adding them to *work* (*works, worked, working*) we indicate something about number and tense, but we do not change the essential meaning of the word. This kind of suffix is a *grammatical* suffix.

Grammatical suffixes are important in grammar, but in vocabulary we are more concerned with the second kind of suffixes—those that make new words. By adding *–ful* to *thank*, we get a different word: *thankful*. Adding *–hood* to *girl* gives us *girlhood*, again a different word. Suffixes that change meaning in this way are called *derivational* suffixes. Notice in the following examples that the addition of a derivational suffix often gives a new part of speech as well as a new meaning.

ROOT	DERIVATIONAL SUFFIX	RESULT
acid (n. or adj.)	–ity	acidity (n. only)
free (adj.)	–dom	freedom (n.)
accept (v.)	–ance	acceptance (n.)

Since derivational suffixes so often determine the part of speech of English words, we can conveniently classify them according to parts of speech. The meanings given for the suffixes are very broad. Often they have little connection with the meaning of the resulting word.

NOUN SUFFIXES	MEANING	EXAMPLES
Old English		
–dom	state, rank, condition	freedom, wisdom
–er	doer, maker	hunter, writer, thinker
–hood	state, condition	childhood, statehood
–ness	quality, state	softness, shortness

NOUN SUFFIXES		EXAMPLES
Foreign (Latin, French, Greek)		
–age	process, state, rank	passage, bondage
–ance, –ancy	act, condition, fact	acceptance, vigilance, hesitancy
–ard, –art	one that does (esp. excessively)	coward, laggard, braggart
–ate	rank, office	delegate, primate
–ation	action, state, result	occupation, starvation
–cy	state, condition	accuracy, captaincy
–ee	one receiving action	employee, refugee
–eer	doer, worker at	engineer, racketeer
–ence	act, condition, fact	evidence, patience
–er	doer, native of	baker, westerner
–ery	skill, action, collection	surgery, robbery, crockery
–ess	feminine	waitress, lioness
–et, –ette	little, feminine	islet, cigarette, majorette
–ion	action, result, state	union, fusion, dominion
–ism	act, manner, doctrine	baptism, barbarism, socialism
–ist	doer, believer	monopolist, socialist
–ition	action, state, result	sedition, expedition
–ity	state, quality, condition	paucity, civility
–ment	means, result, action	refreshment, disappointment
–or	doer, office, action	elevator, juror, honor
–ry	condition, practice, collection	dentistry, jewelry
–tion	action, condition	creation, relation
–tude	quality, state, result	fortitude, multitude
–ty	quality, state	novelty, beauty
–ure	act, result, means	culture, signature
–y	result, action, quality	jealousy, inquiry

ADJECTIVE SUFFIXES	MEANING	EXAMPLES
Old English		
–en	made of, like	wooden, golden
–ful	full of, marked by	thankful, masterful
–ish	suggesting, like	childish, devilish
–less	lacking, without	helpless, hopeless
–like	like, similar	childlike, dreamlike

ADJECTIVE SUFFIXES	MEANING	EXAMPLES
Old English (continued)		
–ly	like, of the nature of	friendly, cowardly
–some	apt to, showing	tiresome, lonesome
–ward	in the direction of	backward, homeward
–y	showing, suggesting	hilly, sticky, wavy
Foreign		
–able	able, likely	capable, affable
–ate	having, showing	animate, separate
–escent	becoming, growing	obsolescent, quiescent
–esque	in the style of, like	picturesque, statuesque
–fic	making, causing	terrific, soporific
–ible	able, likely, fit	edible, possible, divisible
–ose	marked by, given to	comatose, bellicose
–ous	marked by, given to	religious, furious

ADJECTIVE OR NOUN SUFFIXES	MEANING	EXAMPLES
–al	doer, pertaining to	rival, animal, autumnal
–an	one belonging to, pertaining to	human, European
–ant	actor, agent, showing	servant, observant
–ary	belonging to, one connected with	primary, adversary, auxiliary
–ent	doing, showing, actor	confident, adherent
–ese	of a place or style, style	Chinese, journalese
–ian	pertaining to, one belonging to	barbarian, reptilian
–ic	dealing with, caused by, person or thing, showing	classic, choleric
–ile	marked by, one marked by	juvenile, servile
–ine	marked by, dealing with, one marked by	marine, canine, divine
–ite	formed, showing, one marked by	favorite, composite
–ive	belonging or tending to, one belonging to	detective, native
–ory	doing, pertaining to, place or thing for	accessory, contributory

VERB SUFFIXES	MEANING	EXAMPLES
Old English		
–en	cause to be, become	deepen, darken
Foreign		
–ate	become, form, treat	populate, animate
–esce	become, grow, continue	convalesce, acquiesce
–fy	make, cause, cause to have	glorify, fortify
–ish	do, make, perform	punish, finish
–ize	make, cause to be	sterilize, motorize

Some of the words in the above lists make independent sense without the suffix (*employee, employ*). Others, however, do not (*delegate, deleg–*).

Because the English language has been exposed to so many different influences, the pattern of adding suffixes to form related words is often inconsistent. Things made of wood are *wooden*, but things made of stone are not *stonen*. We do have some regularities: verbs ending in *–ate* usually have a related noun ending *–ation* (*prostrate, prostration*). We have such regular patterns as *differ, difference, differential, exist, existence, existential*, etc., but we have many other examples that are not so systematic. This irregularity is one reason why it is so important to learn related forms of the new words you add to your vocabulary. You cannot derive the noun form of *reject* (*rejection*) by knowing the noun form of *accept* (*acceptance*). You have to learn it separately. In a sense, you do not really know a word until you know its important related forms.

EXERCISE 8. Writing Related Nouns of Specific Verbs. What nouns, if any, are companion forms of the following verbs? Write the noun after the proper number. Do not use gerunds.

EXAMPLES   1. convene   2. decode
               1. *convention*   2. *decoder*

1. cavil
2. collate
3. demur
4. disburse
5. intercede
6. intervene
7. prescribe
8. proscribe
9. stultify
10. verify

EXERCISE 9. Writing Related Verbs for Specific Nouns.
Number your paper 1–10. Give a related verb for each noun below if
there is one. If there is no verb form, write 0 after the proper number.

1. asperity
2. austerity
3. complaisance
4. defection
5. notation
6. raillery
7. remission
8. remuneration
9. turpitude
10. decision

**EXERCISE 10. Writing Related Adjectives for Specific Nouns
and Verbs.** Number your paper 1–10. Give a related adjective for
each of the following nouns and verbs.

1. austerity
2. complaisance
3. deduce
4. increment
5. environment
6. essence
7. excess
8. prescience
9. prescribe
10. vituperate

Roots

A root is the core of a word—the part to which prefixes and suffixes are
added. To find the root, you have only to remove any affix there may
be. For example, removal of the affixes *a–* and *–ous* from *amorphous*
leaves us with *–morph–*, a root meaning "form or shape." The root
–clysm, meaning "falling," remains after we remove the prefix *cata–*,
meaning "down," from *cataclysm*.

Roots have more specific and definite meanings than either prefixes
or suffixes and appear in fewer different words. The following list
contains some of the common foreign roots in English words.

ROOT	MEANING	EXAMPLES
Latin		
–ag–, –act–	do, drive, impel	agitate, transact
–agr–	field	agriculture, agrarian
–am–, –amic–	friend, love	amatory, amicable
–aqu–	water	aquatic, aqueduct, aquarium

ROOT	MEANING	EXAMPLES
–aud–, –audit–	hear	audible, auditorium
–ben–, –bene–	well, good	benefit, benediction
–brev–	short, brief	abbreviate, breviary
–cand–	white, glowing	candor, incandescent
–capit–	head	capital, decapitate
–cent–	hundred	century, centennial
–cid–, –cis–	kill, cut	suicide, regicide, incision
–clin–	bend, lean	decline, inclination
–cogn–	know	recognize, cognizant
–cred–	belief, trust	incredible, credulity
–crypt–	hidden, secret	crypt, cryptic
–culp–	fault, blame	culpable, exculpate
–duc–, –duct–	lead	educate, conductor
–equ–	equal	equation, equanimity
–err–	wander, stray	erratic, aberration
–fac–, –fact–, –fect–, –fic–	do, make	facile, manufacture, defective, efficient
–fer–	bear, yield	transfer, fertile
–fid–	belief, faith	fidelity, perfidious
–fin–	end, limit	final, indefinite
–frag–, –fract–	break	fragment, fracture
–fus–	pour	transfuse, effusive
–gen–	birth, kind, origin	generate, generic
–jac–, –ject–	throw, hurl, cast	adjacent, eject
–jud–	judge	prejudice, adjudicate
–jug–	join, yoke	conjugal, conjugate
–junct–	join	junction, disjunctive
–jur–	swear, plead	adjure, perjury
–leg–, –lig–, –lect–	choose, read	eligible, legible, lectern
–loc–	place	locus, locale
–loqu–, –loc–	talk, speech	colloquial, locution
–magn–	large	magnitude, magnify
–mal–	bad	malady, malevolent
–man–, –manu–	hand	manicure, manual
–mit–, –miss–	send	remit, emissary
–mor–, –mort–	die, death	mortuary, immortal
–omni–	all	omnipotent, omniscient

ROOT	MEANING	EXAMPLES
–ped–	foot	pedal, quadruped
–pend–, –pens–	hang, weigh	appendix, suspense
–pon–, –pos–	place, put	postpone, interpose
–port–	carry, bear	transport, importation
–prim–	first, early	primitive, primordial
–punct–	point	punctuation, punctilious
–reg–, –rig–, –rect–	rule, straight, right	regent, incorrigible, rectangular
–rupt–	break	rupture, interrupt
–sang–	blood	sanguine, consanguinity
–sci–	know, knowledge	omniscient, prescience
–scrib–, –script–	write	inscribe, proscribe, manuscript
–sent–, –sens–	feel	presentiment, sensitive
–sequ–, –secut–	follow	sequel, persecute, consecutive
–son–	sound	consonant, sonorous
–spir–	breath, breathe	expire, inspiration
–string–, –strict–	bind tight	constrict, stricture, stringent
–tract–	draw, pull	traction, extractor
–uni–	one	unify, universe
–ven–, –vent–	come	intervene, supervene
–verb–	word	verbal, verbiage
–vid–, –vis–	see	evident, television
–vit–	life	vitality, vitamin

Greek

–anthrop–	man	anthropology, misanthropic
–arch–	ancient, chief	archaeology, monarch
–astr–, –aster–	star	astronomy, asterisk
–auto–	self	automatic, autonomy
–bibli–	book	bibliography, bibliophile
–bio–	life	biology, autobiography
–chrom–	color	chromatic, chromosome
–cosm–	world, order	cosmos, microcosm
–cycl–	wheel, circle	cyclone, bicycle
–dem–	people	democracy, epidemic
–gen–	kind, race	eugenics, genesis
–geo–	earth	geography, geology
–gram–	write, writing	grammar, epigram
–graph–	write, writing	orthography, geography

ROOT	MEANING	EXAMPLES
–hydr–	water	hydrogen, dehydrate
–log–	word, study	epilogue, theology, logic
–micr–	small	microbe, microscope
–mon–	one, single	monogamy, monologue
–morph–	form	amorphous, metamorphosis
–neo–	new	neologism, neolithic
–orth–	straight, correct	orthodox, orthography
–pan–	all, entire	panorama, pandemonium
–path–	feeling, suffering	apathy, pathology sympathy
–phil–	like, love	philanthropic, philosophy
–phon–	sound	phonology, euphony
–poly–	many	polygon, polygamy
–proto–	first	prototype
–psych–	mind	psychology, psychosomatic
–soph–	wise, wisdom	philosophy, sophomore
–tele–	far, distant	telegram, telepathy
–zo–	animal	zoology, protozoa

EXERCISE 11. Writing Words with Specific Roots. List two English words (other than those given as examples above) containing each of the following roots.

EXAMPLES   1. –verb–
                    1. *adverb, verbose*

1. –aud– (hear)
2. –crypt– (hidden, secret)
3. –duc– (lead)
4. –fin– (end, limit)
5. –junct– (join)
6. –man–, –manu– (hand)
7. –mor–, –mort– (death)
8. –port– (carry)
9. –vid–, –vis– (see)
10. –vit– (life)

EXERCISE 12. Writing Words with Specific Roots. Follow the instructions for Exercise 11.

1. –arch– (chief)
2. –auto– (self)
3. –bio– (life)
4. –chron– (time)
5. –cycl– (wheel, circle)
6. –dem–, –demo– (people)
7. –gram– (write, writing)
8. –hydr– (water)
9. –mega– (large)
10. –poly– (many)

REVIEW EXERCISE A. Using Prefixes, Suffixes, and Roots to Define Words. Using slanting bars (/) to mark each separation, divide the following words into their parts. Then, referring to the preceding lists of prefixes, suffixes, and roots—or, if necessary, to your dictionary—write a brief definition for each. Be prepared to explain how the parts produce the total meaning.

EXAMPLE   1. zoology
                1. *zoo / log / y (study of animals)*

1. achromatic	8. extortion	15. nominee
2. autonomy	9. geology	16. proponent
3. bibliophile	10. ineligible	17. pseudonym
4. cosmic	11. incapable	18. subsequent
5. cryptogram	12. infidel	19. transmission
6. deduction	13. judicious	20. vociferous
7. evoke	14. lucid	

Limitations of Word Analysis

Knowing something of the way in which prefixes, suffixes, and roots combine to form words provides insights into the history of our words and into their meanings. However, it would be misleading to suggest that the original meanings of the parts are always clearly reflected in a modern word.

It may happen that following the method of word division will lead you to a meaning that is so far from the modern one as to be of little help. For example, the words *admonition* and *monetary* have an element (*–mon–*) in common. The first means "warning" and the second "pertaining to money." What is the connection? There is one, but it is remote: in ancient Roman times, money was coined in or near a temple of Juno, a goddess known as "the warner." This is interesting, but not much of a clue if you do not already know the meaning of both words. Word analysis can often help you to make a plausible guess at what a word may mean; it can rarely be absolutely depended upon.

Semantic Change

One obvious reason that word analysis does not always work as a way of finding meaning is that words change their meanings. This change in meaning—called *semantic change*—is extremely common.

There are several ways in which this change comes about. Sometimes a word that has had a general meaning comes to have a specific meaning. The word *starve* once meant "to die." It only later took on the special meaning of "to die from lack of food." In Old English, any crawling creature—including the dragon in *Beowulf*—could be called a *worm*. Now the word is used only to mean earthworms and the like.

Words also take on new meanings in the opposite way—from specific to general. Originally *barn* meant "a storage place for barley," and *lord* meant "loaf guard or bread keeper."

When a word acquires a new meaning, it may lose the old meaning, as *worm, starve,* and *lord* have. When this situation takes place, the word has become detached from the root meaning, although it retains the original root form. The *–jure* of *adjure* is related to *jury* and originally had to do with swearing in a legal sense. But usually the word now means "to entreat," and the meaning connection with the root has been lost.

Auspices literally means "looking at birds." The ancient Romans believed that they could tell from studying the entrails of sacrificial birds whether or not an enterprise would be successful. The word came to be used for any combination of favorable signs and then, as it is now, for a combination of protection, guidance, and patronage.

Sometimes both old and new meanings are retained. Indeed, often it works out that a word will have six, eight, or ten meanings. Some of these meanings may be close to the original meanings of the word elements; some may vary from them considerably. The word *aegis* meant originally a shield or breastplate, especially one associated with the goddess Athena; then it came to mean also "protection" and "patronage, sponsorship." Depending on the context, it can mean any of these things in modern English. As a result, we may say that a lecture or exhibit is held under either the auspices—originally, bird watching —or the aegis—originally, shield—of a certain group. *Insular* means "pertaining to an island," but it has also come to mean "isolated, detached" and also "narrow, provincial." *Sanguine* may retain the root meaning and indicate "bloody," but it is more likely to mean "quite optimistic." Because there are so many situations involving semantic change, careful use of context clues or steady use of the dictionary is likely to give a more accurate sense of word meanings than word analysis alone.

EXERCISE 13. Writing the Original Meanings of Specific Words. List the following words and write after each its original meaning as given in the dictionary: *abeyance, challenge, derive, detriment, dirge, farce, glamour, knave, lampoon, melancholy, monster, pedigree, sabotage, scandal, vegetable.*

Synonyms

Word borrowing, word derivation by affixes and roots, semantic change, and other processes keep going on all the time, making English rich in synonyms. Synonyms are words that may be interchanged in given contexts. We may say "a hard task" or "a difficult task," because *hard* and *difficult* are synonyms. We may say that New York is a large city or a metropolis, and *city* and *metropolis* are therefore synonyms.

It is often said that there are very few pairs of words in English that are entirely interchangeable, because there are usually slight but important differences between synonyms. Sometimes one synonym is noticeably more learned than another; *edifice* is more learned and pretentious than *building, domicile* more so than *home* or *residence. Daily* is the ordinary English word, *diurnal* and *quotidian* quite learned. Sometimes one of a pair of synonyms is noticeably informal; *smidge* or *smidgeon* is less formal than *particle.* Often learned words are rather specific in their suggestions; the sphere in which they can be used is narrow. It is possible to analyze both *terrestrial* and *mundane* as "pertaining to the world." But *terrestrial* is likely to suggest contrast between our world and other heavenly bodies, described by words like *lunar* and *solar*, and *mundane* carries with it suggestions of the practical, routine, everyday affairs of this world, as contrasted with more spiritual matters. Synonyms may differ, too, in expressing value judgments; to be *resolute* is a virtue; to be *determined* expresses no value judgment; and to be *obstinate* is a fault.

The wealth of synonyms in English gives us a variety of ways of expressing ourselves, but challenges us to decide on the most appropriate of them.

EXERCISE 14. Writing Synonyms for Specific Words. Find three synonyms apiece for each of the following words. Use your dictionary if necessary. Be prepared to discuss differences between your synonyms.

1. sick	5. dangerous	9. dislike
2. expensive	6. talk	10. work
3. pleasant	7. walk	11. enjoyment
4. hard	8. see	12. knowledge

EXERCISE 15. Understanding the Difference Between Pairs of Synonyms. Be prepared to discuss in class differences between the following pairs of synonyms.

1. donation, gift
2. venomous, toxic
3. reverent, pious
4. lean, gaunt
5. meditate, ruminate

6. vapid, inane
7. void, vacuum
8. gracious, cordial
9. congenital, hereditary
10. handle, manipulate

Early in this chapter, you were advised to keep a vocabulary notebook in which to list new words and their meanings. If you have done so, your notebook should contain a number of new words drawn from this chapter and from the word list that follows it. Do not be content, however, to have these words in your notebook. Listen for them, and watch for them in your reading. Observing how a new word is used is the best way of learning to use it yourself. Your vocabulary notebook is like the address books people use to remind them of the names and addresses of people they don't encounter often. No one needs such a book for close acquaintances. Get into the habit of making old friends of new words.

REVIEW EXERCISE B. Selecting the Definitions of Words. Number your paper 1–20. After the proper number, write the letter of the word or expression that comes closest to the meaning of the italicized word.

1. *amorphous* clouds
   a) formless
   b) romantic
   c) jar-shaped
   d) commonplace
2. under the *auspices* of the state
   a) protests
   b) sponsorship
   c) opposition
   d) observation
3. struggle for *autonomy*
   a) fair treatment
   b) self-esteem
   c) survival
   d) self-rule
4. the last chance to *capitulate*
   a) turn the tide
   b) surrender
   c) negotiate
   d) compromise
5. *circumspect* behavior
   a) improper
   b) cautious
   c) surprising
   d) praiseworthy
6. to *collate* two documents
   a) preserve
   b) seal up
   c) duplicate
   d) compare

7. feeling no *compunction*
   - a) satisfaction
   - b) ambition
   - c) remorse
   - d) pride

8. to *conjecture* about a motive
   - a) guess
   - b) mislead
   - c) lie
   - d) find out

9. the soldier's *defection*
   - a) weakness
   - b) decoration
   - c) desertion
   - d) wound

10. not daring to *demur*
    - a) whisper
    - b) appear
    - c) object
    - d) tell the truth

11. *devoid* of sympathy
    - a) full
    - b) without a trace
    - c) deserving
    - d) undeserving

12. without *divulging* the answer
    - a) guessing
    - b) revealing
    - c) suspecting
    - d) peeking at

13. to *expiate* a crime
    - a) profit from
    - b) witness
    - c) atone for
    - d) facilitate

14. a *judicious* choice
    - a) illegal
    - b) required by law
    - c) wise
    - d) laughable

15. a *minute* creature
    - a) short-lived
    - b) quickly moving
    - c) very small
    - d) very young

16. *mundane* concerns
    - a) worldly
    - b) tedious
    - c) religious
    - d) dishonest

17. *parasitic* followers
    - a) loyal
    - b) living off others
    - c) disloyal
    - d) fanatical

18. a *propitious* start
    - a) proper
    - b) false
    - c) sudden
    - d) favorable

19. an unusual *pseudonym*
    - a) last name
    - b) antonym
    - c) pen name
    - d) honorary title

20. an act of *temerity*
    - a) cowardice
    - b) rage
    - c) uncertainty
    - d) foolish daring

Word List

In many of the following vocabulary words you will recognize the Old English, Latin, and Greek word parts you have just studied. Make it a habit to learn unfamiliar words from this list regularly; ten each week is a practical number. When you consult a dictionary for the meaning of an unfamiliar word, make sure you find the meaning that fits the context you have in mind, or ask your teacher to verify the meaning.

aberration
abeyance
abject
abnegation
abscond
absolve
abstruse
acrimonious
adjudge
adjure

admonish
adroit
affront
allay
amorphous
anarchy
antipathy
antipodes
apostasy
artifice

ascetic
ascribe
aspersion
assiduous
assimilate
atrophy
augury
auspices
austerity
avarice

aver
banal
bauble

bellicose
benevolence
biennial
blazon
bode
bravado
broach

buffoon
bullion
burnish
cadaverous
cajole
calumny
candor
capitulate
capricious
captivate

caricature
cessation
charlatan
chastise
chauvinism
chicanery
choleric
circumvent
civility
clandestine

coerce
cognizant
colloquy
commensurate
commiserate
commodious

conciliate
confer
configuration
connoisseur

consign
consternation
contingency
copious
corollary
corroborate
cosmopolitan
dearth
decorum
deduce

demagogue
denizen
deplore
desist
detriment
devoid
differentiate
dirge
discrepancy
discursive

disparity
dissent
distraught
diurnal
doggerel
dogma
duress
effusion
elegy

elicit

elocution
emaciate
emanate
empirical
engender
enigma
ennui
epitome
equanimity
equivocal

erudite
esoteric
espouse
ethereal
ethnology
eulogy
euphemism
euphony
evanescent
exhilaration

exhort
expatriate
expound
extant
extenuate
extol
extort
extraneous
extricate
facetious

facile
farcical
feign
festoon
fiasco
finesse

firmament
fissure
foible
foment

fortuitous
fresco
frugal
gambol
gauntlet
germane
glib
gratuitous
gregarious
guffaw

guile
hackneyed
harbinger
herculean
hiatus
homily
homogeneous
humdrum
hyperbole
idiosyncrasy

ignominy
illicit
immutable
impair
impassive
impeccable
incarcerate
incognito
inconsequential
incorrigible

indigent
indulgent
inexorable

infringe
ingenuous
iniquity
inordinate
inscrutable
intercede
introvert

inundate
inveigle
iridescent
irrevocable
lampoon
litigation
longevity
loquacious
ludicrous
lugubrious

magnanimous
maim
malign
malinger
maudlin
menial
mercurial
mesmerism
mete
misnomer

mollify
moot
mottled
mundane
munificent
nadir
nebulous
nefarious
nemesis
nettle

nondescript
nonentity
obese
obnoxious
obsequious
officious
omniscient
opulence
ostensible
pallor

paragon
parsimonious
patrimony
pecuniary
perfidious
pervade
pestilence
phlegmatic
poignant
precocious

precursor
predispose
prerogative
prevaricate
primordial
proffer
progeny
prognosis
promontory
propitious

proponent
propriety
prosaic
protégé
pseudonym
punctilious
purloin
quell

querulous
quiescent

rampant
recant
refute
regimen
remonstrate
remuneration
renounce
repository
reprisal
residual

restitution
retaliate
retroactive
retrospect
revile
sagacity
salient
saline
sanguine
scathing

scrupulous
scurrilous
sedentary
seraphic
solicitous
sonorous
specious
strident
subjugate
subversion

sumptuous
sundry
tacit
taciturn
temerity

tenable
tenuous
tenure
terra firma
testimonial

treatise
truism
usury
venal
venerate
vestige
vindicate
virulent
vociferous
voluminous

CHAPTER 38

Spelling

IMPROVING YOUR SPELLING

This chapter suggests a number of things you can do to improve your spelling:

1. Be careful.
2. Use the dictionary.
3. Keep a list of your own spelling errors.
4. Learn to spell words by syllables.
5. Learn a few helpful spelling rules.
6. Learn to distinguish between words that sound alike.
7. Learn lists of commonly misspelled words.

GOOD SPELLING HABITS

1. *Be careful.* Care in writing and in proofreading your compositions will eliminate errors in the spelling of simple words like *to, there*, and *its*, which account for so many of the teacher's corrections on students' themes.

2. *Use the dictionary.* Some students apparently think themselves allergic to the dictionary. They would rather take a chance on guessing than expose themselves to the truth. But the only sure way to find out how to spell a word is to look it up.

3. *Keep a list of your own spelling errors.* We do not all misspell the same words. Although it is a difficult habit to establish, the habit of recording in your notebook the words you misspell in your compositions will pay you a large return on the investment of a little time and patience.

4. *Learn to spell words by syllables.* This is the "divide and conquer" technique used with success by invading armies. It is equally effective in attacking a long and troublesome word. Dividing a long word into syllables gives a number of short parts. Short parts are simpler to spell than long ones; hence you can simplify your spelling problem by acquiring the habit of dividing words into syllables and spelling them part by part.

Two common causes of spelling mistakes are the omission of a letter or syllable and the addition of an extra letter or syllable. A student who spells *probably* as though it were *probaly* has made the first kind of mistake. If you spell *lightning* as though it were *lightening*, you have made the second kind. Errors like these are errors in pronunciation which, in turn, are the result of not knowing the exact syllables in the word.

Dividing a word into its pronounceable parts (syllables) will help you to pronounce and to spell the word correctly.

EXERCISE 1. Spelling Words by Syllables. Write each of the following words in syllables—place a hyphen between syllables. When you have completed the exercise and studied the words, take a test on them from dictation. Whether your divisions correspond exactly with the dictionary syllabication is not important, provided the words are divided into pronounceable parts and all letters are included and no letters are added.

1. modern	5. privilege	9. representative
2. similar	6. perspiration	10. entrance
3. library	7. boundary	11. lightning
4. surprise	8. candidate	12. accidentally

EXERCISE 2. Spelling Words by Syllables. Follow directions for the preceding exercise.

1. athletics	5. equipment	9. sophomore
2. disastrous	6. temperament	10. quiet
3. government	7. recognize	11. mischievous
4. undoubtedly	8. business	12. curiosity

SPELLING RULES

5. *Learn a few helpful spelling rules.* Although some spelling rules are hopelessly complicated, a few are simple enough and important enough to justify the effort required to master them. Study the following rules and apply them whenever possible in your writing.

ie and *ei*

38a. Write *ie* when the sound is *ē*, except after *c*.

EXAMPLES believe, thief, fierce   ceiling, receive, deceive
EXCEPTIONS seize, either, weird, leisure, neither

Write *ei* when the sound is not *ē*, especially when the sound is *ā*.

EXAMPLES freight, neighbor, weigh, height
EXCEPTIONS friend, mischief

EXERCISE 3. Spelling *ie* and *ei* Words. Write the following words, supplying the missing letters (*e* and *i*) in the correct order. Be able to explain how the rule applies to each.

1. for&#2;.gn	7. c...ling	13. ach...ve	19. bel...ve
2. br..f	8. gr...f	14. handkerch...f	20. w...rd
3. rel...ve	9. p...ce	15. perc...ve	21. rec...pt
4. conc...ve	10. rec...ve	16. th...f	22. bel...f
5. v...l	11. retr...ve	17. s...ge	23. f...nd
6. n...ce	12. sl...gh	18. s...ze	24. l...sure

–cede, –ceed, and –sede

weird

38b. Only one English word ends in *–sede*: *supersede*; only three words end in *–ceed*: *exceed*, *proceed*, *succeed*; all other words of similar sound end in *–cede*.

EXAMPLES precede, recede, secede, accede, concede

Adding Prefixes

A *prefix* is one or more than one letter or syllable added to the beginning of a word to change its meaning.

38c. When a prefix is added to a word, the spelling of the word itself remains the same.

il + legal = **il**legal

in + elegant = **in**elegant

im + movable = **im**movable

un + necessary = **un**necessary

un + excused = **un**excused

a + moral = **a**moral

mis + understood = **mis**understood

mis + spell = **mis**spell

re + commend = **re**commend

over + run = **over**run

over + eat = **over**eat

Adding Suffixes

A *suffix* is one or more than one letter or syllable added to the end of a word to change its meaning.

38d. When the suffixes *–ness* and *–ly* are added to a word, the spelling of the word itself is not changed.

EXAMPLES   mean + ness = mean**ness**

final + ly = final**ly**

EXCEPTIONS   Words ending in *y* usually change the *y* to *i* before *–ness* and *–ly*: ready—read**ily**; heavy—heav**iness**; happy—happ**iness**. One-syllable adjectives ending in *y,* however, generally follow Rule 38d: dry—dry**ness**; shy—shy**ly**.

EXERCISE 4. Spelling Words with Prefixes and Suffixes.

Spell correctly the words indicated.

1. *rate* with the prefix *over*
2. *habitual* with the suffix *ly*
3. *agree* with the prefix *dis*
4. *green* with the suffix *ness*
5. *material* with the prefix *im*
6. *appoint* with the prefix *dis*
7. *apprehend* with the prefix *mis*
8. *practical* with the suffix *ly*
9. *abated* with the prefix *un*
10. *casual* with the suffix *ly*
11. *natural* with the prefix *un*
12. *stubborn* with the suffix *ness*
13. *legible* with the prefix *il*
14. *appropriate* with the prefix *in*
15. *appear* with the prefix *dis*
16. *movable* with the prefix *im*
17. *construct* with the prefix *re*
18. *animate* with the prefix *in*
19. *similar* with the prefix *dis*
20. *keen* with the suffix *ness*
21. *spell* with the prefix *mis*
22. *use* with the prefix *mis*
23. *avoidable* with the prefix *un*
24. *merry* with the suffix *ly*

38e. Drop the final *e* before a suffix beginning with a vowel.

EXAMPLES   care + ing = caring   use + able = usable

EXCEPTIONS   Keep the final *e* before *a* or *o* if necessary to retain the soft sound
of *c* or *g* preceding the *e*: noticeable, courageous

38f. Keep the final *e* before a suffix beginning with a consonant.

EXAMPLES   care + ful = careful   care + less − careless

EXCEPTIONS   true + ly = truly   argue + ment = argument
acknowledge + ment = acknowledgment [more usual spelling]

38g. With words ending in *y* preceded by a consonant, change the *y* to
i before any suffix not beginning with *i*.

EXAMPLES   funny—funnier; hurry—hurried; hurry—hurrying

38h. Double the final consonant before a suffix that begins with a
vowel if both of the following conditions exist: (1) the word has only
one syllable or is accented on the last syllable; (2) the word ends in a
single consonant preceded by a single vowel.

EXAMPLES   plan + ing = planning [one-syllable word]

forget + ing = forgetting [accent on last syllable; single consonant
and single vowel]

cancel + ed = canceled [accent not on last syllable]

prefer + able = preferable [accent shifts; not on last syllable]

EXERCISE 5. Spelling Words with Suffixes. Write correctly the
words formed as follows:

1. defer + ed
2. defer + ence
3. hope + ing
4. approve + al
5. benefit + ed
6. nine + ty
7. prepare + ing
8. profit + ing
9. write + ing
10. propel + ing
11. desire + able
12. control + ed
13. hope + less
14. move + ing
15. true + ly
16. run + ing
17. singe + ing
18. fame + ous
19. name + less
20. red + est

The Plural of Nouns

38i. Observe the rules for spelling the plural of nouns.

(1) The regular way to form the plural of a noun is to add _s_.

EXAMPLES   chair, chairs   book, books

(2) The plural of some nouns is formed by adding _es_.

The _e_ represents the extra sound heard when –_s_ is added to words ending in _s, sh, ch,_ and _x_.

EXAMPLES   dress, dresses   birch, birches
           box, boxes   bush, bushes

(3) The plural of nouns ending in _y preceded by a consonant_ is formed by changing the _y_ to _i_ and adding _es_.

EXAMPLES   fly, flies   enemy, enemies   lady, ladies   salary, sal-
                                                              aries

(4) The plural of nouns ending in _y preceded by a vowel_ is formed by adding an _s_.

EXAMPLES   monkey, monkeys   donkey, donkeys

(5) The plural of most nouns ending in _f_ or _fe_ is formed by adding _s_. The plural of some nouns ending in _f_ or _fe_ is formed by changing the _f_ to _v_ and adding _s_ or _es_.

EXAMPLES   Add _s_: roof, roofs   dwarf, dwarfs   chief, chiefs

           Change _f_ to _v_ and add _s_ or _es_:
                   knife, knives   calf, calves
                   loaf, loaves   wharf, wharves
                   leaf, leaves

(6) The plural of nouns ending in _o preceded by a vowel_ is formed by adding _s_. The plural of nouns ending in _o preceded by a consonant_ is formed by adding either _s_ or _es_.

EXAMPLES   _o_ following a vowel:
                   rodeo, rodeos   radio, radios

           _o_ following a consonant:
                   hero, heroes   potato, potatoes
                   mosquito, mosquitoes

EXCEPTIONS   Words of Italian origin ending in _o_ that refer to music form the plural by adding _s_: piano, pianos; soprano, sopranos; solo, solos.

(7) The plural of a few nouns is formed by irregular methods.

EXAMPLES   child, children   mouse, mice   ox, oxen
                woman, women   tooth, teeth   goose, geese

(8) The plural of compound nouns written as one word is formed by adding *s* or *es*.

EXAMPLES   cupful, cupfuls
                leftover, leftovers
                strongbox, strongboxes

(9) The plural of compound nouns consisting of a noun plus a modifier is formed by making the noun plural.

In the following examples, the phrases *in-law* and *of-war* and the adjectives *martial, general*, and *by* are all modifiers. It is the nouns modified by them that are made plural.

EXAMPLES   mother-in-law, mothers-in-law
                man-of-war, men-of-war
                court martial, courts martial
                secretary-general, secretaries-general
                passer-by, passers-by

(10) The plural of a few compound nouns is formed in irregular ways.

EXAMPLES   drive-in, drive-ins
                tie-up, tie-ups
                six-year-old, six-year-olds

(11) Some nouns are the same in the singular and the plural.

EXAMPLES   sheep, deer, trout, species, Chinese

(12) The plural of some foreign words is formed as in the original language.

EXAMPLES   alumnus (*man*), alumni (*men*)
                alumna (*woman*), alumnae (*women*)
                datum, data
                crisis, crises

(13) The plural of other foreign words may be formed either as in the foreign language or by adding *s* or *es*.

EXAMPLES   index, indices *or* indexes
                appendix, appendices *or* appendixes

> ☞ **NOTE** In certain words the English plural is the preferred one, for example, *formulas* not *formulae.* Whenever there is any doubt about which plural to use, consult the dictionary.

(14) The plural of numbers, letters, signs, and words considered as words is formed by adding an apostrophe and an *s.*

EXAMPLES   If you think there are ten 5's in that column, you'd better count again.
There are two *s*'s in *necessary.*
My last paper was full of 0's, not +'s.
Don't use too many *I*'s in writing your paper.

EXERCISE 6. Writing the Plural Form of Nouns. Write the plural form of each of the following nouns. Be able to explain your spelling on the basis of the rules.

1. candy	8. chief	15. bench
2. sheep	9. tomato	16. editor in chief
3. piano	10. gas	17. spoonful
4. valley	11. fly	18. hero
5. alumnus	12. alto	19. knife
6. cameo	13. brother-in-law	20. goose
7. torch	14. shelf	

EXERCISE 7. Explaining the Spellings of Words. By referring to the rules on the preceding pages, explain the spelling of each of the following:

1. regretted	8. misstate	15. occurred
2. receive	9. stubbornness	16. writing (*e* dropped)
3. illegible	10. peaceable	17. roofs
4. coming (*e* dropped)	11. ladies	18. weigh
5. conferring	12. conference	19. disappear
6. niece	13. alumnae	20. naturally
7. contraltos	14. leisure	

WORDS THAT SOUND ALIKE

6. *Learn to distinguish between words that sound alike.* These words present problems because they sound alike but have different meanings and different spellings. You probably have had trouble distinguishing between *principle* and *principal, capital* and *capitol,* and other such pairs. Most of the paired words in the following lists sound alike. Some pairs, however, are confused even though they are not pronounced exactly alike.

already	*previously* I had *already* seen the movie twice.
all ready	*all are ready* (or *wholly ready*) Give the signal when you are *all ready.*
all right	[This word really does not belong in this list, but it is included here because many persons think there is a word spelled *alright*, as though *all right* did have a homonym. There is no word *alright*. The correct spelling is always *all right*.]
altar	*a table or stand in a church* or *a place for outdoor offerings* The priest was standing beside the *altar.*
alter	*to change* If we are late, we will *alter* our plans.
altogether	*entirely* She doesn't *altogether* approve of me.
all together	*everyone in the same place* We were *all together* at Christmas.
born	*given birth* When were you *born*?
borne	*carried* He has *borne* his hardships bravely.
brake	*device to stop a machine* A defective *brake* caused the accident.
break	*to fracture, shatter* Try not to *break* any dishes.
capital	*city*; also, as an adjective, *punishable by death* or *of major importance*

Washington, D.C., is the *capital* of this country.
Killing a police officer is a *capital* offense.
That is a *capital* idea.

capitol *building*
The *capitol* faces a park.

---

cloths *pieces of cloth*
Try the new cleaning *cloths*.

clothes *wearing apparel*
Her *clothes* are expensive.

EXERCISE 8. Selecting Correct Spelling Words to Complete Sentences. Number your paper 1–20. Write after the proper number the correct one of the words given in parentheses in the sentences below.

1. The damage has (already, all ready) been done.
2. Mother was (all together, altogether) too surprised to protest.
3. Events have (born, borne) out my predictions.
4. Pete is an (altar, alter) boy at St. Anne's Church.
5. If you (brake, break) a window, you will pay for it.
6. When you are (already, all ready), I will help you.
7. Belgrade is the (capital, capitol) of Yugoslavia.
8. (Altar, Alter) the neckline and I will buy the dress.
9. My mother was (born, borne) in France.
10. Was her work (alright, all right)?
11. We polished the car with (cloths, clothes).
12. We will (altar, alter) the building to suit tenants.
13. The dome on the (capital, capitol) is illuminated at night.
14. The club members were (all together, altogether) only once.
15. Cars are (born, borne) across the river on a ferry.
16. Herbert was wearing his best (cloths, clothes).
17. When did the Supreme Court rule on (capital, capitol) punishment?
18. I applied the (brakes, breaks) immediately.
19. Are you feeling (all right, alright)?
20. The family were (all together, altogether) on my birthday.

---

coarse *rough, crude*
He wore a suit of *coarse* cloth and used *coarse* language.

course   *path of action; part of a meal; a series of studies*
The golf *course* is outside of town.
Soup was the first *course*.
I am taking a *course* in cooking.

---

complement   *something that completes or makes perfect*
The *complement* of 50° is 40°. [*completes* a 90° angle]
His part of the job *complements* mine. [Together they
   complete the job.]

compliment   *a remark that says something good about a person; to say*
   something good
I am pleased by your *compliment*.
She *complimented* me on my backhand.

---

consul   *representative of a foreign country*
The American *consul* in Quito helped us during our visit.

council,   *a group called together to accomplish a job; a member of*
   councilor   *such a group is a councilor*
The *council* met to welcome a new *councilor*.

counsel,   *advice; the giving of advice; one who gives advice is a*
   counselor   *counselor*
I accepted the wise *counsel* of my *counselor*.

---

des′ert   *a dry region*
We flew across the *desert*.

desert′   *to leave*
She *deserted* her friends in their time of need.

dessert′   *the final course of a meal*
The *dessert* was ice cream.

---

formally   *conventionally or properly, according to strict rules*
She spoke *formally* and with great dignity.

formerly   *in the past, previously*
I was *formerly* a member of that club.

---

its   [possessive]
The village is proud of *its* school.

it's   *it is*
It's a long way.

later	*more late* We will arrive *later*.
latter	*the second of two* When given the choice of a football or a tennis racket I chose the *latter*.

lead	[present tense] *to go first* You *lead* and we will follow.
led	[past tense] She *led* the team to victory.
lead	[pronounced **lĕd**] *a heavy metal*, also *graphite in a pencil* The industrial uses of *lead* are many.

EXERCISE 9. Selecting Correct Spelling Words to Complete Sentences. Number your paper 1–20. Write after the proper number the correct one of the words given in parentheses in the sentences below.

1. Our (consul, counsel) in Romania has returned to Washington.
2. I enjoyed the dinner but not the (dessert, desert).
3. Avoid (course, coarse) language.
4. Mr. Abrams was (formally, formerly) vice-president of the bank.
5. No (councilor, counselor) may serve more than three years on the council.
6. I do not enjoy parties conducted as (formally, formerly) as this one.
7. The walls of the room were papered, but (its, it's) ceiling had been painted.
8. Some people are distrustful of (compliments, complements).
9. We are not sure which (course, coarse) to follow.
10. (Desert, Dessert) soil is often fertile if irrigated.
11. Are you sure (its, it's) not too late?
12. I spent five summers working as a camp (councilor, counselor).
13. A golf (course, coarse) requires continual care.
14. I spoke to the mayor and the superintendent; the (later, latter) was more helpful.
15. I can't recall his ever giving me a (complement, compliment) on my writing.
16. The soldiers who (deserted, desserted) were finally caught.
17. The guidance (councilor, counselor) advised me to take the test.

18. During his senior year, Albert (lead, led) the team to a championship.
19. Have you finished your (course, coarse) in hygiene?
20. These supplies will (complement, compliment) those you already have.

---

loose
free, not close together
The animals broke *loose*.
They stumbled in the *loose* sand.

lose
[pronounced **lo͞oz**] *to suffer loss*
When did you *lose* your books?

---

miner
worker in a mine
A *miner's* job is sometimes dangerous.

minor
under legal age; less important
A *minor* cannot marry without a parent's or guardian's consent.
They raised only *minor* objections.

---

moral
good; also *a lesson of conduct*
His good conduct showed him to be a *moral* person.
The class understood the *moral* of the story.

morale
mental condition, spirit
The *morale* in our school is excellent.

---

passed
verb
The Fiat *passed* me at the finish line.

past
noun or adjective or preposition
Some persons prefer to live in the *past* (n.) because *past* (adj.) events seem more interesting than present ones.
I went *past* (prep.) your house without realizing it.

---

peace
opposite of strife
Everyone prefers *peace* to war.

piece
a part of something
They ate every *piece* of cake.

---

personal
individual
He gave his *personal* opinion.

personnel
a group of people employed in the same place
The *personnel* of the company ranged in age from 16 to 64.

---

plain
not fancy; also *a flat area of land*; also *clear*
She lives in a very *plain* home.

We crossed the *plains* in two days.
Our problem is *plain*.

plane   *a flat surface; also a tool; also an airplane*
Plane geometry is a study of imaginary flat surfaces.
The carpenter used a *plane*.
A *plane* circled the airport.

principal   *head of a school; also the main one of several things*
They went to the *principal's* office.
The *principal* cause of accidents is carelessness.

principle   *a rule of conduct; also a main fact or law*
The judge accused the criminal of having no *principles*.
She understands the *principles* of mathematics.

quiet   *still, silent*
A study hall should be *quiet*.

quite   *completely, wholly; also to a great extent or degree*
I had *quite* forgotten her advice.
Angela is *quite* tall.

EXERCISE 10. Selecting Correct Spelling Words to Complete Sentences. Number your paper 1–20. Write after the proper number the correct one of the words given in parentheses in the sentences that follow.

1. My troubles this year have been (miner, minor) ones.
2. Winning three games in a row boosted our basketball team's (moral, morale).
3. All three nations signed a (peace, piece) treaty.
4. Do these printed instructions seem (plain, plane) to you?
5. This store's sales (personal, personnel) are very helpful.
6. The assistant (principal, principle) will make the announcement.
7. The (principal, principle) of solar energy is easy to understand.
8. If you (loose, lose) your concentration, you might (loose, lose) the tennis match.
9. Suddenly the room became very (quiet, quite).
10. D. H. Lawrence often wrote about coal (miners, minors).
11. Can you tell the (principal, principle) parts of the verb "to shrink"?
12. I had a (peace, piece) of pumpkin pie for dessert.
13. One of the bolts was (loose, lose).

14. I filled out a job application form in the (personal, personnel) department.
15. Students should remain (quiet, quite) during a study period.
16. We (passed, past) through Indiana on our way to Illinois.
17. Does every fable have a (moral, morale)?
18. On my way to school I always walk (passed, past) the bakery.
19. If you can vote, you are officially no longer a (miner, minor).
20. She is a person who always tries to live up to her (principals, principles).

stationary	*in a fixed position* The classroom desks are *stationary*.
stationery	*writing paper* I received three boxes of *stationery* at Christmas.
than	conjunction I am stronger *than* she.
then	adverb meaning *at the time* Wear a green hat; *then* I'll recognize you.
there	*a place*; also used as an expletive (see pages 31–32) We were *there* at two o'clock. *There* were four of us.
their	[possessive] The pupils bring *their* own lunches.
they're	*they are* *They're* going with us.
to	a preposition or part of the infinitive form of a verb Give the book *to* me, please. We will have *to* leave early.
too	adverb meaning *also* or *too much* George is a sophmore, *too*. It is *too* late to go now.
two	*one plus one* We had only *two* dollars.
waist	*middle part of the body* She wore a wide belt around her *waist*.
waste	*unused material*; also *to squander* Pollution can be caused by industrial *wastes*. Don't *waste* your time.

who's	*who is, who has* *Who's* coming? *Who's* been here?
whose	[possessive] *Whose* coat is this?

your	[possessive] Is this *your* coat?
you're	*you are* *You're* a true friend.

EXERCISE 11. Selecting Correct Spelling Words to Complete Sentences. Number your paper 1–20. Write after the proper number the correct one of the words given in parentheses in the following sentences:

1. They had neglected to lock (there, their) lockers.
2. I wanted to go to camp, (to, two, too).
3. Tie the rope around your (waist, waste).
4. The platform, we discovered when we tried to move it, was (stationary, stationery).
5. No one could remember (whose, who's) name had been drawn first.
6. This year's annual will be larger (than, then) last year's.
7. Where do you think (your, you're) going?
8. Some students regard the class as a (waist, waste) of time.
9. The work was (to, too) strenuous for me.
10. I used school (stationary, stationery) for my letters.
11. When (you're, your) homework has been finished, call me.
12. I do not know (whose, who's) going to solve the problem.
13. As soon as (their, they're) printed, we will ship the books.
14. Write your letters on business (stationary, stationery).
15. (Your, You're) lucky to have such a good job.
16. I cannot do any more (then, than) I have done.
17. In only a few minutes we earned (to, two, too) dollars.
18. I'd like to know (who's, whose) responsible for this mess.
19. I was surprised at (you're, your) taking that attitude.
20. Chemistry has converted many (waste, waist) products into valuable commodities.

REVIEW EXERCISE. Selecting Correct Spelling Words to Complete Sentences. Number your paper 1–40. After the proper number, write the correct one of the words in parentheses in the following sentences:

1. Columbia is the (capital, capitol) of South Carolina.
2. Everything seemed to be (alright, all right).
3. Mrs. Starkey (complemented, complimented) me on my grades.
4. Have you discussed this problem with your guidance (councilor, counselor)?
5. We were blown several miles from our (course, coarse).
6. The letters have (all ready, already) been mailed.
7. The vegetation in the (dessert, desert) surprised us.
8. Mrs. Crane (formally, formerly) taught here.
9. Every nation must conserve (its, it's) resources.
10. My companion (lead, led) me down a dark passage.
11. We were (all ready, already) to start before dawn.
12. Try not to (lose, loose) your keys.
13. Success is the best (moral, morale) builder.
14. Their (coarse, course) manners were not amusing.
15. We were told not to ask for a second (piece, peace) of pie.
16. The new (altar, alter) is made of white marble.
17. I have read all of Murdoch and Spark, and I prefer the (later, latter).
18. You must go to the (principal, principle) to get a permit.
19. (Its, It's) time to think about getting a job.
20. There was (all together, altogether) no truth in the report.
21. Members of the (counsel, council) are elected annually.
22. A (capital, capitol) offense will cost you your life.
23. Everyone is (all ready, already).
24. (Course, Coarse) wood absorbs more paint than fine-grained wood.
25. My red tie (complements, compliments) my blue suit.
26. Jack (past, passed) the ball to Joe.
27. When you are (all together, altogether), I'll take a group picture.
28. The mission was accomplished without loss of (personal, personnel).
29. The company embarked on the strongest advertising campaign in (its, it's) history.
30. What are the (principal, principle) products of Puerto Rico?
31. We prefer (stationary, stationery) seats in our classrooms.
32. There's a student (whose, who's) going to succeed.

33. His act was not outstanding, but it was (alright, all right).
34. She always uses (plain, plane) stationery.
35. When we had cleaned our lockers, the (waistpaper, wastepaper) littered the floor.
36. The (principals, principles) of democracy are admired.
37. Do you know (they're, their, there) new address?
38. Why didn't the campers follow their (counselor's, councilor's) instructions?
39. (Who's, Whose) pen is this?
40. Mrs. Smith gave our play (complimentary, complementary) reviews.

COMMONLY MISSPELLED WORDS

7. *Learn lists of commonly misspelled words.* Frequent short spelling tests are an effective means of fixing correct spellings in your mind. On the following pages you will find a list of 300 commonly misspelled words. Taking no more than twenty at a time, have these words dictated to you. Study the ones you miss and record them in your list of spelling errors. When you have studied them (divided them into syllables and practiced writing each word several times), write them again from dictation. Spelling tests should be written, not oral.

Three Hundred Spelling Words[1]

abundant	adolescent	attendance
academically	advantageous	awfully
accelerator	aerial	ballet
accessible	allege	bankruptcy
accidentally	allegiance	barbarian
acclimated		basketball
accommodation	alliance	beggar
accompaniment	allotting	behavior
accomplishment	annihilate	beneficial
accuracy	anonymous	bibliography
	apologetically	
acknowledge	apparatus	biscuit
acquaintance	apparent	blasphemy
adequately	arousing	boulevard
admission	arrangement	bracelet
admittance	atheistic	buffet

[1] The list does not include the homonyms listed on pages 930–37.

bureaucrat
burial
calculation
camouflage
capitalism

carburetor
caricature
catalog
catastrophe
cellar
cemetery
changeable
chassis
Christianity
circumstantial

colossal
communist
comparative
competition
complexion
conceivable
connoisseur
conscientious
consciousness
consistency

controlling
controversy
cruelty
curriculum
debacle
decadent
deceitful
deference
descendant
desirable

despair
detrimental
devastation
devise
dilemma

diligence
disastrous
disciple
discrimination
diseased

dissatisfied
division
ecstasy
efficiency
embarrassment
emperor
emphasize
endeavor
enormous
entertainment

enthusiastically
entrance
environment
espionage
exhaustion
exhibition
exhilaration
expensive
exuberant
familiarize

fascination
fascism
feminine
financier
fission
forfeit
fulfill
fundamentally
gaiety
galaxy

gauge
grammatically
guidance
harassment
hereditary

hindrance
horizontal
hospital
hygiene
hypocrisy

hypocrisy

ideally
idiomatic
incidentally
independent
indispensable
inevitable
influential
ingenious
initiative
innocent

inoculate
institution
intellectual
interference
irrelevant
irresistible
kerosene
laborious
larynx
leisurely

license
liquor
livelihood
luxurious
magistrate
magnificence
maintenance
malicious
manageable
maneuver

marriageable
martyrdom
materialism
meadow
mediocre

3 Xerox

Oct 11, '93

Feb 8

melancholy	picnicking	statistics
melodious	playwright	strategic
metaphor	pneumonia	stubbornness
miniature	politician	succeed
mischievous	precede	succession
misspelled	presence	summed
mortgage	prestige	superintendent
mosquito	presumption	supersede
municipal	prevalent	suppress
mysterious	privilege	surroundings
naive	procedure	susceptible
necessity	propaganda	symbolic
neurotic	propagate	symmetrical
noticeable	prophesy	symphonic
novelist	prove	synonymous
nucleus	psychoanalysis	tariff
nuisance	pursue	temperament
nutritious	quietly	temperature
obedience	rebellion	tendency
occasionally	receive	theoretical
occurrence	recommendation	tolerance
omitting	reference	tomorrow
opportunity	referred	tortoise
orchestra	rehearsal	traffic
outrageous	relieve	tragedy
pageant	reminiscent	transcend
pamphlet	remittance	transparent
paralysis	representative	tried
parliament	resources	twelfth
pastime	responsibility	tyranny
peasant	reveal	undoubtedly
pedestal	safety	universal
penicillin	seize	unmistakable
perceive	separation	unnatural
permanent	sergeant	unnecessary
permissible	siege	unscrupulous
persistent	significance	vaccine
perspiration	souvenir	vacuum
phenomenon	specimen	valedictory
physician	sponsor	variation

vaudeville	villain	whistle
vehicle	vinegar	withhold
vengeance	visage	yacht
versatile	welcome	yawn
vigilance	whisper	yield

CHAPTER 39

Test-Taking Skills

COLLEGE ENTRANCE AND OTHER EXAMINATIONS

No matter what your plans for the years following high school, it is more than likely that you will be asked to "take some tests." Many of the most commonly administered tests include measures of verbal fluency, reading comprehension, and/or grammar and composition.

Among the tests of this type used for college entrance, the best known are probably the *Scholastic Aptitude Test—Verbal*, or SAT–V (including the *Test of Standard Written English*), and the *English Composition Test*, or "English Achievement" test. Both of these tests are administered by the College Entrance Examination Board, or CEEB. Another well-known test is the American College Testing (ACT) Program Assessment Test.

Many schools and colleges do *not* require tests for admission but do administer tests for placement in courses and for guidance purposes after you have registered. The military and other employers may also, on occasion, administer tests of English vocabulary, reading, or grammar when such skills can be shown to be important to success in the job.

Tests with the word *aptitude* in their titles are used mainly to predict future success, whether in school or on the job. They do not, on the whole, measure what you have learned in particular courses. They measure the English language skills which you have been developing all your life through your habitual listening, reading, and speaking.

Achievement tests, on the other hand, concentrate on specific skills and understandings which you have learned in the courses taken to complete your academic program.

Cramming is *not* an appropriate or helpful way to prepare for tests of this nature. There are, however, a number of good test-taking practices that will help you to do your best on any examination. These may be summarized as follows:

SUMMARY OF TEST-TAKING PRACTICES

1. *Take a positive approach to the test.*

   a. Try to do your best even though you may be nervous. Don't panic.

   b. Regard lapses of memory as normal. If you "block" on a certain question, go on and come back to it later if you can.

   c. Don't expect to answer every question correctly. Some of the tests we are discussing are built so that the average student will answer only about half of the questions correctly.

2. *Use your time wisely.*

   a. Look over the test before you start to work. Get a feel for its length and difficulty.

   b. Plan your time. If you have a time limit of 20 minutes for a 40-question test, check that you are on or beyond question 21 after 10 minutes. But don't be an excessive clock-watcher. Clock-watching uses up your time and heightens anxiety.

   c. Work rapidly but carefully. Answer the easy questions first. If you don't know an answer right away, leave it and go on. Easy questions "count" just as much as hard ones.

   d. If you have time after finishing the test, try some of the questions you left out the first time. (On the ACT, you are not penalized for guessing.)

3. *Avoid careless errors.*

   a. Pay close attention to directions. Do the sample questions even though you're sure you understand the task.

   b. Read each question carefully. Be sure you know exactly what it is asking you to do.

   c. Look at all the choices before you answer. In many cases the correct answer is not *absolutely* correct; it is the *best* among the choices you have been given. Be *sure* to compare all the choices before picking the one you believe to be the best answer.

d. Avoid careless mistakes in marking the answer sheet. Keep it lined up with the booklet if possible. Be sure you make your mark in the correct manner in the correct row for the question. The scoring machine can't tell when you were "off" by one question or one row.

e. If you change an answer, be sure you erase the first answer thoroughly. If the machine "reads" both marks, it will count the question as unanswered.

One of the best ways to prepare for any test is to become familiar with the types of tasks you will be asked to perform. Many test questions will be similar to those on tests you have taken before. Others may be new to you. The purpose of this chapter is to show you some of these question types. When any test you take makes use of them you will, in a sense, be on familiar ground.

TESTS OF WORD KNOWLEDGE OR VOCABULARY

Vocabulary tests measure your understanding of the meaning of words, either in isolation or in context. Often, the relationships among words—the way they are related in meaning—will be tested. Examples of three types of vocabulary questions follow.

Word Meanings

The simplest type of vocabulary question simply asks you the meaning of a word. Usually, the format is an incomplete statement to which you add one of several choices to complete the meaning. The following is a sample question of this type.

EXAMPLE **A** To whet one's appetite is to ——

    a wean it
    b salve it
    c sharpen it
    d appease it   Answer:[1]
    e dampen it   **A** ⓐ ⓑ ● ⓓ ⓔ

Some questions of this type ask for a choice between *phrases* explaining the word's meaning or use; others offer *single words* and ask you to choose a synonym of the key word.

[1] Answer: © *sharpen it*. When you have marked your answer sheet for © this is the way it will look. You will black in the circle containing the letter of the correct answer. Answers are shown this way for all sample test items throughout this chapter.

EXERCISE 1. Choosing the Correct Meaning. Read the beginning of each sentence below and the choices that follow it. Choose the answer which best completes the sentence.[2]

1 A person who is talkative is ——

    a fervent
    b reticent
    c jocular
    d loquacious

2 To be nimble is to be ——

    a gracious
    b agile
    c numb
    d earthy

3 Material you can see through is called ——

    a opaque
    b potential
    c imaginary
    d transparent

4 Something that is powerful must be ——

    a lavish
    b lenient
    c potent
    d malicious

5 To condense something is to ——

    a abridge it
    b accelerate it
    c abolish it
    d acclaim it

Synonyms and Antonyms

In a test on synonyms or antonyms you are asked to select, from four or five choices, the word *most similar* in meaning (synonym) to the word given *or* the word *most nearly opposite* in meaning (antonym). *Pay attention!* These are sometimes mixed together. Careful reading will

---

[2] Answers for this and all the following exercises will be found on page 967.

help you here. There are very few true synonyms or antonyms in English; the "correct" answer, therefore, is the one most nearly the same or most nearly the opposite in meaning—it need only be better than the other choices.

Following are three sample questions in which you are to find the word *most similar* in meaning (synonym) to the underlined word.

EXAMPLES **A** disclose

    a react
    b darken
    c resound
    d visualize
    e reveal

      B impediment

    a agreement
    b obstacle
    c idiot
    d outline
    e utterance

      C enervate

    a encourage
    b enlarge
    c bemoan
    d weaken
    e cut

Answers:

A (a) (b) (c) (d) ●
B (a) ● (c) (d) (e)
C (a) (b) (c) ● (e)

You will note that in the last question, a common misconception of the word's meaning is included among the choices. Many people are confused as to whether *enervate* means to take "nerve" away or to give it; hence *encourage* is given as an incorrect choice.

EXERCISE 2. Choosing the Antonym.   For each of the following questions, choose the word *most nearly opposite* in meaning (antonym) to the underlined word.

1 abstract

    a extract
    b general
    c concrete
    d ideal
    e difficult

2 chronic   a occasional
             b habitual
             c public
             d unimportant
             e healthy

3 detriment a complement
             b loss
             c damage
             d attribute
             e benefit

4 abate   a fall
             b shrink
             c subside
             d increase
             e release

5 transient a swift
             b permanent
             c polite
             d sure
             e passenger

Verbal Analogies

Analogies are designed to measure your understanding of the relationships existing among words. Here is a sample set of directions and one question.

EXAMPLE   In the items below, the first and second words are related in a certain way. The third word is related in the same way to one of the four words which follow it. You are to choose the word related to the third word in the same way that the second word is related to the first.

   A *Inch* is to *foot* as *ounce* is to ——

      a weight
      b meter
      c yard   Answer:
      d pound   **A** ⓐ ⓑ ⓒ ●

In this sample question, the relationship tested is that of a unit of measurement to a larger unit in the same scale. An inch is a division of a foot. Hence, the correct answer is *pound* since an ounce is a division of a pound. *Weight* is an attractive wrong choice, since an ounce is a unit of weight, but the relationship is not parallel to that between *inch* and *foot*. If the first part of the analogy had been *inch* and *length*, then *weight* would have been the best answer.

Analogies may also be presented as shown in the following example.

EXAMPLE Below is a list of five pairs of related words. Choose the pair of words whose relationship is most like that of the first pair.

A INCH: FOOT::

    a quart: measure
    b weight: peck
    c ounce: pound
    d mile: length   Answer:
    e meter: yard   **A** ⓐ ⓑ ● ⓓ ⓔ

The same relationship is being measured here as was measured in the first example. *Ounce* is related to *pound* as *inch* is related to *foot*. But here you are to find the whole pair. In the first example, the first part of the second pair was given to you. If you are not familiar with analogies, it may help to turn them into sentences such as the one in the first example.

Suppose the first pair of words were *glance* and *gaze*. They are both "ways of looking at something." But a *glance* is a quick look, usually superficial or casual, while *gaze* has the idea of a long, careful, or thoughtful look. Which of these combinations, then, has the same relationship between the words?

EXAMPLE **A** GLANCE: GAZE::

    a blink: scowl
    b glimpse: stare
    c observe: note
    d skim: peek   Answer:
    e peruse: study   **A** ⓐ ● ⓒ ⓓ ⓔ

Option b would be the most similar pair to complete the analogy, since *glimpse* also implies a quick once-over, and *stare* gives the notion of a long and concentrated look. Another way to check your understanding of the analogy is to compare the first and third parts, and then check to see if the second and fourth parts have the same relationship. In the original example, this check would take the form: "*inch* is to *ounce* as *foot* is to ——?"

EXERCISE 3. Completing Analogies. In the items below, the first and second words are related in a certain way. The third word is related in the same way to one of the five words which follow. Choose the word related to the third word in the same way as the second word is related to the first.

1 *Clear* is to *cloudy* as *definite* is to ——

a sunny
b vague
c bright
d positive
e short

2 *Reckless* is to *cautious* as *rash* is to ——

a hasty
b impudent
c careless
d prudent
e smooth

3 *Gaggle* is to *goose* as *pride* is to ——

a lion
b vain
c king
d bear
e eagle

4 *Calm* is to *storm* as *quell* is to ——

a traffic
b crowd
c ink
d riot
e nerve

5 *Encourage* is to *scold* as *chide* is to ——

a punish
b praise
c query
d insult
e forbid

In the following items, choose the pair of words whose relationship is most similar to that of the first pair given.

6 LIMP: WALK::

    a snore: sleep
    b walk: ride
    c whistle: sing
    d stutter: speak

7 QUARRY: STONE::

    a rock: mineral
    b mine: ore
    c soil: field
    d oil: drill

8 SALVE: WOUND::

    a eraser: pencil
    b drink: thirst
    c save: money
    d sword: scabbard

9 LAVISH: STINGY::

    a quick: average
    b late: earlier
    c bright: brightest
    d profuse: grudging

10 RELEVANT: PERTINENT::

    a wasteful: efficient
    b thoughtful: reasonable
    c implicit: explicit
    d quiet: slow

READING ACHIEVEMENT

Your grasp of the meaning of what you read and your understanding of concepts presented in written form are abilities that are often measured in tests for school or vocational guidance. Reading abilities are usually measured in one of the two ways described below.

Sentence Completion

This question format could be called "fill in the blanks." Sentences are presented with one or two blanks, each indicating that a word has been left out. You are to choose, from the possible answers given, the one which fits best in the sentence.

EXAMPLE **A** We laughed at the clown —— he performed funny tricks.

    a but
    b until
    c because
    d unless   Answer:
    e although   **A** ⓐ ⓑ ● ⓓ ⓔ

The sentence clearly calls for a conjunction, but the only one that makes any sense is *because*. Questions like this do not ask for the recall of information. Rather, they look for your ability to recognize the logic and coherence of the sentence—one aspect of comprehension.

Reading Comprehension

The reading tests you are likely to be taking are not concerned with testing whether you understand, word by word, what you have read, but rather how well you draw conclusions about what you read, and how well you make judgments about it. The questions you will be asked about the passage you read should not require outside information, but should be based upon the information found within the paragraph itself. Here is a sample passage followed by three questions.

EXAMPLE   Two days after his sudden death on June 9, 1870, Charles Dickens was honored in a *New York Times* obituary covering more than five of the seven long columns on the front page. The length of this article accurately reflected Dickens' position among the American reading public of a century ago, when entire households waited anxiously from month to month to discover the fate of Little Nell, or Oliver Twist, or whichever Dickensian hero figured in the novel currently being serialized for United States audiences. In later years, the novelist's reputation diminished; critics dismissed him as a "popular" writer rather than a true craftsman. His remarkably vivid characterizations were considered caricatures, even though numerous outstanding writers such as Feodor Dostoevski, Joseph Conrad, and Henry James expressed their indebtedness to "the master." But during the 1940's, writers like Franz Kafka and Edmund Wilson brought readers to a fresh awareness of Dickens' unforgettable delineations of personalities whose very names—Scrooge, for instance—have assumed an independent meaning for people around the world. Readers today are also impressed by Dickens' vision, more than 100 years ago, of what the modern city was to become. For Dickens' London was a place of smoke and filth and a decaying social fabric, rather than the rich, bustling, upper-class London of virtually all his contemporaries.

A The main thrust of this article has to do with ——

    a modern attitudes towards Dickens
    b Dickens' descriptions of London
    c changes in Dickens' literary reputation
    d Dickens' treatment of fictional characters

B Dostoevski, Conrad, and James indicated that ——

    a their writing was influenced by Dickens
    b Dickens wrote for a lower-class public
    c they had learned about London from Dickens
    d Scrooge was a caricature

C Apparently other British authors of Dickens' day ——

    a were upper-class Londoners
    b ridiculed Dickens' London
    c believed Dickens an expert on city life
    d pictured London as an attractive place to live

Answers:

A ⓐ ⓑ ● ⓓ
B ● ⓑ ⓒ ⓓ
C ⓐ ⓑ ⓒ ●

These sample questions are fairly typical of the kinds of questions that may be asked in reading comprehension tests. Question A, for example, asks for the main idea of the passage. Question B asks for a restatement of an idea clearly stated in the passage. And question C asks for an inference which the reader must draw from the passage. Other types of questions often used in this type of test may ask the meaning of a term or phrase as used in the paragraph, a recognition of the author's intent, or the identification of bias, exaggeration, value judgments, or the like.

EXERCISE 4. Drawing Conclusions from Reading. After reading the following passage, answer the questions given at its conclusion.

The computerized age in which we live, while enabling us to
land people on the moon and accomplish vast feats of arithmetical
figuring in seconds, has raised many new problems. One of these,
according to Dr. Lee McMahon, a psychologist at the Bell Tele-
5 phone Laboratories, is the need for communication between computers and between humans and computers. In order to facilitate
such communication, Dr. McMahon developed, in 1966, a new
"language" designed to eliminate computer confusion about the
relation of words in a sentence. The language is called FASE, for
10 Fundamentally Analyzable Simplified English, and although at first
it appears indistinguishable from ordinary English prose, it is
actually quite different, for FASE reduces English to a strict form
in which syntax is absolutely clear and free of ambiguity. The
resulting grammatical structures can be broken down easily by a
15 computer, while ordinary English cannot. For example, consider
how a computer would interpret the phrase "time flies." The
computer would have to decide whether this meant "time speeds
by" or "clock the speed of certain insects," and such a choice,
unaccompanied by human guidance, is beyond the capacity of even
20 the most advanced computers. But a computer programmed to
"read" FASE would have no trouble with the phrase, for FASE is
based on a strictly maintained sequence of subject, verb, and
object, with other parts of speech falling regularly into line. FASE
lacks the beauty of English, then, and its spontaneity, but can be
25 very useful in indexing scientific documents, which would be
punched on cards and stored in a computer until needed. Locating
a particular subject would be a comparatively simple matter for the
computer, since there would be no ambiguity of meaning. "Time
flies," for instance, would be "FASE-indexed" under time, rather
30 than speed or insects.

1 FASE was developed by a ——

a psychologist
b computer programmer
c physician
d linguist

2 A FASE-programmed computer could correctly interpret the phrase "time flies" because ——

   a the phrase is an idiom
   b computers work so speedily
   c the phrase contains a verb
   d the subject comes before the verb

3 Sentences written in FASE are probably rather ——

   a ambiguous
   b idiomatic
   c boring
   d spontaneous

4 The writer implies that a computer's ability to make decisions is ——

   a unlimited
   b limited to choices about grammar
   c nonexistent, even in sophisticated machines
   d controlled by the use of FASE

5 In which of the following lines is a value judgment expressed?

   a line 24
   b line 26
   c line 7
   d line 16

STANDARD WRITTEN ENGLISH

Tests on written English are designed to measure, at least indirectly, your knowledge of standard English. The best way to "test" your writing skill is to have you write. This is not always practical, so multiple-choice tests have been developed to measure your knowledge of correct spelling and usage, your skill in organizing material into a cohesive whole, and your sensitivity to nuances of tone, style, and choice of words. The paragraphs which follow give examples of some of the more commonly used methods of testing skills in standard written English.

Spelling

Spelling may be tested in any number of ways. One of the most common formats consists of five words, one of which may be misspelled. You are to indicate the word spelled incorrectly or mark a choice indicating no errors. Another type of common spelling error derives from the misuse of homonyms—words which sound alike but differ in spelling, such as *to, too*, and *two*. In this sort of test question, four phrases with different homonyms will usually be given, and you will be asked to choose the phrase in which a homonym is used correctly or incorrectly. In the following sample, choose the phrase in which a homonym is incorrectly used:

EXAMPLE **A**   a *too* hot
             b grizzly *bear*
             c *peace* of pie   Answer:
             d rough *seas*   **A** ⓐ ⓑ ● ⓓ

EXERCISE 5. Identifying Misspellings. For each of the following questions, choose the one word which is misspelled. If no word is misspelled, mark the answer N for no error.

1 a seize
   b percieve
   c righteous
   d salutary
   N

2 a ruse
   b laughter
   c explannatory
   d traveler
   N

3 a peaceable
b edible
c salable
d changable
N

7 a *whole* wheat
b *steel* pipe
c ice *floe*
d *idol* hands
N

4 a picnicking
b prejudice
c foreigner
d desiccate
N

8 a bumble *bee*
b *bowl* weevil
c string *bean*
d acting *troupe*
N

5 a mischievious
b grandeur
c gorgeous
d athletic
N

9 a bare *feet*
b boat's *sail*
c *bail* of hay
d filet of *sole*
N

6 a *herd* of elephants
b *berth*place
c mountain *peak*
d apple *core*
N

10 a pint of *beer*
b carving *board*
c *right* to work
d wild *hoarse*
N

Error Recognition

Another way of testing writing skills indirectly is to ask you to detect or correct errors in written passages. Some type of error recognition questions ask you only to indicate that an error has been made; others ask you to specify the type of error it is. Here are samples of three types of questions.

EXAMPLES   TYPE 1.

Mark the letter of the line containing an error in spelling, punctuation, capitalization, grammar, or usage. If there is no error, mark N for no error.

A a Actually, bats are fascinating
b animals. They are the only Mammals
c living today that are able to fly.
N

Answer:
A ⓐ ● ⓒ ⓝ

TYPE 2.

Mark the letter of the underlined part that must be changed in order to make the sentence correct. (Be sure to note whether underlining includes the punctuation.) If there is no error, mark answer space *e*.

B During <u>the colonel period</u>, many colonies had <u>their own flags</u>,
　　　　　　　a　　　　　　　　　　　　　　　　　b

<u>the earliest of which</u> was based on <u>the British flag</u>.　<u>No error</u>
　　　　c　　　　　　　　　　　　　　　　　　　　　　　　e

Answer:

B ● ⓑ ⓒ ⓓ ⓔ

TYPE 3.

Some of the sentences below contain errors; others are correct as they stand. For each sentence, mark your answer sheet:

　a -if the sentence contains an incorrect choice of words (error in
　　diction)
　b -if the sentence is wordy (verbose or redundant)
　c -if the sentence contains an overworked expression (cliché)
　　or mixed metaphor
　d -if the sentence contains an error in grammar or structure
　e -if the sentence is correct as it stands

1 Each day it was a daily occurrence to see the mail truck arrive.

2 The mass of detail is not penitent to the question at hand.

3 The young man was fit as a fiddle as he started work.

Answers:

1 ⓐ ● ⓒ ⓓ ⓔ
2 ● ⓑ ⓒ ⓓ ⓔ
3 ⓐ ⓑ ● ⓓ ⓔ

EXERCISE 6. Identifying Errors in Written English. Following the appropriate set of directions, record your answers to each of the following questions.

TYPE I. Mark the letter of the line containing an error in spelling, punctuation, capitalization, grammar, or usage. If there is no error, mark N for no error.

1 a Russias woman astronaut may have been
   b the first woman to explore outer space,
   c but she wasn't the first woman explorer.
   N

2 a As long ago as 1805, woman were helping
   b men find their dangerous way across
   c the uncharted Rocky Mountains.
   N

3 a Sacajawea whose name means "Bird Woman," was
   b only 13 when she was captured by a tribe of
   c enemies.
   N

4 a She was living with them in North Dakota
   b when Lewis and Clark asked her help
   c in accomplishing this difficult feat.
   N

5 a Charbonneau, her French-Sioux husband,
   b was hired in the autumn of 1804
   c as a guide for the exposition.
   N

TYPE II. Mark the letter of the underlined part that must be changed in order to make the sentence correct. (Be sure to note whether the underlining includes the punctuation.) If there is no error, mark answer space *e*.

6 Sacajawea's geographical knowledge and
            a

   her usefulness as a guide was limited to
       b   c

   her native region of western Montana.   No error.
                d   e

7 <u>Nevertheless</u>, she traveled all the way from
‾‾‾‾a‾‾

<u>Fort Mandan, N.D.</u>, to the <u>Pacific Ocean</u> and
‾‾‾‾‾‾b‾‾‾‾‾‾   ‾‾‾‾c‾‾‾

back <u>again with the exploring</u> party.   <u>No error</u>.
‾‾‾‾‾‾‾‾‾d‾‾‾‾‾‾‾‾‾   e

8 The <u>first-hand reports</u> of the expedition
‾‾‾‾‾‾‾‾a‾‾‾‾‾‾‾‾

<u>by Lewis, Clark, Gass,</u> and others <u>praised</u>
‾‾‾‾‾‾b‾‾‾‾‾‾   ‾‾‾c‾‾‾

<u>her highly but, not her husband.</u>   <u>No error</u>.
‾‾‾‾‾‾‾‾‾‾‾d‾‾‾‾‾‾‾‾‾‾‾   e

9 Shortly before the expedition <u>left to find</u>
‾‾‾‾‾a‾‾‾‾‾

<u>its way</u> to the coast, a <u>healthy son</u> was born
‾‾b‾‾   ‾‾‾c‾‾‾

to Sacajawea <u>on February 11, 1805.</u>   <u>No error</u>.
‾‾‾‾‾‾‾‾d‾‾‾‾‾‾‾‾   e

10 Her son, <u>who was given the name</u>
‾‾‾‾‾a‾‾‾‾‾

<u>Jean-Baptiste Charbonneau</u> made the entire
‾‾‾‾‾‾‾‾b‾‾‾‾‾‾‾‾

<u>trip</u> with his <u>mother</u> and <u>father.</u>   <u>No error</u>.
‾c‾   ‾‾d‾‾   e

Some of the sentences below contain errors; others are correct as they stand. For each sentence, mark your paper with one of the following letters as appropriate:

    a –if the sentence contains an incorrect choice of words (choice in diction)
    b –if the sentence is wordy (verbose or redundant)
    c –if the sentence contains an overworked expression (cliché) or a mixed metaphor
    d –if the sentence contains an error in grammar or structure
    e –if the sentence is correct as it stands

11 Charbonneau was given five hundred dollars for his services as a guide, but Sacajawea received no pay.

12 It was generally agreed by the leaders of the project, Charbonneau mistreated his wife and was unworthy of his pay.

13 Their son returned back to St. Louis, Missouri, with William Clark, who brought him up and paid for his education.

14 After all was said and done, Sacajawea faded from view and, to make a long story short, it is not known what fate befell her in her later years.

15 Though it is a mistake to say that she guided the expedition, it is entirely possible that the roll played by Sacajawea made the difference between its success and its failure.

Error Correction

Error correction questions indicate the inappropriate part of the sentence and ask you to choose a suitable correction from among the choices given you. Here are some samples.

EXAMPLES **A** Eating, drinking, and *to stay up* late at night were among her pleasures.

   a correct as it stands
   b she liked staying up
   c staying up
   d to remain up

B *On the snow-covered branch, two sparrows, they huddled close together.*

   a correct as it stands
   b On the snow-covered branch, two sparrows huddled close together.
   c On the snow-covered branch, two sparrows, huddled close together.
   d Closely, on the snow-covered branch, huddled the two sparrows together.

Answers:
A ⓐ ⓑ ● ⓓ
B ⓐ ● ⓒ ⓓ

Sentence Revision

This type of question requires you to mentally restate a *correct* sentence, using a phrase that is given to you. Using the phrase will require change in other parts of the sentence as well. Then you must choose, from among the choices given you, a word or phrase that will appear somewhere in the restated sentence. (They may not necessarily follow directly after the given revision.) Study the sample given below.

EXAMPLE **A** Sentence: When night came and the temperature fell, my father lit the fire in the bedroom.

> Revision: Begin with "*Each night . . .* "
> > a that the temperature
> > b upon the temperature's
> > c because the temperature
> > d when the temperature

Answer:

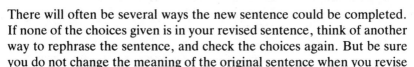

There will often be several ways the new sentence could be completed. If none of the choices given is in your revised sentence, think of another way to rephrase the sentence, and check the choices again. But be sure you do not change the meaning of the original sentence when you revise it.

EXERCISE 7. Selecting the Best Revision. Following the appropriate directions, answer each of the following questions.

Error Correction. Choose the letter which indicates the best correction for the underlined part of each sentence. If the sentence is correct as it stands, mark *a*.

1 Traffic on the highway was blocked for an hour, <u>this causing</u> many drivers to have cold suppers.

a correct as it stands
b causing
c thus having necessitated
d which was responsible for

2 I <u>haven't but</u> a few more pages to write for this report.

a correct as it stands
b have scarcely
c haven't any except
d have only

3 <u>Everyone due to the continued storm sat and sang around the fireplace.</u>

a correct as it stands
b Sitting and singing around the fireplace were everyone, while the storm continued.
c The storm continued while everyone sits and sings around the fireplace.
d Everyone sat around the fireplace and sang while the storm continued

4 Harry, although tired, worked late, <u>typed long</u> into the quiet summer evening.

  a correct as it stands
  b lengthily typing
  c and he typed late too
  d typing long

5 Suppose you tell us exactly where you hid <u>and a thorough report of your precise reasons for doing it.</u>

  a correct as it stands
  b and a report on why.
  c and give us a report of your reasons.
  d and precisely why you did it.

Sentence Revision. Mentally revise each of the following sentences according to the instruction given for each. Then choose the letter of the phrase most likely to occur in the sentence as revised.

6 Sentence: Leaning on the arm of her granddaughter, the old woman slowly entered the room.

  Revision: Begin with: *The old woman leaned*
    a so that she could
    b for her entrance
    c as she
    d to slowly enter

7 Sentence: Aside from his dread of snakes, he was afraid of almost nothing.

  Revision: Begin with: *He had a dread*
    a but otherwise
    b still
    c outside of that fear
    d and so

8 Sentence: What have we been doing all week but preparing for the holidays?

  Revision: Change to a declarative sentence.
    a had done
    b anything all week more than
    c nothing all week but
    d does

9 Sentence: Bonnie told me she hadn't been there and didn't find out about what had happened until the next day.

    Revision: Change the indirect quote to a direct quote.

        a told me, "I'd never been there and didn't find out

        b told me, "I wouldn't have gone and

        c told me, "I wasn't there. I didn't find out

        d told me, "I won't go. I'm not going to find out

10 Sentence: She leapt to her feet and yelled, "I heard you say, 'What are they really worth?' "

    Revision: Make the last direct quote an indirect quote.

        a "I heard you say What are they really worth?"

        b "I heard you ask what they're really worth."

        c "I heard you ask What they're really worth."

        d "I heard you say what they're really worth."

Organizing Paragraphs

Another skill of written English that is often tested is organization. The most frequent exercise designed to measure organizational ability is the scrambled paragraph. This exercise takes a paragraph from any type of subject matter and presents the sentences to you in random order. Your job is to figure out the correct order, the order which will rearrange them so as to make a well-knit paragraph. This you do to some extent by studying the sequence of ideas presented; but primarily you have to concern yourself with the transitional words and phrases.

Here is the way the directions are likely to go:

DIRECTIONS   Each group of sentences in this section is actually a paragraph presented in scrambled order. Each sentence in the group has a place in the paragraph; no sentence is to be left out. You are to read each group of sentences and decide the best order in which to put the sentences so as to form a well-organized paragraph.

      Before trying to answer the questions which follow each group of sentences, jot down the correct order of the sentences in the margin of the test book. Then answer each of the questions by blackening the appropriate space on the answer sheet. Remember that you will receive credit only for answers marked on the answer sheet.

A sample paragraph follows:

EXAMPLE

P As you read, however, concentrate only on main ideas; don't try to remember everything.

Q If you develop an interest in what you read, you are more likely to remember the factual information in a passage.

R Finally, when you have completed the passage, pause to summarize the main ideas in your mind.

S You will have an even stronger motive for remembering those facts if you understand their importance to you.

1 Which sentence did you put first?

a sentence **P**
b sentence **Q**
c sentence **R**
d sentence **S**

2 Which sentence did you put after sentence **S**?

a sentence **P**
b sentence **Q**
c sentence **R**
d None of the above. Sentence **S** is last.

3 Which sentence did you put after sentence **Q**?

a sentence **P**
b sentence **R**
c sentence **S**
d None of the above. Sentence **Q** is last.

Answers:

1 ⓐ ● ⓒ ⓓ
2 ● ⓑ ⓒ ⓓ
3 ⓐ ⓑ ● ⓓ

Note the use of words such as *finally, however,* and *even stronger.* These words refer to previous statements. You may also find clues in sentences using pronouns or adjectives clearly referring to some noun in a previous sentence (*those* facts). Before you answer any of the questions, you should determine the correct order for all the sentences and write it down for your own reference. Most tests, however, will not ask you to give that order all at once. They will be set up so as to give you credit for each correct relationship you detect between the individual sentences. If you were merely asked for the order itself, you would lose all credit for a single mistake.

EXERCISE 8. Organizing Paragraphs. Read the following sentences carefully and write down their correct order before answering the questions related to them. Then choose your answer for each question that follows.

P Swim out and approach the victim from behind in order to avoid struggling.

Q Then go into the special procedure called a "carry," and swim back to shore with the victim.

R In order to save a drowning person, you must jump into the water, keeping your eye on the victim at all times.

S Bring the victim into a horizontal position by pulling back on the chin and resting the body on your hip, using your arms as a lever.

T Stick your elbow in the middle of the victim's back and cup the chin with your hand.

1 Which sentence did you put first?

a sentence P
b sentence Q
c sentence R
d sentence S
e sentence T

2 Which sentence did you put after sentence P?

a sentence Q
b sentence R
c sentence S
d sentence T
e None of the above. Sentence P is last.

3 Which sentence did you put after sentence **Q**?

  a sentence **P**
  b sentence **R**
  c sentence **S**
  d sentence **T**
  e None of the above. Sentence **Q** is last.

4 Which sentence did you put after sentence **R**?

  a sentence **P**
  b sentence **Q**
  c sentence **S**
  d sentence **T**
  e None of the above. Sentence **R** is last.

5 Which sentence did you put after sentence **T**?

  a sentence **P**
  b sentence **Q**
  c sentence **R**
  d sentence **S**
  e None of the above. Sentence **T** is last.

Answers to Exercises

Ex. 1, p. 946	Ex. 2, p. 947	Ex. 3, p. 950	
1-d	1-c	1-b	6-d
2-b	2-a	2-d	7-b
3-d	3-e	3-a	8-b
4-c	4-d	4-d	9-d
5-a	5-b	5-b	10-b

Ex. 4, p. 954	Ex. 5, p. 956		Ex. 6, p. 959		
1-a	1-b	6-b	1-a	6-c	11-e
2-d	2-c	7-d	2-a	7-e	12-d
3-c	3-d	8-b	3-a	8-d	13-b
4-c	4-N	9-c	4-N	9-e	14-c
5-a	5-a	10-d	5-c	10-b	15-a

Ex. 7, p. 962		Ex. 8, p. 966
1-b	6-c	1-c
2-d	7-a	2-d
3-d	8-c	3-e
4-d	9-c	4-a
5-d	10-b	5-d

ESSAY TESTS

Essay questions require that you organize and write down your understanding and analysis of a specified subject in a set time. Your answer is considered deficient if it is not organized according to the directions provided, not supported with sufficient detail, or is incomplete in the treatment of the subject matter.

Studying for Essay Tests

Study for the kind of test you are going to take. The very best preparation for an essay test is to write out questions on your own. You will find in doing this that you must review the material in order to decide what are the most important points to be included in your test questions.

Once you have come up with several questions, close the book and set a time to at least outline the answers. You will be testing your command of the material and exercising the skills you need in the actual test.

Scheduling Your Test Time

Always scan the complete test before you begin to work on any answers. Note the number and types of questions to be answered in the time allowed as well as the point value of each section. Then schedule your time accordingly. Once you get started, use your watch or the classroom clock to keep yourself on schedule.

Be sure to do a further breakdown of the time you set aside for each essay question. As a general rule, count on about two minutes planning and one minute revising for each five that you schedule for actual writing.

Analyzing the Question

Always read an essay question carefully and thoughtfully before you begin your answer. You usually have some choice about what to include; however, teachers often specify the following two points about how you are to treat the material.

Identify Key Terms

Key terms indicate the organizational pattern you are expected to use. Answers that do not use the approach specified in the question may be evaluated as incorrect, even if the information given is correct. For example, if you have been asked to compare two characters in a short story, you must talk about two characters in terms of their similarities and differences. Your discussion of how one character was developed in the story might be accurate but it would not show the comparison that was asked for.

The chart below gives the four main patterns of exposition and key terms associated with each.

PATTERN	KEY TERMS
1. Comparison and contrast	compare, contrast, show the differences, have in common, find likenesses, in what way are . . . similar/dissimilar
2. Cause and effect	analyze, explain, criticize, defend, show why, give factors that lead to, tell the effect of
3. Sequence or placement	list and discuss, trace, review, outline, give the steps, locate
4. Description	describe, identify, give examples of, tell the characteristics of, define

Identify Specific Points to Be Included

Most essay questions require that you complete more than one task. Take time to note carefully exactly what points you must include in your answer.

EXAMPLE   In literature as in life, there are many forms of heroism. One fictional character is a hero because of a single act of valor. Another is heroic because of living a life of quiet endurance. Sometimes the heroic act is one of physical strength and stamina. In other stories, the hero manifests moral courage. How do you define heroism? Choose two characters, each from a different short story read this semester. Evaluate each character in terms of the characteristics of heroism that you included in your definition of a hero. Show by contrast that one character is a hero and the other is not. Use specific details to support your evaluation.

In your answer you must write a definition of a hero which makes clear the characteristics that you consider essential to heroism. You must evaluate two short story characters (each from a different story) in terms of your definition. You must contrast the characters, explaining why one is a hero and the other is not. You must use specific details from each story to support your evaluation.

EXERCISE 9. Analyzing Essay Questions. Read through the following essay questions for a one hour test on computer use. For each (a) tell how much time should be scheduled for the answer; (b) list the key term or terms and identify the pattern of organization called for; (c) identify the number and kinds of examples or support that must be included in a full answer.

1. (30 points) Different programming languages have been developed to meet needs such as scientific calculations, data programming, and games design. Choose one popular programming language (BASIC, Pascal, Assembly, Logo, Fortran, Cobol) and analyze how it is well suited for one of these applications. In your discussion include a comparison with at least one other language.
2. (15 points) Discuss the technical developments that resulted in powerful, small-sized computers.
3. (10 points) List three to five ways a computer might be used in a small business office.
4. (15 points) Show the advantages of word processing programs over traditional typewriters. Include at least three specific points in your comparison.
5. (30 points) Describe how either programmed learning or simulation games take advantage of the computer's capacities. Include three or more examples of specific programs.

Writing Essay Answers

Even though you will be working under time pressure, do not leave out any of the three steps of the writing process.

1. Plan your answer by formulating a thesis statement and very briefly outlining your major points of support. The thesis statement should indicate the pattern of organization you will be using.

2. Write your answer in complete sentences. Use your thesis as the introduction. Judge from the amount of time available whether you should write a single paragraph or if you should develop each of your main points in a paragraph of its own. No matter what the length of your answer, be sure to include specific examples or details from the material that is being tested to support your thesis. Also, use transitional words and phrases to make the development clear.

3. Read through your answer to make sure you have covered all the points specified in the question. Proofread for correctness in spelling, punctuation, and mechanics.

EXERCISE 10. **Planning and Writing an Essay Answer.**
Following your teacher's directions, compose your own essay question
on a topic you are studying in one of your classes. Assign it a point value
in a test meant to take 40 minutes. Exchange questions with another
student or use one you have written. Schedule the appropriate amount
of time and then write a sample answer, including planning and revision.

PART SEVEN

SPEAKING AND LISTENING

CHAPTER 40

Discussion and Debate

TYPES OF DISCUSSION;
ELEMENTS OF DEBATING

It is natural for people to talk things over, either to exchange information or to dispute. The common kinds of discussion and debate are treated in this chapter.

GROUP DISCUSSION

Societies of every kind—school clubs, civic organizations, labor unions, legislative assemblies—use discussion as a means of arriving at a solution to a particular problem or airing the opinions of members before making a decision. This method of problem solving gives each member a voice in deciding matters and ensures the right of everyone to be heard.

40a. Learn how discussion differs from conversation and debate.

Although conversation, discussion, and debate are similar, there are marked differences.

A *conversation* is unplanned and private. It ranges over many topics, casually touching on each. It may have no purpose at all other than fellowship, or it may aim to entertain, instruct, or persuade.

A *discussion* is planned and public. It is focused on one topic, which is examined in depth under the direction of a discussion leader. Its

975

purpose is to consider a problem, evaluate proposed solutions, and arrive at the best solution.

A *debate* considers two sides of a problem. The supporters of each side attempt to defeat their opponents by arguments set forth in carefully reasoned and extended speeches. A debate usually follows a formal procedure and involves a decision by judges.

TYPES OF GROUP DISCUSSION

40b. Learn the various types of group discussion.

Among the many types of group discussion, the most common are the *round table*, the *forum*, the *symposium*, and the *panel*.

A *round table* is an informal discussion in which the participants exchange views around a table—not necessarily round—under the direction of a discussion leader and most often without an audience. The number of participants usually does not exceed a dozen. Members of the group speak without rising and without being recognized by the chair.

The most common example of round-table discussion is the committee meeting. Many organizations conduct a large part of their business through committees. A committee considers business referred to it and reports its findings and recommendations to the entire organization.

In a round-table discussion everyone has a feeling of equality. This type of discussion is most likely to succeed when the participants are well informed and nearly equal in ability.

A *forum* is any type of speaking program that is followed by audience participation. For example, a lecture followed by questions from the audience is a forum.

A *symposium* involves several formal speeches on a single topic followed by audience participation. When the audience is large, audience participation is sometimes limited to questions; expressions of opinion from the floor are usually not allowed.

A *panel* is a discussion among a selected group of persons under a moderator in front of an audience which joins in later. The speakers represent different viewpoints. There are usually no set speeches, but sometimes speakers are asked to set forth their viewpoints in brief preliminary statements.

A panel is really an overheard conversation guided by a moderator. It may consist of four to eight members who face the audience and remain seated while talking. The moderator keeps the discussion moving forward and, at some interesting point, invites the audience to join in. The panel conversation spills over to include the audience. At the conclusion of the discussion, the moderator summarizes what has been said and thanks the participants and audience.

The purpose of a panel is to get important facts and opposing opinions into the open, stimulate audience thinking, and lay a basis for wide participation later.

40c. Select a topic that lends itself to profitable group discussion.

The success of a group discussion depends on the topic. Before selecting a topic, ask yourself:

1. Is it sufficiently limited for the time allowed?
2. Is it related to the needs, interests, and experience of the listeners and speakers?
3. Is it timely?
4. Is it controversial?
5. Is it many-sided?
6. Is it stated clearly?
7. Is it stimulating?

What are good sources of topics for group discussion? Books, magazine articles, movies, and television programs can often stimulate discussion. Newspapers are another source. The discussion of current events, especially of controversial matters, can capture and hold an audience's attention. Topics that are trivial or timeworn, have no audience appeal, do not evoke strong differences of opinion, or can be answered by *yes* or *no* are not suitable.

A topic for discussion should be a question of policy rather than fact. "Have we a supply of energy?" is a question of fact and hence not discussible. The only appropriate reply is a direct, factual answer. "Should we control the use of energy?" is a question of policy which should stir discussion. For suggestions for choosing suitable topics, see page 577.

EXERCISE 1. Selecting Topics for Group Discussion. List five topics suitable for group discussion. Test yours and those submitted by other members of the class against the criteria listed above. The topics may be related to school, community, state, national, or international affairs.

EXERCISE 2. Conducting a Round-Table Discussion. Conduct a round-table discussion on a topic concerning all the participants. The discussion leader, appointed beforehand, will end the discussion after twenty minutes, summarize, and invite class discussion. Suggested topics:

1. City vs. country living
2. Improving the student organization
3. The school yearbook
4. Assembly programs
5. Building school spirit

EXERCISE 3. Conducting a Forum. Conduct a forum. A student will lecture on a current, vital problem and propose a solution for it. At the end of the lecture the class will ask questions.

EXERCISE 4. Conducting a Symposium. Conduct a symposium on discipline. The speakers should represent the viewpoints of a young person, a parent, a law enforcement officer, an educator, and a community leader.

EXERCISE 5. Presenting a Panel Discussion. Divide the class into groups. Each group will select a discussion leader and present a panel discussion before the class on any one of the following topics or a topic of its own. Each panel should meet beforehand to settle matters of procedure and scope.

1. Modern manners
2. Radio and television advertising
3. Youthful crime
4. The ideal school
5. Choosing a career
6. The honor system of conducting examinations
7. Professional vs. amateur sports
8. Vandalism
9. Prejudice—and how to overcome it
10. Student dress
11. The kind of world I'd like to live in
12. Extracurricular activities
13. Our foreign policy
14. Problems of the small farmer
15. Ways of preventing war
16. Selecting a college

40d. Prepare for group discussion by thinking, talking, and reading about the topic.

Many discussions fail because of insufficient preparation by the participants. When the topic is announced, think about it. Do your own thinking. If you simply swallow what you see, hear, and read without analyzing it, you are not acting intelligently. Make sure that there is sufficient evidence to substantiate the truth of every major point. Think things through and avoid making rash or erroneous judgments.

Talk to others about the topic. Discuss it with your friends and parents. Discuss it with someone who is an authority on the topic. Be ready to modify your previous opinion in the light of your new knowledge.

Consult reference books, recent publications, magazine articles, and editorials. Inform yourself as thoroughly as you can about the topic. Investigate the facts before arriving at a decision, for otherwise you may delude others as well as yourself. For other strategies on gathering information, see pages 381–91.

Problem-Solving Discussions

In problem-solving discussions, follow the steps of logical thinking. When you are confronted by a problem, your mind follows certain logical steps. For example, if your ball-point pen fails to write, you ask yourself:

1. What is the trouble? [You define the problem.]
2. What *might be* the cause? [You mentally list various causes: a clogged point, defective mechanism, exhausted ink cartridge.]
3. What *is* the cause? [You consider each of the previously listed possibilities. The point is not clogged, the mechanism works smoothly, the cartridge is used up.]
4. What should be done about it? [Obviously you need a new cartridge or a new pen.]

This simple example illustrates the steps in problem solving. They are as follows:

I. Define the problem.
    A. Limit the problem.
    B. Phrase the problem.
II. Find the possible causes.

III. Propose and examine possible solutions. [What would be the effects of each? To what extent would each solve the problem?]

IV. Select the best solution.

V. Put the best solution into operation. [What obstacles will be encountered and how will they be overcome?]

When participants are familiar with these five steps, they follow them in their individual and group thinking, and an orderly discussion results. The discussion does not remain static and pointless. It marches forward.

EXERCISE 6. Analyzing a Television or Radio Discussion. Listen to a television or radio discussion program and report on it orally to your class. Did the discussion follow the steps in problem solving listed above? If not, what order or sequence did it follow?

Participating in Group Discussion

The success of a group discussion depends on the attitudes of the participants and the quality of their participation, the guidance of the discussion leader, and the response of the audience.

40e. Learn the responsibilities of a speaker in a group discussion.

As a speaker in a group discussion, you should have a cooperative attitude, recognizing that the common good of the group supersedes your own concerns.

Know your topic well. To have an adequate knowledge of the topic, prepare thoroughly by reflecting on it and by talking and reading about it.

Contribute willingly. Some of your ideas will come from previous reflection, and others will come on the spur of the moment, stimulated by what someone else has said. Don't hesitate to express tentative ideas for the other participants to consider, for these ideas may be just what are needed. Be careful, however, not to monopolize the discussion. Everyone should have a chance to be heard.

Listen intelligently. When you agree with another speaker, listen to increase your store of information. When you disagree, listen to accept a different viewpoint if it is supported by sufficient evidence or to refute it by sound reasons if it is fallacious.

Speak so that all can hear—not only the participants but the audience too, if there is one.

Recognize and admit the truth of what others say. There is no need, however, to pass judgment on every statement made by someone else.

Be courteous always. Sarcasm and ridicule are out of place. Self-control is a mark of maturity. Disagree reasonably—and with reasons.

40f. Learn the responsibilities of a leader of a discussion.

The skill and personality of a discussion leader are important. If you are chosen to lead a discussion, consider yourself complimented. Your teacher and classmates have recognized your leadership ability.

You should familiarize yourself with the topic and the special interests and backgrounds of the participants. If the discussion is to be held before an audience, arrange a preliminary meeting of the speakers to decide on procedure and the order in which the various aspects of the topic will be discussed.

Decide on the seating plan. "Set the stage" with an arc of chairs and tables on a slightly raised platform close to the audience. Do not seat members with similar viewpoints together; mix them up.

Introduce the speakers to the audience, telling something of each one's background or point of view.

Arouse the audience's interest in the topic by a brief introductory statement. Say just enough to spotlight the problem and then throw out the first question.

Address your questions to the group as a whole. Don't question individual members, as a rule. Let participation be as free and spontaneous as possible. Ask challenging questions—not the *yes* and *no* kind, but *why?* and *how?*

Dig out points of differences, not as in debate, but in a friendly, united pursuit of a solution. Work to find the common meeting ground.

Take time for occasional summaries. People like to know what progress is being made. In your final summary mention the loose ends, if any.

Keep your own viewpoint out of the discussion. Break in only to ask clarifying questions, bring the discussion back on the track, advance to the next point, or summarize. Be impartial.

Keep the discussion on the track. Encourage the give-and-take of opinion among the participants.

Invite audience participation at a point of high interest, usually about the halfway mark. Speakers from the floor may describe their own experiences, state their opinions, or ask questions. Do not answer questions; refer them to the panel.

Before closing, be sure to thank the speakers and the audience.

40g. Learn the responsibilities of a member of the audience.

By listening attentively, asking questions, and making clarifying statements, members of an audience can help make a group discussion stimulating.

As a member of the audience, you also have an obligation to prepare for the discussion by thinking, talking, and reading about the topic.

Listen with an alert mind. Ask yourself: "What proof is offered in support of each important argument?"

Join in when the discussion leader invites the audience to participate. Speak freely, briefly, sincerely. A discussion in which there is general participation is more stimulating and interesting than one in which only a few take part.

Focus on the main issues. Minor points of fact or opinion should be overlooked.

Speak audibly. While your remarks are addressed to the chair, speak so that all can hear.

Nonverbal Communication

As you may have noticed in your conversations and discussions with others, people often gesture with their hands or use facial expressions to convey meaning. These body movements are examples of nonverbal communication.

Discussion skills should include effective nonverbal habits. For example, hand gestures should not distract listeners; they should support what you are trying to say. Hands can show size, shape, or direction. You can indicate the organization of your remarks by using fingers to count off the points you want to make. In fact, gestures are quite varied. Be sure that those you use convey specific meaning to your listeners. Needless hand waving can indicate nervousness.

EXERCISE 7. **Participating in a Group Discussion.** Divide the class into groups of six to eight members. Each group, under the direction of a leader, will select a question for discussion and phrase it properly. The discussions will be carried on simultaneously in separate areas of the room with the instructor moving from one to another. After a designated time, the class will reassemble, and the discussion leader of each group will report on the problems faced in its discussion, how they were handled, and where improvement is needed.

Listening

As a member of the audience, you must be able to understand and evaluate the ideas of others in the discussion. You must *listen* to what is said, not just *hear* it.

40h. Learn to listen efficiently.

Studies show that the average listener recalls only a little more than half of what a speaker says. By understanding and applying the following points, you can close this communication gap between speaker and listener.

Listen to acquire information and evaluate it. As you hear a speaker present ideas, you interpret them and pass judgment on them as sound or weak. Ask yourself: "Has the speaker presented enough evidence to justify these opinions? Is the evidence from reliable sources? Is the reasoning valid?"

Listen with the right attitude. To listen efficiently, you must be unbiased and cooperative. People with fixed ideas find it difficult to listen to viewpoints different from their own. They develop a mental deafness to ideas that do not sit well with them. An intelligent listener, on the other hand, is fair-minded and receptive to all ideas that are supported by convincing evidence.

Do not strongly agree or disagree with a speaker early in a talk. Withhold final judgment until the topic is developed.

Listen with attention. Concentration is hard work. We all have a tendency to listen for a few minutes, daydream for a while, and then turn our attention again to the speaker. To overcome this tendency, be aware of it and make an effort to concentrate continuously on the speaker's message.

Listen for the main ideas. Usually only a few main points are presented in a discussion, although many minor points and some digressions creep in. Listen with the purpose of discovering the central ideas and fastening attention upon them.

Listen for supporting information. A speaker should support assertions by offering evidence in the form of facts, statements of authorities, and logical reasoning.[1] The evidence must be sufficient to justify what has been said; otherwise the assertion fails for lack of proof. Whatever is asserted without proof can be denied without proof.

Listen for faulty reasoning. In Chapter 25 you learned about errors in reasoning, such as hasty generalizations, cause-and-effect fallacies, and only cause fallacies.

As you listen to discussion, you may hear faulty reasoning of this sort, for this mistake is more common in oral than in written presentations.

Listen for loaded words.[2] The use of emotionally loaded words is natural in free discussion, particularly when the speakers are committed to a viewpoint. The active listener is aware of this danger and discounts arguments that are directed at emotions, not reason.

EXERCISE 8. Listening Critically to a Radio or Television Discussion. Report on a radio or television discussion on a controversial question. Did the speakers present both sides of the question fairly? What evidence did they offer to support their opinions? What objections can you pose?

Evaluating Group Discussion

By considering the merits and deficiencies of a group discussion after it is over, you can learn to improve future discussion programs. In your evaluation, consider the group as a whole, the individual participants, the discussion leader, and the outcome of the discussion.

40i. Evaluate a group discussion by asking key questions about it.

The following questions will help you estimate the worth of a group discussion.

1. Was the discussion purposeful? Were the causes of the problem considered? Were various solutions proposed and analyzed? Did the discussion ramble or did it proceed in an orderly fashion? If the discussion was concerned with solving a problem, did it follow the steps of logical thinking?

2. Was the outcome worthwhile? A group discussion need not reach a solution or agreement. It may be successful if it brings areas of disagreement into the open.

[1] For a discussion of evidence, see pages 588–90.
[2] For a discussion of loaded words, see pages 740–41.

3. Were the participants thoroughly familiar with the problem? Did they present facts, statements of competent and unbiased authorities, and statistics to support their opinions?

4. Was the discussion lively and general? Was there a give-and-take of opinion in an atmosphere of mutual respect? Did all participate? Did anyone monopolize the meeting, or did everyone speak briefly and to the point?

5. Were the audience's questions thought provoking? Did the speakers answer them directly and fully?

6. Was the discussion courteous? Did each speaker exercise self-control by refraining from interrupting when another was speaking? Were statements and objections phrased courteously?

7. Was the discussion leader competent? Did the introductory remarks arouse interest? Did the discussion avoid pointless digressions? Was everyone encouraged to join in? Was there a summary?

EXERCISE 9. Preparing a Rating Sheet for Group Discussions. Prepare a rating sheet for use by class and teacher in rating group discussions.

DEBATING

A debate is a contest in which arguments are used instead of physical strength. It is a form of argument in which two sides publicly dispute a question in a systematic way.

Debating focuses attention on controversial questions, particularly those affecting the public interest. It stimulates thinking, develops ability in speaking, provides training in research, and encourages the habit of suspending judgment until all facts are at hand.

The team supporting the question or proposition is called the affirmative; the opposing team, the negative. Each team consists of two (or rarely, three) speakers, who are called *first affirmative* (or *negative*), *second affirmative*, etc.

A debate is divided into two parts. During the first part (constructive speeches), both sides present their arguments for or against the proposition. After an intermission, both sides try to refute (with rebuttal speeches) the opposing arguments.

The order of speaking may be as follows:

1. CONSTRUCTIVE SPEECHES
a. First affirmative
b. First negative
c. Second affirmative
d. Second negative

2. REBUTTAL SPEECHES
a. First negative
b. First affirmative
c. Second negative
d. Second affirmative

Notice that the affirmative side opens and closes the debate and that the first rebuttal is made by the negative side.

The Proposition

The characteristics of a proposition are discussed in Chapter 25, pages 578–79. The following review should recall the main points in that discussion.

40j. A proposition is a topic stated in debatable form.

It may be phrased either as a question or as a resolution.

EXAMPLES   Should football be prohibited as a high-school sport?
Resolved: Football should be prohibited as a high-school sport.

(1) A proposition should contain only one central idea.

NOT DEBATABLE   Resolved: Fraternities and sororities should be banned in high schools, and every high-school student should be required to participate in at least one extracurricular activity. [two ideas]

DEBATABLE   Resolved: Fraternities and sororities should be banned in high schools.

DEBATABLE   Resolved: Every high-school student should be required to participate in at least one extracurricular activity.

(2) A proposition should be debatable. It should have two sides.

NOT DEBATABLE   Resolved: The automobile has greatly affected the way we live. [This is so obviously true that it cannot be debated.]

NOT DEBATABLE   Resolved: Space flights allow us to obtain valuable scientific information to aid human progress. [Since nearly all the arguments are in the affirmative, this is too one-sided to be debatable.]

(3) A proposition should be stated fairly.

UNFAIR   Resolved: That the unjust and harmful cutbacks in school aid should be rescinded. [This assumes what has to be proved—that school aid cutbacks are unjust and harmful.]

FAIR   Resolved: That the cutbacks in school aid should be rescinded.

(4) A proposition should be timely.

There are hundreds of vital questions relating to young people, schools, local conditions, and state, national, and international affairs that stimulate controversy.

(5) A proposition should be stated affirmatively.

CONFUSING   Resolved: Capital punishment should not be abolished. [The affirmative side would have to argue, "Yes, it should not be abolished," a confusing position.]

CLEAR   Resolved: Capital punishment should be abolished.

(6) A proposition should put the burden of proof on the affirmative.

Anyone who makes an assertion should be ready and able to prove it. The affirmative side, which asserts the truth of a proposition, must present enough proof to establish its case beyond a reasonable doubt.

The affirmative side must show a need for a change; for example, that high-school football should be prohibited or that a government lottery should be established. Existing conditions—called the *status quo*—are presumed to be satisfactory until the affirmative offers sufficient proof to show that a change is necessary.

NOT DEBATABLE   Resolved: That our government should continue to support wildlife conservation. [This makes the affirmative defend the *status quo* and the negative advocate a change.]

DEBATABLE   Resolved: That our government should stop supporting wildlife conservation.

The negative has only to prove that the affirmative case is false or unsound. It does not have to offer an alternative solution.

(7) A proposition should contain no words of uncertain meaning.

For example: "Resolved: That oil is more valuable than steel in modern civilization" is not debatable because "valuable" has no exact meaning. Does it mean essential? Costly? Efficient? Useful?

EXERCISE 10. Composing Propositions for Debates. Compose five propositions for class debate. Be sure that each of your propositions satisfies all the requirements listed above.

The Issue

40k. An issue is a point of disagreement.

The points in a debate on which there are clashes of opinion are called *issues*.[1] A proposition rests on several issues. If they are proved, the proposition is proved. An issue is stated as a question that can be answered by *yes* or *no*.

PROPOSITION   Resolved: That students should participate in the process of selecting high-school principals.

    ISSUE   Is the present method of selecting principals faulty?

Issues often deal with the need for a change, the practicability of a proposed solution, and the desirability of adopting a different solution.

EXERCISE 11. Listing Issues for a Proposition. List at least three issues for one of the propositions you submitted in Exercise 10.

The Brief

40l. A brief is an outline for debate.

In Chapter 25, you learned the principles of argumentation. Those principles are as valid in debating as in writing. Debating is simply oral argumentation.

In a debate, arguments are not written in consecutive prose. They are prepared in the form of a detailed logical outline called a *brief*. A brief is an orderly arrangement of all the arguments needed to prove or disprove a proposition. All the statements in a brief are complete sentences.

The introduction summarizes the history of the questions and defines terms. Sometimes, it sets forth issues and mentions any matters

---

[1] An *issue* in debate corresponds to the minor proposition in other kinds of argument.

that are excluded from discussion by mutual agreement.

In the brief proper the issues are taken up one by one, and the evidence in support of each is given in the form of facts, figures, examples, authority, and logical reasoning.

The conclusion summarizes the main arguments and reasserts or denies the proposition.

The example that follows illustrates the form and content of a brief.

Model Brief

Resolved: That the jury system in the United States should be significantly changed.

Affirmative

I. Jury trials in civil cases cause unfair delay and clog court calendars.
   A. Court calendars are crowded because only a few jury cases can be heard at a time while many others await trial. A national survey by the Institute of Judicial Administration showed that the average delay was 13.3 months.
   B. Delay is a great aid to wrongdoers.
      1. It erases the memories of witnesses.
      2. It may cause wronged parties to give up their cases.
   C. Delay inflicts hardship on the innocent, who have to wait before they can clear themselves.
II. Jury trials waste time and money.
   A. They take up the time of the courts, participants, and jurors.
   B. They increase the cost of court administration, including the payment of jurors' fees.
   C. In New York City alone, jury service each year is equivalent to taking 50,000 people away from their jobs for ten days—an enormous loss of time and money to the jurors' businesses.
III. Juries should be composed of fewer than twelve members.
   A. There is no sound reason for the number twelve.
   B. Many states have smaller juries, sometimes eight, often six, and the administration of justice has not suffered.
   C. If juries were smaller, fewer jurors would have to be challenged, expenses would be cut, and verdicts could be reached more quickly.
IV. Unanimous verdicts should not be required.
   A. Many states require only a majority of some number less than a unanimous vote.
   B. In 1972, the Supreme Court ruled that a criminal jury need not be unanimous. (*Johnson v. Louisiana*)
   C. By removing the need for a unanimous verdict, the time for deliberation would be reduced, and there would be fewer hung juries.

V. Juries should be eliminated in civil cases and verdicts rendered by a single judge.
  A. The quality of justice would be improved if administered by a judge alone.
    1. Judges are trained in law and bring experience and knowledge to each case.
    2. Juries sometimes do not follow the law as explained by the judge but determine a cause by their prejudices or common sense; consequently they create a government by people, not by law.
  B. Juries have been proved to be unnecessary, since thousands of nonjury cases are tried each year, and no one claims that such a procedure is undemocratic.

Negative

 I. The jury system is a safeguard for citizens.
  A. It is a protection against injustice and corruption and against prejudiced judges and overzealous prosecutors.
  B. Experience over a period of 5,000 years has shown that it is necessary for the evenhanded administration of justice.
  C. Although imperfect, some of its shortcomings can be lessened without tampering with its basic structure.
 II. Court congestion is not caused by jury trial alone but by:
  A. Increasing population.
  B. Failure of public authorities to create sufficient judgeships and to provide enough court facilities.
III. The jury system does not waste time, money, and human energy.
  A. Compared with what we spend on education, defense, and other aspects of government, the jury system costs little.
  B. In the Federal courts, jury expenditures constitute only 1/170 of 1% of total costs. (If you paid an income tax of $17,000, only one dollar of it would go to support the jury system.)
  C. A University of Chicago study found that 94% of those who served on juries wanted to serve again, 3% more were willing to do so, and only 3% were unwilling to serve again.
IV. The proposal to reduce the size of juries is fraught with danger.
  A. It would be the first step in doing away with juries entirely.
  B. It diminishes the protection given to those in the minority.
  C. It substantially reduces the likelihood of representation by people of diverse ethnicity.
  D. It would lower public confidence in jury verdicts.
  E. Innocent persons are more likely to be convicted if a jury is composed of fewer than twelve.

V. Unanimous verdicts should be required.
   A. There would still be a reasonable doubt about the guilt of a person convicted by a less-than-unanimous vote.
   B. Most juries are able to reach a unanimous verdict; hung juries occur very rarely.
VI. Justice might be weakened if administered by a judge alone.
   A. If a judge is biased, justice may be thwarted; but if one or two jurors are biased, the effect is diluted among twelve.
   B. On some questions, twelve minds are better than one, no matter how skilled that one is; for example, deciding whether or not a witness is telling the truth.
   C. Jury trials are of a higher quality than nonjury trials.
      1. Attorneys prepare their cases more carefully when they have to present them to a jury.
      2. Cross-examination is more effective.
      3. Attorneys take more trouble to have highly qualified experts present.

The Rebuttal

40m. Plan the rebuttal while preparing the debate.

The rebuttal is the most interesting phase of a debate because it tests a debater's ability to analyze and answer an opponent's arguments. To refute effectively, a debater must be able to think quickly and speak extemporaneously.

Prepare for the rebuttal weeks before the debate, at the time you are gathering material and thinking about your case. As you learned in Chapter 25, you will be in a weak position if you ignore a major argument of the other side. Your success as a debater may rest on your ability to answer your opponents' arguments. As you prepare your brief, consider the arguments they will use, confer with your colleagues about them, and assemble arguments to refute them. Summarize each opposing argument and your answer to it on a separate card. Have your cards available for reference during the debate.

Refutation can start during the constructive speeches. Reply to your opponent's arguments when your turn comes to speak. Because of time limitations, however, most of your reply must wait until the rebuttal period. When refuting, state your opponent's arguments clearly and fairly, quoting your opponent's words if possible. Then present evidence to show that the argument is illogical, misleading, or unproved.

In rebuttal, limit yourself to the main arguments of the opposition. It is wasteful to spend time refuting minor points of fact or opinion. If you can demolish the opposition's main contentions, the minor arguments can be ignored.

Participating in Debate

40n. Observe the conventions of debate.

Address the chair as "Mr. Chairman" or "Madam Chairman." Refer to the judges as "Honorable judges."

Instead of referring to participants by name, use the customary terms: "The first affirmative speaker," "My worthy opponents," "My colleagues," or "My teammates."

Ridicule, sarcasm, and personal attacks have no place in debating. A debate should be won or lost on the basis of reasoned argument and convincing delivery.

40o. The judges' decision is based on the skill of the debaters, not on the truth or falsity of the proposition.

The most common method of determining the winner of a debate is by decision of three appointed judges. The judges base their decision on the merits of the debate and not upon their own views of the question.

Another method is by decision of a critic judge who announces the winning team and gives the reasons for the decision.

A third method is by means of a shift-of-opinion poll. Before the debate, ballots are distributed to listeners to record their opinions regarding the proposition. At the end of the debate another ballot is taken. Only ballots showing a change of opinion are counted. The decision is awarded to the team that caused the greater number of listeners to change their opinion.

EXERCISE 12. Preparing for a Debate; Presenting a Debate. Divide the class into groups of four or six. Each group will decide on a proposition for debate, divide into affirmative and negative teams, prepare briefs, and on the appointed date present the debate in class under a chair, or leader, appointed by the teacher or elected by the class. If desired, another class may be invited to attend the debate. The following topics, which should be phrased as propositions, are only suggestions.

1. Coeducation
2. Homework
3. Jury system
4. Tipping
5. Freedom of the press
6. Abolition of football
7. Government support of TV
8. Electoral college
9. Compulsory voting
10. Eleven-month school year
11. Elective courses
12. Professional boxing
13. Nuclear energy
14. Role of the UN
15. U.S. foreign policy
16. Abolition of interscholastic athletics
17. Federal aid to schools
18. Honor system of examinations
19. Censorship of motion pictures
20. Protecting endangered species
21. Raising (Lowering) the driving age
22. Energy conservation
23. Labor unions
24. Ecology
25. Youthful crime
26. Compulsory military service
27. Lagging school spirit
28. Reorganization of Congress
29. A permanent site for the summer Olympics
30. Mass transit

CHAPTER 41

Effective Speech

PRONUNCIATION AND ENUNCIATION

If you want to communicate your ideas and feelings to others so that they understand, feel, and act as you want them to, you must know how to speak effectively. Poor speech interferes with communication. It diverts attention from *what* is being said to *how* it is being said. "Mend your speech," said Shakespeare, "lest it mar your fortunes."

PRONUNCIATION

The United States has several speech regions, each with its own standard of pronunciation. Fortunately, American regional differences are not great enough to hinder communication. The speech of one region is easily understandable in another.[1]

41a. Be particularly careful about stress or accent.

No pronunciation fault is quite so obvious as stressing the wrong syllable.

It occurs most often with words we encounter in books but rarely hear. For such words, a dictionary is usually a reliable guide to pronunciation. For the pronunciation of commonly used words, of course, careful speakers in your own area are your best guides.

---

[1] For further discussion of the varieties of English, see pages 98–102.

There are a few rules governing stress, but they have so many exceptions that you must be careful in applying them.

Stress tends to be recessive in English; it recedes, or backs away from, the final syllable.

When *automobile* came into English from the French, it was pronounced *automoBILE*. Later it became *autoMObile*. Today it is commonly *AUtomobile*.

Chauffeur and *menu*, once stressed on the last syllable, are now stressed on the first.

Balcony and *confiscate* were formerly stressed on the second syllable only. *Retail*, *detail*, and *address*, formerly accented on the second syllable only, may now receive a stress on the initial syllable.

Words that contain the suffix –able *do not usually put the accent on the syllable immediately preceding* –able.

EXAMPLES ádmirable   inéxplicable
ápplicable   inéxtricable
disréputable   inhóspitable
fórmidable   irréfutable
incómparable   préferable

In words ending in –ity *and* –ety, *stress the third syllable from the end.*

EXAMPLES aménity   satíety
anonýmity   spontanéity
inebríety

The final syllable is stressed in many words taken from the French. In nearly every case these words have not been fully naturalized.

EXAMPLES bourgeoisíe
entrepreneúr
ragóut (rhyme this with "Drag who?")

Words ending in –iacal *have a long* i *sound and are stressed on the* i.

EXAMPLES hypochondríacal   maníacal

Stress is sometimes used to distinguish parts of speech. A word that has the same form when used as a noun, adjective, or verb is usually stressed on the first syllable when used as a noun or adjective and on the second syllable when used as a verb.

NOUNS OR VERBS	ADJECTIVES OR VERBS
affix	absent
compress	frequent
contract	perfect
insult	present
rebel	subject
survey	
torment	

Compound nouns and adjectives usually receive primary stress on the first part of the compound; compound verbs are usually stressed on the second part.

NOUNS bláckbirds, fírefighter, móonshine, síxpence, éarthquake

VERBS outdó, overcóme, counteráct, underráte

EXERCISE 1. Stressing the Correct Syllable(s) in Words.

The following words are often stressed on the wrong syllable. Check each in a dictionary and write it with an accent mark over the stressed syllable. Note that in some cases two pronunciations are permissible.

acumen	decorous	impious	orchestra
admirable	desultory	impotent	peremptory
adult	dirigible	incognito	prestige
alias	eczema	incomparable	recess
awry	equitable	indefatigable	respite
combatant	formidable	inexorable	robust
condolence	gondola	infamous	secretive
contrary	grimace	integral	superfluous
conversant	herculean	lamentable	theater
curator	horizon	mischievous	
debate	hospitable	municipal	

EXERCISE 2. Pronouncing Foreign Expressions Correctly.

Here are some foreign words frequently used in English. Look up their pronunciation in a dictionary.

French: apropos, blasé, bon voyage, cuisine, de luxe, elite, en masse, en route, hors d'oeuvre, lingerie, née, petite, première, rapport, sabotage, trousseau

Italian: adagio, concerto, fiasco, maestro, maraschino, cognoscenti, sotto voce

Spanish: guitar, mesa, rodeo
Latin: ad infinitum, ad nauseam, de facto, gratis, facsimile, status
   quo, data, via, vice versa

EXERCISE 3. **Stressing the Correct Syllable in Words Used as Both Nouns and Verbs.**   Each of the following words can be used as a noun or verb. The accented syllable is shifted to denote the parts of speech. Read the list aloud, accenting the correct syllable in each case.

perfume (n.)	rebel (n.)	refuse (n.)
perfume (v.)	rebel (v.)	refuse (v.)
object (n.)	present (n.)	insult (n.)
object (v.)	present (v.)	insult (v.)
survey (n.)	torment (n.)	contract (n.)
survey (v.)	torment (v.)	contract (v.)

41b. Avoid the omission or addition of syllables and the switching of sounds.

In nonstandard pronunciation, syllables are often omitted; for example, *s'pose* for *suppose, champeen* for *champion,* and *jool* for *jewel.*
   Syllables are also added in nonstandard pronunciation, as in *umberella* for *umbrella; athalete* for *athlete.*
   In certain cases, sounds may be switched or transposed; for example, *calvary* for *cavalry, irrevelant* for *irrelevant, prespiration* for *perspiration,* and *bronical* for *bronchial.*

EXERCISE 4. **Pronouncing Words Without Omitting Any Syllables.**   Careless speakers frequently omit a syllable or a sound in each of the following words. Practice saying this list aloud, taking care not to omit a syllable.

government	giant	poetry	literature
ideal	probably	geometry	particular
library	geography	cigarette	ridiculous
company	police	finally	

EXERCISE 5. **Pronouncing Words Without Adding Any Syllables.**   Practice each of the following words aloud, being careful not to add a sound or syllable.

elm	ticklish	hindrance	grievous
film	extraordinary	banana oil	mischievous
helm	idea	laundry	law
athlete	chimney	burglar	
athletics	lightning	translate	

EXERCISE 6. Pronouncing Words Without Transposing Sounds. Practice each of the following words aloud, being careful not to transpose sounds.

perspiration	prodigy	larynx	irrelevant
southern	modern	poinsettia	prescription
hundred	cavalry	western	bronchial

41c. Learn the rules for pronouncing *ng*.

The *ng* sound causes much confusion. You can eliminate any difficulty by learning three simple rules.

1. All words ending in **ng** *and all words derived from them are pronounced with the final sound in* **sing**.

EXAMPLES   bring, bringer, wing, winging

EXCEPTIONS   Use the sound in *finger* in the following words: longer, longest, stronger, strongest, younger, youngest.

2. The combination **nge** *at the end of a word is pronounced* **nj**.

EXAMPLES   hinge, flange

3. In all other words, **ng** *is pronounced as in* **single**.

EXAMPLES   hunger, anger, single

EXCEPTIONS   gingham, Bingham

EXERCISE 7. Pronouncing Words with Final *ng*. Practice the following words and sentences aloud. In every case *ng* is pronounced as in *sing*.

tongue	slangy	thronging	songbird
ringlet	among	clingy	prongless
springier	fangless	harangue	twangy

The slangy singer sang a song.
The bringer of good news came from Long Island.
He was coming in, not going out.
The youngish singer put the hanger in the closet.
The throng gathered around the bell ringer.
The young and lovely child had a ringlet on her forehead.

EXERCISE 8. Pronouncing Words with *ng*. Practice the following words and sentences aloud. In every case *ng* is pronounced as in *finger*.

anger	longer	younger	spangled
mingle	hunger	stronger	elongate
single	jingle	tangle	angry
bangle	jangle	dangle	
bungle	English	bingo	
linger	language	fungus	

When I was single, my pockets did jingle,
I wish I was single again.
Linger longer.
The English language is difficult to learn.
The angler hurt his finger.
If you are hungry for mangoes, do not linger.

ENUNCIATION

Enunciation is the process of forming, uniting, and separating speech sounds. It has to do with distinctness of utterance.

When you enunciate correctly, your words are clearly shaped and easily understood, yet not overly precise. Here are some typical enunciation errors:

gimme	gunna	wanna
whyncha	dunno	wit' (for *with*)
wonnerful	didja	gover'ment

41d. Enunciate clearly.

To enunciate clearly, you must move your lips, tongue, and jaw.

If your friends often have difficulty in understanding what you say or if telephone operators often ask you to repeat a number or message, your enunciation may be faulty.

The exercises that follow are useful in correcting the habit of mumbling. Practice them with exaggerated vigor, precision, and speed.

EXERCISE 9. Practicing Sound and Word Combinations. Practice the following sound and word combinations.

bah-bay-bee-baw-boh-boo
mah-may-mee-maw-moh-moo
mee-maw, mee-maw

bool-ah, bool-ah
raw beet, raw beet
meat ball, meat ball

EXERCISE 10. Practicing Sounds and Sound Combinations. Place the tip of the tongue on the gum ridge behind the upper teeth. Lightly and agilely practice:

t-t-t   d-d-d   t-t-t   d-d-d

tah-tay-tee-taw-toh-too
dah-day-dee-daw-doh-doo
lah-lay-lee-law-loh-loo

EXERCISE 11. Practicing Word Combinations. Old-fashioned tongue twisters are lots of fun—and good enunciation drills, too. Practice the following, at first slowly and then with increasing speed.

1. The big black bug bit the big black bear.
2. Fanny Finch fried five floundering fish for Francis' father.
3. Lemon liniment, lemon liniment.
4. Prunes and prisms, prunes and prisms.
5. The seething sea ceaseth and thus sufficeth us.
6. She sells seashells by the seashore.
7. The sixth sheik's sixth sheep's sick.
8. Truly rural, truly rural.

EXERCISE 12. Pronouncing Words with Difficult Sounds and Sound Combinations. Pronounce the following lists of words, giving special attention to the enunciation problem indicated for each list.

Initial sounds:

about	electric	exact
America	eleven	huge
because	eraser	remember

Middle sounds:

accidentally	cruel	government	poem
all right	diamond	history	poetry
already	February	interesting	really
automobile	finally	jewel	recognize
champion	geography	library	shouldn't
company	giant	mystery	wonderful

Final sounds:

child	second	chest	past
gold	east side	last	post
hand	west side	meant	left
kind	abrupt	nest	

Difficult consonant combinations:

cts:	conflicts, facts, respects, restricts, tracts
dths:	widths, breadths, hundredths
fts:	lefts, rafts, shifts, tufts
lds:	builds, fields, folds
pts:	accepts, precepts, concepts
sks:	asks, desks, disks, risks
sps:	clasps, lisps, rasps, wasps
sts:	adjusts, frosts, digests, insists, lists, mists, rests, tests

41e. Avoid substituting one sound for another.

The substitution of one sound for another is a frequent fault: *ciddy* for *city, dis* for *this, tree* for *three*.

EXERCISE 13. Distinguishing Between *t–d, t–th*, and *d–th* in Pairs of Words. Practice the following pairs of words, taking care to distinguish between them.

t–d		t–th		d–th	
beating	beading	boat	both	bayed	bathe
bitter	bidder	tree	three	breed	breathe
matter	madder	true	through	dare	there
metal	medal	taught	thought	day	they
latter	ladder	tinker	thinker	doze	those
writing	riding	tin	thin	read	wreathe

INDEX
AND
TAB KEY INDEX

Index

Nothing, no, none, 256
Notorious, famous, 245
Noun, 4–5
  abstract, 5
  case of, 158
  collective, 5
  common, 5
  compound, 5
  concrete, 5
  defined, 4
  gerund, 54–55
  plural in form but singular in meaning, 142
  possessive case of, 827–30
  proper, 5
  proper, capitalizing, 771
  rules for forming noun plurals, 926–29
  used as adjective, 11
  used as adverb, 18
Noun clause, 75–76
  defined, 75
  diagramed, 75, 76
  indefinite relative adjective, 75
  indefinite relative pronoun, 75
  introductory word omitted, 76
  to combine sentences, 344
Nowheres, 239
Number, agreement of pronoun and antecedent, 147–49
Number, amount, 239
Number of, 144, 252
Numbers
  apostrophe for plural, 831
  at beginning of sentence, 761–62
  hyphenated compound numbers, 762
  written as numerals, 762
  written as words, 762

O

Object
  direct, 34–35
  indirect, 35–36
  of preposition, 19–20
  of verb, 34–36, 161–62
  retained, 210
Object complement = Direct object, Indirect object
Object of preposition
  case of, 163
  defined, 47
Objective case, defined, 157
  uses of, 161–62, 163
Objective complement, defined, 36
  diagramed, 36

Objective treatment of topic, 440
Observation, direct and indirect, 382–83
Of, have, 242–43
Off of, 252
Old English, 114–18, 902–04
One, number of, 134
One of those, agreement of subject and verb, 143
Only, but, as negative words, 255
Only cause fallacy, 620
Opinion
  as beginning of expository composition, 489
  as topic for persuasive composition, 577
  debatable, suitable topic for persuasive paragraph, 451
  distinguished from fact, 442–43
Or, nor, 252
  agreement of pronoun and antecedent, 149
  number of subjects joined by, 138–39
Order letter, 719–21
Order of importance, 432
  in persuasive paragraph, 453–54
Organizing paragraphs, tests of, 964–66
Ought, 248
Ourselves, myself, 251
Outlining, 481–84
  debate, 988–91
  model, research paper, 702
  parallelism of topics, 483
  preliminary, research paper, 682–83
  revising, research paper, 687
  rules for form, 482–84
  sentence outline, 481–84
  topic outline, 481, 483

P

Panel discussion, 976–77
Paragraph, 407–60
  adequate development of main idea, 414–15
  alternating method of comparison or contrast, 434–36
  block method of comparison or contrast, 435–36
  chronological order, 427–28
  clincher, or concluding, sentence, 417
  coherence, 423–35
  comparison and contrast, 434–36
  defined, 407
  descriptive, 455–57
  expository, 440–50
  four types of paragraphs, 439–60

Tab Key Index

Key to
English Workshop Drill

To supplement the lessons in *English Grammar and Composition, Complete Course*, there is additional practice in grammar, usage, punctuation, capitalization, composition, vocabulary, and spelling in *English Workshop, Review Course*. This chart correlates the textbook rules with the lessons in *English Workshop*.

Text Rule	Workshop Lesson	Text Rule	Workshop Lesson	Text Rule	Workshop Lesson
1a-c	1	10a-b	2	23f	103
1d-e	2	12a-b	33	23h	104
1f	4	12c	34		
1g	2			25a-k	105
		13a	2		
2b-j	3	13b	39	27a-b	107
		13c	39, 40	27d	107
3a-j	4	13d	41, 43	27g-h	108
				27i	109
4a	5	14a-b	50	27j-l	110
4b	6				
4c	1, 5	15a	47	28a-b	106
4d-e	6	15b	48		
4f-h	5			29b	95
		16a	51	29c-e	94
7a-f	64	16b-d	52		
7g-j	65			31c	1, 10-12
7k-l	67	17b	85	31d	11
7p	64				
7t	68	19a	42-43, 56	32a-g	17
		19b	42-43, 58	32h	21
8a	1, 72-73	19c	42-43, 58	32i-j	20
8b	72, 75	19d	57	32k-l	18
8c	72, 75	19e	43, 59-61	32m	18, 21
8d-e	73, 75	19g	43		
8f	76			33a-c	26
8g	77	21e-h	90	33d	17
				33i	27
9a	82-84	22a-e	90	33l-m	28
9b	82	22f	92		
9c	82, 85	22g	90	34b	107
9d-e	85	22h	91, 93-94, 96-102	34d-e	107